CONFUCIAN ETHICS
OF THE AXIAL AGE

SUNY Series in Chinese Philosophy and Culture
Edited by David L. Hall and Roger T. Ames

CONFUCIAN ETHICS OF THE AXIAL AGE

A Reconstruction
under the Aspect
of the Breakthrough toward
Postconventional Thinking

HEINER ROETZ

STATE UNIVERSITY OF NEW YORK PRESS

Published by
State University of New York Press, Albany

For information, address State University of New York Press,
State University Plaza, Albany, N.Y., 12246

Production by Cathleen Collins
Marketing by Dana Yanulavich

Library of Congress Cataloging in Publication Data

Roetz, Heiner, 1950–
    Confucian ethics of the axial age   :   a reconstruction under the
aspect of the breakthrough toward postconventional thinking   /   Heiner
Roetz.
        p.   cm. — (SUNY series in Chinese philosophy and culture)
    Includes bibliographical references and index.
    ISBN 0-7914-1649-6. — ISBN 0-7914-1650-X (pbk.)
    1. Confucian ethics—History.   I. Title.   II. Series.
BJ117.R64   1993
170'.931—dc20   92-39938
                                                                             CIP

10   9   8   7   6   5   4   3   2   1

Humaneness is a knot
to link the citizen of Paris
with the citizen of Peking

Paul Thiry d'Holbach

Contents

Preface

Confucian Ethics of the Axial Age is based on my book *Die chinesische Ethik der Achsenzeit* published by Suhrkamp in May 1992. The English edition is not just a replica of the German original. During the translation, I took the opportunity to revise the whole text, make a lot of amendments, and take into account some important new publications which appeared in the meantime.

When working on the English edition, I also had to be aware of the difference it makes to address a German- or an English-speaking audience. Western Chinese studies take part in common discourses, and the similarities and divergences of opinions run through the various national traditions. Nevertheless, there are also different historical developments and philosophical habits which leave their marks on the respective receptions of China and her ethics, entailing different preoccupations, interpretations, and evaluations. In the given case, there is not only the analytic Anglo-Saxon heritage. There is also a conspicuous pragmatic tendency in American sinology especially, concerned with "knowing how" as against "knowing that," to use Ryle's terms, which forms a contrast to the Hegelian-Weberian influence still rather prevalent in German analyses. Important exceptions on both sides only prove the rule. Yet, despite their marked divergences, both outlooks have more in common than they appear to have. They show a peculiar complementarity in their neglect of what I will describe as the "postconventional" strain of Chinese moral philosophy, and it is revealing to view one tendency in the light of the other. In my discussion of Chinese ethics, then, I will at the same time enter into some topical problems of Western sinology. Perhaps this may promote the transcontinental encounter of opinions.

The general aim of this study is to give a reconstruction of the ethics of the Chinese "axial age" (c. 600–200 B.C.), especially of the early Confucian school. Instead of providing a chronological presentation of the different thinkers, as is usually found in the well-known histories of Chinese thought, it discusses the moral thinking of ancient China under systematical aspects. Based on a phylogenetic adaptation of Lawrence Kohlberg's cognitive-developmental theory, the respective topics are arranged in such a way that the *genetic structure* of the moral reasoning of the Chinese axial age as the reasoning of an early *epoch of enlightenment* becomes apparent.

This study will not add another doxographical description of "what the Chinese have thought" to the ones already existing. Because of the many lacunae in our knowledge of China's intellectual history, doxography, without any doubt, has not lost its importance today. In this study, however, I shall try to direct the textual work by questions more far-reaching and by an integration of different perspectives, without violating established philological standards. These questions are the result of (a) a critical revision of the reception of Chinese ethics in the West, (b) the Chinese discussion which began in the nineteenth century and continues to the present, as to whether a mediation between China's own cultural tradition and "Western" modernity can be achieved, and if so how, and (c) the philosophical endeavor in ethical universalism.

This book could not have been written without the help of teachers and friends. I thank Professor Chang Tsung-tung for philological assistance. I feel deeply indebted to Professor Karl-Otto Apel, an inspiring and original philosopher, who among other things introduced Kohlberg's cognitive-developmental theory to me. For many helpful conversations, I am grateful above all to Professor Hubert Schleichert, Heribert Lang, and Ole Döring. I thank Farzeen Hussein-Baldrian who took the burden upon herself to go over my English manuscript. Last but not least, I thank Suhrkamp and SUNY Press for making this publication possible. And hadn't it been for Knut Walf and Norman Girardot. . . .

Let me express my gratitude to all who have offered their advice and help to me by a saying of Xunzi (c. 310–230 B.C.):

He who criticizes me and is right is my teacher. And he who agrees with me and is right is my friend.

Conventions

In my quotations from Chinese sources, additions to the text are in brackets, explanations in parentheses.

I have consulted the extant translations of Chinese classics. My rendering can differ considerably from theirs. For comparison, I give page references to standard English translations, unless the texts are quoted by paragraphs.

Romanization follows the pinyin system. I have only occasionally supplied tone marks to distinguish words which could otherwise be confused with homophones or quasi-homophones.

1

The Topicality of the Classical Moral Philosophy of China

After a positive phase during the period of the European Enlightenment, Chinese ethics has for the most part had a rather bad press in the West. This has mainly been due to the influence of late eighteenth- and early nineteenth-century philosophy, especially German Idealism. Even today we still find assessments of Chinese culture which could stem from the pen of Hegel. The corresponding claim that Confucianism as the most influential of the philosophical schools of China represents a mere heteronomous "ethics of accommodation" has found wide and international acceptance through the influential work of Max Weber. Not only in Western sciences including sinology have Weber's theses been of great import, but also in China they have fallen on fertile ground in a time of hypercriticism of the traditional culture.

The *Weberian discourse*, as I would like to call it, describes China in terms of particularism, world optimism, mythos, and heteronomy, as opposed to universalism, world domination, transcendence, and autonomy in the West. Recently, this discourse has entered into a peculiar liaison with another discourse which primarily takes place in the United States—the *neopragmatic* or *contextualistic discourse*. The pragmatic discourse comes to conclusions quite similar to those of the Weberian one, but the assessment is different: the contextualists endorse what the Weberians view as a deficiency. When Weber called the "relentless canonization of tradition" a "barrier to Confucian rationalism,"[1] he unmistakably, despite his postulate of value neutralism, uttered a negative evaluation. In the pragmatic discourse, however, the alleged embeddedness of all thinking and, in particular, ethics, in tradition and cultural context, in the immanence of the "ontology of events," as Hall and Ames have put it in Heideggerian terms,[2] has become an indication of the profoundness and competence of Chinese philosophy. The "sacredness of the secular" (Fingarette), an initially negative topos dating back to Hegel and Schelling and later leading to Weber, is promoted to Confucius' message to present-day modernity oblivious of the rituals and customs of everyday life.

For reasons yet to be shown, the Weberian as well as the pragmatic discourses fail to appreciate the fundamental nature of China's classical philosophy in general and Confucianism in particular. This fundamental nature can be described as a *reflected reaction* precisely to the *crisis of the established context* and the inherited tradition. Hegel and Weber were wrong when they answered in the negative to the question they had posed and which, to me, is of first rate importance: whether ancient China knew of any context-transcending reflexivity. Pragmatist sinology, however, does not reject Hegel's and Weber's answer. It rejects their very *question* as springing from an unjustified generalization of modern Western idiosyncrasies. One of the sinological Hegelians has ridiculed the esoteric sinophilia of our time for "preposterously seeking 'ways to the self' in a culture one of the characteristics of which has been exactly not to develop a self separated from nature."[3] Authors such as Fingarette, Rosemont, Hall, and Ames, however, assure us that China can teach us to recognize that the mentality of self, autonomy, and freedom has run its course. Together with the Chinese, we should recall our "communal rituals, customs, and traditions"[4] and "inherited forms of life."[5] We should abandon the "myth of objective knowledge," and adopt a "thinking that avoids the disjunction of normative and spontaneous thought."[6] Confucius especially presents us a model which for our world is perhaps "more relevant, more timely, more urgent" than it has been even in China herself.[7]

The motivation of these authors and of their appreciation of China presumably is the sense-crisis of modern Western culture. However, in their rejection of modernism and their search for alternative ways of living, they overshoot the mark. Criticizing negative developments, including the development of our own societies, presupposes general normative criteria. Is it not paradoxical, then, to employ Confucius and the Chinese for a contextualism which is no longer interested in questions of right and wrong, of relativity and objectivity?[8] And can this approach really claim the authority of the Chinese texts? Mo Di (c. 480–397 B.C.), one of the earliest Chinese philosophers, already brought forward a striking argument against a contextualistic or holistic ethics: whoever advocates funeral ceremonies (which was rejected by Mo Di) with the argument that they represent an established custom, would ultimately also have to advocate cannibalism and infanticide. Are not cannibalism and infanticide established customs among some peoples, too? Yet, said Mo Di, they contradict humaneness and justice.[9] True, Mo Di was an opponent of the Confucian school, but his insight into the difference between the *normatively valid* and the *merely current* is characteristic of the consciousness of the Chinese "axial age" in general including Confucianism.

It constitutes a remarkable lapse behind this insight, if today we are told, in the name of Confucius, that we should learn and practice the "conventions and traditions we inherit from our culture," "not because we find [them] to be right, but *by virtue of [their] defining for us what we are to value as right,"* as Fingarette says. The "powerful prudential guides" of those conventions and traditions (the Confucian *li*), Fingarette adds, "preclude the need for further awareness, for they have their own autonomous authority *independently of consequences*."[10]

This devotedness to context and tradition, regardless of what the intentions of the various authors may be, is conspicuously blind to the experiences of history. Was not the practice of crippling the feet of women in China, burning widows in India, and enslaving blacks in eighteenth- and nineteenth-century America (not to mention German commonsense half a century ago) sanctified by contexts or traditions? Do not these appearances represent "conventions and traditions we inherit from our culture"? And does not he who, nonetheless, recommends to replace conscious "awareness" by the "autonomous authority *independently of consequences*" of conventions and traditions willy-nilly make himself an accomplice of such developments?

How can we criticize the unspeakable injustice inflicted upon man in the name of traditions and contexts if we leave the final say to both and abandon any ethical reserve? And how can we identify it as injustice in the first place if we do away with the "fact-value dichotomy," as Hall and Ames recommend, again appealing to the alleged authority of Confucius?[11] The indispensability of traditions and contexts notwithstanding, the contextualistic message, in view of the drama of our world, sounds naive, and it is ethically dubious.[12] I doubt in particular that its sane world perspective offers a solution to the problems of today's China.

The new discovery of Confucianism in the West unmistakably bears *postmodernist* traits. Modern Chinese intellectuals, in contrast, occupy themselves with the seemingly outdated question how China can participate in *modernity*. This debate has received new incentives by the return of Confucianism in mainland China during the last decade and the economical success of the East Asian countries. But it already existed in the nineteenth century. Since the shock of the military defeat and political humiliation by Western imperialism and Japan, China has faced the question how to reconcile an age-old form of culture and the new measures of an alien industrial civilization. The Reform movement at the end of the nineteenth century, the founding of the Republic, the May Fourth movement, the introduction of Marxism, and the establishment of the People's Republic constitute various efforts to solve this problem.

Today, a contradictory situation has arisen. On the one hand, it is characterized by the economic progress of the "Confucian" states which seem to meet the Western challenge successfully. For Weber, China served as a contrasting foil to "Occidental rationalism" which laid the fundaments for modernity. Today, however, the question is raised by some authors whether Confucian ethics does not represent a functional equivalent to the Protestant one. They even ask whether it is not superior to the latter as far as the problems of the future are concerned, since this form of ethics could provide correctives for some of the Western developmental errors.[13] China, accordingly, should no longer be measured by the standards of current modernization theories. These theories, it is argued, should be reformulated instead on the basis of the East Asian experiences.[14]

Regardless of whether one subscribes to this opinion—Weber's assumption that China, because of an ostensibly "mythical" attitude towards nature, could not by her own resources achieve a "rational mastery of the world,"[15] but would have to adopt this capability—a thoroughly ambiguous one as we know today—from the Occident, has ever since been a myth itself.[16] The different economic developments of the West and the East can hardly be explained by different worldviews.[17] That Confucian economic ethics are not at all inferior to those of Protestantism was already stated by Keyserling.[18] And Weggel tries to show that Confucanism disposes not only of the virtues advantageous for economic activity, which according to Weber distinguish Protestantism, but of another trump which is lacking in the West: "corporativity."[19] Weggel's "Meta-Confucian" catalogue of values—willingness to integrate oneself, "face," efficiency, submission, thrift, etc.—is tailored to serve the economy. China, however, not only faces economical, but also political and social problems, and there are many contradictions between them. To give an example, how does an alleged value like submission relate to the demands for freedom of expression, human rights, and individualism? It looks plausible that Confucianism has developed an economic ethic which is nearly equivalent to the Protestant one. But what about the political and the social side of the interaction of tradition and modernity, if modernity is not to be understood in merely functionalistic terms? Is there more than political subordination and social adaptation which Confucianism has to offer?

Confucianism seems to enjoy above all the sympathy of conservative circles. In the People's Republic, its return lies in the interest of stability. The Cultural Revolution has not created a new man, but rather demoralized the old one. A rapid economical modernization, orientated towards profit making, competitiveness, and initiative, has deeply affected the old jog trot of the *danwei*-society with its solicitous tutelage by the state. An enormous population growth and a continuing political oppression cause additional stress. Under these circumstances, the Chinese once again recall to mind the efficiency of the traditional ethics. These ethics serve also in Taiwan and Singapore as a counterweight against the sequels of industrialization. It would be astonishing, indeed, if in order to convey the corresponding timeless norms of social behavior such as manners, modesty, solidarity, assiduity, sense of duty, etc., China would not draw upon the well-proven capacities of the one philosophical school which, among other things, specialized in this field. The desire for a stabilizing everyday morality is nothing but normal. It becomes ideological, however, if it merely serves the purpose of consolidating established power structures. This is one of the reasons why the Chinese youth turns a deaf ear to Confucian or other traditional Chinese values and rather adheres completely to Western standards. The statue of liberty on the Tiananmen Square was a clear indication of this attitude. The conservative block of functionaries, however, finds the traditional secondary virtues expedient, and discredits democracy as "foreign," while in Stalinism they have always felt at home. Yet, the People's Republic does not stand alone in East Asia with her inclination to authoritarianism.

The Confucian virtues as a ferment for economy and as guarantors for the stability of authoritarian societies—is this the future potential of Chinese civilization? And is the only alternative the rejection of tradition and the adoption of the Western model? There is a third road already discussed by the nineteenth-century reformers, one of integration of tradition and progress. This road is anything but obsolete, and is probably the only one that can be taken, if China neither wants to perpetuate her traditional authority structures,[20] nor to give up her cultural authenticity and suffer the same loss of identity so many societies of the Third World have witnessed after having been overrolled by the West. China, above all because of her rich intellectual history, can spare herself such a fate. To achieve this goal, a *nonregressive appropriation of tradition* would be necessary which combines the interpretation and adaptation of the intellectual heritage with the modern demands for democracy and change. A formally similar program has been followed by the historians of the People's Republic under the motto of "making the old useful for the present" (*gu wei jin yong*). But their "inheritance of the philosophical legacy" (*zhexue yichan de jicheng*) stood under the auspices of the party, was utilized for the legitimation of the regime, and degenerated into a clumsy and schematic application of Marxist labels to Chinese intellectual history.[21] In the eighties, China was on the way towards a less ideological attitude. After the setback of 1989, it can, for the time being, hardly be expected that the Chinese state will loosen its monopoly of opinion, which it exploits in such a blunt and shameless way, and will tolerate a free public realm.

To appropriate tradition in a nonregressive way,[22] under modern conditions, does not mean to promote a renaissance of traditional modes of thought. The most simple reason for this is that the Chinese tradition is in many respects discredited for good reasons. The People's Republic, to give an example, has not only made use of imported Stalinistic methods of rule, but has also employed traditional devices—the well-proven mixture of legalist *raison d'état* and of conventional obligations from the Confucian canon, which has rendered the Chinese state good services since Han times. But "tradition" is more than this. To appropriate it in a nonregressive manner—which should be the task of the Chinese humanities, if they could develop without regimentation—could well provide the foundations for the modern, imported demands for democracy and codified human rights and subsequently underpin these with autochthonous thought taken from the Chinese intellectual heritage. Ideas of human dignity, equality, and autonomy were developed in China no less than in the Occident. What has to be reconstructed and regained is, therefore, the *universalist potential* of the old culture, which has ever since transcended the narrowness and injustice of the established forms of life and the simple worldview of most of China's leaders. For China, and this is my central hypothesis against Weberian and neopragmatic sinology, has, during the "axial age," gone through an epoch of early *enlighten-*

ment in the sense of a reflective disassociation from everything hitherto valid, and of a breakthrough towards "postconventional," detached thinking. Since then, Chinese culture disposes of a textually fixed and transmitted stock of critical consciousness, the potentialities of which have never been exhausted. On the contrary, the later generations have, on the whole, fallen behind the preexisting level. From the distant perspective of its effective history (*Wirkungsgeschichte*), this potentiality has, therefore, always been underestimated.

The question as to whether or not Chinese philosophy holds a universalist potential is of importance not only for China, but also for ourselves. It cannot be all the same to us whether humaneness and human dignity are nothing but the prejudice of a specific civilization, and have only relative validity in consequence, or whether they are based on interculturally shared convictions. Hence, neither for the Chinese nor for us is classical Chinese ethics a topic of merely archival interest. It is a topic which is in itself ethically relevant. Such a topic needs a specific methodology which can, with Habermas, be called "reconstruction."[23] Reconstruction means to reorganize the ideas of the ancients in a form which is more appropriate to their true intentions—if our interpretation of these intentions is right—than are their quite unsystematic and often unclear arguments, and to make the best of them in the light of the ethical problems of our time. In order to avoid "intentional fallacies," philological exactness is indispensable. Reconstructive hermeneutics does not mean free extrapolation at will, but must always be coupled with the testimony of the text. On the other hand, however, the texts will remain unintelligible, if we do not approach them with a set of well-reasoned questions. I derive these questions, which are decisive for the form of reconstruction, from the current ethical discussion in the West. For reasons yet to be shown, it is especially Kohlberg's theory of the genesis of the competence of moral judgment which offers a promising basis of interpretation.

It could be objected to this approach that we cannot apply a "Western" measure, and the more so a modern one, to "Chinese thought." But in order to decide whether or not "our" categories can be applied, we have to make the test. To get into the "circle of understanding" at all, we have to invest something beforehand. As will be shown in the following chapter, the West has got into the habit of doing this on a level as low as possible. Not only Western philosophy— exceptions only prove the rule—but also some sinologists have adopted an attitude towards Chinese philosophy which could, polemically, be termed "hermeneutic supposition of incompetence."[24] Conversely, I will try my best to treat the ethics of the Chinese axial age from the perspective of a demanding discussion in contemporary moral philosophy. The thinkers of ancient China stood at the peak of their time, and sinology owes them at least the attempt to treat their thought at the peak of ours and give them their due. This also involves evaluation and criticism. To refrain from them would be equivalent to not taking the ancients seriously and ignoring their claim to rightness and truth.[25]

2

Topics of the Western Reception of Chinese Ethics

E thics has often been regarded as the main concern of Chinese philosophy, above all of Confucianism. This prominence, however, has not protected Chinese ethics from really crushing verdicts. Max Weber, to give an example, in his influential study *Konfuzianismus und Taoismus* (*The Religion of China*) imputes to Confucianism a mere *ethics of accommodation* which "intentionally left people in their personal relations as naturally grown or given by relations of social super- or subordination."[1] Weber's judgment has been widely accepted until today, and it stands in the background wherever, with regard to China, interpreters speak of "particularism" and "heteronomy." Weber himself can draw on a long-established tradition of the heteronomous reading of Chinese ethics. His most important source is German Idealism, above all Hegel's philosophy of history. Hegel places China at the "unreflected" beginning of world history where "substance" is not yet dissolved by "subjectivity," and the idea of freedom is not yet known:

> The universal Will displays its activity immediately through that of the individual: the latter has no self-cognizance at all in antithesis to Substantial, positive being, which it does not regard as a power standing against it—as, (e.g.) in Judaism, the "jealous" god is known as the negation of the Individual. In China the Universal Will immediately commands what the Individual is to do, and the latter complies and obeys with proportionate renunciation of reflection and personal independence. . . . The element of Subjectivity is therefore as much wanting in this political totality as the latter is on its side altogether destitute of a foundation in the mental disposition (*Gesinnung*) of the subject. For the Substance is simply an individual—the Emperor—

7

whose law constitutes all the disposition. Nevertheless, this ignoring of moral disposition does not imply caprice, which would itself indicate moral disposition—that is, subjectivity and mobility. Here we have the One Being of the State supremely dominant—the Substance, which, still hard and inflexible, resembles nothing but itself—includes no other element.[2]

Hegel's "unreflected substantiality" of the "Orient" which has not transcended the "unity of mind and nature" is the archetype of many similar formulas to come.[3] Basically, it means that China has not witnessed an epoch of *enlightenment* which would have emancipated thought from nature and institutions. Hegel herewith stands in sharp contrast to the preceding conviction of the philosophers of Enlightenment itself and their admiration for China. Opposing the struggle of the Christian confessions, they had proclaimed a *consensus gentium* to which in particular pre-Christian and extra-Occidental thought was to bear witness. Hence, China became important in a double way. Confucianism was a first-class authority for the moral power of "natural" human reason which the philosophers wanted to substantiate in their own interest. Christian Wolff, one of the great figures of the time, writes in his famous *Oratio de Sinarum philosophia practica*:

> But who will doubt what has been affirmed by so much experience . . . , that one can make the test in this case with no other people better than with the Chinese who have neither a natural nor a revealed service of God and have never paid attention to external reasons. Since they only relied on internal reasons derived from the nature of human action itself, their example can clearly show how far those internal reasons can take us.[4]

For Wolff, China can show us the "capacity of nature," since the Chinese "only used their natural powers and did not receive anything by contacts with other peoples." They simply followed "what according to their insight corresponded with human reason." They insisted on reason, because

> one must have a clear perception of good and evil if one wants to dedicate oneself to virtue without fear of one's superiors and without hope to get a reward by them, but one will not achieve a perfect perception of good and evil if one has not exactly examined the nature and reasons of things.[5]

China herewith became the witness for an autonomous capability of moral judgment and action without relying on external authority. The comparison of Confucius and Socrates suggested itself, and is frequent in the literature of the time.

Ethics stood in the center of the attention that the philosophers of Enlightenment paid to China. Regardless how low their level of exact knowledge may have been, their interest in China was governed by much deeper earnestness than that of many learned researchers of later times. China for them was not more or less a random subject matter, but an ally in a common concern: the victory of reason. Though the Enlightenment was only fascinated by the Congenial of the foreign while neglecting its unyielding aspects—which, among other things, constitutes its "dialectics"—the systematic grounding of the interest in other cultures on the conviction *tua res agitur* remains important.

Under the impact of the later negative assessments and the modern fate of China, it has to be asked whether the Enlightenment's enthusiasm for China was justified at all. Was Confucius any better than a mere authority for a system which secured harmony at the expense of freedom, or for an enlightened despotism after the heart of the French physiocrats? Montesquieu's suspicion that the celebrated spirit of China, like that of Asia in general, in reality was merely the spirit of "slavery"[6] soon became the new consensus of the Western mainstream, after the French Revolution had opened new and hitherto unthought-of perspectives of progress.

Montesquieu for the first time gave a negative evaluation to a topos which has always dominated the Western interpretation of China: the topos of *unity*. The philosophers of Enlightenment were fascinated by the Stoic idea of the unity of the moral man and the order of nature, and it was this idea which they also gathered from the then known Chinese texts. Quesnay, to give an example, hailed the "political and moral constitution of the huge empire of China" as authentic applications of "natural law" which "deserve to serve as a model for all states."[7] In Montesquieu's critique of China, however, nature, as mere physical climate, causes a uniformity of "customs, manners, laws, and religion" which breathes the "spirit of despotism."[8] There is no development in China, since the compactness of the social structure leaves no room whatsoever for the slightest alternative.[9]

Montesquieu's new idea of a *separation* of powers gradually replaced the preceding paradigm of unity as the cipher of the old, exploded despotism. German Idealism and Romanticism later gave the final blow to the China fashion of the eighteenth century. Kant's criticism destroyed the conviction that there is a unity of nature and reason, which had delivered the last basis of the philosophical sinophilia. The Romantic discovery of the individuality of the different "spirits of the peoples" (*Volksgeister*) undermined the Enlightenment's cosmopolitism. Both developments put an end to the Stoicism of the age which lay at the bottom of the esteem for Chinese ethics. Parallel to the decline of the two vogue words of the eighteenth century, "nature" and "cosmopolite," China's star began to wane. Western Rationalism separated itself from an increasingly irrational nature-sentiment. Hegel's "absolute idea" and its historical appearance as *Weltgeist* meant a certain mediation of the Kantian and Romantic distinctions again. In Hegel's new all-embracing system, however, China became the mere starting point of a development which proceeds beyond her and leaves her behind. She is cast off as the iridescent slough of the mind pupated in the East and unfolding and coming to itself in the Occident.

The positive outlook of the Enlightenment, and the negative one of Montesquieu and the German Idealists mark two idealtypes of Western interpretations of China. They have remained fundamental also for later assessments, even if the various authors are not necessarily aware of the heritage.[10] The prevailing paradigm today is the *paradigm of substantiality*, though not merely in negative, but also in neutral or positive variants. It dominates the reception of Chinese ethics in the form of a *heuristic of holism and heteronomy*. It can be divided in four single complexes: The alleged undividedness of the Chinese worldview is (a) attributed to a specific *form of thought*, which in turn can be (b) traced back to the *structure of language*. It is furthermore explained by (c) *socioeconomical and political conditions*, and (d) by *religion*.

A. THOUGHT FORM

"East Asia thinks differently" is a widespread opinion in the West as well as in the East itself.[11] This view, which E. W. Said has labeled as "Orientalism," can go together with quite contradictory evaluations of "thinking differently."[12] Especially at times when weariness of the modern Western way of life is overwhelming, "Chinese thought" has been a cheap object of mystification. Edifying or esoteric approaches have discovered deepest truth and "wisdom" in the same sympathetic "unity of man and nature" which China's critics have held responsible for her "backwardness." Negatively, this alleged characteristic can be termed "a principally magical relation to the world," or "a secularized basic magical relation to nature which has not been overcome."[13] Accounts like these, for the most part late blossoms on the family tree of German Idealism, have ethical relevance. A thinking which does not draw a dividing line between man and nature will also never achieve an independent stance vis-à-vis society. It will be embedded into society in the same way as into the movement of the cosmos, neither recognizing the difference between the two nor its own heteronomy. In its holistic universe, the rules of etiquette coincide with the general course of the world at large. In Granet's words,

> Every being which would violate the smallest prescription of etiquette would be rebellious and instigator of disorder. Etiquette is the only law, by it the order of the universe is realized. It must command every gesture, every attitude of the beings, be they small or great.[14] . . . Both macro- and microcosmos are equally gratified by the preservation of revered customs. The universe is nothing but a system of behavior, and the behavior of the mind is not different from that of matter.[15]

Granet proves to be an exponent of the traditional Western view of China which has received new support by Durkheim's discovery of the numinous nature of institutions. He is guided by the fascination that Chinese society is a classic representation of the operation of Durkheim's "collective unconscious." And the ancestor of the "collective unconscious" is the undivided "general" in the first phase of history which Hegel assigned to China.

Chinese ethics have all too often been interpreted along these lines. And the allusion to the underlying "magical" form of thinking is hardly ever lacking. For Weber, too, this is the key to the understanding of China, when he calls "the unbroken and continued existence of purely magical religion" the presupposition for the Confucian "ethic of unconditional affirmation of and adjustment to the world."[16] Weber is undecided, however, whether Confucianism has only tolerated magic or is itself imbued by it. Rejecting such hesitation, Trauzettel emphasizes that the "magical relation towards the world" was the "collective cultural property of ancient China in which Confucianism also took part."[17] The magical form of thought, according to Trauzettel, has not only been an obstacle to individuation and autonomy. Its existence even forbids one to talk of "ethics,"[18] since the alleged compactness of the Chinese worldview does not permit any stable differentiation of value spheres (ethics, law, art, religion, production, etc.).

A variant of the "magic"- approach is brought forward by Fingarette. For Fingarette, however, "magical" does not denote a worldview which has to be overcome, though he has been misinterpreted in this sense.[19] "Magic" is the miracle of the automatic functioning of everyday life by rituals, habits, and language. Human actions for Fingarette have a "magical quality," and it is Confucius who can inform us about this. Fingarette's topic, then, is not a retarded form of thought, but rather the "invisible hand" (Adam Smith) or the "Autopoiesis" (Niklas Luhmann) by which social relations constitute themselves without any conscious effort on the side of the participants. His topic, then, is the well-functioning *context* in which man already finds himself and which has not first of all to be created by him. Fingarette's thesis documents how negative topoi of the Weberian discourse are taken over and positively reevaluated by the pragmatic discourse.

B. LANGUAGE

Until Romanticism it had been taken for granted that the human languages are nothing but different tools to express the one and the same human thinking. The Chinese, too, shared this conviction. For the Daoists, language is secondary to meaning,[20] and for the *Lüshi chunqiu,* "words are the outer form of what is meant."[21] The Han-Confucian Yang Xiong calls the word the "voice of the heart" (that is, of the mind) and the written word its "picture."[22]

It was Wilhelm v. Humboldt who by his linguistic studies initiated a series of revisions of the "grammatical indifference" of his predecessors. According to Humboldt, there reposes "a unique world-view (*Weltansicht*) in every tongue."[23] Language is "the structural organ of ideas,"[24] rather than a passive tool. Nevertheless, there is a common human thought underlying all languages, which provide different possibilities to express this thought. But there is only one ideal grammar for this task—that of the Indo-European languages, and in particular the Greek one. Every language can express everything, but not every language "inspires" thought:

> Every language remains a likeness of the original predisposition responsible for language, and . . . every language possesses the pliancy to absorb everything and is capable in turn of imparting its own expression to everything. Under no conditions can it become an absolute restriction to man. The difference between languages is only whether the point of departure for the increase of power and expansion of ideas (*Krafterhöhung und Ideenerweiterung*) lies within its very self or is a foreign extraction. In other words, the problem resolves itself as to whether language is inspired or whether it remains more or less passive and resignedly collaborative.[25]

Humboldt seeks the important difference between languages "in the grammatical method of sentence building."[26] Because of its lack of morphology, the Chinese language for him is less capable of inspiring thought than the inflective languages.[27] Herewith for the first time the structure of language is identified as the cause of the difference between China and the West. After the "linguistic turn" in philosophy, Humboldt's theses have developed into a decided linguistic relativism at the expense of his assumption of general human forms of thought. In this connection, the Chinese language has frequently been used for illustrating the various deficiencies which an ostensibly inferior grammar—a nonmorphological one—entails for thinking.[28] Above all, it has been held responsible for impeding science and natural science in particular. But ethical aspects are involved, too. Both dimensions, the scientific and the ethical one, are complementary. Man's ability to conceive himself as a subject and a self will determine his position not only vis-à-vis nature, but also vis-à-vis society. The Chinese language, it is maintained, is handicapped in this respect. Ludwig v. Bertalanffy, who puts the "non-Westerner" on one level with the child and the "wild," writes:

> "Things" and "self" emerge by a slow build-up of innumerable factors of gestalt dynamics, of learning processes, and of social, cultural, and linguistic determinants; the full distinction between "public objects" and "private self" is certainly not achieved without naming and language, that is, processes at the symbolic level; and perhaps this distinction presupposes a language of the Indo-Germanic type.[29]

Ethically relevant assessments about Chinese language concern, above all, its so-called "subjectlessness," the dominance of syntax over morphology, and the nature of words. The fact that a Chinese sentence does not have to contain an explicit subject has been associated with "collectivism" by Forke, and with the "absence of complete individuation" by v. Tscharner.[30] The conclusion, however, that a subject which is not made explicit does not exist has itself much in common with the primitive word magic which it imputes to the speakers of Chinese.

For Johannes Lohmann, one of the foremost Heideggerian philosophers of language, Chinese represents the "form of consistent ontological indifference," the "state of the primitive human language" which stands close to that of the ape and the Neanderthal.[31] The "ontological indifference" of the Chinese language, says Lohmann, is due to its grammar which consists of pure syntax and reduces the linguistic mechanism to the order of words. The "problem of order, not the problem of reflection or sense," however, is "fundamental" "for the thought-form of ontological indifference."[32] The absence of "reflection" in China is a Hegelian topos, and like Hegel, Lohmann wants to show the alleged inability of "Chinese thought" to become conscious of itself and take an independent standpoint against the world. Instead of achieving this "ontological difference," the linguistic principle of pure order represented by grammar has as its complement a pure and unchangeable social order. "In the semantical form of ontological indifference," Lohmann writes, "the order of language is by itself the immediate image of a *real* order to which the speaker adjusts himself."[33]

Granet's analysis of Chinese language centers around the Chinese word. It is an "emblème" of standardized behavior which it immediately calls forth with magical power, simply by being uttered.[34] There is no scope allowing one to distance oneself from the world and to question it. In quest of an empirical counterargument against Habermas' universal validity claims of the human language,[35] Negt ingenuously accepts Granet's view. Chinese, for him, is the model of a purely perlocutionary language. It is not a means of argumentative communication, but of direct evocation of behavior. By uttering words and writing characters, language transports what has always been valid because of historical experience. Magic and myth take the place of ethics.[36]

The fact that this picture from the infancy of ethnosinology is alive and well again is, above all, due to the postmodern criticism of "Occidental" universalism, which is also shared by the influential pragmatistic wing of American Chinese studies. The most ambitious recent attempt to achieve basic insights into Chinese culture by linguistic analysis has been made by Chad Hansen. Hansen does not want to make general statements on "what language can do," but wants to talk about "what was said" in the Chinese texts.[37] However, "what was said" is a matter of interpretation, and in order to achieve a correct interpretation, Hansen favors a "language-focus approach."[38] The nature of Chinese, according to Hansen, has led the Chinese thinkers to assumptions about language quite different from those of Western thought. Assumptions about language, however, says Hansen with the "linguistic turn" in contemporary philosophy, shape philosophical theorizing.

For Hansen, the distinctive characteristic of the Chinese language is the nature of its nouns and its sentence. Chinese nouns, he says, are "mass nouns" in contrast to the "count nouns" of Indo-European languages. They do not denote individuals of a class or of a kind (like the English "horse"), but parts of a whole (like the English "water"). For a speaker of Chinese, the world is a complex of "mereological sets" which "consist of, rather than contain, their members."[39] The function of thinking is to make the right "cuts" in the world stuff: "In learning names we (referring to the Chinese) learn to discriminate or divide reality into the mereological stuffs which names name."[40] This "mass-noun syntax" means that Chinese is lacking a "built-in principle of individuation."[41] Philosophy, too, therefore, remains principally "nonindividualistic."[42] It develops an ethics in which the individual does not play any important role, which has heteronomous and holistic traits, and which loses, in consequence, its very contours as an ethic.[43]

There is another momentous feature of Chinese language which Hansen draws attention to: nearly every word can make a sentence, and complex sentences, because of the lack of morphology, appear to be mere "strings of names."[44] The Chinese, therefore, are merely interested in the words, not in the sentence. It follows that Chinese philosophy has no concept of truth, which can only be attributed to sentences. Instead of on truth, Chinese philosophy focuses on the pragmatic "appropriateness" of language usage.[45]

The priority of language pragmatics, together with the lack of reflection on sentences and on a concept of truth, must keep philosophy, if we can speak of philosophy at all, in dependence of the established ethos. Sentences have a conventional structure, but they are the creation of the individual, whereas words, except neologisms, are the common property of the language community. If the attention is addressed to words rather than to the sentence, the important task will be to "internalize ways of classifying and categorizing things."[46] The preeminent function of language will be a regulative instead of a descriptive one:

> The relative stress on the attitude-forming functions of language versus the content-expressing function is one of the most crucial and most frequently ignored contrasts between the Western and the Chinese traditions.[47]

The orientation marks of the corresponding ethics are

> (1) a naturalistic, holistic conception of the place of humans in nature; (2) a conception of the well-ordered society as a peaceful cooperative structure produced by a *shared moral cultivation;* and (3) a conception of human action which presents that motivation as *socially given*—in particular, through learning how to use words.[48]

Such an "ethics" is only interested in the *effect* it has in influencing people and has no place for autonomous reason. It relies on the conventional "knowing how" of behavior in a society which works "via a harmony of moral judgments."[49] The harmonious system, in which "persons" do not exist, functions on the basis of regulative usage of language. By way of the inherent collectivism of "mass nouns" and "world-focus," it adjusts all members of the community to the standard of the established worldview. Just as in Granet's view, language creates a world after its own image by being adequately used by its speakers. To question this world from the inside would presuppose a knowledge of exactly what is lacking—individuation and detachment from society. And to criticize it from the outside would be pointless, since criticism would require the use of criteria which are not applicable to the Chinese context. For Hansen, there is neither any possibility nor any necessity for evaluation. What interests him is only the contrast of contexts with their incommensurable background assumptions.[50] This is a typical indifference of the pragmatic discourse.[51]

Another language-based interpretation of the specificity of China is brought forward by Bloom. The "low level of social principledness" he claims to have found in Hong Kong, and the "deferential orientation to authority" he attributes to the Chinese, are linked to a "traditional Chinese view" that "no autonomous rational competence exists untied from its action implications."[52] If thoughts cannot be separated from the consequences of action, thoughts have to be brought under control in the same manner as behavior. Moreover, if the Chinese cannot separate thought from action, they would find it difficult to enter into hypothetical thinking. Mental detachment from the perceptual context and the deliberation of alternatives, the presupposition for any "postconventional" reasoning, would become nearly impossible.[53] Bloom suggests that an absence of counterfactuals in Chinese language provides a linguistic basis for the putative Chinese attitude. The Chinese language, he argues, only knows the conditional style "if x, then y" and not the counterfactual style "if x were, then y would be."[54] This claim, however, does not betray familiarity with Chinese ability of reasoning, Chinese language, and Chinese intellectual history.[55] What has to be taken seriously, however, is the atmosphere in which it could flourish: the popular mixture of linguisticism, relativism, and a contextualistic reading of Chinese ethics, which will perhaps be good for further surprises.

How sound are the linguistic theses which treat ethics as a subtopic of a science of *native* language? The following objections concern each of the mentioned theories:

1. The linguistic approach is reductive. It negates the potential of actual social conflicts and crises which motivate the ethical debate, or regards it as secondary compared to the influence of linguistically determined patterns. The preoccupation with the difference of languages blinds the linguisticist to the similarity of problems. It is true that the questions which move the thinkers of the axial age are formulated in specific languages. But they are brought up by a reality which confronts each of the respective cultures with the same challenges—loss of tradition and of nature, tyranny, war, and economic upheaval.

2. The linguistic approach leads to quite arbitrary conclusions. It is

not one whit more plausible, to give an example, to argue with a relative strictness of Chinese syntax for the existence of order-consciousness, than to argue with a relative looseness of Chinese syntax for the existence of monadic individualism.

3. The equations set up by the linguistic relativists like: priority of syntax = preoccupation with order, missing subject in a sentence = collectivism, mass nouns instead of count nouns = stereotyping instead of individuation, and, above all, absence of inflexion = absence of reflection, how sophisticated their presentation may be, are based on a simple analogism. Analogizing, however, in terms of confounding different spheres of reality, and that is, as an "inferior" form of thinking, is by the same token attributed to the Chinese.

4. The elevation of the native language shared by the members of a community to be the decisive factor in forming the worldview goes hand in hand with playing down or ignoring divergences of opinion, alternatives of thought, progress and retrogression, etc., within that community. The linguistic approach inherently tends to a systematics which presses all intellectual complexity into a single scheme. Under this aspect, it sounds problematical and only prima facie convincing, when Hansen presents the "coherence" of his theory as an argument for its correctness. He justifies his claim that "there is no individualism in Chinese philosophy" as follows:

> In claiming that the conceptual structure of Chinese is not individualistic, I thus argue that, other things being equal, we should not choose individualistic interpretations of particular doctrines when we have a choice. . . . Chinese philosophy is nonindividualistic in the sense that it is more coherent to interpret it via a part-whole rather than a one-many contrast. . . . Nonindividualistic interpretations are always possible for texts written in classical Chinese and interesting philosophical theories . . . all reflect elaborate, sophisticated, and coherent nonindividualistic points of view. These theories, originating in the classical period of Chinese thought, all fit most coherently with a part-whole analysis of the structural features of the Chinese language. The burden of proof is thus shifted to any individualistic interpretive theory.[56]

Thus, the uniformity of statements about a culture is declared the criterion for their rightness. But it has also to be examined how homogeneous the respective culture is in the first

place. For an ethical or developmental evaluatio
system, it is important to know how much room it leave⌣
alternatives. The state of thinking, again, is relative to the extent
to which established "background beliefs" become the subject of
discussion and lose their unquestioned certainty. The linguistic
heuristic does not suggest making these distinctions. It aims rather
at homogeneity than at a differentiated portrait. It is of course
important to know the cultural common sense in order to understand the philosophical writings of ancient China. But it has to
be taken into consideration that the *unity of an epoch of enlightenment*—and whether the Chinese axial age is such an epoch, is
at issue—consists in its *diversity* and *complexity*. Its interpretation presupposes an idea of the broad spectrum of opinions that
can be expected to hold ideal-typically in such an epoch.

5. If the final word is left to linguisticism, either ethnocentrism
(example: Lohmann) or relativism (example: Hansen) will be the
result. In both cases, Chinese ethics will only be of limited interest. For the relativist, it becomes an arbitrary contrast program
to other ethical systems. This would mean, however, abandoning
elementary ethical intuitions. Hansen constructs a fantasy state
named "Chinina" modeled after Chinese philosophical thinking.
"Chinina" treats her citizens "as children" and relies on "group
sanctions" and "manipulating others into doing the right act."[57]
To criticize this nightmare in the name of individual dignity
would presuppose measures which do not exist in the target
culture, and would thus "beg the question."[58] By this argument,
we can legitimate virtually anything. To approach Chinese ethics
from a nonrelativistic viewpoint, by contrast, not only takes into
account our own concern for morality, but is the only way to
develop and preserve criteria for denouncing, if necessary, the
injustice inherent in every life world and particularly in that of
Hansen's "Chinina."

C. SOCIOECONOMICAL AND POLITICAL CONDITIONS

In his analysis of Chinese ethics, Weber stresses the importance of social influences. The Chinese literati, the "bearers" of ethics, are not an independent stratum. They aim at "princely service," their mentality being formed by the "relation
to state-office."[59] They are a status group with an "orthodox doctrine adjusted to
the situation"—Confucianism.[60] The entrance into this status group can be reached
by the "assimilation of existing ideas" through "unceasing study,"[61] and by passing
the examinations as a test "in conformity with the prescribed mental outlook."[62]

By the multiple enchainment of education and rule, any interest in casting doubt upon the world is paralyzed. Critical forms of thinking develop more easily among plebeian classes without the possibility for social advancement.

Whereas Weber later qualifies this social explanation of the "specific Chinese attitude towards life" (see below), other authors make it the core of their argument. Stange, for one, who seeks for "historically identifiable causes" for the differences between the East and the West, points out that in ancient China "the courts of absolutist sovereigns were the center of social life," and not, like in Greece, "the people's assembly." The rulers, however, "only understood historical examples" and not the "democratic method of logical argumentation," with considerable consequences for the history of Chinese philosophy.[63] This claim is overstated. Han Fei, to give an example, in his essay *The Difficulty of Persuasion* lists a series of different modes of argument which the speaker must know in order to convince a ruler.[64] What is demanded is not merely the "historical example." Although the wandering scholars of the Zhou epoch are always welcome at the courts of princes and dignitaries, Chinese philosophy does not develop in their audience halls, but in an atmosphere of remarkable intellectual freedom in the controversies of the competing schools. At the beginning of the third century B.C., up to 1,000 scholars stay at the Jixia academy in Qi for the single purpose of discussion.[65] Only for Imperial China it is worth considering to what extent thought has been restricted by political intolerance.

For Wittfogel, too, the socioeconomical conditions of China are the key to her fate. The "hydraulic society," he argues, produces a total despotism which implies taking the given social patterns "for granted."[66] Prusek also holds this form of society responsible for the failure of a liberation of the individual in China.[67] Even if we follow Wittfogel's theory for a moment and leave out its inaccuracies, which have often been proven,[68] we would still have to ask why the alleged Chinese despotism was never overcome. Why were there no checks upon power in the name of other authorities, which in other cultures made "breakthroughs" possible? At this point, socioeconomical theories need further elucidation. Methodically, these theories have an affinity for the normal, the conventional, and the commonsense. A heuristic suitable for the understanding of the Chinese axial age, however, must be prepared for the separation of thought and society.

Weber, too, qualifies the sociological method and the importance of the social status of the "bearers" of the ethical value system. However, he is not motivated by reservations that from the sociological perspective the liberation of thought from institutions remains unrecognizable—he denies that in China this liberation has occurred in the first place. What he wants to avoid is the reductionism of the orthodox Marxist base-superstructure schematism. Therefore, he stresses that social influences remained secondary compared with "religious sources."[69] This leads us to the fourth paradigm important for the understanding of Chinese ethics: religion.

D. RELIGION

In his *Lectures on the Philosophy of Religion*, Hegel treats China under the heading of "nature religion," the antipode to "religion of freedom." "Nature" refers to the "substantial" which Hegel had attributed to China in his preceding *Lectures on the History of Philosophy*. On the level of religion, it means the absence of any "immanent, determinate inwardness" of conscience which is replaced by the "external," "the constitution of the state, the circumstances of being ruled from without."[70] The accompanying conception of God is earthly; "the heaven of the Chinese is not a world that forms an *independent realm above* the earth. On the contrary, everything is *upon earth*. . . ."[71] This world immanence of religion for Hegel is merely a symptom of a general subjectlessness.

In Schelling's *Philosophie der Mythologie*, however, religion does play the decisive role. For Schelling, the key to understanding why "the patriachical principle has maintained its influence and power for thousands of years" in China is the abrupt change of the religion of Heaven into the deification of the state—*"religio astralis in rempublicam versa."*[72] The "absolute secularization of the religious principle"[73] on the one hand ends up in atheism unrecognized as such by the ancient Chinese. On the other hand it bestows a religious aura upon the institutions—an idea which today reappears in Fingarette's formula of "the secular as sacred." How this transition can be explained, is a "dark point" for Schelling.[74] He suspects that the repentance of the "overbearing dragon" which he finds in the *Yijing* describes a fall of the celestial to the earth analogous to the fate of Lucifer.[75] In direct contrast to this fantastical construction, Hegel's explanation for the putative sacredness of the secular in China stands out by its unspectacular motive: the fall from the heights of Heaven is unnecessary, since Heaven and the world are not separated from each other anyway. What distinguishes the Chinese religion of Heaven from the beginning is precisely the *absence of transcendence*.

Weber's analysis of China is an imaginative and consistent explication of this single central idea. Together with the radical transcendence which in the Occident characterizes Jewish religion and, later, ascetic Protestantism, China lacks, according to Weber, a decisive innovatory potential. There is no supramundane creator who could propel man to subdue and master the "material" of creation in ascetic action. And no otherworldly God makes demands in the name of which the given forms of life can be called into question. "Tension with the world" remains foreign to China in the "radical world-optimism" of Confucianism, or is reduced to nothing in the mystical "indifference" of the Daoists with their "minimization of worldly action."[76] The result is an "ethic of unconditional affirmation of and adjustment to the world" without any "eschatology or doctrine of salvation, or any striving for transcendent values and destinies."[77] Talcott Parsons has summarized the consequences and the difference to the West as follows:

. . . ascetic Protestantism . . . was, as Weber succinctly puts it, not a doctrine, like Confucianism, of rational adaptation *to* the world, but of rational mastery *over* the world. Archimedes is reported to have said, "Give me a place to stand and I will move the world." The Confucian ethic failed to move the world precisely because its world-liness denied it a place to stand outside the world. The Protestant ethic, on the other hand, had such a place to stand, its transcenden-tal God and its concept of salvation. In precisely the *ascetic* aspect of its ethic lay its driving force. From this basic difference follow a number of more special differences. On the one hand, from the worldliness of Confucianism followed its acceptance of tradition, even more its sanctification of it. On the other hand, from the transcen-dental basis of the Puritan ethic followed the absolute unsanctity of tradition.[78]

Long before the Protestant ethic, the paradigm of transcendence as the Archimedean point to throw the world off balance was established by the ancient religion of Israel. Here, God is not "Heaven" like in China, but Heaven's creator. "The Heavens declare [his] glory," states Psalm 19.1. His radical otherworldliness means the complete profanation of nature[79] as well as the subordination of political rule under the imperatives of the religious covenant. Against the background of the prevalent stereotypes of the Chinese "unity of man and nature" and sociopolitical authoritarianism, this would mark a fundamental difference to China.[80] Nothing may symbolize the radical nature of Jewish monotheism more than the political destabilization of ancient Israel, which finally collapsed in the continuing conflict between kings and prophets. The unending history of the political institutions in China appears equally symbolic. In spite of all recurring catastrophes, they man-aged to stabilize over and over again. The topos of the eternal and unchanging, *"das Statarische,"* as Hegel has called it,[81] is intimately connected with the topos of religious immanence. Whence it would follow that the politically organized culture of China could only survive because it has itself been "sacred" (Fingarette), instead of having to legitimize itself in the face of another sacred authority.

The common Western picture of the innerworldliness of Chinese religion, as described above, is too simple, and yet has a *fundamentum in re.* As Hang, for one, has noted, the early Zhou concept of God is not without transcendent traits.[82] As we will see, the Chinese "Heaven" is an authority which does have the poten-tial to question the mundane powers. On the other hand, it cannot be denied that this potential has remained relatively weak, perhaps above all because institu-tional support from an independent churchlike organization was missing. Heaven could be appealed to by critical philosophers against the state, but its service remained the prerogative of the king instead of a class of priests.

Regardless of which significance we attribute to religion in the final analysis, and how we evaluate the Chinese forms, in view of Occidental history, a series of heuristically relevant questions concerning the possible dependence of ethics, philosophy, and science on religion comes to mind. These questions can be divided into three complexes concerning:

1. The relation of subject and object: How, unless by means of the concept of an otherworldly god, can nature be "disenchanted" (Weber) in such a way that it becomes the profane object of systematical transformation and conquest by man? How, in particular, can natural science be developed, unless based on the assumption of natural laws, which in turn presupposes the concept of a divine lawgiver?[83]

2. The relation of the subject to other subjects: How, unless in the name of a supramundane authority, can normative standards be obtained which are not merely refinements of the existing order, but transcend it? Where, in particular, is an effective counterweight to family and state?

3. The relation of the subject to itself: How, unless by means of direct communication with a transcendent god, can the identity of an ego be formed which detaches itself from the social role and conceives of the self as more than the microcosm of the one and only world order in its totality?

Points 1–3, termed the "three kinds of conflict" by Russell and "the actor's three relations to the world" by Habermas,[84] concern the entirety of all world relations in which man finds himself. Their differentiation is relative to or constitutes the levels of cultural development. It is the totality of life, then, which is affected by the problem of transcendence. And in each of the three spheres China has been pinpointed with the same deficiencies.

How should the religious approach to the interpretation of China be evaluated? To take recourse to religion is more flexible and less determinate than to ground worldviews in the native language or in unchanging forms of thinking. Moreover, from the vantage point of religion, some sharply pointed questions can be raised which are touchstones of any thinking that can count as "enlightened." Transcendence is an instance which seems to be indispensable to any form of ethics going beyond the conventional. It is a different matter, whether a religion of the type described above is a *conditio sine qua non* for creating a gap between thought and the world. In an earlier study,[85] I have concerned myself with the first of the aforementioned "world relations;" the results show that phrases like "unity of man and nature," "identity of subject and object," etc., are far from describing the reality of China. Contrary to a current stereotype, in China, nature has become the object of human conquest practically on the same scale as in the West, a practice which has given rise to corresponding theoretical reflection by the Daoists and the Confucian Xunzi. There is no decree of a transcendent God which played a role in this process; on the contrary, it was the steady decline of the belief in "Heaven" which favored the profanation of nature.

If we generalize this result, it can be assumed that also with regard to the second "world relation" (subject–society), which is the topic of the present study, there is a sufficient potential for questioning the established social conditions also without radical religious transcendence. This is not to say that religion did not play any role at all. As I have already mentioned above, the Chinese Heaven could unfold a subversive power. Nevertheless, it should be taken into consideration whether transcendence should not first of all be understood in *formal* terms so that different, but functionally equivalent ways of detaching oneself from the world fall within its range. Specifically religious transcendence seems neither to be a necessary condition for an objectifying and detached attitude towards the world nor does it necessarily imply such an attitude.

I have surveyed interpretations which contrast Chinese ethics against "Western" conceptions and consign it on the level of heteronomy. Strictly speaking, the purport of these interpretations is that there is no ethics *as* ethics (rather than: as politics, as cosmology, or as both together) in the first place. They maintain a general undifferentiated compactness of the "Chinese worldview" as a whole. Although these interpretations are undifferentiated for their part, it cannot be denied that they throw a light on some phenomena of the intellectual history of China and also of the history of Chinese ethics. Labels like "holistic" or "coordinative," if they do not merely mean a prereflective state of mind, mark a characteristic of Han and Song Confucianism which had considerable ethical implications. The political and social development, too, especially from the rise of Confucianism to state orthodoxy and the bureaucratization of the intellectual elite, is of outstanding importance. To what extent, again, the religion of Heaven has influenced the ethical thought of the axial age appears to be the most challenging of the questions raised by Weber and his predecessors. Most of the aforementioned theses, therefore, are worth considering. They are, nevertheless, inappropriate for a reconstruction of the ethics of the Chinese axial age, since their point of departure lies within the bounds of a heuristic of heteronomy or stagnation. In the following pages, I shall present a more suitable heuristic: a heuristic of enlightenment.

3

Methodological Considerations: A Universalistic Heuristic of Enlightenment

A heuristic of enlightenment should furnish the methodological presupposition for the reconstruction of Chinese axial age ethics as the ethics of an epoch of enlightenment. The fundamentals of such a heuristic can be derived from an explication of the concept of the axial age and from deliberations on the development of moral reasoning. This should provide us with a universalistic conception of understanding, which avoids the ethnocentric implications or relativistic consequences of recourse to native language and culture specific forms of thought. This universalistic approach implies working with the expectation to find a spectrum of normative ideas in China similar to that of our own tradition. This assumption should be revised if it turns out that it cannot be substantiated by the texts.[1] The texts should, moreover, not only be treated with all the philological accuracy which we owe to their authors and our readers, but also be taken seriously in terms of ethics and normatively evaluated. Last but not least, special attention must be drawn to possible indications of universalism.

This hermeneutical priority of the normative results from the normative content of the subject of ethics itself. Justice would not be done to these normative implications if one were to treat the subject of ethics like any other scientific topic.[2] To understand this priority of the normative in universalistic terms means reentering the deadlocked program of Enlightenment. This program should not be naively copied, but its conviction that the fate of the foreign reflects our own fate can be taken over. Yet, the methodical universalism I propose must continuously be confronted with the complementary problem that every analysis should take into account the authenticity and uniqueness of ancient China. For what use is universalism if it fails to acknowledge the foreign *as* the foreign, too?

In the following pages, I determine the complicated relation of empirical research and normative claims in light of Karl Jaspers' idea of the "axial age" of the ancient high civilizations and Lawrence Kohlberg's cognitive-developmental theory.

A. JASPERS' THEORY OF THE "AXIAL AGE"

In Jaspers' early works, the legacy of historism with its accent on the subjectivity of philosophies is predominant. In his *The Origin and Goal of History*, however, the emphasis is on universality and truth. He is motivated by the intention to overcome national and cultural particularism by means of the idea of communication, thus "opening the horizon in which mankind can grasp the chance of its due solidarity."[3] He wants to "gain possession of something *common to all mankind*, before all differences of creed." Mankind is united by "one single origin and one goal."[4] Despite all the distance which separates them, axial age cultures, upon their encounter, recognize that "the other is also the own."[5] This reminds us of the *consensus gentium* of the Enlightenment. This universalistic ethical context in which Jaspers' theory of the axial age is formulated is crucial, but it has fallen into oblivion with its later instrumentalization by the philological and historical sciences.[6] It is all the more important to bring it back again to recollection. Jaspers' interest does not simply lie in developing criteria for the interpretation of the classical philosophies. For him, foreign cultures, and among them China, are of systematical significance on the underlying basis of the "idea of unity."[7] In a letter to Hannah Arendt from 1957, we find the following provoking lines which challenge sinology as well as philosophy:

> Confucius has made a great impression on me. I did not only want to protect him from most sinologists who declare him banal. To me, he was *fruitful for us.*[8]

To search for the True in individual cultures, Jaspers conceives a "universal history" "empirically accessible," in order to do justice to both the unmistakable uniqueness and the "communication or continuity of humanity."[9] For his "historical Platonism,"[10] the Universal has to be empirically identified in history if it is more than a matter of faith inspired by Christian religion. It appears for the first time in a historical epoch which Jaspers, because of its pivotal importance, calls the "axial age." Between 800 and 200 B.C., in the Near East, Greece, India, and China simultaneous breakthroughs in thought took place. In intellectual developments coming about independent from each other, an epoch of early *enlightenment* with world historical dimensions was born which laid the foundations for everything still to come. The term "axial age" has, therefore, a threefold dimension: The *synchronic dimension* refers to the simultaneousness of comparable progresses in thinking situated along a geographical axis from the Mediterranean to East Asia. The *diachronic dimension* refers to the molding influence it has had for all later developments of each of the respective cultures. The *universalistic dimension* refers to the "challenge to boundless communication,"[11] that is, the perspective of a common future for mankind, which the axial age has opened up for the first time.

Hence, the axial age for Jaspers is not merely an epoch of historical importance. It delivers a *normative point of orientation* for the interest in history and for the concern with the foreign. To think from the common horizon of the axial age means getting rid of the Hegelian-Weberian perspective of the de facto subjugation of the rest of the world under the Western supremacy without handing ourselves over to a postmodernist delight in haphazardness.

Although, at times, there are gloomy-dramatic undertones which befit the *Existenzphilosophie* more than the unembarrassed atmosphere of the epoch itself, Jaspers draws an impressive portrait of the axial age. It contains a great variety of formal criteria which can serve as the foundation of a more detailed analysis: loss of substantiality and of the closedness of life by reflection and transcendence (what Hegel had denied for China),[12] the overcoming of mythos by reason, the discovery of the individual, the questioning of everything previously accepted, the deliberation of the most contradictory alternatives, spiritualization, consciousness of history, etc.[13] Because of their fundamental importance, these categories are at the same time yardsticks for regressions and renaissances.

Jaspers inquires into the "historical reasons" for the events of the axial age. Diffusionist theories overlook that the "spiritual movement" of the period, with the "sublimity of its content," is not accessible to migrations and exchanges.[14] For Jaspers, the only "methodologically arguable hypothesis" so far advanced has been put forward by Alfred Weber. Weber believes in a turning point of history brought about by nomadic Indo-European equestrian peoples from Central Asia who invaded the surrounding high civilizations.[15] This shocklike existential experience of catastrophes jolted thought, which had to cope with the "problematic character of existence" and took on tragi-heroic traits.[16] Yet, migrations and conquests, Jaspers objects, had taken place for millenniums without causing a phenomenon like the axial age and do not suffice, therefore, to explain it. The "mystery of the simultaneous inception" remains unsolved.[17]

I suspect, however, that this "mystery" is merely a superficial problem. For why, we can ask, did a great number of cultures *not* take part in the developments of the axial age? In this case, the fact of the nonsimultaneity would require an explanation. Instead of trying to solve the problem of contemporaneousness, it seems more fruitful to ask why the breakthrough towards a period of enlightenment in any culture can happen in the first place.[18] There is no historical necessity for such a development. But the fact that it occurs can well be interpreted in terms of the *logical possibility* of a sequential evolution. For this idea, I am indebted to Kohlberg's cognitive-developmental theory.

B. KOHLBERG'S COGNITIVE-DEVELOPMENTAL THEORY

The "cognitive-developmental theory" is a theory about the ontogenesis of moral judgment competence. According to Kohlberg, the development of this competence follows a logical sequence of irreversible stages which can be described as definite, consistent, and relatively stabile types of moral outlooks. The formulation of the stage sequence is based on philosophical considerations, mainly in the Kantian tradition, and on longitudinal empirical research. Kohlberg confronted subjects with hypothetical theoretical dilemmas such as: Heinz's wife is near death from cancer. A druggist has discovered a drug that might save her life. But since Heinz cannot get together enough money, he would not sell it to him. Should Heinz break into the store and steal the drug to save his dying wife? And why, or why not? The responses to problems and questions like these that were given from childhood to adulthood indicate the following chronological sequence of stages of moral reasoning:[19]

Level A. Preconventional Level
Stage 1. The stage of punishment and obedience orientation. The physical consequences decide whether an action is right or wrong. Obedience to authority is guided by the egocentric interest in benefits and the avoidance of physical harm.
Stage 2. The stage of instrumental exchange. What is right, is, like at Stage 1, that which satisfies one's own immediate needs while strategically also recognizing the interests of others. The orientation is towards elementary rules of reciprocity and concrete exchange like "you scratch my back and I'll scratch yours."
Stages 1 and 2 together form the "preconventional level" of early childhood. Action and judgment are directed by a naive hedonism and not by internalized expectations of others, group solidarity, or general ideas of justice. Moral evaluation is hardly separated from physical experience. In the first maturity crisis, the child then turns away from the hedonistic principle and reaches the level of internalized conventional morality.

Level B. Conventional Level
Stage 3. The stage of interpersonal concordance and expectations or "good boy–nice girl" orientation. The right is what "pleases" and what is motivated by the rules, values, and expectations of groups.
Stage 4. The stage of law and order orientation. The right is what is in accordance with the prescriptions of one's role in state and society. Action and judgment are motivated by the respect for authority and doing one's duty as a value per se.
Stages 3 and 4 together form the "conventional level" of role morality with the focal points of family and state loyalty. In contrast

to the preconventional level, action and judgment are directed in an alienated way (especially at Stage 4) by means of self-identification with heteronomous rules and norms. The aim is not only adjustment to a given order, but its maintenance for its own sake. In the second maturity crisis (the adolescent crisis), the adolescent transcends the conventional level and proceeds to the postconventional stages:

Level C. Postconventional Level
   Stage 4¹/₂. The stage of "anything goes," the phase of youthful protest. What is the right is a question of arbitrary subjective decision. This stage is characterized by a radical rejection of the alienated conventionalism of Level B and the recourse to the naive pleasure principle of Level A. Instead of new normative rules, this stage proclaims a provocative "beyond good and evil." It is "postconventional but not yet principled."[20]
   Stage 5. The utilitarian, relativistic social contract orientation. What is right is not predetermined, like on Level B, by the existing institutions and social conditions. It is first of all a matter of personal, relative values and opinions. Beyond this it is defined in terms of standards that have been agreed upon by free and equal individuals and that can be changed by regulated procedures.
   Stage 6. The universal ethical principle orientation. The right is what is in accordance with abstract, consistent, and universally valid principles. It is based on the autonomous decision of conscience.
   The Stages 4¹/₂, 5 and 6 form the "postconventional level" which views society from outside and independent from the values of other individuals, groups or institutions. Conventional morality is not necessarily rejected (except at Stage 4¹/₂), but its acceptance is accompanied by a clear awareness of the possible conflict between conventions and law on the one hand and morality on the other.

Such is the core of Kohlberg's model.[21] Which stage an individual may achieve is open ended.[22] The sequence, however, is invariant, it's guiding thread being the growing capacity of *role taking*, the adoption of the perspective of the other in a process of increasingly complex reciprocity. Hence, the unfolding of reciprocity is the basic measure for moral progress.

The extraordinary resonance Kohlberg's theory has found is, above all, due to the fact that it introduces the new possibility of a *complementarity* into the old debate about the relationship of "is" and "ought," of the empirical and the normative—which was the problem that occupied us with Jaspers.[23] Hence, "is" and "ought" are neither torn asunder, like in the Platonic-Kantian tradition, nor identified with each other, as is the tendency of the Aristotelian-Hegelian tradition. Yet, Kohlberg has called a lot of critics to the scene, especially from the camp of cultural relativism.

What makes the "cognitive-developmental theory" truly significant for a reconstruction of Chinese ethics can be discerned in the following complexes:

1. The cognitive-developmental theory makes the claim to intercultural validity and to the refutation of ethical relativism. To substantiate this claim, Kohlberg points out his research in a number of Third World countries, among them Taiwan. The data showed the same tendency as in a highly developed industrial society, though the postconventional level in most of the lesser developed countries was reached less often. Thus, Kohlberg can speak at least of a *universal tendency* of development. This means:

   > Moral development is not merely a matter of learning the verbal values or rules of the child's culture, but reflects something more universal in development, something which would occur in any culture.[24]

   Different and supposedly cultural specific moral orientations, then, might not necessarily represent incommensurable normative systems, but different stages of one and the same universally valid scheme, their common basis being the cognitive development which underlies the moral one (Kohlberg with Piaget). If this is sound, the cognitive-developmental theory would offer systematic grounds that the application of "our" own normative concepts to the interpretation of foreign cultures is at least not in and of itself biased or problematic. A fundamental problem of comparative philosophy, often felt in sinology, too, though mostly passed over and seldom discussed, could be brought nearer to a solution which corresponds to our common intuitions. This does not dispense one from the necessity of doing justice also to the singularity and specificity of a culture. Ethical universalism not only is compatible with a plurality of individual and collective cultural life-styles, it would also be meaningless without them. Reversely, it is the precondition for recognizing them as authentic expressions of human existence.[25] This is implicitly acknowledged, paradoxically, by most cultural relativists themselves, when they plead for tolerance of foreign cultures. Tolerance is obviously laid claim to as a principle which can logically not be relative itself.[26]

   Nevertheless, many critics deem Kohlberg's theory (in particular the assertion of postconventional stages) a mere bias of the modern Western male intellectual. R. Shweder, to give an example, declares Stages 5 and 6 to be "culture specific." "If they are advocated at all," he writes, "and they rarely are, it is among Western educated middle-class adults."[27] Objections are especially raised against the testing methods (the dilemma approach), the formulation of the test questions, the rating of the responses, and the universalistic framework as such.[28] China, too, is named as a proof. Bloom doubts on account of his research in Hong Kong that moral autonomy can be the condition of the highest stage.[29] And for Dora Dien, the cognitive-developmental theory misses the Chinese value system. Kohlberg's methodology, she argues, is based on the "prevailing Western conception of man as an autonomous being, free to make choices and determine his destiny," while in China the individual is integrated into the universe and subordinated to the group and the ideal of harmony.[30] Dien is quoted as an authority by other skeptics such as Vine.[31]

Rejecting the critique from the camp of relativism, it can firstly be pointed out that Kohlberg's theory has been welcomed in China by prominent representatives of contemporary "New Confucianism." Liu Shuxian assents to Kohlberg's universalism as well as to the idea of a development towards autonomous morality.[32] What he misses, however, keeping faith with the ancient Confucian Mengzi, is a normative grounding in human nature.[33] This sympathy for Kohlberg's approach can partly be explained by what Metzger calls the "optimistic this-worldliness" or "epistemological optimism" of Confucian thought—the belief in an "objectively valid moral consensus," in moral knowledge and human reason, and in the attainability of "highest moral-political goals," which is at odds with what he identifies as the Western relativistic, historicist, and skepticistic mainstream.[34] Unlike Metzger, who merely describes the disparity and does not want to evaluate the different discourses,[35] I think there is at least one decisive argument which speaks in favor of the Confucian position: without a rationally justifiable normative goal, the course of history, in the final analysis, would be handed over to the blind arbitrariness of the marketplace and to the rule of might makes right. This "optimism," however, can, under modern conditions, only be upheld as a *regulative* one—referring to something that *can* and *ought to* be—without the typical ontological and cosmological assumptions of the Neo-Confucians.[36]

Secondly, the results of empirical research can be referred to. Meanwhile, a great number of ontogenetic studies have been carried out, among them quite a few about the cultures under Confucian influence, which at least substantiate Kohlberg's central thesis that there is a tendency towards postconventional thinking.[37] Gielen has received among Taiwanese students even higher scores for the postconventional stages than in comparable social layers of the U.S.[38] But even if such an empirical corroboration had not taken place, this would not mean a refutation of the cognitive-developmental theory. "Cultures" are more complex than a synchronic cross section would possibly show. Whether they hold a universalistic potential or not cannot be decided by the fleeting impression of a questionnaire. Of equal importance at least is a look into their history. As the case may be, this look will prove that what today pretends to be the authentic form of life is, in fact, retrogressive. If we leave aside the special problem of preliterate societies, apparently original "patterns of culture"[39] can be the outcome of regressions. In this case, they do not bear the normative criteria which have been established by the respective tradition itself and should be looked upon rather as a subject matter of *Ideologiekritik* than as sanctified cultural assets.

2. The cognitive-developmental theory, originally conceived in ontogenetic terms, is *mutatis mutandis* applicable to the *phylogenesis* of the human race. It provides a yardstick for measuring and evaluating in its specific variations the cultural evolution of mankind. The basic idea of this adaptation is simple: the ontogenetic stages represent ways in which men communicate with each other, and these ways in turn mold the appearance of societies. By its application to phylogenesis, the cognitive-developmental theory returns to the starting point from where it received its inspiration—the theory of social evolution.[40] Onto- and phylogenesis stand in a close reciprocal relationship. The level of social evolution determines the possibilities of individual development just as much as the outstanding contributions of individuals who are ahead of their time—like the philosophers of the axial age—can influence the future of their society. Onto- and phylogenesis are not complementary, however. Composed entities like societies "learn" in a different way than individuals do. They consist of layers and subentities in which a great variety of different moral outlooks can be found. These outlooks compete with each other far more than they may do within one individual. Thus, the "breakthroughs" of the axial age concern a small yet influential stratum of intellectuals.

     This nonsimultaneousness is an important presupposition for another difference between onto- and phylogenesis: the different probability of *regressions*. Progress in history is less stable than it normally is in ontogenesis. As the case may be, it has to be regained in renaissances, since it can easily be shattered by historical events such as war, ethnic subjugation, migration of peoples, political chaos, and economic impoverishment. Kohlberg's sequence, then, does not describe a necessary, but possible yet partially realized progress in phylogenesis. It delivers a standard for measuring social evolution if it does take place. It does not describe (like nineteenth-century evolutionism) the actual dynamics of history.

A further difference between onto- and phylogenesis concerns the presence of the different stages. Associations of individuals to social units cannot be conceived without assuming some rules and conventions which will normally be followed. Phylogenesis, then, can hardly begin with the preconventional stages.[41] As complex systems encompassing groups with different interests and having to hold their own against other systems of their kind, societies will, moreover, never reach the highest stage possible in individual development. The remaining stages refer to chiefdoms (3), centralized states (4), and constitutional states with an institutionalized possibility of change (5). The topic of the present study, however, is not the course of Chinese history in its entirety. The aim is to reconstruct the inner logic and genetic structure of the ethical discourse in a specific yet formative phase of Chinese history.

3. Kohlberg's theory combines the supposition of a normative Universal with the idea of a gradual development. It can thus serve as a connecting link between the aforementioned two main poles of the traditional Western reception of China—the contradicting positions of the Enlightenment and of Hegel, while allowing to abolish their specific weaknesses to the advantage of their strong points. The philosophers of Enlightenment discovered in Chinese culture the Kindred which confirmed and reinforced their own identity—the perfectibility of man, a morality by pure reason without revealed religion, confessional freedom, etc. Rejecting the churches' claim to power they proclaimed a consensus of all peoples testified by Jesus as well as by Socrates and Confucius. This consensus, however, was rooted in an ahistorical "natural reason." Hegel took history into account, but at the expense of that consensus. He depreciated foreign cultures as mere footboards of the "world spirit" (*Weltgeist*). The cognitive-developmental theory allows a productive integration of both conceptions. By its theoretical postulation and empirical corroboration of one and the same interculturally valid humane telos, it helps to save the Enlightenment's normative egalitarian idea of the

semper idem while at the same time stripping it of its naivety and differentiating it. This telos is universal, but it can only be realized over certain steps and in tendency, without any "historicistic" assertion of a historical necessity. Which stage will be reached is open-ended and not, like in Hegel's system, long settled from an ethnocentric retrospective.

Hence the cognitive-developmental theory can deliver a new foundation for a systematic interest in the foreign which does not exhaust itself in the search for contrast foils. It allows to reconcile philological sincerity with the orientation by a complex theoretical framework and a universalistic moral perspective. The necessity of such a "postconventional" perspective can hardly be doubted after the catastrophic failure of conventional group moralities, not least in our century. This incorporation of our own fate and moral concern into scientific research does not at all obstruct the view on the subject matter. On the contrary, it makes the reconstruction of Chinese ethics possible while taking its claim to normative validity seriously.

Herewith, we have reconstituted and incorporated into our study what was the essence of the "breakthrough" of the axial age: regulative thinking no longer tied up in established contexts. This is the deeper reason why Jaspers' concept of the axial age can be conceived in a new and rich systematic by Kohlberg's theory. The program of the cognitive-developmental theory inherits the legacy of the axial age. Conversely, China's entrance into the axial age can be described as the transcending of Kohlberg's conventional level in an "adolescent crisis" of society which leads to a breakthrough towards postconventional consciousness in the intellectual layer of society. The cognitive-developmental theory makes us sensitive to the typology of such an era of enlightenment which can be expected to hold ideal-typically. At the same time, the complementarity of "is" and "ought" in Kohlberg's system can fulfill Jaspers' idea of an "empirically accessible universal" and restore its meaning. Both approaches are linked together by the attempt to start thinking from a normatively designated peak of development instead of leaving the final say on the course of history and the communication of cultures to a relativistic arbitrariness.

4

The Heritage of the
Pre-Confucian Epoch

The breakthrough towards postconventional thinking presupposes not only a high civilization with state organization, literacy, division of labor, and education, but also a degree of maturity in which traditional, established methods of integration no longer suffice. Without the challenge of crises, there will be no demand for new models of organization. Without a highly developed culture, there will be no means to acquire them. In both respects, the pre-Confucian epoch laid the foundations for the axial age enlightenment.

A. POLITICAL AND SOCIAL CHANGES

Chinese philosophy was the answer to the political and social changes which had their roots in the Western Zhou and Chunqiu eras. The background of these processes was the decay of the central power of the Zhou king and the dissolution of the patriarchal feudal system. Along with the decline of the house of Zhou, local power centers emerged. By the middle of the millennium, China had split into a number of principalities led by former vassals. Their territories developed into de facto independent states. This political polycentrism laid the seeds of war, but at the same time it was culturally extraordinarily fertile. It is not by accident that the peak of Chinese philosophy fell into the "warring states period" (481–221 B.C.). War was the most evident expression of the crisis which tore the world asunder and which the philosophers tried to overcome in the free controversies of the "hundred schools," without any tutelage by a strong political center.

The new states found fewer and fewer traditional ways of government. In the sixth century, Zheng and Jin introduced written penal codes. Lu as the first of the states proceeded to collect land tax instead of corvée in 594 B.C. A free peasantry emerged which in turn enlivened commerce and trade. China's entrance into the Iron Age led to a further intensification of agriculture. For the first time it became possible to ascend from the lower layers of society by accumulation of wealth, whereas the Western Zhou only knew social descent according to the rules of primogeniture. Together with former nobles who had dropped out of the declining nobility, the parvenues formed a new middle class. Its members became the clients of private teachers who imparted education needed in the newly emerging administrations, which increasingly relied on "capable men" (*xian, neng*) instead of assigning hereditary ranks.

These developments not only promoted social mobility, but they also changed the view of the world. They challenged the system of propriety (*li*) which had held together the old hierarchical society. For the new times, novel normative concepts had to be found. The search for these concepts constituted the different lines of Chinese philosophy. The philosophers, however, did not only overcome the past, they also took up its legacy in various ways. What is this legacy, and where does the break with tradition, which allows us to speak of a "pre-Confucian epoch," lie in the first place?

As far as the break is concerned, whenever pre-Confucian literature talks about ethical matters, it refers to the established detailed code of conduct known as *li*, the noble rules of propriety. There is no real center of ethics beyond the multiplicity of the *li* and the "virtues" (*de*). Confucius is the first to seek for a "*one*" that "pervades all," and this is what constitutes his fundamental philosophical achievement. He seeks for a basic moral norm. His predecessors, in contrast, select rather unsystematically from the traditional catalogue of virtues. This difference can be understood as the difference between a prephilosophical ethics and, at least in tendency, a philosophical one.

In contrast to the later moral philosophy of the axial age, pre-Confucian ethics is, moreover, decidedly aristocratic. It is the second great achievement of Confucius—at least he has a great part in it—to ethically sublimate originally social concepts (the outstanding example is the *junzi*, the "prince's son," who now becomes the "gentleman" with character), and to enlarge the scope of moral responsibility to man as such.

As far as the heritage is concerned, in the pre-Confucian epoch a series of changes took place which were of far-reaching consequence for the later axial age. I will discuss the most important of these developments in the following sections.

B. THE EARLY CHECK UPON FAMILISM

How the state came into existence has been a moot point for centuries.[1] If we follow the cognitive-developmental theory, however, the phylogenetic transition from Stage 3 to Stage 4 should, among other factors, be understood as a process of historical learning. The background of this process was presumably a crisis of the archaic kinship system under the conditions of continuing population growth. Because of its inherent particularism, the kinship system was unable to solve the structural problems of the early societies. The answer to this was the state as a relatively permanent, suprafamilial, and territorial system of institutionalized social control and management by a specialized hierarchical machinery of government and legal devices.[2] Its nucleus may have been the successful and accepted stabilization of conflict settlement by an impartial judge.[3] It was most probably population pressure which necessitated the discovery of a way out of the particularism of the "closed societies" of the kinship groups.

The centuries before the age of philosophy were characterized by the emergence of political, suprafamilial structures which gradually supplanted the neolithic particularism of clans. From around the end of the third millennium B.C., chiefs of federations of tribes and founders of dynasties appeared whose functions centered around conflict settlement, jurisdiction, and, if necessary, the military enforcement of internal peace. They are said to have promulgated and executed penal laws about which we know little. They built roads, constantly toured their country, divided the territory into geographical regions, and set up administrative roles. In these activities, a *political* milieu was established which for the first time broke the limits of blood ties. A clear document for this is Pan Geng's (one of the most outstanding Shang kings, around 1400 B.C.) announcement that he will "punish by death all those who commit crimes and display the goodness of those who show virtuous behavior, regardless of how distant or near they stand [to me]."[4] Pan Geng demands that his subordinates "fear" him, the "one man,"[5] and accept his authority, since otherwise the whole state would break into parts and "we will all together sink in ruin."[6] Hence, everybody is admonished to "fulfill his business and get his position in order."[7] If the chapter *Pan Geng* from the *Shujing* is authentic, and I assume that basically it is, it indicates that Stage 4 reasoning—orientation towards role and upholding of the system instead of preference for kin—was fully present in the last centuries of the second millennium.

Thus, the establishment of a political order sets free a moral potential, in that it brings into effect a higher and more general interest than that of the archaic kinship groups. This supersession has never been complete, to be sure. The public and general interest which is in principle embodied in the political institution of the ruler gets under the control of a clan or a class again and may, thereby, be distorted past recognition. Moreover, the state overcomes the internal group morality of the kin groups, but as a new system of self-preservation constitutes another group morality against new "aliens"—like, in the case of China, against the Qiang, the preferred human victims of the Shang. The moral philosophy of the axial age has to rediscover the import of the state against the political reality of the time.

C. THE EXPECTATION OF POLITICAL RECIPROCITY

The same applies to the motif of reciprocity. Comparative ethnology has shown the "notoriously archaic attitude"[8] of reciprocity to be the most important mechanism of integration of the early societies before the emergence of the state.[9] Reciprocity secures the bond within the groups and regulates the relationships between them.[10] With the emergence of political rule, it suffers an asymmetrical shift, but is not abolished. Together with his power, the ruler takes upon himself a ritualized responsibility for his subjects, as Tang, the founder of the Shang dynasty. In the later lore, he offers himself as sacrifice to obtain rain in a drought. "If the myriad regions have any fault, may it rest upon my person; but if I have any fault, may it not extend to the myriad regions," Mo Di lets him speak to the God on High.[11] And the Zhou king Wen Wang interprets an earthquake as a personal penalty by Heaven and gives presents to his subordinates in order to redress his guilt.[12]

Accounts like these seem trustworthy. The actions described express the acknowledgment of reciprocity between ruler and ruled. The motif of "giving away the throne" (*rang wang*), a favorite idea of the early Daoists, fits into this context. Yielding the throne pays a demonstrative tribute to the expectation of reciprocity with its equilibrium of giving and taking. "Often, in fact," says Sahlins, referring to the Stone Age in general, "high rank is only secured by o'ergrowing generosity; the material advantage is on the subordinate's side." Cooper has traced out the tracks of archaic potlatch rituals in ceremonies described in the *Yili* and the *Liji*. Felber has shown that the exchange of presents remained a basic form of communication not only socially but also economically even until the Western Zhou era.[13]

This does not mean to say that the emergence of political rule, which little by little superseded the dominance of kinship relations by the institutionalization of suprafamilial fixed administrative roles, has been a process of pure reciprocity involving no violence. Violence does play its role in the history of the state, but it does not explain its stabilization. In order to be *accepted* as a new method of integration and to be more than a transient phenomenon, there must be, as social contract theories have always stressed, at least some sort of a consensus on the advantages political rule is going to provide for a relevant number of people. This is precisely what is reflected in the persisting expectancy of reciprocity. When the political philosophers of the axial age emphatically underline that everybody will be just in case the ruler is just, but that the ruler will be treated by his subjects as an enemy in case he treats them as mud and weed,[14] this is not merely a belated attempt to moderate the government. It is a reminder of the conditions of origin of the state. Fighting against the tendency of rule to make itself independent, the thinkers of the Zhou rediscover the topic of reciprocity in politics and make it the center of their theories.

D. THE INFLUENCE OF LAW AND THE DISCOVERY OF THE MENTAL ATTITUDE IN JURISDICTION

The accomplishment by which political rule under the conditions of population pressure and warlike conflict recommends itself as a promising solution is probably conflict settlement by the ruler as a mediator and a judge.[15] Since early

Chinese accounts on history obviously contain later moralizations, idealizations, and systematizations, they cannot count as undisputable sources to verify such a thesis. Nevertheless, many accounts fit well into the proposed theory. The *Shiji* presents Huang Di as a peacemaker among the fighting clans.[16] He surpressed the rebellion of Chiyou which, according to the *Lü xing*, had "extended to the peaceful people," so that "there were none who were not robbers and bandits."[17] The *Shangjunshu* states that Huang Di was at the same time the initiator of the penal system, which because of rare population had not been necessary under his predecessor Shennong.[18] Obviously Huang Di established and administered a novel legal system. His great-grandson Di Ku, according to the *Shiji*, "held the middle," a reference, I suppose, to his just jurisdiction.[19] At the time of Shun, we read in the *Hanfeizi*, farmers tresspassed on each other's fields, and fishermen disputed about shoals. Shun went there and lived among them until he had adjusted their quarrels.[20] He succeeded Yao instead of Yao's son Danzhu, because "those who had to try a lawsuit did not go to Danzhu, but to Shun."[21] Later, by the same procedure, Qi was chosen to be successor of his father Yu.[22] Again Shun appears in the *Shujing* as promulgator of penal laws which he administered through Gaoyao as "judge."[23] And Yu and Tang, the founders of the Xia and Shang dynasties, according to the *Zuozhuan* enacted legal codes.[24] Nothing of these codes has survived, and they are hardly imaginable without writing. Yet, it is possible that archaeological finds will some day show that the emergence of Chinese writing has to do with law, and not merely with divination.

All this information from Zhou sources seems reliable in that it corresponds very well with the gradual transition from archaic gentile law to monopolized jurisdiction by central authority that seems to stand behind the emergence of the Chinese state. The intimate relationship between political rule and juridical power is also illustrated by etymology. The character *wang*, "king," according to Lin Yun, is the pictograph of an ax as a symbol of the power of sentence.[25] *Pi* has the double meaning of "penalty" and "ruler." The identification of *yi*, "justice," and *yi*, "prestige" or "authority" by the *Shuowen jiezi* becomes intelligible from here, too.[26] The same applies to the identification of "just" and "public" in the word *gong*.

More than anything else, the maintenance of internal peace and external security by the disposition of the two methods of sanction, justice and the military, makes the lasting establishment of the institution of a ruler plausible.[27] This institutionalization of the dual function of ruler-judge is a very relevant phase of moral evolution. Prior to the introduction of public law, the legal system, as comparative ethnography has shown, is characterized by the principles of revenge, redress in accordance with the *lex talionis* (an eye for an eye, a tooth for a tooth), and collective responsibility.[28] The emergence of a suprafamilial power center, equipped with juridical means of sanction, draws a limit to the destabilizing and never ending mechanism of feud and retaliation. It allows a separation of the levels of conflict and jurisdiction respectively. Relieved from the obligation of taking revenge, a more differentiated and, therefore, a more just view of the "other" becomes possible. This liberation from the narrowness of the social milieu, in the long run, means a step towards individualization and an expansion of the range of positive reciprocity. The natural orientation towards the primary group and kinship is for the first time broken in favour of a *political* orientation towards the population of a certain integrated territory. The territorial instead of kinship orientation becomes manifest in the extensive construction of roads that the *Shiji* already attributes to Huang Di,[29] and in the long tours of inspection which all of the early emperors constantly made around their country.[30] Furthermore it is seen in the division of the land into geographic political regions initiated by Shun and completed by Yu.[31] The tendency of these events is the gradual establishment of a public domain transcending the boundaries of blood ties. The most striking document for this is the aforementioned announcement of Pan Geng to his clansmen that he will punish the evildoers by death, but display the goodness of the virtuous, "regardless of how distant or near they stand."

The jurisdiction of the emerging state is not primarily interested in subsequent retaliation, but in enforcement of inner peace. This requires a catalogue of deterrent punishments aiming at the psyche and motivation of every single person, something that does not play a role in gentile law. The damage that has been inflicted becomes less important in comparison with the delinquent's consciousness and the mental element of the offense. This in turn makes it possible to discriminate, regardless of the material consequences, between objective and subjective guilt or innocence. The first explicit record of this idea, which is certainly older, can be found in the *Kang gao.* Zhou Gong, King Wu's younger brother, advises the Prince of Feng on the occasion of his enfeoffment in Kang:

> If somebody has committed a small offense, and if it was not by mishap, but he persists in doing so and is unlawful by his own initiative, then, even if his offense is small, you cannot but kill him. If someone has committed a great offense, but does not persist in doing so and has only done it by mishap and by chance, then you cannot kill him when he entirely confesses his guilt.[32]

In this passage, the mental attitude of the offender decides upon pardon or increase of punishment. In principle, this also means calling into question the system of collective responsibility. The *Da Yu mo* demands that "punishments should not be extended to the descendants."[33] The *Zuozhuan* quotes the *Kang gao* again:

> If the father is unmerciful, the son devoid of reverence, the elder brother unkind, and the younger brother disrespectful, then theses offenses are not transferable.[34]
>
> The guilt of father, son, elder brother, and younger brother is not mutually transferable.[35]

Like the distinction between illegal acts committed with intent, and those which happen out of a momentary weakness, the rejection of the joint liability of relatives, too, implies a conception of individual responsibility and the value of the individual person.[36] It documents the early overcoming of "moral realism" (Piaget)[37] and belongs to the prehistory of the internalization of morals and the concept of "independent action" which later stands in the center of axial age ethics. Thus, although it has been underestimated in favor of divination and ritual, law plays a decisive role for the history of Chinese institutions and thought.

E. THE RELIGION OF HEAVEN

In the middle of the eleventh century B.C., the Zhou people overthrew the dynasty of the Shang. They justified their rebellion by an argument which can count among the most efficacious of Chinese history: Heaven, *Tian*, they argued, probably under the influence of older ideas of the Shang,[38] confers a dynastic mandate for rule (*tian ming*) to the most virtuous. If the dynasty becomes tyrannical, it loses its legitimation. It will be removed by a rebel who acts in Heaven's name and founds a new dynasty. Since "Heaven" is an ethical deity, the mandate theory subordinates political rule to morality. But it does not appeal to moral norms which should be followed for their own sake. The early Zhou rather believed that the good will earn the reward, and the bad will earn the punishment of Heaven. "Whether Heaven will send calamity or happiness," the *Shujing* states, "depends on one's virtue."[39] The physical consequences, hence, recommend one to be virtuous. In later Confucian ethics, however, morality is detached from personal advantage.

Human, and especially political fortune, therefore, depend on a demeanor well pleasing to Heaven. Man is thrown back upon his own acts. Heaven as the power which decides on misery and happiness is directly dirigible by him. The catastrophe of the eighth century, however, which is reflected in many poems of the *Shijing*, lastingly upset this conviction.[40] Earthquakes, famines, and political chaos—the royal domain was overrun by nomads in 771 B.C.—raised the question how Heaven, as an ethical power, could tolerate these calamities which also struck the innocent. The long-term result was the loss of dignity of Heaven, the growing emphasis on its dysteleological, natural side, and a "humanistic" turn in thinking. Finally, the failure of the divine power led man to direct his attention to himself. Religion lost ground to new speculations. It occupies a rather secondary role in the philosophical systems of the axial age, without completely forfeiting its significance. When Confucianism subordinates politics to morality, it overtakes the legacy of the belief in Heaven. The traces of this belief are especially visible in the work of Mengzi. Here, *Tian* represents a moral region beyond the human world from where the earthly rulers are put in their place.

F. THE IDEA OF ECUMENE

That Heaven only rewards virtue does not merely imply the replaceability of a ruling house. The mandate for power is ethnically neutral, too. The Zhou melted their god *Tian* with *Shangdi*, the "God on high" of the Shang, stressing that *Shangdi* himself, too, charged them to overturn the Shang. Thence the idea of an ecumene evolved comprising the whole inhabited world and reaching beyond the states (*guo*). It is called *tianxia*, "(all) under Heaven." Herewith, the germ for ethical universalism was laid which was later to sprout in the egalitarian anthropologies of the axial age. Yet, the prephilosophical age also knows a cosmological, sacral geography in which the world is divided into regions of increasing ontological importance with the royal domain as their center. According to Cassirer and Eliade, cosmological geography indicates a "mythical," archaic mentality.[41] This cosmological geography has survived the axial age—one only has to think of geomancy (*fengshui*)—although it actually had already been overcome by it. For the philosophers, there is no longer any center marked out by sacral meaning. For the "pandaoistic" line of Daoism, to give an example, the *Dao* is present even in the lowest things.[42] And in a time when the old order declines, the Confucians establish a new, unmythical center of the world: the *junzi*, the "gentleman," whose very presence, wherever he might be, is an assurance of the existence of morality and culture.[43] The political fragmentation of China has surely contributed to the demythification of the conception of the world.

G. THE DISCOVERY OF THE EGO

"I the only one" (*yu yi ren*) is the formula by which the king from Shang to Zhou times emphasizes his exceptional rank. The subjectivity of the rulers is delimited by their intermediate position between the ruled and the divine power to which they are responsible for their deeds. When addressing their followers or their subjects, they normally appeal to a religious order or to the sacred tradition of their ancestors. In the late Zhou period, however, many princes, supported above all by the Legalist school, liberate themselves from the commitment to religion and tradition. The axial age philosophers, too, stand out by their pronounced self-awareness. It is only in constant reference to his "self" that the Confucian "gentleman" finds his identity which makes him independent from the judgment of others.

Next to the self-consciousness of the rulers, lyrics, too, paves the way for this development. The *Shijing* contains quite a lot of markedly self-centered poems which despite their dependence on popular forms give individual expression to feelings like grief, indignation, yearning, and lover's anxiety. These can, in some cases, be attributed to particular authors.[44] The character *wo* ("I," "me," in some lines also "we") is the third most frequent of the anthology.

I have given an overview on some early developments which were not necessarily the determining factor of their time, but, from the retrospective of the successful breakthrough towards postconventional thinking, prove to be of evolutionary importance. The pre-Confucian epoch, moreover, gives birth to the crisis which calls forth the philosophical search for a solution, and it lays the foundations for the social mobility without which the intellectual discourse of the axial age could not have taken place. This epoch thus produces the questions which will occupy the later ages, and already points out ways to possible answers.

5

The Background of the Emergence of Chinese Moral Philosophy: The Dissolution of Conventional Morality in the Mirror of the Lunyu

Chinese moral philosophy in general, as well as Confucianism and the program of its founder in particular, cannot be understood unless one is aware of the problems of the epoch to which an answer had to be found. The challenge faced by the Zhou philosophers which stirred up philosophical thought as a systematical questioning in the first place is the crisis of the established conventional morality. The indicators for this crisis are manifold. There is not a single text in which we do not find the motives of chaos (*luan*), decay (*shuai*), worry (*you*), fear (*ju*), and deliverance (*jiu*)—vocables that reflect the mood of the time and make plain the motivation of the authors. The *Dao*, the true way, has been "lost" and "comes to be torn apart."[1] An agitation has seized the world which is felt to be threatening. The flood engulfing everything becomes a typical metaphor.[2] The *Zeitgeist* can assume tragic dimensions.

Restlessness makes itself felt, accompanied by the loss of intimate surroundings. It ultimately finds its expression in the travels of the philosophers. Like their Greek contemporaries, they tour the country, have discussions with their equals, and receive audiences at the courts of the princes. It is Confucius who establishes the tradition of these wandering scholars. Already advanced in age, he goes on a journey of nearly ten years traversing many of the city-states. When burying his mother, he is said to have erected a mound over her grave contrary to the custom of antiquity. His argument is this:

> I am a man of the East, the West, the North, and the South. It won't do that I don't find the grave again.[3]

The unsettled life of the axial age philosophers is in contrast to the embeddedness in tradition and community which dominated in former times. But the loss of rootedness is not always considered a fateful calamity. The Confucians, assured of their being on the side of culture and morality, find themselves in the right place even in a disintegrating world. Disappointed with the conditions of China, Confucius even wants to dwell among barbarian tribes. When asked how he could put up with their "primitiveness," he answers:

What primitiveness could there be where a gentleman lives?[4]

In the failure of established contexts, the "gentleman" himself becomes the center of a new, unmythical and unbounded world. This self-appreciation remains characteristic of early Confucianism.[5] For Mengzi, morality itself becomes the "abode" of the Confucian intellectual, and his "great road" is justice.[6] As his "territory," the *Ruxing* states, he will consider the "accomplishment of just deeds."[7] And Xunzi proudly proclaims:

A man of Yue feels at home in Yue, a man of Chu feels at home in Chu. A gentleman, however, feels at home in elegance.[8]

The common people, too, lose their sedentariness. Migrations of farmers from a bad state to a better one are not uncommon, not to mention the upswing of commerce. Not only men, but also ideas get into motion as never before. Questioning (*wen*) and thinking (*si*) join tradition-oriented learning (*xue*) and exercise (*xi*).[9] The "spirit of doubt" shapes the atmosphere.[10] "Heaven" has lost its unquestioned dignity, and politics forfeits its aura. In Zheng, one of the most advanced city-states, the citizens politicize each day and discuss the merits and faults of the government, to the annoyance of the nobility. They are defended, however, by the enlightened minister and later chancellor Zichan. He wants toleration, since to forbid critical discussion would be tantamount to damming up a stream, which could lead to much greater danger if the dike should burst. When Confucius hears of this, he praises Zichan as "humane" (*ren*).[11] Yet, Zichan is said to have put to death his opponent Deng Xi, a true personification of the dissolution of certainties, who advises people in lawsuits, "turning wrong (*fei*) into right (*shi*) and right into wrong, so that there was no longer any measure for right and wrong, and what was proper (*ke*) and improper changed every day."[12] The politicizing of the citizens and the general dispute about right and wrong continue to be an important theme. According to Confucius, people discuss because the *Dao*, the true way, does not prevail.[13] Everybody, whether "wise" or "stupid," states Xunzi later, has his own view of what is "proper" (*ke*).[14] And Han Fei, the Legalist, criticizes that the whole world speaks about politics and war and owns the corresponding literature, but nobody would lend a willing hand himself.[15] For the Legalists, corruptors of language, rhetoricians, and all kinds of chatterers have developed into veritable parasites of the state. The fact that "designations" (*ming*) no longer are in accordance with "reality" (*shi*) is a standard topos of Zhou literature.

The traditional certainties disintegrate in the struggle of opinions. "Hundred schools present different teachings," deplores Xunzi. Mengzi laments that "private scholars indulge in discussions," which for him is a sign of decay.[16] In the same passage, he coins the ominous notion of "heresy" (*xieshuo*). But before Confucianism, in a Pyrrhic victory over the other schools, becomes the orthodox teaching under the Han and ossifies, China experiences the intellectually most fruitful epoch of her history. With unembarrassed imagination, without awe of tradition and convention, and full of contempt for the "vulgar world" (or the "customs of the time," *shi su*),[17] novel alternatives are brought forward to find the right answer for the urgent problems of the age. To "change the customs" (*yi su*) and to "establish" new ones (*zhi su*) becomes the motto of enlightened politics.[18]

From the outset, the philosophers do not conform to their society. Like their Greek colleagues, they feel superior to the "multitude" (*polloi, zhong*). Their activity is smiled at or criticized as cadging at the expense of others by their contemporaries, to whom they often appear strange.[19] But neither do they let themselves be distracted from their convictions by the opinions of the majority nor by the perspective of failure. *"To do it, although knowing that it is impossible"* is the ironical formula with which an anonymous gatekeeper in *Lunyu* 14.38 caricatures the stubbornness of the early Confucians. And Mo Di defends himself against the hedonist Wumazi, who reproaches his altruistic teaching for being useless, by pointing out his better motivation (*yi*). Even if one should not achieve one's goal, says he, it would still be better to try to extinguish a fire than to stir it up.[20]

In the middle of the first millennium B.C., China faces the task of newly determining man's position in the world without an unreflected and immediate resort to tradition and religion. How does the Chinese intelligentsia think of getting to the root of the agony of the age? The different diagnoses and therapies that are offered constitute the mainstreams of classical philosophy: For the *Legalists*, alone, the change of times represents the normal state of things. Because of the simple fact of population growth, new solutions for new problems have always been required. In the present situation, the solution is penal law and administrative technique. The *Daoists* identify the separation of man from nature and the process of civilization as such as the cause of all evil and advocate a return to the original conditions. The *Confucians* hold a less radical view: neither in going back to the primordial past nor in a fundamentally new perspective will a solution be found, but rather in laying a new foundation for the inherited mores. Next to these three main alternative positions characterized by the mottoes of *method*, *nature*, and *morals*, we find the utilitarianism of the *Mohists*, who advocate following the "good" in the sense of the "useful," regardless of its being of old or new descent.

From the retrospective of later history, Confucianism is the most influential of the many schools which emerged during the Zhou epoch. This is above all due to its role as the transmitter of China's traditional heritage and style of life. It was this affirmative attitude which more than anything else was responsible for the victory of Confucianism over its competitors, whose relationship to Chinese culture was indifferent or iconoclastic. Mo Di regards the expenditure for etiquette and music as a useless waste of resources. In the law-and-order state of the Legalists, culture is a perilous foreign body, and the radical Daoists proclaim its destruction. All of these pointedly anticultural stances, which in all sharpness reflect the crisis of China—they belong within Kohlberg's Stage 4½—explain why the success of the corresponding schools, their popularity in the Zhou era notwithstanding, had to fall short of that of the Confucians in the long run. They were unable, or refused, to make their normative conceptions compatible with the established ethos and commonsense. If Chinese culture could survive as one of the few cultures of antiquity, then in the name of Confucianism.

From the beginning, the conflict with proto-Legalist and proto-Daoist ideas is constitutive for the Confucian position. Nevertheless, it has found its theoretical foundation before its competitors in a representative text: the "Collected Sayings," *Lunyu*, of Confucius.[21] Not only is the *Lunyu* the founding document of the school, which already prefigures all the different directions into which it is to develop afterwards, but it also throws an exemplary light on the crisis of China,[22] the beginning separation of *Sittlichkeit* and *Moralität* which typifies the Chinese axial age as a period of enlightenment.

By *Sittlichkeit* and *Moralität*—"ethical life" and "morality" in the standard English translation—I take over a conceptual distinction from Hegel's critique of Kant. This distinction, however, cannot be applied to China in a simple way, since Hegel himself has explicitly denied this. He places Chinese culture on the level of *Sittlichkeit* and regards it as devoid of any element of *Moralität*. *Sittlichkeit* means to live according to the transmitted customs. It demands "the individual's simple conformity with the duties of the station to which he belongs." Man has "simply to follow the well-known and explicit rules of his own situation."[23] Hegel calls this kind of *Sittlichkeit* "substantial" because it is still embedded in the unquestioned habits of the community and lacks what constitutes *Moralität*: reflection and subjectivity. *Moralität*, for which *Sittlichkeit* as customary rectitude "often seems to be something comparatively inferior," asks for the motives of action, takes its bearing from subjective conscience, and wills that man "himself be in everything he does."[24] The initiator of this separation is Socrates, the "inventor of morals."[25] In China, however, according to Hegel, *Sittlichkeit* does not encounter the rivalry of *Moralität*.

This basic assumption remains characteristic of Weberianism. It can also be found among the sinological contextualists. When Rosemont, to give an example, assures us that ancient China does not know the word "moral" as well as the accompanying vocabulary of autonomy, decision, duty, freedom, ought, etc., but that she well disposes of an "ethics" concerned about right "conduct,"[26] this differentiation reminds one of the one made by Hegel, and it makes sense, to me, only in such context. Rosemont stands up for *Sittlichkeit*, appealing to A. MacIntyre, who pleads against the "disordered" modern culture of enlightenment for the ancient virtue-ethics guided by tradition and role-orientation.[27] Rosemont takes it still one step further. For him, in China, "moral" is not only absent in comparison with "ethical," but also with nonmoral.[28] Yet, Xunzi already explicitly distinguishes between "action for the sake of profit" called *shi*, and "action for the sake of justice" called *xing*.[29] Autonomy, decision, and duty, as we will see, are not at all unfamiliar to the ancient Chinese either.

The contradiction of *Sittlichkeit* and *Moralität*, which in many respects is congruent with that of "conventional" and "postconventional," is, contrary to Hegel and a strategy of de-differentiation like that of Rosemont, quite fruitful for a reconstruction of the ethics of ancient China and classical Confucianism. Confucianism, not unlike Hegel, aims at a synthesis of both. Its whole project is dedicated to the task to find a new fundament for "ethical life" by means of "morality," and that is, by way of a reflected internalization of morals. But both of these bearing pillars of ethics conflict with each other. Their tension-filled relation is the philosophical red thread which runs through the pedagogical scenery of the *Lunyu*, a red thread, however, which lies hidden under the form of the text with its protocol-like sentences unsystematically strung together by later compilers. Moreover, precisely at this demarcation line the *Lunyu* is characterized by a typical undecidedness. It becomes apparent in the relationship of *ren*, "humaneness," and *li*, "rites," "propriety" or higher social "etiquette," which remains peculiarly unsettled. This, to my mind, is an important characteristic of the work and one of the secrets of its success. It was possible to adopt its message with quite different accents—in the name of conventional *Sittlichkeit*, or in the name of *Moralität* which comprises *Sittlichkeit* in terms of an ethics of responsibility.[30] What I am talking about is not simply a defect of the *Lunyu*. The openness of the text for interpretation is a challenge and a chance for the nonregressive appropriation of tradition.

The form of the *Lunyu* also reflects the primarily pedagogical, not philosophical activity of Confucius. It is not least due to a method which is good at giving hints in order to prompt the pupils to think and draw their own conclusions.[31] Thus, the form is part of the content itself. The other side of the story is that elaborate argumentation and giving reasons are missing. Both are introduced into the philosophical literature by Confucius' critic Mo Di. Confucius the pedagogue, furthermore, in contrast to Confucius the philosopher, can give different answers to the same question, taking into account the different temperament and receptivity of his interlocutors.[32] His clients are the sons of the lower nobility, dropouts of their class through the system of primogeniture. In some cases, they are members of the low stratum of society. They form a new middle layer of educated intellectuals called *shi*, after the noble rank from which most of them stem.[33] They often aim at a position at one of the courts, where the demand for employees qualified by ability instead of descent increases. In modern terms, it is the services sector for which Confucius, against the honorarium of dried meat,[34] like other private teachers imparts knowledge. He teaches subjects such as the "six arts"—writing, mathematics, archery, charioteering, music, and propriety—which seventy-two of his three thousand pupils are said to have mastered.³⁵ That the *Lunyu*, despite this concrete pedagogical setting, became a text of philosophical importance, is due to the mission with which Confucius feels entrusted by Heaven: to save the Zhou culture and to change the course of the times:

> With King Wen dead, does not culture rest here [on me]? If Heaven were to let this culture perish, then [I as] someone born so late after King Wen would not have got involved in it.³⁶

> Changju and Jieni worked in the fields together when Confucius passed by and sent Zilu to ask for the ford. Changju said, "Who is that man holding the reins?" Zilu said, "Kong Qiu."—"Kong Qiu of Lu?"—"Yes."—"Then he knows the ford already."
> Thereupon Zilu asked Jieni. Jieni said, "Who are you?"—"Zhongyou."—"The disciple of Kong Qiu of Lu?"—"Yes, I am."—Then Jieni said, "A swelling flood, such is all the world, and by whom could this be changed? Moreover, instead of following a scholar who withdraws from men, wouldn't it be better to follow one who withdraws from the world altogether?" Then he carried on harrowing without stopping again.
> Zilu went and reported their words to Confucius. The master sighed and said, "I cannot associate with birds and beasts! But if I do not become a follower of these³⁷ people—whose follower, then, shall I be? *If the world were in possession of the Dao, I would not have to take part in changing its state.*"³⁸

Even if the last story had been invented,³⁹ it aptly reflects the mood of the early Confucians. The idea of dropping out of society like their two proto-Daoist critics is not at all foreign to them. But they decide in favor of their social responsibility in order to lead the world to better times. Since Confucius' political ambitions were obviously frustrated,⁴⁰ it was only by his teaching that he could work for his aim. This embeds his pedagogics into the program of a comprehensive moralization, in the center of which stands a postconventional reconsideration of virtue. It gives a moral coloring also to the term *shi*. A "scholar" in the Confucian sense is not only skilled in the "six arts" and other practical fields, but he also embodies the unity of morality, intellectuality, and courage, the three basic orientations of a "gentleman."⁴¹

Of all the answers which the ancient Chinese have found to the problems of their time, the answer of the *Lunyu* is the least spectacular, since the norms to which it appeals stem from the established canon of the Zhou nobility. Confucius, accordingly, has often been regarded as a mere representative of traditionalism. Indeed, for him, as well as for the Confucians in general, in contrast to their Legalist and Daoist opponents, but not unlike the Aristotelian tradition in Western ethics,⁴² the indispensability of the transmitted conventions is from the beginning beyond doubt. Man has to accustom himself to the established ethos, and by education must be made familiar with it down to the minute details. "If one does not know the rules of propriety (*li*)," we read in the *Lunyu*, "one is *without any standing (li)*."[43] That one has to adapt oneself to the habits of one's social station and to the requirements and duties of one's role belongs in this context. Confucius proclaims:

> Let the ruler be ruler, the subject be subject, the father be father, the son be son.[44]

"Let the ruler be ruler and the subject be subject" does not mean, however, that the power of the princes must never be interfered with by the subordinates. In the final analysis, it even implies that he who expects to be treated in keeping with his position must also behave accordingly. The same holds true for the relationship of parents and children. Only the first element of the above-listed pairs of concepts is descriptive. The second one represents an idealization that stands against the disorder of the empirical world. The persons named by social terms do not necessarily conform with the ideal meaning of those terms.

This experience is in the background, when in the *Lunyu* two of the respective terms are taken out of the social context from which they stem: the *junzi*, originally the "son of a prince," now becomes the "gentleman" in character, and the *xiaoren*, originally the member of a low stratum, now becomes the morally "mean." The old social and the new moral hierarchy can contradict each other: for Xunzi, political power can fall into the hands of a "mean man" (*xiaoren*).[45] And Mengzi points out the possibility that "a king is not a king," that is, a king in power (referring to King Xuan of Qi) is not necessarily a true king as well. He ascribes the predicates "of high standing" (*gui*) and "of low standing" (*jian*) according to the morality of a person and not, as is usual, according to his social position.[46] The corresponding contradiction of *ming* (name) and *shi* (reality) is a recurrent theme of Zhou literature. To rescue the ideal meaning of terms from their empirical degeneration reflects the dissolution of the ingenuous "ethical life." The Chinese teaching of the "correct usage of terms" (*zheng ming*) is, in this respect, equivalent to Plato's idealism, which was, metaphysically overdrawn though, a reaction on the sense-crisis brought about by the relativism of the Sophists.

Hence, *Lunyu* 12.11 formulates an ideal which contrasts with the reality of the time. Rulers no longer behave as rulers should do, and subjects no longer behave as subjects should do. The rules of proper behavior according to the social position have turned out to be fragile and have lost their binding force. Instead of displaying their stabilizing function, they are transgressed everywhere. The decline of the Western Zhou kingdom with its firmly established hierarchies has drawn the ritual rules of propriety (*li*) into the whirlpool of decay. The *li* are no longer resistant to undue usurpation, and at times they become a tool in the hands of ambitious newcomers. The most presumptuous representative of these parvenus for Confucius is the Ji clan of Lu. The Ji arrogate a ritual ceremonial to themselves which is reserved for the Duke of Lu or the Zhou King.[47] In a time of social mobility, in which the social position is no longer decided by descent, and appreciable careers become possible, "speculation" even spreads among the lower classes.[48] The code of conduct is not only violated, but whoever conforms to it might be doing this for reasons of mere self-interest. "If you, in serving your prince, fully observe the rules of propriety (*li*)," Confucius deplores, "you will be looked upon by others as a flatterer."[49] A sophistic doubt about the genuineness of virtuous behavior is spreading. More promising than to be truly virtuous is to be a good rhetorician. Without eloquence, "it is difficult to escape in this age."[50] "With rhetoric and disputation," a saying goes, "one can even delude spirits and gods."[51] Confucius, therefore, repeatedly polemizes against rhetoric.[52]

Parvenus, flatterers, and rhetoricians reveal the decay of the ethical life and threaten the belief in the value of virtue. Confucius likewise detests calculating mediocrities who denounce all those not conforming with the spirit of the times as eccentric dreamers—the "pharisees" (*xiangyuan*), whom he calls "thieves of virtue."[53] *Mengzi* gives a detailed description of a *xiangyuan*. When his pupil Wan Zhang asks him why Confucius, when in Chen, yearned for his "ardent and impetuous" young pupils of Lu,[54] the following conversation develops:

Mengzi: "If Confucius could not associate with men pursuing the way of the mean, then he at least sought the company of the ardent or the cautious. The ardent rush forward, the cautious at least refrain from certain things.[55] Not that Confucius would not have desired the middle way. But since he could not be sure of finding [such men], he thought of the second best."

Wan Zhang: "May I ask what sort of a man can be styled 'ardent'?"

Mengzi: "People like Qin Zhang, Zeng Xi, and Mu Pi[56] were what Confucius styled 'ardent.' "

Wan Zhang: "Why did he style them 'ardent'?"

Mengzi: "Their ambitions were so high! 'The ancients! The ancients!' they said, but when one examines their deeds, they were not congruent with their words. If Confucius could not get such ardent people either, he wished the company of scholars who did not go in on impure things. These are the cautious, and they are yet one rank lower. Confucius said, 'The only people who do not cause me regret when they pass my door without entering my house are the pharisees. The pharisees are the thieves of virtue!'"

Wan Zhang: "What sort of a man can be styled a 'pharisee'?"

Mengzi: "Those who say about the ardent, 'Why aim so high? In their words they do not care for their deeds, and in their deeds they do not care for their words, and yet they say, 'The ancients! The ancients!' Why do they act so peculiarly and reserved? Living in this world, one should take the side of this world. To behave well is all that is needed!'—those who talk like this and court the world's favor are the pharisees."

Wan Zhang: "When the whole neighborhood calls them 'solid' (*yuan*) people, and they are everywhere regarded as such, why then did Confucius consider them thieves of virtue?"

Mengzi: "If you want to blame them, you find nothing to blame. If you want to criticize them, you find nothing to criticize. They conform to the current fashions, they chime with the filthy world. In their conduct, they appear to be benevolent and faithful, and in their actions they appear to be honest and pure. The multitude is delighted with them, and they think themselves right. One cannot embark on the way of Yao and Shun with such people. This is the reason why they are called 'thieves of virtue.' "[57]

The *xiangyuan*, then, is the personification of conformism. The fact that he can become a negative figure indicates the failure of ethical life. Orderly conduct, concord with one's environment, and the applause of the majority are no longer a guarantee against sanctimoniousness and fraud. What is more, they join with the prejudice against enthusiasts who reject cheap compromise with their contemporaries and whose unrealistic exuberance, much more than the resentful malice of the well adapted, meets with the approval of the Confucians. In the figure of the "pharisee," that which is current and generally accepted is distinguished from that which is really valid and acceptable. The solidity of substantial forms of life can no longer be relied upon—a basic insight of postconventional thinking. It can also be gathered from *Lunyu* 13.24:

Zigong asked, "If everybody in the neighborhood likes one, how would that be?" The Master said, "That is not enough."—"And if everybody in the neighborhood dislikes one?"—"That is not enough either. It is better if the good in the neighborhood like one and the bad dislike one."

It is the same idea which motivates this distrust in "public opinion" and the distrust in the *xiangyuan*: it cannot be taken for granted that the community is guided by good standards like by a good instinct. The "good" does not coincide with the general sentiments. Presumably, this is also the conviction underlying Confucius' pedagogical activity, which presupposes a deficit in what it tries to impart.

A similar reservation can be found in *Lunyu* 12.20:

Zizhang asked, "What must a scholar be like before he can be called perfect?"—The Master said, "What do you mean by perfect?"—Zizhang said, "He must enjoy reputation in his country and in his clan."—The Master said, "That is reputation, but not perfection. Perfection means to be straight in one's nature and to love justice, to examine one's words and observe one's countenance, and to be considerately obliging to others. Such a person will surely achieve perfection in his country and his clan. As to reputation, one can give oneself the air of being humane and do the opposite in one's deeds. If one gets settled in this without misgivings, then one will surely achieve reputation in country and clan."

In this passage, too, the good is separated from the generally accepted. Coveting reputation is rejected not only for the reason that this would contradict modesty, but because of the doubts about the moral reliability of public judgment. What arouses the skepsis about the "pharisee" and the majority's applause is the dissolution of the substantial life rooted in propriety and custom. It is only from this point on that the way Confucian ethics will take explains itself: the way towards the interior as a means of finding the only solid basis for ethical life in the individual's inner self.

Faced with the crisis of conventional morality, the Confucians set about securing the meaning of the established ethos which they regard as indispensable. In the *Lunyu*, this is first of all done by a reflection on each individual term from the ethical canon, normally introduced by "What is . . . " questions. Implicitly, this leads to a differentiation of cardinal and secondary virtues. The final result is the attainment of a new center of morality, of a final "one"—*ren*, humaneness, which, however, stands in a complicated reciprocal relation with *li*, propriety. To follow external rules of behavior is from now on accompanied by an inner moral attitude. The aim of this program is to base the fulfillment of singular obligations—to one's family, the ruler, the friends, the cultural tradition—on moral integrity and adherence to higher moral norms.

Against the background of the social and spiritual crisis outlined above I will now proceed to reconstruct the ethics of the Chinese axial age, above all the ethics of Confucianism. I will try to bring out the inner genetic structure of the ethical discourse, its logical developmental coherence, which not necessarily coincides with the chronological transmission of the various ideas. I will first discuss the two main fields of conventional morality, the family and the state, whose limits will become apparent. Hence the necessity of a higher stage of morality follows, the form of which will be the subject of the next sections. I will then turn to the Confucian concept of the moral person in whose "self" the new morality is rooted, and to the subsequent problem of a reflected return to ethical life in the name of responsibility. Thereafter, I will discuss some proposals for a postconventional grounding of morality. The fact that my analysis is mainly concerned with the Confucian position lies in the reason that the Confucian school has presented by far the most comprehensive and most influential ethical program. Most of its opponents, moreover, did not see themselves as ethicists as such. Nevertheless, the opponents' arguments are important not only for the general appearance of the Chinese axial age, but also for understanding Confucianism. They will, therefore, constantly come up for discussion. Their main ideas will be the topic of a special chapter.

6

The Family and the Virtue of Filial Piety

The shaping of China by the family system and its values has often been described.[1] Even the survival of Chinese culture has been attributed to the influence of *xiao*, filial piety. Xu Fuguan calls *xiao* the "fundamental power on account of which the Chinese nation managed to persist continuously."[2] *Xiao* has also been understood as the paragon of Chinese ethics. Weber calls it "the one basic social duty," "the absolutely primary virtue," which "in case of conflict preceded all other virtues."[3] The classical concept of filial piety, however, is far more complex than a verdict like this, which is motivated by later regressive tendencies, suggests.

Filial piety first of all means a respectful and obliging attitude towards the elders of the family, above all the parents. It comprises the main aspects of *care* and *obedience* and a third important component which is normally not sufficiently accounted for in the literature on China: *moral vigilance*. The child-parent relationship in this connection is in principle a generational one and not bound to a specific age. Care, of course, is due above all to aged parents, and moral vigilance is to be expected primarily of a grown-up son.

A. FILIAL PIETY AS CARE

Most of the explications of the term *xiao* in early Confucianism center around *respectful care*, to which no less than three out of five unfilial forms of behavior mentioned by Mengzi refer.[4] Confucius, too, for whom *xiao* is a quite secondary topic, stresses the concern for the physical and spiritual well-being of the parents:

> While the parents are alive, one should not make a long journey. If one does, then only to a fixed place [known to the parents].[5]

53

One must always be mindful of the parents' years, for one thing to rejoice [at their longevity], for another to be anxious about them.[6]

The careful treatment of the parents must be accompanied by a cheerful disposition and truly felt *respect*:

The difficulty [with filial piety] is presenting a [cheerful] face. If, in case of work to be done, the young take the burden on themselves, and at a meal provide the elders with food, can this already be called filial piety?[7]

What is meant by filial piety nowadays is to be able to care for one's parents. But even horses and dogs can receive care. Where is the difference if one does not show respect?[8]

To maintain a distance to the animals is characteristic of Confucian ethics in contrast to Daoism. This probably reflects the teleological idea that man should behave in accordance with the uniqueness of his being a human as opposed to the rest of nature. The reverse of this is the degradation of the outer nature to the object of human practice.[9]

Unless accompanied by sincere respect, care for parents is of little ethical value. Confucius' disciple Zeng Shen calls it the lowest stage of a filial attitude:

There are three degrees of filial piety: Highest filial piety is to revere one's parents. The second-best is not to bring disgrace to them. The last is to know how to care for them.[10]

Care for the parents also comprises providing a dignified funeral for and making sacrifices to them after their death.

As far as the basic idea is concerned—I do not speak of abuses like those described in the *Ershisi xiao*—filial piety as respectful care can be interpreted as resulting from a natural feeling of responsibility and as an expression of gratitude which makes good the pains the parents took for their child. Such an idea of reciprocity can be found in the *Lunyu* concerning the period of mourning: we give back to the parents the time during which we could not dispense with their arms.[11] *Liji* and *Dadai Liji* go even further: by our respectful service, we only dedicate to the parents what we owe to them—ourselves.[12]

B. FILIAL PIETY AS OBEDIENCE TO PARENTS AND SUPERIORS

The second main aspect of filial piety is obedience, primarily to the father. It is here where the criticism of modern authors who have viewed filial piety as the basic evil of Chinese civilization has set in. For Wu Yu, the radical iconoclast of the May Fourth movement, the Confucian family has also been the school of submissiveness to political power. *Xiao* is the entrance door to *zhong*, loyalty to the ruler, and this makes "the kinship system the basis of despotism."[13] Indeed, in ancient literature, the obedience component of filial piety becomes most apparent in the frequent transition from family- to state-morality. So we read:

> Because a gentleman is filial when serving his parents, he can be loyal to his ruler. Because he shows fraternal deference (*ti*) to the eldest brother, he can be obedient (*shun*) to his superiors.[14]

The *Dadai Liji* attributes a similar statement to Zeng Shen:

> When we can already recognize the loyal subject in somebody, although he does not yet serve a prince, then we speak of a filial son. When we can already recognize the obedient subordinate in somebody, although he does not yet serve a superior, then we speak of a deferential younger brother.[15]

Daxue 9, too, employs the idea of the state as a great image of the family. The locus classicus, however, for the politicization of filial behavior is *Lunyu* 1.2, where Confucius' disciple You Ruo states:

> It rarely happens that someone who as a man shows filial piety and fraternal deference (*ti*) likes to attack his superiors. And it has never happened that someone who does not like to attack his superiors liked to stir up a rebellion. The gentleman devotes his efforts to the basis. Once the basis is established, the *Dao* will grow. Filial piety and fraternal deference, are they not the basis of humaneness?

Ti, "fraternal deference," is more than just a secondary supplement of the intrafamilial principle of authority. Going beyond submission to the will of the eldest brother, *ti* also refers to the respect for all elders or superiors (*zhang*) outside the family.[16] "Indoors *xiao*, outdoors *ti*" is a standard formula of Zhou literature going back to *Lunyu* 1.6. *Ti*, therefore, can be seen as the link between *xiao* and *zhong*, loyalty towards the ruler.

It is not difficult to imagine why Chinese rulers—like Han Wu Di, who looked for filial sons to fill high offices;[17] Yang Jian, the founder of the Sui dynasty, whose "favorite handbook" was the *Xiaojing*[18] and who intended to "rule the empire by means of filial piety";[19] and the Qing emperors with their moral edicts[20]— were so fond of *xiao* and its correlate *ti*. Even the Zhou Legalists, in general the declared enemies of familism, have no objections to a filial piety which does not strengthen the family against the state, but supplies the state with submissive subjects:

> The subject must serve the ruler, the child must serve the father, and the woman must serve the husband. If these three [rules] are observed, the world will be in order, but if they are acted against, the world will be in chaos. If this becomes the immutable way of the

world, neither altered by enlightened kings nor by worthy ministers, then no subordinate will dare to usurp the throne even if the ruler is a good-for-nothing.[21]

The Legalist calculation is clear: the naturalness of the parent-child relationship shall be smoothly transferred to the quite unnatural relationship between ruler and subject. Hence, not only political power will be accepted as naturally given, but even the ordinary mediocrity of a ruler, which the Legalists, in their cynical realism, declare normal. If this calculation miscarries, Han Fei deplores, then it could only be because of the Confucians. They praise the heroes of the past which, as sons, harassed their father or, as rebels, dethroned their lord.

This criticism indicates that the Confucian notion of *xiao*, even in its reading as obedience, is more versatile than is desirable for a pure morality of submission. The Confucians have linked filial behavior to a concept of the moral person which is more than a mere subject of role obligations. Rather than a mere tool in the hands of family and state, the individual is the most fundamental social unit:

> The state is the basis of the world, the family is the basis of the state, and the self is the basis of the family.[22]

Filial obedience, accordingly, must be rooted in self-respect. "I have never heard of anybody," Mengzi says, "who, having lost his self, was able to serve his parents."[23] The inner attitude addressed in sentences like this not only renders *xiao* a specifically *moral* obligation. It also sets a limit to obedience.

C. THE LIMITS OF OBEDIENCE: FILIAL PIETY AS MORAL VIGILANCE

This leads us to the third and often overlooked main aspect of filial piety: moral vigilance expected from a son when fulfilling the wishes and instructions of his parents.[24] This task, however, has not always come easy to the Confucians. To urge one another by remonstrance to be good, Mengzi says, is "the way of friends," but it estranges father and children from each other. In antiquity, therefore, people exchanged their sons for fosterage.[25] The Confucian ideal doubtless is the harmonious family where the young can fulfill their duties without misgivings. In such a family, the old would not give grounds for complaint in the first place by adhering to the virtues destined for them—*ci*, kindness, the counterpart of *xiao* on the side of the parents, and *you*, friendship, the counterpart of *ti* on the side of the eldest brother.

Family harmony based on moral foundations, however, was an ideal far from reality. The standard case was rather that the authority which claimed obedience was not morally justified. According to the testimony of the *Zhuangzi*, to consent to everything the parents say or do was even in the popular opinion of the "vulgar world" regarded as unworthy and as flattery.[26] One had to take into consideration, then, that the parents, like all the other authorities, did not meet the moral requirements themselves. The problem is drastically formulated by Confucius' critic Mo Di:

> Whoever wishes to achieve something in the world cannot do without norms (*fa*) and standards (*yí*). . . .
> What should be the norm for government?
> What about everybody taking his parents as a norm? There are many parents in the world, but only few of them are humane. If everybody would take his parents as a norm, this would mean taking inhumanity as a norm.
> What about everybody taking his teacher as a norm? There are many teachers in the world, but only few of them are humane. If everybody would take his teacher as a norm, this would mean taking inhumanity as a norm.
> What about everybody taking his ruler as a norm? There are many rulers in the world, but only few of them are humane. If everybody would take his ruler as a norm, this would mean taking inhumanity as a norm.
> Neither the parents, nor the teacher, nor the ruler, therefore, can be taken as a norm for government. What, then, can be taken as a norm for government? Nothing is better than to make Heaven the norm.[27]

The Confucians, too, had to face these problems, and the case of the immoral parents occupied their mind hardly less than that of the immoral ruler. They are far from advocating unconditional obedience. To reduce moral reservation to nothing reflects a regressive tendency within Neo-Confucianism. In order to elucidate the contrast, here is one of the most astonishing relevant statements documented by Zhu Xi:

> Li Tong said, "The fact that Shun could help Gusuo (his criminal father) to achieve delight[28] was simply because he fulfilled the way of serving the parents to the utmost, discharged the duties of a son,[29] and shut his eyes to the wrongdoings of the parents."
> Luo Zhongsu (Luo Congyan) once remarked to this, "It was simply because *there are no parents in the world who are not right.*"[30]
> When Liaoweng (Chen Guan) heard this, he found it excellent and said, "Only then the roles of father and son in the world were fixed.[31] Whenever subordinates have murdered their rulers and sons have murdered their fathers, this has always started with their finding fault with them."[32]

Luo Congyan and Chen Guan are students of the second generation of Cheng Yi's (1033–1107) school, Luo is the teacher of Li Tong who in turn is the teacher of Zhu Xi (1130–1200). The three philosophers quoted here thus are important connecting links between two of the main figures of Neo-Confucianism. It is all the more remarkable that the father-child relationship is reduced to a schematic subordination of the younger, and the potential of moral conflict is without hesitation done away with. The exculpation of the criminal father, who had tried to kill Shun,[33] leads to the imputation that the child ready for criticism is a possible murderer. A commentator of Zhu Xi's *Xiaoxue* named Zhen adds:

> To blame oneself and not to find fault with one's parents, this is the heart of a humane person and a filial child. To harbor resentment against one's parents and not to look into oneself, this is the heart of a rebellious subject and a criminal child.[34]

This perverts the old Confucian idea that "the gentleman blames himself"[35] to the justification of wrong on the side of the parents. A slightly more moderate position is taken by Sima Guang (1019–86):

> Regardless how great or small the matter, no member of a younger generation may act independently. By all means one has to consult the head of the family. Whenever a son receives an order of the parents, he must write it down, carry it with him, look at it regularly and put it into practice quickly. When the order is carried out, he has to report it to the parents. In case the execution of the order should not be admissible, then he should with a friendly countenance and in a gentle voice[36] entirely explain what is right or wrong, advantageous or disadvantageous with that order. Then he has to wait for the approval of the parents, and after that the order can be changed. But if they disagree, he should put up with following the order, provided that it does not do great harm to the matter in question. If, however, regarding the order of the parents as wrong, he directly puts into practice his own will, then he will be considered to be a disobedient son, even if everything he maintains is right.[37]

In this passage, at least the possibility is taken into account that one has to contradict the parents in the name of morality. Yet, this concession remains without consequences if the parents do not come round.

It would be much too undifferentiated to rate these Neo-Confucian statements as a simple retrogression behind the early philosophers.[38] The words of the ancients are for the most part anything but clear, often timid, and always subject to interpretation. Generally speaking, they are characterized by the conciliatory attitude which shapes the Confucian relationship of role and morality as such and which is not easily translated into practice. We can distinguish, nevertheless, two lines. A short statement of Confucius in *Lunyu* 4.18 can count as the starting point of the controversy. The text is equivocal and allows for two main variants of translation:

(Variant A): In serving your parents, you may remonstrate with them gently.[39] If you see that they do not follow your will, then keep on being respectful, and do not resist (*wei*). Even if they harass you (*lao*) you must not resent them.

In this translation, the mood of the parents is a more deciding criterion than the concern of the child. The demand on the child simply neglects the cause for criticism, the moral dubiety of the parents' behavior. The moral objection falls flat in the face of the unequal distribution of roles. But *Lunyu* 4.18 can be interpreted differently:

(Variant B): In serving your parents, you may remonstrate with them when there is an opportunity. If you see that they do not follow your will, then keep on being respectful, but do not abandon (*wei*) your purpose. Keep on exerting yourself for them (*lao*), and do not resent them.

In this reversal of the accents of variant A, which is possible because of the unclear reference of the verbs *wei* and *lao*, more significance is attached to the admonition of the parents by the child. The child's moral firmness in the conflict is now just as important as a tactful tone and a sympathetic understanding which reflect its subordinate position in the family and probably increase the chances of the moral engagement. In this way, both the imperative of the role and that of morals would be abided by, in the typical endeavor of the Confucians to make the two normative systems compatible with each other as far as possible. Although one might be skeptical about the possible success, it remains important that the moral imperative is not revoked in favor of the final priority of role.

The two versions of interpretation—still other variants are conceivable[40]—diverge considerably under the aspect of moral evolution: the first one is conventional and restrictive, the second one is postconventional in tendency. Yet, both readings can be reconciled to a certain degree. In view of the restrictions still imposed on the child in the "postconventional" reading, it has not yet reached what Rosenzweig calls the "established unity of defiance" protecting the self from "suffocating in its misfortune."[41] In the "conventional" reading, again, not every moral reservation is lost. For all fraying on its patient obedience, the child still harbors the ulterior motive that the parents might be moved by its willingness to suffer. The paradigm case for such a salutary effect is Shun:

He daily cried with tears to compassionate Heaven and his parents, taking to himself all guilt and charging himself with the parents' wickedness. Reverently he appeared before his father Gusuo, trembling with awe, until Gusuo came round. Highest sincerity even moves the Gods. . . .[42]

The motif of the son "crying with tears" reappears in the *Liji*:

According to the rules of propriety for a minister, he should not re-monstrate with his ruler openly. If he has three times remonstrated and is still not listened to, he should quit service. In the service of his parents by a son, if he has three times remonstrated and is still not listened to, he should follow [the parents] crying with tears.[43]

It is uncertain whether emotional manifestations like these, except for the case of Shun, made any impression. It is not less questionable if not loud lament, but silent humility is to evoke the parents' remorse. An example of this is Confucius' student Min Ziqian. His stepmother discriminated against him in favor of her own sons. In winter she provided him with such thin clothes that one day when driving the chariot he got his hands frostbitten and let go the reins. When his shocked father wanted to dismiss his wife, Min Ziqian put in a good word for her. Accord-ing to the *Ershisi xiao*, the behavior of her stepson touched her heart, and she mended her ways.[44] Shun's and Min Ziqian's filial piety may be moving, but an ethic which suppresses anger in the face of injustice and instead relies on self-accusation or passive readiness to suffer hardly imparts the competence for postconventional action. Those Confucians, it seems, who praised these attitudes as exemplary, evaded a moral decision in favor of a moral exaction.

How limited the possibilities of the child as a moral corrective of the parents were also becomes apparent from a passage of the *Liji* which resembles *Lunyu* 4.18:[45]

If the parents have a fault, one should with bated breath, bland aspect, and gentle voice admonish them. If the admonition does not take effect, one should be the more respectful and filial. When the parents are pleased, one should repeat the admonition. If the parents are displeased, rather than allow them to make themselves guilty of an offense against neighbors and fellow citizens, one should admonish them in a well thought-out manner. If the parents get angry then and are displeased, and beat one till the blood flows, one should not dare to complain and be resentful, but be still respectful and filial.[46]

Again the vacillation between role and morality. Under the unequal conditions given by the authority structures within the family and not suspended for a mo-ment, the moral engagement of the child becomes a risky performance. To come in for a thrashing, however, rather belongs to the normal expectations of the child.[47]

In view of these restrictions, "moral vigilance" does not seem to have been worth much in practice. Yet another limitation has to be mentioned: *Lunyu* 13.18 finds it laudable that father and son conceal each other's wrongdoings from the government authorities.[48] In public, too, the mistakes of the parents, in contrast to those of the ruler, should be hidden:

In serving one's parents, one should, if the occasion arises, conceal their faults and not stand up to them. . . . In serving one's ruler, one should, if the occasion arises, stand up to him and not conceal his faults. . . . In serving one's teacher, one should, if the occasion arises, neither stand up to him, nor conceal his faults.[49]

What is left over then, of a moral consciousness which well grants a special importance, but not an exceptional status to the family? As pointed out in connection with *Lunyu* 4.18, it was possible to develop Confucianism into another direction than that of the ideologists of Chinese conventional mores. Not to speak of the concept of the "great fellow" who, if necessary, "makes his way alone,"[50] there are other utterances on the problems of family ethics which proclaim more than imposed harmony. Compared with the constrained half-heartedness of the quoted passages, where just a small path is paved for morality into the family, they are like a fresh breeze relieving one from stuffy air. We read with satisfaction that Mengzi contradicts a certain Master Gao from Lu who disparagingly calls the poem *Xiao pan* the work of a "mean man." According to a tradition, in this poem Yijiu, the son of the tyrannic King You (reigned from 781–71 B.C.), complains about his father. Contrary to the usual tendency of Confucian literature to wag an admonishing finger as soon as a child might be "resentful" (*yuan*) of a parent,[51] Mengzi here defends the displeasure of the presumable author:

> Not to resent the parents in case of a major wrong would only increase the distance to them.[52]

Yijiu, the legitimate heir apparent, had to yield to the son of the cunning lover of his father. After the downfall of the father, however, he was appointed king by the feudal princes. He numbers among the positive figures of the past who, given the Confucian esteem for antiquity, often became models to be emulated. The fact that most of them had stood against the current or had even been rebels has time and again put a radical twist on Confucian ethics. Han Fei has recognized this with the flair of the law-and-order ideologist.[53] Mengzi takes pains to reconcile the historical reports with the topical political and moral convictions of the school. His student Xianqiu Meng confronts him with one of the many legends about Shun:

> A saying goes: *A scholar of abundant virtue may neither be treated as a subject by his prince nor be treated as a son by his father.* When Shun was facing south (was on the throne), Yao, at the head of the feudal princes, faced north to pay homage to him, and so did his father Gusuo. When Shun saw Gusuo, he knit his brow. Confucius commented, "At that moment, the empire was in critical condition!" I do not know whether this was really so.[54]

How could Yao as a ruler pay homage to his successor Shun? And how could Gusou as a father be the subject of his son? The true topic of these questions is not history, but the superiority of virtue over authority, and the answer of the quoted motto is: because outstanding morality suspends the obligations of the role. Since Xianqiu Meng obviously identifies himself with this radical motto, he is irritated by the answer put into Confucius' mouth. Mengzi himself tries to dismiss the story as gossip. Yao, he says, was never Shun's subject, and Shun could have done no greater honor to his father than to become ruler. If we consider, however, the separation of the Heavenly realm of virtue from the profane human realm of political ranks which Mengzi himself proclaims elsewhere,[55] this explanation is not satisfying. Mengzi rejects conclusions which can be drawn from his own teaching.

Despite Mengzi's objection, the sentence that "a scholar of abundant virtue may neither be treated as a subject by his prince nor be treated as a son by his father" shows that there must have been a free and outright discussion on family and state among the early Confucians, and that they not only knew meticulous considerateness and appeasement. Shun is now no longer the Shun we know from other passages. The model of submissive filial piety has turned into the hero of the scholars (*shi*), the "freely suspended" intellectuals falling out of all preconceived roles.

To appreciate the importance of some of the ethical and political conceptions circulating in the Confucian school, a look into the writings of their opponents is often helpful. The explosiveness of Xianqiu Meng's motto, too, becomes more apparent from the *Hanfeizi* than from the *Mengzi* itself:

> The old records say: When Shun saw his father Gusuo, he changed his aspect. Confucius remarked, "What a critical moment! The world was on the verge of disaster! Anyone who possessed the *Dao* could definitely not be treated as a son by his father or as a subject by his ruler!"
>
> I comment on this: Confucius has not understood the way of filial piety, fraternal deference, loyalty and obedience in the first place. If he were right, would not this mean that anyone who possesses the *Dao* would not be the subject of his ruler[56] when in office, and would not be the son of his father when at home? The reason why a father wishes to have a worthy son is that the son can make a poor family rich and make the father's bitter life pleasant. The reason why a ruler wishes to have worthy subjects is that they can put a chaotic state into order and make a mean ruler honored. Now supposing there is a worthy son and he is not there for his father, then the father in managing the family will get into trouble. And if there is a worthy subject who is not there for his ruler, then the ruler's position on the throne will be endangered. It can be outright regarded as a damage, then, if a father has a worthy son and a ruler has a worthy subject. Which benefit would they have by them? And what would it mean, then, that a loyal subject does not endanger his ruler, and a filial son does not neglect his parents?

Now, Shun, by his worthiness, took his ruler's state, and Tang
and Wu (the rebels who founded the dynasties Shang and Zhou),
because of their sense of justice, banished and murdered their rulers. They all endangered their rulers by their worthiness, and yet the
world honors them as worthy. The glorious heroes of antiquity at the
court did not serve their rulers as subjects, and at home did not care
about their clan. . . . This is the way to put the age into chaos and cut
off posterity. Therefore, to honor Yao, Shun, Tang, and Wu as worthy
and to approve of the glorious heroes is a method to throw the world
into chaos.[57]

The *Hanfeizi* attributes the statement about the moral person who may "not
be treated as a son by his father and as a subject by his ruler" to Confucius
himself. This in turn allows to play off the Confucian virtues against the Confucian picture of history and the consequences resulting from it. If one praises the
giants of the past, one also approves of the transgression of the limits defined by
the social station. The Legalist polemic discloses the latent potential of Confucian
ethics. Yet, it has to be stressed again that the final goal of the Confucians is not
the playing off of morality against the role, but the harmonizing of both.

This fundamental motif is again discernible in the following quotations from
the *Zi dao* (*The Way of the Son*), chapter 29 of the *Xunzi*. The *Zi dao* is a small
collection of short texts which as far as their content is concerned rate among the
most important of classical Confucianism, although they have seldom attracted
proper attention.[58] I first quote the second passage:

Duke Ai of Lu asked Confucius, "Is it filial if a son follows the order
of the father, and is it loyal if a subject follows the order of the
ruler?" Three times he asked, but Confucius did not answer.

Confucius, after having tripped out (the gait before a superior),
reported this to his student Zigong . . . and asked him about his opinion. Zigong said, "If a son follows the order of the father, this is
already filial piety. And if a subject follows the order of the ruler, this
is already loyalty. But what is the answer of my teacher?"

Confucius said, "What a mean man you are! You do not know
that in antiquity, if there were four frank ministers in a state with ten
thousand war-chariots, its territory was never diminished. If there
were three frank ministers in a state with a thousand war-chariots,
that state was never endangered. And if there were two frank subordinates in a clan with one hundred war-chariots, its ancestral temple
was never destroyed. If a father has a frank son, he will not do
anything that contradicts propriety. If a scholar has a frank friend, he
will not do anything unjust. *How, then, could a son be filial if he
follows the order of the father? And how could a subject be loyal if*

he follows the order of the ruler? One can only speak of filial piety and loyalty after one has examined the reasons why they follow the order."[59]

Xiaojing 15 contains a somewhat shorter version of the same conversation which ends with the proclamation:

Therefore, faced with an injustice, a son cannot but quarrel with his father, and a subordinate cannot but quarrel with his ruler. *Faced with an injustice, one has to take up the quarrel.* How can it count for filial if one . . . simply follows the order of the father!

More important than the question of authorship—we can be certain that Confucius' name, like in so many other passages, is only used to give authoritative weight to the words—is the content of these straightforward commentaries on obedience, which were found so attractive that, with a further version in the *Kongzi jiayu*,[60] they were handed down thrice. Uncompromisingly and unequivocally, the duty of obedience is subordinated to higher criteria. These criteria are not exclusively postconventional in kind. The survival of the state and the continuity of the family, as well as the interest in a good reputation, represent only conventional imperatives. The mere observance of the rules of propriety is not necessarily an expression of morality either. In the criterion of "justice" (*yi*), alone, the duty of obedience is fully submitted to the moral vigilance which is an indispensable constituent of filial piety. In the *Xiaojing*, which demands a quarrel with father and ruler in case of injustice, this moral accent becomes all the more plain than in the *Xunzi*. The *Xunzi*, however, adds an essential conclusion missing from the *Xiaojing*: filial piety becomes a truly moral virtue only if the *reasons* of the actor are moral themselves. Whence follows that a mere performance of roles, without considering the underlying inner attitude, can be morally indifferent or even wrong.

Hence, conventional role-morality and a postconventional reflection which examines and, if the case may be, does not acknowledge the motives for conventional action, are distinguished from each other. The same applies to the opening passage of the *Zi dao*:

To practice filial piety at home and respect the elders in public, this is the *minor conduct* of man. To be compliant towards one's superiors and exert one's energies towards one's subordinates, this is the *medium conduct* of man. *To follow the Dao and not the ruler, to follow justice and not the father, this is the great conduct of man.* When [in doing so] the will of man rests in propriety and his words are uttered only in accordance with the kind [of the given case], then the way of a Confucian is already complete. And even an ideal ruler like Shun would not be able to add anything.

There are *three conditions under which a filial son does not follow an order:* If obedience brings his parents into danger, but disobedience means security for them, then it is honest if the filial son does not follow the order. If obedience means disgrace to the parents, but disobedience means honor, then it is just (*yi*) if a filial son does not follow the order. If obedience means *animality*, but disobedience means embellishment, then it is an expression of respect (*jing*) if the filial son does not follow the order.

Therefore, not to follow an order which may be followed would mean not to behave like a son. But to follow an order which may not be followed would mean to be dishonest. To get clear insight into the *principle of when to follow and when not to follow*, and then to translate this insight into action with courtesy, respect, loyalty, trustworthiness, uprightness, and guilelessness, this can be called *great filial piety*. This is meant when it is said in the ancient records: *Follow the Dao and not the ruler, follow justice and not the father.*

In hardship and exhaustion to manage not to lose one's respect, in calamities and disaster to manage not to lose one's [sense of] justice, and, when one is not loved, but hated because of disobedience, not to lose one's own love—this is only possible for a man who has humaneness (*ren*). This is meant when it is said in the Songs that "a filial child is not wanting in anything."[61]

This passage is a highlight of ethical reflection in Zhou Confucianism. It distinguishes several stages of morally relevant action. Conventional role observance, the "minor conduct" (*xiao xing*) in the family, and the "medium conduct" (*zhong xing*) in an office, only represents the two lowest stages (Stages 3 and 4 in Kohlberg's system). The classifications at the same time refer to the chronology of ontogenesis and the normative evaluation of the stages. The highest stage of "great conduct" (*da xing*) transcends the limits of convention. For one closed moment, the actor now sojourns in pure commitment to the *Dao* and justice (*yi*), and, after that, *reflectedly returns* to ethical life. Now he knows about the moral relativity of any conformity with role expectations and about the necessity to scrutinize the duties he is obliged to perform. When doing this, he orients himself by principles (*yi*). Three of these principles are mentioned. Two of them, the security and the reputation of the family, stay within the limits of group morality and are conventional in kind. The last one, however, is abstractly moral—it evaluates whether an order is not beneath human dignity as such. It is only from this detached point of view that the meaning of conventional role observance is secured. Thence, not a single virtue has to be struck off the conventional codex, nor have the respective social bodies of family and state to be called into question. But now, "courtesy, respect, loyalty, trustworthiness, uprightness, and guilelessness" are no longer the same virtues they were before—they are accompanied by an autonomous consciousness that scrutinizes the motives for any action and, if necessary, makes a moral reserve.

To summarize, the attitude of early Confucianism to family morality, the most characteristic content of Kohlberg's Stage 3, is as follows: The family, not only as a natural community, but also as that social body which has to secure education, nutrition, and survival of its members largely by itself, is a place of special ethical commitment. The family ethos imposes upon the young the duty of respectfully serving the elders, above all the parents. The basic virtue *xiao* demands care and obedience. Nevertheless, the family is not a realm beyond higher moral norms. It is not only that the elders are expected to be benevolent and kind towards the younger. As the case may be, filial piety itself demands to remonstrate with the parents in the name of morality, or to refuse obedience.

The virtues practiced in the family shall also prepare for the role of the loyal citizen. Yet, as we will see, the relationship of family and state is also marked by a deep aporetic conflict. Moreover, commitment to the family has to be integrated with commitment to the general public. In several respects, then, there is a contradiction running through family solidarity. Moral development must not neglect it, but has to proceed beyond.

7

The State

N ext to the family, the state is the second of the great reference systems of
conventional morality. The Confucian attitude towards both is positive, in
contrast to the radical line of Daoism which rejects the state, and the Legalists
who want to subjugate the family under political power. Family and state, however, also conflict with one another in Confucian philosophy. Far more bluntly
than the family, the state is, moreover, submitted to the dictate of morals. Its
legitimation depends on the achievement of social and ethical purposes. This
has serious consequences for practice.

A. THE THEORY: THE LEGITIMATION OF THE STATE

Mengzi's sentence, directed against Yang Zhu, "to know neither ruler nor father
is the state of beasts,"[1] can claim the consent of all Confucians. They have given
different reasons for the necessity of the state. According to Mengzi, without
the establishment of a political order by the heroes of the past, the civilized
human world could never have emerged amidst a hostile natural surrounding.
The state, a product of the "anxiety" of sages and hence from the beginning
conceived as a monarchy, continues to be indispensable. It is the guarantor of
order, because the mass of the people, this is the common conviction of all
Confucians, does not by itself find the right course. "The people can be made to
follow something, but not to understand it," says Confucius. Mengzi agrees on
this point.[2] For him, the division of mental and physical labor, hence the separation of society into those who govern and those who are governed, is the "general norm in the world."[3]

In his legitimation of the state, Mengzi refers to the desolation of outer
nature. For his antipode Xunzi, the state is called into action not only because

the external natural world has to be brought under control, but also because of the badness of man's inner nature. In the state of nature, men can exist neither with nor without each other. Xunzi writes:

> Without a ruler to control the subjects, and without superiors to control the subordinates, the world would be harmed because everybody would give reign to his desires. Men's desires and dislikes are directed towards the same things. But desires are many, and things are few. Because of the scarcity of things, there will inevitably be strife. The products of a hundred crafts are necessary to support a single individual. Even an able person could never be skilled in all of them together. One man, moreover, cannot occupy several offices at once.
>
> If men live isolated from and do not serve one another, they will live in poverty. But if they live in societies without distinctions (*fen*), there will be strife. To live in poverty is a disaster, and strife is a calamity. In order to rescue people from disaster and eliminate calamity, nothing is better than to make plain the distinctions and let people form a society.[4]

How is it that cattle and horses are used by man, though his strength and his pace are not equal to theirs? I say: Men are able to form societies, but those are not. Why are men able to form societies? I say: because of the distinction of roles (*fen*). And how is it that the distinction of roles can work? I say: by justice (*yi*). Therefore, if the distinctions are organized on the basis of justice, then there will be harmony. Harmony means unity, unity means great power, great power means strength, and strength means being able to win over nature. Hence it became possible for men to live in houses. To arrange works according to the four seasons, to control the myriad things, and to be equally profitable to the whole world[5]—there is no other reason for this than distinctions and justice.

Therefore, human life is impossible without social organization. Social organization without distinction of roles, however, would lead to strife. Strife leads to chaos, chaos to disintegration, and disintegration to weakness. In a state of weakness, one cannot win over nature.[6]

Left to their own devices, this is the message of these lines, men would be hopelessly inferior to nature. But if they unite with their fellows, they can profit from one another, because they have different abilities which complement each other. At the same time, however, because of the insatiability of human desires and the scarcity of the goods at hand, strife is inevitable and, together with it, hardship again. This initial constellation is the same as in Protagoras, in the Anonymos Iamblichi, and later in Hobbes.[7] The solution, too, is similar: It consists in the well-planned establishment of a sociopolitical organization which is not natural, but artificial (*wei*). For Xunzi, it is characterized by a strict hierarchy and a rigid division of roles (*fen*) which puts everybody in his place. A ruler is an "expert in social organization" (*shan qun*) and the "cardinal point from where the division of roles is administered."[8]

Thus, Xunzi has not only legitimated the existence of the state, but at the same time that of a stratified society. This society is dominated by the principle of male seniority, but it shall also provide chances for promotion for all who are really capable. The legitimation has a crucial reverse side: The fact that the state, together with the strictly organized social differentiation, came into existence in order to put an end to the misery of all, gives it a function for the fulfillment of which it can be made accountable. It is no end in itself. Rulers "are there for the people," not the other way round.[9] They administer power upon trust.

For Xunzi, whether the state meets its task of safeguarding a peaceful and carefree living together of its citizens depends on the *justice* of the social order. Order is just if, in keeping with the initial consideration why the state came into existence, the necessary inequality of men is to the advantage of all, instead of merely being utilized for the profit of the better-off and the powerful. This social-utilitarian postulate means that any detachment of rule from the interests of the commonwealth not only deserves moral condemnation, but undermines its own raison d'être: to increase the benefit of all in orderly ways. This basic idea of Xunzi's political philosophy is also expressed by the *Lüshi chunqiu* in a long passage clearly indebted to the Confucian:

> Man's nature is such that his nails and teeth do not suffice for his self-defense, his skin does not suffice to protect him from cold and heat, his sinews and bones do not suffice to pursue his benefit and to escape from harm, and his courage does not suffice to oppose wildness and to put a stop to aggressiveness.[10] If he, nevertheless, disposes of the myriad things, tames wild animals and brings cowed vermin under his control, and if cold and heat, drought and wetness cannot harm him, is not this simply because he takes corresponding precautions and forms societies? The fact that societies can be formed is for the reason that one can *mutually benefit* from it. And the fact that benefit results from society is due to the establishment of the way of the ruler. . . .
>
> In high antiquity, there was no ruler. Men lived in hordes, they knew their fathers, but not their mothers.[11] There were neither the distinctions of kinship between elder and younger brother, husband and wife and the sexes, nor the ways of superiors and subordinates, old and young. One did neither know the etiquette of tact and courtesy, and the convenience of clothes, shoes, belts, houses, cattle breeding, and stockpiling, nor the devices of tools, mechanisms, ships,

carts, inner and outer city walls, and natural bulwarks. This was the evil of not having rulers. Therefore, the just relationship between ruler and subject has to be made clear.

Since remote antiquity, a great number of states has perished. The reason that the way of the ruler has nevertheless not been abandoned is that it means an advantage to the world. Therefore, the false rulers should be eliminated (!), and those who [truly] walk the way of a ruler should be brought into power. But what is the way of a ruler like? It is beneficial, and the benefit of all beings becomes manifest.

(After listing a number of peoples without rulers the text continues:) These are the regions without rulers. Their people live like beasts, the young command the elder, and the elder fear the strong. He who uses his physical strength is regarded as worthy, and the brutal and proud are honored. Day and night they do violence to each other without interruption, wiping out their race.

The sages *(shengren)* made profound observations of this misery. Therefore, they made long considerations for the world and found that nothing would be better than to establish a Son of Heaven. They made long considerations for the single states and found that nothing would be better than to establish princes. That the princes were established was not in order to flatter the princes, and the establishment of the Son of Heaven was not in order to flatter the Son of Heaven. And the installment of officials and superiors was not in order to flatter them. When virtue declined, however, and the world sank into chaos, the Son of Heaven used the empire to his own advantage, the princes used the states to their own advantage, and officials and superiors used their posts to their own advantage. This is the reason why states flourish and perish, and chaos and catastrophes regularly appear. Therefore, loyal subjects and honest scholars should, internally, criticize *(jian)* the mistakes of their rulers, but, outwardly, [be willing] to die for the just duty of a subject.[12]

Man as a deficient being compared with the biological equipment of the animals, his ability to nevertheless dispose of the "myriad things" by means of social cooperation, the coming to an end of the natural strife by the deliberation of the sages and the establishment of the state, the obligation of politics towards public welfare—these are typical tenets of Xunzi's teaching. The core of his political theory, too, is brought out clearly: The "just" subordination of the subjects to the ruler is bound to a utilitarian understanding of the tasks of the state.

Xunzi, then, advocates an order in which the distribution of roles with its imposed inequalities does not lose its meaning as the "original benefit *(ben li)* for the world."[13] This is presumably based on the idea that the social order must be acceptable to those who are affected, which is hardly possible without a material incentive, given human nature with its desires. "The early kings and the sages," Xunzi states against Mo Di's philosophy of thrift, "knew that a ruler can never unite the people if he does not enhance and embellish their living, and that he can never rule the subjects if he does not make them rich and is beneficial to them."[14] This is more than a tactical advice to the calculating self-interest of those in power. It is the adoption of the archaic motif of *reciprocity*, which has not become obsolete after the emergence of rulership, but has stayed alive and is rediscovered in the axial age, above all in the form of the incorporation of the *Golden Rule* into political theory.[15]

In individual cases, however, it often does not stand to reason that the alleged participation in public benefit makes up for a low status. This holds true for example for the subordination of women under men, or for Xunzi's ingenuous remark that the celebrated social division of labor "brings ease and pleasure to the one and toil and labor to the other."[16] Nevertheless, Xunzi's central idea remains important and even topical today: the idea that social inequality on the one hand, and the equality of all in terms of the safeguarding of their living and their equal deliverance from the fight for the resources on the other are coupled with each other.[17] Xunzi writes:

When a humane person is in power, farmers will labor with all their energy to get the utmost from their fields, merchants will with their observant mind do everything for their business, artisans will with all their skill throw themselves into the production of utensils, and all stations from the low nobility via the grand officers up to the feudal lords will without exception fulfill their official duties with humaneness, generosity, wisdom, and ability. This is called *highest equability* (*ping* = justice). So the one may have as his emolument the whole empire, and yet he will not think it too much (since he has to exhaust himself for it). And the other may be a gatekeeper, a travel servant, a border guard, or a night watchman, and yet he will not think this too little. When it is said, "fissured yet equal, bent yet fitting, unequal yet uniform,"[18] this refers to human social order.[19]

Again, in his essay on *The Institutions of a King* (*Wang zhi*), Xunzi writes:

If all roles were equal, there would be no universality. If all positions were equal, there would be no unity. If the masses of people were equal, no one could be employed. Since there was heaven and earth, there has been the distinction of above and below. But only since enlightened rulers have been on the throne, there has been a system to govern the state. It is a natural fact that two men of equally high position cannot serve and two men of equally mean position cannot employ each other. If positions and posts are equal while desires and dislikes are the same, strife will be inevitable, because the [limited number of] goods cannot satisfy all desires. Strife will lead to chaos, and chaos to poverty. The early kings hated chaos, and hence they established propriety and justice to assign different roles to the people, so that there would be the ranks of poor and rich, high and low. This guarantees a *mutual supervision*. This is the foundation to support the whole world. This is meant, when the *Book of Documents* says that *"equality is not equality."*[20]

In view of the parallels to Occidental theories about the genesis of the state, the question presents itself whether Xunzi's dialectical legitimation of the inequality of a hierarchical order by the equal advantage of everybody to escape chaos is based on a notion of *social contract*. By his assumption of the human mind's autonomy to choose freely according to its own discretion,[21] Xunzi has laid a necessary foundation for such a contract theory. Neither in his works nor in those of other Zhou philosophers, however, do we find its clear formulation. The existence of a contract theory has even been explicitly denied for ancient China, for example by Hsiao Kung-chuan.[22]

There are a number of reasons, however, which support the assumption that for Xunzi, who is certainly indebted to Mo Di in this respect, the acceptance of rulership is indeed based on a kind of covenant. His theory of language already shows that the idea of social agreement is not alien to him: language functions by "agreements" (*yue, qi*) of the speakers which make up for its arbitrariness.[23] An indication that he also knows the idea of social contract in the political sense is his quoted statement that the just order guarantees a "mutual supervision" of the different social stations, obviously in order to secure that privilege never dissociates itself from responsibility. This fits in with the frequent assertion in Confucian literature that the subordinates will not refuse to follow their superiors as long as these will meet their own duties.[24] The attitude in question has much more in common with the expectation of reciprocity inherent to an agreement than with a belief in a "magical" effect of exemplary behavior on the side of the superiors.

In view of the general circumstances of the time, too, the appearance of the idea of contract, contrary to the established sinological opinion, is quite plausible. Western Zhou investiture can already be interpreted as contractual in nature.[25] Some Eastern Zhou states know certain forms of political participation, for example Chen, where in 494 B.C. the citizens decide by division whether to take the side of Wu or of Chu in warfare.[26] In agriculture, contractual relations replace paternalistic ones,[27] and similarly in the employment sector. Moreover, since the decline of the central power, the establishment of hegemonies in the seventh century, and the development of an independent foreign policy of the former fiefdoms, conferences (*hui*), agreements, covenants, and contracts (*meng, yue*) are everyday occurrences in Zhou China. In retrospect, the *Huainanzi* has even identified them as the typical feature of the age:

In ancient times, the people were obedient under Shennong without regulations and edicts. Under Yao and Shun there were regulations and edicts, but no punishments. The Xia kept their word. The Shang swore. The Zhou made covenants (*meng*). And nowadays one tolerates abuse and takes disgrace lightly, covets after gain, and does hardly know shame.[28]

According to the *Huainanzi*, in high antiquity it was completely superfluous to take institutional precautions for loyalty—a Daoist picture of the original condition contradicting Xunzi's view. In the time of Yao and Shun, there were such regulations, but they did not yet need the threat of sanctions. The Xia had to give their word in order to achieve confidence, and the Shang even swore oaths. The Zhou made covenants which were sealed with blood[29] in order to ensure their being performed at all. Under the Han, finally, any form of obligation has been lost.

For the *Huainanzi*, the contract as a means to ensure confidence is an indication of a declining world. Xunzi, too, is far from believing that an explicit contract would be the preferable solution to achieve political and social order. The idea of contract is present in his work, but not without some important reservations.

Xunzi distinguishes three forms of political rule: The rule of an ideal king (*wang*) based on justice (*yi*), the rule of a hegemon (*ba*) based on confidence (*xin*), and the rule of a regent doomed to ruin based on power (*quan*) and schemes (*mou*).[30] The last form shows that power alone does not legitimate rule. Whereas the ideal form refers to the utopia of a pure kingdom of virtue without any institutional controls, the second form which, in contrast to Mengzi, is judged favorably by Xunzi, obviously has a contractual basis. With a hegemon, Xunzi says, "subordinates and subjects know clearly that he can be made accountable (*yao*)."[31] *Yao*, used as a verb here, as a noun means contract or agreement. Hegemony, then, has its origin in agreement. It is based on "confidence," since otherwise the agreement could not be ensured. This nexus of agreement and confidence is also apparent in the following passage:

When both parts of a tally or a wooden contract document match, this is a sign of confidence (*xin*). If the ruler loves power and schemes, the deceitful among his subordinates and officials will take the opportunity, and there will be fraud. . . . But if the ruler loves propriety and justice, if he promotes the virtuous, employs the capable, and has no covetous mind, then the subordinates will become very polite and yielding, too. They will show loyalty and confidence and heed their duties as subjects and sons. Then there will be confidence even among the lowest people without first having to put together the sides of tallies and wooden contract documents.[32]

In the picture of the tally and the contract document,[33] Xunzi incorporates the idea of contract into the relationship of ruler and subjects. Yet, at the same time, it becomes plain that for him a contractual understanding of politics represents a merely deficient form of social integration. Ideally, there should be no necessity at all to make agreements and to supervise their performance. The Confucians have never abandoned their utopia for the sake of sober *Realpolitik*.

The idea of an agreement between the ruling and the ruled inherent in Xunzi's legitimation of the state, furthermore, does not imply that there would be any institutionally guaranteed opportunity for a free shaping of the society by all its members. This opportunity would presuppose that the opinions of all are taken seriously as a factor in decision making. Xunzi does accept that the opinions of men about what is right diverge, and herewith pays tribute to the general atmosphere of the Chinese axial age—the decline of the unquestioned certainties, and the discussion of alternatives. But unlike some Daoists,[34] he does not draw relativistic conclusions from this. The discrepancy of opinions for him does not at all imply their relativity:

> Different grades of men live together, sharing the same desire yet differing from each other in their ways, and sharing the same likings yet differing from each other in their knowledge. This is their nature. All of them, the intelligent like the stupid, have [an idea of] what is proper (*ke*). But the difference between their ideas of the proper makes up the difference between the intelligent and the stupid.[35]

Among the ideas of what is "proper," only those of the intelligent are worth considering. A broad plurality of opinions which would necessitate accord by consent is not conceivable for Xunzi. The Confucians, after all, are no democrats. They criticize the politics of their time in a sharp and uncompromising manner because of its cruelty and injustice. They do not criticize it for not tolerating a public realm of free discussion which would eventually influence the political decisions and, at least in tendency, include the people. Nevertheless, this does not rule out that Xunzi has an idea of social contract. Quite similar inconsistencies can be found in Hobbes' contractualism. For Hobbes, what follows from the contract—a contract of submission—is not democracy, but the absolute state. After the social hierarchy has once been established by the fictitious rational agreement of all, there is, for both philosophers, no further possibility to call it into question again like the conditions which preceded it. For Xunzi, the tacit agreement "merely" persists as the obligation of the higher ranking to a just and benevolent treatment of their subordinates. The only quasi-institutionalized control is the right to "admonish" (*jian*) the superiors.[36] In spite of their numerous reservations against politics (to be discussed in the second half of this chapter), and in spite of a suggestion in the *Lunyu* that a world of culture might not require rulers,[37] the Confucians are far from formulating any alternative to monarchy. And before they conceive an institutional framework for change, they try to make change unnecessary by humanizing the existing system as far as possible and putting strong moral obligations on the powerful. Considerations, however, about how to find a procedure for abdication in order to bring a better ruler to the throne are explicitly rejected by Xunzi. Whereas Mengzi thinks of a changeover within the ruling family,[38] Xunzi evades the question: the case of abdication would not occur in the first place, "if the duties defined by propriety and justice are fulfilled."[39]

Nevertheless, the Confucians have to face the fact that rule despite all efforts can turn into tyranny. Where a legal device for getting rid of a bad ruler is missing, an extra-institutional and exceptional means has to be tolerated—tyrannicide. Xunzi and Mengzi justify it with reference to the rebels of the past:[40]

> King Xuan of Qi asked, "Is it true that Tang banished Jie, and Wu made a punitive expedition against Zhòu?[41]" Mengzi said, "It is so in the records."—"Then it is permissible that a subject murders his ruler?" — "He who does damage to humaneness is called noxious, and he who does damage to justice is called cruel. He who is noxious and cruel is called an isolated fellow. I have heard that an isolated fellow named Zhòu has been executed. I have not heard that a ruler has been murdered."[42]

> To execute the ruler of a tyrannous state is like executing a lonesome fellow.[41]

A tyrant has forfeited his dignity as a ruler. He is not "murdered by a superior" (*shi*), but "executed" (*zhu*) like a normal criminal.[44] He has become an "isolated, lonesome fellow" by losing the consent of his people. This consent for Mengzi as well as for Xunzi is the basic condition for legitimate rule. Heaven, Mengzi says, bestows its mandate only after a candidate has been "exposed to the people and the people have accepted him," because Heaven "sees with the eyes and hears with the ears of the people."[45] For Xunzi, who does not refer to Heaven any longer, the acceptance by the people directly becomes the mandate for power. The tyrants lost it since they lost the people:

> He to whom the world turns is called king (*wang*). He from whom the world turns away is called lost (*wang*). Therefore, Jie and Zhòu did not possess the world, and Tang and Wu did not murder a ruler.[46]

The world's turning to and turning away from a ruler through a "vote by feet" again recall the implicit agreement and its denunciation. True, the people are no really free contractors. They pass a sentence which is executed by somebody else in their name. Their vote, moreover, only refers to the person of the ruler, or the ruling house, and not to the structure of the system. Still, the overthrow of a dynasty is an extraordinary historical moment reminiscent of the fictitious social stipulation.

Great parts of Xunzi's political theory, then, can be interpreted by the heuristic of an implicit social contract. At the same time, it becomes apparent that he does not really think the idea of contract to the end—or that he rejects it, recognizing that no stable social order can be achieved in this way. This hesitation might be less motivated by Xunzi's conviction that there is no equality of opinions in the empirically given world, and that opinions are not merely relative. Anyway, the point of the contract theory is not that the contract is *in reality* concluded by all who are affected. It only assumes that the state and the social order are artificial institutions established under the terms of the general interests of men, which can in principle—though not necessarily de facto—be appreciated as rational interests by everybody.[47] This rational insight, for Xunzi, first of all is the vicarious insight of the sages (*shengren*) who by deliberation and art (*wei*) create institutions and morals.[48] It is reproduced in the likewise vicarious understanding of the intellectual elite, to which Xunzi himself belongs. Yet, the sages, as well as the members of the intellectual elite, for Xunzi merely personify human reason per se which is also possessed by the "man in the street" if he exerts himself.[49] Xunzi's skepticism, then, may result from a specific weakness which is inherent in contractualism as such: it has no satisfactory answer to the question how the *observance* of the contract can be guaranteed without having to contract again.[50] This crux is well known to the ancient Chinese. The *Zuozhuan* comments on a covenant (*meng*) which ends up in war (700 B.C.):

> A gentleman would say: If confidence is not secured, a covenant is of no use. When it is said in the *Songs*, "The son of the prince has frequently made covenants, and the disorder is thereby increased," this refers to the want of confidence.[51]

I assume that misgivings like these make Xunzi hesitate to view a social contract as the final basis of human order. The same self-interest that now advises one to enter into the agreement might at another time recommend the breaking of it. Confidence is not established by the agreement, but is presupposed for the latter. Presumably, this is also the reason why Xunzi calls a hegemony dependent on trust, whereas ideal rulership can be seen as constitutive for it.

Xunzi, then, plays with the idea of contract, although he neither systematically discusses it nor makes it the foundation of his political teaching. What can be interpreted in terms of contract is, first of all, his basic idea that the justification of social inequality lies in safeguarding the existence of all and delivering them from the fight for resources. What can be interpreted in terms of contract is, furthermore, the coming into existence of the state, if we take into consideration that the ingenious creative act of the sages is little more than a metaphor for the rationality and profitableness of the stratified social order based on human insight as such. After the irrevocable artificial emergence of the state in the interest of all, however, it is impossible to remodel the form of human existence once again.[52] The idea that politics is based on agreement leads to the conception of a welfare state in which the upper classes know that with their social position they have also taken over a special responsibility, and that in the final analysis they are supported by nothing but the consent of the people. In case they do not meet the expectation of reciprocity of the lower classes, they run the risk of rebellion.

Unlike a republican constitution which draws institutional and formal juridical conclusions from the idea of contract, this system remains fundamentally dependent on the insight and good will of the powerful, as well as on a segment of society which continuously reminds them of their duties. This is the educated elite equipped with a rigid humanist ethic and claiming the right of uncompromising judgment. The scholarly elite is the true actor of politics, to which the rulers, ideally, are ready to listen.[53] Only in exceptional cases the decisive voice is that of the "multitude," the people themselves. One should listen to their opinion,[54] but in general they remain the object of politics.[55] The Confucian idea of equality and Xunzi's concept of agreement thus collide with an elitist intellectualism aware of its distance to the "stupid masses."[56] On the other hand, the people should be the *cui bono* of all political activity, which requires care for public welfare.[57] The contradiction can best be characterized by a formulation of Maruyama meant for the Neo-Confucian Ogyu Sorai (1666–1728): ". . . although the conscious aim of Sorai's concept of invention[58] was a *Gemeinschaft*, this concept is clearly permeated with the logic of a *Gesellschaft* (ultimately of a Verein)."[59]

Xunzi's outlined justification of political rule and social inequality is a typical case of an antique postconventional legitimation of the state at Stage 5 of Kohlberg's sequence. "Antique" I call the merely halfhearted acknowledgement of the equality of all and of the importance of their opinions, as well as the predominance of elitism. Genuine representations of Stage 5 are the social utilitarian position that order does not exist for its own sake, but for reasons of general utility, the view of the state as a product of deliberation and art, the idea—however implicit—of social agreement, and furthermore the "prior-to-society perspective"[60] inherent to Xunzi's whole theorizing. Xunzi's anthropological assumption that man, with his "heart," his faculty of reason, disposes of an autonomous organ of choice and decision[61] fits well into this picture.

The orientation to public welfare, however, has never been the final purpose prompting Confucian political teaching. The participation of all in social wealth is rather the precondition for realizing yet a higher ideal: the cultivation of man, which above all means his moral elevation. Politics thus is subordinated to a moral goal. This implies that the utilitarian legitimation of the state must not be confused with a utilitarian grounding of morality. Morality in Confucianism is an end in itself and not merely an expedient for a good life.

Politics is not only submitted to morality by the detour of social utility as a precondition for moral cultivation, but also in a direct way. This is already the core of the early Zhou teaching of the "mandate of Heaven" (*tian ming*), and if any of the later philosophical schools inherited this idea, then it was Confucianism. Succeeding the religion of Heaven, Confucianism has developed a religious legitimation of the state, next to the pragmatic one by Xunzi, which draws on the early conception of the appointment of the ruler by moral Heaven. This conception is missing in the *Lunyu*, but is emphatically supported by Mengzi. It is never the ruler, Mengzi stresses, who hands over power to his successor, but only Heaven itself.[62] Thus, political rule is at the same time legitimated and obligated to fulfill the moral will of Heaven.

Mengzi's adherence to the religion of Heaven has an even deeper dimension. The fact that Heaven has endowed every man with one and the same *good nature*,[63] which distinguishes him from the animals and makes him a being of intrinsic dignity with an "honor in himself,"[64] *directly* indebts politics to the interests of the people. There is no other reason for politics than to provide the best external conditions possible for developing man's innate goodness. If the state fails in doing this, it loses the right to demand services from the people or to punish them for offenses:

> After a clash between Zou and Lu, Duke Mu of Zou asked Mengzi, "Thirty-three of my officers have died, and none of the people would die in their place. If I put them to death, the executions will not come to an end. But if I do not put them to death, they will maliciously watch the death of their superiors without rescuing them. What is the best thing to do?"
>
> Mengzi answered, "In years of calamity and famine, the old and weak of your people weltered in the gutter, and the able-bodied were scattered in all directions by thousands. All the while, your granaries and magazines were full, and none of your officials touched the problem. This shows how rude the superiors are and how cruelly they treat the subjects. Zengzi said, 'Beware, beware! What proceeds from you will come back to you!' It was only now that the people could pay back [what they had suffered]. You cannot blame them for that! If you will practice a humane government, the people will love their superiors and die for them."[65]

> To have a constant mind without a constant livelihood—only a scholar is capable of that. As to the people, if they have no constant livelihood, they will abandon themselves to every unrestraint, eccentricity, depravity, and excess. When they get into crime then, to punish them accordingly would mean entrapping the people.[66]

If we add his moral anthropology on which these arguments are based, Mengzi in these passages presents a functional equivalent to Western theories of natural rights. The state is legitimated only by devoting itself to the service of the moral possibilities which every human being is endowed with by his very nature. The ruler has to submit himself to this cause.[67] "The people," Mengzi can therefore say, "are the highest, the spirits of territory and grain (= the state) are next, and the ruler is the most unimportant."[68]

B. THE PRACTICE: BETWEEN LOYALTY AND NONCOMPLIANCE

The reclamation that the state fulfils its tasks is the reverse side of its legitimation. The theoretical definition of the raison d'être of rulership has considerable practical consequences. The gamut of behavior reaches from loyal cooperation under the reserve that a moral regime is pursued, to the vindication of a guardianship of politics, and finally to the withdrawal from public activity, refusal of cooperation, and inner or outer emigration.

The necessity of the state first of all means the duty of everybody to respect the laws and to "serve his ruler in loyalty."[69] The ruler may expect that a subject "respectfully discharges his duties and puts his emolument last," and that he "devotes himself" to him.[70] One must, moreover, not go beyond the boundaries of one's competence and meddle with matters outside the responsibility of one's office.[71] Loyalty (*zhong*) is the basic political virtue the state may demand.[72]

Exactly in this willingness to devotion and putting self-interest last, however, there is a crucial ambiguity. As the case may be, it could become the source from which not only the loyal subject, but also the nonconformist oppositional can draw his strength. A Confucian lives with the possibility, or even probability of conflict. How tension-filled his attitude towards the state is becomes apparent from two short passages from the *Lunyu*:

> The Master said, "Can you be loyal to anyone without instructing him?"[73]

> Zilu asked how to serve the ruler. The Master said, "Do not deceive him, but stand up to him."[74]

One may argue that "standing up" to the ruler and "instructing him"—both certainly stand for the idea of "admonition" (*jian*)—are not necessarily motivated by moral, but strategic considerations. *Lunyu* 13.15, indeed, recommends Duke Ding of Lu to allow contradiction in his own well-understood interest, for otherwise he might lose his power. The Legalist school has reduced the notion of criticism to the function of upholding the system. The *Lunyu*, however, gives sufficient evidence that the genuine Confucian idea is different: rulership and power are not the purpose which criticism has to serve. Criticism, reversely, is dedicated to the aim to make rulership the means for yet a higher goal: the goal of culture, interpreted in terms of morality. The ethics of the official as founded by Confucius rests on two pillars: the pillar of loyalty to the ruler and active service to the state, and the pillar of loyalty to morals. The relationship of both "pillars" is more complicated than it appears to be in this confrontation, since serving ruler and state is itself a moral obligation. Nevertheless, a collision is possible. In case of doubt, morality is the more binding orientation. "If a ruler is correct himself," Confucius stresses, "his government will be successful without orders being issued. If he is not correct himself, orders may be given, but they will not be followed."[75] He furthermore says:

> He who is called a great official serves his ruler according to the *Dao*. If this is not possible, he will quit his service.[76]
>
> It is a shame to remain poor and of low position in a state which has the *Dao*. It is likewise a shame to be rich and of high position in a state which does not have the *Dao*.[77]

Similarly, we later read in the *Mengzi*:

> He who is called a "good official" today would have been called a parasite of the people in antiquity. To seek to enrich a ruler who is not inclined towards the *Dao* and does not set his mind on humaneness is to enrich a Jie (a tyrant).[78]

The crucial criterion of decision here is the *Dao*. The Confucian concept of *Dao*, like the Daoist one, often refers to something not realized in the given human world. The *Dao* is the most important cipher of the postconventional perspective of classical Chinese philosophy. Its otherness compared to the empirical reality can explain why the concept remains vague in many paragraphs of the *Lunyu*. We are told that the *Dao* does not succeed, and that the world is devoid of it.[79] In *Lunyu* 4.8, it gets an utopian, nearly redeeming dimension:

> If I could hear of the *Dao* in the morning, I would be willing to die in the evening.

The utopian dimension of the *Lunyu* is often overlooked in view of the orientation to the past which Confucius attests himself, for example in his famous dictum to "transmit, but not to innovate."[80] This dimension can be found, however, exactly in his attitude towards the state and the *shengren*, the sage, in Confucianism the personification of intellectual and moral greatness and ideal rulership. In *Lunyu* 6.30 we read:

> Zixia asked, "If there were somebody who granted extensive benefits to the people and were able to assist the citizens, how would he be like? Could he be called humane?" The Master said, "That would not [only] be a case of humaneness. Such a person would surely be a sage. Even Yao and Shun were still not perfect in this respect."

The reserve against Yao and Shun[81] is remarkable, because the two predynastic rulers, the earliest mentioned in the *Lunyu*, represent the idealized antiquity. The future, we might conclude, is open for developments which are neither realized in the present nor are simple repetitions of the past. Nevertheless, it cannot be overlooked that the Confucian utopia is normally projected back to a Golden Age.[82] But regardless of whether it takes its orientation from vividly depicted memories or from vaguely described expectations, the tension with the given reality as such remains important. How Confucius conceives of a state in which a *shengren* puts the *Dao* into practice, is left unclear in the *Lunyu*. The hints it gives show that the ideal is a monarchy with a virtuous, benevolently caring ruler who behaves in an exemplary manner and does not depend on administrative techniques.

When Confucius speaks of "states which have the *Dao*," therefore, he hardly refers to the political situation given in his times. "To have the *Dao*" is either an ideal-typical assumption, or means that a state is at least on the right way and therefore deserves support. Yet, the early Confucians are not confident that the possibility of practicing the *Dao* in a state could also become reality. It is only Xunzi who, in his conviction that strong institutions are necessary, grants a greater bonus to the state. He, too, has a distinctive awareness of the conflict situation in which an official can find himself. But in this conflict, he stresses yet another tension which overlaps and complicates the one between service and morality: the tension between serving the ruler and serving the state. This tension, which is also known to Mengzi,[83] is especially emphasized in Xunzi's essay *The Way of the Official* (*Chen dao*), where he writes:

> *Obedience* is to obey an order and to benefit the ruler thereby. *Flattery* is to obey an order though it will do harm to the ruler. *Loyalty* is to disobey an order if this benefits the ruler. *Usurpation* is to disobey an order and to harm the ruler thereby. A *robber of the state* is called he who does not care for the ruler's glory or disgrace or whether or not the state is prospering, who conforms with a speculative mind, and is opportunistically complaisant (*tou he gou rong*) in order to maintain his sinecure and to support his relations.
>
> In case the ruler plans or does something wrong, so that the state and his clan are endangered and one has to fear for the existence of the country, then, among the high officers and elders, one calls an *admonisher* the one who is able to speak to the ruler, and who lets the matter rest if the ruler uses his advice, but otherwise takes his leave. One calls a *fighter* the one who is able to speak to the ruler, and who lets the matter rest if the ruler uses his advice, but otherwise [even is willing] to meet his death. One calls a *helper* the one who is able to call the intelligent together, to unite all forces, and to lead all officers and clerks in order to force and bend the ruler, so that the ruler, even if it does not please him, cannot but comply, and who, in doing this, rescues the state from a great calamity and damage, and manages to procure honor to the ruler and security to the state. One calls *resistant* the one who is able to resist the ruler's order, usurp his authority and counter his activities in order to

remove the threat to the state and the ruler's disgrace, and whose political and military efforts suffice to establish the greatest benefit for the state.

Therefore, the admonisher, the fighter, the helper, and the resistant are the true officials for the country and the ruler's treasures. They are honored by enlightened rulers, but regarded as their personal enemies by ignorant and deluded ones.[84]

Xunzi distinguishes several types of officials among which the four last mentioned, the admonisher, the fighter, the helper, and the resistant, are of special importance. They defy the ruler in the overriding interest of the state. In the well-ordered country which Xunzi has in mind, however, the Confucian ethical norms are taken care of too, and in his quoted essay he frequently changes over to the normal moralizing diction of the Confucian school. Xunzi moreover distinguishes three kinds of rulers who should be treated in different manners:[85] The ingenious and exemplary ruler (*sheng jun*) deserves more than mere loyalty (*zhong*)—he deserves obedience (*shun*) without admonishment (*jian*) or even strife (*zheng*). Loyalty, which unlike obedience can imply opposition,[86] and admonishment are in place when serving an average ruler (*zhong jun*). Conflict, hence, is nota bene no exception, but normality. Towards a despotic ruler (*bao jun*), finally, a psychological strategy is appropriate if one cannot leave him. One should praise his strong points and not talk about the weak ones, one should remain kind and make use of his fears and anxieties, his pleasures and outbursts of rage. So one may succeed by patient endeavor to bring the ruler back to the right path.

How a ruler has to be classified is obviously left to the judgment of the subordinate. This means that even the submission which is the due of a sage ruler is based on preceding scrutiny and decision. Xunzi can, therefore, generalize:

Follow the Dao, do not follow the ruler![87]

This one sentence, which we also found in the *Zi dao* (*Xunzi* 29), where it was complemented by the exhortation to "follow justice and not the father," reflects the whole postconventional identity of the Chinese axial age. It is remarkable that it is to be found in the *Xunzi*, a text which in some respects stands close to the authoritarianism of the Legalists. Yet, the ideologists of Legalism themselves, as we will see, are also above the servility they demand of others.

"Follow the *Dao*, do not follow the ruler" is a postconventional maxim which can be sure to meet with the approval of all Confucians, though Confucius has avoided such a pointed generalization of the experiences with political rule. The maxim can be interpreted differently, however. Xunzi asks for the *how* of political service. For other Confucians, the more fundamental question was *whether* a state is worth cooperation at all. The insight that the *Dao* as the incarnation of moral fulfillment and the policy actually pursued contradict one another could lead to diverging conclusions. One alternative is to provide the official with a firm ethos that he can serve as a corrective of power. In this case, the hope of realizing the *Dao* is, in spite of all difficulties, not yet abandoned. The other alternative is that of the dropout who is more than skeptical about the chances of the *Dao* and from the beginning rejects taking office. Both positions can be found in Confucian literature. The standard case is the attempt to meet one's social and political responsibility and yet, remaining true to oneself, to maintain the option for withdrawal. This withdrawal implies renunciation and a life outside the protection of the institutions of the state. The unconditional readiness for a humble and ascetic existence and even the sacrifice of one's life becomes part and parcel of the Confucian ethos. For only he who fortifies himself against his egoism will not be obsequious to power.

The rejection of political activity can first of all refer to rebellious and endangered countries, where one should not dwell.[88] But since the whole world lies in agony, the exception threatens to become the rule. In early Confucianism, especially in the *Lunyu*, we therefore find a pronounced tendency towards inner or outer emigration which the school has in common with the Daoists. "A wise man retires from the world," *Lunyu* 14.37 states, and in *Lunyu* 5.6, the "Master" says:

> The *Dao* does not succeed. When I go out to the sea on a raft, it will be Zilu who follows me.

The conviction to fight for a lost cause in a time of striving for profit and power runs through the early classics. Many "scholars" turn their back on the world and prefer a private life in poor circumstances to an official career, like Yan Hui, Confucius' favorite disciple. His teacher praises him:

> How able Hui is! A bowlful of rice, a calabash of water, and a living in a mean alley—no other would endure this distress. But Hui does not lose his happiness. How able he is![89]

In Yan Hui, the ascetic and yet joyful intellectual became an exemplary figure authorized by Confucius himself. Mengzi later tries to preclude a misinterpretation, when he defends Yan Hui as well as Yu and Ji, the untiring cultural heroes of the past.[90] The abstinence of the one and the activity of the others, he argues, were justified by the different conditions of the respective times. The *Zhuangzi*, however, does not miss the opportunity to play off Yan Hui against the normal social engagement of the Confucians.[91]

According to the *Shiji*, two other disciples personify the withdrawn way of life secluded from the world even more typically than Yan Hui: Yuan Xian, Confucius' steward, and Gongxi Ai (Jici), about whom the *Kongzi jiayu* reports:

> Gongxi Ai . . . saw with contempt how the whole world went into the service of clans of high officials. He therefore never bent his moral integrity and never became another's subordinate. Confucius was full of admiration for him.[92]

The *Shiji* makes the two disciples the leading figures of an unconventional and antipolitical, yet—in contrast to the Daoists—decidedly intellectual line within Confucianism:

> As far as those Confucians are concerned who because of their skill held the positions of chancellors, minsters, and high officials, and who assisted the rulers of their time, their merits and glory have already fully been recorded in the annals of the states and therefore do not have to be discussed further here. As to Jici (Gongxi Ai) and Yuan Xian, they lived in common alleys, studied their books and cherished the virtue of the gentleman who makes his way alone. On principle (*yi*) they refused opportunistic adaptation to their contemporaries, and these in turn laughed at them. Therefore Jici and Yuan Xian lived all their lives in barren dwellings with bramble-woven doors, wearing felted clothes[93] and eating coarse food,[94] and they never grew weary of this.

To make one's way in loneliness and independence (*du*), not to seek opportunistic adaptation, and not to care about the opinions of the world marks a free and fearless attitude which can count as the collective possession of all Zhou philosophers. The subcultural symbolism of disintegration, too—coarse clothes, the primitive dwelling, the bramble-woven door—stems from a common stock of metaphors which graphically reflects the consciousness of the epoch. Although normally this symbolism is rather associated with the Daoists than with the Confucians, who always attach importance to form, it can quite often be found in Confucian contexts.[95] Zeng Shen says in proud words breathing the unconventional spirit of the axial age:

> Therefore, the gentleman will not be distressed if he lives in poverty, and he will not quarrel over a humble position. It does not matter for him if he enjoys no reputation. His clothes are worn out, his coarse food does not make him sated,[96] his door is bramble-woven, and his window is just a hole. Yet, he is diligent day-to-day and cherishes humaneness.
>
> If I am known I am not delighted, and if I am unknown I do not feel distressed. Therefore, the gentleman is direct in his speech and action. He will not talk with twisted words to become rich, and he will not resort to crooked action to get a post. That the humane are persecuted and the knowing are killed can never bring him into difficulty.
>
> To bend himself and do something inhuman, to use twisted words and act against his knowledge—the gentleman will not do that. Even if his words are not listened to, he will remain loyal—this is what the *Dao* means. Even if his actions are not accepted, he will remain loyal—this is what humaneness means. And even if his criti-

cism is ignored, he will remain loyal—this is what knowledge means. If the world is void of the *Dao*, he himself will continue to follow the *Dao*. And if he remains lying in the street without a refuge to hide and anything to cover his limbs, this is not the gentleman's fault. It is the shame of those who own the country.[97]

Therefore, the gentleman considers humaneness the highest. What is rich with what the world regards as rich? He regards humaneness as richness. And what is valuable with what the world regards as valuable? He regards humaneness as valuable.[98]

Such defiant declarations of an independent, unyielding, and yet ethically responsible attitude are typical of the early Confucians. It is especially characteristic to state at the same time one's commitment to loyalty and one's claim to moral integrity. The proudest manifestations of a free and steadfast mind can be found in Mengzi, whose sharp rhetoric is supported by the conviction to speak in the name of the innate good nature conferred to man by Heaven. Mengzi is the prototype of the free intellectual dedicated to his moral ideals and travelling all over the world to read the feudal lords, whenever possible, a lecture. He coins the figure of the "great fellow" (*da zhangfu*) who, averse to obedience, "makes his way alone and cannot be debauched by wealth and honors, led astray by poverty and mean conditions, and bent by authority and power."[99] Mengzi, who also says that one should "despise the great and disregard their lofty position when one gives counsel to them," and for whom, quoting Zeng Shen, it is "worse to toady and grin fawningly than to toil in the fields in summer"[100] has in mind no less than a guardianship of the politicians. When in Qi, he expects that the ruler visits him in person instead of inviting him to his palace. Justifying himself, he distinguishes three kinds of authority:

> Zengzi has said, "The wealth of the states of Jin and Chu cannot be equalled. Let them adhere to their wealth—I adhere to my humaneness! Let them adhere to their ranks—I adhere to my sense of justice! Why should I be dissatisfied, then?"
> There are three kinds of achievable honors in the world: *rank*, *age*, and *virtue*. At court, nothing equals rank. In the neighborhood, nothing equals age. But for helping the world and promoting the people, nothing equals virtue. If one has only one of them (i.e. rank), how can one treat rudely the other two? Hence a ruler who is to achieve great things must have subordinates he does not summon. If he wants their advice, then he goes to them. The ruler, however, who has not gone far in honoring virtue and delighting in the *Dao*, is not worthy cooperating with.[101]

In order to keep the critical distance which is in place when dealing with a ruler, Mengzi rejects the idea that a feudal lord and an intellectual could make friends with each other:

Duke Mu often visited Zisi (Confucius' grandson). Once he said, "Ruling over a state with one thousand war chariots, in antiquity one made friends with scholars. What do you think about that?" Zisi was displeased and said, "The ancients had a saying 'Render service to him.' How would they have said, 'Make friends with him'?"

Was not Zisi's displeased answer as if he had said, "With regard to position, you are the ruler, and I am the subject. How could I dare to make friends with you? But with regard to virtue, you are the one who has to serve me! How could you become my friend, then?"[102]

Rank and virtue in this passage are irreconcilable, and Mengzi will ontologically separate them from each other by the fundamental categories of *tian* (Heaven) and *ren* (man). Elsewhere, he works himself up into the following proclamation of confident superiority over political power:

The gentleman has three delights, and to be king over the world is not amongst them. That his parents are both alive and his brothers give no cause for anxiety, this is the first delight. That, looking up, he need not be ashamed before Heaven, and, looking down, he need not be ashamed before other men, this is the second delight. To win the flourishing talents of the world and to teach and educate them, this is the third delight. The gentleman has three delights, and to be king over the world is not amongst them.[103]

A great land and a numerous people—the gentleman may desire this, but his [true] delight is not here. To stand in the center of the empire, to bring peace to the people within the four seas—the gentleman may delight in this, but what makes up his nature is not here. What the gentleman has as his true nature cannot be added to even by the greatest deed (rulership) and cannot be diminished even by a dwelling in poverty. This is because he is certain about his task. What the gentleman has as his true nature—humaneness, justice, propriety, and knowledge—is rooted in his heart. When they thrive, they suddenly manifest themselves in his face, fill his shoulders, and spread all over his four limbs. Without words, his whole posture illustrates his nature.[104]

Family, morality, and *culture,* these are the three great competitors of political power, uncompromising ones, if necessary. If we consider Mengzi's words, Mo Di's claim that the Confucians are rebels might subsequently become understandable. Mo Di quotes Yan Ying, the chancellor of Qi, saying that "Confucius racks his brain over and summons up all his intelligence to commit depravity, encourages the subordinates to rebel against their superiors, and tells the subjects to kill their ruler."[105] It is difficult to substantiate such reproaches.[106] The Confucians have always understood themselves, even in their role as critics, as loyal subjects. What they insist on is the moral reservation, and if the powerful do not meet their moral standards, they turn their back on rather than work against them. Their concern is the unrestricted independence of their judgment, and this is more valuable for them than power itself. For, as Xunzi says,

> He who cultivates his will and motivation looks down upon wealth and eminence. Where the *Dao* is of importance, kings and dukes will be despised.[107]

Nevertheless, Mengzi's provocative pride, much more than the rather cautious statements of the *Lunyu*, invites radical consequences. Perhaps this is the reason why Mengzi, who for himself does not mince his words, puts a spoke in his pupil Wan Zhang's wheels:

> Wan Zhang asked, "May I ask what is the attitude of mind in social intercourse?"
> Mengzi: "Politeness."
> Wan Zhang: "Why is it that the insistent refusal of a present counts as impolite?"
> Mengzi: "When a man of honorable rank grants you a present, and you only accept it after having asked yourself whether he has got it by just (*yi*) or unjust means, this in my eyes is impolite. Therefore, you should not refuse it."
> Wan Zhang: "When one does not explicitly refuse the present, but rejects it in one's heart, saying to oneself that he has taken it unjustly from the people, and when one then does not take it by offering some excuse, would not this be acceptable?"
> Mengzi: "When he deals with one in a well-mannered way (lit.: according to the *Dao, yi dao*), and receives one according to propriety (*li*), then Confucius would have accepted the present."
> Wan Zhang: "Suppose there is a waylayer outside the gates of the city, and he too would deal with one in a well-mannered way and would make one a present according to propriety—would not it then be acceptable to receive robbed goods as a present?"
> Mengzi: "No, it would not. When the *Kang gao* says,[108] 'They kill others for their goods, and when one feels pity with them, they will even not shrink from death; among all the people there are none who would not hate them,' then this means that such people may be executed without trying to give them instruction first. . . . How, then, could one accept a present from them!"
> Wan Zhang: "The feudal lords of today rob the people like waylayers. I dare to ask how you would explain, then, that a gentleman accepts something from them if they only treat him with apt propriety?"

Mengzi: "Do you think that if a true king should arise he would execute all the feudal lords of today? Or would he give instructions to them, and execute them only if they do not change? Indeed, to say that everybody is a robber who takes something which is not his own, is not this an extreme generalization?"[109]

From archaic times, the granting of presents by superiors has belonged to the ritual of power. Generosity is the service in return for the privileged position. Against this background, to reject a present in the name of justice (*yi*) is more than a personal affront.[110] It questions no less than the status of the donor. This is exactly what Wan Zhang is doing, taking up the "sophistic" argument that the observance of established manners in accordance with propriety (*li*) can go together with a cunning mind.[111] Again, we come across the basic surmise of the axial age here. It is most drastically brought forward by the Daoists, but it is remarkable how many of the Daoist motives are also to be found in Confucian literature or are anticipated in it. This not only holds true for the comparison of the powerful to waylayers. It likewise goes for the susceptibility to occupation of a behavior "according to the *Dao*" (here meaning "well-mannered") by a robber, which is not only maintained by the radical chapter 10 of the *Zhuangzi*, but already by Wan Zhang.[112] True, Mengzi contradicts the opinion of his disciple. But the latter corners him with arguments which could stem from himself. Mengzi, too, calls the feudal lords murderers. He says that it does not make a difference to kill a man by a blade or by politics, speaks of the "greed for murder" of the rulers of his time, and proclaims that militarists deserve the highest punishment—death.[113] So strong is his protest that Zhu Yuanzhang (1328–98), the founder of the Ming dynasty, had his work censured on the grounds that "these are not the words appropriate to a subject."[114] Mengzi tries to lay the ghosts he evoked himself. He has picked the rulers to pieces, but refuses the consequences—a typically Confucian dilemma.

Another determined representative of still untamed Confucianism is the unknown author of the *Ru xing* (*The Conduct of a Confucian*), a text transmitted by the *Liji* and the *Kongzi jiayu*. Opposing the Confucianism of his time, which was already smiled at as weak and conformist, the author's obvious intention is to regain the original spirit of the teaching.[115] He adopts such a proud tone that his words have been rejected by some later Confucians as arrogant and unworthy of being included in a classic.[116] The *Ru xing*, however, stands entirely in the tradition of the proclamations of independence we have found in so many other documents of the Confucian school. Using Confucius as his mouthpiece, the author says, among other things:

> The Confucian may not consider gold and jade to be treasures, but benevolence and trustworthiness. He does not request the possession of a territory, but regards the accomplishment of justice as his territory. He does not request to heap up goods, but regards as

wealth to have studied many texts. He is difficult to engage, but easy to remunerate, he is easy to remunerate, but difficult to retain. If it is not the proper time, he will not enter the picture—does not this mean that he is difficult to engage? If it contradicts justice, he will not cooperate—does not this mean that he is difficult to retain? He puts effort first and remuneration last—does not this mean that he is easy to remunerate? Confucians can be like this in their dealing with others. . . .

The Confucian may neither submit above to the Son of Heaven nor serve below a feudal lord. He cares for his tranquility and appreciates freedom (*rong*, or: leisure). He is strong and resolute, yet companionable, he has broad learning and yet knows to submit [to other opinions]. He keeps to culture and style,[117] he sharpens his moral edges. And even if a ruler wished to share the country with him, it would not be worth a cent for him, and he would never become someone else's subordinate or take office for it. Such norms can a Confucian establish for his action. . . .

The Confucian may not be dejected by poverty and humble position. Wealth and eminence will not go to his head nor will he let himself be defamed for them. Yet, he will not make a fool of rulers and kings, he will not be a burden for superiors, and he will not pity the officials.[118] This is why he is called a Confucian.[119]

In this passage, prior to the subjection to political rule, morality and culture set the orientation marks for the Confucian "gentleman." Nonetheless, what the *Ru xing* formulates is not a blunt renunciation of any cooperation in politics, but the conditions for the latter. The ideal-typical Confucian proclaims his freedom in principle and shows how far he *may* be willing to go. In case of conflict he will "not cooperate." But he may also accept the dignified occupation of a post and perform loyal service if this is possible without betraying his moral ideals.

The early Confucians, then, are ready for an extreme disassociation from the role of the obedient subject. Open proclamations of noncompliance and refusal unite them with the Daoists, who merely resort to even more radical formulations. This affinity notwithstanding, what separates the Confucian from the Daoist is the basic impulse not to turn his back on society, an impulse which can be described in terms of an ethics of responsibility.[120] The Confucian tries, in spite of all disillusionment, to continue his social engagement, although knowing that he fights for a cause which is nearly lost. The price for this is the inner loneliness of the unrecognized, an essential constituent of the Confucian *person*.

There is yet another competition the state has to face—the competition of culture. One of the "three delights" which Mengzi played off against rulership was the education of the "flourishing talents of the world. The dropouts Jici and Yuan Xian immerse themselves in their books. The *Ru xing* regards as true wealth to "have studied many texts." Yan Hui, who does not seek office, outstrips his fellow students in his "love for learning."[121] Intellectual education for the Confucian is not merely a tool tailored to fulfill administrative roles. Still in the late Han, Wang Chong uses the term *ru* or *ru sheng*, commonly used for the members of the Confucian school, for the unemployed scholar as distinguished from the civil official (*wen li*).[122] When Confucius' disciple Zixia says that "he who excels in his studies should take office,"[123] he is demanding influential positions for the educated elite rather than recommending striving for a post by all means. Zixia himself makes this clear when he declares that the aim of learning is the *Dao*:

> The artisans stay in the bazaar in order to make their business. The gentleman studies in order to reach the *Dao*.[124]

Xunzi later points out that education is the condition for taking office, but to take office is not the aim of education:

> It is not that someone who studies must also occupy an office. But the one who occupies an office must set to study.[125]

And the "Master" himself states:

> To study for a number of years without aiming at a salary—this is not easily to achieve.[126]

Education, for the Confucian, is not merely an accumulation of knowledge, but the foundation for a cultivated life and for the self-formation of the person. "The men of antiquity," Confucius says, "learned for themselves; the men of today learn for others."[127] The interest in education, hence, is part of the endeavor to protect the self against foreign domination. In view of the fate which Chinese culture has witnessed from the side of the state, there is good reason for the dissociation of education and civil service. Only a few decades separate the maybe greatest cultural achievement ever performed by the Chinese state, the founding of the Jixia academy in Qi, from the disaster of 213 and 212 B.C., when the First Emperor of Qin ordered the burning of all privately owned books and the execution of 460 insubordinate scholars.[128] In view of this catastrophe, a sentence in *Lunyu* 3.5 sounds like a dark premonition of the danger which can accrue to culture from the side of uncontrolled power:

> Even if the Yi and Di (the Barbarians) have their rulers, they do not equal the lands of the Xia (the Chinese) without rulers.

In free translation, this sentence would go: A number of civilized countries without rulers should be preferred to a barbarian state with intact rule. What is at issue is the primacy of culture. Power as such may be a sign of barbarism. Chinese interpreters, however, disagree on the meaning of *Lunyu* 3.5. For some of them, Confucius wants to point out the lack of culture of the Yi and Di rather than the intimate relationship of barbarism and power. Thus, Confucians of the Chinese middle ages have quoted the sentence against Buddhism as a "barbarian" teaching.[129] For the Neo-Confucians Cheng Yi and Zhu Xi, however, Confucius praises the barbarian tribes for their functioning system of rule in order to pillory the political chaos of the Chinese states.[130] This construction presupposes the arbitrary reinterpretation of *bu ru*, "not equal," as *bu xiang*, "not be like." The motive for this is presumably to preclude consequences from Confucius' statement like the one drawn in the nineteenth century by Kang Youwei:

> When Confucius speaks of the Yi and Di and of China, he presumably means what nowadays is called primitive and civilized. Primitive communities are so splintered that they need a despot to hold them together, in accordance with what is appropriate in a world of chaos. In a civilized world, however, human rights are flourishing. All men are under the reign of public law, there is public discussion, democracy, and no ruler. Both methods of government are indispensable for the world, and they both have advantages and disadvantages. Yet, the primitive method of government by a ruler for times of chaos does not equal the civilized one without a ruler in times of peace.[131]

Liang Qichao repeats Kang Youwei's interpretation in a speech for the defense of Confucius against a fictitious skeptic who takes the reading of the Neo-Confucians for granted.[132] Liang and Kang herewith give an example of the "non-regressive appropriation of tradition" I have mentioned in Chapter 1. Doubtless the idea of the *Lunyu* is not democracy, which, in the form envisaged by Kang Youwei, can only be a *cura posterior*. But nevertheless, it opens a door in this direction when it relates power not legitimized by morals and culture to barbarism, and for a moment even conceives of the possibility of a civilized life without reign. This construction fits in well with the aforementioned reserves against the state. And where, if not in questioning Stage 4 law-and-order-morality, lies the difference which distinguishes genuine Confucianism from Legalism? The radical Daoists, by the way, would have rejected this alternative. For them, civilization and reign are just complementary appearances of one and the same denatured artificiality.

The attitude towards the state and state morality of the early Confucians can be summarized as follows: In general, the Confucians legitimize political rule as the precondition of a safe, peaceful, and civilized living together of men in a hierarchical society organized by division of labor. Political power, however, is not there for its own sake. By the assurance of public welfare, it has to fulfill a social function, and the politician is (in Mengzi) under obligation to the natural moral destination of man. Thus politics is under the purview of utilitarian and moral standards. The exercise of power must imply social responsibility and moral exemplariness. A criterion for legitimate rule is the consent of the ruled; the acceptance of social inequality and subordination presupposes that those in power fulfill their function for the whole of society and put their personal interests last. This expectation of reciprocity is implicitly contractualistic. A tyrant isolates himself by violating it and hence provokes his legitimate overthrow.

Under normal conditions, the state deserves loyal and active support. When taking office, the intellectual elite is obliged to bring politics on to a morally justifiable course. The educated official, ideally, is not merely a reliable bearer of assigned roles, but also a trustee of culture and morality. The moral authority of the "gentleman" is the loyal opposing power of the ruler. However, since it is not unlikely that the mighty prove to be robbers and murderers and deprive the state of its raison d'être, a true Confucian lives with the perspective of conflict and failure. Leaving society, leading a secluded and ascetic existence, and even sacrificing his life are within the range of possibility.

Ideally, a Confucian tries, at the same time, to do justice to his moral conviction, to appease his desire for education, to care for the well-being of his family, and to fulfill his social and political responsibility. But the accents placed on each of these goals differ according to the various representatives of the school. On the "right," their positions can come close to those of the Legalists, and on the "left," to those of the Daoists. In any case, the chosen attitude results from a detached consideration which weighs the imperatives of competing normative systems one against the other and presupposes reflection and choice.

8

The Conflict between Family and State and the Problem of Tragedy

In Confucianism, family and state stand in a close relationship. Nevertheless, both not only reach moral limits, but they also conflict with each other. The family, we read in the *Yijing*, came into existence before the state.[1] For many Confucians, it has not only genetic but ethical precedence. In his famous "five social relations" (*wu lun*),[2] Mengzi places the father-son relationship before that of ruler and subject:

> Xie ... instructed men in social relations: There should be love between father and son, justice between ruler and subject, a division of functions between husband and wife, an order of rank between old and young, and faith between fellow students and friends.[3]

The state, hence, is of lower dignity than the family. This order is reversed in the *Zhongyong*, however, and this remains valid to a large extent for Imperial China.[4] Not all Confucians, then, have accepted Mengzi's ranking. Nevertheless, it remains typical of Confucianism to have reserves against politics from the viewpoint of the family. We find an example of this in Mengzi's quoted distinction of the "three delights" of a gentleman; and when Mengzi roots morality in children's love for their parents, this, too, is a clear hit at the state.[5] Zeng Shen, too, in case of conflict, takes the side of the family:

> When Qi wanted to appoint Zeng Shen minister, he refused, saying, "My parents are old. To live on the pay of another means that one has to care for the other's affairs. I cannot bear to abandon my parents and become another's slave."[6]

Zeng Shen is famous for his filial piety. His problem can be called the *conflict of care*. For him, civil service would rule out caring for his parents. Many

93

Confucians have brought forward this argument to quit service, though it some-times has served as a pretext if one tried to escape one's obligations to the state on other grounds. Filial piety was also invoked in the reverse case, when it was argued that only by taking office could the family be sustained.[7] In this case, the state was served, but not for its own sake. In the *Shuoyuan*, a certain Tian Guo declares to the annoyed King of Qi that he only "serves the ruler in the interest of his parents."[8]

The Confucians have not only, whenever necessary, evaded the state on behalf of their parents, but they also have, conversely, demanded a policy in favor of filial piety. The state has to guarantee living conditions to the family which allow the aged to be cared for. The argument that old people are no longer able to spend their last years free from worry and need is central to Mengzi's criticism of the disastrous consequences of the politics of his time.[9] Mengzi recommends his utopia, a subsistence economy for small family units of eight people, by the assertion that this would safeguard the support of the aged with meat and silk (for warm clothes).[10]

The second and more important conflict between state and family is the *legal conflict*. Although later Chinese law has found filial piety worthy of special protection,[11] there is a tension between the demands of the family and public law. Filial piety, in fact, is ambiguous—it can enter into a liaison with *zhong*, political loyalty, but it can also be played off against the state. Classic evidence for the latter case can be found in *Lunyu* 13.18:

> The Prefect of She said to Confucius, "In my county there is a man called 'Upright Gong.' When his father stole a sheep, he as the son testified this." Confucius said, "The upright people in my own county are different. The fathers cover up for the sons, and the sons cover up for the fathers. Uprightness is already to be found in this."

Loyalty to the state, or, to be more precise, the acknowledgment of its title to criminal prosecution—and that is, of its raison d'être, the safeguarding of public order—ends at the doors of the family. Western law, too, knows the privilege of declining to give evidence against relatives. Yet, in view of the role the family has played in Chinese social history, the message of *Lunyu* 13.18 deserves special attention. In spite of some efforts to play down its importance,[12] Confucius' statement has been frequently quoted as a proof for the so-called dominance of the clan not only in Confucianism, but in Chinese culture as such. Han Fei already interprets the case along these lines.[13] For Bertrand Russell, the anecdote illustrates how "Confucian emphasis on filial piety prevented the growth of public spirit."[14] And Trauzettel quotes the passage to corroborate his thesis that "the clan organization, which was legitimately represented by Confu-cianism, . . . became the crystal nucleus of *all* moral norms."[15] As will be shown, these judgments are all too rash. Nevertheless, they prima facie seem to be supported by the following passage from *Mengzi* 7A35:

Tao Ying asked, "When Shun was Emperor and Gaoyao judge, what would they have done if Gusou (Shun's father) murdered a man?" Mengzi answered, "Gaoyao would simply have arrested him." Tao Ying: "Then Shun wouldn't have prevented that?" Mengzi: "How could he? Gaoyao had received the mandate for that." Tao Ying: "What would Shun have done, then?" Mengzi: "For Shun, to abandon the empire would have been the same as to throw away worn-out sandals. He would have stolen away with his father on the back, settled somewhere at the coast, lived there happily to the end of his days, and would have forgotten the empire."

The predynastic ruler Shun is a frequent topic in the *Mengzi*, among other things, because he gave an outstanding example of filial piety under extreme conditions. Although his half brother Xiang together with his father Gusou made several attempts on his life, Shun continued to treat them with love.[16] According to Mengzi, he even enfeoffed Xiang with a place called Youbi.[17] Wan Zhang objects to this, wondering how Shun could promote the wicked brother while others were punished for their crimes without hesitation. And what was the guilt of the people of Youbi that they should be treated in this way? Wan Zhang asks the same question which is discussed in *Mengzi* 7A35: Are there different rights for relatives and foreigners? Mengzi answers that "a humane person never harbors anger or resentment against his brother, but simply loves him."[18] As for the rest, he maintains that Shun had taken care that Xiang had no real power in his fief. The point of his argument is probably that Xiang's crimes were directed against Shun himself, and it is up to Shun to forgive him. In *Mengzi* 7A35, however, Gusou is supposed to have killed another man. Now the role of the ruler, who has delegated his function as impartial judge to his minister of justice, has become incompatible with that of the son. Forced to make a decision, Shun takes the side of his father. Nota bene, he does not bend the law in favor of the father. He dispenses with the position in which his solidarity with the father would mean a violation of law.

The reverse case of a crime of the son was obviously regarded as less complicated. That Shi Que from the nobility of Wei ordered his son, who had made common cause with an assassin, to be killed, meets the approval of the *Zuozhuan*. It comments that "great justice (*yi*) exterminates kinship."[19] "Great justice" in this radical sense can overrule all kin relations, with the exception of the commitment to the parents, in favor of public interest.

The conflict between family and state comes to a head in the question of *blood revenge*. Blood revenge seems to have been quite common in Zhou China. In *Mengzi* 7B7, we read:

If somebody kills another's father, the other will also kill his own father. And if somebody kills another's brother, the other will also kill his own brother. This is nearly the same as to kill one's father and brother oneself.

Mengzi describes the reality of his times. His own opinion about blood revenge is unclear, and the same holds true for the *Lunyu* and the *Xunzi*. Other texts show that revenge was approved of to a large extent, but that it was also discussed controversially. A well-known topic of Zhou literature is the renunciation of private feud in favor of the commonwealth. To recommend a personal enemy for a high position counts as exemplary not only for the Legalist Han Fei,[20] but also for many others. The *Zuozhuan* calls such an attitude impartial, and Confucius, according to the *Lüshi chunqiu*, praises it as an expression of public spirit (*gong*).[21] The *Shuoyuan* considers it "humane" when a prince of Wu disclaims the throne instead of taking revenge.[22] And when Shuxiang from the high nobility of Jin justifies the assassination of his brother, a corrupt judge, by one of his victims, Confucius is said to have commended him for "not covering up for his relative."[23]

Votes for blood revenge are to be found in the following passages:

There is no common life with the murderer of a parent. One does not share the country with the murderer of the brother. One does not share the village with the murderer of a friend. One does not share the neighborhood with the murderer of a member of the lineage.[24]

Zixia asked Confucius how to behave in case one has to take revenge for the parents. The teacher said, "One sleeps on straw[25] with the shield for a neck support, and does not take office, so as not to live with the murderer under the same heaven. If one meets him in the market place or at court, one attacks him with the weapon always kept at hand."

"And how should one do with reference to the murderer of the brother?"—"One does not take office in the same state. If one is sent on a mission by one's ruler and meets the murderer, one does not fight with him."

"And how should one do with reference to the murderer of the cousin?"—"In this case one does not take the lead. If he who is chiefly concerned is able to take revenge by himself, one supports him from behind with the weapon in the hand."[26]

When the *Liji* demands immediately attacking the murderer of a parent even at the court, it values the kinship duty of revenge higher than the service to the ruler. But already in the case of the brother, the reverse is true. A similar vacillation between family and state can be found in the *Zhouli*, which tries to find a legal framework for revenge. In case the avenger makes a written notice to the governmental authorities in advance, he should not be punished. The *Zhouli* moreover conceives the office of an arbitrator who separates the conflicting parties geographically.[27]

A specially explosive question is whether the son can also take revenge in case of the execution of the father. The *Gongyangzhuan* offers a middle course.

It cites Zishenzi, an authority of the Gongyang school, stating "not to take revenge for the father is not to behave like a son."[28] But elsewhere, it quotes Confucius' contemporary Wu Zixu who took revenge for his innocently executed father:

> In case the father has not deserved to be executed, it is admissible that the son avenges his death. But in case the father has deserved to be executed, the taking of revenge by the son would lead to butchery, and the evil would not be removed by it.[29]

Together with the *Gongyangzhuan*, Wu Zixu's words became canonic. Still Liu Zongyuan (773–819) quotes them in defence of Xu Yuanqing who had killed the judge of his executed father.[30] Hence, it is not least the distrust of the arbitrary or corruptible jurisdiction which has made many Confucians hesitate to grant an unrestricted monopoly of force to the state. It is neither guaranteed that every crime is prosecuted, nor is judicial murder impossible. On the other hand, it has been clear to them that the responsibility of the state for jurisdiction cannot simply be called into question, since this would lead to an endless chain of mutual retaliation. The Chinese state for its part has left nothing undone in its attempts to prohibit private revenge—albeit the foundations for this were laid by the Legalists and not the Confucians.[31] But the state has also made extensive use of collective punishments, regardless of individual guilt, and has thus helped a rival principle from the archaic world of the clans closely related to blood feud to survive, although rather for pragmatic than for ideological reasons. Xunzi's remarkable polemic against this practice has not met with much success:

> In antiquity, penalties did not exceed guilt, and ranks did not exceed virtue. So it could happen that the father was killed and his son was made minster, or that the elder brother was killed and the younger was made minister. . . . In our chaotic age, however, things are different. Penalties and fines exceed guilt, ranks and rewards exceed virtue. Clan punishments are inflicted, and the capable are raised to hereditary positions. Thus, one man makes himself guilty, and yet all the members of his clan to the third degree suffer the same fate. And even if someone would have the virtue of Shun, he would be punished along with the others. This means to inflict punishments according to the clan principle.[32]

Where family and state claim mutually exclusive rights, conventional morality disintegrates into two conflicting ethical powers. According to Hegel, the corresponding collision of duties, which makes the actor guiltlessly guilty whatever he may do, is the essence of the *tragic*.[33] Greek tragedy—the model is, above all, Sophocles' *Antigone*—for Hegel represents the "outbreak . . . of opposing forces from the undivided consciousness of life and the godlike"[34] as a decisive stage of the Occidental worldview. In its aporetic rupture, the limits of ethical life are experienced in such an elementary way that they can subsequently be transcended. Tragedy, therefore, is significant for moral evolution. Its lack would be an indication of the unquestioned continuing existence of "substantiality," and it is in this sense that the Orient remains nontragic for Hegel.[35]

Thus Hegel has again passed a judgment which later became a stereotype. For Alfred Weber, China is "the anti-tragic country per se."[36] The impulse of the waves of equestrian peoples from Central Asia, which, according to Weber, caused a tragic shock in other civilizations, subsided in China's "chtonic" soil. Whereas elsewhere, he says, the "mantical-magical" was shattered under the impact of the tragic experience, in China it was merely sublimated and de-demonized, and transferred into a harmonistic cosmology.[37] Similarly, Rosenzweig and Trauzettel have denied that China knows the tragic.[38]

Ancient China has not developed tragedy as a dramatic genre. The lack of the dramatic form, however, does not necessarily imply that the *tragic motif* as such is absent, too. Let us understand this motif in terms of Hegel's collision of rights, thus attributing to it an evolutionary significance which can be related to the transcending of Kohlberg's conventional level. From the retrospection of the postconventional breakthrough of the axial age, we have to reckon, then, with an accumulation of problems during the preceding period in which we find the tracks of the tragic dilemma. That the moral evolution in China indeed encountered the tragic hurdle, is demonstrated not by a Chinese Sophocles, but by scattered evidence in the historiographic and poetic literature. The *Lüshi chunqiu* and the *Hanshi waizhuan*, for example, contain episodes from the Chunqiu and Zhanguo eras of genuinely tragic dimensions, like the one about Shizhu of Chu:

At the time of King Zhao of Chu (r. 515–488 B.C.), there was a scholar named Shizhu. He was impartial, upright, and unselfish by character. The king gave him an office in his administration. Once a man was killed in the road. Shizhu pursued the assassin, and when he brought him to bay he turned out to be his father.

Shizhu turned the carriage and drove back. Standing in the court, he said, "The assassin was the servant's father! I cannot bear to administer penal law to my father. But it is also impossible to bend law in favor of a culprit. To submit to punishment when having disregarded law is the duty of a subordinate." Thereupon, he prostrated himself before the axe and the execution block and asked the king for his death. The king said, "You pursued the assassin, but did not catch him—why should you have to submit to punishment, then? Just go on with your work!" But Shizhu declined, saying, "He who is not partial to the father cannot be called a filial son. But he who, in service of the ruler, bends law cannot be called a loyal subject. That Your Majesty now grants me pardon, is the grace of a superior. But not to dare disregarding law is the conduct of a subject." He did not leave axe and execution block, until he died in the king's court.[39]

Whereas Shizhu is hopelessly trapped in the conflict between the obligations to family and state, Qing Bing of Zhao is caught in the collision of loyalty and friendship. While travelling with his lord Zhao Xiangzi, he finds his former friend Yu Rang lying in ambush to kill Zhao. Neither being able to disclose the plan of his friend nor to betray his lord, he commits suicide.[40] Again, Zhuang Zhishan of Chu falls victim to the collision of loyalty and filial piety. Foreboding his impending death, he goes to war for his ruler against rebels (479 B.C.). When taking leave of his mother he tells her that he can only support her by the salary he gets from his lord, but for the same reason owes allegiance to him. Although his knees fail him before the fight, he does not recede. Saying that he cannot put his private interests above public duty, he meets his death.[41] A fourth episode takes place 481 B.C. in Qi:

After Tian Chang had assassinated Duke Jian, he made a covenant with the citizens, saying that those who would not covenant with him would be put to death along with their families. Shituo said: "In ancient times, those who served their ruler also died for them. To abandon one's ruler in order to preserve one's family is disloyal. To abandon one's family in order to die for one's ruler is unfilial. [Both] I cannot do. If I do not covenant, I will kill my family. But if I covenant, I will repudiate my ruler. Alas! *Born into disordered times one cannot achieve correct conduct.* And compelled by brutes it is impossible to maintain justice. How deplorable!"

Thereupon he covenanted so as to spare his father and mother. Then he withdrew and threw himself on his sword to die for his ruler. Those who heard of this said, "What a gentleman he is! How he submits to his fate!"[42]

The *Hanshi waizhuan* comments on the *Shijing* by historical anecdotes or episodes with moral overtones. Shituo's fate is to illustrate the line *jin tui wei gu*, quoted in the poem *Sang rou* as a proverbial saying.[43] The poem, perhaps from the eighth century B.C., laments the times of war and rebellion, where—this is the most plausible interpretation of the quoted sentence—"to go forwards or backwards alike leads into an abyss." The expression *jin tui wei gu*, nearly three thousand years of age, is still in use in modern Chinese for "being caught in a dilemma." The *Hanshi waizhuan* defines this dilemma as the mutual exclusion of practical alternatives after one has got between the two fronts of family and state morality. In the *Shijing* itself, however, the dilemma remains unspecified. That it might relate to the aforementioned moral conflict can be concluded from the poem *Si mu*,[44] which bewails that military service makes it impossible to care for one's parents. The conflict is in the air, but is not expressed in a trenchant manner. But even before the episodes from the *Lüshi chunqiu* and the *Hanshi waizhuan*, it becomes aporetic in the story of Shensheng, the prince of Jin, in the first half of the seventh century B.C. When his father falls in love with the concubine Li Ji who wants her own son to become heir apparent, Shensheng gets the target of a well-devised psychological intrigue. Finally, he has to choose between saving the state, which is disrupted by the affair, and fulfilling the duty of the obedient son. Feeling "guilty" in the conflict of the two ethical obligations, there is no way left to him but suicide (656 B.C.).[45]

We do find the tragic motif, therefore, in Zhou China, though not in the forcible manner of the Greek tragedy. The tragic figures of China take softer contours than the defiant heroes of the Greeks. When in the throes of moral conflict, they prefer to lay hands on themselves rather than commit a determined though faulty deed.[46] The psychological effect of their fate, therefore, may be less spectacular. But it is touching enough to motivate steps towards a morality which no longer fails in the conflict between family and state. Thus the episodes of Shensheng, Shituo, Shizhu, and the other victims of conventional morality[47] probably deliver a missing link between the ethos of the early Zhou and the postconventional philosophical ethics. Chinese philosophy, after all, bears the stamp of a deep crisis in which, in the words of the *Zhuangzi*, "the art of the *Dao* comes to be *torn apart*."[48] The motif of division indicates tragedy. Still in the Daoist return to the "undivided" (*pu*), there appears the endeavor which, in China like in Greece, helps to constitute philosophy as a *posttragical* project:[49] not to leave the last word to the tragic. When Heaven, as Mengzi says, "exercises a man's mind with bitterness and his sinews and bones with toil, exposes his body to hunger, exhausts him and confounds his undertakings," then it is to "confer a great task on him."[50] And "principled heroes," according to Kohlberg, "do not make a tragedy."[51]

9

The Search for Postconventional Norms and Principles

Family solidarity and loyalty to the state both find their limits. A higher level of morality turns out to be as indispensable as the conventional ethos itself, in order to protect the latter against corruption and to find a way out of aporetic conflicts. How can this higher level be defined? In what follows, I will discuss candidates which *prima facie* come into consideration for a more than conventional orientation and a principled ethic. But first I want to show that the notion of principle is not alien to China in general and to Confucianism in particular, as has been maintained.[1]

A. THE *DAO* AND THE ONE

An important and much-used cipher for the orientation to a something which does not coincide with the empirical world is the *Dao*. I speak of a "something" because the word *dao*, except for a number of concrete meanings like "way," "method," "teaching," refers to an entity which is vague and undefined and distinct from the familiar. This is supported by the etymology of the character: it shows a deer path, not a broad road known to everybody.[2] The introduction of this term into Chinese thought means a detachment from the social and natural world similar to that implied in the Indian *brahman* or Anaximander's *apeiron*, despite efforts to bridge the gap again. The positions reach from the monism of the Daoists and Confucius' sentence that he would be willing to die in the evening if he could hear of the *Dao* in the morning[3] on the one side, to the "pandaoistic" reconciliation of the *Dao* with the world,[4] or its limitation to the "way of man" (*ren dao*) in Xunzi on the other.[5] The *Dao* has a more metaphysical coloring in

Daoism and a more ethical one in Confucianism. But as far as its distance or closeness to the world is concerned, the conflict of opinions runs through either school.

As a representation of everything still missing in the given state of things, the *Dao* is too abstract to provide a maxim for everyday life. Chinese philosophy has, therefore, made other attempts to find practical standards for moral action beyond mere conventionalism and fulfillment of role obligations. The search is directed to abstract norms or to a moral principle in the sense of a *first* and *one* which is not dependent on something else. That the expression "principle" in this sense, for which classical Chinese knows the term *yi*,[6] is not out of place here, is evidenced by *Lunyu* 15.3:

> The Master said: "Ci (Zigong)! Do you think I am one who has come to knowledge by learning much?"—"Yes, I do! Or is it not so?"— "No, it is not! I pervade (*guan*) all by one."

To learn and become acquainted with many things is in agreement with the Confucian ideal of knowledge. But "if one learns without thinking, one gets entangled."[7] A unifying perspective is necessary in order to systemize what one has experienced and studied and to draw conclusions on the still unknown. The topic as such transcends ethics. It concerns a methodic postulate of general relevance which is also addressed in *Lunyu* 7.8 and 5.9, and in many passages of the *Xunzi*.[8] In *Lunyu* 4.15, however, the context is ethical:

> The Master said, "Shen! My way (*dao*) is pervaded (*guan*) by one." "Yes!" said Zengzi. When the Master had gone, the disciples asked, "What does he mean?" Zengzi said, "The way of our teacher is *zhong* and *shu* (benevolence and fairness), and that is all."

Yet, it has been called into question that Zengzi's concretization of the "one pervading all" has to be understood in terms of ethics. According to Hu Shi, such an understanding would be a misinterpretation, since, as he says, the two terms *zhong* and *shu* have not only an ethical, but also an epistemological meaning.[9] The founder of this modern view is Zhang Taiyan (1869–1936):

> The way (*dao*) is to "pervade all by one," and *zhong* and *shu* are its cardinal points. . . . When the mind is able to draw analogies, this means *shu*. To examine things from all sides, this is *zhong*. To "know ten by hearing one," and to "answer with the other three corners after one has been pointed out" is, therefore, a matter of *shu*.[10] . . . To examine things from all sides, to point out their phenomena and to analyze their structures, this is a task of *zhong*. Hence, "to have a thorough understanding and know the distant" is *shu*, and "systematics and meticulous scrutinizing" is *zhong*.[11] To "observe something oneself" is *zhong*, and when "the location is no barrier" we deal with *shu*.[12]

By the last two definitions, Zhang Taiyan refers to the Mohist canon. The Mohists distinguish three kinds of knowledge: knowledge by hearing (*wen*) taken over from others "by transmission," knowledge by explanation (*shuo*) won by arguments "without the location's working as a barrier," and personal knowledge (*qin*) achieved by "one's own observation."[13] *Zhong*, then, would be detailed knowledge by personal observation and experience, and *shu* theoretical knowledge gained by abstract inferences without having to occupy a certain place in the chain of transmission or a special observation point.

Zhang Taiyan's interpretation of the term *zhong* is far fetched. In my opinion, *zhong* in *Lunyu* 4.15 serves to specify *shu* in a specifically ethical sense.[14] *Shu*, however, indeed implies the logical operation of analogizing. Yet, this does not justify questioning the ethical reading of *Lunyu* 4.15 in favor of a general epistemological one.[15] The point of the passage, like that of the operation *shu*, is exactly to introduce a formal and abstract procedure into ethics—the procedure of analogizing, measuring, and inferring from the self to the other. This procedure, as we will see, constitutes the systematical core of the ethics of the *Lunyu*.

Confucius, then, does not intend to establish a mere catalogue of virtues. He searches for a center, a thread of his ethic.[16] The highlighting of this *one* separates his moral teaching from the pre-Confucian one, which loosely connects virtues without a clear center, or imbeds them into the broad code of propriety.

In Confucianism, several concepts have been elaborated, or taken over from tradition and developed further, which may come into consideration for the coherent and unifying orientation in question: the concepts of the *mean*, of *justice*, and of *humaneness*. In contrast to the material virtues of the conventional stages—filial piety, loyalty, obedience, etc.—they have, at least in some of their readings, a formal and abstract trait. Regressive modifications of these orientations can exactly be understood as re-concretizations. A special role is, furthermore, attached to *friendship*, which owns a potential not always in accordance with conventional standards.

B. FRIENDSHIP

Friends, music, and books—these were the things on which, from the nostalgic retrospection of the Song-Confucians, the ancients set their hearts.[17] As a matter of fact, friendship is given much attention in the early writings, above all in the *Lunyu*.[18] The very second sentence of the work is dedicated to it:

When a fellow student (*peng*) comes from far away, is not this a joy?[19]

For Mengzi, "faith between fellow students (*peng*) and friends (*you*)" is one of his quoted famous "five social relations." Friendship ranks last among them.[20] Yet, what is remarkable is its discovery and acknowledgment as an independent social relation with its own profile, which, in contrast to the other four relations, is based on equality.[21]

The most important aspect of friendship is an ethical one. One should "seek the company of humane people" and "go to those who possess the *Dao* to be corrected by them," says the "Master." A friend should "benevolently be admonished and led in the right direction." Zeng Shen calls friendship a "support for humaneness."[22] Hence it is of true value only when struck up with the good:

> Confucius said, "Three kinds of friendship are advantageous, and three kinds are harmful. To make friends with the upright, the considerate, and those who are very knowledgable is advantageous. To make friends with lackeys, people without spine, and flatterers is harmful."[23]

Everything depends on finding the right friends, and, as Xunzi stresses, one cannot be careful enough in choosing them.[24] But "if one makes friends with a good friend," he asserts, "then one will experience a benevolent, faithful, reverent, and modest conduct."[25] Friendship, then, presupposes the *good*, just as much as to reach this good can hardly be achieved without friendship. Friends are as important as a good teacher,[26] who likewise can become a good friend.

Friendship is already important in the forefield of moral goals. It is indispensable for studying, for "if one learns alone without a friend, one will remain lonesome, on a low level, and uninformed."[27] Now the friend becomes the fellow student, and *pengyou*—fellow students and friends—is a much used composite in Zhou literature.

The company of good friends is desirable also for its own sake, for example when one wants to enjoy nature and leisure far off from the bustle of the world. When Confucius asks some of his pupils with what kind of a task they would like to be entrusted, they express their wishes. Zilu pictures himself as the savior of a state of a thousand war chariots, Ran You would like to help a suffering people to a safe existence, and Gongxi Hua aspires after the office of a ceremonial assistant. Finally, the question goes to Zeng Xi, Zeng Shen's father, who is still half absorbed in playing his zither:

> "And you, Dian, what are your wishes?" Zeng Xi let his music die away, laid the zither aside, rose, and said, "My choice is different from that of the others." The Master said, "What harm is there in that! Each of you should just tell his ideal."
>
> Zeng Xi then said, "In late spring, when the spring clothes have just been made, I should like, together with five or six young men and six or seven boys, to bath in the river Yi, to feel the breeze at the rain altar, and return home singing." The Master sighed and said, "I go with Dian!"[28]

Again we come across the motif of leaving society, of withdrawal from the political tasks which a Confucian, strictly speaking, is committed to. This inclination seems to have been personified and romantically cultivated above all by Zeng Xi, who was called "ardent" by Confucius.[29] However, the "Master's" answer is not without wistfulness. He knows that another reality is waiting for him. Remarkably enough, he gives preference to Zeng Xi over his fellow students who aim at official services. The idyllic being together in the circle of friends gains its own legitimacy vis-à-vis the engagement for the world.

As a more than passing and casual relationship which occupies an independent position among the basic social constellations, friendship can display a dynamic which brings it into conflict with other norms. This conflict can end up tragically, like the one between family and state.[30] The important fact for moral evolution is that friendship runs athwart to all the other social patterns of order. As Mengzi says,

> One strikes up friendship without presuming on age, position, or kinship relations. Friendship is friendship by virtue, and one must not presume on anything else.[31]

Mengzi gives examples of friendships between people of unequal rank up to friendships between rulers and commoners where the social station did not count. In Zhou literature, however, the opposite becomes a topos—the refusal of such ties with the powerful by the intellectuals. In order to bask in their high position, Chinese rulers liked to gather scholars around them and enjoy their respects. He who evaded this embrace became a heroized figure. The prototypes of the proud intellectual "whom no ruler can gain as a friend" are Zeng Shen and Zisi, praised for their conduct by Confucians and Daoists alike.[32] The Legalists, however, regard such an exemplary affront against power as intolerable. It deserves to be punished by death. Han Fei approves of the execution of the two private scholars Kuangyu and Huashi who lived self-sufficiently, refused to take office, and were proud of "neither serving the Son of Heaven as a subject nor making friends with a feudal lord."[33]

Who, then, is the partner of friendship, if not the mighty? Mengzi answers this question as follows:

> He who is an outstanding scholar of a village will make friends with the other outstanding scholars of the village. He who is an outstanding scholar of the whole land will make friends with the other outstanding scholars of the land. He who is an outstanding scholar of the world will make friends with the other outstanding scholars of the world. And if this friendship with the outstanding scholars of the world does not satisfy him, he goes beyond that and discusses the men of antiquity. He will recite their songs and read their books. But

is this possible if he does not know these men? Therefore, he will consider their times. This is highest friendship.[34]

The community of friends, in the final analysis, is the more and more expanding, place and time transcending community of the wise of the world— an elitist club of nonconformists which would also have found its members among the Hellenistic Greeks.

By undermining all hierarchies, friendship harbors an egalitarian potential. In China, this potential could not unfold without subversive consequences. It appears symbolic that the thinker who, to my knowledge, was the first to call friendship the highest form of communication and to declare all other "social relations" (*lun*) deficient in comparison to it, He Xinyin (1517–79), was slain in jail.[35] About 300 years later, the reformer Tan Sitong (1865–1898) was executed. He, too, celebrated friendship as superseding the other four social relations as their "guiding rule."[36]

Yet, however high friendship may rank, it cannot deliver the foundation of morality. The "gentleman," after all, seeks his friends among the virtuous. This not only presupposes a concept of the morally good. It also implies making a selection which does not exclude particularism.

C. MEASURE, MEAN, AND HARMONY

To find the right measure and avoid hubris is a fundamental idea of ancient ethics. In ancient China, too, the number of warnings against greed (*tan, duo yu*), excess (*yin*), eccentricity (*pi*), unrestraint (*fang*), immoderateness (*guo du, wu jie*), etc., is legion. They have been unanimously brought forward by all schools. For the Daoists, the anthropocentrism of the Confucians itself is the embodiment of presumptuousness. For their own position of mimesis to nature, they claim the "mean" resting in itself, while haste and audacity are ascribed to the unleashed human ratio and its Confucian protagonists. Reversely, the Daoists appear eccentric to the Confucians who are always concerned about forms and manners.

The idea of measure played an important role not only in ethics, but also in politics and economy. Confucian texts, especially the *Yijing*, frequently demand to consider the "right moment" (*shi*) for all measures.[37] Confucius recommends that statute labor should only be performed "in accordance with the season."[38] Xunzi and Mengzi demand restrictions on felling trees and fishing.[39] The *Yueling* ("Monthly orders") presents a well-balanced program for state activities and the use of natural resources.[40] In all of these cases, the idea of measure is brought forward against a world which has become immoderate—countries are struck with war, the people are plagued by corvée and taxes, and nature has suffered severe damage in the surrounding of the settlement centers.

But what is the right measure? Confucius, for whom to "go beyond is like falling short of the mark,"[41] has understood it as the *mean*. He recommends the mean (*zhong*) as a general maxim:

> The application of the mean as virtue—this will be the highest! It has been rare among the people for a long time.[42]

The "application of the mean" (*zhong yong*) has become prominent by the writing of the same name,[43] which Zhu Xi later has included in the *Four Books*, the basic texts of classical Confucianism, as he saw it. The *Zhongyong* is, above all, known for the cosmological exaltation of the Confucian moral values—a quite questionable fame, though. It gives disappointingly little information about the topic of its title. For all that, we find the following explication:

> When pleasure, anger, melancholy, and joy have not yet been stirred, this is called the mean (*zhong*). When they have been stirred and yet hit the right measure (*jie*), this is called harmony (*he*). The mean is the great fundament of the world. Harmony is the universal path of the world. Let the mean and harmony come, and heaven and earth will find their hold in them, and all things will be nourished by them.[44]

The *Zhongyong* projects ethical concepts into the cosmos, thus making the mean an ontological entity. I will deal with this aspect of the *Zhongyong* later; here I want to discuss the ethical content of the passage in the narrower sense. The first sentence refers to the original condition of human nature (*xing*) which shortly before has been defined as "what has been endowed by heaven" (*tian ming*). To hit the right measure when the emotions arise preserves this original constitution in everyday life. To hit the measure, then, means the controlled operation of emotions, the avoidance of excess as well as of too much reserve. The ideal is to "take hold of the two extremes," like Shun in the days of yore, which reminds one of the preference the *Lunyu* gives to the mean over ardency and caution.[45] The affinity with the Greek idea of *mesotes* is obvious, though a systematic presentation like that in Aristotle's *Ethica Nicomachea* is missing.[46] The *Zhongyong* merely gives some scattered hints towards a more detailed understanding. A gentleman, we read, "stands in the middle and does not incline to the side."[47] Similarly, Xunzi confronts the "mean" and "one-sidedness" (*pian*).[48] *Zhongyong* 6, moreover, praises Shun for "using the mean when dealing with the people." And Mengzi says that Tang, the founder of the Shang dynasty, too, "held fast the mean."[49] The mean, in these cases, refers to just and balanced government.

The principle of the mean has often been regarded as a kind of national wisdom of China. According to Liang Qichao, Confucianism met with such success exactly since it represented this characteristic trait of the Chinese people.[50] Wing-tsit Chan has recently recommended the idea of the mean, for him the quintessence of the Confucian teaching, as a framework for the current discussion on China's modernization.[51] As the authentic wisdom of "the" Chinese, however, the way of the mean would become a general maxim of prudence, of the avoidance of extremes, of the mediation of opposites, and of a reasonable thoughtfulness in every possible situation of life. Although this would suffice to prevent excesses—for example of politics—and, insofar, must not be thought little of, the specific "moral point of view" would be lost in such a broad and far reaching practical advice. It would be problematical, therefore, to locate a moral principle like the Golden Rule within the general setting of the observance of the mean, as Liang Qichao has suggested.[52] For, the mean, much more than the Golden Rule, contains problems which make doubtful whether it can serve as an ethical, let alone postconventional maxim in the first place. First of all, it can fall under suspicion of mediocrity. E. v. Hartmann, to give an example, under the influence of Nietzsche, rebukes Aristotle for an "apotheosis of mediocrity" which does not go well with Greece, but with the "manneristic ceremonial" of China, where "society in its insipid and characterless leveling resembles a lacquered tea tray."[53] And for Weber, the "correct mean" is the "supreme good" of the "ethic of social adjustment" which he imputes to Confucianism.[54] The mean, then, would simply coincide with the normal.

The Confucian mean, however, is not to be misunderstood as an easy adaptation to general consent. When Confucius breaks a lance for the "ardent," it is because he cannot find "men pursuing the way of the mean."[55] The "mean," here, is even more far away from normality than ardent exuberance. And the *Zhongyong* emphasizes:

> It is possible that the whole empire, a country, or a clan are brought to order. It is possible that one declines rank and emolument. It is possible that one treads on a naked blade. And yet, it might be impossible that one understands to use the mean.[56]

> A gentleman is harmonious, but he does not swim with the tide. How strong he is and proud! A gentleman stands in the middle and does not incline to the side. How strong he is and proud! When the *Dao* prevails in the country, he does not change the bastion [of his conviction]. How strong he is and proud! When the *Dao* does not prevail in the country, he does not change his course to death. How strong he is and proud![57]

In these passages, the mean is the absolute opposite of averageness. To keep to the mean helps to find an inner balance which immunizes against the temptation to establish oneself in convenient adjustment. For all of this, it has to be asked whether the "mean" can really accomplish the "extraordinary"[58] which Confucius and the *Zhongyong* associate with it. The mean, and this is the crucial problem, can only be thought of as the middle between something, in a similar way as every measure presupposes a unit of measurement. Who furnishes the parameters for this? And is not, furthermore, the harmony of emotions aimed at in *Zhongyong* I neutral in relationship to a broad variety of practical goals, too? The mean, then, is relative to something else. Mengzi has pointed out this weakness:

> To hold a mean without weighing is like holding one side. I hate this one-sidedness, since it injures the *Dao* and means choosing one point and discarding a hundred others.[59]

In order to provide valid moral orientations, an additional criterion is necessary. Otherwise the normality of a merely relative community itself will define the limits, instead of being transcended, if necessary. It is in this sense that Xunzi associates the "stream of the mean" (*zhong liu*) with propriety (*li*), which "trims what is too long, stretches out what is too short, diminishes what is too much, and adds to what is insufficient."[60] And the *Zhouli* proposes "checking the falseness of the people and teaching them the mean by the five domains of propriety."[61] Utterances like these have aroused a suspicion of ideology against the Confucian "mean."[62]

An analogous problem is constituted by the concept of *harmony* (*he, tiao, xie*). Like the mean, harmony is often extolled as the quintessence of Chinese "wisdom."[63] Allegedly, it especially characterizes the relation of man and nature, which is actually one of the many myths about the East. Nature for most Chinese was primarily an economic resource, and Chinese civilization has done its best to exploit and utilize it for human interests. True, there have been "ecological insights."[64] But they are found in Daoist rather than in Confucian literature, and they were, with bitter words, formulated against a reality which was already in Zhou times marked by the subjugation and beginning destruction of nature. The Confucians have, at least in principle, welcomed this separation of the human world from that of nature.[65] From the perspective of Chinese history, China's modern ecological disaster is thoroughly homemade.

Harmony, in relation to the individual as well as to society, doubtless is a Confucian ideal. When the Confucians appreciate music, it is not least because of its power to form a harmonious character in a harmonious society.[66] But what should harmonize with each other, and at what costs? Again, a criterion is necessary for setting limits. If this criterion is propriety, harmony can assume a conventional coloring:

> Master You said, "Of the functions of propriety, harmony is the most precious, and of the ways of the former kings, it is the most beautiful. One should follow it in matters small and great, but there is one restriction: To be harmonious for harmony's sake, and not to set a limit to it by the rules of propriety—this cannot be done."[67]

For Confucius' disciple You Ruo, harmony is subordinated to the social bounds defined by propriety. It needs just a slight modification of this idea to make harmony an ideological concept of reifying social inequality and upholding rule. For the Han-Confucian Dong Zhongshu, harmony serves as a means to keep the social order, which is based on a strict separation of rich and poor, in a manipulated balance. As he writes, drawing on Xunzi and the *Liji*:

> Great richness leads to arrogance, great poverty leads to worry. The feelings of the multitude are such that from worry one gets a robber, and from arrogance a tyrant. The sages recognized these feelings as the source of chaos. Therefore, they conceived the way of man (*ren dao*)[68] and distinguished high and low, so that the rich had enough to display their high position without getting arrogant, and the poor had enough to make their living without getting into worry. With this as a norm, harmony (*he*) and balance (*jun*) are achieved. Therefore, wealth is not exhausted, and high and low live in peace with each other, Hence, it is easy to rule.[69]

Harmony, then, can go together with extreme inequality. It is a secondary value and relative to the preconditions under which it operates, and to the aims which shall be achieved by it. Just as the mean is neutral in comparison to the poles, harmony is neutral in comparison to the parts between which it establishes a balance. The problem was recognized in early Confucianism, for we find efforts to put a moral and not merely a social constraint on harmony. As Xunzi states, it is indifferent towards good and evil:

> To harmonize with others for the sake of goodness is called adaptability. . . . To harmonize with others for the sake of evil is called toadying.[70]

A "gentleman," therefore, will see to it that his strife for harmony does not end up in opportunism. He "harmonizes, but does not conform (*tong*)," says Confucius. He "is harmonious, but does not swim with the tide," we read in the *Zhongyong*.[71] Xunzi condemns officials who "conform with a speculative mind and are opportunistically complaisant (*gou rong*)."[72] The *Hanshi waizhuan* quotes this passage, substituting *tong* (conform) for *rong* (complaisant).[73] *Bu gou tong*, "not to conform opportunistically," has remained a Chinese ideal till today.

As a counterbalance to harmony, therefore, Confucianism knows the readiness to quarrel, not only with people of lower or equal rank, but also with authorities like father and ruler, as described in previous chapters. Far more dangerous than such defiance is unconditional harmony. Rather than creating "conflict by concord," the moral actor should seek "concord by conflict," as the *Huainanzi* says in a trenchant formulation which in essence will meet with the approval of the genuine Confucians.[74]

D. JUSTICE

Yi is a central concept of classical Chinese ethics which is frequently translated as "justice." This translation suggests itself already because of the modern composite for "justice," *zhengyi*. *Yi* has, furthermore, been rendered as "righteousness," "sense of duty," "oughtness," "integrity," or, in Boodberg's neologism experiment—distortingly—as "selfshipful compropriety" and "nostritude."[75] More than any other concept, *yi* confronts us with the basic difficulty of translating classical Chinese—the right translation of the terms. In the given case, the variety of proposals coincides with actual variations in the meaning of *yi*,[76] which can be aptly explained by the difficulty to determine what the "just" is in the first place. But our term "justice" is intricate, too. When "justice" recommends itself as a translation of *yi*, it is above all for the reason that the basic intuition in both cases is the same: the point at issue is the *due* and the *fitting* or *appropriate*. *Yi*, therefore, is frequently identified with the homophonic *yí*:

> *Yi* means *yí* (appropriate). To honor the wise is the greatest exercise of it.[77]

> *Yi* is that everybody does his due (*yí*).[78]

> *Yi* means that there is a relationship of service between ruler and subject, superior and subordinate, that there is a distinction between father and son, and high and low, that there is contact between acquaintances, fellow students, and friends, that there is a difference between relatives and strangers, and the family and the public. It is appropriate (*yí*) that the subjects serve the ruler. It is appropriate (*yí*) that the subordinates are devoted to the superiors. It is appropriate (*yí*) that acquaintances, fellow students, and friends help each other. It is appropriate (*yí*) that relatives belong to the inner and strangers to the outer circle. The just *yi* means the appropriate (*yí*).[79]

The coincidence with the due or the appropriate (*yí*) is a very common connotation of *yi*, the just, and it is quite characteristic of the antique understanding of justice. The Chinese identification of *yi* and *yí* corresponds to Plato's and Aristotle's notion of *dikaiosyne* (justice). For Plato, justice is "the having and doing what is a man's own and belongs to him," and "doing one's business and not being a busybody."[80] For Aristotle, justice is "the virtue through which everybody has his due, in accordance with the law."[81] What this means becomes plain in Aristotle's *Politics*: "It is clear, then, that some men are by nature free, and others slaves, and that for the latter slavery is both expedient and just (*dikaion*)."[82] To translate *yi* as "justice," then, does not prejudge the content of the notion of justice and leaves room for interpretation. Relative to the moral stage, what is "just" can be understood quite differently. When Rawls and Kohlberg, to give an example, speak of "justice *as fairness*," or "justice *as reversibility*," they refer to the highest stage of moral competence. Justice, for them, comprises the idea of general *equality*. In antiquity, however, the combination of justice and equality is not at all self-evident. For Aristotle, the just can go together with equality and inequality alike:

> For all men cling to justice of some kind, but their conceptions are imperfect, and they do not express the whole idea. For example, justice is thought by them to be, and is, equality, not, however, for all, but only for equals. And inequality is thought to be, and is, justice, neither is this for all, but only for unequals. When the persons are omitted, then men judge erroneously.[83]

Their conviction that all men are equal by nature has protected the Chinese philosophers from such a discrimination of "unequals by birth," for example slaves, as in Aristotle's *Politica*. Nevertheless, despite their egalitarian anthropology, the social bounds and separations predetermined by the given inequalities of their society do play a role in their idea of justice. This holds true for example for Mengzi's occasional definition of justice as "respect for elders," or his defense of the rule of the brainworkers over those who work with their physical strength as "general justice of the world."[84] It is even more typical of the *Xunzi* and the *Liji*, where we find the following passages:

> To be honored as Son of Heaven and be so wealthy as to possess the whole world—this is something that the human feelings of each man desire. To give free reign to human desires can neither be tolerated from the vantage point of power, nor would the material goods be enough to satisfy the desires in the first place. The early kings, accordingly, have established propriety (*li*) and justice (*yi*) for men, in order to assign different roles to them, creating thereby the ranks of high and low, the disparity between old and young, and the separation of roles between the wise and the stupid, the able and the incapable. They made sure that each man would assume his tasks and receive his due (*yi*). After that, they cared for well-balanced emoluments.[85]

> That the young serve the old, the inferior serve the superior, and the incapable serve the wise—this is the all-pervading justice of the world.[86]

> Justice inside (in society) sets measures among men, and outside sets measures in the world of things. Above it gives peace to the ruler, and below it creates harmony among the people. To set measures inside and outside, above and below, this is the essence of justice. Therefore, as far as the essentials for managing the world are concerned, justice is the fundament, and confidence is the next important.[87]

What is the just for man? That the father is kind and the son is filial, that the elder brother is good to the younger brother and the younger brother respects the elder brother, that the husband is just *(yi)*[88] and the wife is obedient, that the elder are gracious and the young are docile, that the ruler is humane and the subject is loyal—these ten things are called the just for man.[89]

The gentleman calls justice that high and low have their tasks in the world.[90]

These quotations[91] share a notion of justice which is oriented to the particular social station. The meaning of justice is the maintenance of a hierarchical order with a strict division of roles in which everybody fulfills his duty,[92] that is, does his "due," and only this. *Yi*, accordingly, is often used in connection with the vocabulary of social differentiation *(bie, fen, cha, deng, lei)*. This corresponds with the Confucian teaching of the "correct use of terms" *(zheng ming)*. When the *Lunyu* demands that "the ruler be ruler, the subject be subject, the father be father, the son be son,"[93] it makes use of the conventional concept of justice. *Yi* in this connection is close to *li*. To do the just in the sense of the appropriate to the station is the preliminary stage of propriety. "Propriety is the fruit of justice," we read in the *Liyun* and similarly in the *Guanzi*.[94] The most clear indication of the conventional content of this idea of justice is the fusion of *yi*, justice, and *li*, propriety, to the compound meaning "morals." *Liyi* is frequently used in the *Xunzi*, the *Liji*, and the *Guanzi*. They give preference to it over the compound *renyi* which is coined by Mo Di and also preferred by Mengzi. Perhaps the best way to construe the co-occurrence of *li* and *yi* is to view *yi* as representing the *general* structures of the hierarchical social relations—like the subordination of the subject under the ruler, and the son under the father—and *li* as describing the *detailed* code of the corresponding appropriate forms of behavior.[95] At the same time, in the compound *liyi*, justice becomes human etiquette itself as the characteristic which distinguishes human society from the animal kingdom. "The absence of distinctions and justice is the way of beasts," says the *Liji*,[96] and Xunzi differentiates:

Fire and water have energy, but no life. Grass and trees have life, but no knowledge. The animals have knowledge, but no justice. Man has energy, life, knowledge, and, moreover, justice. Therefore, man is the highest being in the world.[97]

If *yi* is a conventional rule in the sense of "everybody his due," why, then, regard it as a candidate for a postconventional principle? The reason is that in Confucian literature *yi* is not always relative to the social position. That the "appropriate" could be more than the orientation to the prescriptions of the station is evidenced by many passages I have quoted already. When Mengzi puts virtue above rank, he appeals to Zeng Shen's proud rebuff of the powerful of Jin and Chu: "Let them adhere to their ranks—I adhere to my sense of justice!" In Wan Zhang's question on the conditions of accepting a present from a ruler, *yi* can only be understood in a nonconventional sense. Convention would prescribe the acceptance of the present, not its rejection in the name of justice. The notion of justice in the *Zidao*, too, is nonconventional, since justice overrides the duty of obedience.[98]

The postconventional content of the notion of justice *(yi)* in these and similar cases is obviously this. Now no longer the internal perspective of the prescriptions of the specific role is decisive, but the external perspective of the advocate of morality on the *social order in its entirety*. Now, justice can even imply, in view of the injustice done by the powerful, transcending the limits defined by the role. The Chinese intellectuals have always justified their existence as a stratum subsisting on the material producers by this engagement for the justice of the whole. Mo Di, to give an example, claims to benefit the world by teaching it justice much more than a farmer or a weaver ever could by their handwork.[99] Confucius' admonition to his disciples that it would be "cowardice not to interfere when justice is at stake"[100] has always been understood as a call to civil courage in the interest of the underprivileged. The *Lunyu* attributes such a sense of justice, above all, to the "gentleman."[101] This does not mean, however, that partisanship for justice would be the gentleman's "due" in terms of, again, a duty of station. The reverse is the case: the intellectual elite constitutes itself as a distinct social body by its self-interpretation as the advocate of justice, also on behalf of those who are unable to help themselves. In the quasi-station of the intellectuals, which forms itself right through the social classes, justice loses its character of a duty of station.

A just order, which is also binding for the powerful, is characterized *negatively* by the renunciation of being set on one's own advantage. Mengzi identifies the "feeling of shame and dislike" as the innate root of the sense of justice, forming the negative counterpart of the active impulse of humaneness.[102] Bo Yi, Yi Yin, and Confucius, he stresses, "would never have committed a single injustice or killed a single innocent person in order to achieve the power over the world." Chen Zhongzi, he says, would have "declined the rule over the state of Qi offered to him contrary to justice," and would not accept a revenue from his brother, because he considered his emolument to be "unjust." When told that a planned abolition of taxes shall still be postponed, Mengzi says, "Knowing that something is unjust, one must put an end to it quickly—why wait till next year?" And he generalizes, "To take what is not one's own is unjust."[103]

It is obvious whom this restrictive, negative reading of justice is directed against: the powerful of the time. Their greediness obstructs the raison d'être of the state which exclusively consists in safeguarding a just order. The *positive* side of such an order can be inferred from Mengzi's attitude towards war. When Qi in 314 B.C. attacks and occupies its neighbor Yan, where a tyrannic government has provoked civil war, Mengzi supports the annexation of Yan provided that "the people of Yan are pleased with it."[104] If we additionally take into account his verdict that there has not been a single "just war" in the whole Chunqiu era,[105] we can conclude that the possible "justice" of an offensive war depends on whether it is to the advantage of the people in the attacked state. This criterion is *utilitarian* inasmuch as it aims at public welfare as distinct from the private interests of the warring parties. As we have seen, such a utilitarian idea stands in the center of the Confucian legitimation of the state. It has, above all, been elaborated by Xunzi, and his arguments sound like an explication of the concept of justice. For Xunzi, the direct outcome of just politics is "shared benefit" and general profit for the world:

> Tang and Wu (the founders of the Shang and Zhou dynasties) followed their *Dao* and practiced their justice. They promoted the shared benefit (*tong li*) of the world, abolished its shared harm (*tong hai*), and the whole world turned towards them.[106]
>
> To arrange works according to the four seasons, to control the myriad things, and to be equally profitable (*jian li*) to the whole world—there is no other reason for this than distinctions and justice.[107]

In his ingenious dialectical theory of society, Xunzi combines the conventional reading of justice with the idea of the just order in its entirety, in terms of general welfare and benefit. Propriety and justice, he points out repeatedly, were created by the sages of the past to establish social order. This order is to guarantee, above all, a regulated access of all to the scarce resources. Although Xunzi from the beginning assumes an asymmetry of the rights of disposal, the just order is not meant to privilege some at the expense of others. In order to give a share to everybody, the shares have to be unequal, since it is only by social difference that all can escape from the wearing struggle in the natural state. Social difference, at the same time, makes careers possible and is a stimulus to exert oneself. The secret of a well-functioning and productive order for Xunzi lies in the mediation of unity and difference.[108] Justice, then, integrates inequality and equality, the task of the hierarchical order being to safeguard the existence of everyone. This idea reminds one of Rawls' "principle of difference," and modifying a sentence of his we could define: *Justice consists in inequalities which are to the benefit of all.*[109]

This double character of justice helps to explain many of the divergences in the use of *yi*. The stress can be laid on its conventional, restrictive aspect as well as on the abstract one aiming at the interest of the greater whole. Both sides can conflict with one another if the general interest necessitates suspending what would be appropriate according to the social station. The paradigm cases for this conflict are the rebellions of Tang and Wu Wang against the tyrants Jie and Zhòu. For Xunzi, they exemplify how "justice is achieved only by the usurpation of power, humaneness by killing, and loyalty (*zhen*) by exchanging the positions of superiors and subordinates."[110] In both cases, the basic idea remains the same: justice has to bring into effect the interest of all against the egoism of individuals and groups. In the name of justice, Chinese philosophers constantly polemize against the search for private profit. In the *Lunyu*, the terms *yi* and *li* (profit) already contrast with each other:

> A gentleman listens to the argument of justice, a mean man listens to the argument of profit.

> He who seeing a profit yet thinks of justice . . . can be regarded as a complete person.[111]

The book *Mengzi* starts with a moral lecture to King Hui of Liang who wants to hear something "profitable" and is, instead, referred to humaneness and justice. Xunzi, too, never grows weary of denouncing the greed for gain and attacking *li* in the name of *yi* while defending the benefit for all. The campaign against egoism and the partly implicit and partly open identification of justice and "geometrically" distributed advantages for all are two sides of one and the same public-utilitarian basic idea. They explain themselves by the political direction of assault of many of the Confucian statements on justice, which aim at the ruling classes and their indolence to the suffering of the people. Against this group of squanderers and despots, who have been a constant nuisance to all of the axial age thinkers, it is necessary, at the same time, to condemn private selfishness and demand public utility. In political justice, both aspects are reconciled with each other. The *Daxue* drives this point home when it makes us consider that what matters in a state is "not to regard profit (*li*) as profit, but to regard justice (*yi*) as profit."[112] The Confucian usage of the term *yi*, therefore, can be understood within the general context of discussion of the Zhou era, in which the linkage between the two concepts of *yi* and *li* is quite common. From the pre-Confucian thinkers via Mo Di to the late Mohists, *yi* and *li* are communicating terms.

In its public-utilitarian dimension, *yi* is related to another notion expressing "justice" in classical Chinese: the notion of *gong*. The basic meaning of *gong* is "public." As the opposite of *si* (private, selfish) and *pian* (one-sided, partial), it stands for impartiality, public spirit, and neutrality. *Gong* means justice, inasmuch as justice implies putting one's personal advantage and group interests last in favor of objective and general goals. In order to distinguish *gong* from *yi*, I have chosen the translation "impartiality." What was meant by *gong* is most evident from the chapter *Appreciation of Impartiality* (*Gui gong*) of the *Lüshi chunqiu*. We read:

> When in ancient times the sage kings ruled the world, it was indispensable for them to put impartiality first. By impartiality the world comes to peace. . . . In general, the stability of rule is an outcome of impartiality. Therefore, the *Hongfan* says, "Do not be one-sided, do not be partial, the way of a king is vast. Do not be one-sided, do not be prejudiced, follow the justice (*yi*) of a king. Never give yourself over to your predilections, follow the way of a king. Never give yourself over to your dislikes, follow the road of a king."

The world is not the world of a single person, it is the world's world. The harmony of Yin and Yang does not merely let one single species grow. Sweet dew and timely rain do not give preference to a particular being. And the ruler of all the people must not favor a single man.

When leaving for his fief Lu, Boqin asked how to govern. Zhou Gong (his father) said, "Be beneficial, but do not seek [your own] benefit!"

A man of Jing lost his bow. Instead of seeking it, he said, "A man of Jing has lost it, a man of Jing will find it. Why should I seek it, then?" When Confucius heard about it he said, "If he leaves out *Jing*, it will be all right." When Lao Dan heard of it, he said, "If he leaves out *man*, too, it will be all right." Thus Lao Dan was the most impartial.

Heaven and earth are great. Yet, they do not treat as their children what they produce, and they do not take possession of what they accomplish. All things experience their kindness and get their benefit, but no one knows from where it comes. Such was the virtue of the Three Majesties and the Five Emperors.[113]

The fact that this passage from the *Lüshi chunqiu* collects Confucian as well as Daoist materials shows that the idea of impartial justice belongs to the shared cultural heritage of the ancient Chinese.[114] The exemplification of an impartial attitude by heaven and earth and metaphors from nature, too, hits on the commonsense.[115] Opinions differ, however, when it comes to decide who is to enjoy the benefits of impartiality. The parable of the lost bow shows that for the "substantial" ethical life of the normal people, the moral boundary coincides with the boundary of the own country. For the Confucians, all men as men, regardless of their origin, belong into the range of application of impartiality. The macroethics of the Daoists, represented by Lao Dan, expands the community of equals to the entirety of nature.

More than the term *yi*, which often pays tribute to the restrictions of the specific social standing, *gong* implies the idea of treating everybody as equal. *Yi* is a concept of justice which, at least in one of its typical readings, can accept *inequality* in favor of the well-being of all (not to be misunderstood as the well-being of the majority). *Gong*, however, is a concept of justice which assumes the *equality* of all. The *Lüshi chunqiu* calls the father of an assassin impartial (*gong*) who, saying that anyone who kills another has to be put to death, rejects mercy for his son.[116] According to the same chapter, Confucius praised Qi Huangyang from Chu as impartial (*gong*), because he recommended a personal enemy for a high position.[117] The capable, hence, have to be given equal chances, regardless of our relationship towards them. Xunzi illustrates the idea of equal chances by making "drawing sticks and throwing hooks"—casting lots—the model case of an impartial (*gong*) attitude.[118]

When *gong* does not refer to action, but to judgment, it can be rendered as "objective." Xunzi demands to "speak from a humane heart, listen with readiness to learn, discuss in an impartial (*gong*) spirit, and not let oneself be moved by what the multitude criticizes or praises,"[119] and he expects the feudal lords to be "impartial in their judicial decisions."[120]

Another concept of justice is *ping*, "equability." According to Xunzi, the people go to where "punishments and administrative measures are equable." As "highest equability" he praises what he considers the just society, conceived as the dialectical unity of equality and inequality.[121]

The terms *zheng* (upright, straight, correct), *zhi* (straight, direct), and *zhong* (mean), too, have an affinity to justice. All of these terms are combinable with each other and frequently build compounds, of which *gongzheng*, *zhengyi*, *gongping*, and *zhengping* have become modern standard expressions for "justice."

I have presented a number of conceptions which hypothetically come into consideration for postconventional norms or principles, in order to compensate the insufficiencies of mere role morality. It is doubtful, however, whether the discussed concepts meet the demand of a "one pervading all": *Friendship* harbors an egalitarian potential, but it concerns a selected circle of people and presupposes a criterion for choosing friends. The adherence to the *mean* prevents excesses, but is relative to the extremes and, therefore, is dependent on additional determinations. *Harmony* may secure peace, but it does, by itself, not preclude to harmonize with the bad, or to harmonize for opportunistic reasons. The discussed concepts of *justice* have a broad range of variation. The "just" (*yi*) can be the conventionally appropriate as defined by the social status. Other ideas of justice are postconventional in that they do not refer to what is due to the role, but to the just organization of the society as a whole. Xunzi, however, shows that the concept of justice bound to the social station, too, can have a postconventional substratum. To make plain the necessity of a hierarchical order, he refers to the general interest of all men in securing their existence. This view of society under the aspect of general utility, as well as the corresponding concept of justice, represents Stage 5 of moral evolution. Nevertheless, the idea of equality inherent in it suffers from a hierarchical distortion and comprises inequality. But it needs only one step further to identify the just directly with the general interest. This is done in the idea of impartiality (*gong*). Whereas *yi*, at least in a typical reading of the term, demands the *due* for everyone according to his position, *gong* demands the *same* for all of them. Both notions of justice come close to a generalizable basic principle of ethics. Confucianism, however, knows yet another moral concept which looks even more suitable for a "one pervading all"—the concept of humaneness.

10

Humaneness (ren)

I f we seek for a concept which represents Confucian ethics more than other concepts do, this is *ren*, "humanity" or "humaneness." Because of the etymology of the character, which contains the elements "man" and "two," the translation of *ren* appears to be less difficult than that of other terms. The concrete meaning of *ren*, however, is already for the ancients a topic of discussion. And when today opinions diverge about the *Lunyu*, this relates in most cases to different evaluations of "humaneness" and of its rank in the hierarchy of values. In the final analysis, the fundamental question of the debate is whether humaneness or propriety (*li*) stands in the systematical center of the work. In the People's Republic, Confucius has either been praised as the advocate of humaneness—unless *ren* has been understood in terms of group morality of the nobility—or been condemned as the ideologist of conventional etiquette.[1] Sympathies for Confucius as the philosopher of *li* can be found in the political conservatism of East Asia, but also, remarkably, in contemporary American Chinese studies.[2]

A. THE POSITION OF HUMANENESS (*REN*) IN THE SYSTEM OF THE *LUNYU* AND ITS RELATION TO PROPRIETY (*LI*)

If one compares the *Lunyu* to other Zhou texts, a first impression already indicates the role it ascribes to humaneness. *Ren* is by far the most frequent ethical term, while in pre-Confucian literature (including *Zuozhuan* and *Guoyu*), characteristically, *li* takes the first place.[3] In the *Lunyu*, humaneness appears in about 60 of its nearly 500 passages. The quantitative change corresponds to a qualitative one. In the words of Wing-tsit Chan, *ren* from a "particular virtue along with other particular virtues" develops into a "general virtue which is universal and fundamental from which all other particular virtues ensue."[4] This development,

119

however, remains incomplete in the *Lunyu*, partly because of the unsystematic and protocol-like nature of the text. We find a lot of disjointed statements, a great amount of which consists of performative speech acts like eulogies and counsels[5] or touch upon, as I see it, secondary implications of a "humane" attitude. There are only few passages which refer to essential characteristics of humaneness. Its decisive role in the system of the *Lunyu*, as well as this system itself, largely remains implicit and is hidden under the work's fragmentary surface.[6] Nevertheless, there is such a system, and the *Lunyu* is not a model case of a merely situational ethics.

If we take into consideration the passages in which Confucius directly answers questions regarding humaneness, five accounts attract attention: the accounts of humaneness as a return to propriety, as love, as respect, as the Golden Rule, and as a clamp encompassing other virtues.[7] The last of these accounts indicates the place which humaneness occupies in Confucius' ethical system. When *ren* is viewed in the *Lunyu* as a combination of "reverence (*gong*), tolerance (*kuan*), trustworthiness (*xin*), keenness (*min*), and kindness (*hui*)," or of "reverence (*gong*) in private life, respect (*jing*) when entrusted with a task, and benevolence (*zhong*) when dealing with others,"[8] this shows its "inclusive"[9] character. If one achieves *ren*, one at the same time masters other virtues, also including courage, prudence, cautiousness in talking, and propriety.[10]

In many passages of the *Lunyu*, humaneness is a nearly unattainable ideal which even Confucius himself, as he says, has failed to realize.[11] To become a "gentleman" (*junzi*) and not to remain a "mean man" (*xiao ren*), however, is a realistic goal of his pedagogics. Humaneness ranks higher than the *junzi*-ideal, as is evident from the sentence, "It can happen that as a gentleman one does not have humaneness."[12] Yet, just like humaneness, the "gentleman," too, is an ensemble of virtuous behavior which encompasses, among other things, justice, solidarity, impartiality, and harmony.[13] The specific nature of humaneness, then, must be found in something other than in its "inclusive" character: it is the top of an ethical hierarchy which "gives meaning"[14] to all the other norms. This hierarchy—which is only implicit in the *Lunyu*—has the following structure:

1. Social virtues like trustworthiness (*xin*), reverence (*gong*) harmony (*he*), and giving precedence (*rang*) are either restricted by concrete prescriptions of propriety or subordinate to justice (*yi*) and humaneness. As the *Lunyu* says:

    Reverence without propriety is lost labor.

    When humaneness is at stake, one does not give precedence to the teacher.

    (Youzi:) When reliability is in agreement with justice, a word given can be made good. When reverence is in agreement with propriety, one will escape disgrace.

(Youzi:) To be harmonious for harmony's sake, and not to set a limit to it by the rules of propriety, this cannot be done.[15]

2. The militant virtue of courage *yong* is subordinate to propriety, justice, and humaneness:

Courage without propriety leads to rebellion.

A gentleman regards justice higher than courage. If he has courage, but does not know justice, he will become a rebel. A mean man, under the same circumstances, will become a robber.

A humane person will surely also have courage. But a courageous person does not necessarily have humaneness.[16]

3. The intellectual virtues of prudence (*zhi*), and eloquence (*ning, you yan*) are subordinate to virtue (*de*) in general, or to humaneness:

A humane person rests in humaneness. A prudent person [only] regards humaneness as profitable.

I do not know why Yong (a disciple) should need eloquence if he is already humane.

A virtuous person surely will also be eloquent. But an eloquent person is not necessarily virtuous.[17]

In this order, a higher level does not exclude, but includes what on a lower level, taken for itself, is only of relative validity. The different virtues shall not be played off against each other. They come into their own each at its proper place, and there should be no conflict between them, if possible. This harmonizing tendency explains itself by the task Confucius is facing: to find a new moral basis exactly for rescuing the ethical life. Mediation, not conflict, but not mediation at any cost, is the main option of this program, and it is here that success and decline of Confucian ethics is rooted. When Confucius' teaching exerted fascination, it was because it promised the integration of a moral attitude (*Moralität*) and a socially responsible ethical life (*Sittlichkeit*). At the same time, it suffered, like all of the great ethical conceptions of mankind, from a loss of substance, which is perhaps due to the fact that *Moralität* and *Sittlichkeit* are too smoothly reconciled with each other, and that their latent potential of conflict is not brought out in a trenchant manner. This becomes most apparent in the relationship of the two cardinal terms *ren* and *li*.

The *li* are originally the unwritten rites and customs of the prestate communities and tribes comparable to the Greek order of *themis*.[18] Along with the political supremacy of specific peoples, lastly the Zhou, they become the code of demeanor of the nobility. In the middle of the Zhou era, the process is reversed: the *li* gradually filter down from the higher stratum of society, developing into the refined etiquette of "the" Chinese. From eating and drinking, clothing, sacrificing, and waiting upon guests up to birth and death the *li* regulate the daily life with detailed prescriptions, each of them tailored to station, role, and gender. The *li* lay restrictions upon communication. They set limits to social intercourse and do not stress the equality, but the inequality of men. They separate high and low, create an order of rank, and "consolidate the roles."[19] The *li* act as barriers in the inner of man, too, serving as "dikes" against excessive emotions.[20]

In the sense crisis of the mid-Zhou era, however, the *li* are increasingly seen as superficial and forced. "The highest propriety (the great conventionalists)," *Laozi* 38 states, "takes action, and in case no one responds, it turns up its sleeves and drags one near." The *li* also get suspected of being used for immoral purposes. Whoever sticks to them, might solely calculate his profit, or even be a robber.[21] Nevertheless, for the Confucians, the rules of propriety are indispensable. These rules not only distinguish man as a civilized being from animals,[22] but without them, the *Lunyu* stresses in anti-existentialist phrases, he would be "without any standing."[23] The fact that man needs transmitted conventions for finding his orientation does not mean, however, that he could exclusively rely on them. It is a prevailing fashion to reduce the ethics of the *Lunyu* to an aesthetic program of refined style, the patterns of which are described by the *li*.[24] The architecture of this ethic is more complicated than this, because it has taken into account the experienced fragility of established conventions, and has recognized that the conventional ethical life must be based on the new foundation of an inner morality.[25] *Li*, thus, is supplemented by *ren*.

In the two terms *li* and *ren*, the ethical life, the ritual forms of behavior and of intercourse of the traditional society of the Zhou with its emphasis on social difference, and the new "postconventional" dimension of the *Lunyu*, a morality of love and fairness, face each other. Yet, the two following quotations show that Confucius does not see any fundamental contrast between both:

> Yan Yuan asked about humaneness. The Master said, "To overcome one's self (*ke ji*) and to return to propriety (*fu li*) is humaneness. If one day one will overcome the self and return to propriety, then the whole world will turn towards humaneness. Humaneness can only come from the self—how could it come from others?"
>
> Yan Yuan said, "I beg to ask for the concrete steps." The Master said, "Do not look at what is contrary to propriety! Do not listen to what is contrary to propriety! Do not speak what is contrary to propriety! Do not put into action what is contrary to propriety!"
>
> Yan Yuan said, "Although I am not smart, I wish to serve these words."[26]

> If, as a man, one does not possess humaneness, what is propriety good for, then?[27]

Ren and *li*, here, stand in a peculiar circular relation. *Lunyu* 12.1 identifies *ren* with conduct in accordance with *li*, while *Lunyu* 3.3 declares *li* meaningless without *ren*. It is, above all, this contradiction[28] which has divided the opinions of Confucius' interpreters. For Confucius himself, however, exactly the vacillation seems to be characteristic. It shows that humaneness is not to be played off against the conventional ethos, but is to safeguard it. Both are indispensable. Individual rules of propriety may be suspended, if the situation demands it,[29] but *Sittlichkeit (li)* as such is not replaceable. It is the ethical etiquette which constitutes human culture as distinct from mere nature, and without it there would be no human society. *Ren*, however, is the necessary corrective which is to protect the conventional ethos against degenerating into a superficial and exploitable formalism once again.[30] The much discussed question as to which of the two concepts is given precedence in the *Lunyu*, does not make sense, then, if one asks for the more important concept. But we can evaluate both by Kohlberg's stage sequence. Humaneness is the *higher* norm, inasmuch as is helps to keep propriety uncorrupted, and it is in this sense that it is also the center of the *Lunyu*. "Confucius regards humaneness the highest," testifies the *Lüshi chunqiu*.[31] And Mengzi, who himself views *ren* as the highest of the "Heavenly ranks," lets Confucius say, "There are only two ways: humaneness and inhumanity."[32]

But what can humaneness add to a life embedded in the transmitted rules of decency and good manners? This is love, active sympathy, and respect for the other as a being like myself. But who is the "other"? In order to understand the nature of humaneness, *ren*, we have first of all to clear the notion of "man," *rén*. This is all the more necessary, since it is the concept of man which those authors who reproach Confucian ethics of *group morality* mostly refer to.

B. THE CONCEPT OF "MAN"

The most fundamental objection to Confucian ethics is that it does not recognize an abstract concept of man. This is an old topic of its Chinese opponents. It has been a standard argument in the discussions of the People's Republic that Confucius by "men," *rén*, only meant the members of the ruling classes as distinct from the "people," *min*. The doyen of this criticism was Zhao Jibin with his radical general thesis that all seemingly abstract terms used in the *Lunyu*, particularly the ethical ones, must in reality be understood sociologically and class specifically.[33] To search, like Zhao's target Feng Youlan,[34] for ethical universalism in the early Confucian writings, and that is, for abstract and timeless meaning adoptable still today, would, therefore, be absurd.

Zhao's opinion became authoritative to a large extent in the People's Republic. But since the rehabilitation of Confucianism, it has been regarded as overdrawn or misleading. Nearly all authors—including Cai Shangsi, one of the most prominent contemporary critics of Confucius—now regard *rén* as an abstract concept, thus coming closer to their collegues from Taiwan.[35] One could, therefore, consider the debate closed. Yet, in some *Lunyu*—passages the term *rén* does have a concrete sociological meaning, and the opinion that *rén* should generally be understood as "person of rank" is still held by some authors.[36] I will, therefore, enter into the problem, since the reproach of group morality should be taken seriously.

Whereas in the oracle inscriptions of the Shang *rén* even counts sacrificed prisoners of war, *rén* and *min* in Western Zhou texts, indeed, sometimes refer to different social layers.[37] The Zhou, as the ruling people living mainly in the towns, called themselves *rén*. *Min* was the subjugated autochthonous rural folk whose male members, according to Guo Moruo's explanation of the graph, had one eye gouged out in order to put them out of action.[38] These conceptual distinctions, however, were not strictly observed even in the Western Zhou era.[39] In the middle of the first millennium B.C., parallel to the decline of the nobility, the lower classes experienced a general revaluation. Eastern Zhou society was characterized by a growing social mobility. The result was the gradual merging of the terms *rén* and *min* into the compound *rénmin*, "people."

On which stage of this process of convergence is the *Lunyu*? *Lunyu* 1.5 recommends to "be lenient (*ai*) with the *rén*, and call in the *min* to statute labor [only] in accordance with the season." *Rén* here does not denote "men" as such, but the inhabitants of the cities, while *min* denotes the rural people.[40] Mengzi, too, now and then distinguishes the two terms.[41] Yet, there is no consistent and thoroughgoing opposition between both. *Rén* is far more often used as a generic term meaning "man" than as the name of a specific layer—an abstraction Chinese writing has made from the beginning by using *rén* as a classifier. Confucius uses *rén* as the opposite term of animal or ghost,[42] and in many passages it denotes the *other* in contrast to the "self" (*ji*). Mengzi speaks of *yerén*, "men out in the country" who are governed by the "gentlemen" and support them, hence are hardly persons of rank. He distinguishes the affairs of the "great men" from those of the "mean men," referring to the division of mental and physical labor. Here, too, *rén* is no social term. That the animals of the feudal lords are well fed, but the people *min* starve to death, Mengzi furthermore says, amounts to "letting animals eat men (*rén*)." And elsewhere, he implicitly uses *min* as a generic term for "man," saying that "a sage (*shengrén*) is of the same kind as the people (*min*)," just as "the phoenix is of the same kind as the birds."[43]

Min, to summarize, normally refers to the lowest, rural layer of society, and in exceptional cases to man as a species. *Rén*, conversely, normally refers to man as a species and in exceptional cases to the higher layers living in the cities. The references of both terms, then, do not provide an argument for reproaching group morality.

If we analyze the ethical statements themselves, the result is similar. *Ren*, humaneness, is not simply the essence of a group morality of "persons of rank," but is, in two respects, also valid for the people. First of all, the people are the object of a "humane" government. Mengzi's slogan of "humane politics" means, above all, to care for the well-being of the people.[44] For Confucius, humaneness consists, among other things, in "employing the people as if performing a great sacrifice." Among the attributes of the humane person is *hui*, kindness, which should be shown for the people.[45]

Is humaneness, then, not an expression of particularism, but still not universally valid, because it is only a duty of superiors? *Ren* has often been interpreted as such a "vertical" virtue.[46] It is, indeed, now and then assigned to the ruler as the virtue proper to his position.[47] In the *Lunyu*, too, it is sometimes discussed in the context of rule, because many of Confucius' pupils aimed at influential posts. But this does not mean that *ren* is exclusively tailored to the ruling elites. When Confucianism insist on a "humane" attitude of those in power, it is because a special responsibility rests upon their shoulders, and not because humaneness would be in good hands particularly with them. And to become a humane person, even if this can hardly be achieved, is in principle a desirable goal for anybody. This concerns first of all the Confucian "scholars," who see themselves, not the rulers, as the defenders of *ren*, and who desire humaneness for its own sake, regardless of political ambitions. The only disciple of Confucius who is said to have achieved humaneness for a period of time is Yan Hui, who abhorred an official career.[48] For many followers of the schools, humaneness is the ideal of the independent intellectual who cannot be "bent by power and force."[49] *Ren*, then, is not the specific virtue of rulers or superiors. When the Confucians demand that it should become the binding principle of politics, they expect, in this way, to raise the people themselves to the level of *ren*.[50] "If the superiors love humaneness," we read in the *Liji*, "the subordinates will compete to surpass one another in it."[51]

Confucian anthropology, correspondingly, denies any relevant natural distinction between men. In his famous sentence that "men by nature are close to one another, and by daily practice (or: by custom) diverge from one another,"[52] Confucius is rather cautious to generalize, but in his Golden Rule he all the same implicitly supposes the sameness of the basic desires and wants of men. "A sage and I are of the same kind," and "Anybody can become a Yao or a Shun," Mengzi afterwards proclaims.[53] And Xunzi adds that even a "man in the street" has the makings of a Yu, the founder of the Xia dynasty.[54] When Mengzi proves the innateness of humaneness by the love of children for their parents and the spontaneity of the impulse of compassion, he refers to a realm prior to any class- or culture-specific socialization. Although his ethic is characterized by a certain asymmetry, he does not exempt the lower layers of society from the responsibility for humaneness. The feeling of compassion, which for him is one of the fundamental expressions of humaneness, increases in importance the higher the power to inflict harm on others. But, basically, everybody can find himself in the position of the one on whom the other's fate depends.

Although humaneness is generally valid, the chances for realizing it are different. In practice, it especially remains beyond the reach of the common people. Normally, they can only "be made to follow something, but not to understand it."[55] Confucian ethics reaches a limit here, which is not a principle, but an actual one. To be more precise: it is a political one, since the Confucians are no democrats. It is characteristic of their moral philosophy to transcend their political viewpoint, that is, their adherence to the monarchic corporative state. Political rule should be lenient, kind, just, and generous, and should rely on the confidence of the people,[56] but the latter continue to be its object.

Humaneness applies also to the "barbarian" non-Chinese tribes. In Zhou literature, they are always refered to as "men" (*rén*). Yet, the *Zuozhuan* writes that "it is by virtue that the central states (China) are soothed, and it is by severe punishment that the tribes around are awed."[57] In a noteworthy contrast to this sentence, we read in the *Lunyu*:

> Fan Chi asked about humaneness. The Master said, "Be reverent in private life, be respectful when entrusted with a task, and be benevolent when dealing with others. Even among the Yi and Di you cannot put aside this."[58]

The cultural gap which the Chinese saw between themselves and their neighbors, then, did not imply for a Confucian that in dealing with "barbarians," regardless of their own habits, he could abandon his moral attitude.[59] Confucius' willingness to settle among the Yi can count as a further indication of this.[60] It shows that for him there is no distinct demarcation line between realms of principally different moral responsibility in the then-known world. I also interpret the famous statement of Confucius' disciple Zixia that "all within the four seas are brothers" in this sense.[61] All Chinese philosophers of the axial age have assumed the natural equality of men regardless of social position or ethnic descent and have ascribed the differences between them to education, custom, and external circumstances alone.[62]

Another possible limitation of Confucian ethics concerns women. In the conventional role morality, they are assigned a place on which they are, more or less, servants of their husband. The patriarchalism of the conventional morality, however, contrasts with the fact that none of the essential postconventional achievements of the classical ethics—the Golden Rule, the egalitarian anthropology, and even less the idea of compassion—can earnestly be considered as an expression of "male" ideals. It is rather in the name of those achievements that the injustice which the officially Confucian Chinese society allowed to happen to women should be criticized.

To understand "humaneness" as a postconventional principle is, therefore, not already excluded by the very reference of the terms *rén* and *ren*. Yet, we will have to deal with the objection of group morality also in the content analysis of "humaneness" that follows.

C. HUMANENESS AS A FEELING:
LOVE, FAMILY LOVE, AND COMPASSION

One of the most conspicuous accounts of humaneness is love. The first direct identification of both is found in *Lunyu* 12.22:[63]

Fan Chi asked what humaneness is. The Master said, "To love men (*ai rén*)."

Consequently, after the *Lunyu*, identifying humaneness with love became quite common and was also taken over by the opponents of Confucianism. Here are some examples from Zhou and Han literature:

Ren means to embody love.[64]

A person of *ren* loves others (or: loves men).[65]

To love men and to be advantageous to things, this is called *ren*.[66]

Ren means love.[67]

When superiors and subordinates love each other, this is called *ren*.[68]

A person of *ren* makes love his task.[69]

To love all men together in one's heart, this is called *ren*.[70]

Ren means love.[71]

"Love" (*ai, qin*)[72] denotes a gentle attitude of care, a well-tempered benevolence for others, and the endeavor not to do harm to them. When humaneness is called "internal" in Zhou literature—sometimes in contrast to "external" justice[73]— this refers to its rootedness in feeling.

The Confucian concept of love has met with two objections. The first objection concerns the lack of an equivalent to the Christian demand of loving one's enemy.[74] *Lunyu* 14.34 has often been quoted as a proof for the alleged inferiority of Confucian ethics compared to Christian standards:[75]

Someone asked, "What do you think of repaying enmity with virtue?"[76] The Master said, "With what, then, shall virtue be repaid? Repay enmity with straightness (*zhi*), repay virtue with virtue."

Why should enmity not be repaid with virtue? A pragmatic answer reads that this normally would bring about nothing.[77] Another answer would be that direct retaliation must be exercised as a matter of principle. The answer of the *Lunyu* is different: *Zhi*, straightness, is by itself a virtue, which can also be rendered as "justice." To repay enmity with straightness, then—and not with enmity[78]—is obviously meant to keep up an element of *justice* within benevolence. The following quotation can be interpreted similarly:

It is only the humane person who can like or dislike others.[79]

Chinese commentators have always read this statement as an expression of the impartiality and the sense of justice of the humane person. This insistence on justice is necessary, since the idea of an otherworldy last judgment is absent. In this world, however, justice does not take its course by itself. Although Confucian literature now and then assures us that the good will also be the successful, on the whole, the belief that every deed will entail its appropriate retribution, as well as the confidence that the moral person will find recognition, have been shattered. But Christianity has not gone without the idea of justice either. It dismisses the idea of retribution in demanding love for one's enemy, but only to let it reappear the more frighteningly in the world to come. This indicates that love cannot really be played off against justice.[80] And even if the loving person can renounce justice for himself, he will still have to demand it for others.

Given the lack of an otherworldly paradise or hell, for the ancient Confucians there is only one alternative to redeem this claim—to incorporate the righteous anger at inhumanity into humaneness itself. In the *Liji*, justice and humaneness are the two sides of a coin, and he who has humaneness without justice will "be loved, but not be honored," while in the reverse case he will "be honored, but not be loved."[81] For Xunzi, humaneness is even compatible with war, for "since a humane person loves men, he hates to see others injure them."[82] Not all Confucians were ready to draw such radical conclusions from the ethical dilemma of responsibility which is the issue here. Mengzi, who anyhow stresses the element of love, plays humaneness off against war.[83] And Xunzi himself is confronting the question of his disciple Chen Xiao how humaneness, which demands love, and war, which aims at conquest, can be reconciled with each other at all.

It is likewise owing to the problem of justice that the *Lunyu* counts knowledge or prudence (*zhi*) among the constituents of humaneness.[84] As a corrective, knowledge is obviously to protect moral action against indiscrimination. The linkage of humaneness and knowledge is found several times in Zhou Confucianism.[85]

The second objection against Confucian love concerns the importance of the family. It is here where Mengzi draws the demarcation line between the Confucian and the Mohist teachings. Mo Di's principle of general "co-love" (*jian ai*) for all men, he argues, neglects the family and degrades men to animals.[86] Probably based on *Mengzi* 3A5, the *Shizi* defines, "Humaneness is, when distinctions are made in love."[87] And when *Zhongyong* 20 explains that "humaneness means to be a man, and love towards parents (*qin qin*) is the greatest [expression] of it," this likewise goes back to Mengzi:

The reality of humaneness is the service to the parents.

To love the parents (*qin qin*) is humaneness.

Among the children still babbling like babies and carried on the arm, there is not a single one which would not know how to love its parents (*ai qi qin*). . . . To love the parents (*qin qin*) is humaneness.[88]

Family love holds a special status here, and it even seems to be the very essence of humaneness. Yet, the priority of the family can be of a different nature. It can be a priority on grounds of principle, with the result that humaneness would become a particularistic attitude, setting limits and excluding strangers. This is, for example, claimed by the *Shangjunshu*, which suspects mere clan egoism (*si*) behind family love (*qin qin*).[89] The priority in question can also be a genetic one. In this case, the family is of special importance as the place of the first exercise of virtue, but it is not ruled out to gradually expand the range of the ethical commitment. What Mengzi has in mind is doubtlessly the second of these alternatives. The family remains a place of primary responsibility, but it is not the only one. On the contrary, the affection which grows naturally in it shall become the model for treating others in general, though never at the price of abandoning one's parents.[90] If family love would not be open to this enlargement, we could never explain why humaneness at so many places is defined as "love for men" (or "love for the other," *ai rén*), as quoted above, and why it frequently appears in contexts which do not relate to the family, like in Mengzi's program of "humane politics" (*ren zheng*), or his idea of compassion. Even *Mengzi* 4A11, a passage which declares family love a sufficient principle of order, does not, on close examination, advocate ethical particularism:

> The way lies so near, and yet it is sought in what is far off. The task is so easy, and yet it is sought in what is difficult. If only every single man would love his parents (*qin qin*) and treat his elders like elders, the world would be at peace.

Family morality is no end in itself, here, but is meant to achieve—as it were, by means of division of labor—the well-being of all. If this model would work, even "humane politics" would become superfluous. In contrast with this ideal conception of Mengzi, the *Liyun* (*Liji* 9) has regarded family love as a product of decay of the original Golden Age of the "great community" (*da tong*). At that time, the *Liyun* lets Confucius speak, "men did not love only their own parents (*qin qin*), and did not treat only their own children as children." It is only "now that the great *Dao* is hidden" that the family counts.[91]

The significance of the *Liyun* can hardly be overestimated, since it offers a direct access to the Universal, instead of winning it, like Mengzi, by the detour of the family, which might, after all, involve losses. The *da tong* passage from the *Liyun* is not atypical of Confucianism, inasmuch as the frequent praise for the predynastic heroes involves an antifamilistic element, too. It is only under the Zhou that the family is esteemed, we read in *Liji* 24, while under Shun its position was held by virtue.[92] As far as phylogenesis is concerned, this argument is untenable, however. The early communities tied together by affinities of blood would hardly have survived without the feeling of kin solidarity. Mengzi can, therefore, claim some primordiality for his motto *qin qin*. He moreover gives empirical arguments for his position and points out the actual distribution of affection. He asks whether the Mohist Yizhi, for whom "love has no distinctions or degrees," "seriously believes that one loves one's nephew just like the infant of a neighbor."[93] If in love, however, distinctions are natural, one can reasonably doubt that it can serve as a grounding of morality at all. To the same degree that Mengzi's argument against the Mohists is empirically right, its normative content decreases. But

Mengzi thinks he knows a way out. The unequal primary distribution of love shall not entail a restriction of morals to the family—if it did, love would a second time prove blind to the problem of justice, for there is an ethical commitment also to strangers. Mengzi, therefore, advocates the transition from the family to the general public, which he conceives as the "extension" of affection or of the feeling of care.[94] As he writes:

> Treat the aged of your own family as is due to the aged, and then include (*ji*) the aged of others in this treatment. Treat the young of your own family as is due to the young, and then include (*ji*) young of the others in this treatment. Then you can make the world go round in your palm. When it is said in the Songs, "[King Wen] was a model for the queen and also for his brothers, and so he ruled in clan and land," this means: Take this heart (attitude), apply it (*jia*) to what is over there, and this is all. Therefore, if one extends (*tui*) one's kindness, it will suffice for the protection of the whole world. If one does not extend one's kindness, it will not even suffice to protect wife and children. It is just one thing in which the ancients greatly surpassed others: they knew how to extend what they did, and this is all.[95]

> What man is capable of without having learned, is his good capacity (*liang neng*). What man knows without having to think, is his good knowledge (*liang zhi*). Among the children still babbling like babies and carried on the arm, there is not a single one which would not know how to love its parents (*ai qi qin*). And when they have grown up, there is not a single one which would not know how to respect the eldest brother. To love the parents (*qin qin*) is humaneness, and to respect the elders is justice. There is nothing else, and this should be extended (*da*) to the whole world.[96]

> A humane person extends (*ji*) [his attitude towards] those he loves to those he does not love. An inhumane person extends (*ji*) [his attitude towards] those he does not love to those he loves. (Criticizing King Liang of Hui who sacrificed his own son in war).[97]

Mengzi wants to take the primary experience in the family as a basis for further steps to finally include all others into the range of ethical responsibility—a model, however, the problems of which he does not account for.[98] That moral development is conceived as the extension of family love is, on the one hand, to prevent the impairment of general interests by the egoism of clans. On the other hand, it is to guard against neglecting the care for one's own family in a world without public welfare. Yet, once having come into existence, humaneness can also liberate itself from the family, and it is not out of question that it stands against kin solidarity: that Shun enfeoffed his criminal brother Xiang, counts as an offense against humaneness for Mengzi's disciple Wan Zhang.[99]

To conclude: The emphasis on family love within the general "love for men," as is especially found with Mengzi, does not aim at a limitation on, but at a *foundation* of morality. Confucianism does not promote ethical particularism, as is assumed in Weberian literature.[100] A further proof of this is another reading of humaneness, likewise to be found in Mengzi, in which humaneness like love falls under the emotions, but from the beginning is outside the kinship context—compassion. Humaneness is an extension of the natural compassion which every man will feel in view of the hardship and misfortune of others. Not to be able to endure their misery and to feel fundamentally alarmed when witnessing it—the most impressive picture is that of the child about to fall into a well[101]—becomes a starting point of ethics just as fundamental as the natural affection for kin. Every man, says Mengzi, has such an innate feeling of compassion, and must only develop it to the full. When King Xuan of Qi does not have the heart to sacrifice an ox trembling with fear of death, Mengzi calls this a "humane attitude." What remains to be done is to also let the people enjoy such an attitude.[102]

To share the suffering of others, to be overwhelmed by their pain, and to feel alarm and compassion in view of the fundamental vulnerability of man—these are the spontaneous emotions of a humane heart, which Mengzi and, together with him, the ancient literature[103] have ascribed to a person of *ren*. These emotions do not remain passive, but turn into care and help for all those who are in need. Both aspects of humaneness can be found in Mengzi's ideal of "humane politics" (*ren zheng*), which is, among other things, characterized by abstaining from force and war, by mild jurisdiction and taxation, and by sharing all wealth with the people.

Compassion, nevertheless, as Mengzi himself involuntarily proves, does not carry far if the direct personal experience of the suffering of others and hence the sensory perception to release the innate impulse is lacking.[104] Together with love, which turned out to be in want of supplements because of the problem of justice, compassion shares typical weaknesses of an ethics of sentiment. Ethics cannot be solely grounded on natural affections which might not arise for everybody and whenever necessary. There are two conceptions in Confucianism which can show a way out of this difficulty: the conceptions of humaneness as *respect for the other* and as the *Golden Rule.*

D. HUMANENESS AS RESPECT FOR THE OTHER

On one of the questions regarding humaneness, Confucius answers:

> Outside your door (in public), behave as if you were receiving a high guest. Employ the people as if you were performing a great sacrifice. What you do not wish done to yourself do not do to others. [Then you will] be free from enmity in land and clan.[105]

Except for the Golden Rule, which will be discussed later, the definitions of *ren* given here seem to be inconspicuous. Yet, the sentence "Outside your door, behave as if you were receiving a high guest" is an outstanding example of the intricacy of the *Lunyu*. It refers to an episode reported in the *Zuozhuan* under the year 627 B.C.:

> Jiu Ji passed Ji on a mission and saw Ji Que weeding in the field. When his wife brought him food, Ji Que was very respectful (*jing*) to her, and they treated one another like high guests. Jiu Ji took Ji Que back with him to the capital. He told what he had seen to Duke Wen, saying, "In respect all virtue gathers. He who can show respect is sure to have virtue, and virtue is the means to govern the people.[106] I therefore ask you to employ this man. I have heard: Outside the door to behave as if receiving a high guest, and to attend a business as if performing a great sacrifice, this is a pattern of humaneness."[107]

Lunyu 12.2, then, implicitly relates humaneness to the motif of respect.[108] Respect (*jing*) is an attitude of seriousness, honesty, and attentiveness when dealing with others. It is won by the ceremonial paragon of the nobility, but now has become valid also for the "Master's" pupils. It is true that respect often has a hierarchic trait. In the *Lunyu*, it frequently denotes a demeanor towards superiors. From this, one could conclude that respect, in Confucianism, is exclusively due to status and role, and not to the "person."[109] But there is a passage in the *Xunzi* and the *Hanshi waizhuan* which shows that although respect always concerns the bearers of roles, since everyone occupies a certain social position, one can, in its name, also abstract from the concrete social determination as well as from the specific abilities of the other, and treat him or her as a person as such:

> A humane person will by all means respect (*jing*) others. For respecting others there is a way. If one deals with a capable person, one will esteem and respect him. If one deals with an incapable person, one will fear and respect him. One will respect a capable person with intimate affection, but will respect an incapable person from a distance. *Respect is the same in both cases, but the feelings are different.* If one is loyal, trustworthy, upright, and guileless, and does not injure the other, then one will behave right *with whomever one comes into contact*. This is the disposition of a person who has humaneness.[110]

In the context of *Xunzi* 13, respect for the incapable refers directly to a ruler and is also motivated by the protagonist's interest in self-protection, hence by strategy. Nevertheless, Xunzi's wording is so abstract that the passage can nearly literally be taken out of its context and quoted as a general maxim in the *Hanshi waizhuan*.[111] The passage from *Xunzi* 13, then, interpreted in the light of the *Hanshi waizhuan*, purports that humaneness as respect does not make distinctions between men, but precedes any status- and role-specific treatment of others. It is also independent of the sentiment one may feel for the concrete person.

In view of respect, every human being, regardless of his or her capa̲ ̲.̲.̲.̲ and ethical qualities, is of the same value. It is this abstraction of "man" which makes up the moral substance of the concept of humaneness in the first place. If we take into consideration the episode from the *Zuozhuan*, then in *Lunyu* 12.2, too, a form of respect independent of role and status is associated with humaneness, since Ji Que and his wife treat "each other" respectfully.[112] That humaneness stands above the social hierarchies becomes still more clearly apparent from its identification with the *Golden Rule*. The Golden Rule, as to be found in the *Lunyu*, provides nothing else than a *formal basic pattern of horizontal respect*.

E. THE GOLDEN RULE: FORMS AND PROBLEMS

As a maxim neither appealing to tradition nor to the values of concrete contexts, and aiming at symmetry in communication, the Golden Rule[113] is a typical identification sign of the ancient enlightenment civilizations. Its ubiquity[114] is one of the most significant empirical arguments against ethical nominalism, since it seems to represent a basic human moral intuition which is not merely culture specific. As a concise, intuitively plausible and generalizable formula for moral conduct, it also plays an important role in philosophical ethics until today, despite criticism that has to be taken seriously and to which I will return.

Some of the earliest and most remarkable formulations of the Golden Rule can be found in the *Lunyu*.[115] Among the ancient protagonists of the Golden Rule, Confucius is, moreover, obviously the first one to recognize its systematical ethical relevance. If we seek for a center of the *Lunyu*, this center will be humaneness in its reading as the Golden Rule. The Golden Rule stands out not only by its identification with the cardinal concept of humaneness,[116] but there is also a direct indication of its special status in Confucius' ethical program: it counts as the "one pervading all,"[117] and as a general maxim of action:

> Zigong asked, "Is there something which consists of a single word and which can, because of its nature, be practiced for all one's life?" The Master said, "I should say this is *shu*: What you do not want for yourself, do not do unto others."[118]

Zigong's question as such is remarkable. What he wants to hear is not a rule for a specific type and sphere of action, but a *general maxim*. This maxim should be as simple and cogent as possible and at the same time so elastic, stable, and comprehensive that it can serve as a general guide to conduct for a whole lifetime. For such a maxim, Confucius recommends *shu*, in everyday language "forgiveness" or "indulgence." In the *Hanfeizi*, *shu* is the cardinal virtue of the pacifist Song Xing and synonymous with *kuan*, "tolerance" or "leniency."[119] In sinological literature, *shu* has mostly been rendered as "reciprocity."[120] This is in accordance with the explication of *shu* in terms of the Golden Rule in the *Lunyu* and other texts, but is somewhat far from its normal meaning and can, moreover, foster the misinterpretation that the Golden Rule recommends a *do ut des*. I suggest, therefore, the translation "fairness"—fairness in the sense of the renunciation of prerogatives for oneself, and the granting of everything one thinks appropriate for oneself to the other. Yet, the meaning "forgiveness" is sometimes still recognizable in the usage of *shu*.

Shu, then, is used in the *Lunyu* for the negative version of the Golden Rule. The maxim is repeated in *Lunyu* 5.12 and 12.2:

> (Zigong): What I do not wish others to do unto me, I also wish not to do unto them.

> (Confucius): What you do not wish to be done to yourself do not do to others.

The negative "Do not do unto others what you would not have them do unto you" has also been called the "Silver Rule," because it ostensibly does not match the positive "Do unto others what you would have them do unto you," as found in the New Testament. Correspondingly, the negativity of the quoted formulations from the *Lunyu* has given rise to a devaluation of Confucius' ethics as compared to that of Jesus.[121] Yet, firstly, the active attitude towards the other as expressed in the positive version does not necessarily represent the "higher" form of behavior.[122] Secondly, the ethically essential abstraction represented by the Golden Rule, the establishment of a reciprocal relation between the self and the other, is also accomplished by the negative version. It is not of prime importance whether the self is playing the active or the passive part. The crucial point is that it puts the other in its own position, and itself into that of the other, regardless of whether the other is the object of actions or nonactions. Thirdly, in *Lunyu* 6.30, we do find the idea to treat others like ourselves not only in the sense of refraining from action, but also in our active doing:

> A humane person, wishing to establish himself, will also establish others. And wishing to achieve perfection, he also perfects others. To be able to take the near as analogy, this can be called the method of humaneness.

To generalize what is "near," that is, one's own wishes, is the core of the Golden Rule. "To establish oneself" and "to achieve perfection," moreover, are such comprehensive goals that *Lunyu* 6.30 de facto presents a positive version of the Golden Rule, though no own expectations are mentioned.[123] In later usage, *shu* has been used for the positive and the negative version of the Golden Rule as well.

What is so remarkable about the Golden Rule and about the fact that it holds a systematically significant position in Confucius' moral teaching? Remarkable is, first of all, what we do *not* find in the Golden Rule—all those instances, namely, which are normally referred to in the Western descriptions of Confucian ethics: tradition or a casuistry which tells us to act like certain models from the past did in comparable situations, parental authority, the judgment of the community, or the conventional normality of what "one does" or "one does not do." This does not mean to say that those instances would be unimportant for Confucian ethics. But they do not have the status of the "one pervading all" which is explicitly assigned to the Golden Rule.[124] The Golden Rule replaces, or, better, supplements them by the fictitious changing of positions of the self with the other on the simple basis of the self's generalized wishes. Herewith, it is for the first time recognized that the moral nature of an action relates to its generalizability, although the given basis of generalization, as we will see, does not appear solid. At the same time, the Golden Rule opens novel paradigms in Chinese axial age ethical reasoning—the paradigms of the immediacy of volition, which leads to Mengzi, and of timeless reflection, which leads to Xunzi.

Next to its content—the self's likes and dislikes—which can in principle be determined free from traditional values, the Golden Rule contains the *formal* element of role taking[125] in the sense of changing the perspectives, or making oneself the *measure* for dealing with the other. In ancient Chinese literature, the formal operation of measuring is several times associated with the Golden Rule:

Shu means to make oneself the measure (*du*).

To measure (*liang*) others by oneself is called *shu*.[126]

Lunyu 6.30, referring to a positive version of the Golden Rule, calls analogizing the "method of humaneness," and *Daxue* 10 describes the Golden Rule as the "method of the measuring-line and the measuring-square." The formalism is so conspicuous that modern Chinese intellectuals acquainted with Western epistemology such as Zhang Taiyan and Hu Shi have even argued that the respective utterances do not refer to an ethical, but to a general logical rule.[127] This means overlooking the very point of the Golden Rule which consists precisely in incorporating a formal, abstract procedure into ethical reasoning—although moral reversibility, as we will see, cannot be reduced to logical reversibility, but only presupposes the latter.

The Golden Rule, or the principle of "fairness" (*shu*), then, is designed to deliver a measure for moral conduct. It represents a formal procedure rather than a virtue. This procedure—and this is important for moral evolution—does not depend on any tradition-impregnated casuistry nor on conventional values. It only depends on imaginatively putting oneself in the place of the other on the basis of the actor's generalized wants, without specifying these beforehand. This grounding of morality, at least as far as the possibility is concerned, in a region beyond social and historical values in a timeless formal rationale corresponds with the starting point of all classical Chinese ethical reasoning: the crisis of the inherited forms of life and of established convictions.

Next to the negative and (quasi-)positive standard versions, the Chinese Golden Rule appears in other forms which modify the one and the same basic intuition. The *Shizi* mentions three of them together:

Fairness (*shu*) means making oneself the measure:
What you do not wish for yourself, do not do unto others.
What you dislike in others, reject in yourself.
What you wish in others, seek in yourself.
This is fairness.[128]

The *Shizi*, a heterogeneous text which is in many respects influenced by Confucianism, is probably not free from Han-time revisions.[129] But the quoted formulations, which betray familiarity with the complicated figure of argument embodied in the Golden Rule, are certainly old. The first version is, of course, taken from the *Lunyu*, and the other two can be found, for example, in the *Mozi* and the *Daxue*:

Do not reprove in others what you show yourself. Do not demand of
others what you do not show yourself.[130]

A gentleman will only demand of others what he shows himself. And
he will only reprove in others what he does not show himself.[131]

The following forms of the operation *shu*, then, can be distinguished in Chinese axial age literature:

Do not do unto others what you do not wish (be done to) yourself.
Let also others achieve what you want to achieve for yourself.
Do not show yourself what you reprove in others.
Do not reprove in others what you show yourself.
Show yourself what you demand of others.
Do not demand of others what you do not show yourself.

Despite its plausibility, the Golden Rule raises a number of serious problems. After it was looked upon for centuries as the "most unshaken rule of morality, and foundation of all social virtue" (Locke),[132] its unquestioned validity has become uncertain. Locke demands a ground of deduction for it because it could not count as innate. For Leibniz, it presupposes the measure of a "volonté juste." Kant, finally, rejects it as "trivial" and replaces it by the categorical imperative.[133] We do not have to follow Kant's scathing criticism of the Golden Rule to find some weaknesses in it and accordingly check the Chinese forms. These weaknesses are related to the very formulation of the Golden Rule, which, in Singer's words, "neither says what it means, nor means what it says,"[134] and concern its actual position and meaning in the overall ethical, social, and political program of the one who advocates it. The four most important points that need to be discussed concern (a) the problem of group morality—who is the "other" in the first place?—(b) the relationship of the Golden Rule to the hierarchical structures of society, (c) the problem of the subjectivity of likes and dislikes, hence the dependence of the Golden Rule on a preceding concept of the "good," and (d) the possibility of a strategical, nonmoral reading of the Golden Rule.

The Golden Rule and group morality

The first serious problem of the Golden Rule concerns the range over which it is valid. If we follow the cognitive-developmental theory, a particularistic version of the Golden Rule is already possible at Stage 3.[135] In our discussion of the reference of the term *rén*, however, it has become clear already that the prominent representatives of classical Confucian ethics do not subscribe to particularistic, but to universalistic assumptions. The genuine Confucian Golden Rule can, therefore, hardly be understood in terms of group morality. None of the readings known to me exclude a universalistic interpretation or even enforce a contextualistic one. What speaks in favor of universalism is, to repeat, the inclusion of the "barbarians" into the domain of *ren*, the concept of *ren* as general respect, the egalitarian anthropology of the later Confucians, and Mengzi's attempt to prevent a particularistic restriction of moral responsibility by the model of "extension." The most explicitly universalistic version of setting as equal the self and the other, however, is not found in Confucian texts, but in the *Mozi*, with utilitarian overtones.[136]

The Golden Rule and the social and political hierarchies

But even taken for granted that the domain of the Golden Rule, at least in principle, is unlimited and not restricted to certain in-groups—does this entail that all men are, in a strict sense, partners of horizontal reciprocity? Obviously not, for, the Confucians, like Mo Di and most of the other Chinese philosophers, have always defended the necessity of a hierarchical social and political order. Nevertheless, the Golden Rule is found particularly in political contexts. Its first proto-formulation in the middle of the seventh century B.C.—if we believe the testimony of the *Guoyu*—by Neishi Guo, "writer of the interior" at the Zhou court, already refers to politics. Neishi Guo reproaches the Duke of Jin, who neglects his people, of offending against a virtue which later stands in a close relationship with the Golden Rule and here almost represents it: the virtue of benevolence (*zhong*). The ruler should govern the people, Guo says, by "scrutinizing what is inside and measuring the heart," and that is, by "benevolence." This reminds one of the aforementioned explanation of the maxim *shu* by "making oneself the measure for others." A ruler, then, should concede to the people what he finds in himself upon scrutiny—his own wishes.[137] To disregard this principle consists in doing to others what one dislikes for oneself:

> To inflict to others what one dislikes means doing away with benevolence.[138]

In similar accounts of later texts, the formal pattern of the Golden Rule, which has been familiar since the *Lunyu*, becomes explicit. In the *Guanzi*, Guan Zhong recommends Duke Huan of Qi to follow the Golden Rule when dealing with his subjects:

Do not inflict to others what you do not feel comfortable about yourself.[139]

Not to do unto others what one does not wish for oneself is humaneness.[140]

Again, the chancellor Yan Ying admonishes Duke Jing of Qi:

What is demanded of subordinates should by all means also be striven for in the position of the ruler. And what is forbidden to the people [the ruler] should not do himself.[141]

In *Daxue* 10, finally, a whole series of maxims after the pattern of the Golden Rule is formulated which explain the political device "bringing peace to the whole world depends on bringing order to one's state":

Therefore, the gentleman has the method of the measuring-line and the measuring-square:
What you dislike in your superiors, do not therewith burden your inferiors.
What you dislike in your inferiors, do not therewith burden your superiors.
What you dislike in those before you, do not therewith precede those behind you.
What you dislike in those behind you, do not therewith follow those before you.
What you dislike at the right, do not give to the left.
What you dislike at the left, do not give to the right.
This is called the method of the measuring-line and the measuring-square.

The political application of the Golden Rule reveals an understanding of politics in which, the acknowledgment of the necessity of rule notwithstanding, an archaic motif of reciprocity has been preserved. Reciprocity was the fundamental mechanism of integration of the early communities, and it still remained present after the coming into existence of political rule.[142] Stable political power can never be based on mere violence, but must bring some advantages to the governed. The acceptance of rulership with all its prerogatives presupposes a return service.[143] Yet, rule shows a constant tendency to set itself free from the general consensus—a tendency which has regularly led into despotism and the subsequent downfall of dynasties.

In view of these disastrous developments, the political thinkers of the axial age rediscover the importance of reciprocity in politics and society. They stress that, in order to be accepted, rulership must not detach itself from its rational function which consists in safeguarding public peace and welfare. Political rule is measured by the standard of a just give and take. This idea fuels the Confucian legitimization of tyrannicide, and when Zhou literature keeps on repeating that subordinates will behave just as their superiors do, this, too, is a reminder of the archaic expectation of reciprocity.[144]

Applied to politics, the Golden Rule may have a moderating and humanizing effect. It helps to remind the powerful that the ruled are human beings with feelings and expectations like themselves, and should be treated as such.[145] All the same, society remains organized on the basis of hierarchy and reign. Whereas the Golden Rule rests on the idea of a horizontal reciprocity, the Chinese life world is organized on the basis of vertical difference of status and hierarchy. This tension can be dissolved in two directions: in the direction of a gradual extension of the egalitarian dimension—in the final analysis, of the democratization of the life world—or in the direction of the dismantlement of the idea of equality in the Golden Rule itself and its tailoring to the actual inequalities of society. What is of primary importance, then, the equality of human aspirations, or the difference of status in the social vertical order? Xunzi would have rejected this alternative, since for him the inequality of status is the precondition for the equal liberation of all from strife and misery. Yet, in his dialectical model for solving the problem of social justice, Xunzi puts all too strong an accent on inequality. The proposed integration of equality and inequality thus leads him to a dubious reformulation of the Golden Rule:

> Confucius said: A gentleman knows three kinds of fairness (*shu*). Being unable to serve one's lord, yet to demand service from a subordinate is not fair. Being unable to repay what the parents have done for one, yet to demand from the son to be filial is not fair. Being unable to respect the elder brother, yet to demand obedience from the younger brother is not fair. If a scholar is clear about these three kinds of fairness he can make himself upright by that.[146]

If we compare these concepts of fairness to the Golden Rule of the *Lunyu*, a remarkable shift becomes apparent. The dual constellation of the self and the other has been changed into a triple one, and the formal reciprocity of claims has underhand been infiltrated by a material inequality of status and roles: ego is to demand only those services from alter$_2$ which ego itself renders to alter$_1$. Nevertheless, there is still some kind of mutuality between the different levels of status when it is said that one should not demand services from a subordinate which one is not willing to perform oneself to one's own superiors. In the following passage from *Zhongyong* 13, however, where Confucius serves as the mouthpiece again, the responsibility towards the lower level is no longer mentioned:

> Benevolence (*zhong*) and fairness (*shu*) are not far from the *Dao*. What you do not like when done to yourself, do not do to others.
>   There are four ways of a gentleman, and not one of them am I already capable of. To serve the father as I require my son to serve me—of this I am not yet capable. To serve the ruler as I require my

subordinate to serve me—of this I am not yet capable. To serve my elder brother as I require my younger brother to serve me—of this I am not yet capable. And to grant to fellow-students and friends in advance what I require them to do for me—of this I am not yet capable.

Except for the relation between friends, the actor here stands in the center of a constellation that links unequal poles. *Shu* no longer means direct reciprocity, since the symmetry of the sides is abolished. The maxim is now, "Treat a superior as you expect to be treated by an inferior." It is still the ego that sets up the expectations. But the reciprocity involved is shifted into the hierarchical space and deferred into the biographical lifetime. Only after working one's way up the ladder of a career and passing through the different stages of age will one, if at all, benefit from the system of fairness. This model ensures that giving and taking on the whole are balanced. It reconciles with and takes the edge off social inequality. But the openness of the original dual relation of the self and the other for status is lost. Of course, this dual relation is designed for its expansion into society, the living together of all. If, however, from the beginning the hierarchical structures of the concrete life world are incorporated into the Golden Rule, it may have a humanizing effect on society, but it will not unfold its egalitarian grain.

Thus, the other side of the remarkable moralization of politics is a questionable politicization of morality. In the *Lunyu*, however, the abstraction of the "other" is not yet called back into the order of unequals, as by the "misplaced concreteness" of later texts. What is valuable in its formulations is precisely the briefness of expression, the abstract fashion, and the lack of any specific social context (at least in *Lunyu* 5.12 and 15.24)[147] which is decisive for the ethical substance of the Golden Rule. This difference—which will be lost if we do not distinguish between the *Lunyu* and the *Zhongyong*—can also be expressed as follows: in the formulations of the *Lunyu* at least the possibility remains open to conceive of the Golden Rule as a principle from which more specific rules for different spheres of action can be derived. In *Xunzi* 30, and even more in *Zhongyong* 13,[148] however, the Golden Rule has become a rule in the narrower sense which only determines what should be done within the given framework of unquestioned concrete social conditions.[149]

Exactly this difference, however, is called into question by authors such as Kuang Yaming, Opitz, and Nivison, who are of the opinion that also with regard to the *Lunyu*, the Golden Rule is from the beginning embedded into inequality and must not be interpreted in terms of horizontal reciprocity.[150] In such a view, the specific tension is lost which exists between the moral and the political assumptions of the early Confucians and which is not always resolved in such a problematical way as in the quoted passages from the *Xunzi* and the *Zhongyong*. They moreover are not accordant with an analytical interpretation of *Lunyu* 5.12 and 15.24. Nivison tries to corroborate his thesis by *Lunyu* 4.15, a passage, however, which I will interpret differently. This leads me to the third problem of the Golden Rule—the subjectivity of the likes and dislikes to which it refers, which has to be compensated by a concept of the "good."

The Golden Rule's dependence on a preceding concept of the "good"

The Golden Rule's adaptation to the hierarchical structures of society, by which the gain in political and social commitment may entail a loss in ethical substance, involves a problem of application. Another difficulty results from the Golden Rule's very wording. It is obvious that in positive as well as in negative reading, the Golden Rule fails to operate in case of conflicting subjective desires. If the other does not share my own inclinations and disinclinations, how can it be imperative to spare him what I do not like and let him share what I enjoy? Or, if I happen to be a masochist—a standard argument since Leibniz—do I have to beat others, then, because I myself enjoy being beaten? The Golden Rule should be supplemented by a ceteris paribus clause here which ensures the similarity of the starting conditions and circumstances. The problem is of different importance for the different formulations of the Rule, because not all of them speak of own inclinations. In the two versions "Do not show yourself what you reprove in others," and "Do not do unto others what you do not wish yourself" (instead of: what you do not wish *be done* to yourself), the crucial criterion is not necessarily my own immediate likes and dislikes. The attitude of the other can be evaluated irrespective of my interest to remain unharmed or to receive benefits.

But even taken for granted that the other holds the same wants as I and is in similar momentary conditions, and I would not project wants into him or her which they do not share, the reversibility of the Golden Rule would still not ensure morality. For our shared wants themselves could be of a morally problematical nature. In order to have moral validity at all, the Golden Rule, therefore, presupposes some acceptable notion of the *good*.

Classical Chinese ethics has operated with two models which can help to meet this difficulty. Firstly, it has specified the *object* of the likes and dislikes in such abstract terms that there can be no conflict of values, and problematical desires are excluded. The universalizability of the maxim *shu* depends on the general nature of the goods in question. *Lunyu* 6.30 speaks of goals in life in a most general way. In the *Hanshi waizhuan*, the recourse to basic human desires instead of individual predilections becomes explicit:

> In ancient times they knew the world without going out of doors. They perceived the way of Heaven without looking out of their windows.[151] Not that their eyes could have seen and their ears could have heard as far as thousand miles. It was because they measured [others] by their own feelings. From their own dislike of hunger and cold they knew that the whole world desired food and clothing. From their own dislike of toil and suffering they knew that the whole world desired peace and ease. From their own dislike of decay and

poverty they knew that the whole world desired wealth and satisfaction.[152] It was the knowledge of these three things by which the sage-kings put the world into order without descending from their mats. Hence the way of the gentleman rests solely on benevolence and fairness (*zhong shu*).[153]

Food and clothing, peace and ease, wealth and satisfaction, as well as the wish to "establish oneself," remind us of a catalogue of *natural rights*, which has also played a role in the Western discussion of the Golden Rule. But who is to define the legitimate "natural" desires of man? Their introduction into the ethical debate is a step forward, and yet, as the example of wealth shows, weighing is necessary which again presuppose an idea of good and bad, right and wrong.

Another possibility to specify the Golden Rule is indicated by the expression *zhong shu* used at the end of the last quotation. This possibility does not concern the object of volition, but the mental attitude of the *subject*,[154] as in Leibniz' presupposition of a "volonté juste." In *Lunyu* 4.15, we read:

The Master said, "Shen! My way (*dao*) is pervaded by one." "Yes!" said Zengzi. When the Master had gone, the disciples asked, "What does he mean?" Zengzi said, "The way of our teacher is benevolence and fairness (*zhong shu*), and that is all."[155]

The expression *zhong shu* is also found in *Zhongyong* 13, from where we know that it stands for the Golden Rule.[156] The fact that in *Lunyu* 4.15 the Golden Rule is identified with the "one" and seen in affinity with the *Dao*, again underlines its function as an ethical principle. But what does the supplementation of *shu*, fairness, with *zhong*, "to wish the best for the other," "benevolence," mean? Feng Youlan and other modern Chinese interpreters have proposed understanding *zhong* as the positive and *shu* as the negative Golden Rule.[157] This all too elegant construction is far fetched from a philological point of view, since there is no evidence for such a usage of *zhong*. According to Nivison's interpretation, *zhong* refers to "duties towards superiors or equals," while *shu* refers to "dealing with equals and superiors."[158] This would imply that hierarchy does not come in only in the context of application, as I have argued above, but is from the very beginning inherent to the Confucian Golden Rule. Nivison's argument, however, is based on the invalid claim that *zhong* exclusively refers to relationships with equals or superiors and is not used regardless of the social station.[159]

I do not see any reason not to interpret *zhong* in its ordinary meaning "loyalty" or "benevolence."[160] If we consider the aforementioned weakness of the Golden Rule which consists in the ethical underdetermination of logical reversibility, we can give a very plausible explanation for the supplementation of *shu* with benevolence: benevolence provides the principle of reciprocity with the necessary moral framework. This solution has already been brought forward by the Neo-Confucian Cheng Yi who construes *zhong* as "to exhaust one's self" (*jin ji*, = to give one's best), and *shu* as "to extend one's self" (*tui ji*).[161] Cheng Yi views *zhong* as "the *Dao* of Heaven" (*tian dao*) and as "substance" (*ti*), and *shu* as "the *Dao* of man" (*ren dao*) and as "application" (*yong*). Zhu Xi's late disciple Chen Chun (1159–1223) explains:

> Without benevolence (*zhong*), from where should the extension be done? Without benevolence, fairness would become arbitrary leniency and would no longer be what is called to reach others from inside.[162]

I think that this attempt to secure the moral nature of the Golden Rule is in accordance with the original intention or intuition of Zeng Shen in *Lunyu* 4.15. *Zhong*, then, is a specification of *shu*.[163] As "benevolence," it provides the framework within which *shu* can work as an ethical rule of reciprocity. Without it, the changing of roles of the self and the other might end up in a moral debacle.

The possibility of a strategical reading of the Golden Rule

The fourth objection that can be raised against the Golden Rule concerns possible nonmoral interests of the one who follows it. Even if we suppose that it aims at the "good" for the other, it is still not excluded that the final motive is something else than respect. After what has been said until now, it is not quite plausible that the Golden Rule represents nothing but an elementary idea of retaliation, as Dihle, and, referring to the *Lunyu*, Weber have argued.[164] Although its genetic descent from the principle of talion is probable, this does not decide on the Golden Rule's philosophical validity. The idea of retaliation, which, of course, is present in Zhou literature, is not inherent to it, since the changing of positions is a merely fictitious and not a real one.[165]

Yet, in practice, the Golden Rule might go together with a subliminal strategical self-interest, thus losing its moral nature and becoming a device of prudence.[166] If I treat the other well, the other will treat me well likewise—this, then, would be the proposed calculation. It is exactly in this sense that Pang Pu has interpreted the Confucian principle of *shu*.[167] The Golden Rule or related forms of argument, indeed, are not seldom intermingled with such considerations of utility. This not only holds true for Mo Di, but also for Confucian texts.[168] In *Lunyu* 12.2, the Golden Rule is followed by the notice that one can avoid enmity in land and clan.[169] *Xunzi* 30 recommends the "gentleman" to be generous, saying that "he who does not give as long as he has something, will not be given anything when in misery." *Xunzi* 11 quotes Confucius' warning to "consider well that others will treat me as I treat them."[170] In most cases, statements like these are directed towards the politicians. Mengzi, especially, does not grow weary of reminding the powerful that they must expect to get back from their subjects what they give to them.[171]

These appeals to self-interest are, on the one hand, due to the moral incompetence of the addressed. Their own value system has to be taken into account, as long as the final goal is not betrayed. On the other hand, political justice is conceived in terms of beneficial reciprocity, and it is not surprising, therefore, that in political contexts the Golden Rule is sometimes amalgamated with reasons of prudence. For a convinced Confucian, however, such arguments hardly count. He will expect that his conduct should influence others and provoke a positive reaction in them, but for pedagogical and never for strategical reasons, and in order to get a confirmation that he himself is on the right path. Confucian literature emphasizes again and again that the "gentleman" should not look for his own advantage. Confucius already tries to free morality from strategy. Knowledge or prudence *zhi* belongs to humaneness, but as far as the search for profit is concerned, both notions are distinguished:[172]

> A humane person rests in humaneness. A prudent person regards humaneness as profitable.[173]

The prudent who finds humaneness profitable is the type of person that fits the strategical adaptation of the Golden Rule. Humaneness for him is only of hypothetical value, while for the humane person it is an end in itself. Not unlike Socrates' dictum that to suffer injustice is better than to inflict it,[174] Confucius proclaims:

> A decided scholar and a humane person will never try to save their lives at the expense of humaneness. It may happen that they give their lives in order to accomplish humaneness.[175]

Together with the will to survive, all forms of egoism are ruled out. Morality, when it comes to a decision, is independent of self-interest, however refined. It is postulated as a duty, as is most forcibly expressed by Zeng Shen:

> A scholar cannot do without greatest resoluteness, for the duty is heavy, and the road is long. To make humaneness one's duty—is this not heavy? And a road which comes to an end only with death—is this not long?[176]

More evidence for the unconditionality of humaneness is provided by the *Hanfeizi* in its explanations of the *Laozi*:

> Humaneness means to love others from one's innermost heart. When a humane person rejoices in the happiness of others and cannot endure their misery, then this comes from an uncontrollable emotion. It is not because he would expect any reward. Therefore, it is said in the *Laozi*, "[A person of] highest humaneness shows humaneness without any [other] purpose."[177]

The Legalists themselves are anything else but apostles of humaneness. For the *Laozi*, humaneness as a positive ethical norm is already an indication of the decay of the original natural virtue. The real protagonists of humaneness as an end in itself are the Confucians, and it is their concept which the *Laozi* and the

Hanfeizi explicate. The demarcation of humaneness from every nonmoral purpose is in accordance with the Confucian intention.

The deontic context of the Confucianism, then, precludes a merely strategical reading of the Golden Rule. The calculus of personal benefit, and the search for one's own material happiness, are dismissed from morality. Here, a paradox seems to arise: if the moral person must not strive for private happiness and, on the contrary, takes a heavy burden of duty upon himself, is he not forced, then, by the very logic of the Golden Rule, to impose duties and sacrifices on the other? We have to bear in mind, however, that Confucianism approves of sacrifice not for its own sake, but in the case of conflict. Moreover, it is not the meaning of the Golden Rule to absolutize one's own course of life, but, conversely, to forestall the release of egoism. To treat the other as equal does not mean to force him into conformity. "To make oneself the measure" is not a dictating, but a conceding maxim. That one should apply a more rigorous yardstick to oneself than to others is required anyhow.

In the overall context of early Confucian ethics, then, the Golden Rule turns out to be a universalizable and nonstrategical principle of action. Yet, because of its ambiguities, it cannot serve as the self-sufficient orientation of conduct as which it recommended itself. Designed as a "measure," it presupposes one. As we have seen, in order to be a generalizable moral maxim, it must be based on an abstract concept of the "other," a concept of the morally good, and a nonstrategical volition. If these conditions are given, the Golden Rule will serve to transform the readiness for doing good into a stable attitude (*Haltung*) of respecting the other as a being like myself. And although the criterion which the Golden Rule delivers for moral conduct is, taken by itself, not sufficient, it is nevertheless a necessary one. Not every action or nonaction that is based on the fictitious changing of the positions of the actor and the affected is moral. But it is no less evident that actions which are not reversible, that is, actions where it does make a difference for me whether I am at the giving or at the receiving end, cannot be moral.[178] In this sense, then, the Golden Rule itself contributes to the development of the moral framework on which it depends.

In early Confucianism, there is only one way out of the described ambiguities of the Golden Rule: the way into the moral cultivation of the inner "self."[179] The versatile program of the formation of the moral person, which will be the topic of the next chapter, hence can be seen as directly deriving from the difficulties of the Golden Rule. The moral self and its inwardness cannot be substituted by imaginatively taking the place of the other. I emphasize this against Graham's assumption that the maxim *shu*, in that it lets one perceive "the other man's likeness to oneself," implies that one is "spontaneously unselfish."[180] This argument, which Graham needs to support his "quasi-syllogism,"[181] is not sound. A robber, too, must take into consideration "the other man's likeness to oneself" and, in his imagination, put himself into his chosen victim's place as objectively as possible, in order to increase his chances. The mental identification with the other, hence, taken by itself, can *constitute* an ethical problem instead of already offering the solution.[182] It is an element not only of moral, but also of strategical action. In order not to lapse into the latter, any communication with the other has, therefore, to be accompanied by the internal self-examination of *conscience*.[183] This is the way of the *Lunyu*, where we find Zeng Shen daily examining himself:

> Have I not been benevolent, when I gave advice to others? Have I not been trustworthy when communicating with my fellow students and friends?[184]

The indispensability of conscience, however, does not dismiss the Golden Rule as secondary. On the contrary, the formation of the self and its conscience is based on the very mutuality which is expressed in the Golden Rule. The above-mentioned preconditions for making the Golden Rule a specifically moral device should not be viewed as external prerequisites either, since the development of morality in turn depends on communication with the other. I will return to this interdependence in my discussion of the Confucian "self."

The Golden Rule, as we have seen, poses quite a lot of difficulties. Yet, rather than restrict its validity, they provide a chance to deepen the insight into the problems of morality. Nevertheless, one might be tempted to ask hypothetically whether morality cannot be achieved in a less complicated way. If the Golden Rule is in want of a concept of the "good" or an unselfish volition, why not directly refer to the latter instead of making a sophisticated thought operation? As Confucius' favorite disciple Yan Hui says in the *Hanshi waizhuan*:

> If somebody does good to me, I will also do something good to him. And also if he does something bad to me, I will do good to him.[185]

Mengzi, too, who, remarkably, does not explicitly mention the Golden Rule, sets up a more simple principle which I will call the "negative imperative":

> Do not do what you do not do. Do not will what you do not will. This is all.[186]

Like the Golden Rule of the *Lunyu*, Mengzi's negative imperative does not refer to conventional rules. But now, the ego does not reflect on what it wishes to be done or not to be done to itself, in order to generalize this afterwards. It directly listens to the voice of the good within itself. It calls into mind what it intrinsically does not want to do, and Mengzi presumes that every man by virtue of his very nature possesses such a moral basis of judgment, the "feeling for right and wrong," or the "good knowledge."[187] Morality here does not constitute itself over a complicated sequence of deliberations and in the mutuality of the self and the other, but in the mobilization of a spontaneously good impulse. Man finds its measure, as it were, not *at*, but *in* himself. What I refrain from is simply what I do not want to do according to my innate moral sense, not what I do not want be done to me. The Golden Rule could now be reduced to "fairness towards one-self." Such a mediation between Confucius' Golden Rule and Mengzi's negative imperative can be found in the new formula of Liu Zongzhou and Chen Que (seventeenth century):

Do not do unto yourself what you do not wish.[188]

If one does not do to oneself, that is, to one's moral nature, what one does not wish on grounds of this very nature, the interests of the other are already taken into account, because nature is understood in moral terms.

In spite of such a reconciliation, the tension between the Golden Rule and Mengzi's ethic of spontaneous love and compassion remains important. In Chinese history, the Golden Rule did not play the role one would have wished, given the ethically relevant abstractions of the axial age which it represents—the abstractions of the ego and the other, and the abstraction from status, context, and custom. To conceive of humaneness as love or compassion, instead of as the formally complicated Golden Rule, proved to be the more direct and intuitive way. What is more: whereas the Golden Rule did not quite suit the hierarchies of the Chinese society, Mengzi's ethics of feeling was well tailored to it, as well as to the self-conception of the educated elite. The Golden Rule, fictitiously, assumes a symmetry in relations, while there can be a great asymmetry in love and particularly in compassion. True, Mengzi, too, advocates *shu*—though it is not quite clear what he means by it—as the best way for achieving *ren*,[189] but he does not identify both concepts. For him, the archetype of humaneness is not the consideration to grant to the other the same which I claim for myself, but the unconscious, spontaneous reaction to save a child from imminent death. The basic ethical constellation is not equality, but the difference of indigence between the strong and the weak, the powerful and those at their mercy—an indigence which demands an emotional answer.

Hence, the social perspectives of the two basic models of humaneness fall apart. Yet, we should not dramatize the difference.[190] The Golden Rule does by no means rule out imagining oneself in the situation of the helpless, and acting accordingly. It does not imply an actual expectation of a return service, but only the thought experiment to be in the other's position. The sameness of conditions is only imaginative. Mengzi's assumption of an innate impulse of helpfulness, on the other hand, albeit tailored to the inequality of human possibilities, has a strong egalitarian trait: by the very possession of one and the same good nature capable of sympathy, every man is a moral being deserving *direct* respect.

Humaneness, to come to a conclusion, is the core of the ethical teaching of Confucius and Mengzi. It stands above propriety with its emphasis on social difference, not suspending, but embedding it into a basic attitude of sympathy and benevolent respect for the other. Regardless whether it is conceived as the rational Golden Rule or as emotional love and compassion, the range over which it is valid is, at least in principle, unlimited. It neither ends at social nor at ethnic boundaries. Even Mengzi's emphasis on kin affection does not aim at a particularistic restriction of humaneness. What Mengzi intends is a gradual "expansion" of a moral feeling first to be experienced in the family to all men.

Under the aspect of moral evolution, among the different conceptions of humaneness, the Golden Rule deserves special attention. Whereas the idea of compassion is the corollary of a society with strong vertical differentiation and in accordance with every hierarchy, the Golden Rule in nuce assumes an abstract horizontal reciprocity and in tendency goes beyond the given life world. Although it poses several problems which are only solved within the overall context of Confucian ethics, it introduces a formal principle into moral reasoning which can rightly claim to "consist of a single word and can be practiced for all one's life." As a formula, it takes no account of context, status, casuistry, and tradition, and represents the abstraction of the "other" as a being of equal dignity like myself. Humaneness, in the reading of the Golden Rule, therefore, is a candidate for a Stage 6 principle of general reciprocity. When translated into action, however, it is all too quickly reconciled with the existing social inequalities. Thus it has a humanizing and moderating effect, but it cannot really unfold its egalitarian potential.

All the same, of all the ethical conceptions China has developed, the Golden Rule is the most promising if we search for potentials for further moral evolution. It roots morality for the first time in the formal procedure of role taking, not in traditional virtues, allowing to transcend the horizon of one's own cultural heritage. It declares the self-reflected ego the "measure" for conduct and thus comprises the elements of *autonomy* and *freedom*. It recognizes the other as a human being like myself and thus comprises the element of *equality*. It implies the acknowledgment of universal human aspirations and hopes and thus comprises the element of *solidarity*. Sufficient reasons, I suppose, to assign central significance to the Golden Rule for the future development of a democratic and solidary China on the basis of her own indigenous values.

11

The Moral Person

With the principle of humaneness, Confucian ethics makes great demands on moral conduct. The tension of their ideals with the empirical world—a tension which Weber denied—is keenly felt by the axial age "scholars." In the *Lunyu*, the sense of failure is omnipresent. Confucius remarks that so far he has at best met "gentlemen," and that only his disciple Yan Hui has succeeded to live up to *ren* for some months. Yan Hui himself, however, has the impression "that something piles up before me, though all my talents are exhausted." Confucius, too, feels he has fallen short of his own teaching. He rejects for himself not only the predicate *sheng*, "ingenious," but also the predicate *ren*, "humane." And Zeng Shen deplores the heavy burden which he has taken upon himself with the duty of humaneness.[1]

To Mengzi's disciples, too, the goals of their teacher appear all too lofty. Mengzi tries to reduce the remoteness of the Confucian ideals and bring them into the immediate reach of human volition.[2] All the same, his pupil Gongsun Chou asks whether the *Dao*, which is as high as heaven to him, could not be made more attainable. Mengzi defends the necessity of principal yardsticks with his usual pathos.[3]

There is no agreement in the texts as to the lot of the moral person and of his ideal. The pessimistic tune of the *Lunyu* disappears in the *Daxue*, which conceives a confident program of pacification of the world and promises success and prosperity to the "gentleman." For Zeng Shen, by contrast, it is clear from the beginning that humaneness will have a hard time and that persecution and loneliness await the good.[4] Xunzi at one time links honor and disgrace nearly mechanically to morality and vice, but at another time follows the skepticism of the *Lunyu*.[5] Mengzi now and then sounds optimistic about the recognition of the good person, but much more often accuses the world for its moral deafness. In what follows, I will, above all, trace the one line within Confucianism which, for all its devotion to the community, maintains a skeptical distance. It is the more original line and is an authentic representation of the pride and independence of the axial age intellectual. It is the line on which most of the genuine Confucians meet.[6]

The topic of this chapter is the Confucian ideal of the moral person that results from the tension of their aspirations with a world which all too seldom listens to them. Within the logical reconstruction of Confucian ethics, the concept of the moral person follows, moreover, from the ambiguities of the Golden Rule as discussed above.

By using the term "person," I anticipate an outcome of my discussion: that the protagonist of the Confucian ethic is positively a "person" in the sense of a self-responsible autonomous being with his own dignity. This autonomous being will do his best to fulfill his social role, but he is more than that. "The gentleman," Confucius puts it laconically, "is no utensil."[7] The subject of Confucian ethics is not essentially or even exclusively defined by the social role, as Rosemont, Sun Longji, and similarly Wawrytko have argued.[8] A role-morality like the one recommended by Rosemont as an alternative to American individualism[9] would, besides, itself be morally deficient, because it does not have any criterion at its disposal to keep the game of roles within a moral framework.

Ethics, of course, would not make sense without reference to the empirical context of life. This does not mean, however, that one can immediately take one's orientation from this context and the roles assigned to one in it. This illusion, which is blind to the experiences of history, was no longer shared by the ancient Chinese. Yet, it controls some of their modern interpreters. One of the prolocutors of this view is Fingarette, who is full of sympathy for the Confucian "ideal community" where, as he says, "all cooperate spontaneously in a mutual respectful harmony defined by the dao."[10] The idyll has its price: Fingarette has—with Confucius, as he assures—banned any "personal self" from the community as well as from ethics. He admits that Confucius knows a "particular self, as distinct from all other selves," which is "self-observing and self-regulating."[11] But this type of self is a mere contingent shell of the impersonal *Dao* without "inner" or "subjective" states.[12]

It is true that for Confucianism the morally right way cannot be a different one for each individual. But this does not imply, as we will see, that the individual self does not have to choose that way in ever new decisions. The "ego" hence is not only present in the will of the egoist, as Fingarette maintains, but also in that of the "gentleman." I think that much of the confusion about the Confucian "self" results from mixing up *individualism* and *autonomy*, a fundamental shortcoming of the debate about Chinese ethics. The Confucians, indeed, have not aspired to be individualists in the modern sense of originality and uniqueness—although Han Fei, remarkably enough, accuses them of vain efforts to differ from others[13]—and have not viewed morality as a private affair. But they have, as a rule, insisted on the autonomy of their judgment, exactly because this has become the indispensable presupposition for the *Dao* to survive in a world not favorably inclined to it. Fingarette, however, cannot admit this, since he from the beginning imputes the unbroken belief in the well-functioning social context to the Confucians—the *proton pseudos* of pragmatistic sinology. In the following paragraphs, I will describe the inner portrait of the moral person. I will discuss the requirements the Confucian must meet in order to come up to the ideals of the school: competence of decision, autonomy of judgment, self-respect, self-strengthening, self-examination, autonomy of action, and a motivation independent of external sanctions.

A. COMPETENCE OF DECISION

To put the Confucian program into practice constantly requires decisions and choices. They are not only necessary for not straying from the right path, despite all adversities, and often against self-interest, but they must also be taken in case conventionally preshaped and long practiced patterns of behavior fail and must be suspended. Even in possession of postconventional norms, decision and choice do not become obsolete. Yet, that decision and choice are important at all for Confucianism has often been denied, the denial being linked to the assumption that the notion of an individual capable of free decisions is lacking. Like with so many Western stereotypes about China, Hegel has contributed to this one, too.[14] Influential today is Fingarette, who says about choice and responsibility:

> Confucius (and his contemporaries) . . . had no significant concern with these moral realities so central to their contemporaries, the peoples of Greece and the Near East. — [The] task is not conceived as a choice, but as the attempt to characterize some object or action as objectively right or not. The moral task is to make a proper classification, to locate an act within the scheme of *li*. . . . In short, the task is posed in terms of knowledge[15] rather than choice.[16]

For Fingarette, Confucius' way is a "way without crossroads."[17] The problem of decisions does not occur, because a "self" or an "inner psychic life" where the process of decision could take place is absent.[18] Choice, moreover, is not regarded as necessary in the first place. In Fingarette's Confucianism, it suffices to base decision "upon familiar and accepted moral or prudential principles that inhere in the *li*." The *li* "describe for me what I am to find good and worthy," unburdening the actor of finding his own judgment.[19] The conscious choice between alternatives is replaced by the acquisition of predetermined patterns in order to classify actions by the yardstick of conventional propriety.

Rosemont and Hansen, no longer confining the discussion to the *Lunyu*, strike the same note as Fingarette,[20] and Dora Dien contests, against the universality claim of Kohlberg's theory, that choice is a valid topic with regard to

China. The playing up of hypothetical dilemmas, she says, represents "the prevailing Western conception of man as an autonomous being, free to make choices and determine his destiny." According to Dien, this misses the "Chinese value system" characterized by "group orientation," "harmonious interdependent social existence," and "primacy of the collective over the individual," and aiming at "reconciliation" instead of "choice."[21] This criticism, however, does not refute Kohlberg. It simply reifies China's conventional morality. It does not take into consideration whether any immediate appeal to the "Chinese value system" would not mean falling behind the reflected and critical attitude of the classical thought of the formative period of Chinese culture itself. What is missing, moreover, from Dien's statements, as in those of Rosemont, Hansen, and Fingarette, is an awareness of the shortcomings of ethical contextualism.

Judgments like the aforementioned, regardless of whether they are critical or affirmative in nature, forget the very historical background of the emergence of Chinese moral philosophy: the crisis of the established conventions. In the loss of traditional certainties, the problem of decision becomes crucial, not only concerning the theoretical designing of new alternatives, but also concerning everyday practice. For practice, the problem poses itself on several levels: Choices and decisions have to be made (a) when morality conflicts with one's material self-interest,[22] (b) when ethical norms conflict with each other, or are prima facie not applicable because of the difficulty to interpret the situation, and (c) when moral efforts leave no impression on the world. In each of these cases, the matter in question is *weighing* (*quan*). Its significance in the ethical context is already emphasized in *Lunyu* 9.30:[23]

> That one can study together with somebody does not mean that one can also walk the same way with him. That one can walk the same way with him does not mean that one can have a common stand with him. To have a common stand with him does not mean that one can also share one's *weighings* with him.

The standard case of decision is that between accustomed bad behavior and the well-known right course. Most of Confucian literature is dedicated to the aim to help the actor overcome this obstacle and to make the hard-boiled, the indifferent, and those afraid of renunciation change their ways. Xunzi recommends a kind of balancing of benefit in order to choose morality:

> If the balance beam is not adjusted, something heavy will go up, and one will think it is light, and something light will sink down, and one will think it is heavy. In this way, one will be misled about weight. If the sliding weight is not correct, then misfortune will appear in disguise of the desired, and one will take it for fortune. And fortune will appear in disguise of the detested, and one will take it for misfortune. In this way, one will be misled about misfortune and fortune, too.

The *Dao* is the correct sliding weight, in the past as well as in the present. He who, departing from the *Dao*, at pleasure makes arbitrary choices has not understood what fortune and misfortune depend on. If a man exchanges one for one, people will say that he has neither gained nor lost. If he exchanges one for two, people will say that he has not lost, but gained. But if he exchanges two for one, people will say that he has not gained, but lost. He who calculates will choose what is more, and he who plans will follow that which is possible. And when nobody exchanges two for one, this shows that people know how to count.

To take one's starting point from the *Dao*, this is like exchanging one for two. What loss would there be in it? But, departing from the *Dao*, at pleasure to make arbitrary choices, this is like exchanging two for one. What gain would there be in it? To give away the aspirations of a hundred years for a single moment of satisfaction, this would mean not to understand the proportions.[24]

Xunzi recommends giving precedence to the *Dao* over arbitrary goals, because this would be to one's own advantage. This utilitarian argument for morality may be connected with his assumption that human nature is bad, whence it appears implausible that man might choose morality for other reasons than utility. But if man in fact is a selfish being, the Legalists will say, why put one's trust in morality in the first place? The utilitarian defense of morality, however, is neither typical of Confucianism in general, nor of Xunzi himself. Xunzi characteristically advocates a dualism of the "evil" physical human nature and of the mind (*xin*) which in the final analysis chooses morality independent of any material self-interest. The motivation for this free choice is self-respect, and it is achieved by rational insight into the good.

For the voluntarist Mengzi, on the other hand, to choose morality is immediately linked to intuitive volition. Mengzi's work is a single appeal to finally stand up for the way which this moral will show us anyhow. The fact that he does not yet rule over the whole empire as an ideal king, he tells the ruler of Qi, is not due to inability, but only to inactivity. And in order to become a "great man," everybody has the possibility to develop the "great" endowed to him by Heaven.[25] Mengzi also takes into account the oppressive external conditions of life, which time and again throw back human volition to naked self-preservation. But even under extreme conditions, decisions remain possible, as long as the "original heart" (*ben xin*), the innate moral sense, has not completely been lost:

Fish is something that I want, and also bear's palm is something that I want. If I cannot have both together, then I will let the fish go and take the bear's palm. Life is also something that I want, and justice, too. When I cannot have both together, then I will let life go and choose justice. Life indeed is something that I want, but among the things I want there is something more important than life. Therefore, I will not try to preserve it at all costs.

Death indeed is something I dislike, but among the things I dislike there is something worse than death. Therefore, there are evils which one does not avoid. If among the things which man wants nothing could be more important than life, why, then, does he not use every possible means to preserve it? And if among the things which man dislikes nothing could be worse than death, why, then, does he not use every possible means to avoid [this] evil? Thus it can happen that one does not use means which would lead to the preservation of life or to the avoidance of evil.

Therefore, among the things which one wants there is something more important than life, and among the things which one dislikes there is something worse than death. It is not that only worthy people would have this heart. It is common to all men, and the worthy simply understand not to lose it. But even a common man in the street will not take a small basket of rice or a bowl of soup which can save his life if they are offered to him with insulting words. And if you give them to a beggar with a kick, [even] he will not do so much as to look at them.

Yet, when it comes to ten thousand measures of grain (a high emolument), then one will take them without pondering on propriety and justice. But what can ten thousand measures give to me? Do I take them for the sake of a beautiful house, the services of wives and concubines, or that I can be generous to the needy among my acquaintances? What was not accepted in the former case even at the risk of life, is now accepted for the sake of a beautiful house, the services of wives and concubines, and generosity to the needy acquaintances. If there is no way to stop this, then this is a case of having lost one's original mind.[26]

Man, then, can in principle choose his way freely, because he is even capable of suspending his very interest in self-preservation. Every Confucian has stressed this possibility of the basic moral decision, the elementary yes or no with all consequences. A "decided scholar," we have read in *Lunyu* 15.9, will, as the case may be, "give his life for humaneness." And for Xunzi, "a gentleman does not avoid death for the sake of justice."[27]

With the basic resolution in favor of morality, the subject matter of choice and decision is not yet settled. The actor must also come to a decision in case his moral values conflict with each other or do not show a way out of intricate situations. As we have seen in Chapter 8, this dilemma can even assume tragical dimensions. Under such exigent circumstances, the moral will has to be supplemented by theoretical and practical competence of right choice.

According to Cua, in this case the "analogical projection" takes place. In his in many respects illuminating study about Xunzi's "moral epistemology," Cua inquires into the problem of what to do in situations in which "established rules"—in particular the rules of propriety (*li*)—do not work. "In normal circumstances," Cua interprets Xunzi, "established rules suffice for guidance. But in exigent circumstances, one must engage in *t'ui-lei* or analogical projection."[28] "Analogical projection" first of all means to extrapolate from a stock of material ethical knowledge and to solve actual problems in the light of cases known from the past. It is the cultural tradition, then, which decides on the right action in a concrete context. Cua writes:

> The Confucian emphasis on the role of historical knowledge, given the backward character of analogical projection, is a useful reminder that any piece of ethical reasoning, if it is to claim interpersonal significance, though in itself occasioned by a present perplexity, must have some contact with the cultural-historical experience of the people. It is in culture and history that an analogical projection finds its anchorage and not in rules and principles of *a priori* ratiocination. In this basic way, the prospective significance of analogical projection is rooted in retrospective ethical thinking.[29]

"Analogical projection," then, does not come into play after ethical principles have failed. It takes the place of such principles, which according to Cua are alien to Confucian ethics:

> For the Confucian, duty and obligation are tied to roles and positions of persons in the community. . . . There are, strictly speaking, no abstract principles that enjoin the individual in resolving his value predicament.[30]

The analogical projection, however, leads into an aporia which, as I see it, is not paid attention to by Cua. It becomes necessary because "established rules" fail, but it takes its orientation from the same past which has already entered into those rules—an obviously circular procedure. A casuistry like that which Cua attributes to Confucianism, moreover, would have to find out which of the many examples from the past is relevant in the specific case. The analogical projection, hence, as Cua himself writes, "depends crucially upon a *prior judgment* as to the similarities of the items in the analogy."[31] It cannot suffice, however, to identify similarities by careful analysis. An additional criterion would be necessary in order to determine in the first place why we should act as it was acted in the past. Moreover, there might be a series of similar exemplary cases among which we would have to make a justified choice. Analogical projection, then, not only proves to be extraordinarily complicated and ponderous, but also ethically deficient and in want of supplementary considerations.[32] In Xunzi's work itself, incidentally, we do not only find appeals to the models of the past, but also some skepticism concerning their import.[33]

Cua presents yet another version of analogical projection which claims validity for Confucianism as such. It is again conceived as a general guideline for conduct, and again replaces principles which are said to be absent:

> Apart from the prescriptions of *li* (ritual propriety) or conventional rules of proper behavior, there are, for the Confucian, no additional action-guiding universal principles that can serve as a basis of conduct.[34]

Concerning Xunzi, "analogical projection" meant the orientation to exemplary cases from history. Now, for Confucianism in general, it is supposed to mean the transference of familiar habits tied to roles and stations to new situations and surroundings. Analogizing of cases is supplemented by "analogizing of status,"[35] which tells us, for example, to act towards another's father like towards our own father. Confucianism, herewith, is willy-nilly once again brought down to the level of role ethics where the abstraction of the "other" regardless of status is not known.

This is not to deny that "analogical projections" of both kinds, as described by Cua on an outstanding analytical niveau, are important methods of decision finding in Confucianism. What I question is the exclusiveness Cua ascribes to them. In Zhou literature, decisions are discussed and deliberated upon in which projections of status do not take place, or would fail, and in which obviously more abstract criteria are involved. These are cases in which conventional rules and higher norms conflict with each other. According to Cua, they cannot occur in the first place, since there are no norms beyond the "conventional rules of proper behavior." But if there are no such norms, by what criterion, to give only some examples, do some of Confucius' disciples reject princely service? By what criterion does the filial son in *Xunzi* 29 refuse to obey his father and his ruler? By what criterion does Wan Zhang reject the present of a feudal lord? By what criterion does Mengzi refuse "compliance"?[36] In each of these situations, an attitude is chosen which contradicts a conventional duty and appeals to a higher authority. The same is true of the case of rescuing life even if the act of rescue violates propriety:

> Chunyu Kun asked, "Is it propriety that men and women must not touch each other when giving or receiving anything?" Mengzi said, "Yes, it is."—"If the sister-in-law is drowning, does one rescue her with one's hands?"—"When the sister-in-law is drowning and one does not rescue her, this is to be a jackal or a wolf. That men and women should not touch each other in giving and receiving is propriety. But that the sister-in-law is rescued with the hand is *weighing* (*quan*)."[37]

Mengzi makes curtailments in propriety in order to give precedence to a conflicting principle (the principle to save life). In most cases it is propriety which falls victim to "weighing" because prescriptions of form naturally balk at flexible reactions. Dong Zhongshu defends the general Zifan of Chu who made peace with Song because of compassion for the starving people, thus violating the order of his lord. This act against propriety in favor of humaneness is justified, Dong Zhongshu says, by Confucius' saying "When humaneness is at stake, one does not give precedence to the teacher."[38]

In the *Huainanzi*, too, which, referring to Confucian and Daoist sources, gives a lengthy discussion of the problem of weighing propriety has to give way in the case of conflict:

Only a *shengren* understands how to weigh.
Always to be reliable in one's words, and always keep agreements, this counts as eminent conduct in the world. When his father had stolen a sheep, Upright Gong testified this. Student Wei died because of an appointment with a girl. To testify against the father because of uprightness, and to drown because of reliability—who would appreciate this, despite all their uprightness and reliability?[39]

In the whole army, to fake an order is regarded as one of the greatest crimes. When Duke Mu of Qin raised troops for a surprise attack on Zheng and, passing Zhou, went eastwards, Xian Gao, a merchant from Zheng, was on his way to the west in order to sell cattle. Xian met the army between Zhou and Zheng. He thereupon pretended an order of the Earl of Zheng and feasted the troops with twelve cattle. So he rescued Zheng by making the army of Qin (which believed itself detected) retreat. Thus there are situations in which reliability turns out to be a mistake, and extravagant talk turns out to be meritorious.

What does it mean to earn great merits by violating propriety? Anciently, King Gong of Chu fought [against Jin] near Yinling [and was taken prisoner]. Pan Wang, Yang Youji, Huang Shuaiwei and Gongsun Bing liberated him by a surprise raid. King Gong was so scared that he broke down, whereupon Huang Shuaiwei gave him a kick. Now the king realized the situation. Furious at this offense against propriety, he got on his feet again. The four nobles took him on their chariot and drove away. . . .

Therefore, a *shengren* considers the complexity of a case and accordingly bends or stretches himself, bows down or looks up. He does not know any fixed appearance. Now he bends, and then he stretches himself. Sometimes he is humble and weak like rush, but not because somebody would have got hold of him. Sometimes he is hard and rigid and of a determined will as high as the clouds, but not because of arrogance. In doing so, he wants to seize the moment (*shí, kairos!*) and react to change.[40]

That in intercourse between ruler and subject one bends the knee and humbly bows in order to honor one another, is propriety. Yet, to kick the ruler in a state of emergency cannot be condemned by anybody in the world. Hence, when loyalty (*zhong*) matters, the argument of propriety does not suffice to bring one into difficulty.

When a filial son serves his parents, he shows a kind face and a humble posture. [In the morning] he reverently presents the girdle and brings the shoes. But if the father is about to drown, then he will pull him out of the water by his hairs.

To call the personal name of the ruler when praying for him [means breaking the name taboo], but is dictated by the circumstances.

This is what weighing is made for. (The quotation from *Lunyu* 9.30 follows). Weighing is something the importance of which only a *shengren* realizes. Therefore, he who reaches *concord by conflict* can be said to understand weighing. But he who creates conflict by concord can be said not to understand weighing. If one does not understand weighing, good changes to evil.

Therefore, propriety is mere tinsel[41] and the veil of falseness. In sudden distress and urgent need, it is of no use. A *shengren*, therefore, communicates with the world in a cultivated manner, but he does what is fitting according to the specific situation. He is not inflexibly bound to a road with only a single track. Therefore, his failures are few and his successes are many. His command goes through the world, and nobody can find fault with it.[42]

The case examples of the *Huainanzi* demonstrate the detours of morality which have become necessary. For a just conduct, it no longer suffices to rely on accepted, established rules. On the contrary, as the case may be, these rules have even to be violated. Similar compulsions have always existed to some extent, of course. What is typical of the axial age is to discuss them as a central problem of ethics, and to emphasize unconventional solutions. Yet, from a Confucian viewpoint, to discharge propriety from the outset and not only in exigent circumstances would be a much too radical conclusion. The *Huainanzi*, moreover, leaves it open what propriety should be replaced by. It seems that a *shengren* simply gives himself over to his momentary intuitions. In *Mengzi* 4A17, however, it is quite obvious what takes precedence over *li*: "jackal" and "wolf" indicate that the alternative in question is humaneness, which is also in *Mengzi* 2A6 described as the impulse of rescuing another. The decision and its legitimation are linked to the hierarchy of values. This does not eliminate the task of choice, however, since it has still to be considered when another virtue has to come second to humaneness.

Decision and choice, then, are significant topics in Confucianism and Chinese philosophy in general. They must be made when self-interest is about to lead one astray from the right path, or when the latter is unclear. And instead of disappearing in the detailed and minute instructions of the *li*, they are required where these instructions fail. Warning the rulers of his time, who surround themselves with the wrong advisors, Xunzi emphasizes the importance of the right decision in his picture of Yang Zhu lamenting at the crossroads:

> Yang Zhu lamented at the crossroads, "If I now make a single wrong step, I will sometimes realize that I have missed the way for a thousand miles!" In this case, too, the crossroad between glory and disgrace, security and danger is at issue, and it is even more deplorable than in the case of Yang Zhu. Alas, how deplorable! The rulers do not recognize that a thousand years are at stake![43]

The problem of decision has yet another aspect. In the arduous and tricky terrain of everyday life, the moral actor will continuously meet with tough obstacles, for the world in which he lives is not the world of his ideals. Nevertheless, he has the ethical obligation to face its sobering conditions and to mediate his abstract standards with his concrete social duties. This problem is related to that of moral conflict discussed above. But it has yet a special dimension, which because of its crucial importance will be the subject of a separate chapter: the dimension of *responsibility* of postconventional action in a conventional and unprincipled world.[44]

B. AUTONOMY OF JUDGMENT

The fact that decisions have to be and can be taken is related to man's freedom to actively form his surrounding, choose alternatives, and escape from established ways. This kind of choice presupposes an autonomous basis of judgment in man. It is already implicitly referred to in *Lunyu* 9.26, where Confucius says:

> It is possible to deprive a whole army[45] of its generals. But it is not possible to deprive even a common man of his will.

Man has his own convictions and is not a mere agent of collective worldviews. He is ready to learn from others and to submit to their criticism, yet never unconditionally, but in choosing "the good" from their words.[46] Mengzi distinguishes "submission by power" from "submission by heart" based on winning the other's conviction as well as his feelings.[47] A classic grounding of the freedom of judgment and decision is later to be found in Xunzi in the following description of the "heart" (*xin*), the organ of thinking:

> The heart is the ruler of the body and the master of the wondrous intelligence. It gives commands, but it does not receive any from anywhere. It prohibits and permits by itself, it decides and chooses by itself, it becomes active and stops by itself. Thus the mouth can be forced to be silent or speak, and the the body can be forced to bend or stretch itself, but the heart cannot be forced to alter its opinion. If it regards something as right, then it accepts it, and if it

regards something as wrong, then it rejects it. Therefore I say: *The heart is free and unrestricted in its choices.* It sees all things for itself. And although its objects are complex and manifold, in its innermost essence it is undivided itself.[48]

The human mind's autonomy to choose and reject according to its own discretion can hardly be expressed more clearly. Whereas the mouth can be silenced and the body be bent—insinuations of oppressive rule—the "heart" is a bulkwark of independent judgment. It is another story that Xunzi is far from recommending free reign of this autonomy. What is "right" and what is "wrong" must in the final analysis be decided by the heart. Nevertheless, it is, objectively, not a mere matter of one's own convenience. One should, therefore, impose a kind of self-restriction on freedom. As quoted above, Xunzi polemizes against "departing from the *Dao*, at pleasure making arbitrary choices." Right and wrong should rather be "hit adequately."[49] There are some orientation marks for them— the norms of the Confucian school. Xunzi, therefore, would have taken the side of Confucius against the disciple Zilu:

> Zilu asked Confucius, "I want to abandon the way of antiquity and only follow my own opinion. Is that acceptable?" The Master said, "It is not acceptable. . . . How do you know that your opinion does not turn right into wrong and wrong into right?"[50]

Zilu wants to substitute the autonomy of the "heart" for the "way of antiquity," the transmitted ethical life. The typical Confucian point is the reverse one: Man should, as far as possible, stick to the established rules, yet out of his own conviction, and guarded against opportunistic consent by his independent mind.

C. SELF-RESPECT AND SELF-STRENGTHENING

In a decaying world which does not promise too many chances to realize one's moral goals, the Confucian program requires a strong ego of its adherents. The reference to the "self" (*ji, shen*)[51] is a basic and general theme of the axial age which has, in the lyrics of the *Chuci*, also found a poetic expression.[52] True, the Confucian self is not an atomic isolated entity, but stands in interdependence with its social environment. This is not only a sinological truism. That self-formation is an essentially social process, is, after G. H. Mead, not denied by modern social psychology either. This does not rule out that the self can detach itself from the society to which it owes its existence, and conceive of still other and better forms of living.[53]

It is in such a dialectical constellation, as was already present in the relationship of reciprocity and conscience,[54] that we find the Confucian self.[55] If we read Confucius' sentence that "virtue is not alone, but surely has a neighbor"[56] as referring to the moral person's situatedness in a context, there is still a tension-filled interrelation between both, and the self never gets absorbed by the social environment. When reading the relevant texts, one even gets the impression that much greater stress is laid upon self-realization than on community orientation. Despite the interdependence of both, the accent is unequivocally put on the active part on the self, and not on the influence of the community which it lives in and depends upon, and to which it dedicates its moral efforts. The reason is, again, the community's sobering condition. The *principium individuationis*, as it were, is a negative one—the isolation of the morally knowledgeable in a disintegrating world.

It is his "self," then, which for the Confucian intellectual becomes the constant point of orientation of all moral action. The self is the internal basis which takes over functions of the failing guidance from outside, not in the sense of a mere internalization of the heteronomous, but of a *reflected affirmation of ethical life*. In *Lunyu* 12.1, a key passage of the work, Confucius says:

> To overcome one's self (*ke ji*) and to return to propriety (*fu li*) is humaneness. . . . Humaneness can only come from the self—how could it come from others?

I interpret the "return" to propriety in terms of the conscious reintegration into the transmitted ethical life. The fact that this reintegration is only achievable by "overcoming one's self" expresses the *alienation* inherent in conventional morality, which has been experienced prior to and during the step towards the postconventional.[57] The same "self," however, which again faces the alienating adjustment to society, must *decide* to do this, because the natural and unquestioned orientation provided by substantial forms of life has long been lost.[58] The autonomy drawn on here is so detached that it can even completely disassociate itself from the latter. It is in this sense that the freethinker Li Zhi (1527–1602) has later appealed to *Lunyu* 12.1 against the Confucian orthodoxy of his time.[59]

Self-respect, *self-strengthening*, and *self-examination* can already be identified in the *Lunyu* as the three steps to make the "self" the unconquerable fortress in which morality shall find its new foundation.

Self-respect (*jing ji*, *gong ji*,[60] also *jin* and *zi ai*) is the precondition of all moral action. It is the decisive fundament of Confucius' ethics, since unlike his successors he does not know any other grounding of morality. He who does not feel respect for himself will never be able to feel respect for others—this is the crucial idea which Confucius has above all brought forward in a political context. He praises Zichan, the chancellor of Zheng, for being "respectful (*gong*) in his attitude towards himself (*ji*)."[61] Shun, too, "showed respect for himself" (*gong ji*), and a "gentleman," in order to "bring peace to all citizens, cultivates himself with respect (*jing*)."[62] Self-respect is not only indispensable for those engaged in political action, but to "be respectful (*gong*) in private life" is a constituent of humaneness valid for everyone.[63] Mengzi later states that "he who bends himself can never make others straight."[64] For Xunzi, self-respect (*jing ji*) is one of the characteristics of a *shengren*. It contrasts with the "virtue of the people," who "regard as good to follow the customs."[65] And Confucius, Xunzi says, praised Yan Yuan an "enlightened gentleman" for his sentence "a humane person cherishes himself (*zi ai*)."[66] Here, too, self-respect counts as the fundament of morality.

By *self-strengthening* I mean the effort, starting from self-respect, to grow into a person of imperturbable moral will regardless of success or failure, acknowledgment or hostility. For self-strengthening, too, the classic passages are found in the *Lunyu;* later texts have, if at all, only explicated what the "Master" has outlined. Making oneself independent of the applause of others and maintaining one's self-reliance counts among his most obvious concerns. As he says:

> Not to be annoyed if others ignore you—is this not gentlemanly?

> A gentleman is troubled by his inability, not by being ignored by others.[67]

Always mindful of his independence, the "gentleman" already precautionarily keeps a distance:

> A gentleman is solidary, but not cliquish. A mean man is cliquish, but not solidary.

> A gentleman has self-respect (*jin*), but does not wrangle. He is sociable, but not partisan.

> A gentleman harmonizes, but does not conform. A mean man conforms, but does not harmonize.[68]

Zhongyong 10 adds:

> A gentleman is harmonious, but does not swim with the tide.

In a world which is often experienced as senseless or hostile, the Confucian "gentleman" must show readiness for poverty and *asceticism*. They are not aspired after for their own sake; an honorable, uncorrupted life in prosperity would at any time be preferred. Renunciation has to be put up with, because the moral goal can hardly be achieved, but cannot be abandoned either. Confucius says:

> A scholar sets his heart on the *Dao*. But he who is ashamed of poor food and poor clothes does not deserve to speak with him.

> A gentleman's concern is the *Dao*, not his food. . . . A gentleman worries about the *Dao*, not about his poverty.

> To live on coarse food and water, and to have the bent arm for a neck support—joy is also in this. But wealth and high position, attained by unjust means, for me are like passing clouds.[69]

Modesty is the precondition of freedom. It includes the readiness for death and signals the resolution to immunize oneself against that weakness in which complaisance and submissiveness have their root: material self-interest. The motif can also be found in Daoist mysticism and is typical of the axial age. But it is suspicious to the ideologists of law and order. Han Fei attacks the spreading linguistic confusion according to which "those who despise rank and emolument" are called "heroic," and "those who make light of the laws and shun neither punishment nor death" enjoy the name of "courageous men."[70] And nobody should be called "honest" who "belittles rank and emolument, and takes lightly to give up or desert his post in order to choose his ruler."[71] Han Fei, therefore, also polemizes against the anchorets: "To leave the world, live in seclusion, and thereby reprove the ruler, this I do not call just."[72] To fortify oneself against egoism and shed one's fear of authority directly undermines the fundaments of the Legalist system, which loses the most effective handle to make its subjects tractable. If not by "rank and remuneration, punishments and fines," Han Fei quotes Taigong Wang, who has put to death two private scholars refusing to take office, how, then, could he ever "employ others" as their ruler?[73]

Next to preparedness for asceticism, *mourning* plays a decisive role for finding the path to oneself. As Zeng Shen says:

> I have heard from the teacher that if a man has not yet found the path to himself he will do so when he mourns for his parents.[74]

The elementary experience of the parents' death serves as moral catharsis. Mourning doubtless has a social function, which accounts for its ritual, ceremonial aspect. For Confucius, however, the inner concern is more important than the external protocol.[75] Yet, it is not solely the grief over the loss of the parents which leaves its impression on the mourner. It is, above all, the long mourning period, the strict retirement from all intercourse for more than two years, the turning away from the others which leads to a withdrawal into the inner self.[76] He who has gone through this exercise will return as a man who has, together with the misery of his most intimate relatives, experienced his self.

Music, too, serves the self-strengthening of the Confucian. Music creates ties with tradition, and it has a positive social effect, since it can contribute to the integration into the community and to the cultivation of the emotions.[77] In *Lunyu* 14.39, however, it has yet another meaning:

> The Master played on the musical stones in Wei, when a man with a basket on his shoulder passed by the door and said, "A determined scholar, indeed, who is playing there!" But after a while, he added, "How vulgar this tinkling is! If one is ignored by others, one should simply give up. 'When the water is deep, cross it with all your clothes on; when the water is shallow, you may hike up your garment.' "[78]
> The Master said, "How resolute! That man cannot be embarrassed!"

The subject matter of this parable is the decision between taking responsibility for the world and resigning in view of its deplorable condition. For the stranger, who reminds one of the door keeper from *Lunyu* 14.38, the endeavor of the Confucians is comparable to hiking up one's garment in a flood although one will be thoroughly drenched in it. Music, here, is obviously not the means for stimulating social feeling in the rhythm of the society. It is rather the refuge of a lonely fighter, and only interpretable by a congenial thinker. The harmony it causes is an inner one in outward disharmony. It serves to strengthen the self in a world which, as it were, has got off time.

This motif is elaborated in the *Zhuangzi*, where music and singing are steady accessories of the protagonists of the Confucian school. Yuan Xian, living in deliberate poverty, plays the zither in his desolate dwelling and pours forth contempt for his rich fellow student Zigong. Zeng Shen hikes all over the world, sings the old odes of the Shang that his voice "fills heaven and earth," and denies the Son of Heaven and the feudal lords service and friendship. And Yan Yuan, supported by the inner stability he gets from his music and from the teaching of his master, rejects the life of an official.[79] Confucius himself, last but not least, remains unswerving and staunch by the help of singing and playing the lute when he is brought to the verge of death, surrounded by the armies of Chen and Cai.[80] This relationship to music which the *Zhuangzi* attributes to the Confucians is the same which distinguishes some protagonists of Daoism itself.[81] The unconventional foible for music belongs to the common repertoire of many of the critical thinkers of Zhou China.

Nearly all of the learning exercises of Confucianism can be related to the formation of the "self." The aim is a double one: to make man a sociable, but at the same time self-reliant moral person. The self has to be stabilized and cultivated (*xiu*) in order to exert influence on the world instead of getting controlled and absorbed by it. As we read in *Mengzi* 7A9:

> Mengzi said to Song Goujian, "Are you fond of travelling [to the courts]? I will tell you something about it. If you are recognized, regard it as fuss, and if you are not recognized, regard it as fuss."— "How can one achieve this kind of attitude?"—"Honor virtue, and delight in justice, then you can achieve it. Therefore, even if a scholar gets into misery, he will not let go of justice, and if he prospers, he will not leave the *Dao*. If in misery he does not let go of justice, he finds himself in it. And if, prosperous, he does not leave the *Dao*, the expectations of the people will not be disappointed. If the men of antiquity were promoted to high positions, their bounty was conferred upon the people. If they were not promoted, their self-cultivation still became manifest for the whole world. In misery, they perfected themselves in solitude. Prosperous, they perfected the world as well.

Inner strength by the conscious profession of morality is the condition for avoiding being despondent when unsuccessful and getting corrupted by prosperity. "The way of the gentleman," the *Zhongyong* stresses, "is based on the self."[82]

D. SELF-EXAMINATION, MOTIVATION, AND CONSCIENCE

The formation of the moral person requires, furthermore, constant self-examination.[83] Thus one should seek the reasons for failure in oneself:

A gentleman seeks in himself, a mean man seeks in others.[84]

If you love others, but they are not attached to you, then you should reflect (*fan*) upon whether you are humane. If you rule others, but they do not adhere to the order, then you should reflect upon whether you are wise. If you treat others according to the rules of propriety, but they do not respond, you should reflect upon whether you are really respectful. Whenever you fail in your action, reflect upon and seek in yourself. When you are correct yourself, the world will turn to you.[85]

To fail oneself, but attribute it to others—is this not devious![86]

Mengzi and the *Zhongyong* compare the commended attitude with archery. Archery, a favorite exercise to learn fair play,[87] can teach in particular to make oneself responsible for failure:

Humaneness is like archery. The archer concentrates himself and then shoots. If he misses, he does not murmur against the one who defeats him. He simply reflects upon and seeks [the reason] in himself.[88]

Archery resembles the [way of] the gentleman. If the archer misses the target, he reflects upon and seeks [the reason] in himself.[89]

Not solely in case of failure has one to put critical questions to oneself, but success and acknowledgment, as we have seen, are things that the moral actor can hardly expect anyhow. Similarly, the successful are not necessarily the good. Self-reflection, therefore, does not simply examine the causes of possible frustration. It examines the *motives* of action, regardless of whether or not they have the desired result. In general, the Confucians place the inner attitude above the outer observance of prescriptions. Thus Confucius stresses that care for parents without "respect" would not differ from care for animals, and he declares true grief as more important than perfection in mourning ceremonies.[90]

In the context of heteronomous interpretations of Chinese ethics, however, it has been called into question that Confucianism distinguishes between motive and action in the first place. Trauzettel writes that Confucianism—if not ancient China in general—"does not concede positive value to motivation as such" and does not separate behavior from its effects.[91] To ascribe such a "moral realism" (Piaget)[92] to China may, if at all, find some support by later Chinese law, which in case of killing a parent did not attach great significance to intent.[93] Yet, Chinese law in general does know the distinction between intent and accident. It is already present in Zhou law and legal thought,[94] and definitely in Zhou philosophy. In the *Mozi*, we find a clear differentiation of the actor's intention and the result of his effort:

> In the matter of justice being beneficial and injustice being harmful, one has to distinguish between intention (*zhi*) and effect (*gong*). . . . Intention and effect cannot be seen as following one another (as coinciding).[95]

This distinction is quite common in Zhou philosophy. Confucius distinguishes the "prudent" who finds humaneness "profitable" from the really "humane" person who "rests in it."[96] The *Liji* adds a third possibility: to practice humaneness because of fear of punishment. The three kinds are "similar in effect, but different in essence," the difference in essence being due to the different motivation. True humane motivation can be seen not from success, but from failure:

> As long as his success is the same as with [true] humaneness, it cannot yet be decided whether somebody is humane. Only when his mistakes are the same as with true humaneness can one know that he is humane.[97]

Xunzi 29, too, stresses the importance of the motives, when it is said that "one can only speak of filial piety and loyalty after one has examined the reasons why somebody follows an order."[98] And Mengzi points out that from a "great man" it cannot be expected that "his words are always reliable and his actions always show results. It is only that his point of view is justice."[99] Thus, in many cases, the good motives are the only thing left for the moral actor, and their value becomes apparent just by their being denied success. "What does it matter, not to be accepted?" Yan Yuan asks his Master, when in deadly peril between Chen and Cai. "*Only by not being accepted does one prove to be a gentleman!*"[100]

In Confucian literature, the events between Chen and Cai often serve as an example of the moral person's lot. For the *Xunzi*, on the one hand, they show that there is no success without the right moment (*shi*). On the other hand, they symbolize that a "gentleman" does not exert himself because he is sure to succeed.[101] When Zilu asks why Heaven brings such misery upon the good, the *Xunzi* lets Confucius answer:

> Iris and orchid live in the depths of the forest, and it is not so that they would not be fragrant since nobody smells them. When a gentle-

man studies, it is not in order to make his way, but to avoid getting into anxiety in hardship and letting his motivation (*yì*) be thwarted in worry.[102]

Motivation as such is decisive here. What is more: Since no justification of Heaven is given, the good motivation is the only support left for the moral act. Hence, when the Confucian gentleman examines himself, this is not only because positive feedback from his surrounding fails to come. Such a feedback can only be expected in the long run, if at all. If the moral endeavor is hardly rewarded by the given world, it can even less be expected that the latter offers an external orientation for it. What is really good no longer coincides with what is generally accepted, and any "moral realism" has fallen apart. Neither is an externally correct demeanor per se an expression of inner moral convictions, nor can the applause of the majority be trusted.[103] It is the given condition of the community, then, which directs the "gentleman's" attention inwards, and not simply individual failure. And only in the inner of man will it finally be decided whether the bad is refrained from and the good is done. However indispensable tradition and manners may be, man for a moment is alone with himself, *a fortiori* since religious controls are lacking to a large extent.[104]

The Confucian must find the moral control within himself. What does it look like? I first will discuss the concept of "watchfulness when alone" (*shen du*), which tries to solve the problem, also debated by the Greeks,[105] how one can be moral without being under observation. Whether the concept *shen du* resolves this task, remains to be seen. *Daxue* 6 states:

> To make one's motivation (*yì*) sincere (*cheng*) means not to deceive oneself. It should be [as natural] as hating a bad smell or loving a beautiful woman. This is called to find one's satisfaction in oneself. Therefore, a gentleman must be watchful when he is alone. A mean man, however, does evil things in private without knowing a limit. Only when he sees a gentleman becomes he weary of his attitude. Then he conceals his evil and highlights his goodness. But when others observe him, it is like seeing his lungs and liver. Of what use, then, is his dissimulation?
> This is called what is truly within becomes apparent without. Therefore, the gentleman must be watchful when alone. Zengzi said, "When ten eyes watch you, and ten hands point at you—is not this a strong [examination]!" Wealth adorns such a person's house, and virtue adorns his self. When his heart is broad, his body is at ease. A gentleman, therefore, must make his motivation sincere.

The *Daxue* hopes that disgust for evil and love for the good become as natural as being part of the biological constitution. This fits in with the eudaimonistic promise of well-being at the end of the passage. It has to be repeated, however, that this is not the characteristic tone of the early Confucian writings. It is also no generally shared conviction that inner badness becomes manifest outside.[106] But most probably, the eyes and hands which catch the "mean man" are those of the "gentlemen" and hence belong to an idealized audience and not to the general public. Nevertheless, self-control because of fear of being unmasked in the end,[107] would be morally underdetermined. I cannot follow Santangelo's claim, therefore, that *Daxue* 6 contains a "strictly personal" notion of conscience independent of "social and external expectations."[108] The formula *shen du* itself can perhaps be interpreted in this way, and also its later history goes in this direction.[109] Its specific justification in the *Daxue*, however, tells something else. It is likewise questionable to view "watchfulness when alone" (*shen du*) as the prospective counterpart of retrospective "self-examination" (*xing shen, nei xing*, etc.), as has been suggested by Xie Youwei.[110] The main difference between both concepts is rather that in the latter case no imagination of an external public is involved (there is no evidence, moreover, that it exclusively refers to past deeds). "Self-examination," therefore, seems to be the ethically more far-reaching and radical concept. It is to be found in particular in the *Lunyu*. Zeng Shen says:

> I daily examine (*xing*) myself (*shen*) on three points: Have I not been benevolent when I gave advice to others? Have I not been trustworthy when communicating with my fellow students and friends? Have I not practiced what has been transmitted to me [by my teacher]?[111]

Instead of the expression *xing shen*, "examine one's self," which is used here, *Lunyu* 12.4 speaks of *nei xing*, "inner examination":

> If [the gentleman], after inner examination (*nei xing*), does not feel qualms [of conscience] (*jiu*), what worries and fear should he have?

In *Lunyu* 5.27, Confucius presents the inner examination as a kind of lawsuit:

> I give it up! I have not yet seen anyone who could perceive his faults and inwardly indict himself.

Inner examination (*nei xing*) is to be thought of as self-indictment (*zi song*) wherein "the heart blames itself without the mouth's speaking," as Zhu Xi comments.[112] The blaming voice is certainly that of *conscience*, which has also been understood as the "consciousness of an inner court in man" in the Western tradition.[113] This concept of conscience is of evolutionary significance because it is linked to the development of personal responsibility and a self-reflective ego.[114] The *Lunyu* operates with this notion of conscience without using a term for it. It is the source of the expression *nei jiu*, used today for "qualms of conscience," while *liang xin*, the common Chinese equivalent of "conscience," is first to be found in the *Mengzi*. *Liang xin* is the innate "good heart," which shows man the right path, but can get lost, just as the trees on a mountain can be felled. *Liang xin*, however, is not necessarily reflective, since the term *xin* is used ambiguously in this respect by Mengzi.[115] It seems to be closely connected with *liang zhi*, the "good knowledge," which intuitively and "without having to think" knows the good.[116] If we make use of a distinction suggested by Rüdiger,[117] the kind of consciousness found in the *Lunyu* can be called "rational conscience," while that of the *Mengzi* falls into the category of "vox-dei-conscience" (or, rather, *vox naturae*). But in the *Mengzi*, too, we find a self-examination resembling the one of the *Lunyu*.

If we follow the established sinological opinion, however, the early Confucian concept of conscience at best represents two other types which Rüdiger mentions—the heteronomous types of "rule-" and of "guilt-conscience," if we should not drop the notion of conscience at all. This has in particular been brought forward by B. Nelson. The problem of conscience is Nelson's crucial point in his polemic against Needham. In the West, he says, the "image of human action and world changed dramatically in the 12th and 13th centuries," when "collective consciousness gave ground to the individual conscience."[118] In China, on the other hand, the power of old faith-structures remained unchallenged till the Cultural Revolution.[119] Together with the individual conscience, the Chinese also lack its correlate, ethical universalism, and the bearer of both, the moral person.[120] There is no breakthrough towards an "objective universal." China remains rooted in "sacro-magical" consciousness characterized by "collective acceptances of responsibility" and oriented to "prescriptive etiquettes" and "cosmic orders."[121] We can agree with Nelson that ethical universalism must be bound to a concept of the person, for only the moral person can be the agent of universal norms which transcend the collectively shared convictions of empirical communities. Nelson's presentation of China, however, is not based on research into the sources, but simply on the debatable theses of Weber.

Contrary to Nelson's skepticism, conscience is already a discovery of antiquity.[122] Yet, this does not rule out the possibility that there are relevant differences concerning the status and nature of conscience in ancient and modern times, in the Orient and the Occident. When Hegel, to give an example, calls conscience "the ground of the modern world," this is because only now it has become the embodiment of the "spirit of the time," while it was not representative for antiquity.[123] Modernity, however, has not only taken up the vantage point of conscience. It has also raised questions about its genesis which concern the moral relevance of conscience itself. British empiricism has pointed out the role of the external milieu for the formation of conscience. Sociology, in particular Durkheim, has interpreted conscience as a representation of collective norms (Rüdiger's "rule-conscience"). Psychoanalysis, finally, has exposed conscience as internalized parental authority (Rüdiger's "guilt-conscience"). This disclosure of external causes is relatively justified. But it merely genetically complicates the problem of conscience and does not make it obsolete. We should rather distinguish an autonomous form of conscience from a genetically earlier heteronomous one, as developmental psychology has suggested.[124]

As to China, what happens in the conscience of the Confucian when examining his self is not merely a kind of puppet play with external dramaturgy. The very social constellation—a society in crisis—within which the gentleman turns his attention to his inner self, speaks against such an interpretation. The reflection on the self at the same time means turning away from what is outside. "In inner examination," Xunzi says, "external things become unimportant."[125] The clearest answer to our question as to the status of the classical Chinese conscience, however, could be given by some unequivocal textual evidence that the good conscience strengthens the individual against the community, and that the moral person's introspection leads to a demonstrative rebuff of the consensus of the multitude or of external expectations. Such evidence is present in *Mengzi* 2A2. In *Lunyu* 12.4, it has already been assured that a "gentleman" who on an inner examination does not feel qualms of conscience knows neither worries nor fear. The gentleman feels anxious when the *Dao* is at stake,[126] but not as far as his own steadfastness is concerned. Mengzi has developed this idea with the pathos characteristic to him. He claims for himself an "imperturbable heart" which raises him above a hero like Meng Ben and which, as he says, his contemporary Gaozi has achieved even before him. When asked whether there is a way to attain this imperturbable heart, he answers:

> Yes, there is. Beigong You has nourished his courage in a way that he does not flinch under a touch and does not turn his eyes aside. But if anyone harms a single hair of his, he considers it the same as being flogged in the market place. He would not stand anything from a common man in rags nor from a notable in wide garments nor from the ruler of a state of ten thousand war chariots. He views stabbing such a ruler as stabbing a common man. He has no awe before the feudal lords, and if anyone bawls at him, he will always return it.
>
> Meng Shishe nourished his courage as follows. He said, "To lose or to be victorious is all the same for me. He who advances only after he has measured the enemy's forces, and engages the latter only after he has calculated the chances of victory, must stand in awe of a great army. How could I be certain of victory? It is simply that I can stay without fear."
>
> Meng Shishe resembles Zengzi, and Beigong You resembles Zixia. I do not know which of the two is the superior one with regard to courage, but Meng Shishe has [more likely] grasped the essential.
>
> Zengzi once said to his disciple Zixiang, "Do you like courage? I have heard of my teacher (Confucius) what great courage is: If, on self-reflexion (*zi fan*), I find that I am not upright, shall I not be in fear [of any one] regardless of whether he is a common man or a notable? *But if, on self-reflection, I find that I am upright, then I will go forward against thousands and tens of thousands.*"
>
> The way how Meng Shishe retained his energy (*qi*) does not yet equal Zengzi's grasp of the essential.[127]

Beigong You probably belongs to a Confucian faction which goes back to Confucius' pupil Qidiao Kai. Han Fei gives a description of Kai which resembles that of Beigong You by Mengzi:

> According to Qidiao, one should not flinch and turn one's eyes aside. If he has acted wrong, he gives way even to a slave. But if he has acted right, he lets loose his anger even before a feudal lord.[128]

The *Hanfeizi* throws additional light on the connection between the "imperturbable heart" and Beigong You's extraordinary courage. The inner conviction to have acted "right" gives one the guts to oppose even the most mighty, while in the reverse case one cannot even face the most humble person—an impressive description of the power of conscience which is presumably based on self-observation. I assume that the topos stems from the earliest phase of Confucianism, since Han Fei and Mengzi attribute it to direct disciples of Confucius. Zeng Shen's "great courage" is the clearest embodiment of the inwardness of conscience, while Beigong You is still under the sway of a heteronomous feeling of honor. His aggressive pride, which does not shrink back even from regicide, is registered by Mengzi, nota bene, not without admiration. But Beigong You makes himself dependent on the will to assert himself and to avoid disgrace, and that is, on something external.[129] Meng Shishe, however, has already freed himself from the constraint of success and from strategy. He rests in courage as such and represents a higher degree of inwardness. He is congenial with Zeng Shen in that neither is interested in triumphing over others, but only in nourishing his conviction.

Yet, Zeng Shen's way towards courage is the most simple and effectual one: Self-examination with the result to be sincere lets the individual confront even thousands of enemies. Any external criterion is missing here. It is evident that the conscience involved cannot be understood as the controlling organ of the community, but only as a power which gives strength to the individual in its unavoidable conflict with the many. The point at question is the *autonomy* of conscience as the organ of self-examination. Mengzi's aforementioned "negative imperative," with its demand "Do not do what you do not do, and do not will what you do not will!"[130] translates this autonomy into an abstract, albeit negative[131] instruction to volition and action. Undoubtedly it is the *liang xin*, the "good heart," which knows what man does not "will," since it is the embodiment of the original morality. Mengzi's negative imperative is the antique counterpart of the more elaborate formulation of the principle of conscience by Wang Yangming (1472–1529). Instead of *liang xin*, Wang uses Mengzi's related term *liang zhi*, "good knowledge":

> That one point of your good knowledge is your own standard. What you are thinking rests in it. If something is right, it knows that it is right, and if something is wrong, it knows that it is wrong. And it is impossible to keep anything from it. Just do not [try to] deceive it, but sincerely act in accordance with it. Then the good will be pre-

served, and the evil will be removed. What security and joy there is in it![132]

This affirmation of conscience is a legacy of Mengzi. Wang Yangming has supplemented his principle of conscience by a principle of logos,[133] which adds to the prereflective knowledge of *liang zhi* a reflective mind:

> In learning it is of highest regard to find something in the heart (the organ of thought). If I examine a word (*yan—logos!*) in the heart and find it to be wrong, then I will not dare to accept it as right, even though it comes from Confucius, let alone if it comes from people inferior to him. But if I examine a word in the heart and find it to be right, then I will not dare to regard it as wrong, even though it comes from an ordinary man, let alone if it comes from Confucius.[134]

Wang Yangming's appeal to the autarky of mind is indebted to axial age Confucianism. Its "effective history" (*Wirkungsgeschichte*), then, underlines the autonomous and postconventional nature of the early Confucian inwardness. Intellectual history, of course, cannot give an unequivocal testimony since its course is variable and subject to all kinds of vicissitudes. In order to support the thesis of autonomy, I will, therefore, discuss further aspects of the early Confucian conception of the "self."

E. AUTONOMY OF ACTION

A very frequent motif in ancient Chinese literature is *independent action*, the practical counterpart of self-reflection. It was already heard in *Mengzi* 2A2. In the following passage, Mengzi celebrates the unbending "great fellow" who, if necessary, "strides his way alone" (*du xing qi dao*):

> To regard compliance (*shun*) as correct behavior is the way of wives and concubines.
> But he who dwells in the wide house of the world (in humaneness), has his stand at the correct position in the world, and walks the great path of the world (justice), who if he reaches his ambitions, makes his way together with the people, but if he does not reach his ambitions, *strides his way alone*, who cannot be led to dissipation by wealth and high position, led astray by poverty and mean conditions, and bent by authority and power—such a man is called a great fellow.[135]

If we leave aside the sexist bias, Mengzi's words are one of the most proud and emphatic of classic proclamations of uncompromising and resolute action exclusively dedicated to general moral norms. The "great fellow" later became a figure of identification of Wang Yangming's school.[136] In the axial age already, *du xing*, "stride alone" or "act independently," together with the related expressions *gua li, du li*, or *te li* ("stand alone"), became an honorable distinction of the free and dauntless intellectual.[137] It is not surprising that the Legalists strongly criticize "the so-called glorious fighters who separate themselves from the majority, act independently (*du xing*), and want to differ from others."[138]

Partisanship for freedom of judgment and autonomy of action is numerous in Zhou literature. I have quoted many of the respective passages in my discussion of the Confucian attitude towards the state. In Xunzi, we find more exemplary evidence, which is the more important since the author is always ready to break a lance for the institutions:

> There is superior, medium and inferior courage.
>
> To stand upright courageously in the midst of the world, to act out courageously the meaning of the way of the former kings, to follow neither decadent rulers nor join a chaotic people, not to remain poor and in misery where humaneness prevails, but to have neither wealth nor high position where humaneness is missing, to share bitterness and joy with the world when one is recognized by it, but to stand proudly and independently (*du*) between heaven and earth without fear, when the world does not recognize one—this is *superior courage*.
>
> To show propriety and reverence and be moderate in one's intents, to think great of levelling and reliability and not think little of wealth, to courageously promote the capable and remove the good-for-nothings—this is *medium courage*.
>
> To think little of oneself and think wealth important, to calmly let calamity take its course, to seek for comfortable solutions and opportunistically evade difficulties, not to care for right or wrong and true and false, just in order to triumph over others—this is *inferior courage*.[139]

The picture which Western literature has all too often presented of China corresponds to what Xunzi calls "medium courage"—to observe moderation, to adapt oneself, to behave properly—and even to the lowest stage of self-denial. In the highest form of courage, however, we find all those values which the genuine axial age Confucian really strives for—independence, incorruptibility, and unbendingness, but also the selfless dedication to the "world" wherever it deserves it. Elsewhere, Xunzi adds:

> When justice is at stake, not to bow one's head before power and look after one's own benefit, and not to change one's conviction even if the whole empire is offered to one, to uphold justice and not to bend oneself, though taking death seriously—this is the courageousness of the scholar and gentleman.[140]

Xunzi's illustrations of courage and Mengzi's ideal of the "great fellow" belong to the most impressive antique pleadings for the "upright walk." It is deplorable that Bloch, the philosopher of the "upright walk," in his interpretation of China has not left behind the biased perspective of the nineteenth century, namely the perspective of Schelling. For Bloch, Confucian ethics represents a mere "rationalist myth of moderation" in which any real notion of "person" would just be "disturbance."[141]

F. NEGATIVE SANCTIONS: PUNISHMENT, GUILT, SHAME, AND DISGRACE

The question of the autonomy of conscience and action is closely connected with that of the sanctions expected for offenses against norms. The East Asian societies have often been described as "shame-cultures" in contrast to the Occidental "guilt-cultures." This distinction relates to that of heteronomy and autonomy, "tradition-oriented" and "inner-oriented."[142] Shame is understood as an external sanction, executed at the pillory of the collective, while guilt is regarded as a personal inner feeling.[143]

These quite common distinctions are unsuited for a reconstruction of China's classical ethics. Neither is the feeling of guilt lacking in China, nor does she know a merely external concept of shame. Only if we distinguish external from internal shame, the concept can be used for our purpose. This differentiation is well-known since Piers and Singer at the latest,[144] but it has not at all been generally recognized. As a rule, it is characteristically ignored whenever "shame" instead of "guilt" is attributed to Confucianism. For Fingarette, to give an example, shame "looks 'outward,' not 'inward,' " and is oriented to "traditionally ceremonially defined social comportment, rather than to an inner core of one's, the 'self.' " Hall and Ames call shame "ritual-orientated in that it describes a consciousness of how one is perceived by others."[145] Shame here is directly related to offenses against status, role, and etiquette, which set external expectations to the individual. A similar external concept of shame is current in what Metzger has called the Chinese "May Fourth sociology."[146] An external form of shame is also face-saving, which in sociological and cultural anthropological studies has often been described as a characteristic of China.[147]

A merely external sanction of moral offenses is *punishment*. According to Hegel, with whom Trauzettel agrees,[148] in the "oriental world," "moral distinctions and requirements are expressed as Laws, but so that the subjective will is governed by these Laws as governed by an external force."[149] To act immorally, hence, is a violation of external prescriptions of law and requires punishment which should more exactly be understood as chastisement: "The Chinese do not recognize the subjectivity in honor; they are the subjects rather of chastisement than of punishment—as are children among us."[150] Punishment as such would not exclude a consciousness of the "inwardness of wrong." In "chastisement," however, the deterring principle is only "fear," and there is no "reflection upon the nature of the action itself."[151]

Just as for Hegel, for Hansen, too, "Chinina," his hypothetical state built after the alleged model of the classical Chinese political and ethical theories, treats her citizens "like children." Punishment in the strict sense would presuppose an idea of the individual, which is lacking in China. Its place it not taken by chastisement, but by "group sanctions" and "manipulating others into doing the right act."[152]

I have introduced some variants of the thesis that the Confucian, or Chinese, sanctions for moral failure are external and heteronomous. In the final analysis, this thesis would mean that morality proper does not exist in China, for it is the essence of morality to be aspired after for its own sake and not to stand under alien laws.[153] Hansen, therefore, suggests ascribing a "non-moral point of view" to Confucianism.[154] Does Confucianism, or China as a whole, not know the "moral point of view," then? To clear this crucial problem, I will address two questions which result from the above discussion: Can we distinguish internal from external shame in the Chinese texts? And what is the relationship of morality to guilt and punishment?

Confucianism, indeed, brings forward an ethics rather of shame than of guilt. But this does not mean that guilt is of no importance. Contrary to standard developmental assumptions, the first millenium B.C. shows a clear development from guilt to shame. The first elaborate ethical teaching of China, the early Zhou idea of the "mandate of Heaven" (*tian ming*), which is later mutatis mutandis inherited by the Confucian school, already implies a pronounced ethics of guilt. A dynasty loses its mandate if it violates the moral standards of Heaven, thus getting guilty before him. "Heaven entrusts the virtuous . . . and punishes the guilty," says Gaoyao, Shun's minister of justice. The rebel Tang relies on the order of Heaven to punish Jie, the last king of the Xia, who has burdened himself with "much guilt."[155] The words attributed to Gaoyao and Tang express typical topoi of the *tian ming* doctrine.

In the *Lunyu*, too, we read that one can "make oneself guilty before Heaven."[156] Yet, Confucius is cautious in drawing on religion for developing his ethics. When a "gentleman" feels the qualms of conscience, there is no indication that his conscience is acting as the voice of a divine power, for Heaven "does not speak."[157] It is, moreover, characteristic of Confucius to build on shame rather than guilt, and this remains typical of later Confucianism. Mengzi counts among the "three delights" of the gentleman that he "need neither be ashamed before Heaven nor before other men."[158] He again appeals to the religion of Heaven, but makes it consonant with the idea of shame.

Man can not only acquire "guilt" (*zui*) before divine regulations, but also before the laws of the state. What relevance has institutional punishment for morality? Trauzettel, following Hegel, maintains that there is an "identity in principle of law and morals" in the "Confucian worldview."[159] True, we find efforts in ancient China to subject morality to jurisdiction, and they have exerted influence on later Chinese law.[160] But these efforts must not be generalized. There is not only a tension between law and the ethical prescriptions of propriety and filial piety, but also between law and morality in the ancient texts. For several reasons, therefore, it is not justified to attribute to Confucianism a general confounding of legal and moral or ethical norms. The founder of the school already explicitly doubts that penal law is a way to morality:

> If the people be led by means of administration and kept in line by means of punishment, they will try to evade [control] and will become shameless (*wu chi*). But if they be led by virtue and kept in line by propriety, they will have a sense of shame and will turn towards [the ruler].

> Ji Kangzi asked Confucius about politics. He said, "What about killing the immoral and seeking the association of the moral?" Confucius said, "With you in power—what need is there to kill? If you wish the good, then the people, too, will be good. The virtue of the gentleman is the wind, the virtue of the mean man is the grass. The wind over the grass is sure to bend it."[161]

Instead of depending on the sanction of punishment, Confucius recommends building on the exemplary effect of virtue. Severe punishments could even be discarded with when politics were based upon moral standards in contrast with mere administration:

> If the state were governed for a hundred years by good men, cruelty (corporal punishment) could be overcome and killing (death penalty) could be abandoned.[162]

The first argument against legal punishment, then, concerns its ineffectiveness to promote morality. The second argument submits the given juridical practice of jurisdiction itself to moral evaluation. The Confucians have never questioned that there are offenses which deserve legal atonement. Even death penalty is, in spite of the quoted passages from the *Lunyu*, not rejected in principle, although it is furnished with a lot of reservations.[163] The penal jurisdiction of the time, however, becomes subject to severe criticism. Often enough, the same power which imposes punishments is the actual culprit. The wickedness of politics, then, compels the people to break the law. This idea already appears in *Lunyu* 12.18 when Confucius tells Ji Kang, the chancellor of Lu, that if he were "not so covetous" himself, he would not have to complain about robbers in his domain. Arguments of this type are especially typical of Mengzi, who is all the more obliged to explain the existence of crimes by external factors, since he claims the natural goodness of man. He emphasizes that it is above all inhumane government which drives men into illegality. To punish them afterwards for their crimes is equal to "entrapping the people."[164] The truly "highest guilt," therefore, is to be attributed to the mighty, especially to the military strategists, who, already at that time, have inflicted most harm to men.[165] Their guilt is so great that "it cannot even be atoned for by death."[166] Xunzi, again, lets Confucius speak:

> To fail above and to punish below—is this acceptable? Not to educate the people, but to sit in judgment upon them, means killing the innocent. If an army suffers a great defeat, you cannot behead the soldiers for it. And if jurisdiction is not in order, you cannot punish. The reason is that the guilt is not with the people. He who is neglectful in his regulations, but meticulous in punishing, is a vermin. He who recovers taxes at any time although the grain matures only in season is a tyrant. And he who presses for success without educating the people is cruel.[167] Only if these three things are abolished can one proceed to inflict punishments.[168]

The various doubts concerning the effectiveness of punishment and the moral legitimation of penal jurisdiction lead to a third tension between law and morality. As the case may be, it is precisely the moral person who must be prepared for getting into conflict with law. The most striking evidence for this can be found with Xunzi who calls corporal punishment "disgrace by circumstances" as distinguished from "just disgrace." Punishment does not necessarily say anything about the true character of the punished. A "gentleman" can be caught in the maze of jurisdiction and yet deserve "just glory."[169] The fact that law, by the same token, can be broken in the name of Confucian morality is indirectly confirmed by the Legalist polemic according to which "kindness (*ci*) and humaneness (*ren*) are the mothers of the transgression of law."[170] In the Legalist state, law and morality are irreconcilable enemies. The split between the Legalist and the Confucian schools is the most conspicuous indication of the falling apart of the two spheres of law and morality in Zhou thought and society.

In early Confucianism, more important than guilt sanctions, be it the punishment by Heaven or legal institutions, be it an inner feeling of guilt, is the sanction of *shame*. When we examine the usage of the respective terms, we find that the internal reading of shame is definitely the prevailing one. It is true that the graph of the most common term for "shame," *chi*, indicates the heteronomous descent of the concept of shame. It contains the two parts "heart" and "ear," the ear perhaps standing for the blushing of the one whose deed has come—a further connotation—to the others' ears. Similarly, the expression to "wash off" shame or disgrace (*xi chi, xue chi*),[171] which is still alive in contemporary Chinese (*xue chi*), shows the traces of moral realism which does not distinguish between physis and psyche. Shame, here, is not an object of inner work, but of outer purification.[172]

In the teaching of the Zhou Confucians, however, shame is an inner-orientated process. Nevertheless, we still have to differentiate between two possible forms of internal shame. It can be aroused by the internalized judgment of the empirical community, or be felt before oneself or an idealized audience. Hence, next to external shame, we have a second, internalized form which no longer takes its orientation from the actual but from the imagined judgment of others, and a third, autonomous form related to self-chosen ideals instead of alien expectations. An example of the internalized and genetically earlier form is found in the *Yue ming*, where it is said about Tang's chancellor Yi Yin that he would "be ashamed as if he were flogged in the market place" in case he would not succeed to make Tang a ruler like Yao and Shun.[173] Beigong You, too, as we have read above, orientates himself by an imagined sanction of this kind. Shame as an internalization of public norms furthermore appears in the *Guanzi*, where it counts, together with propriety, justice, and honesty, among the "four threads" essential for the continuance of the state. He who has shame will not follow the "crooked," so that he will not "go beyond measure," and there will emerge "no heresy."[174]

The third form of shame is implied in *Lunyu* 4.9:

A scholar sets his heart on the *Dao*. But he who is ashamed of poor food and poor clothes does not deserve to speak with him.

Poor clothes can constitute a violation of etiquette, and yet, together with poor food, they are a symbol for the moral person not acknowledged by the world. Not to be ashamed for such poverty does not mean to feel oneself in accord with public judgment, but to remain untouched by it and only feel committed to the *Dao*. This idea becomes clearer when Mengzi says that a "gentleman will be ashamed if his reputation transcends his true [merits]."[175] Reputation reflects public opinion. Yet, it says little about the true qualities of a man. Shame, therefore, should not internalize public opinion, but counterbalance it. In *Xunzi* 6, too, it has exactly this function:

The gentleman can do something that is honorable, but he cannot cause others to honor him for certain. He can do something that deserves trust, but he cannot cause others to trust him for certain. He can do something that is useful, but he cannot cause others to use (employ) him for certain.

Therefore, a gentleman is ashamed of not cultivating himself, but not of being dragged through the mud. He is ashamed of not being trustworthy, but not of not being trusted. He is ashamed of lacking in ability, but not of not being employed. Therefore, he can neither be deluded by praise nor does he fear slander. He follows the *Dao*, uprightly corrects himself (*zheng ji*), and cannot be led astray by material things. Such a man is called a true gentleman.[176]

As the judgment of the community or of the authorities is not reliable, the Confucian "gentleman" chooses the way of "self-correction" (*zheng ji*). His shame does not relate to the reproach of others either, but to something not realized in the empirical world—a moral view of man, or an ideal of character, which he finds recommended in the teaching of his school and tries to give shape to in himself.

Not to meet this ideal violates self-respect,[177] the basis of all moral action. Shame, then, is a reaction on this violation of self-respect.[178] He who need not feel it within himself will not need to feel it before others either, whatever his fate may be. Xun Yue (149–209) has brought the different stages of shame into the following ranked order:

Somebody asked, "If the cultivation of conduct is not done for the sake of others, then shame before the divine intelligence is the highest?" Xun Yue answered, "Not yet. The fundament is to have *shame before oneself*,[179] and shame before the divine intelligence is second best. But to feel shame before others is external. He who merely takes his orientation from external things will accumulate evil inside. Hence the gentleman cares for the shame before himself (*zi chi*)."[180]

With few exceptions,[181] the feeling of shame is positively evaluated in Confucian texts as well as Chinese axial age literature in general. For Mengzi, shame belongs to the distinctive characteristics of man himself. It is one of the four innate "starting points" of morality. The feeling of "shame and disgust" is the prefiguration of justice, which Mengzi understands as refraining from certain actions.

In comparison with shame, *disgrace* (*ru*) is a primarily external sanction imposed by the public. The Confucian attitude towards disgrace is ambiguous, as can be expected from a teaching which always refers to the community of men, but at the same time knows about their susceptibility to failure and misjudgment. First of all, disgrace should be avoided by acting morally. Mengzi assures us that "he who is humane will gain glory, and he who is inhumane will gain disgrace."[182] Similarly, Xunzi, in his essay on *Glory and Disgrace* (*Rong ru*), promises glory for justice and disgrace for selfishness.[183] Nevertheless, it is not ruled out to get into disgrace without deserving it, just as one can enjoy undue glory. Therefore, it is necessary to distinguish between different forms of disgrace. Xunzi develops this point in his polemic against Song Xing.

Song Xing is one of the famous wandering philosophers of the axial age.[184] Famous and much discussed is his untiring plea for tolerance and pacifism. Forke has assigned to him a "slave morality" devoid of "manliness, pride, and honor"[185]— a formulation which reveals a lot about Forke, but little about Song Xing. Song Xing wants to show the dubiousness of such atavistic measures, but not without the sovereign pride of an axial age freethinker. Song Xing, says the *Zhuangzi*, delighted in the way of the ancient followers of the *Dao* who "did not feel bound by custom," and it left him cold "whether the whole world praised or condemned him." For he "was certain about the difference between the internal and the external, and was versed in the judgment about the limits of glory and disgrace."[186] This distinction of "internal" (*nei*) and "external" (*wai*) reflects the general postconventional conviction of the insufficiency of the conventional which characterizes the epoch. Despite his polemic against Song Xing's maxim "to suffer insult is no disgrace,"[187] this conviction is also shared by Xunzi. It is just for this reason that Xunzi, contradicting Song Xing, distinguishes two kinds of glory and disgrace:

> There is *just glory* and *just disgrace*, and there is *glory by circumstances* and *disgrace by circumstances.*
> A cultivated motivation, many virtuous acts, brilliant knowledge and thoughts—this is glory coming from *within*. This is called *just glory.*
> High rank, rich tributes and emoluments, superiority over others in outer appearance and position . . . —this is glory coming from *without*. This is called *glory by circumstances.*
> To be licentious and filthy, to transgress one's duty and bring into confusion the rules of order, to be arrogant, cruel, and greedy— in these cases disgrace comes from *within*. This is called *just disgrace.*
> To be scolded and insulted, be pulled by the hair and beaten, be punished by flogging or smashing the kneecap, be beheaded and mutilated, be exposed as a corpse, be quartered and have the tongue cut off (?)—in these cases disgrace comes from *without*. This is called *disgrace by circumstances.*
> These are the two extremes of glory and disgrace. As a gentleman, one can get into disgrace by circumstances, but not into just disgrace. As a mean man, one can enjoy glory by circumstances, but not just glory. Disgrace by circumstances does not hinder from getting an [ideal ruler like] Yao, and glory by circumstances does not hinder from getting a [tyrant like] Jie. Only the gentleman can have both just glory and glory by circumstances, and only the mean man can have both just disgrace and disgrace by circumstances. This is the difference between glory and disgrace.[188]

This passage shows undoubtedly that external and internal disgrace are explicitly distinguished already in Zhou Confucianism. Xunzi uses yet another differentiation which reminds one of Mengzi's separation of the "Heavenly and human ranks":[189] the qualitative differentiation of "within" (*nei*) and "without" (*wai*), belonging to the spheres of morality and political power respectively. Institutional punishment, as such, is ethically irrelevant, and it even can affect the truly honorable. This viewpoint reflects the fundamental problematic of the axial age—the falling apart of the empirically current and the morally valid. It can also be found in Daoism. The ostentatious liking of the *Zhuangzi* for the mutilated and humiliated victims of penal justice, whom it presents as having a privileged access to truth,[190] is an indication of the postconventional spirit not only of Daoism, but of ancient philosophy in general. Xunzi's evaluation of corporal punishment as mere "disgrace by circumstances," moreover, is a consequence of an inner-Confucian development which starts with the doubts in the *Lunyu* concerning the reliance on legal devices.

Different from what the stereotype of shame- and guilt-cultures tells us, the genuine Confucian concept of shame and disgrace, then, is by no means an expression of moral heteronomy. It is based on a clear distinction of, to use Kohlberg's terms, "self respect" and "self disrespect" on the one hand, and "community respect" and "community disrespect" on the other, a distinction which is constitutive for any postconventional ethics.[191] As the corrollary of sovereign self-respect, instead of internalized heterosuggestion, the feeling of shame is no less efficient for a postconventional morality than the inner experience of guilt. Unlike guilt, it even "leads not to a morality of austere command but to an ethic of mutual respect and self-esteem."[192]

G. THE REWARD OF VIRTUE: FAME AND REPUTATION VERSUS INNER HAPPINESS

The negative sanctions discussed above have their positive counterparts. Again we have to distinguish internal and external forms, as has already become plain from Xunzi's differentiation of "just glory" and "glory by circumstances."

To enjoy glory (*rong*), praise (*yu*), reputation (*wen*), a good name (*ming*), etc., is a very popular ambition in China like elsewhere in antiquity.[193] The philosophical literature, too, with the exception of Daoism, gives in general a positive evaluation of these concepts. Especially in political passages, the hint to glory and disgrace is seldom lacking, surely because one wants to tickle the vanity of the powerful. The *Mozi* emphasizes that "the name follows upon accomplishments" and "name and praise cannot be obtained by false pretenses."[194] And the *Guanzi* assures:

> If one is really trustworthy and sincere in the heart, one's name and praise will be fine. If one is careful and respectful in the cultivation of one's conduct, honor and excellence will follow immediately. But if one is not honest in the heart, one will enjoy a bad name and a bad reputation. If one is lazy and lax in the cultivation of one's conduct, one will get into insult and disgrace.[195]

I have quoted similar statements from Confucian sources already. It is not astonishing to find them also in Aristotle's ethical life philosophy. For Aristotle, "honor is the prize of virtue, and it is to the good that it is rendered."[196] Presumably, the aspiration after a well-known and honored name is acknowledged since it is an incentive to surpass oneself. The good name obtained by a virtuous life has, furthermore, a special importance for posthumous fame. "A gentleman," we read in the *Lunyu*, "would deplore his name not being praised in the world after he has left it"[197]—a "very human weakness,"[198] which is quite understandable, since there is no otherworldly justice. According to Shusun Bao, a noble of Lu who counts among the predecessors of Confucianism, "not to decay after death" consists in leaving behind "virtuous deeds," "merits," and "words."[199] Fame is important, then, as the "antique form of immortality."[200] Yet, neither posthumous fame nor fame and honor as such are unconditionally aspired after by the Confucians. Mengzi makes the following distinction:

> To desire honor (*gui*, also high standing, position) is an aspiration
> which all men have in common. But every man has an honor within
> himself which he only does not think of. What men [in general]
> esteem as honor (*gui*) is not the good honor (*liang gui*). Those whom
> [a potentate like] Zhao Meng can honor, Zhao Meng can also de-
> grade. When it is said in the *Songs*, "Drunk we are with wine al-
> ready, sated we are with virtue already,"[201] this means that for him
> who is satiated with humaneness and justice, the taste of the fat meat
> and the fine millet of others is undesirable. A good reputation and
> far-reaching praise are [already] with him, and therefore the elegant
> embroideries of others are undesirable for him.[202]

Mengzi contrasts "good honor" against high standing based on social rank, which comes and goes together with the favor of the powerful. "Good honor" results from goodness alone and is already present in man's moral nature without any further need for acknowledgment by others.

The Confucians have not contented themselves with this distinction of honor and career. It is not only that the social and political ranks, which Mengzi sharply separates from the "Heavenly" ranks of morality, are external to true honor. But reputation and praise, too, which Mengzi still promises to the moral person in the last quotation, cannot be expected for sure. As the *Lunyu* in particular repeatedly emphasizes, the "gentleman" must not think that his virtuous conduct will find recognition. He must rather be prepared to be ignored and must, therefore, make himself independent of the judgment and applause of others. However, this presupposes a nearly superhuman effort. According to *Zhongyong* 11, "only a *shengren* is capable of retiring from the world and remaining unknown without regretting it."

The good name and the good inner attitude or conduct, then, are not necessarily connected with each other. It is possible to gain reputation even as a wicked person, and that name (*ming*) and reality (*shi*) often fall apart is a standard theme in Zhou literature. The name which one makes for oneself, thus, not only loses relevance, but it can be positively dubious. Corresponding doubts concerning the value of fame and reputation are well-known from Daoist literature.[203] Mangoude ("he who is contended with what he has accidentally got"), a figure from the *Zhuangzi*, points out that only success, but not the real qualities of a man determines to whom the world pays homage.[204] Fame is enjoyed, then, by the coincidental victors and successful assassins. A much earlier document for this skepticism is the *Lunyu.* It points out that the bearer of a good name can, in his heart, be a crook. He can pretend humaneness and yet secretly act contrary to it.[205] Mengzi has, therefore, warned not to be taken in by great gestures. The real value of a man shows itself in minute and inconspicuous things, like in the matter of "a dish of rice or a platter of soup."[206] The audience, moreover, before which one enjoys reputation, might dispose of criteria for judgment which are, on their part, problematical. After all, what should be aspired after is not applause as such, but the applause of the good.[207]

Name and fame, then, and the related distinctions up to success cannot count as positive sanctions morally valid without closer inspection, just as shame could not be regarded as a negative sanction of this quality. Because any promise of a future justice after death is lacking, a single unsuspected reward remains which is the counterpart of the inner feeling of shame and which the moral person can only win from himself and not from others: the inner happiness (*le*) that despite all adversities one has behaved like a human being. This happiness is not an indication of cheap optimism. It is exactly to help the gentleman not to lose heart in difficulties and renunciation. I quote again Confucius' praise of Yan Yuan:

How able Hui is! A bowlful of rice, a calabash of water, a living in a mean alley—no other would endure this distress. But Hui does not lose his happiness. How able he is![208]

Like Kant's "cheerfulness which accompanies virtue,"[209] the happiness of the Confucian is a means to cope with obstacles and take upon oneself the moral duty with calmness. In his inner happiness, the moral person finds tranquility and self-confirmation imperturbable from without. And there is no greater happiness, Mengzi says, than to "find, on self-reflection, that one is sincere."[210]

I have reconstructed a portrait of the moral person in early Confucianism which contradicts the theses of the Weberians and the pragmatic contextualists. The essentials of this portrait can be summarized as follows:

The tension between the Confucian ideals and the empirical world presupposes a strong person as their agent. To devote oneself to morality demands an existential choice. Afterwards, difficult decisions must still be taken to find the right way in the intricacy of everyday life. Not to get disheartened and adapt oneself opportunistically requires constant work on one's "self." For morality means overcoming oneself or—in Mengzi—at least the active defense of one's natural good dispositions against their disruption by comfort and external circumstances. In order to achieve this, one must develop self-respect which is the presupposition also for respecting others. The self, moreover, must be strengthened so that it can remain independent of the opinions of the world, bear up against misjudgment or hostility, and act autonomously. Finally, one has to submit one's motives and reasons for action to a constant control in terms of an examination of conscience. That this conscience is not simply an internalization of external prescriptions is evident from the sanctions which early Confucianism knows for conduct. External sanctions like punishment and disgrace and their positive counterparts like name and fame, in the final analysis, have no decisive moral relevance. Instead of relying on them, the Confucian builds upon an inner feeling of shame and the self-reward of inner happiness. For the genuine Confucian, there is no abode in the world without the seclusion in his self.

12

The Problem of Responsibility

Humaneness in the reading of the nonstrategic Golden Rule, an abstract concept of man not restricted in terms of group morality, and a moral individual free from heteronomy and guided by his self-respect—is the achievement of this *triad of principle, universalism, and autonomy,* which characterizes Kohlberg's Stage 6, equivalent to accomplishing the tasks of a postconventional ethics? The answer is no. The concrete life world itself calls the moral actor back from the realm of abstract ideals and forces him to face its sobering imperfection. A problem has to be confronted which Apel has highlighted as that of the highest stage of a developmental logic of morals: the *"situation-centered application of postconventional morality."*[1] This problem is especially conspicuous in antiquity, where the educated elite stands opposite to the great majority deeply rooted in traditions and conventions.

A pragmatic alternative to a position entailing this difficulty seems to be offered by an ethics of common sense which relies on a judicious, experienced capacity of judgment.[2] Confucianism is usually discussed on this level rather than on that of a principled morality burdened with the complicated task of the application of abstract standards. To substantiate this view, three passages from the *Lunyu* have frequently been quoted. In *Lunyu* 18.8, Confucius rejects strict moralism as well as a quick readiness for adaptation, stating that for him there is "nothing that may be done or may not be done [in each case]." *Lunyu* 9.4 notes that he avoided "strictness" (*bi*) and "inflexibility" (*gu*). *Lunyu* 4.10, finally, says that a gentleman "does not pursue or reject anything, but is committed to the just (*yi*)." According to Cua, Hall, Ames, and Perenboom, these statements advocate the situational creativity of judgment as against the introduction of objective measures into decision-finding.[3] They thus help to avoid a "tyranny of principles."[4] *Yi,* the just, is to be understood, then, in terms of creative spontaneous adjustment to the situation, or even of "aesthetic" choice.[5]

In this type of argument, the ethics of principles seems to be mistaken for the so-called ethics of the moral mental attitude (*Gesinnungsethik*)[6] which places the purity of moral standards above everything and rejects any curtailments even in extreme exigent circumstances. It is furthermore overlooked that such an ethics of the moral mental attitude is by no means alien to Confucianism. It can even be traced back to the *Lunyu*, though it is not typical of it.[7] A quite inflexible position concerning basic moral norms, however, can be found in the *Mengzi*. For Mengzi, normative yardsticks remain incontestable regardless of whether or not the world understands and accepts them:

> A great carpenter does not alter or do away with the plumb-line for the sake of a stupid craftsman, and Yi (a famous archer) does not alter the tension of his bow for the sake of a stupid archer.[8]

In case of doubt whether an action should be performed, one should, according to Mengzi, orient one's decision to the protection of the meaning of the corresponding norm, which relates to its demarcation from other values (in the given case, from polite readiness to accept favors, generosity, and martyrdom):

> When it is proper both to take and not to take, taking would harm honesty. When it is proper both to give and not to give, giving would harm kindness. When it is proper both to die and not to die, dying would harm courage.[9]

Up to this point, Mengzi's outlook still sounds compatible with an ethics of responsibility. But he takes a further step: even for the presumed sake of the good cause, no deviation from the basic standards is allowed, since this might distort the final aim. Chunyu Kun, one of the wandering philosophers of the time, states that in order to rescue the "drowning" world a quick compromise is in place, just as one grasps the drowning sister-in-law by the hands to pull her out of the water, violating the prescriptions of propriety. Mengzi answers:

> When the world is drowning, one rescues it with the *Dao*. When the sister-in-law is drowning, one rescues her with the hand. Do you want to rescue the world with the hand?[10]

In order to understand Mengzi's answer, we have to consider that Chunyu Kun, unlike Mengzi himself,[11] views saving life not as a matter of principle, but of compromise. It is against this background that Mengzi, in his rhetorical question, rejects treating the two cases as analogous. To rescue the world is a long-term task which need not be confronted in the first place if one thinks that principle measures can be suspended. Any tactical relenting would betray the project as a whole and is even less justified for the sake of the self-protection of the protagonist. A "determined scholar" has to take into account anyway that he "might end in a ditch."[12] The pragmatic maxim to "bend a foot for straightening a yard" meets with a strict rebuff:

To bend a foot for straightening a yard is said for the sake of utility.
But if it is for utility, may we not also bend a yard for straightening a
foot?[13]

To preserve the purity of the "good," Mengzi is ready to dismiss every kind
of practical realism from politics. Hearing that his disciple Yuezhengzi shall become chancellor of Lu, he cannot sleep because of joy. Yuezhengzi, however,
lacks everything one would expect from a responsible and considerate *Realpolitiker*:

Gongsun Chou asked, "Is Yuezheng forceful?" Mengzi: "No." — "Is
he deliberate?" — "No." — "Is he experienced?" — "No." — "Why
then, were you so glad that you could not sleep?" — "He as a man
loves the good." — "Is loving the good sufficient?" — "Loving the
good is more than enough for the whole empire, not to speak of Lu!"[14]

Gesinnungsethik, however, is only one of the ways for a postconventional
thinking which, discouraged by the conditio humana, does not want to relapse
into conventional morality or enter into too far-reaching compromise. Another
alternative, which is typically chosen by the Daoists, is to leave society. It is
intimately connected with the endeavor to stay "clean" at any cost.[15] Although this
alternative is now and then coquetted with by the Confucians, the *Lunyu* polemizes
against the search for "purity" and "cleanness" (*qing, jie*). In *Lunyu* 18.7, Zilu calls
to account the son of a hermit who evades official service:[16]

Not to take office is not just! . . . How is it that your father sets aside
the just duty between ruler and subject? In order to stay clean (*jie*)
himself, he brings into confusion the great social relations. When the
gentleman takes office, it is to fulfill his duty. That the *Dao* is not put
into practice, he knows all along.

Zilu advocates an ethics of responsibility. Even if we know that the world
does not stick to the measure of the *Dao*, we should not cold-shoulder it just in
order to keep our own hands clean. Although the Confucians are prepared to
withdraw from society, this is not their primary option. They stay anxious to avoid
the breach. *"To know that it is impossible, and yet do it"*—this became the serious
motto (ironically brought forward by a proto-Daoist in *Lunyu* 14.38), of all those
who have not been contented with upholding a candid motivation, and yet have
seen through the badness of the world to which they have offered their services.

Confucianism, then, in spite of some tendencies which remind one of
Gesinnungsethik, typically follows the program of a postconventional ethics of
responsibility. Its essential motif is the "return to *li*" in *Lunyu* 12.1, if we understand *li* as the ethical life of the community. It contrasts with the Daoist motto of
"forgetting return," as found in the *Chuci*.[17] Return presupposes turning away
from the polity and its unsettled standards, and the individual's turning the attention inside his self where he finds a new basis for a moral existence. In the course

of *turning away, turning inwards,* and *returning,*[18] the seeming conventionalism of the early Confucians becomes a second order conventionalism. The point is to keep faith to the traditional ethos and yet know its insufficiencies, to perform the conventional duty and yet not hand oneself over to it, to adapt oneself and yet maintain one's moral rectitude, in order to attain a *unity of integration and integrity.* This gives Confucian ethics a characteristic *double structure* embedding all conventionally required action in postconventional awareness.

How can this double goal be achieved? And where is the borderline beyond which the compromise at the expense of morality begins? The Confucians are normally ready to make far-reaching concessions to the "ethical life," and to keep the conflict between *Sittlichkeit* and *Moralität* as low as possible. This harmonizing tendency explains that within their teaching a novel moral philosophy, which even goes as far as assuming a symmetry of human relations, and a political conservatism, which to a large extent leaves the hierarchies of societies untouched, can stand side by side.

The point of breach, then, is quite remote, and yet, it is there. It is impossible, however, to define it beforehand. There is no substitution for the free decision of the individual when to say "no." It is a common misunderstanding that a principled ethic mechanically deduces actions from abstract norms, ignoring the concreteness of the situation and the individuals involved. Not to ignore the concreteness of the case can itself be understood as an ethical principle. It does not make sense, therefore, to play off situation relatedness and commitment to abstract norms against each other. Both are indispensable, because we must not only prevent a "tyranny of principles," but also protect our actions against arbitrariness or heterosuggestion. For how can it be ensured that *yi,* as situational judgment, finds a morally justifiable decision at all if it does not take general measures into consideration?

To take into account the specificity of situations neither justifies nor necessitates abandoning principles. A principled ethic that knows about responsibility will not only acknowledge that flexibility is needed in the concrete application of its norms, but will even admit the possibility of dramatical circumstances in which certain principles may not be applicable at all. To give an example: in a society like the one described by Mengzi which does not provide its people with a "constant livelihood," one may virtually be forced into crime for helping one's aged parents or children to survive. To act, in a straightforward manner, in accordance with abstract principles, and not in favor of group interests, in such a situation would even be morally wrong, since it would endanger the lives of the individuals entrusted to one. Today, the situation deplored by Mengzi is found in wide parts of the world. Under such conditions, moral principles—for example the Golden Rule, referring to a general "other"—can not only not be put into practice directly (as is often imputed to principled ethics by its critics), but it even becomes difficult, in situational decisions, to account for them in the first place. The scope for their practical application is nearly reduced to nothing.

To nonetheless hold fast to them now can only mean demanding to first of all create the conditions under which they can be applied without making the actor guilty against his and her concrete charges. Principles now become a normative orientation point of a *regulative* nature, in order to uphold the perspective for a better world.[19] To do away with them, however, would be equivalent to endorsing the state of things.

Even under dramatic circumstances when situational decisions are far remote from abstract standards, then, a principled framework cannot be abandoned. We can generalize that all moral practice has a concrete as well as an abstract component in the sense outlined above. The suppleness which the *Lunyu* recommends in the passages mentioned at the beginning of this chapter does not necessarily contradict the orientation to basic moral norms either. Quite obviously, the Confucians endeavor to do justice to both sides of a responsible decision simultaneously. Classical literature is full of evidence for this. The complementarity of *ren* and *li* in the *Lunyu*, the effort of the "gentleman" to be "solidary" and "sociable," but not "cliquish," the claim of the *Ru xing* to be "strong and resolute, yet companionable," the demand of the *Zidao* to "follow the *Dao* and not the ruler, follow justice and not the father," but to "translate one's insight into action with courtesy, respect, loyalty, trustworthiness, uprightness, and guilelessness"—all of this shows what the true ideal of classical Confucianism is: the *unity of a moral mental attitude and of ethical responsibility*. To possess status-transcending moral judgment competence and motivation, yet to be sovereign and adaptable enough to avoid a pure *Gesinnungsethik*, and do justice to the responsibility for family and state, for one's living context and the cultural tradition, this is the goal of genuine Confucianism. To achieve this goal, Xunzi has recommended a sympathetic understanding which avoids the provocative strictness of Mengzi:

> The gentleman is tolerant, but not easy to deal with. He is a person of integrity, but is not hurtful. He is ready for discussion, but does not quarrel. He is critical, but not provocative. He is independent, but not aiming at victory. He is hard and strong, but not violent. He is soft and yielding, but does not swim with the tide. . . . He bends and straightens as the time (*shi*) demands. When soft and yielding like reed, this is not because of fear. When hard and strong, vigorous and resolute, and thoroughly straight (unyielding), this is not because of arrogance or recklessness. He simply changes and reacts according to what is proper (*yi*) and knows when it is appropriate to bend or to straighten.
>
> An Ode says, "When moving to the left, to the left, the gentleman does what is proper. When moving to the right, to the right, the gentleman has a grasp of it." This means that the gentleman knows to bend or straighten according to what is proper (*yi*) and to change in response.[20]

With his art of "bending" and "straightening," the proper employment of yieldingness and toughness connected with the recognition of the right moment (*shi*), Xunzi provides the "gentleman" with greater freedom of action than Mengzi. In doing so, he does not abandon the principles of the Confucian school. The title of the quoted writing *Bu gou*, after all, can be translated with "not to be opportunistic." The recommended flexible "responding" does not repeal general measures, but presupposes them:[21]

> What has not been changed under a hundred kings can be called the running thread (the "pervading," *guan*)[22] of the *Dao*. To the ups and downs [of events], respond with this running thread. If one manages to use the running thread, there will be no disorder. If one does not know how to use the running thread, one will not know how to respond to change either.[23]

The *Kongzi jiayu*, too, discusses the intricate dilemma of the protagonist of Confucian ethics. In order not only to abide by the *Dao*, but also to take into account the empirical possibilities of the life world and to prevent heroic failure, a well-considered strategy is recommended:

> Bochang Qian asked Confucius, ". . . If one uprightly practices the correct *Dao*, one will not be accepted by the world. But to hide the *Dao* and act artfully,[24] this cannot be endured. If one neither wants to get into misery oneself nor wishes to hide the *Dao*, is there a way for that?"[25]
>
> Confucius said, "... I have heard: When the gentleman talks about the *Dao*, it will not reach the listener if the listener is not perspicacious.[26] If, then, what the gentleman says is so extraordinary and great that it exceeds any check, the *Dao* will not be given credence to. Furthermore I have heard: When the gentleman talks about practical projects, these will not be accomplished if he does not keep within measures. If in his policy he wants to scrutinize everything [as to its exact accordance with the *Dao*], then the people will not [feel] protected. Furthermore I have heard: When the gentleman talks about his goals, [he takes into consideration that] he who tries to break something with severity will not finally succeed. But he who makes things easy, too, will once and again suffer harm. He who is haughty will not be liked, and he who looks for benefit will solely earn distress. And furthermore I have heard: A gentleman who wants to be beneficial to the world is not the first when tasks are easy and not the last when tasks are difficult. He sets a model, but does not obtrude it upon others. He displays the *Dao*, but does not get angry. These four things are what I have heard."[27]

In this document of the disintegration of the ancient world, the knowing "gentleman" stands opposite to his senseless contemporaries. In order to come out to meet them, and yet not to stake the ideal *Dao*, he needs a capacity of judgment which helps him to steer between the two poles of accommodation and harshness, and a well-considered rhetoric in the service of the good cause which takes into account the limited receptiveness of those he addresses. Just as in Xunzi's art of bending and straightening, the aim is to achieve an *uncorrupted flexibility*. In the *Yijing*, this attitude is represented by the hexagram *sun*, the "gentle" or "soft": "With *sun*, one carries out weighing (*quan*)."[28]

Despite all the optimism which can still be detected in the quoted passages from the *Xunzi* and the *Kongzi jiayu*, early Confucianism is marked by the possibility of failure and isolation in a hostile surrounding. Too many things which we heard about its protagonists—their toying with the idea of leaving society, their conquering their self, their nearly coquettish sentiment of being misjudged, their groaning under the burden of duty—reveal Xunzi's elegant art of bending and straightening as a hardly achievable ideal. In an immoral world, a moral actor may even have to confront much greater obstacles than those discussed among the ancient Confucians. Nevertheless, they suffer enough from the discrepancy between their goals and the compulsions of reality. The deepest of the aporias they have to cope with is perhaps that "humaneness" transcends the very limits which in the given world of inequality and group interests are strictly drawn everywhere. The famous utopia of the *Liyun*, from here on, reads like a craving for a world in which the gap between the general and the particular, the moral mental attitude and the ethical responsibility is finally sealed:

> When the great *Dao* prevailed, the world belonged to the general public. They chose the worthy and capable, were trustworthy in what they said, and cultivated harmony. Therefore, people did not love only their own parents and did not treat only their own children as children. Thus the aged could live out their lives, the grown ups all had their function, the young could be reared, and the widowed, the lonely, the orphans, the crippled, and the sick all found their care. Men had their roles, and women their homes. They hated casting away goods, but not necessarily to keep them for themselves. They hated leaving their strength unemployed, but not necessarily to employ it for themselves. Therefore, schemings had no outlet, and theft, rebellion, and robbery did not arise, so that the outer doors were left unlocked. This is called the Great Community (*da tong*).[29]

The "Great Community" of the *Liyun* would unburden the individual of the restriction to his *morally required* special care for his specific living context, which always throws him back upon the representation of particular interests. The world of his principles would have become his life world itself. Even the deserter of Lu, who is, according to Han Fei, praised by Confucius for his attitude, would defend such a world. For it would nullify his argument that, unless he deserts, his old father would have "nobody who cares for him."[30] Instead of the Great Community, however, the age of "Little Peace" prevails, where "the world belongs to the clans, one loves only one's own parents, and treats only one's own children as children."[31] Thus the Confucian must come to terms with the disparity of the two kingdoms which Mengzi separates as "Heavenly" and "human," and must try to reconcile them as far as possible in his responsible decisions. He knows a final goal, but he is no less aware of the fact that the "purity" of his basic norms belongs to another realm rather than the "murky" scenery of the given world. As the *Lüshi chunqiu*, in one of its ingenious parables, lets Confucius speak:

> The dragon lives from purity (pure water) and roams in purity. The *chi* (a hornless dragon) lives from purity, but roams in the murky. The fish lives from the murky and roams in the murky. Now I, Qiu, do not reach the dragon above, and yet am not like the fish below. I suppose, I am a *chi!* *How could someone who wants to deserve well [of the world] hit the measuring line! He who saves a drowning man will get wet himself.* And he who pursues a flying man must run.[32]

13

Groundings of Morals

C onfucianism does not promise any reward to the moral actor except for safeguarding his self-respect, staying free from shame, and inner happiness. The question as to why we should be moral leads us to the problem of grounding morality. To ground morality is not only important for motivating moral action, however. It is indispensable for an ethics which claims superiority over politics, wants to rise above the merely current, and does not leave the final say to the "ontology of events."

Tradition alone can no longer fulfill this task. Despite the self-conception of Confucianism as the transmitter of the old culture, as expressed in Confucius' claim to "transmit, but not to innovate,"[1] the final fundament of its ethics does not simply lie in tradition. The Golden Rule of the *Lunyu* with its timeless formalism and its reference to general human needs and aspirations no longer pertains to traditional thinking. It paves the way for the new nontraditional and nontimebound paradigm of nature and spontaneity represented by Mengzi. Although Mengzi exalts the ancient sages, they excel by following the innate standards of morality rather than by setting up standards to be followed themselves.[2] Xunzi, last but not least, reconstructs tradition as embodying the rational deliberations of cultural heroes. These deliberations can *hic et nunc* be re-appropriated by any rational being who is ready to learn. Abstract ratiocination replaces any immediate orientation to historical standards. The *Dao*, according to Xunzi, knows "neither past nor present," both of which can "obscure" the mind.[3] Xunzi even goes one step further: he gives epistemological priority to "seeing" over "hearing," and to the "near" over the "distant," and demands that "he who is good at talking about antiquity must have a tally from the present."[4] This lays the theoretical foundation for his pupil Han Fei's elevation of the present over the past.

The Confucians, then, partake in the various doubts cast upon tradition in the Chinese axial age. The corresponding arguments concern aspects like the futility of tradition in the change of time, its inconsistency necessitating criteria for choosing from different messages from the past, the difficulty of transmitting the truth in the first place, the dependence of tradition on innovation, the moral dubiousness of some traditional ways of life, etc.[5] Although the more radical positions can be found among the Mohists and, above all, the Legalists, the Confucians are influenced by these reservations.

For a nontraditional foundation of ethics, alternative models have been developed within the Confucian school. The first elaborate and systematic attempt in this direction, however, is made by Mo Di. For Confucius, the problem does not pose itself as urgently as for his successors. Yet, the *Lunyu* is, at least, negatively important for later development, in that it refrains from a religious and a cosmological grounding of morality.

A. THE ROLE OF RELIGION

In 525 b.c. astrologers predict a fire catastrophe. Zichan, the chancellor of Zheng, refuses to offer a sacrifice to prevent the fire. After the prediction has proven true, the astrologer Pi Zao announces a second fire if no sacrifice is made. But Zichan remains steadfast. This is his argument against Pi Zao, who claims to interpret the signs of Heaven:

> The way of Heaven is distant, but the way of man is near and is nothing which reaches Heaven. How could we know Heaven, then?[6]

Zichan's enlightened words become programmatical for Confucius and Xunzi. Both direct their attention to the "*Dao* of man" (*ren dao*) rather than to the "*Dao* of Heaven" (*tian dao*). As Xunzi explicitly states:

> The *Dao* [I talk about] is not the *Dao* of heaven and not the *Dao* of earth. It is that by which men are guided (*dao*), it is the way (*dao*) that the gentleman takes.[7]

What is the *Dao*? The *Dao* of the ruler.[8]

The course which Xunzi sets for ethics is, in its more cryptical language, already marked out by the *Lunyu*:

> Man can make the *Dao* great. It is not that the *Dao* can make man great.[9]

For Confucius, the *Dao* is not an apriorical fixed point of orientation in a religious or metaphysical realm. Yet, the norm it sets does not coincide with the empirically given either.[10] Its transcendence lies within the human world. Human endeavor for the "great" decides what the *Dao*, the embodiment of everything the world is in need of, will be. Man is what he makes himself—an idea which nicely fits in with the Confucian effort for self-cultivation. Man must develop his morality on his own initiative. It is not prefigured by any otherwordly or ontological norm.

This does not mean that religion is insignificant for Confucius. He even feels a divine vocation in himself.[11] Yet, although he should not be regarded as an atheist[12] or agnostic, it is conspicuous that he hardly ever appeals to religion when developing his moral teaching. Thus his sentence "respect ghosts and gods, but keep a distance,"[13] not only pertains to practice, but also to theory. Heaven remains important as a kind of ultimate backing of ethics, but it no longer comes to the fore like in pre-Confucian literature.

Instead of giving ethics an explicit foundation, the *Lunyu* relies on the evidence and the appealing power of the "Master's" sayings. As far as the religious aspect is concerned, this negative account is important, for it refutes Weber. In general, Confucian ethics obviously gains its "postconventional" critical attitude and its distance from the given world without an appeal, or at least a strong one, to a transcendent god. This is in accordance with the conviction of the European Enlightenment and its interest in China. At the same time, it explains the relative moderateness of this ethics, which has not been marked by too much tolerance for other opinions, but which has been far from bringing down upon China the bloody excesses religions have wrought on Europe and the Near East. As an ethics fueled by the self-respect of the individual in the community of "gentlemen," it lacks the missionary zealous fanaticism and the uncompromising hostility against adherents of different faith which prophetic ethics have regularly fallen into. And it relies on the appeal to insightfulness rather than building morality on strict command.

Nevertheless, we can ask whether the explicit reference to a radically otherwordly authority, in comparison to which the world is vain, would have motivated still more trenchant theoretical distinctions (for example between *ren* and *li*), and would have led to a still greater disassociation from the "is" in favor of the "ought." An authentic Chinese proof for the "radicalism of questioning" which religion can bring about[14] can be found in Mengzi, whose work shows that the forceful appeal to a divine power is by no means entirely missing in early Confucianism. In Mengzi's philosophy, the memory of the Western Zhou religion of Heaven is more vivid than in the *Lunyu*. For Mengzi, Heaven has created the things and the people.[15] It bestows and revokes the mandate for rulership, submitting the candidates to a hard examination and finding its judgment "via the eyes and ears of the people."[16] Mengzi, like Confucius, but even more sure of himself, believes to be in a league with Heaven. If Heaven really wants to bring peace to the world, "who besides me," he proclaims pathetically, would be eligible to be its agent?[17] And he quotes a statement of Yi Yin, Tang's later chancellor, which he obviously identifies with himself:

> When Heaven created the people [its plan was this]: Those who come to knowledge before others should awaken those who come to knowledge later, and those who awaken before others should awaken

those who awaken later. I am one out of the people of Heaven who has awoken before others, and I shall awaken this people by this *Dao*. If I do not awaken them, who will do so?[18]

Yet, despite the prophetical tone of this statement, Mengzi does not really pursue the religious line. "It was the task more than the Giver of the task that occupied his attention," Rowley aptly notes.[19] Mengzi is far from a real resuscitation of the old belief in Heaven. Just as Confucius, in the final analysis, he tends to rely on individual self-control and self-respect rather than on Heaven. He quotes the following passage from the *Shujing* twice:

> Calamities sent down by Heaven can still be escaped from. But calamities caused by oneself will cost one his life.[20]

What has to be feared, therefore, is not Heaven, but the consequences of the actions man is himself responsible for—"self-courted disaster," "self-impairment," "doing violence to oneself," "throwing oneself away," and, last but not least, "self-insult," which makes insult by others possible in the first place.[21]

What is the role, then, within this ethics of conspicuously nonreligious self-cultivation, of the no less striking appeals to Heaven? That Mengzi clings to Heaven is no "archaism," as Hsiao Kung-chuan has called it.[22] The reason is because in doing so he can bring his ethics into a marked contrast with the realities of his time and especially with politics. Heaven becomes an embodiment of moral norms, on which it confers its distance from the world. This gives Confucian ethics a previously unknown radicalism. Its most impressive document is *Mengzi* 6A16:

> There are the *ranks of Heaven*, and the *ranks of man*. Humaneness, justice, benevolence, trustworthiness, and untiring delight in the good—these are the ranks of Heaven. Duke, minister, high officer—these are the ranks of man. The men of antiquity cultivated the ranks of Heaven, and the ranks of man followed. But the men of today cultivate the ranks of Heaven only in order to procure the ranks of man. As soon as they have obtained the ranks of man, they throw away the ranks of Heaven. This is the epitome of delusion! In the end, they are sure to perish.

Through the concept of Heaven, Mengzi can draw an ontological separation between the realm of the moral norms, among which humaneness, as the "most honored of the ranks of Heaven,"[23] holds the highest position, and the realm of the mundane authorities. What he formulates is no less than a counterpart of the occidental teaching of the "two kingdoms."[24] It was this teaching which essentially contributed to the very "tension with the world" that Weber contrasted with the alleged Confucian readiness for adaptation.

Mengzi's ethics thus documents the power of the religion of Heaven, to which it is heir. Although, in the name of the Chinese Heaven, the world is not devaluated as such—which in its rigid form constitutes an idiosyncracy anyway—but in its given form, the created distance is sufficient to invalidate Weber's claim that in China the Archimedean point to move the world is entirely missing. It is this distance between the two realms of the "Heavenly" moral norms and the worldly authorities which makes Mengzi's vehement attacks on the ruling elites possible.

In order to find a foundation for his ethics, Mengzi does not content himself with locating his moral norms in a region beyond the contingencies of the human life world. This higher region is relegated into man himself, in that Heaven endows him with morals in the form of his innate nature, *xing*. "Knowing one's nature," Mengzi says, "one also knows Heaven."[25] Anthropology, then, moves into the center of his endeavors, in order to prove the apriorical existence of morals within man. The core of this anthropology is a phenomenological description of the moral activity of human nature. The program to find a ground for ethics becomes nativistic.

B. MENGZI'S NATIVISM

"One can get to hear about the Master's refinement and style," says Zigong in *Lunyu* 5.13, "but one cannot get to hear words about human nature (*xing*) and the *Dao* of Heaven." Confucius' reticence seems, above all, concerned with the question of evaluating human nature with regard to its goodness or badness. His skepticism is probably motivated by his pedagogical experience. Nevertheless, he makes a moderate generalization:

> Men by nature are close to one another, and by daily practice (or: by custom, *xi*) diverge from one another.[26]

That men are not essentially different by nature came to be the general conviction of the Zhou Chinese which was, in contrast to the Greek mainstream, rather seldom called into question.[27] But how to evaluate human nature as far as its moral potential is concerned was one of the most controversial questions. Mengzi's disciple Gongduzi mentions four different views: (a) Human nature is indifferent to good and evil (Gaozi). (b) Human nature can have good or evil effects, for example in reaction to a good or bad ruler. (c) Some men are good by nature, some are evil by nature. (d) Human nature is good (Mengzi).[28]

In the first century A.D., Wang Chong listed up nine positions: (a) In human nature, there is good and evil alike, and either can be cultivated (Shi Shi, Qidiao Kai, Mi Zijian, Gongsun Nizi, cf. Gongduzi's position b).[29] (b) Human nature is good (Mengzi). (c) Human nature is indifferent to good and evil (Gaozi). (d) Human nature is evil (Xunzi). (e) Human nature has a moral propensity. Man can follow this propensity as soon as he has discovered it (Lu Jia). (f) Man's nature is *yang* and moral, but his emotions (*qing*) are *yin* and base (Dong Zhongshu). (g) Human nature is within, and, therefore, *yin*, while the emotions are manifested without and, therefore, *yang* (Liu Xiang). (h) Human nature is a mixture of good and evil (Yang Xiong). (i) Human nature is different. Whether it is good or evil depends on the quantity of the corresponding dispositions (Wang Chong's own view).[30]

All of the theories mentioned by Gongduzi and Wang Chong, of which we often only know the basic idea, have one thing in common: when they speak about the "good" (*shan*), they think of morals. In doing so, they leave out a trend of ancient Chinese discussion on human nature that is represented by Daoism. According to this trend, *xing* is something normatively "good" prior to and beyond morals, which is just an artificial means to subjugate nature or find a scanty compensation for its loss. This separation of the natural and the artificial, in Greek terms, of *physis* and *nomos*, runs through axial age literature. It has momentous implications. In the name of nature, especially from the perspective of Kohlberg's Stage 4½, it is possible to call into question state, society, technique, and civilization as such.

With Graham, I suppose that the Daoist critics, or their predecessors, started the discussion on nature. The Confucians obviously appropriated it in order to prevent the disastrous consequences it could have on society from their point of view.[31] But it was not before Mengzi that the Confucians found an answer to the challenge of naturalism (represented above all by Yang Zhu), and it is this answer which was responsible for Mengzi's admission into the Confucian pantheon: he declares human nature itself moral in terms of the Confucian values. Mengzi's anthropology, however, is not solely directed against the (proto)Daoist attacks on morality, but even more against the brutal politics of his time which, in his eyes, deprives men of the possibility to develop their inborn moral propensities.[32] Mengzi thus shares the critical impulse of the Daoist concept of nature. Human nature for him, too, is an authority which is opposed to the empirical conditions of life. Its idealization represents in particular a challenge to the political institutions. For, if nature is good, there is no need to reign man in in order to make him a social being in the first place.

Mengzi's famous proclamation that "human nature is good" (*xing shan*) implies a host of problems, however, that are not satisfactorily resolved in the textus receptus *Mengzi*. First of all, it has to be explained why evil does exist in the world. Since China does not know a metaphysical principle of evil (like Zoroastrism), there must be a mundane explanation. Mengzi repeatedly points out the miserable conditions of existence which rob the people of their livelihood. But "without a constant livelihood," it is impossible for them to "have a constant mind."[33] Hence, inhumane politics is identified as a source of evil. But how can it be that the rulers themselves are immoral without being victimized by such material hardship? Mengzi must find an *internal* cause for the good's not prevailing in the world. The external conditions are supplemented by an inner susceptibility of man to vice. He can be led astray by sensual, material desires,[34] he has the aforementioned capability of ruining himself, and he can neglect the nourishment of his *qi*, a vital power which also gives energy for moral action.[35] These explanations of the prevalence of evil refer to the loss or imperfect development of an original good. Evil has no independent existence. Nevertheless, there must be some footing for it in the inner of man. But what does it mean, then, that human nature (xing) is "good"? Mengzi must make some differentiation within the sphere which prima facie can be understood as xing. Such an attempt is made in the following passage:

The relations of the mouth to taste, the eye to color, the ear to sound, the nose to smell, and the four limbs to ease is [also] xing. Yet, inasmuch as there is determination (mìng) in them, the gentleman does not call them xing.

The relations of humaneness to father and son, justice to ruler and subject, etiquette to guest and host, knowledge to the capable, and of a shengren to the Dao of Heaven is [also] determination (mìng). Yet, inasmuch as there is xing in them, the gentleman does not call them determination.[36]

In this difficult passage, Mengzi counts the senses and their desires, and elsewhere even sexuality,[37] among human nature xing.[38] Nevertheless, within human nature, he distinguishes between a constituent which deserves the name xing and another one which does not. I suppose that the difference between both is that between a normative part and a quasi-biological one imposed on man. Mengzi defines mìng as "that which is there without having been brought about."[39] The normative part, too, contains a mìng element, which, however, from the perspective of the "gentleman," does not constitute its essence. The idea is probably that morality, although rooted in emotions (like love), is not subject to the compulsiveness of the senses, but involves, at least in its developed form, decisions.[40] Although Mengzi, to me, is not quite consistent in this respect, this interpretation is corroborated by a second attempt to make a distinction within the natural disposition of man: Mengzi puts the "heart" (xin) as the organ of thought above the senses. The heart in terms of thinking constitutes the "great" within man:

Mengzi said, "The body consists of noble and ignoble, small and great parts. Never injure the great by the small and the noble by the ignoble! He who nourishes the small within himself becomes a small (= mean) man, and he who nourishes the great within himself becomes a great man."

Gongduzi asked, "All are equally men. What is the reason that some are great and some are small men?"

Mengzi answered, "He who follows the great part of himself becomes a great man, and he who follows the small part of himself becomes a small man."

Gongduzi said, "If all are equally men, why do some of them follow the great part and others the small part of themselves?"

Mengzi said, "The organs of hearing and seeing do not think and are only obscured by things. When one thing (a sense) comes into contact with another thing (an object), what happens is mere stimulation. The organ of the heart, however, thinks. By thinking, one can grasp something, without thinking, one will not grasp anything. This is something which Heaven has given to me. If a man first stands fast in the great part of himself, then the small part of himself will not be able to take [the great part] from him. It is merely this what makes a great man.[41]

The thinking heart (*xin*) stands out not only epistemologically, but also morally against the senses which in either respect can be easily deluded. Mengzi, then, speaks of *xing* in terms of *xin*.[42] Yet, this does not mean that thinking is the final location of the "good" in human nature. Thinking is only one of two functions of the "heart" which equally represent the good. The second function is characterized precisely by its independence from thought. In a passage which has always been regarded as a showpiece of Mengzi's moral anthropology, *xin* is described as moral feeling:

All men have a heart which cannot be cruel to others (*bu rěn rén*).[43] The early kings had this heart, and they therefore also had a government which could not be cruel to men. If one practices such a government with such a heart, then one can rule the world as if making it turn round on the palm.

My reason for saying that every man has a heart which cannot be cruel to others is this. Suppose a man suddenly sees a child about to fall into a well. In such a situation, everybody will have the feeling (*xin*) of alarm and compassion. This is not because he wants to enter into good relations with the parents of the child, or because he wants to gain praise in his neighborhood and among his fellow students and friends, or because he dislikes the cry[44] of the child.

In view of this, he who has no feeling (*xin*) of compassion is no human being. He who has no feeling of shame and disgust is no human being. He who has no feeling of courtesy and modesty is no human being. He who has no feeling of right and wrong is no human being.

The feeling of compassion is the beginning of humaneness. The feeling of shame and disgust is the beginning of justice. The feeling of courtesy and modesty is the beginning of propriety. The feeling of right and wrong is the beginning of knowledge. Man has these four beginnings, just as he has his four limbs. He who has these four beginnings and declares himself incapable [of virtue] has done violence to himself. And he who declares his ruler incapable [of virtue] has done violence to his ruler. In general, he who has these four beginnings in himself also knows how to expand and bring to completion all of them, like a spring just welling out, or like a fire just lit. If one knows how to bring them to completion, it will suffice to protect all within the four seas. If one does not bring them to completion, it will not even suffice to serve one's parents.[45]

In his famous example of the rescue[46] of the threatened child, Mengzi's point is the spontaneity of reaction prior to any deliberation. Deliberation would be disturbing here, since it might give grounds for suspecting that the rescue operation is motivated by strategic calculation. The "heart" is now the seat of a prereflective feeling. It is obviously another one than that which stood out in 6A15 as the "great" in man because of its capacity of thinking (*si*). Likewise, the innate "good knowledge" (*liang zhi*), which Mengzi already discerns in infants, stands out by knowing "without having to think."[47]

The search for the good in man has led us to the human "heart" and its two functions of thinking and feeling. There is a contradiction between both functions, and yet they should be seen as a unit, unless Mengzi merely wavers as to where to locate the good. But how to conceive this unit remains unclear. Perhaps we can extrapolate as follows: without an emotional basis in man, morality would just be an idle appeal. Mere feeling, however, is insufficient, since it requires an incentive and only allows for reaction, but not for the weighing of different reactions if such a weighing should be necessary. The rational part of the heart, then, might have to resolve a task which feeling cannot resolve: to take well thought-out moral decisions. Yet, for Mengzi, the ultimate basis of morals doubtless is not thought, but spontaneous inclination.[48] The reason for this conspicuous tendency might be that it is Mengzi's endeavor to refute Daoism on its own ground, the belief in prereflected spontaneity.

How promising is Mengzi's approach to find a foundation of morality within human nature? Let us first listen to how he attacks the counteropinion of his contemporary Gaozi who maintains that human nature is indifferent to good and evil. Mengzi's answers to his opponent throw light on some strong points, but also on some weaknesses of his own moral philosophy. The first round of the somewhat one-sided dispute goes as follows:

> Gaozi said, "Nature (*xing*) is like a purple willow, and justice (*yi*) is like wooden cups and bowls. To make morality[49] out of human nature is like making wooden cups and bowls out of the purple willow."
> Mengzi said, "Can you, following the nature of the purple willow, make cups and bowls out of it? You will have to do violence and injury to it before you can make cups and bowls out of it. But if you have to do violence and injury to the purple willow before you can make cups and bowls out of it, will you, then, not also have to do violence and injury to man in order to make him moral? To let everybody in the world consider morals a calamity—this is surely [the consequence of] your words!"

Gaozi formulates his central thesis: morals are nothing natural, as Mengzi claims, but something artificial, created from outside. Similar arguments, though somewhat more sophisticated ones, will later be brought forward by Xunzi. Xunzi will also address, unsatisfactorily though, the question as to how the raw material "man" can ever take on a moral form at all if it does not at least possess the potential for this. Mengzi, however, does not confront Gaozi with this difficulty. Focusing on the disastrous consequences of Gaozi's teaching, he only sees the factor of deformation and not the factor of continuity in the transition from wood to bowl, and thus gives away an argument.

Yet, although he cannot put Gaozi into an embarrassing position, Mengzi's rejection of the analogies human nature/wood, and morality/cups and bowls, deserves our attention. For, what he attacks nearly programmatically is a conception of social order based on the model of technical engineering.[50] In China, the corresponding technical terminology belongs to the standard repertory of the legalistic camp and its informants Mo Di and Xunzi. Mo Di compares the will of Heaven, which sets the measures for morality, to the "wheelwright's compass and the carpenter's square."[51] Xunzi, among other things, uses the analogy of the straightening board (*yingua*) which bends crooked wood into shape, just like teacher and laws act upon man's bad nature.[52] Han Fei, too, is fond of this picture. He moreover compares politics to hair washing where the loss of some hairs should be accepted for the sake of the growth of new ones.[53] For the Legalists, politics is "technique" (*shu*), and reward and punishment are its two "handles."[54] Mengzi, however, intuitively rejects technomorphism in the following passage also:[55]

> Humaneness, justice, propriety, and knowledge are *not cast into us from outside*. We have them in ourselves originally and only do not think of it. Therefore I say: Seek, and you will find them, give them up, and you will lose them.[56]

Morals, or its "beginnings," should be sought in the "heart." For Gaozi, however, there is nothing of moral relevance to find in the heart:

> Mengzi said, "According to Gaozi, one should not seek in the heart what one does not find in the words (*yan*), and should not seek in the *qi* (the vital energy) what one does not find in the heart. That one should not seek in the *qi* what one does not find in the heart can be accepted. But that one should not seek in the heart what one does not find in the words cannot be accepted.[57]

Mengzi and Gaozi agree that energy (*qi*), which man, according to Mengzi, needs as an *élan vital* for his moral efforts, is a secondary and not a normative factor. But their opinions are divided on the heart's position vis-à-vis the so-called "words" which Gaozi gives priority to. "Words" probably refers to the established set of rules and prescriptions.[58] The heart must not pretend to have any precedence over it. Gaozi's version of the "imperturbable heart" discussed in *Mengzi* 2A2[59] means to accept one's limitations and to reconcile oneself to the restraints of objective conditions. In the words of one of his modern defenders, he advocates a "rational compliance to the dictate of duties."[60] The forced adjustment to these heteronomous rules corresponds to the forging of morals according to the model of technique. The fact that Mengzi, against this heteronomy of the "words," defends the importance of the inner authority of the human heart as the seat of thinking and feeling reflects his ideas of autonomy of judgment and action[61] and the necessity of moral decisions. His own version of the "imperturbable heart" is not the humble submission to the inevitable. It is the basis of a responsible, but critical and, if necessary, insubordinate engagement, safely rooted in and fueled by the conviction to possess the good in one's own nature.

Mengzi's dispute with Gaozi, which has up to now not gone beyond the exchange of statements,[62] enters into the second round:

> Gaozi said, "[Human] nature is like whirling water. Give it an outlet to the east, and it will flow east; give it an outlet to the west, and it will flow west. That human nature is indifferent to good and evil is similar to water being indifferent to east and west."
>
> Mengzi said, "Surely water is indifferent to east and west. But is it indifferent to up and down, too? Human nature is good, just as water flows downwards. There is no man who is not good, just as there is no water which does not flow downwards. Now, letting water splash up by striking it, one can make it jump over the forehead. And by making it faster and directing it, one can force it uphill. But is this the nature (*xing*) of water? It is only because of the circumstances that it behaves in this way. And if man can be brought to do evil— does this make his nature evil, too?"[63]

After the manufacturing of bowls and dishes out of wood, Gaozi presents a second analogy taken up by Mengzi: the flowing of water. Analogies, in ancient China, are a favorite means of argumentation.[64] They can be helpful to clarify points, and even today Mengzi's usage of them sometimes sounds convincing.[65] Yet, the ancient Chinese are aware of the limits of analogical reasoning. Mengzi himself emphasizes that in comparison some measure has to be observed.[66] The later Mohists explicitly formulate the crux of the *metábasis eis állo génos*,[67] the inadmissible transgression of the boundaries between different genera.[68] It implies that analogies as such prove nothing, since the comparability of that which is compared has to be ascertained beforehand. In the given case, however, Mengzi does not reject Gaozi's analogy on the grounds that it would treat incomparable objects—moral and physical facts—as comparable. He accepts the analogy in order to draw the opposite conclusion from it. Whence it is already clear that the analogy water/human nature is worthless, and Mengzi would actually be well advised to content himself with this conclusion. The fact that he uses the analogy himself renders his argument purely rhetorical. In addition, he forgets that a naturalistic analogy, from whatever angle it is construed, speaks in favor of Gaozi, who has a biologistic picture of man, whereas Mengzi has separated "noble" and "ignoble" parts within man's natural constitution. Mengzi, then, has still not made a decisive move against his opponent.

Gaozi and Mengzi now enter into the third round of their dispute:

> Gaozi said, (A) "The inborn (*sheng*) is called nature (*xing*)."
> Mengzi said, (B) "Is *sheng* called *xing*, just as white is called white?"
> Gaozi said, "Yes."
> Mengzi said, (C) "Is the white of a white feather like the white of white snow? And is the white of white snow like the white of white jade?"
> Gaozi said, "Yes."
> Mengzi said, (D) "Then the nature of the dog is like the nature of the ox, and the nature of the ox is like the nature of man?"[69]

It is not easy to find out what constitutes the "cryptical"[70] of this much debated passage, and where Mengzi's decisive argument against Gaozi, or his mistake, lies.[71] C, or the transition from C to D, is usually regarded as the key to understanding, since C appears to be the link between Gaozi's seeming premises and the conclusion suggested by Mengzi. The crucial flaw, then, would be that "white" and "nature" are categories of a different status which cannot be equated in the given form. Lau, for example, calls "nature" "a formal, empty term," whereas "white" has "a minimum specific content."[72] Indeed, a reasonable comparison could only be drawn between "nature" and "color." But even in this case, secondary and essential qualities would be confounded. Obviously, a double category mistake is committed. The question is, by whom—by Gaozi, as Lau maintains, or by Mengzi himself, as Wen Gongyi, for one, argues.[73] Mou Zongsan, too, thinks that the mistake is Mengzi's own, for that nature, *xing*, is identical with the "inborn," *sheng*, does not imply that it must be the same with all beings.[74] This critique is justified. Yet, Mengzi obviously suggests that this absurd conclusion results from Gaozi's statement in the light of his answers to Mengzi's questions. Therefore, we should turn once again to the beginning of the passage.

The idea that *xing*, innate nature, should be understood as *sheng*, the "inborn"—a similar definition will later be given by Xunzi—taken by itself, does not mean much. Mengzi, too, thinks of something inborn when he speaks of *xing*. It has to be clarified, therefore, what Gaozi exactly means by his equation of the two terms. Mengzi wants to know whether Gaozi understands *xing* and *sheng* as synonyms, as identical with each other as "white" and "white."[72] While Mengzi, too—remember his passage on *ming* and *xing*—regards *xing* as *sheng*, something inborn, he himself does not treat it as a synonym, but as a lower term of *sheng*. For Gaozi, however, everything which can be termed *sheng* can also be termed *xing*. "Nature" is biological disposition, and nothing else. It is in this sense that Gaozi can assent when Mengzi asks him whether *sheng* is *xing* just as "white" is "white." Yet, this does not establish the relation on which Mengzi's further argument is based—the relation between "nature" (*xing*) and "white." "White" merely functions as an optional variable in order to clarify the relation of *xing* and *sheng*. Gaozi's affirmative answer to question B merely specifies his statement A—now it has become clear that he really wants to say that *xing* and *sheng* are the same. The sentence "*sheng* is called *xing*, just as white is called white," then, does not introduce a second premise from which question C can be derived.[76] If this is true, the structure of reasoning of *Mengzi* 6A3 is as follows:

Premise (A+B): *Xing* and *sheng* mean exactly the same.
Premise (C): The white of the feather is like the white of snow.
Conclusion (D): *Xing* of man is like *xing* of animals.

It is evident that the conclusion drawn by Mengzi does not follow from the premises, since these do not contain a common *terminus medius*. C, which is suspended in midair, since the seeming connecting link B is canceled, can be deleted from the chain of argumentation. What remains is Gaozi's statement that *xing*, "nature," means the inborn, *sheng*, as such. From this premise it does not follow that human nature is identical with the nature of specific animals. It is claimed that going beyond the biological there is no essential nature in a morally higher sense, but not that the essential nature is the same for every being. Only as far as its ethical substance and no other characteristics are concerned, does Gaozi see human nature in analogy to that of animals. This is consistent with his heteronomous view of morality.

That Gaozi has such an idea of human nature is shown in the sentence with which he starts the fourth round of the dispute, and which reads like an answer to Mengzi's last question:

Gaozi said, "Food and sex, this is nature (*xing*). Humaneness (*ren*) is internal and not external. But justice (*yi*) is external, not internal."

Mengzi said, "Why do you say humaneness is internal and justice external?"

Gaozi said, "If I treat (honor) someone as elder (*zhang*) who is older (*zhang*) than I, it is not because treating someone as elder (*zhang*) is in me. It is just as when something is white and I treat it as white, following its being white on the outside. Therefore I call it external."

Mengzi said, "How strange![77] To treat the white of a horse as white is not different from treating the white of man as white. But I wonder if there is also no difference between treating the elder[liness] of a horse as elder[liness] and treating the elder[liness] of a man as elder[liness].[78] Moreover, does 'justice' refer to the old or to treating them as old?[79]"

Gaozi said, "If someone is my younger brother, I love him, but if he is the younger brother of a man of Qin, I do not love him. Here, I am the one who feels pleasure, and therefore I call it internal. I treat the elders of Chu like elders, and I treat my own elders like elders. Now, the elders are the ones who feel pleasure, and therefore I call it external."

Mengzi said, "To relish the roast of a man of Qin is not different from relishing my own roast, and with some other things it is similar. Is there something external in relishing a roast, then, too?"

Gaozi first gives a drastic concretization of his thesis that *xing* is the inborn and nothing else. He then questions that there is any intrinsic criterion for distinguishing morally relevant from morally irrelevant phenomena. That he, nevertheless, calls humaneness (*ren*) "internal" is no real concession to Mengzi. It shows that *ren* for him is nothing but an instinctive feeling of affiliation between blood relatives. The biological viewpoint is not abandoned. Justice (*yi*), however, here used in terms of the conventionally appropriate ("treat elders as elders"), has no foundation in feeling and is, therefore, external. It is a mere heteronomous prescription.

If we take into consideration that "elders" does not solely refer to the elders of one's own family, to which we are emotionally committed, but to a social group in its entirety, Gaozi's argument contains a rational core. That *ren* is internal (*nei*) and *yi* external (*wai*)—and Gaozi is not alone in upholding this opinion[80]—becomes immediately plausible if we relate *ren* to the family and *yi* to the public realm, thus parallelizing *nei* and *wai* to the standard distinction of *ru* (go in = in the family) and *chu* (go out = in the public). For, the step towards the obligation to the public realm implies a much greater amount of *alienation* than growing into the family—a discrepancy which Gaozi has probably recognized exactly because of his biologism. The point at stake is the difficult transition from a "closed" morality which can still be rated as natural, to an "open" one. I think that this is the clue to understanding the controversy, but because alienation is stereotypically regarded as "alien to Asians" (Nakamura), this aspect has hardly received attention in the various interpretations.

As we have seen, Mengzi believes that the transition in question can be brought about by means of an "extension" of family love. This model is of programmatical importance, since it shall prevent the restriction of morality to the family. But it says nothing about the actual gap which has to be bridged here. Bridging this gap can hardly be achieved by mere emotional impulse, but would need an additional cognitive effort (like that of the Golden Rule). Neither does Mengzi tell us in 6A4 how the obligation to the general public (here: to the elders of others) comes into being. He is content with rhetorically undermining Gaozi's counterposition that respect for older people, inasmuch as they do not belong to one's own family, is external. He tries to prove Gaozi guilty of two logical mistakes. Firstly, he focuses on the equivocality of the word *zhang* and asks whether Gaozi has not confounded the attitude *zhang* (to treat/honor an elder as elder) with the object *zhang* (an older person). Gaozi's answer shows, however, that he is not so simpleminded as to take the externality of the object for the externality of the attitude of the actor.[81] For the same reason, the criticism of the later Mohists, too, who explicate Mengzi's argument, cannot affect Gaozi's position.[82] The criterion for the distinction of internal and external is, in reality, itself an internal one, namely, whether one feels "pleasure" (*yue*) or does not. To love one's brother is accompanied by such a feeling of pleasure, and hence is internal. But to honor an old man of Chu only "pleases" the man of Chu, and hence is external.

In his second objection, Mengzi tries to reduce Gaozi's answer to absurdity. If one follows Gaozi, he maintains, then the desire for a roast must be something external, too. With Mou Zongsan, we can raise the counterobjection of the subjectivity of taste here.[83] This argument would not embarrass Mengzi, however, since he assumes that, with respect to taste, men, in general, share the same preferences.[84] Mengzi's argument is not sound for another reason: when Mengzi, by a *grammatical* operation, exchanges the predicate "treat as elder" for the predicate "relish," and the object "the elder" for the object "roast," he turns the *semantic* content of Gaozi's claim upside down. For, the equation of something natural like "relishing a roast" and something which he regards as artificial like "treating an elder person as elder" has been called into question by Gaozi. Exchangeable, then, are only the predicates "relish" and "love," and the objects "roast" and "younger brother." Gaozi, therefore, may reply to Mengzi that the appetite for the roast is as "internal" as humaneness, understood in terms of love for the brother. That the specifically moral nature of *ren* is lost in this argument is another story. Mengzi himself is not at all immune to the "naturalistic fallacy" either, although to the reverse one. This is already apparent in his analogy of the roast, and in the fact that he merely attacks Gaozi's external concept of *yi*, but not his biologistic understanding of *ren*.

The dispute ends without Gaozi's having been disproven. This is not due to the persuasive power of his reasoning, but mainly to the weakness of his opponent's arguments. Mengzi is not merely guilty of logical inaccuracies. He uses problematic analogies, partly in order to trap Gaozi, partly, like in the analogy of water, in order to corroborate his own view of morals. He uses further analogies which are hardly less dubious. In 2A6, he insists that man has his "four beginnings" for morality just as he has his "four limbs." And in 6A7, he claims that "the basic [moral] patterns and justice please my heart just as the meat of grass- and flesh-eating animals pleases my mouth." These parallels are meant to say that morals are as innate as sensory functions. They do not necessarily identify both in a straightforward manner. Nevertheless, especially in the last analogy, morals and the senses are hardly separated from each other.

Mengzi's analogies can be understood as rhetorical devices to furnish his normative claims with the evidence of constative propositions referring to objective facts. He intends to provide the normative rightness of his teaching with the force of indisputable factual truth.[85] His analogies, however, can also count as an indication that he does not really reflect upon the difference between facts and norms. After all, he wants to derive morality directly from nature. His program is essentially to protect and develop the natural disposition and propensities of man. This reminds one of ethical naturalism which does not distinguish between sentences on "is" and "ought." This holism has been under attack since Hume.[86] It represents a "naturalistic fallacy" (G. E. Moore) which inadmissibly infers norms from facts and describes moral predicates as empirical ones.[87] Mengzi himself, however, certainly does make a difference between empirical predicates like "it is useful" and "it pleases" on the one hand and the normative predicate "it is moral" on the other.[88] In the modern ethical debate, he would rather be on the intuitionists' than on the naturalists' side. His ethics lives on the assumption that man can stay aloof of what is beneficial or desirable to him in terms of self-interest, and that he can, by virtue of his innate "good knowledge" (*liang zhi*), choose a moral alternative. Man even possesses a will for justice which, as the case may be, may suspend his will for life.[89] Presumably in view of this ambiguity of will, Mengzi gives an astonishing answer when asked what he means by "good," a predicate which he has ascribed to one of his pupils:

> Good (*shan*) means what can (*ke*) be willed (*yu*) (or: what is desirable).[90]

With Kant's categorical imperative in mind, one cannot but be alert when reading Mengzi's formulation "can be willed." Mengzi does, nota bene, not say that the "good" is the *willed* or the *desired*—according to Moore the classic case of the "naturalistic fallacy."[91] He says that the good is the desir*able*, that which "*can* (*ke*) be willed" in the sense of "is admissible to be willed."[92] He furthermore sets the good against the beneficial:

> If you want to know the difference between [the sage] Shun and Robber Zhi, it is nothing else but the gap between the good (*shan*) and benefit (*li*).[93]

Does Mengzi, then, put the will under the primacy of an independent "ought"?[94] And does he, in doing so, not go beyond the natural "is"? This would not only be consistent with his political voluntarism, but also with his "negative imperative" which demands "not to will (*yu*) what you do not will (*yu*)."[95] In the duplication of the word *yu*, an intrinsic, self-certain and moral will, and a heteronomous one steerable from outside are distinguished from one another. Similarly, in *Mengzi* 6A10, a moral volition overrules a biological one.

Yet, Mengzi's ethics does not take the dualist direction which appears possible here. There is more of a glimpse than a conscious reflection of the discussed problem in his text anyway. As the aforementioned analogies show, the naturalistic fallacy is not consistently avoided. Mengzi thinks that he can draw the demarcation line between the normative and the factical *within* "nature," probably motivated by the effort to vindicate the hotly debated term *xing* from the Daoists for Confucianism. This leads into considerable difficulties which are reflected for example in the quite arbitrary distinction of *ming*, "determination," and *xing*, the intrinsic nature. Nevertheless, Mengzi's approach has its merit. Ethics must not only distinguish an "ought" against the "is," but it has also to face the question how "ought" can be transferred into "can" and be made the object of will. To achieve this, there must at least be a possibility within the "is" that man acts morally. Mengzi has an answer to this problem which has hardly lost its persuasive power even today. It consists in the phenomenological description of the activity of a natural moral sensorium within man. The *Mengzi* contains a lot of corresponding examples of observation. True, ethics cannot be built upon examples, since these presuppose a criterion of selection. Nevertheless, there are examples of immediate evidence which can intuitively be accepted as cogent, a fact, as Mengzi would have it, which in turn proves the presence of morals in ourselves. Not all of Mengzi's observations can claim such a direct ethical relevance. Thus he notices the effect of a moral mental attitude on countenance and posture.[96] He moreover discovers that the eye is a mirror of the inner disposition of man:

> That which is in man becomes best [apparent] from his pupils. The pupils cannot conceal his wickedness. When he is upright in his breast (= in his heart), his pupils are bright by that, and when he is not upright in his breast, his pupils are cloudy by that. Where, then, can a man conceal himself, if, listening to his words, one watches his pupils?[97]

The betraying changes of the pupils today are the topic of pupillometrics,[98] a natural science which can worship Mengzi as its precursor. Yet, neither to the posture nor the to pupils can we, per se, attribute moral relevance. Nonetheless, if Mengzi's assumption that natural roots of morality exist in man can be accepted for other reasons, his observations can count as an additional support of his thesis.

Another group of examples, however, leads us directly into the moral deeper structure of man if we embark on them from the internal perspective of the first person, instead of merely viewing them from the detached third-person perspective of an uninvolved spectator.[99] Mengzi points out that man can, if need be, give up his life if preserving it would mean committing an injustice.[100] That this decision is based on a moral choice, as Mengzi's supposes, can never be determined from outside by empirical research. We can only confirm the claim by our own thought experiment if we imagine ourselves in the role of the just person who prefers death to doing evil. Mengzi's argument, then, is an invitation for identification and making the test. The same applies to the picture of the hungry beggar who may reject the rescuing meal if he receives it with a humiliating kick.[101] This feeling of hurt when receiving an offense is something which everybody can observe in himself. It shows that we possess of a sensitivity to justice. It becomes fully "moral" as soon as it manifests itself in indignation at the injustice done to others[102]—the very indignation so typical of Mengzi himself, when he deplores the inhumane conditions of his time.

Mengzi's main proof for the existence of a natural moral nucleus in man, which should open the eyes of the most tenacious skeptic, is the spontaneous reaction of alertness and compassion when all of a sudden we see a child falling into a well.[103] This example is well chosen. Due to a certain combination of salient features like head and body proportions and stumbling movements which Lorenz has described as "baby-schema" (*Kindchenschema*), it is in particular the sight of an infant which elicits an instinctive parental drive of care and protection.[104] Jonas has called the spontaneously accepted duty to care for the child "the archetype of all responsible action, which fortunately requires no deduction from a principle, because it is powerfully implemented in us by nature." It bridges "the alleged chasm between 'is' and 'ought,'" for the naked existence of the newborn child is "the elemental 'ought' in the 'is.'"[105]

Although lacking elaboration, Mengzi's example appears more convincing than Jonas' "archetype." What Jonas speaks about, is, first of all, the attitude of caring for *one's own* children. However, whether this kind of care should be understood in moral terms at all (as was also assumed by Lorenz) has been called into question by recent ethology. From the perspective of biological, not moral evolution, the parent-child relationship, in its broad range from brood care to infanticide, can be described as a function of a mere cost benefit analysis for the purpose of optimum gene proliferation.[106] This argument is not new in essence. It is already brought forward by Han Fei who wants to expose family love, for Mengzi and other Confucians a foremost foundation of morals, as mere fiction. According to Han Fei, the killing of newborn daughters shows that even the relationship of parents towards their own children is characterized by the "calculation of long-term benefit."[107] Although the phenomenon of infanticide cannot be sufficiently explained by egoism, its occurrence in many cultures—in China, the killing or exposition of daughters has continued until today—presents some difficulties to a thesis like that of Jonas, and also to Confucianism. Yet, it hardly affects Mengzi's specific example, since the child to be rescued is not one's own. Whence the rescue attempt cannot be suspected of a subliminal gene-biological "principle of selfishness." The point of this principle is, namely, that the care for one's own genes cannot be replaced by an instinctive regard for the species and its members.

Next to the rescue of the child, Mengzi gives another phenomenological proof that man has an innate feeling of compassion: the sparing of an ox being led to ritual slaughter by King Xuan of Qi. The king cannot endure the sight of the trembling ox and orders to sacrifice a sheep in its stead. When the people call him parsimonious, Mengzi defends him:

> That was a humane procedure, after all! You saw the ox, but you did not see the sheep. The gentleman's attitude towards animals is such

that he cannot bear to see them die when he has seen them alive, and cannot eat their flesh when he hears their dying cry. The gentleman, therefore, keeps away from slaughterhouse and kitchen.[108]

In the further course of the audience, Mengzi uses the king's reaction to point out that a ruler who shows such great compassion with an animal has no reason whatsoever to refuse a humane politics for the people. It is remarkable that compassion, like in *Mengzi* 2A6, is again discussed in a political context. I suppose that the reason for this is an experience which has not lost its topicality: the experience that nothing represents a greater threat to man than organized institutional, especially state power out of control. The true subject matter of *Mengzi* 1A7, then, is not the attitude towards animals; the trembling ox is rather a symbol of the elementary vulnerability and need of protection of man in the face of power. Unlike the Daoists and afterwards the Buddhists, the Confucians do not regard an animal as a being deserving special respect. On the contrary, respect is the *differencia specifica* which separates the treatment of animals from that of men.[109] The treatment of animals is, basically, merely subject to the charge of moderation which applies to the use of natural resources in general. One should not "fell a single tree and kill a single animal" if "the proper time" has not come, says the *Dadai Liji*. The violation of this rule is not criticized as a lack of respect for nature, but as "unfilial."[110] The definition of the offense is anthropocentric and refers to the harm done to the interests of the parents. Animals not only are no object of special moral commitment, but they are the counterpart of morality as such. Morality is the "little bit" which separates man from the brute, and he who does not possess the "four beginnings" of morals, says Mengzi, "is no human being."[111] The devaluation of nonhuman nature is the reverse side of Confucian humanism.[112]

We can agree with Mengzi that the story of King Xuan and the ox provides more evidence for the existence of the feeling of compassion in man. But the same story no less forcibly elucidates the limits of compassion. Instead of the ox, a sheep has to die. Mengzi justifies this unsatisfying solution by the only argument possible within the framework of an ethics of compassion: the king *saw* the ox, but he did not see the sheep. The reaction of compassion, then, is obviously blind to the problem of justice which would have to take into account the same interest of both animals in their life. If for the accomplishment of the good deed it is necessary to immediately witness the misery of others, the reaction will fail to appear if the stimulus is missing. It is even possible, as Mengzi involuntarily confirms, to consciously evade the moral appeal by avoiding the relevant situations.[113] Thanks to the division of labor, this self-immunization can even assume the form of a constant, institutionalized habit. The slaughterer does the bloody business of killing, the cook cuts the flesh into bite-sized pieces, and the gentleman, who to the end is spared the indignity of using a knife, enjoys, with his chopsticks, a meal from which any perceivable trace of the sanguinary procedure has disappeared.

Mengzi 1A7, then, proves the limited reach of compassion as well as the rivalry it faces from another side of human propensity: looking the other way, not to mention malignancy and aggression. Because of this limitation, Gehlen has demanded "institutional backing" for the "physiological virtue" of compassion.[114] Mengzi, however, thinks further, for what he has in mind is the harm which can be done to man precisely by those institutions. By his appeal to compassion, he first of all wants to put a curb upon the political authorities. Yet, he is obviously not quite aware of the aporia of his argument.

We can ask, then, whether Mengzi's model of the development of morality, the model of the "extension" of the moral germs in man, is well thought-out in the first place. The thought figure of extension can be found in two contexts. The first one is the transition from family morality towards the commitment to the general public. Family love is conceived as a starting point to gradually include all other men within the range of moral responsibility. Here, we can, for one thing, question the concept of love. For Mengzi, love is a spontaneous feeling of children for their parents. This assumption is hardly sound. As developmental psychology has shown, early childhood is rather characterized by original egoism and the pleasure principle (Kohlberg's Stages 1 and 2). The development of love on the side of the child presupposes the experience of love from the side of the parents.[115] Moreover, the transition from the family to the public realm implies leaving behind the natural feeling of affiliation and is not simply conceivable as its "extension."[116] It was Gaozi who had an idea of the breach and the alienation taking place here, whereas Mengzi does not seem to recognize them. On the contrary, he uses the model of extension not only in relation to family love, but also to explain the development of the "four beginnings" into full moral competence. Thus, innate compassion, which normally needs to be triggered off by sense perception, is transferred beyond spatial borders to events which leave us cold to the present since the immediate stimulus is not given:

> For all men there is something which they cannot bear. To *extend*
> this [attitude] to what they can bear is humaneness. . . . If man can
> bring to the full this inner attitude of not wishing to harm others,
> there will be humaneness in abundance.[117]

I suppose that Mengzi here takes up the challenge posed to the idea of compassion by the problem of the nonperceivable distant effects of actions. This problem has become particularly acute in the era of modern weapon technology, but it has always been a problem of government. But how can the "extension" work if—like in the keeping away of the gentleman from the slaughterhouse— already the primary shock experience can be dodged? The answer might be found in the combination of the emotional element of compassion with the rational achievement of abstraction represented by the Golden Rule. Perhaps this is the kind of combination aimed at in the above quotation. But in the final analysis, the principal focus of Mengzi's ethical theory is on the emotional and spontaneous part of morality, and he continues to be less interested in its rational, deliberative part.

In spite of its problems and weaknesses, Mengzi's theory of the moral "beginnings" in man has struck an important point. His moral phenomenology has, at least, made it plausible that man has the *possibility for morality prior to and independent of education and tradition by virtue of his very self*. And perhaps it is only this that Mengzi really wants to show. The following sentences read like the quintessence of his teaching:

> If one approves of one's essence (*qing*), then one can do good by this. This is what I mean in saying [human nature] is good. And if one does evil, this is not the fault of the natural endowment.[118]

Mengzi's moral philosophy does not fulfill everything that it promises. Nevertheless, it presents strong arguments for the existence of propensities in man which allow him to be moral of his own accord. No human being, then, can reject morality as an exaction. Whoever declares himself incapable of virtue has "done violence to himself." Thus, Mengzi has laid an indispensable foundation for ethics. For, if "human nature" cannot at least meet morality, the latter would just be a hopeless project. Mengzi, moreover, wins a solid basis from where he can deal severely with a politics which, instead of taking its bearings from the moral possibilities of men, treats them worse than animals, drives them into crime, and then subjects them to hardest punishments.[119] It is above all because of these political implications of Mengzi's ethics that his critics come to the fore.

C. XUNZI'S RATIONALISM

The most important of the skeptics who do not follow Mengzi's moral anthropology is Xunzi, the last of the great Confucians of the axial age. Xunzi draws a conclusion from the Confucian conviction that that which is good and right is already basically embodied in the cultural tradition. There is no reason for man to seek for the good in himself, then, where he will not find it anyway. This is because his "nature," *xing*, Xunzi maintains in reply to Mengzi, is "evil." Mengzi's intuitive discovery and spontaneous realization of the good is replaced by the careful and patient acquisition of morals by education and learning. Both lines of Confucianism can be traced back to the *Lunyu* where we find humaneness linked to volition as well as to the intellect.

Xunzi's critique of Mengzi is to undermine the assumption that human nature is good. It thus lays the negative foundation for his own ethics. Let us first turn to this negative side of Xunzi's teaching.

Mengzi, as we have seen, maintains that man disposes of inborn moral intuitions. Since these intuitions are moral, they do not simply count among the senses, although they are inborn like senses. Since they arise spontaneously, they

have to be, strictly speaking, distinguished from deliberation, although the thinking "heart," too, is said to have ethical relevance. In spite of these difficulties to
locate the "good" in man, Mengzi declares that human "nature," *xing*, as such is
"good." Perhaps he does so in the exuberance of the feeling that with man's moral
intuitions he has made an extremely important discovery. Nevertheless, he also
views the senses as a part of that nature. Xunzi replies to this unclear use of the
term *xing* with an exact definition. *Xing* is, like in Gaozi, the sensual, instinctual
disposition:

> That which is as it is from the time of birth should be called nature
> *xing*. *Xing* has come into existence by the harmony [of Yin and Yang].[120]
> The conjugation of semina,[121] reaction upon stimulus, being so by
> itself without effort—this should be called *xing*.[122]

> *Xing* is the natural tendency. The emotions (*qing*) are the substance
> of *xing*.[123]

> *Xing* is the natural tendency. It can neither be learned nor worked
> for.[124]

Xunzi maintains that "nature" defined in this way is not "good," but "evil."
The reason for this is the insatiability of the desires which constitute the essence
of nature. Xunzi's famous writing *Human Nature is Evil* (*Xing e*) starts:

> The nature of man is evil, and the good in him is artificial. The
> nature of man is such that from the time of birth there is the fond-
> ness for profit in him. Following this fondness, strife and rapacity
> arise, and courtesy and modesty get lost. From the time of birth,
> there are envy and hate in man. Following these, cruelty and vio-
> lence arise, and loyalty and faithfulness get lost. From the time of
> birth, the desires of the ears and eyes and the fondness for sounds
> and sights are in man. Following them, licence and chaos arise, and
> propriety, justice, and refined patterns get lost.[125]

In Xunzi's ethical theory, *xing*, nature, corresponds to what Mengzi proposed
to call *mìng*, "determination," in order to distinguish a higher, normative dimension of nature from a lower, sensuous one. Mengzi, therefore, would not have
called this part of man "good" either. Is Xunzi's polemic, as critics have often
argued,[126] not to the point, then, because he uses the term *xing* differently than
Mengzi? For Xunzi, *xing* refers to sensualness and not to the rational "heart." For
Mengzi, it refers to moral feeling and judgment rooted in the "heart," and not, or
only secondarily, to sensualness. Nevertheless, if we take into consideration not
the extension, but the intension of *xing*, Xunzi does not talk past Mengzi. Although Mengzi vaguely ascribes a moral function to thinking, the pivot of his
ethics is prereflective knowledge and feeling. Thus, *xing* for him means basically
the same as for Xunzi: something inborn, spontaneous, prereflective, and intui-

tive. When Mengzi and Xunzi speak about "good" or "evil" "nature," then, both refer to the spontaneous and prereflective in man. Hence, the true point of controversy which is obstructed by the somewhat confusing usage of the term *xing*, would be: is there something in man which can count as "good" prior to all reflection? Viewed from this angle, Xunzi's polemic does make sense and is not the result of misunderstanding.

In order to refute Mengzi, Xunzi, in his essay *Xing e*, brings forward a number of deliberations each followed by the phrase "from this it is evident that man's nature is evil, and that the good in him is artificial." In most cases, however, he presents mere assertions. The first argument which deserves this name is the following:

> To maintain that human nature is good means to find nature beautiful already in its raw state, and to find it beneficial already in its original disposition. The relation of the disposition and the raw state to the beautiful [and the beneficial], as well as the relation of the motivation of the heart to the good, are seen in analogy to the inseparability of the power of seeing from the eye and the power of hearing from the ear. . . .
>
> Now the nature of man is such that when hungry he desires satisfaction, when cold he desires warmth, and when toiling he desires rest. This is the emotional nature (*qingxing*) of man. Now, when he is hungry, and yet does not dare to eat before elders, then this is because there are people to which he must yield. And when he is toiling and yet does not dare to seek rest, this is because there is someone in place of whom he must labor. That the son yields to the father and the younger brother to the elder brother, that the son works in place of the father and the younger brother works in place of the elder brother—acts like these are contrary to nature and run counter to the emotions. And yet, they represent the way of a filial son and the refined patterns of propriety and justice.
>
> Hence, if man follows his emotional nature, there will be no courtesy and modesty. Courtesy and modesty run counter to emotional nature. From this it is evident that man's nature is evil, and that the good in him is artificial.[127]

In the second part of this passage, Xunzi reminds us of the reluctance which often accompanies moral or conventionally expected behavior. This empirical objection against Mengzi, however, can hardly diminish the persuasive power of Mengzi's reference to the spontaneous moral sentiments in man. The fact that conventional morality, which Xunzi talks about, is regarded as a burden—as Confucius already knows, when speaking of "overcoming one's self"—does not affect the immediacy of the feeling of compassion. Xunzi, therefore, cannot really refute Mengzi's basic discovery. Nevertheless, he corrects certain exaggerations of Mengzi's nativism, according to which not only humaneness, but also propriety, justice, and the knowledge of right and wrong count among the innate "four beginnings" of morality. On close examination, Mengzi merely gives arguments for the innateness of the impulse of compassion, of an elementary sense of justice, and, *cum grano salis*, of a feeling for right and wrong.[128] He fails, however, in his attempt to show against Gaozi that the conventionally just in the form of honoring elders is "internal," too, and he does not give a proof for innate roots of propriety. Thus, among the "four beginnings," propriety (*li*) and the conventional form of justice (*yi*) hold a rather weak position—which corresponds to the predominance of humaneness in Mengzi's teaching. When Xunzi talks about morals, he conspicuously uses the compound *liyi*, "propriety and justice."[129] In the above quotation, too, the matter at issue is conventional prescriptions falling under the two concepts. The same applies to a further example which Xunzi presents:

> Suppose that there is some fraternal property to be divided and men follow their emotional nature with its fondness for profit and desire for gain. Then even brothers would quarrel and wrangle with each other. But if they are transformed by the cultivated patterns of propriety and justice, then they [may] even yield to a stranger.[130]

This is the level on which Gaozi already argued when he called justice "external." That Xunzi focuses on *li* and *yi* while ignoring humaneness—he does not try to refute Mengzi's argument for the existence of the feeling of compassion—limits the validity of his own considerations. His subject matter is primarily the conventional virtues. Here, the external perspective indeed has its advantages compared to Mengzi's model of the "extension" of innate "beginnings." We might reproach Xunzi, therefore, of choosing the way of least resistance against Mengzi.[131] But we have to take into account that he most probably is not ready in the first place to grant the same significance to humaneness as Mengzi. This might be due to the aforementioned weaknesses of the concepts of love and compassion.

Xunzi anyway is not primarily interested in giving counterexamples to Mengzi's phenomenology of moral feeling. His principal concern is to draw a clear demarcation between the normative and the natural. This demarcation line should not be drawn within *xing* (as in Mengzi), but beyond it. Mengzi blurs the distinction. Although he assigns the senses to the "small part" of man, he nearly nullifies the disparity between the "small" and the "great" part, the heart, by his analogies. Xunzi, therefore, is not altogether wrong to reproach the teaching of the innate goodness of man of treating morality as a sensory function. But with the automatism of "seeing" and "hearing," he wants us to consider, nature only brings forth selfishness. Normative questions, then, must not be confounded with natural phenomena. Both are "of a different category," to use a phrase by which Xunzi describes the relation of politics and anthropology.[132] Morals are only possible *contra naturam*. Now, a problem is canceled which Mengzi had to face: why man, if his nature is good, does not act accordingly. Xunzi, however, takes upon himself another burden of proof: How can morals come into existence if human nature is evil? His answer is that morals are an invention.

This takes us to the positive part of Xunzi's ethics. Xunzi confronts the problem in question in his answer to an anonymous, perhaps fictitious, skeptic:

> A questioner asks, "If human nature is evil, then where do propriety and justice come from?"
>
> I answer, "Propriety and justice (= morals) come from the art (*wei*) of the sages, and not originally from the nature of man. When a potter molds clay and makes a utensil, then the utensil comes from the art of the workman and not originally from the nature of man. And when a workman carves a piece of wood and makes a utensil, then the utensil comes from the art of the workman and not originally from the nature of man. The sages accumulated thought and deliberation and practiced art and purposefulness,[133] in order to produce propriety and justice and set forth laws and standards. Hence, propriety, justice, laws, and standards come from the art of the sages and not originally from man's nature."[134]

Propriety and justice, then, are not a product of nature, but of "art" (*wei*). Xunzi gives precise definitions of this key term of his moral philosophy:

> What cannot be learned and cannot be worked for, and is in man, should be called "nature" (*xing*). What one can be capable of by learning, and what can be achieved by working for, should be called "art(ificial)" (*wei*).[135]

> When the heart conceives a thought, and one is able to put this thought into action accordingly—this should be called "art" (*wei*). What is achieved after one has accumulated deliberation upon it, and has been able to train oneself in it—this should be called "art" (*wei*).[136]

"Art" is a result of the accumulation (*ji*) of deliberation (*lü*) and practice or training (*xi*). With regard to its relation to morality and nature, a number of questions arise to which Xunzi, in the final analysis, does not give a satisfactory answer. First of all, we can ask what is the function of the material with which "art" works, and which determines its possibilities as well as limitations. Pottery or carving (already used as a metaphor by Gaozi) can only produce a utensil if the artisan uses materials with corresponding qualities. "There is nothing in the world," Huang Baijia objects, "which could be enforced without the material base."[137] Xunzi, in his answer to the questioner, completely ignores this aspect of art. He only refers to three of the four dimensions of the analogies of pottery and carving—human nature, art, nature of the material, product—leaving out the relation of the material to the final product. If he confronted this relation, he would, by the very logic of the analogy, find himself compelled to admit that, just as a tile consists of clay, morality "consists" of human nature. As Hu Yuan says:

> Why does Xunzi not say, the potter produces a tile on the basis of clay, the workman produces a utensil on the basis of wood, and the sages produce propriety and justice on the basis of man? And why does he insist on speaking of "art"?[138]

It is exactly this parallel which Xunzi does not want to draw, though we read in his writing *On Propriety (Li lun)*:

> Nature *(xing)* is the original raw material. Art *(wei)* is the abundant richness of cultivated patterns. Without nature, there would be nothing for art to build upon. But of itself, without art, nature cannot become beautiful. Only if nature and art unite can one acquire the name of a sage and the merit of unifying the world.[139]

It seems that here exactly the connection is established which Xunzi tried to bypass: the connection between human nature as the raw material, and morality, which could not come into existence without this material basis. But strictly speaking, there is no such continuity here. Xunzi is more likely thinking of a form of engraftation, since moral action needs a living, physical bearer, rather than of the stimulation of intrinsic dormant potentials of nature.[140] And even when he speaks of "adorning" *(shi)* nature and "bending it straight" *(jiao)*,[141] what he has in mind is not a change in essence, but an external polish. The point in question becomes plainer from his formula of "transformation of nature" *(hua xing)*:

> Nature is something which I am not able to make *(wéi)*, but which can be transformed *(hua)*.[142]

> Therefore, the sages transformed *(hua)* nature and initiated art.[143]

> What we honor in Yao and Shun and the gentleman is their ability to transform *(hua)* nature and to initiate art.[144]

Hua is explicitly defined by Xunzi as an external transformation which does not affect the essence of something:

> If something becomes different by changing its appearance, but is still the same in reality, we speak of transformation *(hua)*.[145]

To "transform" or "adorn" nature hence leaves its original essence untouched. But how can such a superficial manipulation produce ethically relevant results? I suppose that Xunzi pursues a dialectical idea. Man can neither abolish the fixed rules of outer nature,[146] nor can he change the constitution of his own physis. But just as he can utilize outer nature for purposes which are alien to it,[147] he can purposefully steer his inner nature without doing violence to it. This solution is not elaborated in the *Xunzi*, but it is hinted at in the following definitions:

Nature's likes and dislikes, delight and anger, melancholy and joy should be called "emotions"(*qing*). If an emotion is so, but the heart in its stead chooses another one, this should be called "deliberation" (*lü*).[148]

Here, human nature is played off against itself. Man cannot shake off his sensual desires—he would not be a living being without them. But Xunzi's idea is obviously that the biological impulse can be redirected within the natural emotions. He therefore also speaks of "guiding the desires" (*dao yu*).[149]

Xunzi, then, would not consent that there is any continuum between nature and morals. To "transform" nature and to "adorn" it does not imply that nature itself delivers the "material" for the good. The point is to keep it in check by craft without harming it; the true source of morals, however, is exclusively art and deliberation itself. A similar discontinuity is maintained by the Daoists who surely influenced Xunzi. The main focus of Daoist literature is on the world's disruption in the course of the process of civilization after the awakening of the calculating human "heart." The sharp split which increasingly separates man and nature is described as resulting from a perverse destruction of an ideal original state. Xunzi to a large extent endorses the Daoist description, but he reevaluates it affirmatively. This is not only true of the dichotomy of human art and nature in general, but even of the concrete examples of working clay and wood. Together with the breaking in of horses by the tamer Bo Le, the *Zhuangzi* uses these examples to illustrate the maltreatment of nature by man:

> The potter says, "I am good at handling clay! The round forms correspond exactly with the compass, and the edges with the square." The carpenter says, "I am good at handling wood! Bent wood corresponds exactly with the curve, and straight wood with the measuring line."
>
> But how could the nature of clay and wood wish to correspond with compass, square, curve, and measuring line! Yet, generation after generation has nothing but praise, saying, "Bo Le is good at handling horses! And the potter and the carpenter are good at handling clay and wood!"
>
> The fault of those who handle (govern) the world is the same.[150]

Xunzi can agree with this statement, but his evaluation is to the contrary. Whereas for the *Zhuangzi* the work of the artisan is the negative prototype of a technical model of politics, Xunzi does not hesitate to make it the positive paradigm of his genealogy of morals.

But now Xunzi has to face a new problem. If there is no direct continuity between the natural disposition and morality, and morality emerges from art alone, we can still object that human "art," on its part, must somehow belong to human nature. Again it is the fictitious skeptic who confronts Xunzi with this argument:

Propriety and justice and the accumulation of art are from human nature, and it is for this reason that the sages are able to produce them.[151]

Xunzi's opponent points out two problems. Speaking of "propriety and justice," he again claims the continuous transition from inborn nature to the product of the effort of the sages. Speaking of "accumulation of art," however, he claims a continuous transition from inborn nature to the act of producing. Xunzi's answer is as follows:

When the potter molds clay and produces a tile, is making clay into a tile the nature of the potter, then? When a workman carves wood and produces a utensil, is making wood into a utensil the nature of the workman, then? The relationship of the sage to propriety and justice is such that he produces them like the potter molds [things]. How, then, can propriety and justice and the accumulation of art be the original nature of man![152]

It is remarkable that Xunzi again evades the question as to how clay and wood relate to the products made out of them.[153] He likewise does not present a convincing answer to the problem how man can bring forth art if this faculty is not rooted in his "nature."[154] And why does "art" exactly produce morals? How can man, asks Hu Yuan, "if his nature be evil, know in the first place that the bad can be 'bent straight' and the good can be 'made'?"[155] Does the rational faculty for morality, which Xunzi obviously attributes to man, not constitute a part of his natural disposition?

Inconsistencies like these have frequently been charged against Xunzi. They have even given rise to doubts concerning the authenticity of the *Xing e*.[156] The problem in question is, on the one hand, a terminological one. Xunzi, I suppose, would not deny that man possesses a natural intellectual faculty as the foundation of art and morality.[157] But he does not want to include it under the extension of the term *xing* because *xing* for him is the inborn as the spontaneous and prereflective, as mere "natural tendency." The term *xing*, however, normally refers to the essential qualities of something, as in Mengzi's dispute with Gaozi. Xunzi violates this normal usage of language when he states that the essential quality of man is not to be found in his *xing*:

What is that by which man is a man? I say it is the fact that he knows distinctions. To desire food when hungry, to desire warmth when cold, to desire rest when toiling, to be fond of profit and to hate what is injurious—this is something which man has by birth and which is so without his having to wait for it (or: without depending on something). It is something which Yu and Jie (ideal rulers and tyrants) have in common. . . . But that by which man is a man is not his having two feet and no feathers.[158] It is the fact that he knows distinctions. Now, even though animals have fathers and sons, they do not know the love between father and son. They know female and male, but not the separation of sexes. The way of man is without exception characterized by distinctions. Of the distinctions, none is greater than the distinction of roles. Of the distinction of roles, none is greater than [that by] propriety. And of propriety, none is greater than that of the sage kings.[159]

What separates man from the animals is merely his ability to form a social organization by the standard of propriety. His essence—"that by which man is a man"—has to be distinguished, therefore, from his "nature," which rather links him to the animals. It is worth considering whether another terminology would not have been expedient here. But what is more important is to recognize Xunzi's essential point. His argumentation, although neither convincing in substance nor in terminology, explains itself by a serious strategic goal: he aims at the complete dichotomy of the natural, which for him is compulsive and blind as such, and the specifically human, which is the considerate, rational, and moral. Why this sharp distinction? Does Xunzi pursue an apology of rule, which becomes all the more important the deeper the gap between nature and morality opens?

It is out of the question that Xunzi's ethics has a considerable authoritarian component, as is already indicated by the technical metaphors of the forging of morals. The most striking of these metaphors is the straightening board (*yingua*) which bends crooked wood into shape just as man has to be made "straight" by morals. The Legalists, too, think in technical terms, and their main representatives Han Fei and Li Si are Xunzi's disciples. Xunzi has often been charged with having betrayed the spirit of Confucianism to Legalism. Han Fei, of course, also takes over Xunzi's theory of the evil nature, since it provides a welcome argument for the necessity of strong institutions. And Xunzi himself seems to use his negative anthropology as a means of justifying political rule:

Suppose that the nature of man in fact intrinsically [represented] the right norms and peaceful order—then what use are the sage kings and propriety and justice?[160]

If nature is good, we can dispense with the sage kings and put an end to propriety and justice. But if nature is evil, then we must go along with the sage kings and honor propriety and justice. Therefore, that the straightening board was made is because of the crooked wood. That measuring line and ink arose is because of the unstraight. And that rulers and superiors were established and propriety and justice were elucidated is because nature is evil. From this it is evident that man's nature is evil and that the good in him is artificial.[161]

It seems that Xunzi justifies his theory of the badness of human nature by the necessity of the institutions,[162] thus committing a classic *petitio principii*. In fact, the criticism of Mengzi's teaching that human nature is good has later been brought down to the level of a logic of *raison d'état* by Dong Zhongshu:

> If one says that nature *(xing)* is already good, is this not nearly equivalent to abandoning education? And to follow one's nature *(ziran* = that which is so by itself) is moreover not in accordance with the principle of government.[163]

Yet, although Dong Zhongshu undoubtedly is influenced by Xunzi, such a blunt instrumentalization of moral theory for the interests of political power is not intended by Xunzi himself. I suppose that Xunzi's idea is this. He does not want to say: because the state *must* exist, human nature is evil, but: the fact that the state *does* exist shows that human nature must be evil. His argument is not dogmatic, therefore, but empirical and logical. For him, the very existence of historically grown institutions speaks for the assumption that there must also be a good reason for them. This is consistent with the Confucian conviction that tradition contains reason, and that history, in spite of the present crisis, cannot have been a failure altogether. This conviction not only separates Confucianism from Daoism, but also from Legalism which focuses on the present and is hostile to tradition.

However, that some sort of reason has materialized in history, for Confucius no longer implied that one could trustfully rely on the established ethical life. He instead supplemented the latter by inner morality. This internalization of morals reached its climax in Mengzi. Xunzi partly rescinds it, but he does not, in its stead, simply restore the authority of the traditional institutions and norms. Their mere existence for him is an argument against Mengzi. Yet, Mengzi's nativism is not to be abolished in favor of a merely political or traditional legitimation of morals and institutions. If this were the case, we could never understand Xunzi's determined pleading for autonomous judgment and action.[164] His point, then, is the opposite one: Tradition is reasonable, since, on its part, it is the outcome of *rational efforts* of man. These efforts are first of all those of the ingenious sages and cultural heroes of the past, the *shengren*. But the *shengren* themselves are nothing but the historical embodiment of a general reason peculiar to man as such. From the time of birth, Xunzi stresses, all men without exception are nothing but "mean persons" *(xiaoren)* with the same desires and propensities, and to adhere to the opposite opinion just springs from the resentfulness of those who do not develop their faculties.[165] But anyone who strives earnestly can become a sage:

> Let a man in the street submit himself to method and study, concentrate his mind and focus his will, deliberate and make detailed investigations, day by day over a long period of time, accumulating goodness without stop—then he will gain access to the most wonderful enlightenment and will equal heaven and earth. A sage, therefore, is something which man arrives at through accumulation.[166]

Xunzi, then, is not so much interested in extoling the powers which ensure order, but in the very human reason which they represent. Reason, not history, is his true concern. Not only in phylo-, but also in ontogenesis, not only with regard to the sages, but also with regard to every single person is the emergence of morals the result of intellectual effort. The engagement of the early heroes which gave rise to culture is, at the same time, a metaphor for the constant endeavor to work patiently on oneself. However, whereas the sages had to rely on their own creativity, the later generations, thanks to the cultural tradition once initiated, can dispose of the help of the institutions, especially the institution of the teacher. Institutionalized reason, then, is held in high regard by Xunzi, but contrary to the Legalists it does not make itself independent. Law, to give an example, has no standing by itself, but must be rooted in moral authority:

> There are men who achieve order, not laws which achieve order. . . .
> Law cannot stand by itself. . . . Law is the starting point of order, but
> the gentleman is the source of law.[167]

As many other passages in the *Xunzi* show,[168] institutions are nothing sacred, and they stay open to criticism in the name of the very reason to which they owe their existence. Also, the authority enjoyed by the teacher is not an unconditional one, since that which he imparts must be rationally acceptable. Xunzi says in a formulation which brings to mind Aristotle's famous dictum that he loves his teacher, but that he loves truth more:[169]

> He who criticizes me and *is right* is my teacher. And he who agrees
> with me and is right is my friend. But he who flatters me is my
> malefactor.[170]

Reason, then, is the true pivot of Xunzi's philosophy, the very reason the exact role of which remained unclear in Mengzi's concept of moral nature. That Xunzi sharply distinguishes reason from nature, however, is more due to his opposition to Daoism than to his criticism of Mengzi. For, the Daoists demonstrate the implications of a normative concept of nature in a much more pure and radical fashion than the comparatively harmless Confucian Mengzi. If nature is "good," why read the Confucian catalogue of virtues into it in the first place? Is it not more consistent to ascribe to nature, as the Daoists do, a moral quality *prior* to all positive moral norms and culture and *against* both? Xunzi, therefore, chooses the opposite strategy as Mengzi to cope with the intrinsically Daoist theme of nature. The solution is not to endorse the Daoist claim that nature is good and give "good" a different interpretation. The solution is this. Nature does not provide any normative foundation at all upon which ethics could be built. To make nature a norm not only destroys morals. It is treason to man himself, who is thrown back into the animal kingdom where he, contrary to the assertions of the Daoist utopia, cannot survive. Man's inborn nature is not only "evil" because of its insatiability, but it is also deficient for the reason that it does not equal that of an animal. In contrast to animals, men would sink in misery if they achieved no social agreement.[171] This agreement, together with its most important vice, morals, is necessary in order to compensate the insufficiencies of the natural constitution of man, which is "bad" also[172] with regard to the imbalance and disarrangement of its desires and faculties. It is this deficiency of his "nature" which condemns man to culture. The sages and the "early kings" personify this historical insight which made the survival of the human race possible. By their invention of propriety and justice, they drew the conclusion from the chaos of the original position:

> From where does propriety arise? I say: By birth man has desires. If he desires something and does not get it, then he cannot but seek for it. If he seeks for it without knowing measures and limits, quarrel will be inevitable. Quarrel leads into chaos, and chaos into misery. The early kings hated this chaos. They therefore established propriety and justice, in order to set up a division [of roles between men], meet their desires, and supply their demand. They saw to it that desires were not restrained by [the scarcity of] things, and things were not used up by desires, but that both could grow, supporting one another.[173]

The view of man as a deficient being which is unfinished by nature and has to adopt his ability to survive by careful education and organization is surely a main aspect of Xunzi's theory that human nature is evil. And it is only against the background of this motif of *natura noverca* (also to be found in Greek literature)[174] that Xunzi's following remarks, which prima facie sound counterintuitive, make sense at least to some extent. Xunzi maintains that exactly man's endeavor to be good shows that he is evil:

> In general, the reason that man wants to be good is that his nature is evil. Thin wants to be thick, ugly wants to be beautiful, narrow wants to be broad, poor wants to be rich, low wants to be high. For if one does not have it within oneself, one will inevitably seek it outside. Therefore, when, being rich, one does not long for wealth, and, being in high position, does not long for power, this is because one does not seek outside what one has within. From this we can see that man's desire to be good is because his nature is evil. Now, since man's nature is originally without propriety and justice, he forces himself to study and seeks to possess them. And since his nature does not know propriety and justice, he thinks and deliberates and seeks to know them.[175]

In claiming that "poor wants to be rich" and "low wants to be high" Xunzi forgets the ethos of the nonconformists of his age. Nevertheless, for the sake of argument, we may take his assertion for granted for a while in view of his concept of human nature. The same concept of nature, however, forbids us to say that he who is rich and in high position will not strive for still more wealth and power. Xunzi's statement not only contradicts all experience, but also his own teaching about the insatiability of the human desires. He must, furthermore, explain why the alleged fact that "man wants to be good" does not exactly speak in favor of a good innate propensity. As Hu Yuan and Huang Baijia write, alluding to Mengzi's "four beginnings":

> That man wants to be good is because his goodness does not yet suffice, and he has the disposition to be capable of developing it to the full, and the quality to do this.[176]

> I do not understand how one should have the heart of wishing to be good if nature were really evil. To have this heart already suffices to prove that man's heart is good.[177]

Even more important than these non sequiturs is the category mistake which Xunzi commits. He uses glaring naturalistic analogies which, in view of his general position, he had to dismiss from ethical argumentation. In doing so, he confounds two aspects of the concepts "good" and "bad" (or "evil"): the good (and mutatis mutandis the bad) can be the good in terms of morality as well as in terms of the beneficial and pleasant. Only the good in terms of the pleasant is aspired after like wealth and power—the latter are identical with it in this case. From here to pass on to the morally good revokes the separation of the two realms of morality and desires which Xunzi himself has drawn.

Xunzi's ethics appears essentially utilitarian here. Is this a slip, or is there method in it? To view the bad as the unpleasant fits in with his argument that social morality is a necessary compensation for the imperfect biological equipment of man. Is Xunzi an ethical utilitarian, then?[178] If this were the case, the whole dualism of norms and nature which he has vehemently—though inconsistently—defended would collapse. For, the criterion of goodness would be the satisfaction of the same anarchic desires which Xunzi wants to banish from the realm of morals.

Perhaps we can distinguish here between social and individual ethics in Xunzi. His social ethics, which concerns the orderly living together of men, is indeed utilitarian. We have already seen that Xunzi's legitimation of the state is based on social-utilitarian considerations. The state, for him, is a product of rational human insight for the benefit of all. Reason, however, which has invented the state together with its hierarchical structure as the only expedient and efficacious form of human organization, and which afterwards helps us to understand its meaning and importance, is by itself more than a mere calculus of profit. Contrary to the desires which constitute the nature of man, reason is not bound to self-interest. The "heart," Xunzi states, is absolutely free in its decision. It decides autonomously on right and wrong, and can, as the "ruler of the body," also command over the sensuous nature.[179] His heart, his free reason, allows man to take individual decisions which run counter to his material self-interest, and that is, to any private benefit. The heart normally will choose a life in accordance with the social rules and role prescriptions. But it can also decide, for reasons of principle, to reject service to the parents or to the ruler. It can advise the gentleman to prefer "highest courage" to modest adaptation, and to "stand proudly and independently between heaven and earth without fear." And it can even let him choose "death for the sake of justice."[180]

Xunzi does not tell us, however, from where the "heart," rising far above nature, takes this readiness for a moral upright walk. It is left unresolved why human reason can be moral for other than utilitarian grounds. We can only presume that, in the final analysis, it is fueled by self-respect.[181] It is, likewise, left open why human reason does not aspire to evil. Xunzi would probably answer that in this case, the heart behaves like the slave of the senses and falls back under the yoke of nature. As a matter of fact, he uses the term *xin* in an ambiguous way which reflects this difficulty quite precisely.[182]

In view of his concept of an autonomous human reason capable of morality, it is unjustified to blame Xunzi for the decay of Zhou Confucianism, as was done by many modern Chinese intellectuals who saw Confucius as a democrat and reformer, and Xunzi as an agent of authoritarianism.[183] Such a verdict is all too generous in the case of Confucius and all too rash in the case of Xunzi. None of the early Confucians wanted to be reformers in the sense of innovators, and it was Xunzi who stood closest to the real reformers of the epoch, the Legalists. A democrat, too, can hardly be found among the early Confucians. They sharply criticize the despotism of their time, but it is not their primary concern to advocate, or promote, the participation of the citizens in political affairs or to insist on a free public realm as a forum of general discussion. Among the Zhou Confucians, Xunzi is certainly the most elitist one, a fact which is in full accord with his rationalistic grounding of morality. If a moral attitude presupposes rational insight, a curb has to be put on the "stupid majority"[184] (*yu zhong*). The scholarly elite, however, may claim for itself influence and independence. Nevertheless, the same grounding of morality implies that there is no natural barrier between both social segments. Whether to become a "gentleman" or stay a "mean man" is in the hands of every single human being, who within his "nature" carries the germ of evil, but within his reason possesses the germ of goodness. The postconventional spirit of ancient Confucianism is not yet betrayed. Its real decline falls within the Han dynasty. It is the reverse side of the rise of Confucianism to state orthodoxy.

D. COSMOLOGY

In some texts of Zhou Confucianism, we find a mixture of ethics and cosmology which is often regarded as the Confucian variety as such of grounding morality. The topic has far-reaching implications, since cosmological, holistic reasoning often counts as an indication that a breakthrough towards enlightened thought has not taken place. For Weber, to give an example, cosmology and adaptation are the two sides of a coin:

> Confucianism meant adjustment to the world, to its orders and conventions. Ultimately it represented just a tremendous code of political maxims and rules of social propriety for cultured men of the world. . . . The cosmic orders of the world were considered fixed and inviolate and the orders of society were but a special case it this. . . . The "happy" tranquility of the empire and the equilibrium of the soul should and could be attained if man fitted himself into the internally harmonious cosmos.[185]

Similar accounts can be found in Granet and Gernet.[186] Trauzettel, too, has argued that Confucian ethics is "cosmologically grounded," and according to Weber-Schäfer, "the Chinese speculation on the order of man and world has never made the radical step of a complete break with the compact truth of cosmological symbolism."[187] Eisenstadt, finally, maintains that cosmology is the means to cope with the "tension between the transcendental and the mundane order," which he, contrary to Weber, assigns to China. I would like to dwell on this idea of a unity of transcendence and cosmology for a moment, since it appears to be a variant of the Weberian picture of China going beyond Weber himself. Eisenstadt writes:

> In the classical Chinese belief systems this tension between the transcendental and mundane order was couched in relatively secular terms. . . . This secular definition of such tension and the rationalizing tendencies it involved became here connected with a tendency to an almost this-worldly conception of the resolution of such tension. The thrust of the official Confucian civilizational orientations was that the resolution of this tension was attained through the cultivation of the social, political, and cultural orders, as the major way of maintaining the cosmic harmony. Thus it focused around the elaboration of what Herbert Fingarette has defined as the cultivation of the "secular as sacred" and of "The Human Community as a Holy Rite." . . . Thus the Chinese this-worldly orientation—the Confucian-legal one—did stress the proper performance of worldly duties and activities within the existing social frameworks—the family, broader kin groups, and Imperial service—as the ultimate criterion of the resolution of the tension between the transcendental and the mundane order and of individual responsibility.[188]

This theory does not deliver what the term "transcendence" promises. Maintenance of cosmic harmony by "proper performance of worldly duties within the existing social frameworks" merely reifies the existing order instead of also—the only point of transcendence—calling it into question.[189] Eisenstadt, who wants to correct Weber, but in reality keeps faith with him, overlooks that in axial age China precisely the "proper performance of worldly duties" was in crisis. To what extent he misunderstands the intellectual climate of the epoch becomes apparent, above all, from his appeal to Fingarette. Fingarette's "sacredness of the secular," after all, characterizes a thoroughly affirmative attitude to the given world free of tension and transcendence. Weber's analysis is not in the least affected, since he is one of the authors of the widespread opinion that the Chinese legitimation of political order is based on the maintenance of cosmic harmony. The topic of "tension" loses any significance unless it is related to the topic of the *division* of the world, the separation of cosmos and society.[190]

Similar to Eisenstadt, Huston Smith has located the Chinese concept of "transcendence" in an "organic system of interdependent parts." However, if the "social norms (*li*)" are "sanctioned by the cosmos," and "society, nature, and cosmos combine to function like a beautifully synchronized machine,"[191] the concept of transcendence becomes pointless again. Smith refers to Tang Junyi, pointing out the primary source of this kind of cosmologism: The idea that the world is a holistic whole within which there is no human realm of its own is a typical Neo-Confucian stereotype.[192] The paradigm is clearly one of world immanence. It is quite difficult to construe why the modern Confucians insist on "transcendence" for their philosophy, as long as they stick to their holistic ethical cosmology. The alleged melting of immanence and transcendence appears to be little more than empty verbiage.[193]

The Neo-Confucian approach can merely bar our access to the ancients. True, evidence can be quoted for a connection of ethics and cosmology in Zhou Confucianism. But we have to distinguish between the different texts, and have to examine the exact status of cosmological arguments if these are given. In the *Lunyu*, to begin with, a cosmological foundation of ethics cannot be proven. Hall and Ames, who hold the reverse opinion, must impute an "implicit cosmology" and "tacit intuitions" to Confucius.[194] The presence of a cosmological worldview, however, cannot simply be inferred from alleged background assumptions generally shared by the ancient Chinese. Zichan, after all, who was repeatedly praised by Confucius, already in the sixth century B.C. separated the world of man from the movements of Heaven, thus expressing a conviction which had gained ground since the eighth century.[195] Although Zichan was not quite consistent in this respect,[196] we can, for the successive period, no longer take the existence of cosmologism for granted.

It is even more questionable to deduce a cosmological worldview from the etymology and usage of the character *ren*, humaneness, which is composed of "man" and "two." As Weber-Schäfer argues in his discussion of Confucius, *ren* expresses a "cosmologically bound anthropology." In *ren*, he maintains, man does not become man "by virtue of his own power as an individual" through "participation in the *nous* or incarnation of *pneum*a," but only through the "fellow man" or the "second one." Man continues to be "embedded into the ritual order of a cosmological society."[197] There is a non sequitur in this argumentation. The idea that becoming a human being is a social process presupposing the "other" does not imply any holistic assumption of the kind in question. What Weber-Schäfer, because of his Platonism, regards as a deficiency of mythical thinking, is even remarkable from the viewpoint of a developmental logic of morals based on the unfolding of reciprocity.[198]

The representation of Confucius as a cosmological thinker normally refers to the Confucius of the *Zhongyong*, rather than to the Confucius of the *Lunyu*. In the *Zhongyong*, we find the concept of the "sincere" (*cheng*) which, indeed, bridges morals and the cosmos and brings a cosmological dimension into ethics. The "sincere" is the ontological principle of all development, the "beginning and end of things,"[199] an idea which probably relates to the reliable constancy of the process of nature. Transferred to man, the "sincere" denotes the ability to foresee calamity and happiness, and to "hit what is right without effort and apprehend without thinking."[200] Strictly speaking, *cheng* is no ethical concept in its specific, but refers to a comprehensive highest state of being. The "sincere" is the "way of heaven" only accomplished by the sage; to "make oneself sincere" is the "way of man" who does not yet spontaneously hit what is right and still must "choose the good."[201]

In the *Zhongyong*, "harmony" and "mean," which "heaven and earth find their hold in,"[202] have an ontological dimension similar to that of the "sincere." There is no definite answer to the question as to why the *Zhongyong* incorporates an ontological speculation into ethics. One of the reasons might be to avoid a mere traditional foundation of morality, which is generally regarded as unsatisfactory. Moreover, *cheng* reads like a Confucian answer to the Daoist *Dao*. Nevertheless, it remains unclear whether the *Zhongyong* really aims at ontologizing moral categories in a strict sense, or merely exalts them rhetorically by ontological metaphors.

The same question can be put to other texts transmitted by the *Liji* and the *Dadai Liji*. Thus we read in the *Yueji* that music and propriety came into existence after the model of heaven and earth, yet as a product of the sages.[203] Obviously, the cosmos merely serves as a paragon for human action here. The same applies to the following passage:

> Zixia said, "The virtue of the three kings (Yu, Tang, and Wu) equaled heaven and earth. I dare to ask of what nature virtue must be that it can be said to equal heaven and earth." Confucius said, "[The three kings] reverently received the three impartialities in order to encourage the world." Zixia said, "I dare to ask what is called the three impartialities." Confucius said, "Heaven covers all without impartiality, earth bears up all without impartiality, sun and moon shine on all without impartiality. They reverently received these three in order to encourage the world. This is called the three impartialities."[204]

According to the *Yueji*, the social hierarchies, too, are framed after the model of the cosmos and its hierarchical structures, in particular the supremacy of heaven over earth.[205] We can interpret these and a number of similar arguments as allegorical. In the following eulogy of the *Dadai Liji* on propriety, however, morals evidently becomes the cosmic process itself:

> [By propriety] heaven and earth unite, the four seas are in harmony, sun and moon shine, the stars revolve, the Jiang and the He flow, the myriad things flourish. . . .[206]

Now the cosmos no longer delivers the patterns according to which the human world should be organized. The rules of order of the human world have, reversely, turned into the innermost driving force of nature. Does this represent a substantial cosmology or a rhetorical extolment of Confucian morality? What speaks against the cosmological reading is the fact that the quoted passage in nearly identical wording also appears in the *Xunzi*.[207] Xunzi, however, is an unequivocal proof that we cannot simply deduce ontology from terminology, though this is persistently ignored by the defendants of the cosmology thesis. For, the same author who celebrates propriety as the force keeping heaven and earth in motion, describes it only a few pages earlier with profane arguments as an invention of the early sages. Since Xunzi, moreover, in his writing *On Heaven* (*Tianlun*) develops a thoroughly materialistic view of nature,[208] we can conclude that the cosmological diction is rhetoric and serves the grounding, rather than the exaltation of Confucian ethics.[209]

However, we can not yet conclude the topic of the cosmological foundation of morals. It gets its real significance in post–axial age Confucianism, namely in Dong Zhongshu who merges Confucian ethics into older cosmological speculations of the *yinyang-wuxing* school.[210] Of serious consequences is, in particular, the incorporation of *yin* and *yang* into moral philosophy. Ruler, father, and husband, according to Dong Zhongshu, are *yang*, whereas subject, son, and wife are *yin*. Yang and *yin* cannot exist without each other, but, nevertheless, stand in a hierarchical relation. *Yin* is a mere appendage of *Yang*. As Dong Zhongshu says:

> All things must have a counterpart. . . . *Yin* is the counterpart of *yang*, the wife is the counterpart of the husband, the son is the counterpart of the father, the subject is the counterpart of the ruler. There is nothing which would be without a counterpart, and both parts relate to one another as *yin* and *yang*.
>
> *Yang* is coexistent with *yin*, and *yin* is coexistent with *yang*. The husband is coexistent with the wife, and the wife is coexistent with the husband. The father is coexistent with the son, and the son is coexistent with the father. The ruler is coexistent with the subject, and the subject is coexistent with the ruler. The just relation of order between ruler and subject, father and son, husband and wife stems without exception from the principle of *yin* and *yang*.

The ruler is *yang*, and the subject is *yin*. The father is *yang*, and the son is *yin*. The husband is *yang*, and the wife is *yin*. *On the path of the yin, there is no autonomous action (du xing).* At the beginning of the path, [the *yin*] must not rise alone, at its end, it must not have the merits for itself.[211]

Although there is hardly any idea in Dong Zhongshu which cannot be traced back into the conventional ethics of the Zhou era, his special arrangement is of a new quality. Subordination and inequality are, once and for all, ontologically reified. That every member of society should fulfill the duties of his and her social station was also advocated by the early Confucians. But they set up correctives in order to prevent blind compliance. The most conspicuous expression of their conviction that mere adjustment to the social role is no warrant of a moral life was their concept of "independent action" (*du xing*) not bound to any status. Dong Zhongshu renounces this conviction in that he grants independence only to those who are in command anyway. It is replaced by another regulative stemming from the same realm from where Dong Zhongshu borrows his arguments for the sealing off of the given authority structures: from cosmology. By *yin* and *yang*, human action is directly linked to the movement of the macrocosm. If the ruler behaves improperly, nature will answer with odd portents and, finally, catastrophes which "have their root in the failure of the state."[212]

It cannot be denied, therefore, that in Dong's Confucianism there is still an effective check upon political rule. But he not only reduces ethics to the mechanism of reward and punishment, he also discards the rational view of nature which Zhou philosophy had developed and Xunzi had brought to completion. Nature, for Xunzi a sphere with its own invariant rules (*chang*) and not linked with man by any sympathetic ties, becomes the arena of cosmic judgment. It supplants the "self" before which the Zhou Confucian had to justify his actions. Thus Confucianism pays for its rise to state orthodoxy tailored to the superstition of the powerful with a double regression:[213] Ethically as well as cognitively it falls back on a level which the axial age philosophers had once overcome.

14

The Non-Confucian Schools

Z *huangzi* and *Xunzi* speak of "one hundred schools" competing with each other in the last century of the Zhou era. Their competition counts as a symbol of decay of a world where "the art of the *Dao* comes to be torn apart," and "*Dao* and *de* (primordial virtue) are no longer one."[1] China's political polycentrism produced an extraordinary variety of opinions never found again in later times. The most conspicuous signature of the postconventional breakthrough of the axial age with its dissolution of all certainties is the pluralism of many novel systems of thought. Each of them should be taken into account for a reconstruction of axial age ethics. It is only in the light of diversity and competition that the reflexivity of the respective ideas becomes apparent, and often their essential point is only brought out by the polemic of their opponents.

For understanding Confucian ethics, too, it is indispensable to know the opinions of its competitors. It develops in a constant interaction with their ideas. Moreover, the ethical legacy of the axial age does not solely consist in the Confucian teaching. The various schools think through different models to determine man's position in the world. They furthermore disclose the deficiencies of Confucianism and have never lost their importance as correctives and alternative options, although they were not elevated to the rank of China's official self-understanding.

All of the different schools sprouting in axial age China would hence deserve to be discussed here—the "school of the tillers" (*nongjia*), whose intellectual adherents recommend a plebeian life, the "school of the strategists" (*zonghengjia*), which conceives of political action in terms of deritualized strategical rationality, or the "school of names" (*mingjia*) with its metaethical reflections, to mention only some of them. In the following chapter, I will only focus on the teachings of Mo Di, Yang Zhu, the Daoists, and the Legalists, which constitute the four most important challenges to Confucianism and are representative of some paradigmatic differences in Zhou ethical reasoning.

233

A. MO DI'S UTILITARIANISM

The first great attack on Confucius' ethics is launched by Mo Di (Mozi, Zimozi, c. 480–397 B.C.), the founder of the Mohist school. In his writing *Against the Confucians (Fei Ru)*, he brings forward a number of reproaches. The Confucians, he says, advocate an exaggerated and costly ceremonial, above all for funerals, they believe in fate, indulge in laziness, idolize the past, are disloyal to the rulers, and instigate rebellion. These rather odd charges remarkably enough do not touch upon what Mengzi later highlights as the core of the debate between Confucianism and Mohism—the role of the family, and the motif of utility. Mo Di incidentally remarks that the Confucians "make a difference between relatives and strangers."[2] But in the following, he does not treat this as an ethical problem of fundamental relevance and only speaks about funeral rites. Yet, the opposite reproach, namely, not to acknowledge the family, stands in the center of Mengzi's polemic against Mo Di. Mo Di's principle of "co-love" *(jian ai)*, Mengzi maintains, denies the role of the father. Rejecting the statement of the Mohist Yizhi that "love has no distinctions or degrees," he defends the special status of the family.[3]

As to Mo Di, he neither calls into question the authority structures within the family nor those within the state. Filial piety, for him, is no less important than political loyalty. What he rejects is the idea that one's own family or state should take precedence over the families and states of others. He identifies particularism as the root of all evil of his time and wants to replace it by the reverse principle: to grant to other social units just what one grants to one's own. From the beginning, Mo Di advocates an ethics of absolute reciprocity, which is not confronted with Mengzi's problem how family morals can be "extended" in order to prevent particularism. As he writes,

> It is the occupation of the humane person to strive for increasing the benefit of the world and eliminating its calamities. Now, among all the calamities of today, which is the greatest one? That the large states attack the small ones, that the large clans cause disturbances in the small ones, that the strong rob the weak, that the majority tyrannizes the minority, that the cunning plot against the stupid, that the noble disdain the humble, this is the calamity of the world. And it is moreover a calamity to the world that rulers lack grace, subjects lack loyalty, fathers lack kindness, and sons lack filial piety. And it is moreover a calamity to the world that one man degrades the other, and that they harm each other with weapons, poison, water, and fire.
>
> Let us try to fathom the source of these calamities—from where have they arisen? Have they arisen from loving others and benefiting them? Certainly we will at once say no, and will say that they have arisen from hating others and injuring them. If we classify [these attitudes] by different names, shall we find hating others or injuring them pertaining to inclusion *(jian)* or to exclusion *(bie)*? Certainly

we will at once say they belong to exclusion. Is not this mutually excluding each other, then, really the source of the greatest calamity to the world? Therefore, exclusion should be rejected. . . . Zimozi says, *exclusion must be replaced by inclusion.* But why can inclusion replace exclusion? Now, when one stands up for the state of others as one stands up for one's own state, who alone would mobilize his own state in order to attack that of others? One would stand up for others as one stands up for oneself. When one stands up for the capital of others as one stands up for one's own capital, who alone would mobilize his own capital in order to attack that of others? One would stand up for others as one stands up for oneself. When one stands up for the clan of others as one stands up for one's own clan, who alone would mobilize his own clan in order to attack that of others? One would stand up for others as one stands up for oneself. Now, when the states and capitals do not attack each other, and when the clans do not disturb and harm each other, is this a calamity to the world or a benefit? Certainly we will at once say, it is a benefit.[4]

Humaneness, then, the concept from where Mo Di started, means not to harm others, whoever they might be, but to benefit them as one benefits oneself. Mo Di draws radical consequences from the abstraction of the "other." The point of orientation of a humane person is the "world" (*tianxia*), just as the point of orientation of a filial son is the family:

A humane person plans for the world in the same way as a filial son plans for his family.[5]

Notwithstanding his opposition to the Confucians, Mo Di's concern brings Confucius into mind. The total equality of the "other" (*bi*) and the "self" (*ji*), as well as the principle of "inclusion" (*jian*), read like uncompromising conclusions from the Golden Rule of the *Lunyu* and as a radical unfolding of its universalistic potential. Whatever objections I will raise against Mo Di in the following, he deserves a place of honor in the history of ethical universalism. His position becomes problematic, however, as soon as he tries to find a rational foundation for it.

A moral attitude, for Mo Di, is not the result of a careful cultivation of the person, the development of innate propensities, or the gradual extension of family love. It is rooted in a single rational idea of immediate plausibility: the idea that to be moral is *beneficial.* To be humane and just—the later Mohists directly identify justice and utility[6]—not only increases the benefit of others, but also pays off for oneself. To be immoral, however, will lead to the ruin of all. Mo Di writes:

He who loves others, will, thereby, surely also be loved by them. He who benefits others, will, thereby, surely also be benefited by them. He who hates others, will, thereby, surely also be hated by them. He who injures others, will, thereby, surely also be injured by them. What is so difficult about that?[7]

Mo Di's principle of reciprocity, the positive side of which he calls "exchange of mutual benefit" (*jiao xiang li*) or "co-love" (*jian ai*), is ingenuously built on self-interest. Unlike Confucius' maxim *shu*, it is not understood in terms of moral duty irrespective of personal reward, but recommended as a profitable strategy. Yet, Mo Di does not advocate egoism. On the contrary, he is known for his exemplary altruism and is always ready to do his utmost for the world, "bareheaded and on foot," as Mengzi certifies.[8] But although Mo Di in practice is on the side of unselfish behavior, he builds his case on the quoted strategical reading of the Golden Rule with an extramoral justification of right action when it comes to ground morality in theory. This leads Mo Di into a tragic paradox.[9]

Although Mo Di's hint at the utility of a moral attitude is "well meant"—he wants to put an end to military aggression, oppression, and tyranny—it is counter-productive in the end. For, if it is utility which entices us to be moral, why not wait for the chance to secure it for myself directly and to the disadvantage of the other instead of in cooperation with him? And who can guarantee that the other will really stick to the exchange of benefit and does not likewise harbor the hidden reservation to gain an advantage for himself if the occasion arises? To put the criterion of utility first, Mengzi says, would surrender any norm to arbitrariness and entail "not being satisfied before one has not snatched all."[10] The Daoists, too, call attention to this fundamental aporia of the principle of utility, pointing out that in the final analysis it will only be to the advantage of the most reckless.[11] The *Guanzi* and the *Shangjunshu* formulate the crux of utilitarian reciprocity from a point of view which is itself strategical:

The ruler must not listen to the teaching of humaneness! . . . That I am able not to attack others can be granted. But I am not able to cause others not to attack me.[12]

The humane person may be humane towards others, but he cannot cause others to be humane, too. The just man may show love for others, but he cannot cause others to love, too. From this I know that humaneness and justice do not suffice to govern the world.[13]

The Legalists distrust the stability of an ethics of reciprocity, and instead exclusively rely on the power of institutions. In doing so, they can, paradoxically, refer to Mo Di. For, Mo Di himself implicitly questions the solidity of his principle of utility, when he finds it suitable to back it by additional arguments which reveal its inherent weakness. He first of all restores religion and claims for his ethics the authority of Heaven, which was hardly appealed to by Confucius:

What does Heaven want, and what does Heaven hate? Zimozi says, Heaven's will is such that it does not want that the large states attack the small states, that the great clans cause disturbances in the small clans, that the strong tyrannize the minority, that the cunning plot against the stupid, that the noble disdain the humble. These are what Heaven does not want. But this is not all. Heaven wants that those who have the energy work for each other, that those who know a good method teach each other, that those who have wealth share with each other. And furthermore it wishes that the superiors diligently attend to government and the subjects diligently attend to their work.[14]

Heaven gives emphasis to its will by punishment and reward. To follow Heaven, then, recommends itself for considerations of expediency. "When I do what Heaven wishes, then Heaven, too, will do what I wish," Mo Di affirms. "But if one does not do what Heaven wishes, but does what Heaven does not wish, then Heaven will not do what one wishes either, but will do what one does not wish."[15] Thus, the moral person earns "happiness and emolument," and the evildoer must reckon with "disease and misfortune."[16] This assertion obviously seemed all too ingenuous even to Mo Di's contemporaries. When getting ill, he is asked ironically why the illness strikes him, the sage.[17] Yet, his argument is a consequence of his naive and frank tackling of the idea of utility, which he has discovered as a central theme of ethics.

The same function as Heaven, namely, to bring human self-interest on the right path by reward and punishment, is ascribed to spirits and ghosts. Mo Di writes:

If all the people in the world could be made to believe that ghosts and spirits are able to reward the worthy and to punish the violent, how could the world be in chaos? Now those who maintain that ghosts do not exist say, "Surely there are no ghosts and spirits." From morning till evening they teach this to the world. They bewilder the majority, causing them to be mistaken about the difference which it makes whether spirits and ghosts exist or not. Hence the world is in chaos. Therefore, Zimozi says: If the kings, dukes, nobles, scholars, and gentlemen of the world really want to increase the benefit of the world and remove its calamities, then, as I see it, they must clearly examine the difference between existence and nonexistence of ghosts and spirits. . . .

How must a theory look like by which we achieve this? Zimozi says: This can be achieved by the method by which the world [generally] examines and comes to know whether something exists or not. The criterion must be what the ears and eyes of the majority really know about the existence or nonexistence of something. If it is really so that some have heard or seen something, then we have to regard it as existent. If no one has heard or seen it, then we have to regard it as nonexistent.

If this is so, why not go to a village or hamlet and ask? If from antiquity to the present, since the beginning of man, it has happened that the bodies of ghosts and spirits were seen and their voices heard, how can we say that ghosts and spirits do not exist? And how can we say they exist if none have seen or heard them?[18]

Mo Di then cites a host of reports and anecdotes which are to prove that ghosts and spirits have been seen and heard and hence exist. But finally, he slyly gives us to consider that even if there are in fact no ghosts and spirits, it would still be advisable to believe in their existence. For besides the effect of strengthening morals, the sacrifices to those ghost and spirits will be an opportunity for "having common pleasure, bringing together a lot of people, and making friends with neighbors."[19] Mo Di's defense of religion, then, is itself based on the principle of utility. The belief in ghosts to him is not necessarily sound, but it is healthy and should not be undermined by skeptics. He thus invents the topos of the destructive intellectual, which has stayed alive till our times.

Religion, for Mo Di, is useful for morals, since by its numinous aura it can strengthen the fear of punishment and the hope for reward. This does not mean to say that Mo Di's interest in religion can be reduced to this blunt practical goal. Heaven in particular sets objective and ultimate standards which overrule the social authorities, and hence is more than a means to the pragmatic end of influencing behavior.[20] The problem with Mo Di's position is, again, that when it comes to *giving reasons* why men should follow the religious standards, the argument follows the logic of benefit.

In search of additional support for moral action, Mo Di not only resorts to Heaven and the ghosts and spirits, but yet to another institutional backing: Morality becomes a duty owed to the state, and "co-love" is sanctioned by law:

> If men would practice "co-love" and exchange mutual benefit, this would be beneficial and moreover easily to achieve beyond all imagination. As I see it, this would be the case even without a ruler taking pleasure in it. But if a ruler took pleasure in it, encouraged it with rewards and commendations, and provided it with authority by punishments, then, I think, men would tend towards co-love and exchange of mutual benefit just as fire goes upwards and water flows downwards.[21]

Mo Di's utilitarianism thus ends up in the idea of an authoritarian state. This is quite consistent. Since Mo Di's principle of reciprocity is based upon the unstable foundation of self-interest, it needs a strong guarantor to supervise its observance. Here, Mo Di obviously succumbs to a temptation: If governmental control proves to be necessary, why not simply replace the horizontal reciprocity of "co-love" by a vertical principle of obedience? If morals, moreover, need an institutional safeguard, why not simply substitute the latter for them? And if "co-love," last but not least, is based on self-interest anyway, why not directly justify the state by the existence of human egoism, instead of merely making it the custodian of mutuality? Mo Di draws these conclusions in his writing *Appreciation of Conformity (Shang tong).*[22] Here, it is not the supervision of the "exchange of mutual benefit" which requires a strong state, but the termination of hostile competition between men. Mo Di describes this competition as the original position of mankind:

In ancient times, when mankind had just come into existence and there was yet no law and government, men, presumably, all were of different opinions when they spoke with each other. Thus one man had one opinion, two men had two opinions, and ten men had ten opinions. The more the number of people grew, the more grew the number of what they called their opinion. As a result, everybody approved of his own opinion in order to disapprove of the opinions of others. So they contended with each other in mutually disapproving their opinions. Therefore, resent and hate arose in the families among fathers and sons, elder and younger brothers, and they split, unable to live in harmony. All of the clans in the world caused damage to each other by water, fire, and poison. When they had surplus energy, they were unable to support one another. They would let surplus goods rot before sharing them. They kept good methods secret instead of teaching them to each other. The chaos in the world was just like among beasts.

Then it became clear that the world was in chaos because there were no government and elders. Therefore the most capable and acceptable of the world was elected and set up as Son of Heaven. After the Son of Heaven had been set up, regarding his strength as insufficient, other capable and acceptable men of the world were elected and installed as the three high ministers. After the Son of Heaven and the three high ministers had been installed, the empire was divided into many states where feudal lords and local rulers were established, because the empire was so great that it was impossible to achieve accurate knowledge of the discussions on right and wrong, benefit and harm among the people of the far states and different regions. After the feudal lords and local rulers had been established, regarding their strength as insufficient, capable and acceptable men were again chosen and installed as officials. After all officials had been installed, the Son of Heaven proclaimed his policy to the clans of the empire:

"All those who, upon hearing something good or[23] bad always report it to their superiors, who by all means and always consider right or wrong what their superiors consider right or wrong, who, when their superiors commit a fault, moderately remonstrate with them, who, when their subordinates have certain qualifications, recommend them impartially, and who conform with their superiors and do not form cliques with their subordinates—these shall be rewarded by the superiors and praised by the subordinates.

But all those who, upon hearing something good or bad, do not always report it to their superiors, who do not by all means and always consider right or wrong what their superiors consider right or wrong, who, when their superiors commit a fault, do not moderately remonstrate with them, who, when their subordinates have certain qualifications, do not recommend them impartially, and who form cliques with their subordinates and are not capable of conforming with their superiors—these shall be punished by the superiors and condemned by the people."

On this basis, the superiors made rewards and punishments. They scrutinized with greatest sharp-sightedness to make sure that their examination [of the different cases] was reliable.[24]

The proclamation of the Son of Heaven is followed by similar announcements of the village chiefs, the county elders, and the rulers of the different states. They *uni sono* demand identification with the superiors. *Mozi* 13 additionally incorporates the clan chiefs into the hierarchy, making the families an appendant of the state.

Mo Di hence advocates an authoritarian state which once and for all puts an end to the atomistic disorder of the original position by rigid vertical conformism.[25] His *Leviathan* is the archetype of the later Legalist system which likewise rests on the sparse program of reward and punishment, duty of denunciation, and the *Gleichschaltung* of the families. Yet, Mo Di's horrifying utopia,[26] projected back to the beginning of history, must not make us overlook the novel and extraordinary in his political theory and its progressive elements. In Mo Di, the state is neither a natural fact nor sanctified by a holy tradition. Like later in Xunzi, in accordance with the utilitarian idea, the state is a human invention for the sake of all. Its functionaries should not be members of a hereditary nobility—which some Zhou Confucians, like Mengzi, have not yet abandoned—but should excel by their capabilities.[27] The political elite is elected. The primary election of the emperor, which initiates the establishment of the political hierarchy, deserves special attention. It calls into mind Western contract theories, in particular that of Hobbes, which is likewise formulated in a utilitarian context.[28] This association, of course, implies that the election is done by the conflicting people. In neither version of the *Shang tong*, however, does the respective sentence contain a subject. Many commentators have argued that the subject which has to be supplied can only be "Heaven."[29] Yet although Mo Di indeed puts Heaven above the political hierarchy,[30] there is no philological evidence that it is also the subject of the primary election of the sovereign.[31] According to the usual practice of classical Chinese, it is not necessary to make a given subject explicit if its knowledge is regarded as unimportant or can be concluded from the context. From the context of the opening passages of *Mozi* 11–13, however, only the people themselves and not Heaven come into consideration for a possible subject.

This interpretation fits in with Mo Di's basic ideas. Yet, it forces us to accept some contradictions. How can the superior position of Heaven and the election of the ruler by the people be made compatible with each other? And how can people in conflict with and hostile to each other come to an agreement at all? These inconsistencies, however, reflect typical difficulties of contract theories like the one of Hobbes. They do not necessarily invalidate the assumption that there is an idea of social contract in the *Mozi*. How the agreement in question can be achieved has remained a problem of contractualism even today. It cannot be solved without implicit and, within the context of contractualism, unfounded normative presuppositions, like the supposition of "fairness" conditions in Rawls' "original position."[32] This contradiction is rather characteristic of a contract theory and, contrary to Hsiao Kung-chuan's opinion,[33] no sufficient reason to doubt the presence of such a theory in Mo Di. Instead of "fairness" conditions, Mo Di postulates a divine authority. This does not rule out the existence of contractualism, but veils the problem of the necessary normative presuppositions. It moreover answers the further question, how the *keeping* of the agreement can be secured in the first place.[34]

If we compare the theories of Mo Di and Hobbes, they not only share these characteristic aporias. Both thinkers speak of a chaotic original situation where men harm each other and where there is no generally accepted distinction of right and wrong.[35] For both thinkers, the means to put and end to these disastrous conditions is the state. It comes into existence by an agreement of the conflicting individuals—if we follow the most plausible reading of the *Shang tong*—to establish a ruler. By his coercive power, he decides on what is right and wrong, and punishes offenses.[36] Once having been achieved, there is no further legitimation to revoke the agreement and call again into question the monopoly of rule. Freedom turns into absolute authority.

To solve the problems inherent in the original situation, Hobbes makes use of human self-interest and a calculated reciprocity after the model of the strategical Golden Rule.[37] The same kind of reciprocity is proposed by Mo Di. In the *Shang tong*, too, it is most probably simply human self-interest which motivates men to enter into an agreement. Contrary to Hobbes, Mo Di does neither explicitly mention the contract nor does he speak of "natural rights" of the individual which are surrendered to the state under the condition that all others are also ready to do so.[38] Yet, in asserting his "natural rights," man for Hobbes follows "natural laws" which are in the final analysis mere rules of prudence.[39] Rules of prudence, in turn—the calculation of advantage and disadvantage—for Mo Di, too, in general govern human behavior. They may also underlie the acceptance of the authoritarian state.

It is possible, hence, to construe Mo Di's political teaching as implicitly contractualistic. It disposes of a basic stock of theorems which are part and parcel of standard contract theories.

Mo Di's ethics requires a differentiated evaluation. Compared to Confucius, we can identify three substantial progresses: The *Lunyu* rejects particularism rather implicitly, whereas Mo Di identifies it as the decisive grievance of the time. Decidedly, he makes explicit what was already at the heart of Confucius' teaching: that the entirety of mankind, including the "barbarian" tribes, equally falls within the subject range of moral responsibility.[40] Mo Di is an uncompromising universalist.

Mo Di's thought, secondly, is characterized by a far more radical detachment from tradition and custom than that which we detected in Confucius' Golden Rule. This above all becomes apparent in his problematical hostility to culture, which is already criticized by Xunzi.[41] By the impious, at the same time simple and revolutionary argument of waste, Mo Di stands up against all established customs: music, funeral rites, and the material culture in its entirety get under the dictate of a policy of thrift. Mo Di thus underrates the importance of traditions for the orientation of life, which the Confucians acknowledge, and he may even lack a sense of aesthetics. But what he does, in fact, is to draw wrong conclusions from the right insight into the insufficiencies of a merely customary ethos. This insight was already discernible in the *Lunyu*, but Mo Di is much more outspoken. By a drastic example, he shows that arguments by tradition and custom can entail fateful consequences. He confronts the proponents of funeral rites, who regard these as the traditional "way of the sage kings," with the argument:

> This can be called to consider a habit (*xi*) convenient and regard custom (*su*) as a norm for what is just.
> In ancient times, there was a land named Kaishu east of Yue. Right after birth, the people dismembered the firstborn child and ate it, saying that this was propitious for the younger brothers. When the grandfather died, they loaded the grandmother on their back and abandoned her, saying that they could not live together with the wife of a ghost. The superiors regarded this as the correct order, and the people saw it as a custom. So they carried on practicing these things and did not give them up. But how could this, in fact, be the way of humaneness and justice?
> This means to consider a habit convenient, and to regard custom as a norm for what is just.[42]

In a much clearer language than the Confucians, who are always anxious to mediate and be flexible, Mo Di plays off moral principles against the merely relative authority of convention and tradition. The orientation to time-bound standards, be they old or new, is replaced by the abstract orientation to the "good." Rejecting Confucius' dictum "to transmit, but not to innovate," which soon had become a motto of the Confucian school,[43] Mo Di formulates the novel maxim

> to transmit what is good (*shan*) in the old, and to institute what is good in the present.[44]

Nevertheless, this highlighting of the "good" is, again, anticipated in the *Lunyu*,[45] and Mo Di radicalizes ideas of Confucius rather than altogether discards them.

Mo Di's ethic, thirdly, also formally goes beyond the *Lunyu*. He is the first thinker of the Chinese axial age to recognize the necessity of giving detailed arguments for one's position.[46] The *Lunyu* mainly formulates gentle appeals and gives unsystematic hints to prompt thought. The *Mozi* for the first time presents thematic treatises. They try to convince the reader by long-winded and ponderous chains of arguments, which already at that time gave the author the reputation of lacking eloquence.[47] They, moreover, are interlarded with—at least would-be— evidence. Mo Di even sets up criteria of validity, which has made him the most important precursor of Chinese logic.[48] This form of argument, precisely with regard to its ineloquent clumsiness, its endless repetitions and overaccentuations, is already in itself an indication of the postconventional spirit of the axial age. It demonstrates that at least in the intellectual circles no established conviction was any longer taken for granted.

His formal breakthroughs bring Mo Di very close to an ethics of communication. In his polemic against Confucianism, we find the astonishing sentences:

Humane persons inform each other of the reasons (*li*) why they choose or reject something, or why they find something right or wrong. He who cannot [bring forward] reasons (*gu*) follows the one who [brings forward] reasons. He who has no knowledge follows the one who has knowledge. He who has no arguments (*ci*) submits to the other, and recognizing something good he will change his position. Why then should they quarrel?[49]

Despite this remarkable passage, Mo Di, in the final analysis, does not build his ethics on argumentative reason, but on the calculation of benefit. Here, he falls behind the level reached in the *Lunyu*, in that he reduces the logic of the Golden Rule to a naive strategical expectation of reciprocity (Stage 2). The lability of this profit-oriented reciprocity in the end even leads him to propagating a rigorous moral of institutions. Mo Di's authoritarian state is a logical consequence of the aporias of this elemental utilitarian point of view. Nevertheless, the state is charged with moral responsibilities, which brings Mo Di into a sharp opposition to the regimes of his time. The state is not an end in itself. It should be the representative of the general interest for the sake of securing and promoting the benefit of all. Its legitimation, therefore, in spite of the authoritarian implications, takes place from a postconventional perspective with the "utilitarian overtones" of Kohlberg's Stage 5.

B. YANG ZHU'S HEDONISM

Mo Di's antipode is his younger contemporary Yang Zhu (c. 440–360 B.C.). For Mengzi, both thinkers symbolize the decline of the age. Their teachings, he says, "fill the world," and people follow either Mo Di or Yang Zhu. Mo Di, for Mengzi, by his principle of "co-love" betrays the family—a distorted an unhappy reproach if we think of the universalism inherent in Mengzi's own idea of "extension." And

Yang Zhu betrays the state, for he advocates egoism. He would not have removed a single hair from his body, Mengzi says, even to benefit the world.[50]

Besides these scarce informations, Zhou and early Han literature note that Yang Zhu "valued the self," and taught to "preserve one's inborn nature (*xing*) and protect the true."[51] If we combine these accounts,[52] Yang Zhu advocates a natural life which appreciates the individual existence, values the protection of the natural constitution—the "true"[53]—as the highest good, and rejects any external burden. Whether chapter 7 of the *Liezi*, which bears Yang Zhu's name, can be consulted to complete this scanty picture, is controversial. According to the sinological mainstream, the *Liezi* including the *Yang Zhu* chapter is a forgery from the third or fourth century A.D. Despite this skepticism, I will, in the following, assume that the chapter is basically authentic and later return to the question of its genuineness.

If we leave aside the legendary Lao Dan, a Daoist personage difficult to date, and some bizarre figures from the *Lunyu*, Yang Zhu personifies the first revolt of human nature against the compulsions of the conventional ethos and positive morality which can be fastened to an individual name. As he says,

> Loyalty is not sufficient to give safety to the ruler, but it is just enough to endanger oneself. Justice is not sufficient to protect others, but it is just enough to harm one's own life.[54]

This argument is directed against Mo Di. Morals, in fact, are not beneficial to anyone; all they can do is bring disaster upon oneself. In a provocative antithesis to Mo Di's assertion that morality will gain reward, as well as to Confucius' belief in the inner happiness of the moral person even in miserable external conditions, Yang Zhu maintains that the truly happy were the tyrants, while the just and benevolent have only burdened themselves with hardship. The celebrated ancient paragons of virtue toiled all their lives only to die in distress, and the same happened to Confucius.[55] The tyrants Jie and Zhòu, however, enjoyed their lives to the full and did not "vex themselves with propriety and justice."[56] Yang Zhu himself, too, recommends a hedonism which does not gag the natural drives, satisfies the sensuous desires, and does not care about rank and honor, reputation and glory. These higher goals which allegedly surpass natural happiness fade beside the banal fact of the finality of death. Man, therefore, is well advised to enjoy the brief span of his life as intensively as possible:

> The men of high antiquity knew how quickly life comes and death passes. Therefore, they followed their hearts in their actions and did not act contrary to their spontaneous inclinations. They did not reject what delights the body. Therefore, they were not incited by longing for reputation. They roamed following their nature, without hampering the inclinations of other beings. They did not prefer reputation after death, and so punishment did not affect them. Whether in reputation and praise they came first or last, and whether their destined years were many or few did not count for them.

Yang Zhu says, where all things are different, this is life, and where all things are the same, this is death. In life, there are the capable and the stupid, the noble and the low, and this is that in which men differ. In death, there are stench and rot, putrefaction and extinction, and this is the same to all. . . .

Regardless whether in ten or in a hundred years—we all die. Regardless whether a humane person and a sage or a criminal and a fool—we all die. Those who were Yao and Shun in life, are rotten bones in death. And those who were Jie and Zhòu in life, are rotten bones in death. As rotten bones, they are all the same, and who would still know to distinguish them? Let us, therefore, turn to our present life! Why care about the time after death?[57]

In a culture which does not assume a life to come, the argument of death has the opposite import than it has in the *vanitas* reminders known from the Old Testament or the baroque. What is vain for Yang Zhu is not life, but anything which promises to go beyond it. It is, in particular, the lacking perspective of a future justice in another world which binds all meaning and sense given to human existence to the present. Even if a rewarding and punishing Heavenly authority is brought into play, it must prove its power empirically perceptible in this life. All theodices which Zhou China develops take this direction.[58] But they remain weak in comparison to the Christian teaching of the Last Judgment, and it is their weakness where Yang Zhu's argument sets in.

Yet, Yang Zhu does not advocate any hectic craze for indulgence. In the *Yang Zhu* chapter, such an unrestrained hedonism is attributed to two brothers of Zichan, the chancellor of Zheng, who overindulge in alcohol and sex. When the famous statesman tries to bring them back to the path of virtue by promising them emolument and reputation, he meets with a severe rebuff. Rejecting any attempt to "bend nature straight" (*jiao qingxing*)—a positive motto of Xunzi[59]—in order to "call up a good name," his brothers tell him that their only worry is that "our stomachs flow over and we can no longer give rein to drinking, and that our potency gets exhausted and we can no longer enjoy to the full our feelings in sex."[60]

Yang Zhu's own point, however, is not to emphasize pleasure as such. He rather negatively rejects any restraint imposed upon man by himself or society which demands useless sacrifice. What is important is to be free of inhibitions towards natural desires, and be unconcerned with conventional values and expectations. But it would be wrong, when searching for happiness, to fall back into haste and constraint again:

There are four reasons why people do not find rest: The first is longevity, the second is reputation (*ming*, name), the third is office, the fourth is possession. He who has these four fears spirits, other people, authority, and punishments. Such a man should be called a man in flight [from his nature]. Perhaps he will be killed, perhaps he will stay alive, but his destiny (*ming*) is decided from outside.

But why should he who does not go against destiny yearn for longevity? Why should he who does not want to boast of high position yearn for reputation? Why should he who does not want power yearn for office? And why should he who is not greedy for wealth yearn for possession? Such a man should be called a man in accordance [with nature]. Nothing in the world defies him. His destiny is determined from within.

Hence the saying, "Without marriage and office, man would be relieved of half his desires. Without clothing and eating (material desires), the way of ruler and subject would cease."[61]

The natural joy recommended by Yang Zhu refers to freedom from burden, not to an excessive amount of pleasures. Immoderateness, on the contrary, is the evil of the age, which submits man to external restraints. Even the yearning for longevity *(shou)*—next to family luck *(fu)* and emolument *(lu)* one of the three popular components of happiness—runs counter to nature, since it means quarreling with one's natural destiny. Equanimity towards death is part of an authentic life. This by no means contradicts the quoted testimony of the *Huainanzi* that Yang Zhu taught to "protect the true (one's life)." To protect life does not imply lengthening it at any price. To cling to it would prevent us from enjoying it in due moderation. Yang Zhu, then, does not advocate a hedonism of the Cyrenaic type which sets pleasure as absolute, regardless of the form in which it is aspired to. He depreciates the pleasure afforded by wealth and position and recommends the pleasure of a frugal but carefree existence. In Greece, Epicurean hedonism is characterized by similar differentiations.

Yang Zhu's teaching is based on a normatively loaded concept of nature. Unlike for Xunzi, for him nature is not the insatiable greed for profit. To be in accordance with nature means to enjoy the sweets of life, but also to calmly dispense with all the tinsel that the world idolizes. When Yang Zhu praises the tyrants, therefore, it is not in order to speak for the reckless satisfaction of desires. He merely deplores that it is exactly the wicked rulers who do not restrain themselves, while the heroes of virtue suffer to the end of their lives. He would neither consent that injustice is better than justice, because it gives more pleasure, nor that only justice means true happiness.[62] The given world does not deserve any justification, but it must not be handed over to the law of the jungle either. Yang Zhu's natural life explicitly comprises an ethics of compassion:

There is an old saying that in life we should have compassion for one another, and in death should abandon each other. This word is to the point! The principle *(dao)* of mutual compassion means more than just a feeling. Compassion can bring relief in distress, can satiate when hungry, can bring warmth when cold, and can help to get through in misery. The principle to abandon one another in death does not mean that one would not grieve for one another. It means not to put pearls and jade in the mouths of the dead, not to dress them in elegant brocade, not to lay out sacrificial animals, and arrange grave goods.[63]

Yang Zhu's philosophy of "live and let live"[64] belongs to a number of positions hostile to convention and oriented to the right of the self which pertain to Kohlberg's Stage 4½. These hedonist teachings, which according to the above-mentioned testimony of Mengzi were very influential round 300 B.C.,[65] are typical representations of the postconventional spirit of the Chinese axial age, because they straightforwardly reject the constraint of custom, family, and state. Exposing the alienation inherent in conventional morals, they return to the preconventional rationality of the early stages and appeal to a right of nature. Thus Yang Zhu links his rejection of the established hierarchy of values to a refined pleasure principle and a reciprocity of "compassion" in the manner of Stage 2. This ancient Chinese hedonism is not the symptom of decadence as which modern Chinese critics, above all from the People's Republic, have pictured it.[66] It is rather an expression of a youthful phase of defiance of Chinese philosophy. This youthful protest is certainly wrong in not recognizing the achievements of the conventional ethos and rejecting it altogether. But it is right in exposing its crass shortcomings, and in calling up what in this world all too often comes to nothing: individual happiness.

The ideas of the *Yang Zhu* chapter fit excellently into the intellectual spectrum of the Chinese axial age. Not at all antagonistic,[67] they even hold a position in this spectrum which can be expected to be occupied in an epoch of enlightenment if we follow the logic of the cognitive-developmental theory. From this point of view, the *Yang Zhu* chapter of the *Liezi* basically contains authentic material from the Zhanguo era.[68]

C. DAOIST NATURALISM

A critique of conventional morality similar to that of Yang Zhu can be found in the texts of Daoism. Yang Zhu anyway belongs to the Daoist environment.

Daoism and Confucianism represent two paradigmatically different answers of ancient Chinese philosophy to the formation of a world of man as distinct from the world of nature. Confucianism is the declared advocate of this development, and Daoism is its avowed enemy. For the Daoists, civilization in all its manifestations like technique, rule, morals, and art is nothing but the irreversible destruction of an ideal primordial state. Unlimited fertility, perfect union of all beings, absence of social distinctions as well as of greed and knowledge, these are the constantly recurring topoi of the Daoist descriptions of the lost Golden Age. The original idyll is furthermore characterized by the absence of moral constraints. Still disposing of a natural primordial virtue (*de*),[69] all men act spontaneously and unconsciously good, without needing the guidance of positive values. What in later times morality at best aspires to is in the original position effortlessly accomplished by the natural instinct of the *bon sauvage*:

In the age of perfect virtue . . . people lived like deer in the wild. They were upright and correct without knowing it, and thereby practiced justice. They loved each other without knowing it, and thereby practiced humaneness. They were sincere without knowing it, and thereby practiced loyalty. They acted properly without knowing it, and thereby practiced trustworthiness. They moved like caterpillars in spring and supported each other without regarding this as a favor.[70]

The Daoist philosophy of history allies with an anthropology that views man's original nature as the embodiment of the good. The primordial commune in history corresponds to early childhood in ontogenesis. The infant is a pure and unadulterated representation of nature, and its idealization is one of the most remarkable features of Daoist literature. "He who embraces the fullness of primordial virtue resembles the newborn babe," we read in *Laozi* 55, and *Laozi* 28 gives out the maxim *"Back to infancy,"* a fitting heading of Stage 4½ of moral evolution. It is true that in the *Laozi* the extolment of childhood also serves a strategical goal. When the *Laozi* recommends to "be as weak as a child,"[71] we have to bear in mind that the text in general is dedicated to a dialectical strategy of gaining victory by weakness.[72] Yet, the fact that the child becomes a central topos in the first place can only be explained from the specificity of an enlightened postconventional perspective which turns back to the preconventional past.

A further example of the Daoist preoccupation with childhood is found in *Zhuangzi* 23:

> Laozi said, "This is the canon for preserving life: Can you embrace the One, without losing it? Can you, without consulting the oracle, foretell fortune and misfortune? Can you pause? Can you stop? Can you give up to expect it from others and instead look for it in yourself? Can you be free from restraints? Can you be free from inhibitions? *Can you be a child?* The children cry all day, yet their throat never gets hoarse. This is the highest harmony. The children make fists all day, without grabbing anything. This is partaking in primordial virtue. The children look around all day, yet their eyes do not get heavy, for they have no preferences outside. They move around without knowing where they go. They stay at home without knowing what they do. They cling to things and become one with their waves. This is the canon for preserving life."[73]

To stay free from restraints, inhibitions, and the compulsion to justify one's doings is the antitype to the standardized world of conventions and occupation by heteronomous duties. The *Laozi* strikes the same note:

> How far apart from each other are saying yes and being scolded?[74] / What is the difference between good and evil? / If others fear something, / one should also fear them. / Immense is that which has not yet reached its climax! / The men of the multitude are joyful, / like feasting at the great sacrifice, / or climbing a terrace in spring. / I

anchor[75] where there is no omen, / *like a child* that does not yet smile, / apathetic, like having no goal. / The men of the multitude all possess more than enough, / I alone give away. / I have the heart of a fool / and am like lethargic. / The common people are bright, / I alone am obnubilated. / The common people are punctilious, / I alone am forbearing, / blurred, like the sea, / immense, like having no end. / The men of the multitude pursue their goals, / I alone am stubborn and rustic. / I alone want to be different from others / and value highest *to drink from the mother*.[76]

The exaltation of childlike ingenuousness serves the goal of remaining unaffected by the demands of conventional and generally shared values, which are still unknown to the child. Instead of saying yes and endorsing the current distinction of good and evil,[77] instead of pursuing external goals, increasing one's wealth and playing up the trifles of life, the "I" of the *Laozi*—in no other paragraph does it appear as frequently as here—returns to the ease and unconstrained equanimity of infancy. It yearns for the indeterminate beginning where everything is still open and not yet forced into a specific course.

The topos of the child reappears in Mengzi.[78] For Mengzi, the love of children for their parents is the earliest manifestation of humaneness. And "a great man," he says, "is one who has not lost his heart of the newborn child."[79] Like the Daoists, Mengzi refers to nature as a normative authority which is represented in purity by spontaneous, prereflective action and by the constitution of the child prior to the influence of education. Mengzi claims the *natural spontaneity of morality*, which for him is identical with the specific virtues propagated by the Confucian school. The Daoists, however, advocate a *quasi-morality of natural spontaneity*. The spontaneous naturalness which exemplarily manifests itself in the child is good prior to and beyond all specific virtues. The primordial virtue which the Daoists claim for the beginning of phylo- and ontogenesis does not know any positive values. The *Zhuangzi* defines:

What I call "good" (*zang*) is not humaneness and justice, but *to be good in one's primordial virtue* and nothing else. What I call "good" is not humaneness and justice, but *to give free rein to the essence of one's nature* and nothing else.[80]

The *Zhuangzi* herewith gives a naturalistic definition of the good. Correspondingly, early Daoism does not develop an ethics in the strict sense. It formulates a general naturalism within which the question how man should act answers itself—he should follow nature. The description of nature is at the same time normative prescription. The fact that nature, as Xunzi rightly points out, also knows the fight for existence up to the destruction of the other is passed over by the Daoists without comment. They tacitly presuppose a thoroughly normative concept of nature, and this alone explains their fierce attacks on everything artificial like the state and its institutions. If there is no deficiency at all in the natural constitution, the state has no function to fulfill and can merely destroy the ideal primordial condition.

This destruction has become reality for the *Zhuangzi*. The phylogenetic process of the development of civilization, and, after civilization has made its way, the ontogenetic process of socialization, entail the loss of the original perfection. The "age of highest primordial virtue" perishes with the emergence of technique, the bloody foundation of the state with its physical and psychical means of coercion, and the spreading of overrefined culture. The tragic happening is illustrated in the *Zhuangzi* by the following allegory:

> The emperor of the South was Haste (*Shu*), the emperor of the North was Sudden (*Hu*), and the emperor of the Center was Chaos (*Hundun*). Haste and Sudden at times met each other in Chaos' territory, and Chaos treated them very generously. Haste and Sudden then discussed how they could repay Chaos' kindness. They said, "Men all have seven openings in order to see, hear, eat, and breathe. He alone has none. Let us chisel him some!" Each day they chiseled one opening. On the seventh day, Chaos died.[81]

"Haste" and "Sudden" and their destruction of "Chaos" personify human action in its specific and its disastrous consequences for nature, the chaotic and faceless, which knows neither human measure nor purposes.[82] "Haste" and "Sudden" moreover symbolize the restless movement of the human mind. Like in the Biblical Fall, it is the irruption of human thought which rends the unity of nature, sets free a calculating reason, and destroys the spontaneous self-regulation. From now on, man and nature are divided in a double sense: Man develops into an insatiable enemy of outer nature, and ruins his inner nature in the strife for fame, wealth, and power.[83] And there is "no way to revert to the essence of one's nature and return once more to the beginning."[84]

In view of the disruption and artificiality of the world, the early Daoists feel in a mood which, down to the details, resembles the mood called "sentimental" by Schiller.[85] A world has fallen apart, the unreflected ethical life in unity with nature has dissolved, and philosophy, to speak with Hegel, sets about to reconcile the mischief caused by human thought.[86] The Daoists, however, would neither accept Schiller's alternative of the "ideal" and his solution of a "legislation of reason" transcending nature[87]—which is more in line with Confucianism—nor an optimistic philosophy of history like the one brought forward by Hegel. Except for some attempts to seek a compromise with the trend of the times, their answers to the loss of primordial virtue remain retrospective and resigned. The mystic tries to win back at least individually a part of the lost unity, and a naturalistic philosophy of life aims at mimetically regaining objective traits of nature by discarding intellect, morals, emotions, and activity. Both programs are individualistic and intend the complete detachment from society.

On the basis of their normative concept of nature, and full of indignation about the oppression and violence which have made their entry into the world after the decay of the primordial unity, the Daoists formulate a critique of the given order which in its sharpness is unparalleled in the entire axial age. They in particular attack the state and the ethics of law and order, but also the cardinal virtues of Confucianism. There are, above all, two arguments which the Daoists introduce into the ethical debate of ancient China: Morals are (a) at best a bad compensation for the loss of naturalness, or (b) a mere means to an end.

(a) The very existence of positive moral norms is *index falsi*. The *Laozi* writes:

> When everyone in the world knows the good, this is not good already.[88]

> When the *Dao* was lost, only then came virtue. / When virtue was lost, only then came humaneness. / When humaneness was lost, only then came justice. / When justice was lost, only then came propriety.[89]

The second passage is also found in the *Zhuangzi*.[90] It is remarkable that the appearance of primordial virtue (*de*) already counts as the first symptom of decay, a fact which hardly fits in with its normal idealization. Probably, the mere emergence of the world from the *Dao* is already regarded as the beginning of unstoppable decay. In *Laozi* 18, however, the *Dao* itself holds the place of *de*, and in the *Huainanzi*, too, the opposition of both terms is missing:

> When the great *Dao* declined, there were humaneness and justice. / When prudence and intelligence appeared, there was the great manipulation (*wei*). / When relatives no longer were in harmony, there were filial piety and kindness. / When the states and clans got into disorder, there were the loyal subjects.[91]

> To act according to inborn nature (*xing*), this is called *Dao*. To get one's heavenly nature, this is called primordial virtue. When nature is lost, only then humaneness is appreciated. When the *Dao* is lost, only then justice is appreciated. Therefore, *Dao* and virtue had gone when humaneness and justice were established. When propriety and music were dressed up, the pure simplicity had already dissolved. When true and false took shape, the people were already blinded. When pearls and jades were held in esteem, the world was already in struggle. These four are products of a decaying world and instruments of the last age.[92]

Laozi, *Zhuangzi*, and *Huainanzi* formulate a dialectical compensation theory of morals as a poor substitute for the fatal loss of the primordial condition. The Confucian hierarchy of values appears in exactly reverse order as stages of a continuous decay. This process of decay necessitates ever new compensations ending up in the coercion represented by conventional propriety. Since humaneness (in the reading of the Golden Rule), justice (as underlying Xunzi's concept of social order), and propriety can be related to Kohlberg's Stages 6, 5, and 3 or 4 respectively, the sequence of the cognitive-developmental theory, too, is turned upside down. This confirms Kohlberg's evaluation of the different stages, since the deplored process is one of decay. But for the same reason, the Daoists would never accept that a developmental theory delivers a measure for genuine progress. From the beginning, they stand above the paradigm of a movement towards something higher. They would at best give it a condescending smile, but more probably unmask it as the worst ideology of destruction.

(b) The second argument of the Daoists is that regardless of the illusions of sincere moralists, morals have made their way because they are of advantage for certain nonmoral interests. But precisely the advocates of utility reckon without the host. In their shortsightedness, they resemble "lice on a pig," feeling comfortable between its nipples and buttocks like in a "place of profit," and unsuspecting that one morning the butcher will roast them along with their "house of repose."[93] This reduces Mo Di's utilitarianism to absurdity. If morals are useful, the *Zhuangzi* says, then, in the final analysis, only for those who are the most reckless in seeking after their benefit:

> There are few men who can do without humaneness and justice, but many to take advantage of both. To practice humaneness and justice is not only at best insincere, but even means lending weapons to the wildest greed.[94]

The example of a gang of robbers illustrates this claim:

> Robber Zhi was asked by his followers, "Does a robber, too, have his *Dao* (ethos)?"
> Zhi replied, "Where would the *Dao* not be! Blindly guessing the treasure in a room, this is sageliness. Being the first one in, this is courage. Being the last one out, this shows sense of duty. Knowing whether or not a coup can be made, this is wisdom. And dividing up the loot equally, this is humaneness. Without these five things, no one in the world has ever become a great robber."
> From this we can see that without the *Dao* of the sages no good man can establish himself, and no [robber like] Zhi can succeed. But since in the world good men are few and bad men are many, the benefit which the sages bring to the world is little and the harm is much.[95]

That morals is a creation of the early sages is also maintained by Xunzi. Like in so many aspects, in the genealogy of morals, too, Xunzi proves to be at the same time the pupil and the antipode of Daoism. He endorses Daoist theses, but reevaluates them in affirmative terms. For Xunzi, morals is a positive compensation for the inefficiency of man's natural constitution designed to prevent strife and aggression. For the radical line of Daoism, however, morals are the solder which even keeps together a gang of robbers. They are indifferent, then, to specific goals and also to the egoism of groups. Any virtue is a secondary virtue, morality and group morality cannot be distinguished from each other.[96]

Although this Stage 4½ criticism is surely overstated, it should not be dismissed all too quickly. It is not apt to discredit morality altogether, but it does deliver an excellent criterion for testing ethical programs by a fundamental thought experiment: *Can they rule out my being a member of a gang of robbers?*[97]

For the radical Daoists, the greatest of all gangs of robbers, which utilizes morals as an efficient tool, is the state. Once established as an apparatus of bloody repression,[98] the state together with its laws and norms is a mere instrument in the hands of unscrupulous criminals who call themselves rulers. "The little robber is imprisoned," says Mangoude in the *Zhuangzi*, "but the big ones become feudal lords."[99] The institutions created by the sages do not preserve the state from corruption. On the contrary: They resemble the locks and buckles which protect a trunk—much to the thief's delight, because he steals the whole trunk, which is now protected for himself.[100] The *Zhuangzi* concludes:

> Until the sages are dead, great robbers will not cease to appear. Even if you govern the world redoubling [the efforts of] the sages, this would only mean piling up the profit of robbers like Zhi. Make pecks and bushels to measure things by, and they will take their booty together with the pecks and bushels. Make scales and balances to weigh things by, and they will take their booty together with the scales and balances. Make tallies and seals to certify things by, and they will take their booty together with tallies and seals. Set up humaneness and justice as correctives, and they will take their booty together with humaneness and justice.
>
> How do I know this is so? He who steals a belt buckle is put to death, but he who steals a country becomes a feudal lord. And if there is still humaneness and justice at the courts of the feudal lords, does not this mean that they have stolen humaneness, justice, sagehood, and intelligence?[101]

The Daoist critique of the state does not always sound as categorical as in this passage. There are more moderate voices, too, which at least implicitly acknowledge the necessity of political rule, though they disgustedly reject any cooperation and only accept an unambitious person as ruler.[102] The crux of the more radical line described above is not its lack of readiness for compromise or differentiation, however. The identification of the state with a well-organized gang of robbers, which is also found in Augustine's *The City of God*,[103] can still today marshal a lot of empirical evidence in its favor and is, its generalizing tone notwithstanding, not merely a product of excessive imagination. The real dimension of the outrage upon humanity that has been committed by governmental institutions is even beyond the imagination of the ancients. What is questionable with the sharp criticism of the state brought forward in the *Zhuangzi*, however, is above all the thoughtless leveling of the difference between morality and politics that has been highlighted by the Confucians and Mengzi in particular, as well as the singling out of the intellectuals as actually responsible for the atrocities of the state. Since without the intellectuals neither the establishment of the state nor the formulation of morals would have been possible, *Zhuangzi* and *Laozi* demand the elimination of intelligence:

> Put an end to sageness, cast away knowledge, and the world will be in perfect order![104]

In *Zhuangzi* 10, this appeal culminates in a general call to destroy culture.[105] Unsuspectingly, Daoism herewith hands itself over to the detested institutions. Instead of winning arguments from the cultural and moral evolution against the depravation of political power, it regresses to a level which negates both alike. Ancient Chinese enlightenment turns into counterenlightenment in the same moment it reaches its utmost polemical climax. It was quite easy to deflect the condemnation of the intellectuals, which was, curiously enough, meant to hit the state, into a purposive *policy* of stupefaction. Thus the *Laozi*, which can anyway be interpreted as a strategical utilization of originally critical insights of Daoism, writes:

> Therefore, the sage governs like this: He empties the people's minds, fills their bellies, weakens their ambitions, and strengthens their bones. For ever he causes the people to be without knowledge and pretensions. He ensures that the knowledgeable do not venture and undertake anything, and that is all. Thus there is nothing that is not in order.[106]

> Therefore it is said: He who practices the *Dao* does not want to enlighten the people by it, but wants to stupefy them. That the people are hard to rule is because of their knowledge.[107]

The deeper root of the Daoist hostility to human intellect is the recognition of the ambiguity of reason which has become manifest in the subjugation of nature and man by scheming calculation. Setting as absolute the experience that "there has been no sagehood and intelligence which did not make cangues and chains,"[108] Daoism radically rejects the Confucian belief that by mobilizing moral reason, despite all adversities of the time, an ideal order can once be achieved or regained. "The heart of man is more perilous than a mountain river," writes the *Zhuangzi*.[109] The Daoists do not recognize that human reason itself, dialectically, becomes the medium of critique of the very disaster it has brought about. Paradoxically, their writings themselves excel by an intellectual acumen hitherto unknown. The aporia of Daoism, not to be willing to rely on language and discourse,[110] but to verbosely communicate precisely this message, has been exposed by the later Mohists with transcendental arguments like:

To take all statements as contradictory is contradictory. The explanation lies in [precisely] that statement.[111]

Daoist ethics relies on the mobilization of nonintellectual strata in man, above all on mysticism. In the *Zhuangzi*, two kinds of mysticism can be distinguished, the one aiming at the mystical union with the *Dao* as the final monistic principle of all being, the other aiming at the union with the *Dao* as nature.[112] The second kind of mysticism allies with a naturalistic philosophy of life which by way of mimesis tries to become one with nature. He who achieves this oneness will at the same time embody morality, although—the typical dialectical thought figure—not *as* morality. "Highest humaneness," says the *Zhuangzi*, "is not humane."[113] The submersion in the all-pervading *Dao* present in all things, or the merging with nature, mean making the essence of both one's own. This entails discarding calculation, renouncing using other beings as a means to an end, and acknowledging the right of every single being, not only of man, to live its natural destination to the full. For, the *Dao* and nature do not know any purpose, and to them everything is equal.

Daoist naturalism hence undoubtedly contains the idea of universality. That this universality is not discursively mediated has one advantage: not solely the members of the linguistic community, but everything belonging to nature, also that which cannot speak, apriori falls within in its range. Ethics is macroethics from the very beginning. There are a number of impressive examples of this in the *Zhuangzi*.[114] The most concise document, however, is a parable from the *Lüshi chunqiu*. In ingenious simplicity, it distinguishes conventional group morality, Confucian universal humanism, and Daoist universal naturalism:

A man of Jing lost his bow. Instead of seeking it, he said, "A man of Jing has lost it, a man of Jing will find it. Why should I seek it, then?" When Confucius heard of it he said, "If he leaves out *Jing*, it will be all right." When Lao Dan heard of it, he said, "If he leaves out *man*, too, it will be all right." Thus Lao Dan was the most impartial.[115]

To merge ethics with the ontology of the *Dao* on the one hand enlarges the scope over which it is valid, but on the other it implies a specific restriction. In the same way as the *Dao* is "inactive" (*wuwei*) and nature lets everything happen "by itself" (*ziran*), Daoist ethics does not tell how to act, but how not to act. Within the idealized, counterfactual reference system of a nature which does not know violence, this is quite consistent. In nature, the *Zhuangzi* stresses, everything is perfect as it is, and there is no want of active correction and human standardization.

In view of the severing of the umbilical cord which linked man to nature, and the establishment of a human world of culture, there is something regressive in Daoist naturalism, however interesting it may sound in these times of the modern ecological crisis. Daoism tries to evade development instead of influencing its direction, and it ends up in individualism fleeing society. Here, the Daoist nature mystic meets with other members of the Daoist community who are moved by the concern for their individual physical existence—the "true" (*zhen*). This was already the way of Yang Zhu. But the focus on life can mean something different in detail. Thus the yearning for longevity, which is rejected by Yang Zhu, occurs in some passages of the *Zhuangzi*,[116] and it has become even more important for later Daoism. Reversely, hedonism is rejected in *Zhuangzi* 12 as harmful to life.[117] Robber Zhi, again, proclaims a message which can similarly be found in the *Yang Zhu*. Zhi calls Confucius to account, who has tried to stop him from robbery by promising him the rank of a feudal lord. He counters the homily of his critic by the following creed:

> Now I will tell you about the essence of man: The eye desires to see colors, the ear desires to hear sounds, the mouth desires to taste flavors, and the will desires fulfillment.
>
> The highest longevity man can achieve is one hundred years, medium longevity is eighty years, and the least longevity is sixty years. Take away the time of illness, mourning, and anxiety, then there are no more than four or five days in a month when one can laugh heartily. Heaven and earth are unending, but man's death has its time. Take this time-bound something, put it into the unending, and in a trice it is over, as quickly as a thoroughbred horse gallops past a crack in the wall. Those who are incapable of satisfying their will and intention and of cherishing their destined years all are no experts of the *Dao*.[118]

Opportunism represents yet another way of giving effect to the interest of life. In Chapter 3 of the *Zhuangzi*, entitled *Principles of nourishing life*, we read:

> If you do good, stay away from fame! If you do evil, stay away from punishment! Make to follow the middle your guiding rule! Then you can protect your body (or: your self, *shen*), keep life whole, nourish your parents, and live out your years.[119]

Usefulness for life determines the guide line for human action—a mean between good and evil if not a calculated mediocrity. *Zhuangzi* 33 ascribes this philosophy of adaptation above all to Shen Dao (c. 350–275 B.C.). He is quoted, among other things, with the following statement:

> Unscrupulous and free from responsibilities, I laugh at the world for honoring capable men. Uninhibited and without morals, I disparage the greatest sages of the world. When whip and torture threaten me, I adapt myself to things. I put aside right and wrong if I can stay out of trouble thereby. I neither consult knowledge nor deliberation, I do not know [the strategy] of advancing and waiting, and I yield

myself to the course of things. That is all. Only if pushed, do I begin to move, and only if dragged, do I start on my way.[120]

Merely caring for the physical consequences of behavior, Shen Dao is firmly determined to abandon morality for the sake of remaining unharmed, with the passiveness of a fellow traveler, though, rather than with the aggressiveness of a robber.[121] His attitude radically contradicts the readiness of the Confucians to sacrifice life for morality.

The ethically relevant positions of the Zhou Daoists described above can be interpreted as exemplary representations of Kohlberg's Stage 4½. The gesture of exposing moralism, the nonconformist symbolism the *Zhuangzi* is replete with, the rejection of conventional compulsion and the emphasis on individual life—all this fits well into the phase of youthful protest. From here, the defiant applause for the robber, the glorification of the freedom of childhood, and the defense of opportunism also explain themselves. Such seemingly contrasting topoi like the robber, the child, the opportunist, as well as the hedonist of the *Liezi*, are linked together by one and the same deeper structure of a *postconventional recourse to the preconventional past*.[122] More than any other school, the Daoists personify the adolescent crisis of Chinese society. They are "professional youths" who, defying adjustment and normality, lend their voice to the revolt of nature against its enthrallment, fueled by a deep feeling of alienation with sentimental overtones. And if even today the unembarrassed frankness of the Daoists, much more than the sedate earnestness of most Confucians, appeals to us, it is probably because it evokes reminiscences of the naive spontaneity of childhood.

Yet, the Daoist return to preconventional spontaneity does not establish any substantial new morality. It reflects the yearning for the simple lucidity of the original situation, and tries to escape the puzzling complexity of civilized society.[123] It well succeeds in exposing the crass shortcomings of the conventional ethos and in providing necessary retreats. But in the final analysis, it constitutes a regressive evasion of development—with the danger of being caught up by it in an unexpected way. This tragedy of Daoism manifests itself most strikingly in the fact how easily it can be exploited by Legalism. Exactly because of its special liking for the preconventional, it gets utilized by the very powers which it tries to banish by its "back to nature" ideology.

D. LEGALISM: LAW AND ORDER

For the Legalists, the only way out of the crisis which disrupts China is the establishment of a centralized authoritarian state apparatus to replace the feudal system. As a broad philosophical and political current, Legalism is hardly less diversiform than the other schools. However, the *Hanfeizi*, the last great work of the Zhanguo era, presents a summa which consistently synthesizes the thought of the predecessors while skilfully borrowing ideas from the opponents. The primary rocks of Legalism—Shen Buhai's concept of political "technique" (*shu*), Shang Yang's theory and practice of government by penal law (*fa*), and Shen Dao's apology of institutionalized power (*shi*)—Mo Di's utilitarianism and authoritarian model of state, Xunzi's view of human nature, and the Daoists' hostility to culture together with their enchantment by the self-regulation of nature—these are the main constituents which Han Fei brings into a system of impressing and oppressive consistency. The complexity of his synthetical achievement notwithstanding, Han Fei's thought has a tendency towards simplicity, methodical transparence, and a cold resoluteness which bears the traits of the political utopia he propagates—the absolute state. He starts from a minimalistic anthropology which radicalizes the view of human nature developed by his teacher Xunzi. Whereas for Xunzi man is morally malleable, for Han Fei he remains a thoroughly selfish being only superficially molded by culture, tradition, and social bounds. Mengzi's argument that there is a natural basis of morality in man is voluptuously picked apart by the example of family love:

> The relation of parents to their children is such that they congratulate each other if a son is born, but they [may] kill a daughter. The children equally come out of the parental womb. The reason that one congratulates on a son, but kills a daughter, is that parents merely consider their future conveniences and calculate their long-term benefit. Thus even parents in relation to their children use a calculating mind. How much more holds this true [for politics] where there is no parental kindness.[124]

In the antifeudal program of Legalism, which aims at the elimination of the influence of the noble clans, family and family ties become a major target. State authority can only be enforced against them. Family interests have to be replaced by the absolute obligation towards the prescription of the role assigned by the state. Both are mutually exclusive, as Han Fei illustrates by his version of the denunciation case of Chu[125] and another anecdote about Confucius:

> In Chu there was a man called Upright Gong. When his father stole a sheep, he reported it to the authorities. Thereupon the chancellor ordered to kill the son, thinking that he was upright to the ruler, but undutiful to the father. So the son was punished for his report. From this it can be seen that the upright subject of a ruler is a ruthless son of his father.
>
> A man of Lu followed his ruler to war. In three battles, he ran away three times. When Confucius asked him for the reason, he answered, "I have an old father. If I die, nobody will take care of him." Confucius regarded him as filial, and recommended him for a high position. From this it can be seen that a filial son of his father is a disloyal subject of his ruler.

So it came about that after the chancellor of Chu had put Upright Gong to death, no more crimes were reported to the authorities. And after Confucius had rewarded the deserter, the people of Lu were susceptible to capitulation and desertion.[126]

For Han Fei, family morals and public duty are irreconcilable with each other. The same conviction can be found in the *Shangjunshu* (attributed to Shang Yang's school), where filial piety and fraternal respect count among the "ten evils" or "seven lice" which ruin the state.[127]

Although Han Fei also takes the possibility into account that state morality can be based upon a rigid education in the family,[128] it is far more typical of him to rely exclusively on strong governmental institutions. Such institutions, however, according to Han Fei, have not always been necessary. Man's evil nature notwithstanding, in remote antiquity it was possible to live without the firm hand of the state. Men had to defend themselves against the animals and cope with various kinds of adversities, but they did not have to lead war against each other. For "they were only few, and goods were there in abundance." "That in antiquity people made light of goods," Han Fei continues, "was not because they were humane, but because goods were many. That today they quarrel and rob is not because they are so mean, but because goods are few."[129]

Han Fei herewith rejects his teacher's picture of the primordial condition. According to Xunzi, it was the scarcity of resources which called the sages to the fore, because men had to quarrel for satisfying their basic needs. For this reason, Xunzi considers the traditional ethical values, above all the rules of propriety, as representing the ingenious answer to the age-old problem of distribution, an answer which secured the survival of the human race in the first place. Yet, if such a problem did not exist in the past, the Confucian esteem for the cultural tradition loses its foundation. For Han Fei, morals are not a well-proven precious means of securing existence, but mere normality in a time when no real problems had to be solved.[130] The main factor which renders the "way of antiquity" irrelevant for the present is population growth. It necessitates new methods of politics. Han Fei, therefore, proclaims:

A sage expects nothing from cultivating the past. He does not take as a model what was proper for a long time. He speaks about the tasks of his age and accordingly takes his measures.[131]

He who still believes that one should emulate the example of the idealized rulers of remote times resembles a stupid peasant who, instead of working in the fields, keeps standing by a stump where a hare has once broken his neck.[132]

Regardless of what may have been valid for antiquity, the men of the present live under constrained conditions which require disciplining them by force. They should be molded into willing peasants and soldiers, the two pillars of a rich and powerful state. A systematic policy of stupefaction, as also suggested by the *Laozi*, is indispensable for this goal.[133] The basic handle, however, to make man a compliant tool, is to get hold of him by his very selfishness. Even more than the family, the state is held together by the mere logic of profit. "The relation of ruler and subject," Han Fei states, "consists in *calculation*."[134] Hence, reward and punishment can become the two main instruments of politics. In one of the numerous passages on this theme, Han Fei writes:

> In general, when governing the empire, one has to follow human feelings (*qing*). Human feelings have likes and dislikes. For this reason, reward and punishment can be applied. If reward and punishment can be applied, then prohibitions and orders can be set up, and the method of government is already perfect.[135]

The causally conditioning[136] principle of reward and punishment must by no means, in wrong sentimentality, be diluted by benevolence and generosity. How tough-minded and merciless the Legalists are on this point becomes apparent from an episode reported approvingly by Han Fei. During a famine, the King of Qin rejects the proposal to give out food to the starving people. His argument is this:

> According to the law of Qin, he who has merits shall be rewarded, and he who commits a crime is punished. If I now give out the vegetables and fruit from the five parks, I would equally reward those who have merits and those who have none. This would be the way to chaos. Instead of giving out the food of the five parks and inviting chaos, we better throw it away and maintain order.
>
> According to another source, the king said: . . . Better they die, and we maintain order, than that they live, and we invite chaos.[137]

Rewards should be rather scanty, but punishments should be severe even for small offences.[138] The most efficacious method is to "institute what people hate."[139] Punishment serves exclusively for deterrence; the archaic idea of retaliation is alien to the Legalists. By way of deterrence, crime can be nipped in the bud, and finally it will be possible to "abolish punishment by punishment." This frequent motto of Legalist literature[140] throws light on the utopian gist of the Legalist program: The Legalists are guided by the temptation to at one stroke and once and for all get rid of all problems of human living together. Punishment is the ultimate way to virtue:

> Punishment produces force. Force produces strength. Strength produces authority. Authority produces virtue (*de*). Virtue thus has its origin in punishment.[141]

The Legalist "virtue," however, is nothing but efficiency in the service of the state.[142] The final goal is not that the good is done, but that the evil is prohibited. Politics must not be guided by neat ideals, but by the recognition of the shabby mediocrity of man:

When a sage rules a country, he does not count on people's doing him good, but relies on making it impossible for them to do him wrong. If he counts on people's doing him good, then in the whole country there will not be a dozen of such men. But if he relies on making it impossible for them to do him wrong, he can uniform the whole country. Those who govern must take the majority into account, and not the minority. Hence their devotion not to virtue, but to law.... Therefore, a ruler who knows method does not follow the good which might be there by coincidence, but follows the way of necessity.[143]

Morality which would be more than mere self-interest is not only unexpectable. Any trace of it would be like sand in the mechanism of power, a mechanism only kept in motion by its ingenious simplicity. What fascinates the Legalists is the automatism of a system which plays off human egoism against itself, utilizing and paralyzing it at the same time. Morality in the Confucian sense, therefore, is a foreign body in the Legalist state. This not only holds true for humaneness, which for Shang Yang together with kindness (*ci*) is the "mother of transgression [of law],"[144] or for other public values like sincerity, integrity, and justice.[145] It even concerns loyalty to the ruler (*zhong*):

Order and strength result from law, weakness and rebellion result from bending law. If the ruler understands this, then he will be correct in his rewards and punishments without having to show humaneness to his subjects. If rank and emoluments result from merits and executions and fines from crimes, then the subjects, as soon as they understand this, will exert all their strength without having to be loyal to the ruler. If the ruler is versed in not being humane, and the subject is versed in not being loyal, then it is possible to become king of the empire.[146]

Only if the system is not built on morals can it be solid. But the seemingly paradoxical sentence that a subject should be "versed in not being loyal"[147] has a still deeper meaning. The Legalist idea is that, in general, relations between men should be replaced by the orientation to the prescription of the specific role. Any personal bonds would be a weak point, where imponderable morals might strike roots again. Wherever morals become visible, they should be suspected of calculation. Institutionalized suspicion is the very fundament of the Legalist system. Like the ruler himself, the subject, too, is well-versed in *concealed strategical action*—"seeing without being seen, hearing without being heard, knowing without being known"[148]—which even more than open strategical action becomes the basic problem of Legalist politics, and to which Han Fei dedicates his whole acumen.[149] The only efficient counterdevice of the ruler is a strictly supervised delimitation of competence which keeps the scope of action of the subordinates as narrow and controllable as possible. The execution of a valet who protected his lord by a garment against cold when he lay there drunk is exemplary—the valet was only responsible for the headdress and thus had trespassed his duties.[150]

Anxious about protecting the state against the old rival powers of private and group interests, family, and morality, the Legalists finally end up in an apotheosis of evil:

> If the good are employed, the people will love their relatives. But if the wicked are employed, the people will love the institutions. To seek consent and shield others, this is what the good do. But to disassociate oneself from others and spy on them, this is what the wicked do. If the good are accorded decorations, transgressions will be hidden. But if the wicked are employed, crimes will be punished. If transgressions are hidden, the people will be stronger than the law, but if crimes are punished, the law will be stronger than the people. If the people are stronger than the law, there will be rebellion in the state, but if the law is stronger than the people, military power will be great.
>
> Therefore I say: Using good people in government surely leads to rebellion and loss of territory. But using the wicked in government surely leads to order and strength.[151]

Even the most sober modern procedural rationality lives on the tacit assumption that the functionaries on which it depends will not only act according to the legal prescriptions of their roles, but, in general, will also show a "good will." The Legalists do not rely on such a fiction. Their system is designed not only to do without goodness—it builds on badness, convinced to control it thereby for all times.

In the Legalist state, there is not merely no place for the "good." A whole bunch of "parasites," too, has to be eliminated—intellectuals and rhetoricians, wandering knights who on their own initiative fight for justice, malingerers, traders, and artisans who cheat the peasants.[152] Even innkeepers are on the list[153]— the only mobility in the Legalist state is that of the army going to war. And he who still wants to learn something should "take a clerk as his teacher" and study the laws.[154]

Yet, we should not misunderstand the Legalists. When Han Fei recommends "not to be humane," and Shang Yang demands to govern with the "wicked," there are not necessarily sadistic nihilists at work. The Legalists doubtless stand out by their marked cynicism. But this is a quite secondary concomitant of the logic of system optimizing which they carry to an extreme, and which, as they see it, shows the only way out of the crisis of China. If politics is to function at all, then it has not only to be radically separated from morality, but has to completely subdue the latter. The Confucian guardianship of morality over politics is turned upside down. The Legalist state is solely governed by law as decreed by the ruler, clearly formulated, put down in writing, and furnished with sanctions. Formally, the ruler stands above law, but on close examination he himself is nothing but a functionary in a depersonalized order, which—a typically Legalist topos—only knows the soberingly normal. Like the great majority of men, the ruler is usually just a mediocre scoundrel,[155] relieved of the burden of originality, initiative, and exemplariness by his laws, prescriptions, and means of power. He should let law govern, and set aside his "self" as much as possible.[156]

But what is the source of law? The moral authority of the "gentleman," which Xunzi brings into play here,[157] is canceled by the Legalists. Han Fei in its place at best knows the paragon of the Daoist *Dao*. That the ruler should stick to the *Dao* as the ultimate "standard of right and wrong,"[158] however, may at best prevent despotism, but only seemingly provides political rule with a higher normative backing. It rather shows how normatively underdetermined Daoist naturalism is, a naturalism which Han Fei, the first commentator of the *Laozi*,[159] can smoothly incorporate into his program. The indifferent attitude of laissez-faire to the processes of nature, which distinguishes the *Dao*, is mimetically repeated in the silent and unexcited supervision of society by the ruler. Rather than being shaped by the conscious efforts and aspiration of its members, society is forced back into a quasi-natural blind self-regulation.[160]

Why can Daoism in such a blatant manner be pocketed by the detested Legalist raison d'état? The reason is because the Daoists pay homage to the same preconventional rationality which the Legalist strategically make use of. The logic of reward and punishment, after all, is the reversal of hedonism, of the yearning for "natural" happiness, and of the emphasis on physical existence.

In view of the horror picture of the blind automatism of a system paralyzing and manipulating deindividualized agents of strictly defined roles, it is not easy to do justice to the political philosophy of the Legalists. Their utopia stands comparison with any other model of reasons of state like the ones conceived by Plato, Kautilîya, and Machiavelli. With archaic vigor, a train of thought of rigid consistency is presented which in many aspects sounds temptingly modern. That morals should keep out of politics is a thesis of great topicality, although the Chinese Legalists alone have relentlessly accounted for its implications and consequences. These consequences are already inhuman, by Zhou standards.

Yet, the mercilessness of the Legalists unduly discredited many of their ideas. They stand on the side of the state, vindicating a more general point of view than that of the family. They try to restrain private relationships (*si*) in favor of public interests (*gong*).[161] They seek for a device to relieve politics of the risk which lies in the personality of the ruler. And fighting the old hereditary aristocracy, they proclaim the equality of all, the "high minister" and the "commoner," the "distant and humble" and the "near and loved one," before the impartial law of reward and punishment.[162] Yet, for the Legalists, politics is mere technique, the public realm which they defend is a parade ground of stupefied recipients of orders, and their equality is the equality of standardized cogs in the state machinery. In the end, the society they have in mind is no more than a barbaric distortion of an alternative to personal rule, familism, nepotism, and corruption.

From the point of view of the cognitive-developmental theory, Legalism advocates an extreme law-and-order "morality" of Stage 4 which is not built on conventional virtues, but on the naked preconventional orientation to the physical consequences of behavior (Stage 1). This conception itself, however, is only possible by a cool reflection from the detached postconventional perspective of Stage 4½. The Legalist is well aware of this difference. He demands of others unconditional subordination, but he himself sees through the hermetical system from outside. He "exalts law, but is himself without," as Xunzi aptly notes.[163] And Shang Yang proudly proclaims:

> Ordinary people feel well in old habits, and the scholars immerse in what they have heard [from their teachers]. Both are good for filling offices and maintaining law. But one cannot discuss with them *things beyond the law*.[164]

Hence, Legalism is itself a most outstanding indication of the free and uninhibited spirit of the axial age—the same age which its political representative, the state of Qin, finally put an end to by the unification of China.

15

Conclusion and Prospect

In a systematic interpretation, I have reconstructed the formation of ancient Chinese moral philosophy as a breakthrough towards enlightenment in the sense of the emancipation of thought from tradition, convention, and institutions. In spite of the many differences between the competing schools and within them, we can speak of an overall consciousness of the epoch which can be characterized by Kohlberg's term as "postconventional." China's entrance into the "axial age," then, means the transcending of conventional morality and the transition towards postconventional thinking. By means of an heuristic of ontogenesis, this development can be shown as emerging from a crisis of state and family morality and established ways of life. In the following, I will recapitulate its genetic structure.[1]

The fact that China becomes the scenery of an ethical debate of such dimensions is due to the historical decline of what Hegel has termed *substantielle Sittlichkeit* (ethical life), and its main pillars, the family, the state, and the conventional ethos of propriety. The inner logical development of this process can be subsequently traced from the crisis of these fundamental orientation marks of *Sittlichkeit* (Kohlberg's Stages 3 and 4) via the breakthrough to critical consciousness (Stage 4 1/2) towards the search for new norms (Stages 5 and 6).

Relative to the specific school, *family* conflict is dealt with quite differently in axial age literature. Except for the Legalists, it is not a salient topic, and in general it is fought out less resolutely than the conflict with the state. This is certainly due to the fact that contrary to the state the family still has natural emotion on its side. Yet, there are a number of frictions which, for the axial age thinkers, necessitate asking some critical questions about family morality. Blood revenge, one of its most striking and atavistic expressions, is a destabilizing factor because of its inherent logic of endless retaliation. Family solidarity may also support nepotism which prevents the really capable and worthy from taking office. This is detrimental to effective and just government, and contradicts impartiality. Moreover, one has to cope with the possibility that the parents are immoral. Together with the other once firmly established social authorities, the teacher and the ruler, the parents share the susceptibility to "inhumanity," as Mo Di says. None of these authorities hence can set up an unconditionally binding norm.

The most pointed antifamilistic stance can be found among the Legalists. They measure family morals by public interest, which they identify with the interest of an authoritarian state. Yang Zhu and the Daoists, too, reject being tied into the family, though they would still prefer this to submitting to the state. The Confucians are notoriously well-disposed towards the family, but their attitude, too, is ambiguous. Confucius faces the necessity of admonition, though in a moderate form. Mengzi criticizes "not to murmur when the parents' fault is great." In the *Xunzi* (similarly in the *Xiaojing*), we find an emphatic corroboration of this preparedness for admonishment. It demands to "follow justice and not the father," encourages a "fighting" attitude, and lays down conditions for following or rejecting orders.

In spite of these reservations, family morals can still claim to express a natural sentiment. Obedience to the *state* (Stage 4) is much less self-evident. Chinese philosophers, with the exception of the Legalist apologists of law and order, assume a far more skeptical attitude towards the state than towards the family. The state gets under the pressure of legitimation and becomes subject to severe criticism—in Daoism as a rapacious institution, in Confucianism for the wicked politics de facto pursued. Confucius condemns taking office in a state devoid of the *Dao*. Mengzi calls the feudal rulers murderers and, like Xunzi, justifies tyrannicide. Generally, the Confucians support a moral restraint on politics. Their readiness to loyal cooperation is restricted by their insistence that a policy in the interest of the people and in accordance with their moral ideals be pursued.

The state not only evokes moral resentment, it also collides with the interests of the family. This conflict can be fatal if the obligations towards both exclude each other. Suicide might be the only way out of this hopeless contradiction. Perhaps this tragic aporia constitutes one of the motives to search for criteria which go beyond conventional morality.

The limits of conventional morality are also apparent in the crisis of propriety (*li*). From a Confucian viewpoint, conventional propriety is indispensable, for without it man would be "without any standing," as the *Lunyu* states. Yet, the rules of proper behavior have lost their binding force since the decline of Western Zhou society. People no longer keep to the boundaries defined by the *li*, and whoever does, is, as Confucius deplores, suspected of "flattery." For the Daoists, *li* is nothing but the final state of decay of the primordial unity of nature and an incarnation of constrained artificiality. Confucius advocates a "return to propriety" (*fu li*), which is only possible if man "overcomes himself." Although not in Daoist anger, he hereby expresses the quality of alienation inherent in conventional role observance.

Along with the vanishing belief in the conventional demeanor and in the community's long established inherited forms of life, faith in the community itself and its judgments suffers decay. The "good" ceases to be identical with the general consensus, and to enjoy reputation is no longer a guarantee for being a truly respectable person. On the contrary, a Confucian "gentleman" must be prepared to be misjudged by the others. All philosophers of the axial age, the Chinese like the Greek, feel superior to the opinions of the majority and the "vulgar world." There is no familiar intimate context in which they would any longer feel at home. They wander around restlessly, their unsettled life standing against the rootedness of former times. Morality itself becomes the "abode" of the Confucian intellectual.

To *turn away* from the world, to *turn inward into the self*, and finally to *return (fu li)* to society or break with it forever—this is the pattern of response of Chinese thinkers to the crisis of ethical life. A key indication of the step towards a postconventional perspective can be found in the numerous attacks on culture and custom, especially by the Daoists. These attacks, which stand out by their radical diction, can be identified as exemplary representations of Stage 4½, in ontogenesis the phase of youthful protest against everything that has previously been blindly accepted. At this stage, conventional morality is typically exposed as artificial. Nature, life, and individual happiness are played off against the despotism of custom by appealing to the preconventional rationality of Stages 1 and 2. As in the teaching of the Greek Sophists of the fifth century B.C., the fundamental idea is to lay stress upon the natural against the "made." The Chinese opposition of *nei* and *wai* (the inner and the outer), and of *xing* (inborn nature) and *wei* (artificial, false) corresponds to the Greek opposition of *physis* and *nomos*.

In China, protagonists of Stage 4½ can be found above all among the Daoists and their predecessors. Provocatively, they welcome anyone who does not conform to the conventionally accepted standards—madmen, cripples, people mutilated by corporal punishments, and eccentrics, who in the *Zhuangzi* come forward as having a privileged access to knowledge. The Daoists coin downright classic topoi for the recourse to preconventional freedom: the unaffected child, not yet corrupted by education, the Hedonist giving free vent to his inclinations, and the Hedonist's most striking manifestation, the robber. The opportunism of Shen Dao, who views norms as a physical compulsion and bows to behavioral expectations solely in order to remain unharmed, fits well into this picture. All these figures are linked together by one and the same deeper structure: a postconventional recourse to the preconventional past. And if today the frankness of the Daoist "professional youths" with their special liking for a subcultural symbolism of disintegration still strikes a sympathetic chord in ourselves, it is most probably for reminding us of the naive spontaneity of childhood.

However, the Daoists do not show a way out of the crisis of China. In the final analysis, they merely succeed in exposing the deficiencies of conventional morality, its injustice and its neglect of individual happiness. And from their radical critique, we can win a criterion which can count as a touchstone for testing any ethical system: could it prevent my being a member of a gang of robbers, in the widest sense of the word?

Yet, the Daoists fail to recognize that the conventional ethos also has its achievements, and they do not establish any stable new morality. They shy away from the task that the Confucians try to face up to: to provide a new, inner foundation for the indispensable conventional ethos, although the Confucians, too, know that the *Dao*—the postconventional cipher per se for a state beyond the here and now—"does not succeed." The weakness of the Daoist position manifests itself most strikingly in its exploitability by Legalism. In order to enforce a heteronomous conduct, the Legalist ideologists of a Stage 4 defense of law and order make strategic use of the same preconventional rationality, especially of Stage 1, to which the Daoists pay homage. Thus they have little difficulty in usurping the latter. The fact that both schools, in spite of originally totally divergent aims, can enter into the peculiar affiliation documented by the *Laozi* and the *Hanfeizi* rests upon their shared preference for one and the same "natural" interests of man. Whereas the Daoists play these off against the institutions, the Legalists view natural interests as reliable tools to functionalize man for an authoritarian state machine based upon punishment and reward.

Daoism and Legalism throw a piercing light on the intellectual milieu of the Zhou era. Because of their pointedly anticonventional stance, they document the breakthrough in thought much clearer than Confucianism with its outwardly rather conventional profile. The reason for this is that the Confucians typically try simultaneously to *keep faith with the conventional ethos and yet not surrender to it.* The Confucians accept the role obligations towards family, community, state, friends, etc., but impose restraints on these to prevent their degeneration into blind conformity. Although there is a tendency among the Confucians, too, to evade society, in the final analysis they take pains not to shirk *Sittlichkeit*, but to provide a new basis for it.

If one follows Kohlberg's logic, this basis may first be found in ascribing the rules of social life to an *agreement* for the *benefit* of all. Now what is right is no longer predetermined by tradition or the mere factual existence of concrete norms (as on the conventional level), nor is it revealed by physical nature. It is the outcome of the stipulations of free contractors with relative opinions and interests. This is the Stage 5 in Kohlberg's scheme, and it appears to be a logical continuation of the Stage 4½ insight into the arbitrariness of social norms. Contrary to Greece and, above all, modern Anglo-Saxon political philosophy, relativistic contractualism does not belong to the striking features of Chinese thought. The relativity of opinions is only assumed by one Daoist school, and this school does not believe that there can ever be an agreement between the different points of view. Those philosophers, on the other hand, who view the state as an institution for the benefit of everybody, are no relativists. From an external perspective, the Chinese axial age presents itself as a free forum of controversy of ideas which holds Kohlberg's "lawmaker's perspective." But no thinker has really seen an advantage in this actuality of dispute and has envisaged the chance for progress via agreement achieved by general discussion, though now and then one catches a glimpse of the idea. In general, every philosopher is convinced that there is only one right way, his own or the one of his school, and they do not draw positive conclusions from the intellectual climate they all thrive in.

Yet, ideas of agreement and contract in the interest of mutual benefit after the model of Stage 5 do play a role in Mo Di's and especially in Xunzi's legitimation of the state. Both assume a chaotic "original position" in which men fight each other to assert their own opinion or secure their living. According to Mo Di, a ruler is "selected" to put a stop to chaos by setting up an administration. For Xunzi, ingenious cultural heroes (*shengren*) create morals and institutions in order to guarantee a well-regulated access of all to the scarce resources. This seems to exclude the idea of an agreement. Yet, for Xunzi, in the final analysis a *shengren* is little more than a personification of human reason as such. The idea that the *shengren* have created political order as the only means to secure stability is, therefore, equivalent to stating that order is based on rational insight. The state is not simply sanctified by tradition or a body to be upheld for its own sake (Stage 4). It is a product of reasonable deliberation that can in principle be shared and approved of by everybody. This deliberation is in turn based on a utilitarian rationale: to adapt oneself to the order is useful, while to reject it will lead to the ruin of all. But only—and this is the point of Xunzi's idea—by conceding rule, hierarchy, and a division of unequal roles will order endure. Stating that "equality is not equality," and characterizing social order as "fissured and yet equal," Xunzi proposes a kind of subtle "principle of difference" reminiscent of Rawls designed to make the necessity of social inequality plausible. Dialectically, inequality is the condition for the possibility of an order that guarantees a living equally to everyone. The reverse of this idea is that inequality is only acceptable if in return social care and public relief are provided for by the powerful.

Thus the basic idea of legitimation of the state is derived from public benefit and prosperity, and the state is obliged to fulfill this its own raison d'être. Reciprocity becomes the reverse of hierarchy. A tyrant who violates this principle can be killed like an "isolated fellow," because he has lost the necessary approval of his subjects.

Xunzi's legitimation of political order, which is related to his concept of justice, is hence based on the idea of an implicit utilitarian agreement. If we consider, moreover, the "prior-to-society perspective" (Kohlberg) which his legitimation program presupposes, and if we add his fundamental anthropological assumption that man has a mind to choose and reject freely at his own discretion, Xunzi's political theory as a whole, in spite of its great amount of elitism, represents Stage 5 of Kohlberg's scheme. The fact that he does not explicitly formulate the idea of a social contract might relate to a specific weakness of contractualism: a contract itself cannot guarantee its observance, which requires trust, and thus an additional safeguard. The same calculation of profit that now advises one to enter into the agreement might at another time recommend the breaking of it. The crux is clearly exposed by Zhou thinkers. Mengzi points out that there is no norm whatsoever that would withstand the principle of profit, and that under its auspices one will "not be satisfied before one has not snatched all." And the Daoists emphasize that this principle will in the final analysis only be to the advantage of the most reckless one. These arguments give us to consider that the principle of profit is not generalizable. Mo Di, who tries to base social intercourse on a self-regulating "exchange of mutual benefit," seems to realize the problem, too: he advocates a strong institutional control, which would not be necessary in the first place if the pursuit of mutual benefit alone could provide a solid basis of society. The ambiguity of the principle of benefit is also noted by the Legalists. They emphasize that one can well offer the exchange of benefits to others, but can never be sure that they on their side will really enter into a lasting relation of reciprocity. Legalism, therefore, from the outset stakes everything on the card of institutionalized distrust.

But there is another answer to the aporias of utilitarian contractualism which transcends these instead of lapsing back into an external control of human self-interest. It can only be found within man and beyond his egoism. This is the way of Socrates in Greece, who puts up the rule that it is better to suffer injustice than to inflict it. At the same time, he appeals to the inner voice of his *daimonion* and to the principle to "obey to nothing else of myself but to the *logos* which upon reflection appears to me the best." Socrates hence disposes of a *nonegoistic fundamental norm* and a *principle of autonomy* in which this norm is anchored. Together with the claim to *universality* (the fulfillment of which by Socrates, a sympathizer of slave-holding Sparta, is uncertain), both are central aspects of Kohlberg's highest Stage 6.

A step similar in substance to that of Socrates in Greece is made by Confucius in China. The *nonegoistic fundamental norm* is represented by the concept of humaneness, *ren*, though, as I see it, in the final analysis only in its reading as the Golden Rule. As "the one pervading all" and a maxim that "consists of a single word and can be practiced for all one's life," it is obviously thought of as a last fundament of morality requiring no further justification. Humaneness, in terms of the Golden Rule, introduces into ethics an abstract and formal principle of role-taking (the quintessence of Stage 6), of putting myself in the other's place and conceding to him anything that I would claim for myself. A hidden strategic reservation when following this principle is ruled out by the overall deontic context of Confucian ethics. Although in Confucian literature the motif of profit-oriented reciprocity is not entirely absent, in general humaneness is accepted for its own sake and not for any personal advantage.

As to the *universality claim,* critics have repeatedly argued that the Confucian concept of *ren* is designed only for a closed social group, namely, the family or the ruling aristocracy. But there is no real evidence for this claim. Undoubtedly, for most Confucians the family is a place of major responsibility. But when Mengzi occasionally identifies humaneness with "love towards one's relatives," he does not seek for a limitation on, but a foundation of morality that later should be "extended" to all others. The common people, though hardly able to act on behalf of themselves, should be "raised to the level of humaneness" (Confucius) and be subject to a "humane regime" (Mengzi). Consequently, there are many efforts to make the Golden Rule a political principle by reconciling its horizontal symmetry with the necessities of hierarchical rule. Humaneness, furthermore, does not lose its binding force when a "gentleman" stays among barbarian tribes. It is, therefore, not merely a convention within a specific ethnic or social group. There is at least no principal boundary that would curtail the range over which it is valid. Xunzi and the *Hanshi waizhuan* define *ren* as "respect" due to anyone one gets in contact with, regardless of who he might be. Their support of the hierarchical social order notwithstanding, all anthropologies developed by the Confucians and their opponents are egalitarian in their basic assumptions. The Greek idea that some men are slaves by nature is alien to them, and they do not proclaim the group morality of a closed polis. The most conspicuous avowal of universalism, however, is not found in Confucian literature, but in Mo Di, who uncompromisingly replaces "exclusion" by "inclusion."

The *principle of autonomy*, the third condition of Stage 6, which makes action and judgment independent not only of self-interest, but also of heteronomy, first appears in the *Lunyu* and is later explicitly formulated by Xunzi. The *Lunyu* knows the concept of a "self" that stands its ground against the misunderstandings and the hostility of others. It reflects on and "sits in judgment on itself," knowing a private seclusion analogous to conscience. For Mengzi, critical self-reflection which leads to the realization that one has been upright will enable one to "withstand thousands or tens of thousands." Xunzi declares the human mind an absolutely sovereign organ of decision that at its own pleasure "chooses and repudiates," judges what is right and wrong, and "cannot be forced to alter its opinion." And like Aristotle in his famous dictum that he loves his teacher, but loves truth more, Xunzi proclaims as his teacher the one who "criticizes me and is right." Confucianism herewith disposes of a principle of autonomy which is equal to that of the Greeks. Autonomy is not only claimed for judgment, but also for the far more difficult task of practice. A Confucian gentleman, says Mengzi, "strides his way alone," if necessary, and cannot be "led astray by poverty and mean conditions and bent by authority and power." If the world does not recognize him, Xunzi adds, he will "stand proudly and independently between heaven and earth, and will not let himself be intimidated." He is not guided by the fear of death, institutional sanctions, or community disrespect, but by a feeling of inner shame and a commitment to his ideals and to his self-respect. This motivational orientation corresponds to the postconventional substratum of Confucian ethics and to the principled reading of humaneness.

All aspects of Stage 6 are thus present in early Confucian ethics. This is not to say that Confucianism as such, or any of the other schools, stands on this level.

It means no more and no less than that in systematically important passages in the works of its ancient main representatives, the conventional orientations, in order to meet their insufficiencies, are transcended in the direction of a postconventional universal principled morality.

Even if such a principled morality is not elaborated in detail, we can at least speak of its first anticipation. That it lacks sharp outlines is above all due to the fact that the Confucians, from the vantage point of postconventional thinking, *turn back* to the social context with its conventional rules of propriety and its obligations towards the family, the community, and the state. If they do not want to withdraw from society, then it is because what ethics is there for in the first place is this world of men. This can be seen from the peculiar reciprocal relationship of *li* and *ren* in the *Lunyu*. Propriety without humaneness is empty formalism or even an expression of strategical calculation, but humaneness without propriety is meaningless. The polity would perish if conventional duties were no longer observed with due respect. But their fulfillment must be accompanied by a vigilant consciousness which knows about their corruptibility and limits and, if necessary, raises protest in the name of morality and refuses to follow. The Confucian hope is that both, moral mental attitude and ethical responsibility, can be made compatible with each other—a hope which culminates in the utopia of the "Great community" (*da tong*) where the specific care for the individual context of life no longer obstructs the interest of the greater whole. But since the normative goal remains an ideal, reality enforces flexibility and compromise. *Return* becomes the key metaphor of the *postconventional ethics of responsibility* to which the classic Confucian is committed. The seeming boundedness by context and convention of this ethics is a second order one and relative to its double structure.

Chinese ethical reasoning of the axial age can thus be brought into a Kohlbergian system that shows its logical structure and provides criteria for the evaluation of the different positions. China's entrance into the "axial age," then, means the transcending of the conventional level of *Sittlichkeit* and a breakthrough to the "postconventional" perspective from where the conventional ethos is either rejected or, with new restraints, reestablished. This breakthrough is the outcome of a crisis of Chinese society and of the experience that the traditional ways have failed in the process of decline of the old aristocratic order. The salient characteristic of the intellectual atmosphere is that alternatives become imaginable and are discussed and reflected upon. The thinking of the intellectual elite as such reflects a Stage 5 point of view, and the epoch in its entirety holds the "lawmaker's perspective." "To change the customary" is a recurrent typical motto of the time.

How is the breakthrough achieved? Since Weber and already since Hegel and Schelling, who doubt the existence of such a breakthrough in China, the *transcendence* hypothesis has been prevalent. It supposes that without referring to a transcendent authority the Archimedian point is missing to move the world and to ask radical questions. Usually, transcendence is interpreted in religious or metaphysical terms.[2] At this point, the Chinese material shows two things:

(a) If transcendence is understood as the viewpoint from which the empirical world can be called into question, the concept should be specified in such a way that it can comprise different, functionally roughly equivalent contents. At least, one cannot deny the Chinese breakthrough with the reverse argument that a strictly religious or metaphysical conception of transcendence would be a *conditio sina qua non* for such a development. For, the Chinese thinkers distance themselves from the inherited customary forms of life by categories which, in general, do not presuppose a strong ontological conception of another world. Their most important cipher is the *Dao*, in the *Lunyu* an incarnation for a state beyond the here and now which stands out precisely because it lacks concrete specification. The Daoists appeal to the *Dao* not only as a metaphysical concept, but also as *nature*. In either case, the normative standard for living which it provides can entail radical criticism of culture and rule. Also, the *cosmos* with its constant harmony can serve as an antitype for the chaotic human world, although cosmology hardly plays the role which often has been assigned to it. In Mo Di, the argument of *utility* by a single stroke crosses out a whole cultural tradition. The Legalists make use of pure *strategical calculation* to brush aside everything that has previously been accepted. For the Confucians, another "Archimedian point" becomes important: the inner *self* which knows that a noble mind "shows itself only in its not being accepted." Not in conversation with God, but in self-reflection and self-cultivation does this inner self achieve an imperturbable strength which helps to refuse accommodation to the injudicious world.

All of these different accounts represent "breakthroughs" which are, with the possible exception of the metaphysical reading of the *Dao,* not based on the assumption of a religious or metaphysical "other world." However, the achievements of the Greek Sophists and of Socrates, too, cannot be understood if a too narrow conception of transcendence is declared indispensable for liberating thought from established contexts.

In order to explain the phenomenon of the worldwide breakthrough of the axial age, it is, therefore, necessary to enlarge the concept of transcendence. It should be reformulated in *formal* or functional terms as the standpoint which allows one to distance the given human life world without predetermining the specific content of the corresponding perspective. In this sense, Schwartz has aptly called transcendence "a kind of standing back and looking beyond, a kind of critical, reflective questioning of the actual and a new vision of what lies beyond."[3]

(b) Despite the necessary specification of the concept of transcendence, it still makes sense to attribute to the prototypical religious form a special "leverage." This leverage can be demonstrated by the disenchanting power of the old Israelite conception of God, and it is here where Weber localizes the difference between Occident and Orient. But in contrast to Weber, the idea of religious transcendence also comes into play when we have to explain the postconventional breakthrough in China. Chinese moral philosophy is after all heir to the religion of "Heaven" (*Tian*) of the early Zhou. Even if the "Heaven" of the Zhou is less otherworldly than the God of the Israelites, yet, all human and especially political action can, in its name, be brought into a sharp contrast to "virtue" (*de*). The belief in *Tian* thus leads to a detachment from the empirical human world which can later, after the decline of Zhou religion, be inherited by the philosophers. The fact that by means of the aforementioned different motives the thinkers of ancient China can challenge their age, is owing to the distance between the course of events on the one hand and the truly right on the other which has for the first time been created by the religion of Heaven. This heritage most conspicuously lives on in Mengzi who sets up the distinction of the two realms of human and Heavenly "ranks," in order to subordinate the political hierarchy to the hierarchy of virtues with humaneness at its head. It is certainly this dichotomy which explains the outstanding and uncompromising passion with which Mengzi raises his voice against the potentates of his time.

Religion, therefore, does play a role, although the philosophers of the Chinese axial age in general put forward nonreligious arguments. Mo Di's appeal to religion has a utilitarian coloring. And even Mengzi's radical diction cannot conceal that Confucianism remains a teaching dedicated to the profane world of man and self-cultivation. When Mengzi makes use of the perspective of "Heaven," he does not intend to devalue this world of man as idle, but to rescue the earthly, secular ethos—not in order to fall back into it, but to provide it with a new foundation from a higher point of view. This return is typical of Confucianism. But we must not overlook the preceding withdrawal.

We have seen that classical Chinese ethics can, with remarkable plasticity, be interpreted by the cognitive-developmental theory up to the postconventional stages. This not only confirms, refuting Weber and his followers who underestimate China's potential for ethical rationalization,[4] that the Chinese axial age has been an epoch of enlightenment, but it also corroborates the universalistic claim and the heuristic power of Kohlberg's theory. Kohlberg's evaluation of the stages of moral reasoning is even explicitly shared in some of the ancient texts. The *Xunzi* distinguishes "small conduct" (service to the family, Stage 3), and "medium conduct" (doing one's duty in an office, Stage 4), from "great conduct" consisting in following neither the father nor the ruler, but justice and the *Dao*. The final stage in sequence, which transcends family and state, is at the same time the normatively highest. *Zhuangzi*, *Laozi*, and *Huainanzi* present a similar sequence, although the Daoists do not have in mind the ascent towards an ever higher competence, but the descent from the idealized primordial unity with nature via humaneness, justice, and propriety. The Daoists even know the idea of a parallel between phylo- and ontogenesis. The development of man as a species from the member of the primitive commune embedded in nature to the harassed citizen of civilized society repeats itself in the education of the individual from the free and spontaneous infant to the competitive, ambitious adult.

As a result of this study, it is no longer tenable to maintain, as Kohlberg's critics do, that Western universal and principled ethical conceptions like the cognitive-developmental theory are not applicable to China, because China knew another, namely, collectivistic, conformist, or nonprincipled paradigm. It is quite easy to prove the existence of social conformity pressure, group morality, and leveling of opinion both in traditional and present-day China. But this certainly does not represent the quintessence of Chinese culture. On the contrary, that which has prevailed often fails to embody the ideas of the ancients and is regressive compared to the standards once established. Whoever, regardless for which reason, appeals to Chinese tradition, must confront the likewise transmitted criteria of the axial age enlightenment.

But we also have to explain why the discrepancy between the original potential and the actual historical development of China came into existence in the first place. This is the more important since "official," order-conformist China, also, has appealed to the authority of the Zhou Philosophers, above all of the Confucians, as its intellectual foundation. Every explanation, of course, must remain tentative and vague, because unequivocal and definite causes are not accessible to historical analysis. But we can well relate the ideas of the axial age in a plausible way to their "effective history" (*Wirkungsgeschichte*), or to the absence of that history.

That East and West would develop as they did was not the necessary and predetermined outcome of their respective "innate" potentials. The common *ex post*–perspective of the progress that did or did not take place bars the insight into the contribution of contingencies to history. It cannot be doubted that the West would be different today without the Greek and Jewish-Christian foundations. But no less important for its course were the accidents, the favorable geography, the mixture of peoples, and even the unforeseeable regressions. The political fragmentation of Europe fostered the exchange and diffusion of ideas. The permanent shifting of the cultural centers enabled a very productive competition. Yet, there was no lineal progress. On the contrary, Europe suffered enormous setbacks which then created the preconditions for new breakthroughs. The greatest of these setbacks was the barbaric invasion of the Germanic peoples which put an end to ancient civilization. Not until after hundreds of years was it possible to rediscover classical antiquity, to pick up its threads anew, and finally even to surpass the level once achieved. In the meantime, there had emerged a new challenge for the Western mind which allowed for a hitherto unachieved sharpening of thinking and philosophical argument: the challenge to make Christian religion, something prima facie unyielding to logic and rationality, accessible to reason. Of paramount economic, political, and intellectual importance was, last but not least, the discovery of America which widened and liberated the Western world perspective in an unthought-of way.

By this I only want to hint at the fact that the development of the Occident was the result of a confluence of factors, some of them inherited from classical antiquity and some of them accidental, and not simply the logical unfolding of unique cultural foundations. Yet it was the illusion of its own uniqueness which led the West to discredit the East.

In China, too, in the final analysis, a combination of circumstances, contingencies, and cultural roots determined the course of history. What was perhaps decisive was the absence of some favorable conditions which were important for the West. Chinese culture developed largely on its own and could not participate in a broad exchange of ideas comparable to the one between the Occidental countries. In China, except for Buddhism which caused a step forward in philosophy, foreign influences came primarily from nomadic peoples which stood on a much lower cultural level. They reinforced regressive tendencies, for example in law, rather than exerting fertilizing effects.

What China lacked in comparison with the West was the rivalry of a great number of different and yet equally developed cultures closely adjacent to each other which stood in communication and competition, could make use of the novelty effect of changes of environment, and could, if necessary, provide alternative places of refuge for ideas and thinkers. Whereas the axial age especially is a proof for the productivity of polycentrism, the early political centralization of China entailed a cultural setback, though it had paradoxically been demanded by the philosophers and institutionally was a progress. The philosophers had called for the unifier of China who would end the chaos of the "warring states," and their hopes were fulfilled in a fatal manner. The unified empire gave the death-blow to the free exchange of opinion of the "hundred schools." It was replaced by an amalgam of Legalism, Confucianism, and cosmology, which under the name of Confucianism became the quasi-official state-ideology with a monopoly on opinion. The centralization of power, the establishment of an effective apparatus of government, the abolition of birth privileges, and last, but not least, the introduction of a system of governmental examinations which ought to bring the really worthy and capable into power—all this helped to control and absorb a considerable part of the intellectuals. They made a far-reaching compromise with the state, although the critical impulse of the axial age was never completely lost and time and again found a vent.

Zhou philosophy, however, has not simply been betrayed by later generations for their participation in power, and has not merely met with unfavorable conditions. While this is true to some extent, the fate of classical philosophy also has to do with classical philosophy itself. What is the inner relationship, then, between classical ethics, especially the Confucian one, and its "effective history"? What is the potential of this ethics in the first place, and where did it fail to succeed, and for which *internal* reasons?

Obviously, it was possible to adopt Confucianism with quite different aims, and also to utilize it for purposes which originally would not have found its consent. None of the great ethical conceptions of mankind, however, has been immune against this kind of functionalization and loss of substance. The crux of Confucianism in this connection is perhaps the close relation of the two sides of its ethics which I have termed, with Hegel, *Sittlichkeit* and *Moralität*: *ren*, *Moralität*, is not played off against *li*, *Sittlichkeit*, since it is meant to strengthen the latter. On the one hand, Confucius defines *ren* as "return to propriety" and omission of everything not in accordance with *li*. On the other hand, he denies that *li* has any intrinsic value by itself if "as a man one has no humaneness." The secret of this seeming paradox lies in the effort to superimpose the imperatives of a general "humane" morality over the social role obligations without neglecting these. The tension between both is, characteristically, not expressed in a trenchant manner.

This entails the possibility of referring to the founding text of Confucianism with opposite intentions. For the genuine Confucian, the fascination of the old teaching was obviously derived from the expectation to achieve a true moral life with due commitment to one's social responsibility and willingness to adjust oneself to the bounds of one's context, yet in integrity and proof against opportunistic consent. But since in the *Lunyu* all too much remains unclear and undecided, it could, on the basis of a corresponding selective reading, also be used as a mere catechism of accommodation and subordination. This has determined to a large extent Confucius' "official" influence in China. In the course of this development, Confucianism has been overtaken by the same world of *Sittlichkeit* which it recognized as in need of *Moralität*. Here, it has to pay for what can be viewed as its *proton pseudos:* to leave the mundane hierarchies largely untouched.

Confucianism accepts the given world, but tries to moderate its injustice by appeals to the mighty and conceptions like Mengzi's "humane politics." To call into question the established form of society with all its hierarchies as little as possible, and yet to humanize it to the extreme, this can count as its general program. Fundamental change is beyond imagination. Confucianism develops a morality in the postconventional center of which we find the symmetry of human relations and the abstraction of the "other," but which, in a peculiar constellation, at the same time permits at its side political and social conservatism. In spite of the Golden Rule of the *Lunyu* and of Mengzi's and Xunzi's anthropology, and in spite of all its partizanship for the weak and poor, Confucianism cannot really take its leave of the world of subordination and inequality. Wherever necessary, it restrains the ruling powers, but it hardly disputes their position which invites abuse. This means that the potential of its postconventional, egalitarian, moral side does not really win out over the conventional side which basically accepts the given structures as they have always been.

This is indicated, for example, by the fate of the Golden Rule. The Golden Rule is originally formulated in abstract terms as a principle of horizontal reciprocity of the self and the other. But in connection with its concrete adaption for social action, the idea of equality is distorted by all too quickly incorporating the hierarchies of society into it. It seems that under the condition of a hierarchical world with great social differential, the second characteristic expression of humaneness, the ethics of compassion in the *Mengzi*, was the more successful program in comparison to the Golden Rule with its abstract supposition of equality. The Golden Rule neither came upon promising historical conditions nor could it exert effective influence on these. This is the more deplorable since it represents a culmination of all essential achievements of abstraction of the axial age which could have revolutionized politics, law, and society: the abstractions of the ego and the other, and the abstractions from status, role, and mere custom.

A negative burden for the future of the axial age enlightenment was no doubt the intolerance with which the majority of the Confucians, like the majority of the other philosophers, used to react to their competitors. There is hardly any thinker who would acknowledge the culture of competition which characterizes the epoch and constitutes its richness, and which all of them in fact live on. For the naturalistic Daoists, this goes without saying—as mystics, they do not believe in discourse, and they eloquently declare that words are null and void. For the Legalists, intellectuals are parasites, and he who in their ideal state still wants to learn something shall "take a clerk as his teacher and study the laws." Mo Di, in a truly enlightened moment, formulates an ethical principle of communication according to which only the better argument shall count. He moreover knows the validity criterion of the convictions of the majority, a problematical criterion, however. But then he devises, with all minuteness of detail, the nightmare of bringing into line all opinions by adjustment to superiors. Confucius speaks highly of Zichan, the chancellor of Zheng, who against the resistance of the nobility tolerates public discussion on politics. But Confucius also states that "the citizens would not discuss if the world were in possession of the *Dao*." Although he is the most willing to listen to other opinions, for him too, then, the actuality of discussion is disturbing. Mengzi, who coins the term *xieshuo*, "false doctrine" or "heterodoxy," wants to "put an end" to the respective philosophies, and declares that he "discusses only because there is no alternative." Xunzi expects from a "gentleman" to be ready for discussion, but he also demands to prohibit the theories of twelve renowned philosophers and to penalize "criminal teachings."[5]

The list could be extended, but one thing has already become sufficiently clear: The great majority of the Chinese philosophers lay claim to the intellectual freedom of their postconventional thinking primarily for themselves or for the position of their school, and have difficulties to grant it also to their opponents. The society that most of them have in mind is authoritarian in one way or the other and not republican in the sense of a free general public. The much discussed problem of Chinese democracy[6] begins here and not only with the question whether the "people" actively participate in politics, a participation, after all, which could hardly be expected in Zhou times. If anywhere, then it is here that China's ancient philosophy contains the germ of its later degeneration.

Yet, it also contains the means for its own rectification and further development, because it fell below its own possibilities. Even the intolerance described above is, after all, the reverse side of the claim to one's own moral and intellectual independence and is due to the dialectics of the autonomous "self." What would be necessary, therefore, is to preserve the postconventional content of the classical teachings and to direct it against their own shortcomings and inconsistencies. For, the ethical insights of the ancients in many respects contradict their political and social ideas and have never really materialized. In the case of Confucianism, this concerns, above all, the egalitarian anthropology, the concept of the autonomous yet social-minded "self" with its implications of independent judgment and action, the idea that politics is accountable for morality and the interest of the commonwealth and the Golden Rule as a culmination point of all ethically essential abstractions of the axial age.

Herewith, Confucianism disposes of the ideas of equality, autonomy, social responsibility, and reciprocal respect. It moreover knows the utopia of a "Great Community" where such ideas might become reality. Yet, this potential is hardly employed to bring about structural change, but primarily to make the *given* world more human and prevent the necessary fulfillment of customary duties from its degeneration into opportunism and corruption. It does not come to mind that on the basis of those ideas another world would be possible—a republican world without monarchs and subordination, which would be defined by giving everybody the equal right and the equal chance to participate in the fundamental decisions concerning the course of the system in which he or she lives. The idea of the New is only pursued by the Legalists. Anyhow, it could only be put into practice with the additional idea of institutionalization, which likewise belongs more to the Legalist than to the Confucian tradition. The Confucians trust in the moral essence of the person and his bearing, not in institutional safeguards. This is one of the reasons why their conceptions of equality, autonomy, responsibility, and respect have not led to the explicit formulation of human rights guaranteed by a constitution. However, whether the person-oriented outlook is really inferior to the institution-oriented one is difficult to determine.[7] The mere legal guarantee of freedoms alone may matter little. Today, all too many states decorate themselves with such constitutions, only to trample upon them in practice. But no less removed from reality is the Confucian hope that power can be controlled primarily—though not exclusively—by furthering the moral insight of its wielders and engaging moral advisors, even though we now and then find a "humane" ruler in Chinese history. Both the personal and the institutional element seem to be indispensable and should be integrated with each other. Generally speaking, the only philosophically consistent form of such integration would be a free republic.[8]

Such integration is, theoretically, quite conceivable on the basis the indigenous possibilities of China. Imagine, for example, an alternative historical convergence of Confucianism and Legalism to that which took place. In China, the conventional side of Confucianism actually entered into a solid historical liaison with the socio-technical side of Legalism, that is, the conceptions of administrative technique and control by penal law. The converse model would be: a society based on guaranteed rights, legal equality, and institutional checks on power, and sustained by autonomous moral individuals with a strong sense of social responsibility. Such a society did not evolve in China—nor, strictly speaking, elsewhere—

but it is, as a regulative goal, imaginable within her intellectual tradition. It would be a preeminent task of a really free Chinese intelligentsia to work at such a new construction of the "philosophical heritage," instead of finding novel perspectives merely outside the borders of China. This does not mean supporting the idea of a nationalist self-sufficiency bound up in its narrow horizon. The point in question is to continue precisely the *universalist legacy* of tradition which from the outset has reached beyond the limits of Chinese culture. For in China, too, the *project enlightenment* began more than two millenniums ago. And in China, too, this project, in spite of all its problems, difficulties, and setbacks, must not fail.

Endnotes

NOTES TO CHAPTER 1

1. Weber 1951, p. 164.
2. Hall and Ames 1987, pp. 15 and 16.
3. Trauzettel 1977, p. 353.
4. Rosemont 1986, pp. 208–9: "The *Lun Yu* (Confucius' "Collected Sayings," H. R.) is not merely a window on the world of late *Chun Qiu* China; it can also serve as a mirror of the contemporary United States. . . . Confucius can teach us, then, that to attempt to abandon communal rituals, customs, and traditions altogether is madness, because they can only be replaced by the ethical, psychological, social, and spiritual void, into which far too many autonomous, individual-oriented Americans are already gazing. . . . I believe . . . that the conceptual framework of modern morals, with its concomitant notions of duty, autonomy, rights, freedom, self, and choice, has run its course, and is now a hindrance rather than an asset to our continuing search for how better to get along with one another in the world. We need new, or older, presuppositions. Of course, the 'What else?' question now intrudes, which is where Confucius comes in again."
5. Fingarette 1972, p. 69.
6. Hall and Ames 1987, pp. 73 and 43.
7. Fingarette 1972, p. 70.
8. It is part and parcel of the pragmatic interpretation, to deny the existence of a concept of truth in Chinese philosophy which is not exclusively pragmatic (cf. for example Hall and Ames 1987, p. 57). Cf. p. 14 below, and Roetz 1993a.
9. Cf. p. 242 below.
10. Fingarette 1991, pp. 218 and 219, italics added. Cf. Chapter 10 below, n. 182. For the *li*, cf. Chapter 10A below.
11. Hall and Ames 1987, p. 39, similarly Graham 1989, p. 29. Cf. also Graham 1983.
12. I of course do not deny the importance of traditions or of what I call "conventional morality" in this book. The accomplishments of both for making a cultivated and civilized human existence possible are beyond doubt. The point in question is whether they provide orientations for conduct which guarantee moral results without any closer inspection, thus nullifying the necessity of individual decisions by other than conven-

tional standards. Moreover, a single look into a great number of today's Third World countries and First World cities shows that even conventional morality or orientation by traditional ways of life are not options which are simply available at any time. Under the present conditions of our world, it amounts to a "postconventional," context-transcending claim that every human being should have a context in which conventional rules can and will be practiced in the first place. In any case, to abandon the fact-value dichotomy for the sake of abiding by cultural contexts is thoughtless.

13. Cf. for example Weggel 1985.

14. Cf. Tu Wei-ming 1990, pp. 53-54.

15. Weber 1951, p. 248.

16. Cf. Roetz 1984.

17. After Joseph Needham's monumental work *Science and Civilization in China* it can hardly be disputed that the fact requiring explanation is not the nonoccurrence of a Chinese development in the direction of "rational mastery of the world." What has to be explained is why that development ultimately came to a deadlock in comparison to that of the West. The causes for this can be found in the one domain which seemed irrelevant in this respect to Weber, namely, economy. Elvin (1973) has, in this connection, advanced the theory of the "high-level equilibrium trap": The fact that an innovative period from the tenth to the fourteenth centuries, towards the end of which China had the world's most advanced mechanized industry, was succeeded by technological stagnation is due to a throroughly rational economic attitude. Population growth on the one hand and shortage of resources on the other lowered the per capita income. The cheapening of labor and the soaring prices of the resources inhibited further technical innovations. Wallerstein (1974) argues that the absence of expansion was responsible for China's fate. Europe was condemned to expand because of shortage of space (cattle breeding and wheat cultivation demand more space than rice cultivation), whereas in China the motive for expansion was lacking in the relevant layers of society. Similarly, Yu Yingshi (1987a, pp. 171–72) points out the absence of economic incentives. For Yu, the modern success of capitalism in East Asia proves that it was not for ethical or religious reasons that it did not develop earlier. With R. H. Tawney, he argues that modern Western industrial capitalism came into being because of the discovery of America and not primarily because of ideological factors.

18. Keyserling 1919, pp. 384–86.

19. Weggel 1985, pp. 313 and 315. See also McElderry 1986. For the topic of tradition and capitalism see moreover Harrell 1985.

20. The relationships between the traditional and the modern regimes in China have often been described, though not without some distortions of the traditional social and political conceptions. See for example Pye 1968, pp. 12ff., and Baum 1982.

21. The basic documents can be found in Zhexueyanjiu bianjibu 1957, pp. 273–441.

22. Cf. for this topic Apel 1971.

23. Cf. Habermas 1982, p. 9.

24. The "hermeneutic supposition of competence" is according to H. G. Gadamer (*Truth and Method*) a presupposition of interpreting texts.

25. That this claim is raised in the first place is denied in the "pragmatic discourse." Cf. Roetz 1993a.

NOTES TO CHAPTER 2

1. Weber 1951, p. 241.
2. Hegel 1956, pp. 120–21, trans. Sibree modified.
3. Like "universism" (De Groot), "mythical thinking" (Cassirer), "nature fetishism" (A. Weber), "a-diheretical thinking" (Lohmann), and so on.
4. Wolff 1740, pp. 219–20.
5. Ibid., pp. 211–12.
6. Montesquieu 1949, vol. 1, p. 269.
7. Quesnay 1965, p. 636.
8. Montesquieu 1949, vol. 1, p. 302. "Manners" for Montesquieu relate to the "interior conduct," "customs" to the "exterior" (ibid., p. 300). In China, for him, both are confounded.
9. Cf. ibid., p. 303: "We shall now show the relation which things in appearance the most indifferent may bear to the fundamental constitution of China. This empire is formed on the plan of a government of a family. If you diminish the paternal authority, or even if you retrench the ceremonies which express your respect for it, you weaken the reverence due to magistrates, who are considered as fathers; nor would the magistrates have the same care of the people, whom they ought to look upon as their children; and that tender relation which subsists between the prince and his subjects would insensibly be lost. Retrench but one of these habits and you overturn the state. It is a thing in itself very indifferent whether the daughter-in-law rises every morning to pay such and such duties to her mother-in-law; but if we consider that these exterior habits incessantly revive an idea necessary to be imprinted on all mind—an idea that forms the ruling spirit of the empire—we shall see that it is necessary that such or such a particular action be performed."
10. The direct appeal to the founders of our view of China is rather seldom. Examples are Trauzettel, who professes his loyalty to Hegel, (1977, p. 350) and Gernet, who keeps faith in Montesquieu, for him "without any doubt the first person in the West to have an intuition so correct concerning the spirit of the Chinese customs" (1982, p. 222).
11. "East Asia thinks differently," *Ostasien denkt anders*, is the title of a well-known book by the Swiss author Lily Abegg (1948).
12. In his *Orientalism* (1978), Said describes the history of the prejudice of Western Oriental studies against the "Near East." He defines "Orientalism" as "a style of thought based upon an ontological and epistemological distinction between 'the Orient' and (most of the time) 'the Occident'" (p. 2). It has "less to do with the Orient than it does with 'our' world" (p. 12).
13. Trauzettel 1977, p. 345, and 1979, p. 395.
14. Note the similarity with Montesquieu (note 9 above).
15. Granet 1934, pp. 388 and 389.
16. Weber 1951, p. 229.
17. Trauzettel 1977, p. 345.
18. Ibid., p. 347. Cf. Chad Hansen's view, note 43 below.
19. Cf. Hansen's review of Fingarette's book (Hansen 1976), p. 199, and Fingarette's answer (1980), p. 264.

20. *Zhuangzi* 13, p. 217 (Watson p. 152): "There is something more valuable than words. What is more valuable than words is meaning." *Zhuangzi* 26, p. 407 (Watson p. 302): "Words exist because of meaning. Once you have got the meaning, you can forget the words." Another good example of this conviction is Fayun's *Fanyi mingyi ji* (1157), preface to fasc. 1 (Behr 1993).

21. *Lüshi chunqiu* 18.4, p. 225.

22. *Fayan* 5, p. 14.

23. Humboldt 1971, p. 39, trans. Buck and Raven modified.

24. Ibid., p. 34.

25. Ibid., p. 197.

26. Ibid., trans. Buck and Raven modified.

27. Humboldt 1906, pp. 322 and 323.

28. Cf. the critique in Lang 1981. Before Humboldt, only the complicatedness of the Chinese writing had counted as an obstacle to the development of science.

29. Bertalanffy 1968, pp. 212–13.

30. Forke 1927, p. 19, v. Tscharner 1969, p. 245.

31. Lohmann 1965, pp. 173 and 172.

32. Ibid., p. 172.

33. Ibid., p. 183.

34. Cf. Granet 1934, pp. 38–43.

35. Habermas 1984, pp. 301–19.

36. Negt 1988, pp. 283–89.

37. Hansen 1983, p. 37, and 1985a, pp. 492–93.

38. Hansen 1983, p. 56.

39. Hansen 1985b, p. 37. For a criticism of the mass-noun hypothesis see Harbsmeier 1989 and 1991.

40. Hansen 1983, p. 41.

41. Hansen 1985b, p. 41.

42. Ibid., *passim.*

43. Cf. Hansen 1985c, p. 362, where he suggests attributing a "nonmoral point of view" to Confucianism.

44. Hansen 1983, p. 46, and 1985a, p. 496.

45. Hansen 1985a, p. 514 and *passim.*

46. Hansen 1985c, p. 366.

47. Hansen 1983, p. 61; cf. also p. 59, and Hansen 1985a, p. 503.

48. Hansen 1985c, p. 379, italics added.

49. Hansen 1985c, p. 370.

50. According to Hansen "contrastive analysis must replace comparative analysis in comparative philosophy" (1972, p. 169).

51. This applies also to Fingarette, Hall, Ames, and Rosemont. They style Confucius as a model for the West, but—paradoxically—only in order to remind us of our embeddedness in the *specific* context.

52. Bloom 1977b, pp. 77 and 78.

53. This would also invalidate Kohlberg's "cognitive-developmental theory" (see below).

54. Bloom 1977b, p. 79.

55. Cf. Harbsmeier 1981, pp. 272–87, Garbern Liu 1985, Wu Kuang-ming 1987, and Roetz 1993c.
56. Hansen 1985b, p. 54.
57. Hansen 1985c, pp. 375–78.
58. Ibid., p. 377.
59. Weber 1951, p. 112.
60. Ibid.
61. Ibid., p. 163.
62. Ibid., p. 121.
63. Stange 1950, pp. 389 and 390.
64. *Hanfeizi* 12. For the whole topic cf. Kroll 1987.
65. The Jixia academy ("Under the gate of the god of grain") was founded by Duke Huan (reigned from 376–356) and flourished under King Xuan (319–300). King Xuan bestowed high offices to seventy-six intellectuals, "not for assisting in government, but for discussion" (*Shiji* 46, p. 1895). The academy became the intellectual center of China, and the number of scholars soon rose to one thousand (ibid.). For the academy cf. Hu Jiacong 1981.
66. Wittfogel 1957, p. 136.
67. Prusek 1970, p. 34 (following Wittfogel).
68. Cf. for example Pulleyblank 1958 and Mote 1961.
69. Weber 1920, pp. 240–41.
70. Hegel 1987, p. 561.
71. Ibid., p. 550, note 105.
72. Schelling 1957, p. 531.
73. Ibid., p. 539.
74. Ibid., p. 537.
75. Ibid. See *Yijing*, *Shang jing* 1a (Legge p. 58).
76. Weber 1951, pp. 235, 229, and 187.
77. Ibid., pp. 227 and 145.
78. Parsons 1956, pp. 548–49.
79. This is not necessarily implied in the belief in creation and transcendence, however. It is the final outcome of a development at the beginning of which there were alternatives for another attitude towards nature (for example in Genesis 2). Cf. Kessler 1990.
80. Rosenzweig's sharp polemic against China explains itself from here. According to Rosenzweig, China denies "spiritual powers," since for her "it is precisely the fulness of the world which alone counts as real" (1972, pp. 58–59). For Rosenzweig's attitude towards China, cf. Ben Yosef 1988.
81. "Fixedness" in Sibree's translation (Hegel 1956, p. 116).
82. Cf. Hang 1987 (referring to *Shujing*, *Hongfan*) and 1988, p. 217 (referring to *Shijing* 235.1).
83. An important point in Needham's interpretation of Chinese natural science. The idea is already present in Whitehead. Cf. Roetz 1984, p. 242.
84. Russell 1951, p. 18: "The contests in which men are engaged are of three kinds—they are conflicts of: (1) Man and nature. (2) Man and man. (3) Man and himself." Habermas 1984, p. 100: "Such relations hold between an utterance and 1. The objective world (as the totality of all entities about which true statements are

possible). 2. The social world (as the totality of all legitimately regulated interpersonal relations). 3. The subjective world (as the totality of the experiences of the speaker to which he has privileged access)."
  85. Roetz 1984 (on the relationship of man and nature in ancient China).

NOTES TO CHAPTER 3

  1. For such a hermeneutic of rationality, cf. the arguments in Habermas 1984, pp. 54–55.
  2. This not only holds true for ethics, but for the history of philosophy in general. Cf. Hösle's remarks against "a merely philological history of philosophy" which "cannot justify its interest in the past" (1984, pp. 151–52).
  3. Habermas 1981, p. 89.
  4. Jaspers 1953, pp. 19 and xv.
  5. Ibid., p. 9, trans. Bullock modified after the German original.
  6. For contributions from various field such as sinology, Oriental and Judaic studies, Indology, etc., see *Daedalus* 1975, and Eisenstadt 1986.
  7. Jaspers 1953, p. xv.
  8. Köhler and Sahner 1985, p. 361, italics added.
  9. Jaspers 1953, p. xvi.
  10. Habermas 1981, p. 92.
  11. Jaspers 1953, p. 19.
  12. Jaspers objects to Hegel (Ibid., pp. 10–11): "It is precisely this series of stages from China to Greece whose reality we deny; there is no such series, either in time or in meaning. The true situation was rather one of contemporaneous, side by side existence without contact. . . . There are three independent roots of one history which later . . . become a single unity."
  13. Ibid., pp. 2–6.
  14. Ibid., p. 17.
  15. A. Weber (Max Weber's brother) 1943.
  16. Jaspers 1953, p. 16.
  17. Ibid., pp. 14 and 18.
  18. If one excludes, with Jaspers, diffusion theories, the relative simultaneity of the different breakthroughs in the axial age can only have been by coincidence. Yet all of these breakthroughs represent late results of a development which started with the "neolithic revolution," led to the coming into existence of states, and came to maturity after a long incubation period.
  19. Kohlberg has given several formulations of the stage sequence with slight shifts in accent. See above all Kohlberg 1971, pp. 164–65, and 1981, pp. 409–12.
  20. Stage $4\frac{1}{2}$ normally does not appear in the schemes of the stages, because it counts as unstable and transitional (cf. Kohlberg 1971, pp. 203–04). Yet the Chinese material suggests (as does the philosophy of some Greek Sophists) that a form of Stage $4\frac{1}{2}$ reasoning prevailed among some of the ancient "professional youths" and is of great phylogenetic importance.
  21. Here I skip the problem of a *seventh* stage (cf. Chapter 12) which should be formulated in terms of communication and responsibility (cf. Habermas 1982, pp. 83–

85, Kohlberg's answer in Kohlberg 1983, pp. 155–64, and Apel 1988, pp. 306–69. Cf. also Kohlberg 1981, pp. 311–72, and 1984, pp. 375–86.

22. According to Kohlberg, most people stop at Stage 4. Even if one reaches the postconventional stages, theoretical competence not necessarily encompasses practical one.

23. Cf. Kohlberg 1984, pp. 222–23, Apel 1988, pp. 312–16.

24. Kohlberg 1971, p. 171.

25. Cf. Apel 1980a, pp. 49–51.

26. On the inconsistencies of the relativistic approach and for another plead for "evaluative universalism" cf. also Nathan 1990.

27. Shweder 1982, p. 424

28. Cf. Kohlberg, Levine, and Hewer 1983.

29. Bloom 1977a. Cf. my remarks in Roetz 1993c.

30. Dien 1982, pp. 339 and 334–36.

31. Vine 1986, p. 443.

32. Liu Shuxian 1986.

33. Similarly Lee 1987. For an unequivocal Chinese support for Kohlberg's approach, see Lei and Liu 1991.

34. Metzger 1990, pp. 278, 288, and *passim.* Cf. also Metzger 1987.

35. Metzger 1990, pp. 279–80.

36. I do not agree, therefore, with Metzger's tendency to view modernity as based on relativistic pessimism while wondering how Confucian "optimism" can be made compatible with this. The "modern" point of view—ideal-typically—is to no longer draw on heteronomous instances which secured premodern identity—tradition, religion, cosmology, etc.—but not necessarily to abandon all normative standards. What distinguishes the modern epoch from pre-modern ones is that these standards can only be derived from the self-assertion of the epoch itself and not from older models (which does not rule out that traditions may still be accepted as important for a number of nontraditional reasons). They have to take into account the plurality of ways of life, which is surely a signature of the modern age, and will therefore be found on a formal level (providing a framework for unity in difference) rather than on a material one (recommending or prescribing ways of life).

37. Cf. Gielen 1987a, 1987b, and 1990.

38. Cf. Gielen 1987b. For Taiwan, cf. also the several reports by T. Lei (listed in Gielen 1987a and 1990).

39. Benedict 1935.

40. In the works of Piaget and Kohlberg, this descent becomes occasionally apparent. Piaget refers to Durkheim's analysis of the dissolution of segmentary societies (1932, pp. 107–8). Kohlberg, in order to explain the absence of postconventional stages in preliterate or semiliterate cultures by a "mild doctrine of social evolutionism," refers to Hobhouse, who advanced a theory of stages of moral evolution (Kohlberg 1971, p. 178). Whereas Piaget and Kohlberg confine themselves to ontogenesis, other authors have set their hands to apply his theory to phylogenesis (Elfenbein 1973, Döbert 1973, Habermas 1982, pp. 171–86, Eder 1980, Apel 1980b, Rosenberg, Ward, and Chilton 1988, pp. 127–60).

41. Cf. Apel 1980b, p. 28. Elfenbein (1973), Rosenberg, Ward, and Chilton (1988), and Lei and Liu (1991), however, assume a preconventional beginning of phylogenesis.

NOTES TO CHAPTER 4

1. For an overview of the debate, cf. Service 1975, pp. 21–46, and Service 1977, pp. 177–99.

2. I follow the definition in Service 1977, pp. 173–74.

3. Cf. Habermas 1982, p. 177, Eder 1980, pp. 158–66.

4. *Shujing, Pan Geng*, p. 170b (Karlgren p. 23).

5. Ibid., p. 169b (Karlgren p. 21).

6. Ibid., p. 170c (Karlgren p. 23).

7. Ibid.

8. Gehlen 1964, p. 197.

9. Cf. Mauss 1966, and Lévi-Strauss 1949, chapter V.

10. Cf. Sahlins 1972, p. 199.

11. *Mozi* 16, p. 76–77 (Mei pp. 93–94). Cf. *Shujing, Tang gao*, p. 162b, *Guoyu, Zhouyu shang*, p. 35 (quoting *Shujing, Tang shi*), *Lunyu* 20.1, *Xunzi* 27, p. 331, *Shizi* p. 10b, *Lüshi chunqiu* 9.2, p. 86, *Lunheng* 19, p. 51, *Lunheng* 55, p. 181.

12. *Lüshi chunqiu* 6.4, p. 60.

13. Sahlins 1972, p. 205, Cooper 1982, Felber 1973, pp. 63 and 75–89.

14. Cf. *Mengzi* 4A21 and 4B3.

15. Cf. Habermas 1982, p.177: "Legitimate power crystallizes itself around the function of jurisdiction and around the position of the judge, after law has been reorganized in a way that fulfills the characteristics of conventional morality."

16. *Shiji* 1, p. 3.

17. *Shujing, Lü xing*, p. 247c (Karlgren p. 74).

18. *Shangjunshu* 18, p. 31 (Duyvendak p. 285): Huang Di "at home applied sword and saw, and abroad used mailed soldiers."

19. *Shiji* 1, p. 14.

20. *Hanfeizi* 36, p. 264 (Liao II, p. 142).

21. *Mengzi* 5A5, *Shiji* 1, p. 30.

22. *Mengzi* 5A6.

23. *Shujing, Shundian*, pp. 128c and 130c (Karlgren pp. 5 and 7). Cf. also *Shiji* 1, pp. 77–78, *Shiji* 2, p. 81, and *Zhushu jinian*, p. 197. Mengzi later transforms this division of functions into a division of power, declaring that Shun himself had to submit to his own law (7A35, cf. p. 95 below).

24. *Zuozhuan* Zhao 6.2, p. 360 (Legge p. 609). Cf. *Mozi* 32, p. 160 (Mei p. 180).

25. Lin Yun 1965.

26. *Shuowen jiezi* 12b 17, p. 267.

27. Water control (Wittfogel), if at all, historically plays a role only for the transition to dynastical rule. Yet, I think that only superficially the formation of the first dynasty by Yu was the reward for successfully fighting a flood disaster. It is better understood from the logic of the stabilization of rulership. Together with the consolidation of the role, person and character of its occupant become less important (a process later fought by the Confucians, but welcomed by the Legalists), and hereditary succession provides a stable procedure for the maintenance of power.

28. Cf. Hobhouse 1956, Chapter III, Trimborn 1950, Eder 1980.

29. *Shiji* 1, p. 3.

30. *Shiji* 1, p. 6 (Huang Di); *Shujing, Shundian*, p. 127b–c (Karlgren pp. 4–5), and *Shiji* 1, p. 24 (Shun); *Shujing, Yugong*, pp. 146–52 (Karlgren pp. 14-17), and *Shiji* 2, pp. 52–75 (Yu).

31. *Shujing, Shundian*, p. 128c (Karlgren p. 5), *Shiji* 1, p. 24, *Shujing, Yugong*, pp. 146–53 (Karlgren pp. 14–18), *Shiji* 2, pp. 52–75.

32. *Shujing, Kang gao*, p. 203c (Karlgren p. 40). The speech is formulated in the typical diction of Zhou Gong, but the authorship is disputed. The speaker might as well be King Wu, or his successor King Cheng. Cf. Creel 1970, pp. 450–51.

33. *Shujing, Da Yu mo*, p. 135c (regarded as apocryphal).

34. *Zuozhuan Xi* 33.8, p. 143 (Legge p. 226) (not in the extant *Kang gao*). With reference to this quotation, Ji Que receives an office from Duke Wen of Jin in 627 B.C. (*Zuozhuan* Xi 33.8, p. 143 [Legge p. 226], *Guoyu, Jinyu* 5, p. 393). Since *Lunyu* 12.2 alludes to this episode (cf. Chapter 10 D below), it can be assumed that Confucius, too, rejects collective responsibility. Likewise referring to the *Kang gao*, the Han emperor Zhang Di in A.D. 84 grants amnesty to detainees who are imprisoned for offenses of their relatives (*Houhanshu* 3, pp. 147–48).

35. *Zuozhuan* Zhao 20.3, p. 401 (Legge p. 682) (not in the extant *Kang gao*).

36. The principle of collective responsibility could survive, however, not least because of the Legalist reason of state. Cf. for this topic Hobhouse 1956, p. 87. Cf. also Xunzi's position, p. 97 below.

37. Cf. Chapter 11, n. 92.

38. Cf. Chang Tsung-tung 1970, p. 215.

39. *Shujing, Xian you yi de*, p. 166a. The chapter is regarded as apocryphal. For similar statements in other chapters cf. Roetz 1984, p. 122.

40. For this and the following cf. ibid., pp. 129–35.

41. Cassirer 1969, pp. 104–28, Eliade 1959.

42. Cf. Chapter 9, n. 4.

43. Cf. p. 44 below.

44. Cf. Bauer 1990, pp. 36–45. According to Granet's influential interpretation (1919), however, the *Shijing* rather contains rural folk songs embedded in communal custom and ritual.

NOTES TO CHAPTER 5

1. *Zhuangzi* 16, p. 244 (Watson p. 173), *Zhuangzi* 33, p. 464 (Watson p. 364, Graham p. 275).

2. *Lunyu* 14.39 and 18.6, *Mengzi* 4A17.

3. *Liji* 4, p. 1275a (Legge I, p. 123), *Kongzi jiayu* 44, p. 288.

4. *Lunyu* 9.14.

5. Cf. Tu Wei-ming 1986, p. 365.

6. *Mengzi* 7A33, 3B2, and 4A10.

7. *Liji* 41, p. 1669a (Legge II, p. 404). Cf. p. 88 below.

8. *Xunzi* 4, p. 39 (Dubs, p. 59, Knoblock I, p. 191, with very different interpretations).

9. *Lunyu* 2.15.

10. Hu Shih 1963, p. 296.

11. *Zuozhuan* Xiang 31.7, p. 336 (Legge pp. 565–66).

12. *Lüshi chunqiu* 18.4, p. 225. Cf. Knoblock I, p. 165.

13. *Lunyu* 16.2.

14. *Xunzi* 10, p. 113 (Dubs p. 151).

15. *Hanfeizi* 49, p. 347 (Liao II, p. 290).

16. *Xunzi* 21, p. 258 (Dubs p. 259, Watson p. 121), *Mengzi* 3B9.

17. Cf. for example *Zhuangzi* 12, pp. 199–200 (Watson pp. 138–39): "When a filial son does not flatter his parents and a loyal subject does not flatter his ruler, they are the most excellent of subjects and sons. But he who consents to everything that his parents say and regards as good everything that his parents do, is [even] by the vulgar world called an unworthy son. He who consents to everything that his ruler says and regards as good everything that his ruler does, is [even] by the vulgar world called an unworthy subject. . . . Yet, he who consents to everything that the vulgar world says and regards as good everything that the vulgar world regards as good is not called a flatterer. Does the vulgar world command more authority, then, than the parents or the ruler?"

18. An outstanding example of such an understanding of politics is King Wuling of the northern state Zhao. In order to build up a cavalry which can cope with the equestrian peoples of the north, he decrees in 307 B.C. that his subjects have to dress themselves like nomads. The justification which he and his advisor Fei Yi give for these measures is reported in *Shiji* 13 (pp. 1806–11) and *Zhanguoce* 19 (*Zhao* 2, pp. 653–63): "He who speaks about highest virtue does not harmonize with the customs (*su*), and he who wants to achieve great things does not confer with the majority (*zhong*)." (Similarly *Shangjunshu* 1, p. 1, Duyvendak p. 169). In order to "surpass the age," one has to "leave the customs behind." And the "wise," the king states, "discuss the customs, while the good-for-nothings are restrained by them."

19. For the popular reproach that the intellectuals merely "eat without tilling the soil" cf. *Mozi* 49, pp. 286–87 (Mei pp. 249–50), *Zhuangzi* 29, p. 428 (Watson p. 324, Graham p. 235), *Lüshi chunqiu* 18.6, p. 229. Cf. also *Mengzi* 3B4.

20. *Mozi* 46, p. 257 (Mei p. 214).

21. The dating of the *Laozi* before the *Lunyu* is regarded as problematic since Liang Qichao 1922. The debate is not closed, however. The *Laozi* probably consists of layers of different periods. The *Lunyu* is mainly a compilation of notes made by Confucius' pupils and most probably collected by pupils of the second generation (cf. *Hanshu* 30, p. 1717).

22. The deep sense crisis of the Zhou era becomes apparent already in the *Lunyu* and in the *Mozi*. It does not only date from the fourth century B.C. (as is suggested by Graham 1989, pp. 107–10, and Elvin 1986, p. 336).

23. Hegel 1952, § 150.

24. Ibid., §§ 150, 121 (addition), 137, and 107 (addition).

25. Hegel 1940, p. 350.

26. Rosemont 1988, pp. 61 and 64.

27. MacIntyre 1981.

28. Rosemont 1988, pp. 60–61. Cf. Rosemont 1976, pp. 51 and 31, and Hansen 1985c, p. 362 (cf. Chapter 2, n. 43).

29. *Xunzi* 22, p. 275 (Dubs p. 282, Watson p. 140).

30. Cf. Chapter 12 below.

31. Cf. *Lunyu* 7.8: "I will not enlighten anyone who is not anxious for it. I will not inspire anyone who does not already struggle for words. When I have pointed out one corner and one does not answer with the other three, I will not repeat my words."

32. Cf. for example *Lunyu* 11.20.

33. Yu Yingshi (1987a, Chapter 1) has described the emergence of this intellectual layer. He relates its rise to the "breakthrough" in thought. In accordance with the new function of the group, I render *shi* as "scholar," though the aristocratic connotation "fighter" now and then is still recognizable in the use of the term.

34. *Lunyu* 7.7: "I have never refused instruction to anyone who, of his own accord, has tied dried meat up into a bundle in order to present it to me."

35. *Shiji* 47, p. 1938.

36. *Lunyu* 9.5.

37. Contrary to the standard interpretations (e.g., Legge 1893, p. 334), I take the pronoun *si* (this) as referring to Changju and Jieni and not to mankind in general.

38. *Lunyu* 18.6.

39. Cf. Vervoorn 1990, p. 252, n. 38.

40. Later records, however, have presented Confucius as a successful politician, and the younger the records, the higher his position. What above all speaks against these embellishments of his career is that they cannot be substantiated by the *Lunyu*. The *Zhuangzi* may understate when it calls Confucius an "impoverished commoner" (*Zhuangzi* 29, p. 433 [Watson p. 332, Graham pp. 239–40]), but he most likely never occupied a position of real influence. Precisely "his lack of success," Canetti writes (1979, p. 171), is "highly impressive in Confucius. . . . One could hardly take him seriously if he had actually become and remained a government minister somewhere. He ignores power as it really is, he is interested solely in its possibilities."

41. *Lunyu* 14.28, also *Zhongyong* 20.

42. Cf. Aristotle, *Ethica Nicomachea* 1095b 1-9.

43. *Lunyu* 20.3, similarly *Lunyu* 8.8 and 16.13.

44. *Lunyu* 12.11, cf. *Xunzi* 9, p. 104 (Dubs p. 136, Watson p. 45), *Yijing, Xia jing*, p. 23b (Legge p. 242). Cf. also *Lunyu* 8.14 and 14.26.

45. *Xunzi* 18, p. 218 (Dubs p. 193).

46. *Mengzi* 1A7 and 6A17 (cf. p. 182 below).

47. *Lunyu* 3.1, 3.2, and 3.6, cf. also *Lunyu* 2.24 and 3.22.

48. *Lunyu* 8.2: "If a gentleman (here: a member of the aristocracy) devotes his attention to his relatives, then the people are raised to the level of humaneness. If he does not neglect the old relations (the old-established families), then the people will not speculate." This passage presumably means that official ranks should remain reserved for the aristocracy. This would prevent members of lower classes from "speculating" on attaining influential positions. *Lunyu* 8.2 is an example of the political conservatism of the work.

49. *Lunyu* 3.18.

50. *Lunyu* 6.16.

51. Quoted by the *Yinwenzi, Da dao xia*, p. 9.

52. *Lunyu* 1.3, 14.4, 17.15.

53. *Lunyu* 17.11. *Yuan* in adjectival use means "original." It connotes genuineness, solidity, and honesty. A literal translation of *xiangyuan* would be "the solid people of the neighborhood."

54. *Lunyu* 5.22.

55. Cf. *Lunyu* 13.21.
56. Zeng Xi is Zeng Shen's father. Nothing reliable is known about the other two.
57. *Mengzi* 7B37.

NOTES TO CHAPTER 6

1. Cf. e.g. Ch'ü 1961, and Hsieh 1967. "Family" in this chapter primarily refers to the "nuclear family" (parents and offspring).
2. Xu Fuguan 1983, p. 168.
3. Weber 1951, p. 157.
4. The three forms of behavior which impair the care for parents are (a) laziness, (b) gambling and drinking, and (c) greed and preferential treatment of wife and children. They are supplemented by (d) bringing disgrace to the parents by sensual dissipation, and (e) endangering them by quarrelsomeness. In *Mengzi* 4A26, Mengzi speaks about "three unfilial things," but only one of them is mentioned: to be without offspring and not to assure posterity.
5. *Lunyu* 4.19. Wu Yu (1985, p. 176) comments, "America would never have been discovered, then." *Liji* (1, p. 1234a, Legge I, p. 69) and *Dadai Liji* (50, p. 165) forbid a filial child to "climb heights."
6. *Lunyu* 4.21.
7. *Lunyu* 2.8.
8. *Lunyu* 2.7.
9. Cf. Roetz 1984, *passim*.
10. *Dadai Liji* 52, p. 175, *Liji* 24, p. 1598b (Legge II, p. 226). For the highest form cf. *Mengzi* 5A4.
11. *Lunyu* 17.19. Cf. *Shuoyuan* 19, p. 674.
12. *Liji* 24, p. 1598b (Legge II, p. 226), *Dadai Liji* 52, p. 176.
13. Wu Yu 1985, pp. 61–66.
14. *Xiaojing* 14.
15. *Dadai Liji* 51, p. 173.
16. Cf., e.g., *Lunyu* 13.20, *Mozi* 35, p. 167 (Mei p. 185), *Lüshi chunqiu* 16.8, p. 196.
17. *Hanshu* 6, p. 160.
18. Cf. Wright 1978, p. 65.
19. A motto from the *Xiaojing*; cf. *Xiaojing* 8 and *Suishu* 42, p. 1208.
20. In his *"Sacred edict" (Shengyu)*, an impressive compendium of Chinese conventional morality (in: Wieger 1913), Emperor Kangxi inculcated sixteen rules of demeanor upon his people with explanatory comments by his son, Emperor Yongzheng. At the head of the list, which Wieger, quite misleadingly, calls the "quintessence of Confucianism," stands filial piety. "The message of the Sacred Edict is: keep your place, respect authority, obey the laws, pay your taxes," writes Stover (1974, p. 89).
21. *Hanfeizi* 51, p. 358 (Liao II, p. 312).
22. *Mengzi* 4A5.
23. *Mengzi* 4A20.
24. In the subsequent passages, I shall deal mainly with the father-son relationship. The moral failure of the elder brother is a special case which is briefly treated in

the *Dadai Liji* (53, p. 185). The role of the daughter at best coincides with that of the son. The *Nü xiaojing*, written under the Tang by a "born Zheng" after the model of the *Xiaojing*, has described the task of the wife with regard to "remonstrance" (*jian*) in analogy to that of the son in *Xiaojing* 15 and *Xunzi* 29 (cf. below).

25. *Mengzi* 4A19 and 4B30.
26. Quoted in Chapter 5, n. 17.
27. *Mozi* 4, pp. 11–12 (Mei pp. 13–14).
28. *Mengzi* 4A28.
29. *Mengzi* 5A1.
30. This sentence appealed to Emperor Kangxi, for he quotes it in his *Shengyu* (Wieger 1913, p. 14).
31. *Mengzi* 4A28.
32. Zhu Xi, *Sishu jizhu*, commentary to *Mengzi* 4A28. Similarly Zhu Xi, *Xiaoxue jizhu* 5, p. 14b, and Huang Zongxi, *Song Yuan xuean* 39, 10, p. 63.
33. Cf. p. 95 below.
34. Quoted in Zhu Xi, *Xiaoxue jizhu* 5, p. 15a.
35. Cf. p. 165 below.
36. *Liji* 12, cf. p. 60 below.
37. Zhu Xi, *Xiaoxue jizhu* 5, p. 14a–b.
38. As far as Zhu Xi's *Xiaoxue* is concerned, one should take into account that the text serves the "lesser learning," the education of children from eight to fifteen, as distinguished from the "great learning" of adults. While the difference between both does not consist in an essentially different nature of the ethical commitment, but in knowing the task and in additionally knowing the reasons for it (Zhu Xi, *Zhuzi yulei* 7, p. 1b), Zhu Xi's concept of education contains much more than merely authoritarian elements (cf. de Bary 1983, pp. 21–42).
39. That a filial person should "not grow weary of gentle remonstration" is also demanded in *Liji* 30, p. 1620 b (Legge II, p. 290), and *Dadai Liji* 51, p. 171.
40. *Baihutong* 16, pp. 625–26, for example, interprets *wei* as "to leave." It quotes *Lunyu* 4.18 in support of the demand that a son in any case must stay with his parents, while an official can just leave his immoral ruler.
41. Rosenzweig 1972, p. 76.
42. *Shujing, Da Yu mo*, p. 137b, for the translation cf. Legge/Waltham 1971, p. 25. Cf. *Mengzi* 5A1 and 5A4.
43. *Liji* 2, p. 1267c (Legge I, p. 114).
44. *Ershisi xiao*, p. 156. Min Ziqian is called filial in *Lunyu* 11.5. In *Xunzi* 23, p. 295 (Dubs p. 311, Watson p. 165), he is mentioned as an exceptional case of filial behavior. His filial piety obviously underwent a touching amplification in later times. To my knowledge the story quoted above is missing from Zhou literature.
45. Zhu Xi has treated the following passage in analogy to *Lunyu* 4.18 (*Sishu jizhu, Lunyu jizhu*, pp. 23–24). It has thus become a quasi-official construction of *Lunyu* 4.18.
46. *Liji* 12, p. 1463a (Legge I, p. 456).
47. The respective literary evidence is not without a curious note: One should not let oneself be beaten with a thick stick, but only with a small one—not in order to spare oneself pain, but not to make the father a murderer. This is at least the message of an anecdote from the *Kongzi jiayu* (16, p. 101, cf. also *Shuoyuan* 3, p. 80): Zeng Shen,

after having unintentionally chopped through the root of a cucumber, lets his father knock him unconscious. Confucius condemns this attitude, pointing out that Shun, too, let himself be beaten by his father, but only with a thin stick, and that he was right to take to his heels at the sight of a thick one. Zeng Shen, however, nearly made his father commit a great injustice by killing him, and there is no impiety greater than this. In *Shuoyuan* 3, p. 81, we read: "When Boyu committed a wrong, his mother beat him with a stick. When he cried, she asked, 'You never cried when I beat you. Why do you cry now?' Boyu answered, 'When you beat me formerly, because I did a mischief, it hurt. But now the mother has grown so weak that she cannot hurt me any longer. That's why I'm crying.'"

48. Cf. p. 94 below.

49. *Liji* 3, p. 1274a (Legge I, p. 121).

50. Cf. Chapter 11 E.

51. Cf. *Lunyu* 4.18, *Mengzi* 5A1, *Liji* 12, p. 1463a (Legge I, p. 456), *Liji* 24, p. 1598c (Legge II, p. 228), *Dadai Liji* 52, p. 180.

52. *Mengzi* 6B3.

53. Cf. pp. 62–63 below.

54. *Mengzi* 5A4.

55. *Mengzi* 6A16, cf. Chapter 13 A.

56. I follow Wang Xianshen's conjecture.

57. *Hanfeizi* 51, p. 359 (Liao II, pp. 313–14).

58. W. Bauer is one of the few authors who have appreciated the importance of the *Zidao*. According to Bauer (1971, p. 90), the chapter shows that "there were much more germs in Confucianism than could freely develop later."

59. *Xunzi* 29, pp. 347–48.

60. *Kongzi jiayu* 9, p. 58.

61. *Xunzi* 29, p. 347. The quotation is from *Shijing* 247.5.

NOTES TO CHAPTER 7

1. *Mengzi* 3B9.

2. *Lunyu* 8.9, *Mengzi* 7A5. Cf. also *Xunzi* 22, p. 280 (Dubs p. 289, Watson p. 146).

3. *Mengzi* 3A4, similarly *Xunzi* 7, p. 71.

4. *Xunzi* 10, pp. 113–14 (Dubs p. 152).

5. *Jian lì*, "to be equally profitable to," is parallel to Mo Di's *jian ai*, "equal love" or "co-love." Cf. Chapter 14 A.

6. *Xunzi* 9, pp. 104–05 (Dubs pp. 136–37, Watson pp. 45–46).

7. For Protagoras, cf. Plato, *Protagoras* 322a–323a, for the Anonymos Iamblichi, cf. Freeman 1959, pp. 415–16, and Kerferd 1981, pp. 127–28, for Hobbes, cf. *Leviathan* 12 and 17.

8. *Xunzi* 9, p. 105 (Dubs p. 137, Watson p. 46), and *Xunzi* 10, p. 116.

9. *Xunzi* 27, p. 332: "That Heaven gave birth to the people was not for the sake of the ruler. Heaven installed a ruler for the reason that he should be there for the people."

10. Cf. *Liezi* 7, quoted in Chapter, 13 n. 174.

11. Cf. *Zhuangzi* 29, p. 429 (Watson p. 327, Graham p. 237).

12. *Lüshi chunqiu* 20.1, pp. 255–56.

13. *Xunzi* 10, p. 116.

14. *Xunzi* 10, p. 120.

15. Cf. pp. 137–39 below.

16. *Xunzi* 10, p. 116.

17. The idea reappears, with the accent on equality, in John Rawls' "two principles of justice." Cf. Rawls 1972, pp. 60–65.

18. Quoted as a traditional saying in *Xunzi* 13, p. 171.

19. *Xunzi* 4, p. 44 (Dubs p. 66, Knoblock I, p. 195).

20. *Xunzi* 9, p. 96 (Dubs p. 124, Watson p. 36). The quotation is from *Shujing, Lü xing*, p. 250c (Karlgren p. 77). In the context of the *Lü xing*, the quoted sentence (*wei qi fei qi*) should rather be construed as a predicate-object clause "to equalize the unequal." The *Lü xing* does not discuss Xunzi's social problem, but the juridical question how to find a rule for a flexible punishment of equal offenses under unequal circumstances.

21. Cf. Chapter 11 B.

22. Rejecting Feng Youlan's comparison of Mo Di and Hobbes (1961, p. 133, Fung I, pp. 100–101), Hsiao Kung-chuan states (1979, p. 240, note) that "there is simply no possibility of such a concept's having been produced in the Spring and Autumn and Warring States Periods." Unfortunately, Hsiao does not give any reasons for this mere assertion. H. Smith (1967, p. 192) and B. Schwartz (1985, pp. 144 and 295–96), too, have ruled out the existence of contractualism in ancient China.

23. Cf., e.g., *Xunzi* 22, p. 279 (Dubs p. 286, Watson p. 144): "Designations are not by themselves appropriate, they are agreed upon (*yue*) by determination. Only when the agreement is fixed and a habit has been established do we speak of appropriate designations, and that which differs from the agreement is called inappropriate." Cf. also ibid., pp. 274 and 276 (Dubs pp. 281 and 283, Watson pp. 139 and 141). The arbitrariness of language is a typical theme of the axial age also to be found in Greece (cf. Barnes 1982, pp. 466–70, and Plato, *Cratylos* 384d).

24. Cf. *Lunyu* 13.4, *Mengzi* 4A21 and 4B5 (cf. Chapter 10, n. 144).

25. Hsu and Linduff 1988, pp. 177–79.

26. *Zuozhuan* Aigong 1.2 pp. 465–66, (Legge p. 795). For Zheng, cf. p. 44 above. For Qi, cf. p. 99 below.

27. Hsu Cho-yun 1965, pp. 115–16.

28. *Huainanzi* 13, p. 215.

29. The character for *meng* consists of a phonetic and the classifier "bowl." The bowl is used to hold the blood of a sacrificial animal. Cf. Dobson 1968.

30. *Xunzi* 11, p. 131.

31. Ibid., p. 133. For Mengzi's position, cf. *Mengzi* 2A3.

32. *Xunzi* 12, pp. 151 and 152.

33. A tally, one-half of a cut through object (in the military a small bronze tiger), was used by a messenger to prove his identity for the receiver of the message who had the other half. Wooden contract documents, likewise consisting of two halves, recorded the leasing conditions. With the halves of the landlord on their cart, the collectors regularly went to the tenants to get in the rent. In the third century B.C., Feng Xuan, a client of the Lord of Mengchan, became famous for burning the documents on such an

occasion. His justification was this. His lord had asked him to bring something from his journey which was not already existing in his house. This, however, was justice (*yi*). Cf. *Zhanguoce* 11 *Qi* 4, p. 389, similarly *Shiji* 75, pp. 2359–61.

34. Cf., e.g., *Zhuangzi* 2, pp. 43–44 and 50–51 (Watson pp. 45–46 and 48, Graham pp. 58 and 60).

35. *Xunzi* 10, p. 113 (Dubs p. 151).

36. Cf. Hucker 1959, pp. 193–207.

37. Cf. p. 90 below.

38. *Mengzi* 5B9.

39. *Xunzi* 18, p. 222 (Dubs p. 200).

40. Mo Di, too, justifies the rebellions against the tyrants Jie and Zhòu, cf., e.g., *Mozi* 19, pp. 94–95 (Mei pp. 112–13). Cf. also *Guoyu, Luyu shang* 15, p. 182, where the Grand Histographer Lige from Lu justifies the assassination of Duke Li of Jin (573 B.C.) because of his betrayal of the people. Cf. furthermore *Huainanzi* 15, p. 252, and Roetz 1984, pp. 165–67.

41. Tang and Wu are the founders of the Shang and Zhou dynasties, Jie and Zhòu are the last rulers of the Xia and the Shang.

42. *Mengzi* 1B8.

43. *Xunzi* 18, p. 216 (Dubs p. 190).

44. For a similar argument cf. Locke 1823b, §§ 232–39. For a comparison of the positions of Locke and the Confucians cf. Schleichert 1990, pp. 379–82.

45. *Mengzi* 5A5, referring to *Shujing, Gao Yao mo*, p. 139c (Karlgren p. 9), and *Shujing, Tai shi*, p. 181c.

46. *Xunzi* 18, p. 216 (Dubs p.191).

47. Similarly, the original position is primarily to be thought of as a fiction. It is rather an assumed worst case possible of human existence than the actual starting point of history.

48. Cf. pp. 217–24 below.

49. Cf. p. 222 below.

50. Cf. Apel 1982, pp. 86–92.

51. *Zuozhuan* Huan 12.9, p. 39 (Legge p. 59). The quotation is from *Shijing* 198.3.

52. It is, nevertheless, not unlikely that Xunzi's political philosophy, despite its limits, introduced the idea of social arrangement also into everyday politics. When Liu Bang, the founder of the Han dynasty, conquered the Qin capital in 206 B.C., he convened the notabilities of all districts and "stipulated" (*yue*) with them the replacement of the cruel penal code of the Qin by three simple laws: He who kills another man shall be killed, he who hurts another is liable to pay compensation, and likewise he who steals something (*Hanshu* 1, p. 23, and 23, p. 1096). Bünger (1952, p. 199, n. 26) points out that this model later found emulators. He calls it a "novelty, the ideological origin of which has yet to be ascertained" (ibid.). The search for the "ideological origin" doubtless leads back to the politics of the Zhou era and to the teachings of Mo Di and Xunzi.

53. Cf. for example *Mengzi* 1B9.

54. *Mengzi* 1B7, *Daxue* 10.

55. For the ascent of the lower classes, which was in the final analysis without democratic consequences, cf. Liang Qichao 1984, Chapter *Min ben sixiang*, and Roetz 1984, pp. 179–87.

56. *Xunzi* 15, *passim.*
57. *Xunzi* 9, p. 97 (Dubs p. 126, Watson pp. 37–38), *Xunzi* 10 *passim, Lunyu* 13.9, *Mengzi* 7A23.
58. *Sakui* (*zuo wei*), a clear reminiscence of Xunzi's *wei* (art).
59. Maruyama 1974, p. 228. Sorai has sometimes been compared with Xunzi. Maruyama, however, stresses the differences which show that "the modern consciousness germinating in Sorai's system was completely absent from Xunzi" (Ibid., p. 113 n. 107). Yet, if the novelty in Sorai's thought is a concept of society as a contractual unit, he would indeed be indebted to Xunzi exactly in his central idea. By his differentiation of *"Gemeinschaft"* (community) and *"Gesellschaft"* (society), Maruyama draws on F. Tönnies. For Tönnies (1922 pp. 5 and 39), *"Gemeinschaft"* is an "organism" and "essentially connected." *"Gesellschaft"* is a "mechanical aggregate and artifact" and "essentially separated."
60. Kohlberg 1981, pp. 412 and 152–55.
61. Cf. Chapter 11 B.
62. *Mengzi* 5A5.
63. Cf. Chapter 13 B.
64. Mengzi 6A17, cf. p. 182 below.
65. *Mengzi* 1B12.
66. *Mengzi* 1A7, similarly 3A3.
67. Precursors of this view reminiscent of a natural right philosophy can be found among the political thinkers of the Chunqiu era. Zang Wenzhong, to give an example, in 639 B.C. rescued a shamaness and a hunchback who were held responsible for a drought from being burnt. "If Heaven," he says (*Zuozhuan* Xi 21, p. 217, Legge p. 180), "wished them dead, it should not have given them life."
68. *Mengzi* 7B14.
69. *Lunyu* 3.19.
70. *Lunyu* 15.37 and 1.7.
71. *Lunyu* 8.14 and 14.26, *Mengzi* 5B5.
72. As a political virtue, *zhong* is the fundamental norm of Stage 4. Nevertheless, it also plays an important role on the postconventional level. In its basic meaning "benevolence" (to do one's best for the other), it is not simply a virtue directed upward. It can also characterize a ruler's attitude towards the people (cf. Chapter 10, n. 160).
73. *Lunyu* 14.7.
74. *Lunyu* 14.22 (cf. *Liji* 3, quoted pp. 60–61 above). This sentence is the more remarkable since Zilu, the daredevil among Confucius' pupils, normally gets rather soothing answers to his questions.
75. *Lunyu* 13.6.
76. *Lunyu* 11.22.
77. *Lunyu* 8.13, similarly *Lunyu* 14.1.
78. *Mengzi* 6B9.
79. *Lunyu* 5.7, 18.7, and 18.6.
80. *Lunyu* 7.1. Cf. p. 193 below.
81. Cf. also *Lunyu* 14.42.
82. Cf. p. 191 below.
83. *Mengzi* 7B14, cf. p. 79 above .
84. *Xunzi* 13, pp. 165–66.
85. Ibid., pp. 167–68.

86. Cf. pp. 63–64 and 79 above.
87. *Xunzi* 13, p. 166 (quoted as a traditional saying).
88. *Lunyu* 8.13.
89. *Lunyu* 6.11.
90. *Mengzi* 4B29.
91. *Zhuangzi* 28, p. 421 (Watson p. 317, Graham p. 229).
92. *Kongzi jiayu* 38, p. 225.
93. A symbol for a plebeian life also worn by the followers of the "school of the tillers" (*nongjia*, cf. *Mengzi* 3A4). "To put off the filth" (*shi he*) later came to mean to enter civil service.
94. Cf. *Lunyu* 7.15.
95. The bramble-woven door, to give an example, first appears in the *Zhuangzi* (28, pp. 419–20, Watson p. 315, Graham p. 228), characteristically enough in an anecdote about Yuan Xian. It is also found in the *Liji* (41, p. 1670a), the *Xinxu* (7, p. 235), the *Hanshi waizhuan* (1, p. 11), the *Shangshu dazhuan* (3, pp. 12a–b), and the *Kongzi jiayu* (5, p. 22).
96. Cf. *Lunyu* 6.11.
97. Read *tu* for *shi* (*Shuoyuan* 16, p. 528).
98. *Dadai Liji* 55, pp. 196–98.
99. *Mengzi* 3B2, cf. Chapter 11 E.
100. *Mengzi* 7B34 and 3B7.
101. *Mengzi* 2B2.
102. *Mengzi* 5B7.
103. *Mengzi* 7A20.
104. *Mengzi* 7A21.
105. *Mozi* 39, p. 184 (Mei p. 207). Cf. ibid., p. 188 (Mei pp. 210–11).
106. Guo Moruo (1956, pp. 71–84) regards Mo Di's claims as credible. Confucius for him is the head of progressive subverters, while Mo Di is a conservative.
107. *Xunzi* 2, p. 16 (Dubs p. 47, Knoblock I, p. 154).
108. Cf. *Shujing* p. 204b (Karlgren p. 42).
109. *Mengzi* 5B4.
110. Cf. also *Kongzi jiayu* 20, p. 140 (similarly *Shuoyuan* 4, p. 106): "Zengzi (Zeng Shen) in his worn out clothes worked in the fields in Lu. When the Duke of Lu heard of this, he offered him a domain. Zengzi refused it with polite, yet determined words. Somebody said to him, 'The ruler wants to give it to you by his own initiative without your having asked for it. Why do you refuse it so determinedly?' Zengzi said, 'I have heard: He who accepts the favors of another, will always live in awe before him. And he who gives something to another will always look down upon him. And even if the ruler graciously should not look down upon me—would I myself be free of awe before him?' When Confucius heard of this he said, 'Shen's words suffice to keep his moral integrity intact.' "
111. Cf. p. 50 above.
112. Cf. p. 253 below. I assume that the *Mengzi* is older than the *Zhuangzi*. The critical Confucians attack the predatory rulers who deprive the state of its meaning, while the critical Daoists aim at the state itself as a predatory institution.
113. *Mengzi* 1A4, 1A6, and 4A15.
114. *Mingshi* 139, p. 3982, cf. Jiang Guozhu 1981.

115. Guo Moruo (1954, p. 146) supposes that the author belongs to the school of Qidiao Kai, a disciple of Confucius. Cf. p. 171 below.
116. For the example of Wang Fuzhi cf. Hu Chusheng 1986, pp. 33–34.
117. Cf. *Lunyu* 5.13.
118. The structure of these sentences is active, yet the commentators agree that they should be understood as passive (Hu Chusheng 1986, pp. 137–39) and hence be translated: "He will not let rulers and kings make a fool of him, he will not let himself be troubled by superiors, and he will not let himself be pitied by officials."
119. *Liji* 41, pp. 1669a, 1671a, 1671b (Legge II, pp. 404–09).
120. Cf. Chapter 12.
121. *Lunyu* 6.3, 11.7.
122. *Lunheng* 34, pp. 118–19.
123. *Lunyu* 19.13.
124. *Lunyu* 19.7.
125. *Xunzi* 27, p. 335.
126. *Lunyu* 8.12.
127. *Lunyu* 14.24.
128. *Shiji* 6, p. 258. Literature on medicine, pharmacology, divination, agriculture, and forestry was exempted from the burning (ibid., p. 255).
129. Cf. De Bary 1960, vol. 1, p. 277.
130. Cheng Yi 1984, vol. 4, p. 1136; Zhu Xi, *Sishu jizhu*, commentary to *Lunyu* 3.5. Legge (1893) and Waley (1938) have followed this interpretation.
131. Kang Youwei 1984, pp. 32–33.
132. Liang Qichao 1938, vol. 4, p. 199.

NOTES TO CHAPTER 8

1. *Yijing, Xu gua* 2, p. 53a (Legge pp. 435–36).
2. The "five relations" have often been generalized as the core of Confucian ethics, which has then been epitomized as mere role morality. The present book is dedicated to the rejection of this view. Cf. also the critique in Hsü Dao-lin 1970–71.
3. *Mengzi* 3A4.
4. Cf. *Zhongyong* 20, *Baihutong* 8, p. 442, *Chunqiu fanlu* 12.53, p. 6a.
5. *Mengzi* 7A20 (quoted p. 86 above) and 7A15 (quoted p. 130 below).
6. *Kongzi jiayu* 38, p. 223.
7. Cf. Nivison 1960, pp. 178–81, Masson 1985, pp. 69–70.
8. *Shuoyuan* 19, p. 676.
9. *Mengzi* 1A5.
10. *Mengzi* 1A3, 7A22.
11. Cf. Ch'ü 1961, Chapter I. That offenses against filial piety should be punished by penal law is already demanded in the *Shujing* (*Kang gao*, p. 204b–c, Karlgren p. 42). According to *Xiaojing* 11, Confucius calls want of filial piety the greatest of all crimes deserving corporal punishment (cf. *Lüshi chunqiu* 14.1, p. 138). The *Zhouli* (10, p. 707c) counts want of filial piety among the eight crimes liable to "municipal punishments." Under the Han, it is punished by death (Ch'ü 1961, p. 42), and in the Sui code, which became the model for Tang law, it is one of the ten capital crimes (*Suishu* 25, p.

711). On the other hand, the father, especially under the last three dynasties, had extensive power over the life of his children (Ch'ü 1961, pp. 23–26).

12. J. Wu (1979) stresses that Confucius does not intend to identify uprightness with the covering up of crimes by relatives, but that he rejects the identification of giving evidence against relatives with uprightness.

13. *Hanfeizi* 49, cf. pp. 258–59 below.

14. Russell 1922, p. 40.

15. Trauzettel 1977, p. 342, italics added.

16. *Mengzi* 5A2.

17. *Mengzi* 5A3.

18. Ibid.

19. *Zuozhuan* Yin 4.6, p. 11 (Legge p. 17).

20. *Hanfeizi* 33, pp. 228–29 (Liao II, pp. 81–83).

21. *Zuozhuan* Xiang 3.3, p. 255 (Legge p. 420), *Lüshi chunqiu* 1.5, p. 10. Cf. also *Liji* 41, p. 1670 b (Legge II, p. 407), *Shuoyuan* 14, p. 485.

22. *Shuoyuan* 14, p. 467.

23. *Zuozhuan* Zhao 14.6, p. 387 (Legge p. 656), cf. also *Kongzi jiayu* 41, p. 246. Even if we take into consideration the unequal constellations, this account contradicts *Lunyu* 13.18. Cf. Zhang Hengshou 1980, p. 38, with sympathies for the Confucius of the *Zuozhuan*.

24. *Dadai Liji* 54, p. 191.

25. A prescription of propriety when mourning for a parent. Cf. *Liji* 22 B, p. 1581a (Legge II, p. 191).

26. *Liji* 3, pp. 1284c–1285a (Legge I, p. 140), *Kongzi jiayu* 43, p. 274. Cf. also *Liji* 1, p. 1250b, (Legge I, p. 92).

27. *Zhouli* 35, p. 878c, and 14, p. 732a–c.

28. *Gongyangzhuan* Yin 11.4, p. 22. Another famous case of such a revenge happened at the beginning of the fourth century B.C., when a certain Niezheng killed the chancellor Kui of Han. Kui had put his father to death, because he had defaulted on the delivery of a sword. The long story of the revenge became the topic of the famous suite *Guanglingsan*, which M. Dahmer has analysed (1988). The last movement of the suite is entitled "hopelessness" (*wu ji*)—an allusion to the aporetic nature of the conflict between family and state?

29. *Gongyangzhuan*, Ding 4, p. 443. Cf. also *Baihutong* 5, p. 262.

30. Liu Zongyuan 1961, (*Bo fuchou yi*). Liu polemizes against Chen Ziang (661–702) who had recommended to execute the avenger in the name of law (*fa*) and to decorate his grave and the gate of his village by a banner of honor in the name of propriety (*li*) (Chen Ziang 1961 [*Fuchou yizhuang*])—a crass expression of the aporetic nature of this conflict.

31. Cf. Ch'ü 1961, pp. 80–87. In 359 B.C., Shang Yang forbids private feud in Qin (*Shiji* 68, p. 2230). For Han Fei, too, revenge is an offense against law (*Hanfeizi* 49, p. 344 [Liao II, p. 284]).

32. *Xunzi* 24, p. 301. Confucius, too, obviously rejects collective sanctions. Cf. Chapter 4, n. 34.

33. Hegel 1962, pp. 63–76, 274–86, 291–98.

34. Ibid., p. 67.

35. Ibid., p. 59.

36. A. Weber 1943, p. 97.

37. A well-known topos since Schelling, cf. p. 19 above.

38. Rosenzweig 1972, pp. 74–77, Trauzettel 1977, p. 359. Cf. also Fingarette 1972, pp. 23 and 26, and Hawkes 1964, p. 114. For similar statements by Jaspers and modern Chinese authors cf. Roetz 1992.

39. *Lüshi chunqiu* 19.2, pp. 240–41. Cf. also *Hanshi waizhuan* 2.14, p. 58 (Hightower pp. 52–53), *Shiji* 119, p. 3102. According to the *Hanshi waizhuan* and the *Shiji*, Shizhu (called Shishe in both texts) committed suicide.

40. *Lüshi chunqiu* 12, p. 123, also *Zhanguoce* 18, *Zhao* I, pp. 597–98.

41. *Hanshi waizhuan* 1.21, pp. 23–24 (Hightower pp. 29–30).

42. *Hanshi waizhuan* 6.12, p. 248 (Hightower pp. 202–03).

43. *Shijing* 257.9.

44. *Shijing* 162. For an interpretation of the *Si mu* in connection with the topic of tragedy cf. Qian Zhongshu 1979, vol. 1, pp. 134–36.

45. *Guoyu, Jinyu* 1–2. Cf. Roetz 1992.

46. Sometimes there is a solution which helps to avoid a decision by a substitutional symbolic action. Yugong Zhisi knocks off the tips of his arrows, before, in accordance with the order of his lord, shooting at his teacher's teacher (*Mengzi* 4B24). Since the teacher has to be honored like the father, the conflict is between Stages 3 and 4.

47. Victims whom S. Wawrytko forgets when, in a comparison of the tragic motif in *King Lear* and the concept of filial piety in the *Xiaojing*, she recommends filial piety as a way out of the moral dilemma. If Cordelia, she argues, would have followed filial piety, the "all or nothing dilemma" would not have occurred at all (1986, p. 401): "Cordelia could have satisfied her father's emotional needs without doing violence to her own self-respect." In contrast to this harmonious picture, filial piety could well lead into hopeless situations.

48. *Zhuangzi* 33, p. 464 (Watson p. 364, Graham p. 275).

49. For Ch'ien Chung-shu, the Confucian hierarchical arrangement of values (cf. Chapter 10A below) prevents the tragic dilemma (1935, p. 44): " . . . the defect (!) seems to arise from our peculiar arrangement of virtues in a hierarchy. Every moral value is assigned its proper place on the scale, and all substances and claims are arranged according to a strict 'order of merit'. Hence the conflict between two incompatible ethical substances loses much of its sharpness, because as one of them is of higher moral value than the other, the one of lower value fights all along a losing battle. Thus we see a linear personality and not a parallel one. The neglect of the lower ethical substance is amply compensated by the fulfillment of the higher one so that it is not 'tragic excess' at all."

50. *Mengzi* 6B15.

51. Kohlberg 1981, p. 391. Nevertheless, the tragic situation might reappear in a new form on the postconventional level in connection with the necessary suspension of principles in an unprincipled world, as required by an ethics of responsibility. Cf. Chapter 12, and Roetz 1993c, n. 24.

NOTES TO CHAPTER 9

1. Cf. Chapter 12.

2. Cf. the interpretation of the graph in Chang Tsung-tung 1982, p. 23.

3. *Lunyu* 4.8, cf. p. 80 above.

4. Cf. above all *Zhuangzi* 22, pp. 326–27 (Watson pp. 240–41, Graham p. 161), with the famous statement that the *Dao* is everywhere, even "in shit and piss." I borrow the term "pandaoism" from Wang Yu 1979, p. 245.

5. Cf. p. 194 below.

6. Cf. *Xunzi* 29, p. 347 (cf. p. 65 above): "To get a clear insight into the principle (*yi*) of when to follow or not to follow an order;" *Hanfeizi* 50, p. 353 (Liao II, p. 301): "As a matter of principle (*yi*) he does not enter an endangered town . . . ;" *Shiji* 64, p. 3181 (cf. p. 84 above): "On principle (*yi*) they refused opportunistic adaptation to their contemporaries." Cf. also Wang Xianshen's commentary to *Hanfeizi* 34, p. 237, sentence *yi bu chen tianzi bu you zhuhou.*

7. *Lunyu* 2.15.

8. For *Lunyu* 7.8, cf. Chapter 5 above, n. 31. In *Lunyu* 5.9, Confucius attests to Yan Hui to "know ten by hearing one." For the *Xunzi*, cf. Chapter 13 below, n. 4.

9. Hu Shi 1920, p. 107.

10. Quoting *Lunyu* 5.9 and 7.8, cf. n. 8 above.

11. Quoting *Liji* 26, p. 1609c (cf. Legge II, p. 255), and *Zhongyong* 31.

12. Zhang Taiyan 1977, vol. I, p. 185.

13. *Mozi* 42, p. 211 (Graham 1978, p. 327, A 80, with a different interpretation).

14. Cf. pp. 142–43 below.

15. As is proposed by Hu Shi 1920, pp. 107–12, Wen Gongyi 1983, pp. 192–93, and Mao Ting 1984, pp. 83–84.

16. For the quoted passages from the *Lunyu* cf. also Xu Fuguan 1983, pp. 226–34. Rejecting the empiricism of the Qing interpreters Wang Niansun and Ruan Yuan, Xu stresses that Confucius is interested in an ultimate principle.

17. *Jinsilu* 5, p. 182.

18. Cf. Metzger 1987, pp. 108–09.

19. *Lunyu* 1.1.

20. Similarly in *Zhongyong* 20.

21. The character *peng* shows two strings of pearls of equal length, hence its meaning "to equal" (e.g., in *Shijing* 117.1). According to the commentaries of Bao Xian to *Lunyu* 1.1 and Zheng Xuan to *Zhouli* 10, p. 706c, *peng* means "fellow student" (*tong men, tong shi*). *You* (originally the helper in time of need; the character shows two hands) according to Zheng Xuan (ibid.) means "like-minded person" (*tong zhi*).

22. *Lunyu* 1.6, 1.14, 12.23, and 12.24.

23. *Lunyu* 16.4.

24. *Xunzi* 27, pp. 337–38.

25. *Xunzi* 23, p. 299 (Dubs p. 317, Watson p. 170).

26. Ibid.

27. *Liji* 18, p. 1523b (Legge II, p. 86).

28. *Lunyu* 11.24. Although the authenticity of the passage has been questioned, it very well reflects the mood of many of the early Confucians.

29. According to *Mengzi* 7B37, quoted p. 50 above.

30. Cf. p. 99 above.

31. *Mengzi* 5B3.

32. Cf. *Zhuangzi* 28, p. 421 (Watson pp. 316–17, Graham p. 229), and *Mengzi* 5B7, quoted p. 86 above. The topos is also found in *Zhuangzi* 21, p. 317 (Watson p.

232) (referring to the "men of the true," *zhenren*, of antiquity), and in *Lüshi chunqiu* 12.2, p. 116, and 12.5, p. 122.

33. *Hanfeizi* 34, pp. 236 and 237 (Liao II, pp. 95 and 96–97). Huashi's execution is also justified in *Xunzi* 28, p. 342.

34. *Mengzi* 5B8. For the hermeneutic implications of this passage, cf. Roetz 1993a, p. 101.

35. In his short essay *On Friendship* (*Lun you*), He Xinyin writes (1981, p. 28), "When heaven and earth communicate, this is called the highest. Communication, however, is complete in friendship. . . . It is not that elder and younger brothers would not communicate with each other, but their communication is cliquish and nothing which would correspond to the communication of heaven and earth. . . . In the relationship of husband and wife, father and son, ruler and subject, communication is not absent, either. But in these relations, the point at issue is sexual intercourse, familiarity, or 'to tread from above and press from below' (*Zhongyong* 14). It is not that there would not be communication in the world of the family or among the people, but it is inferior to [true] communication."

36. Tan Sitong 1954, p. 67 (Chan Sin-wai 1984, p. 178).

37. Cf. Rao Zongyi 1978, pp. 91–93.

38. *Lunyu* 1.5.

39. *Xunzi* 9, p. 105 (Dubs p. 138, Watson p. 47), *Mengzi* 1A3.

40. *Liji* 6. The text has also been transmitted in the calendar chapters of the *Lüshi chunqiu*. A shorter version appears in *Huainanzi* 5. Cf. Roetz 1984, p. 72.

41. *Lunyu* 11.16, cf. also *Zhongyong* 4.

42. *Lunyu* 6.29, cf. also *Zhongyong* 3. The second sentence can also be translated "The people seldom achieve this for a long time."

43. The translation of the title is disputed. I follow the explanation by Zheng Xuan (*Liji* 30, p. 1625b).

44. *Zhongyong* 1.

45. *Zhongyong* 6 and *Lunyu* 13.21, cf. p. 50 above.

46. For a comparison of Aristotle and the *Zhongyong* cf. Motegi 1963.

47. *Zhongyong* 10.

48. *Xunzi* 9, p. 109 (Dubs p. 145, Watson p. 51).

49. *Mengzi* 4B20.

50. Liang Qichao 1981, p. 57.

51. Wing-tsit Chan 1988.

52. Liang Qichao 1981, p. 55.

53. E. v. Hartmann 1879, p. 122.

54. Weber 1951, p. 163.

55. *Mengzi* 7B37, quoted pp. 50–51 above.

56. *Zhongyong* 9.

57. *Zhongyong* 10.

58. Jaspers 1959, p. 169.

59. *Mengzi* 7A26.

60. *Xunzi* 19, pp. 242 and 241 (Dubs pp. 233 and 232, Watson pp. 101 and 100). Cf. also Roetz 1984, p. 340.

61. *Zhouli* 10, p. 708a. The five domains of propriety are concerned with sacrifice, mourning, reception, the military, and festivities.

62. Motegi, to give only one example, calls the concept of the mean as developed in the *Zhongyong* a source of "oriental despotism" (1963, p. 27).

63. The most impressive document is Thomé Fang 1980, an example of the raptures Neo-Confucians fall into when they speak about harmony. For "harmony" cf. also Bodde 1953, Cheng Chung-ying 1977, Creel 1977, Liu and Allinson 1988.

64. According to Tu Wei-ming, there is an "ecological insight" in the Chinese idea of harmony. "Promethean defiance and Faustian restlessness," Tu writes, "are not at all compatible with the cherished value of harmony, as both societal goal and cosmic ideal, in East Asian thought." This is, at best, an overstatement. The idea of *social* harmony was quite compatible with the subjugation of nature, and even the maintenance of *cosmic* harmony—inasmuch as it was advocated—must not be confounded with an "ecological" relationship towards the flora and fauna of the human biosphere. Cf. Roetz 1984 *passim*, especially § 5.

65. Cf. for example *Mengzi* 3A4 and the passages from the *Xunzi* quoted in Chapter 7 A.

66. Cf. *Xunzi* 20, *passim*, *Zhouli* 10, p. 708a, *Zhouli* 22, pp. 787–88.

67. *Lunyu* 1.12.

68. The specific principle of order of the human world, as distinguished from *tian dao*, the "way of heaven" or the way of nature. Cf. p. 194 below. Cf. also Roetz 1984, pp. 76–77, 199, and 344.

69. *Chunqiu fanlu* 8.27, p. 1 a. Cf. *Liji* 30, p. 1618b (Legge II, pp. 284–85).

70. *Xunzi* 2, p. 14 (Dubs p. 16, Watson p. 25, Knoblock I, p. 153).

71. *Lunyu* 13.23, *Zhongyong* 10.

72. *Xunzi* 13, cf. p. 81 above.

73. *Hanshi waizhuan* 4.3, p. 150 (Hightower p. 126).

74. *Huainanzi* 13, p. 223, cf. p. 158 below.

75. Boodberg 1953, p. 331.

76. *Yi* can, furthermore, stand for "principle" (cf. n. 6 above) or "meaning."

77. *Zhongyong* 20.

78. *Guanzi* 36, p. 221 (Rickett 1965, p. 175).

79. *Hanfeizi* 20, p. 96 (Liao I, p. 171).—Cf. also *Liji* 24, p. 1598c, *Dadai Liji* 52, p. 176, *Lüshi chunqiu* 14.1, p. 139, *Yinwenzi*, *Dadao xia*, p. 7, *Shizi*, *Chuozi*, p. 11b, *Huainanzi* 11, p. 176, *Xinshu*, *Daoshu*, p. 928, *Yantielun* 55, p. 56, *Fayan* 4, p. 10, and 10, p. 31, *Baihutong* 30, p. 452.

80. *Republic* IV, 433.

81. *Rhetorica* 1366b, trans. Roberts modified.

82. *Politica* 1255a 1, trans. Jowett modified.

83. Ibid., 1280a 10. Strictly speaking, Aristotle distinguishes "arithmetical" and "geometrical" justice. Arithmetical justice ("the just in transactions") "treats the parties as equal, if one is in the wrong and the other is being wronged, and one inflicted injury and the other has received it." Geometrical justice ("the just in distribution") treats men "according to merit" rather than as equal (*Ethica Nicomachea* 1132a 5 and 1131a 25).

84. *Mengzi* 7A15, p. 130 below, 6A4, p. 205 below, and 3A4.

85. *Xunzi* 4, p. 44 (Dubs p. 65, Knoblock I, p. 195). Cf. also the quotations from *Xunzi* 9, p. 96 and 19, p. 231, pp. 71–72 above and 224 below.

86. *Xunzi* 7, p. 71 (Dubs p. 8).

87. *Xunzi* 16, p. 204. That justice "sets measures in the world of things" means, on the one hand, that it regulates the access to the resources. On the other hand,

justice is the basic pattern of human activity which imposes a kind of second order on nature, thus making it possible that man as a civilized being can utilize nature in the first place. Cf. Roetz 1984, pp. 331–36.

88. The explicandum *yi* appears again in the explication. Such circularity is now and then found in the ancient texts. It is normally due to the equivocality of words and sometimes to inexact argumentation.

89. *Liji* 9, p. 1422c (Legge I, pp. 379–80).

90. *Liji* 34, p. 1640c (Legge II, p. 338).

91. Cf. also the eulogy on justice in *Guanzi* 10, p. 48 (Rickett 1985, p. 196).

92. *Yiwu* is the modern Chinese expression for "duty."

93. *Lunyu* 12.11, cf. p. 49 above.

94. *Liji* 9, 1426c (Legge I, p. 390), cf. also p. 1427a (Legge I, p. 390), and *Liji* 11, p. 1456c (Legge I, p. 440), *Guanzi* 36, p. 221 (Rickett 1965, p. 175).

95. Cf. for example *Guanzi* 36, p. 221 (Rickett 1965, p. 175): "Yi is that everybody does his due. Li is to give rhythm and form to this, following the feelings of man, and according to the patterns of *yi*." Cf. *Mengzi* 4A27. Cf. also p. 216 below.

96. *Liji* 11, p. 1456c (Legge I, p. 440).

97. *Xunzi* 9, p. 104 (Dubs p. 136, Watson p. 45).

98. Cf. *Mengzi* 2A2, p. 85 above, *Mengzi* 5B4, p. 87 above, *Xunzi* 29, pp. 64–65 above.

99. *Mozi* 49, p. 287 (Mei pp. 248–49), cf. also *Mozi* 47, p. 265 (Mei p. 222).

100. *Lunyu* 2.24.

101. *Lunyu* 4.16, 15.18, and 17.21.

102. *Mengzi* 2A6, cf. p. 200 below.

103. *Mengzi* 2A2 (similarly 5A7), 7A34, 3B10, 3B8, and 7A33.

104. *Mengzi* 1B10.

105. *Mengzi* 7B2.

106. *Xunzi* 11, p. 147.

107. *Xunzi* 9, p. 105, cf. p. 68 above.

108. Cf. pp. 69–72 above.

109. Rawls characterizes his idea of justice as follows (1972, p. 62): "All social values—liberty and opportunity, income and wealth, and the bases of self-respect—are to be distributed equally unless an unequal distribution of any, or all, of these values is to everyone's advantage. Injustice, then, is simply inequalities that are not to the benefit of all." As a democrat, Rawls puts the accent differently than Xunzi: His primary option is equality.

110. *Xunzi* 13, p. 170.

111. *Lunyu* 4.16 and 14.12. Cf. also *Lunyu* 16.10 and 19.1.

112. *Daxue* 10.

113. *Lüshi chunqiu* 1.4, p. 8. For the quotation from the *Hongfan*, cf. *Shujing* p. 190b (Karlgren p. 32); for Lao Dan's statement, cf. p. 255 below. The Three Majesties are Fu Xi, Shen Nong, and Huang Di, the Five Emperors are Shao Hao, Zhuan Xu, Di Ku, Yao, and Shun.

114. Cf. Bauer 1971, pp. 168–70.

115. Cf. also *Guanzi* 64, p. 329 (Rickett 1985, p. 74), *Zhuangzi* 6, p. 139 (Watson p. 91, Graham p. 93), *Lüshi chunqiu* 1.5, p. 10.

116. *Lüshi chunqiu* 1.5, pp. 10–11.

117. Cf. also *Zuozhuan* Xiang 3.3, p. 255 (Legge p. 420), and *Shuoyuan* 14, p. 485.

118. *Xunzi* 12, p. 151.

119. *Xunzi* 22, p. 282 (Dubs pp. 291–92). Cf. also *Shizi, Guang ze*, p. 9b. Cf. for this topic Paul's comprehensive analysis of "concepts of criticism and critical discussion" in Confucianism (Paul 1990, Chapter 2).
120. *Xunzi* 4, p. 37 (Dubs p. 56, Knoblock I, p. 189).
121. *Xunzi* 14, p. 172, and *Xunzi* 4, p. 44 (quoted p. 71 above).

NOTES TO CHAPTER 10

1. For a detailed overview of the modern debate, see Staiger 1969. For a short survey of traditional and contemporary positions, see Cai Shangsi 1983.
2. Although Li Zehou (1986, pp. 15–16) states that the great majority of scholars today views *ren* and not *li* as the core of Confucius' teaching, the minority position should not be underestimated. It still has prominent advocates (in China, for example, Cai Shangsi). Moreover, normally representing *postconventional* and *conventional*, hence paradigmatically different readings, both interpretations of the *Lunyu* will always remain important.
3. A comparably frequent use of *ren* is only found in the *Mengzi*. In the *Liji* and the *Xunzi, li* is dominating.
4. Wing-tsit Chan 1975, p. 107. For the shift in meaning cf. also Lin Yü-sheng 1974–75. The term "virtue" it not apt to describe all of the meanings of *ren*, however. In its reading as the Golden Rule (cf. below), *ren* represents a procedure to find right conduct rather than a virtue.
5. Cf. Mahood 1971, pp. 180–81.
6. For the form of the *Lunyu*, cf. p. 47 above.
7. *Lunyu* 12.1 (return to propriety), 12.22 (love), 12.2 (respect, cf. Chapter 10 D), 6.30 and 12.2 (Golden Rule, cf. Chapter 10 E), 13.19 and 17.5 (encompassing other virtues).
8. *Lunyu* 17.5 and 13.19.
9. Cf. Wing-tsit Chan 1969, p. 5, Cua 1971, pp. 128–29.
10. Cf. *Lunyu* 14.4 (courage), 5.19 (prudence, implicitly also in 6.26), 12.3 (cautiousness in talking), and 12.1 (propriety).
11. *Lunyu* 7.34.
12. *Lunyu* 14.6.
13. *Lunyu* 4.16, 15.18, 17.21 (justice), 2.14, 6.3 (solidarity), 7.31 (impartiality), 13.23 (harmony).
14. Tu Wei-ming 1979, p. 6. Cf. also Tu 1976, pp. 83–84.
15. *Lunyu* 8.2, 15.36, 1.13, 1.12.
16. *Lunyu* 8.2, 17.21, 14.4.
17. *Lunyu* 4.2, 5.5, 14.4.
18. The pre-history of the *li* has been discussed by Noah Fehl (1971, Chapter I).
19. *Hanfeizi* 20, p. 96 (Liao I, p. 171), *Xunzi* 10, p. 115, *Liji* 9, p. 1422a (Legge I, p. 378).
20. *Liji* 30, p. 1618b (Legge II, p. 285).
21. Cf. *Lunyu* 3.18 (p. 87 above), and *Mengzi* 5B4 (p. 50 above).
22. Cf. p. 113 above.
23. *Lunyu* 8.8, 16.13, 20.3. Cf. p. 49 above.

24. This is the tendency in Fingarette 1972, Hall and Ames 1987, and Graham 1989.

25. Cf. Chapter 5.

26. *Lunyu* 12.1.

27. *Lunyu* 3.3.

28. Cf. also Dawson 1981, pp. 30–31.

29. Cf. pp. 156–57 below.

30. To view *li* as the outer manifestation of *ren*, however, as is often suggested (cf. Kuang Yaming 1985, p. 196, Tu Wei-ming 1979, p. 10, Cua 1971, p. 133), would blur the distinction. Not propriety itself is a manifestation of humaneness, but how and with which inner attitude one acts within its framework. Mengzi is right to identify different sources for both (*Mengzi* 2A6, cf. p. 200 below).

31. *Lüshi chunqiu* 17.7, p. 213.

32. *Mengzi* 2A7 (p. 196 below) and 4A2.

33. Zhao Jibin 1976, vol. III, part 1. Zhao's *Lunyu xintan* is a revised edition of his *Gudai rujia zhexue pipan* from 1948.

34. Feng Youlan 1957, pp. 273–80, 281–85.

35. Cf. Cai Shangsi 1984, p. 104. For some other examples, cf. also Zhang Dainian 1981, pp. 55–56, Yang Bojun 1984, p. 254, and Pang Pu 1984, p. 17. When Zhao Jibin looked over his book again in 1981, he felt "like in another world" (Zhao 1983, p. 49, note).

36. Cf., e.g., Gassmann 1985, pp. 163–64.

37. For example in *Shujing*, *Gaoyao mo*, p. 138b (Karlgren p. 8), and *Shijing* 249.

38. Zhou Fagao 1975, vol. 13, p. 6882.

39. Cf. Munro 1969, pp. 208–9, n. 1.

40. *Ai rén* in *Lunyu* 1.5, hence, does not mean "to love men," as normally translated. In *Lunyu* 1.6 Confucius does not speak of love for all men either. Although *ai* should now be translated as "love," the object *zhong* most probably means the same as *rén* in *Lunyu* 1.5—"citizens." Cf. however, *Lunyu* 12.22, quoted p. 127 below.

41. *Mengzi* 1A2 and 3A4.

42. *Lunyu* 8.4, 10.11, 18.6, 11.12.

43. *Mengzi* 3A3 (cf. also 7A16 and 5A4), 3A4, 1A4, and 2A2.

44. *Mengzi* 1A5, 1A7, 1B12, 3A3, 7A45.

45. *Lunyu* 12.2 and 17.5.

46. Cf., e.g., Dubs 1951, p. 49.

47. Cf., e.g., *Daxue* 3, *Liji* 9, p. 113 above.

48. *Lunyu* 6.7, cf. p. 83 above.

49. Cf. Chapter 11 E.

50. *Lunyu* 8.2, quoted in Chapter 5, n. 48.

51. *Liji* 33, p. 1648a (Legge II, p. 354).

52. *Lunyu* 17.2.

53. *Mengzi* 6A7, 6B2.

54. *Xunzi* 23, pp. 295–96 (Dubs p. 313, Watson p. 166).

55. *Lunyu* 8.9. Cf. p. 67 above.

56. *Lunyu* 5.16, 6.30, and 12.7.

57. *Zuozhuan* Xi 25.1, p. 126 (Legge p. 194).

58. *Lunyu* 13.19, cf. also 15.6.

59. This is in accordance with the general claim that one should orientate one's conduct by one's own standards and not by the attitude of others (cf. Chapter 11 *passim*). Cf. the position of Mo Di, p. 242 below.

60. *Lunyu* 9.14, cf. above, p. 44.

61. *Lunyu* 12.5 (cf. also *Xunzi* 8, p. 77 [Dubs p. 95], *Xunzi* 9, p. 102 [Dubs p. 133, Watson p. 43], *Xunzi* 15, p. 185 [Dubs p. 166, Watson p. 68]: "All within the four seas become a single family."). Although the expression "within the four seas" *si hai zhi nei* can refer to the Chinese territories in their specific, it is normally used to express generality, not distinction.

62. Cf. Munro 1969, pp. 11–22.

63. The association of both concepts can be found already in the *Guoyu*, but the age of the respective passages (*Zhouyu xia*, p. 96, *Jinyu* 1, p. 275, *Chuyu shang*, p. 529) is difficult to determine.

64. *Mozi* 40, p. 191 (Graham 1978, p. 270, A 7).

65. *Mengzi* 4B28, cf. p. 165 below. Cf. also *Mengzi* 7A46.

66. *Zhuangzi* 12, p. 183 (Watson p. 127).

67. *Xunzi* 27, p. 324, similarly *Xunzi* 15, p. 185 (Dubs pp. 167 and 168, Watson p. 69).

68. *Liji* 26, p. 1610a (Legge II, p. 257).

69. *Shangjunshu* 7, p. 16 (Duyvendak p. 226).

70. *Xinshu, Daoshu*, p. 928.

71. *Shuowen jiezi* 8A1, p. 161b. Cf. also *Hanfeizi* 20, p. 96 (Liao I, p. 171), *Dadai Liji* 39, p. 15, *Chunqiu fanlu* 8.29, pp. 7a, 7b, and 8.30, p. 10a.

72. *Ai* also means "treat carefully" or "be sparing with," *qin* also means "intimate," "parents," "relatives," "love like a relative." *Ai* and *qin* are frequently used synonymously.

73. Cf. pp. 205–6 below.

74. Cf. Luke 6:27, 6:35.

75. Cf., e.g., Legge 1893, p. 288: "How far the ethics of Confucius fall below our Christian standard is evident from this chapter. . . . " Cf. also Weber 1951, p. 162.

76. "To repay enmity with virtue" is recommended in *Laozi* 63, though not in a moral but in a strategic context. Chen Guying (1988, p. 44) is of the opinion that *Lunyu* 14.34 quotes the *Laozi*, thus delivering an "iron proof" that the *Laozi* is the older text. However, the sentence can as well have been taken over into the *Laozi* from the *Lunyu* in order to provoke contradiction.

77. Cf. *Guoyu, Chuyu xia*, p. 586, where Zigao (probably the Prefect of She from *Lunyu* 13.18) argues that giving up enmity, because one experiences virtue from the part of an enemy, can only be expected from a humane person.

78. As is proposed in *Liji* 31, p. 1639a (Legge II, p. 332).

79. *Lunyu* 4.3, cf. *Lunyu* 17.6 and 17.22, and *Daxue* 10.

80. Cf. Kohlberg 1981, p. 351: "Rather than replacing principles of justice, agape goes beyond them in the sense of defining or informing acts of supererogation, acts that cannot be generally demanded or required of all people, acts that freely give up claims the actor may in justice demand. The attitude of agape presupposes an understanding and acceptance of the logic of duty and justice for its own definition."

81. *Liji* 32, p. 1639a (Legge II, p. 333).

82. *Xunzi* 15, p. 185 (Dubs p. 168, Watson p. 69).

83. *Mengzi* 7B1, cf. p. 130 below.

84. Humaneness and knowledge for Confucius are independent values which are also contrasted with each other (*Lunyu* 4.2 [cf. p. 144 below], 6.23, 9.29). On the other hand, humaneness comprises knowledge (*Lunyu* 5.19, 6.26). Next to the intellectual type, there is a voluntaristic variant of humaneness in the *Lunyu* (cf. Chapter 11, n. 2). Both forms later become important for Xunzi and Mengzi respectively.

85. *Mengzi* 2A2, *Xunzi* 12, p. 158, *Xunzi* 21, p. 261 (Dubs p. 263, Watson p. 124), *Xunzi* 29, p. 350. Cf. also *Chunqiu fanlu* 8.30.

86. *Mengzi* 3B9. For Mo Di, cf. Chapter 14 A.

87. *Shizi, Fen*, p. 5a. For *Mengzi* 3A5, cf. p. 129 below.

88. *Mengzi* 4A27, 6B3, 7A15, cf. also 7B24, p. 199 below.

89. *Shangjunshu* 7, p. 16 (Duyvendak p. 226).

90. That other virtues can be conceived of as expansions of family morality is already suggested by Confucius' disciple You Ruo who views filial piety and fraternal deference as the "foundations of humaneness" (*Lunyu* 1.2, p. 55 above). For *Xiaojing* 1, filial piety is the "foundation of virtue and the starting point of education," and according to *Guanzi* 26 (p. 156, Rickett 1985 p. 380, the chapter shows Confucian influence) "filial piety and fraternal deference are the ancestors of humaneness." Zeng Shen, finally, identifies other virtues with filial piety (*Liji* 24, p. 1598b–c, Legge II, pp. 227–28, *Dadai Liji* 52, p. 176, similarly *Lüshi chunqiu* 14.1, p. 138).

91. *Liji* 9, p. 1414a–b (Legge I, pp. 365 and 366).

92. *Liji* 24, p. 1599b (Legge II, p. 229, cf. also *Kongzi jiayu* 41, p. 257): "Anciently, the clan of Yu (Shun) honored virtue and esteemed age. The clan of the rulers of the Xia honored rank and esteemed age. The Yin (Shang) honored wealth and esteemed age. The Zhou honored kin and esteemed age."

93. *Mengzi* 3A5.

94. Cf. Gehlen on the "enlargement of the ethos of kinship," Gehlen 1969, Chapter 9.

95. *Mengzi* 1A7. The quotation is from *Shijing* 240.2.

96. *Mengzi* 7A15.

97. *Mengzi* 7B1. Cf. also 7B31, p. 212 below.

98. Cf. pp. 206 and 212 below.

99. *Mengzi* 5A3. Mengzi defends Shun (cf. p. 95 above). An interesting passage in this connection is found in *Shujing, Taishi*, p. 181c, where the rebel Wu Wang says about Zhòu, the last king of the Shang, "Although he has solidary relatives with him, they do not equal humane men (*ren rén*)." (The *Taishi* is generally regarded as a late document. In an early Zhou document, *ren* would rather mean "noble." In the "genuine" chapters of the *Shujing*, *ren* only appears once in the *Jinteng*, p. 196b, where it likewise should be translated as "noble.") The sentence appears also in *Lunyu* 20.1 and, slightly modified, in *Mozi* 15, p. 70 (cf. Lin Yü-sheng 1974–75, pp. 174 and 197). That it could invite an antifamilistic adaptation becomes apparent from *Shizi, Chuozi*, p. 10 b: "Wen (sic.) Wang said, 'If one has humane men, why insist on solidary relatives?' He did not favor his kin, but the states. It is not that the early kings had no favors, but what they favored was different from what other men favor."

100. According to Trauzettel, Confucianism advocates a "pure ethics of near relations (*reine Nah-Ethik*)" (1977, p. 244). According to Schmidt-Glintzer, Mengzi and Xunzi defend "kin particularism" (1983, p. 306). According to Seiwert, Confucianism is dedicated to the family "whereas the well-being of others does not fall within the realm of one's own responsibility" (1984, p. 16).

101. *Mengzi* 2A6, cf. p. 200 below.
102. *Mengzi* 1A7, cf. pp. 210–11 below.
103. "If a ruler sheds tears when corporal punishments are inflicted in accordance with law, this shows his humaneness," Han Fei mocks (*Hanfeizi* 49, p. 342 [Liao II, p. 281]). *Baihutong* 8, p. 452, defines, "*Ren* means 'not to bear' (*bu rěn*), to grant life, and to love men."
104. Cf. pp. 211–12 below.
105. *Lunyu* 12.2.
106. Cf. *Lunyu* 2.3.
107. *Zuozhuan* Xi 33.8, p. 143 (Legge p. 226). Cf. *Guoyu, Jinyu* 5, p. 393.
108. Cf. also *Lunyu* 13.19, p. 126 above.
109. As is, e.g., suggested in Wawrytko 1982, p. 237.
110. *Xunzi* 13, pp. 169–70.
111. *Hanshi waizhuan* 6.8, p. 242 (Hightower p. 198).
112. The difference between the two possible forms of respect—the vertical and the horizontal one, or in Piaget's words, "respect unilatéral" and "respect mutuel" (1932, pp. 93 and 98)—is crucial, since it concerns two types of social relations described by Piaget as based on "contraint" or "coopération" respectively (ibid., p. 58).
113. The popular "Do not do unto others as you would not have them do unto you," or, positively, "Do unto others what you would have them do unto you." According to Philippidis 1929, p. 15, the expression "Golden Rule" was used for the first time by the English historian Edward Gibbon (1737–94) in his *The History of the Decline and Fall of the Roman Empire*.
114. In Greece, the Golden Rule is already attributed to both Pittakos and Thales, two of the "seven sages" of the sixth century B.C., in the formulation "Do not do yourself what you disapprove of with your neighbor" (Diehls/Kranz 10 e 4, Diogenes Laertius I.36). In the Old Testament, it appears in Tobit 4.15 (first century B.C.): "Do not burden another with what you disapprove of yourself." In the New Testament, it is found in Matthew 7:12 ("Therefore all things whatsoever ye would that men should do to you, do ye even so to them: for this is the law and the prophets"), and Luke 6:31 ("And as ye would that men should do to you, do ye also to them likewise."). In India, the epos *Mahābhārata* (Book 13, section 113, p. 235) demands, "One should never do that to another which one regards as injurious to one's own self. This, in brief, is the rule of Righteousness. One by acting in a different way by yielding to desire becomes guilty of unrighteousness. In refusals and gifts, in happiness and misery, in the agreeable and the disagreeable, one should judge of their effects by a reference to one's own self. When one injures another, the injured turns round and injures the injurer. Similarly, when one cherishes another, that other cherishes the cherisher. One should frame one's conduct according to this." Most impressive is the ontological tenet "tat twam asi," "that thou art" from the *Chāndogya-Upanishad* (6.8.7), in which Schopenhauer (1977, VI, pp. 310–11) has seen a metaphysical foundation for all morality. For a host of other examples from ancient sources see Philippidis 1929 and Dihle 1962.
115. The explicit formulation of the Golden Rule in China is probably a personal innovation of Confucius. Negative evidence for this is the lack of the explicit Golden Rule in earlier literature. The fact that the two accounts of humaneness occuring in the quoted passage from *Zuozhuan* Xi 33 are supplemented by the Golden Rule in *Lunyu* 12.2 may serve as positive evidence.

116. In *Lunyu* 12.2, p. 131 above, and *Lunyu* 6.30, p. 134 below. The *Shuowen jiezi* (10b 11, p. 218a) later equates *ren* with *shu*, "reciprocity" or "fairness," the short form of the Golden Rule. *Shu* thus is a convincing explication of the etymological signification of *ren.* The Golden Rule and humaneness are also identified in *Guanzi* 51, cf. pp. 137–38 below.

117. *Lunyu* 4.15, cf. p. 102 above, and p. 142 below.

118. *Lunyu* 15.24.

119. *Hanfeizi* 50, p. 352 (Liao II, p. 300).

120. Other translations are "sympathy," "altruism," "empathy," "mutualness," etc.

121. Cf. Legge 1893, p. 177: "The Golden Rule of the Gospel is higher. . . . " That the Golden Rule in the *Lunyu* is merely negative is also held by Allinson (1985). Rejecting such interpretations, Wing-tsit Chan has stressed that the Golden Rule in China has never been solely understood as negative (1969, pp. 6–7, 1975, pp. 120–21).

122. For Allinson, the alleged negativity of the Golden Rule is consonant with the basic "attitudes of modesty and humility" of Confucian ethics (1985, p. 306).

123. Exactly in the reference to one's own expectation, however, there is a specific ambivalence. Cf. p. 141 below.

124. *Lunyu* 4.15, cf. p. 102 below.

125. Kohlberg defines role taking, among other things, as "the tendency to react to others as like the self and to react to the self's behavior from the other's point of view" (Kohlberg 1971, p. 190).

126. *Shizi, Shu*, p. 7b, and *Xinshu, Daoshu*, p. 928.

127. Cf. Chapter 9 A.

128. *Shizi, Shu*, p. 7b.

129. Cf. Zhang Xincheng 1954, pp. 833–34.

130. *Mozi* 45, p. 251 (Graham 1978, p. 482, NO 11).

131. *Daxue* 9. *Daxue* 9 discusses the political device "To bring the state into order depends on regulating the clan."

132. Locke 1823a, p. 37.

133. Locke, ibid., Leibniz 1959 III/I, p. 56, Kant 1981, 430 (BA 68) (p. 37, n. 23).

134. Singer 1963a, p.16.

135. Cf. Kohlberg 1971, p. 197. A strategical anticipation is already present at Stage 2. Stages 2–6 can be reconstructed as forms of the Golden Rule.

136. Cf. pp. 235–36 below.

137. *Guoyu, Zhouyu shang*, pp. 35–36.

138. Ibid., p. 36.

139. *Guanzi* 66 (late Zhou or later), p. 341 (Rickett 1985, p. 141).

140. *Guanzi* 51, p. 275.

141. *Yanzi chunqiu* 3.18, p. 89.

142. Cf. above, pp. 35–36.

143. For some examples from ancient Chinese literature, cf. ibid.

144. Cf. for example *Mengzi* 4A21 and 4B5: "If the ruler is humane, everybody will be humane. And if the ruler is just, everybody will be just."—"If the ruler regards his subjects as his hands and feet, they will regard him as belly and heart. If the ruler regards his subjects as his dogs and horses, they will regard him as a commoner. If the ruler regards his subjects as mud and weeds, they will regard him as a robber and an enemy."

145. The Golden Rule can also have consequences for foreign policy. In 712 B.C., King Huan of Zhou receives four settlements from Zheng. In exchange he gives twelve

settlements of his own which he cannot control because of rebellions. The *Zuozhuan* (Yin 11.3, pp. 21–22, Legge p. 33) criticizes this as an offense against "fairness" (*shu*). That fairness should be a principle of foreign policy is also stressed by the Song reformer Wang Anshi (1021–86) (cf. Wang 1974, vol. 1, p. 305, Williamson 1937, vol. 2, p. 347).

146. *Xunzi* 30, pp. 352–53, similarly *Kongzi jiayu* 9, p. 53. The quotation is not necessarily from Confucius (cf. p. 64 above). The passage fits well into the context of Xunzi's own social philosophy.

147. There is an implicit reference to politics in *Lunyu* 12.2 and 6.30.

148. Cf. also *Dadai Liji* 51, p. 170.

149. Cf. Singer 1963b, pp. 294–95, and Singer 1963a, Chapter V § 2.

150. Kuang Yaming 1985, p. 224, and Opitz 1990, pp. 529–30. For Nivison, I follow Ivanhoe 1990a, pp. 21–22, since his paper "Golden Rule Arguments in Chinese Moral Philosophy," presented at the inaugural address of the annual W. Y. Evans-Wentz Professorship in Oriental Philosophies, Religions and Ethics, Stanford University, 13 February 1984, was not available to me.

151. Cf. *Laozi* 47.

152. Cf. *Yanzi chunqiu* 1.20, p. 28: "When the wise rulers of antiquity were satisfied, they knew that others were hungry. When they felt warm they knew that others felt cold. And when they were at ease they knew that others were toiling."

153. *Hanshi waizhuan* 3.38, p. 147 (Hightower p. 123).

154. Cua (1984, p. 232) in this connection speaks of the necessity to interpret "volition" in *Lunyu* 5.12 and 12.2 as a "second-order desire."

155. *Lunyu* 4.15, cf. Chapter 9 A above.

156. Quoted p. 139 above.

157. Feng Youlan 1961, pp. 99–100 (Fung 1952, vol. 1, p. 71), and Feng 1962, pp. 116–17. Cf. also Yang Bojun 1965, p. 42, Zhou Yutong and He Zhuojun 1979, p. 12, Gao Heng 1980, pp. 411–413, Zhu Bokun 1984, p. 29. Note that in *Guoyu, Zhouyu shang*, p. 36 (cf. p. 137 above), *zhong* is implicitly associated with the negative Golden Rule.

158. Quoted in Ivanhoe 1990a, p. 22.

159. Cf. ibid., p. 31, n. 23. Cf. Ivanhoe's own claim, ibid., p. 25: "A person can never be *zhong* to a subordinate." Ivanhoe modifies Nivison's thesis in relating *zhong* to propriety (*li*). *Zhong* thus means to "do one's duty, as prescribed by the *li*, in service to others" (ibid.). This likewise gives priority to the hierarchical commitments. Contrary to Nivison's and Ivanhoe's claim, *zhong* behavior is not socially specified. An unequivocal example that *zhong* can also refer to subordinates is found in *Zuozhuan* Huan 6.1, p. 31 (Legge p. 48): "When the ruler thinks of benefiting the people, this is *zhong*." Cf. also *Guoyu, Zhouyu shang*, pp. 35–36, quoted p. 137 above.

160. Cf. the definition in *Xinshu, Daoshu*, p. 929 (trans. Graham 1989, p. 21): "Concern for and benefiting issuing right from the centre of you is called *zhong*."

161. Cf. Chen Chun, 1983, p. 28.

162. Ibid., pp. 29 and 30.

163. For this interpretation, cf. also Fingarette 1979b. Fingarette interprets *zhong* as a specification of *shu* which by itself would remain "morally directionless" (p. 392). *Zhong*, according to Fingarette, is loyal respect of the other's integrity (p. 389). Cua, however (1984, p. 232), understands *zhong* as "loyalty to and conscientious regard for the moral standard of the ideal of *ren*." He thus relates *zhong* not to persons, but to

humaneness. *Zhong* is, furthermore, construed as loyalty to oneself or self-respect. Of these interpretations, Fingarette's, to me, for philological reasons is the most plausible one. I nonetheless doubt whether the model proposed by Cheng Yi is tenable. There is a correlation of moral norms and communication rather than a one-sided dependence of the latter on the former (cf. pp. 146 and 160–61 below).

164. Dihle for this reason has assigned the Golden Rule to "vulgar ethics" (1962, p. 80). According to Weber's interpretation of the Confucian "gentlemen ideal" (1951, p. 162), "all ethics in this sphere go back to the principled mutuality of the neighborhood association of peasants, 'I shall do unto you as you do unto me.' That is the 'reciprocity' which the Master, when questioned, presented as the very foundation of social ethics."

165. Cf. Singer 1963b, p. 294, Reiner 1974, p. 354, Wimmer 1980, pp. 255–56.

166. Cf. Reiner 1974, pp. 376–77.

167. Pang Pu 1984, p. 54 and *passim*.

168. For Mo Di cf. Chapter 14 A. It need not be emphasized that in China, like elsewhere, the *do ut des* has always enjoyed great popularity in everyday life. Cf. Yang Lien-sheng 1957, pp. 291–92.

169. Quoted p. 131 above. Cf. also *Lunyu* 4.12.

170. *Xunzi* 30, p. 353, *Xunzi* 11, p. 148.

171. Cf. n. 144 above, and *Mengzi* 1A1, 1B4, 1B12 (quoted p. 78 above), and 4B3.

172. For Li Zehou, the ascetic, unselfish element of Confucian ethics belongs to its "feudal" aspects and to the "severe obstacles on China's road to industrialization and modernization" (1986, p. 37). The fact that Confucius "makes the moral and not the material the yardstick of value" should not be welcomed from an ethical, but be criticized from an economical point of view (ibid., p. 36). When Li does not distinguish between the rejection of self-interest, which is typical of the ancient Confucians, and their claim for general welfare, this fits the economic policy of the People's Republic of the post-Mao era. This policy has rehabilitated the search for private profit as the foundation of public utility and plays down the contradictions between both as far as possible.

173. *Lunyu* 4.2.

174. Plato, *Crito* 49.

175. *Lunyu* 15.9. Cf. Mengzi 6A10, quoted pp. 152–53 below.

176. *Lunyu* 8.7.

177. *Hanfeizi* 20, p. 96 (Liao I, p. 171). The quotation is from *Laozi* 38.

178. Cf. Baier 1969, p. 108.

179. This accounts for the problem which Kant (1981, BA 68, p. 37, n. 23) has seen in the neglect of "duties to oneself" in the Golden Rule.

180. Graham 1989, p. 385.

181. Graham's "quasi-syllogism" is a formula that tells us to act as we feel spontaneously inclined when fully aware of all relevant circumstances. According to Graham, the "quasi-syllogism" underlies all Chinese ethical reasoning. It goes like this (Graham 1989, pp. 29, and 383): "In awareness from all viewpoints, spatial, temporal and personal, of everything relevant to the issue I find myself moved towards X; overlooking something relevant I find myself moved towards Y. In which direction shall I let myself be moved? Be aware of everything relevant to the issue. Therefore let yourself be moved towards X."

182. Cf. Roetz 1991, p. 414. That Graham's "quasi-syllogism" is not a *moral* device is, for other reasons, also argued by Kachi (1990, p. 393). I should like to defend Graham against Fingarette, however. "Awareness" is no guarantee for the moral nature of an action. But it cannot simply be excluded from the constituents of a moral act and replaced by the guidance of the rules of propriety, which "define for me what I am to find good and worthy, and thus preclude the need for further awareness" (Fingarette 1991, p. 219, cf. p. 3 above). Graham fails to take into account the possibility of strategical action, but he is right to uphold the concept of a conscious actor (although he is not quite consistent on this point). This concept can only be abandoned if one is blind to the dangers of contextualism.

183. Cf. for this topic Apel's justification of Kohlberg's Stage 6 (1988, pp. 350–57).

184. *Lunyu* 1.4, cf. p. 168 below.

185. *Hanshi waizhuan* 9.7, p. 372 (Hightower p. 296).

186. *Mengzi* 7A17. Cf. p. 171 below. I do not believe that this passage contains Mengzi's idea of "extension" (as is suggested by Nivision 1980, pp. 106–7), since the access to moral action is a far more immediate and direct one here than in "extension." For some other interpretation of 7A17, cf. Nivison, ibid. For the idea of extension cf. p. 130 above and p. 212 below.

187. *Mengzi* 2A6, 6A6, 7A15. Cf. p. 130 above and p. 200 below.

188. Chen Que 1979, vol. 1, p. 259 (referring to *Mengzi* 7A17).

189. *Mengzi* 7A4.

190. For a sharp contradistinction of both outlooks cf. Jonas 1984, p. 39.

NOTES TO CHAPTER 11

1. *Lunyu* 7.26, 6.7, 9.11, 7.34, and 8.7 (quoted p. 144 above).

2. The voluntaristic line within Confucianism can be traced back to *Lunyu* 7.30: "Is humaneness really far away? If I only want it, it is here!" This statement, however, is rather atypical of the *Lunyu*.

3. *Mengzi* 7A41, cf. p. 186 below.

4. Cf. p. 84 above.

5. Cf. pp. 178, 179, and 180 below.

6. For Neo-Confucianism, cf. Nivison 1960 and Metzger 1977.

7. *Lunyu* 2.12.

8. Cf. Rosemont 1986, p. 207, Sun Longji 1983, p. 11, Wawrytko 1982, p. 237.

9. Cf. Chapter 1, n. 4.

10. Fingarette 1979b, p. 254.

11. Fingarette 1979a, p. 133.

12. Fingarette 1972, Chapter 3. Cf. Schwartz's criticism, 1985, pp. 72–75.

13. Cf. p. 173 below.

14. Cf. Hegel 1956, p. 120, quoted pp. 7–8 above.

15. A "knowing how," not a reflected "knowing that." Cf. Roetz 1993a, pp. 75 and 76.

16. Fingarette 1972, pp. 19 and 22.

17. Ibid., p. 18, similarly Hall and Ames 1987, p. 265.

18. Fingarette 1979a, *passim*, 1972, p. 45; cf. also Whalen Lai 1984, p. 151. For a criticism of Fingarettes' position similar to mine, cf. Schwartz 1985, pp. 78–80, and Ruskola 1992.

19. Fingarette 1991, p. 219.
20. Rosemont writes (1976, p. 57), "... it is not simply that the early Confucians explicitly *denied* that there were any moral dilemmas. On the contrary, ... they never even *entertained* the idea of genuine conflict involving moral questions, and we must therefore conclude that the concept of moral dilemmas does not play a role in the Confucian moral theory of human action." In an older essay on Xunzi, however, Rosemont writes (1970–71, p. 75), "... it should be noted that the individual must *choose* to have the *li* govern his behavior. ... The young Confucian scholar must make a basic moral choice, whether or not to assume responsibility for following the *li;* and the choice, once made, requires constancy and effort on his part thereafter." According to Rosemont 1986, p. 210, n. 15, he corrected his view under the influence of Fingarette. This shows that Fingarette's theses claim to be valid not only for the *Lunyu*, but for classical Confucianism in general. According to Hansen, the Confucian teaching of the "rectification of terms" serves for transferring conflicts within the established code of behavior into questions of appropriate language usage (Fingarette's "proper classifications"!): "The purpose of the rectification is to create an ideal language for moral discrimination, evaluation, and action. It is supposed to eliminate the problematic ethical questions." (Hansen 1983, p. 77). In Hansen, too, the denial of problems of decision is linked to the claim that a concept of a rational moral individual is missing (1985c, p. 364; cf. also 1985b). Reflection is replaced by the "knowing how," the skill in following established habits.
21. Dien 1982, pp. 339, 334, 335, and 336.
22. In terms of Confucian ethics, Nanrong Zhu has expressed this dilemma as follows in the *Zhuangzi* (23, p. 340, Watson p. 252): "If I am inhumane, I will harm others, but if I am humane, I will, on the contrary, make trouble for myself. If I am unjust, I will injure others. But if I am just, I will, on the contrary, make trouble for myself. How can I escape from this?" The Daoists, in general, criticize the commitment of oneself to morality as a senseless sacrifice of the "true"—the individual life.
23. Weighing is the central concept of decision making also in strategic and instrumental contexts. Cf. *Xunzi* 22, p. 285 (Dubs pp. 296–97, Watson p. 153): "As far as human predilections are concerned, in general man does not purely get what he desires, and is not completely spared what he hates. Therefore, there is no activity which would not require weighing."
24. *Xunzi* 22, p. 286 (Dubs p. 297, Watson pp. 153–54). For the translation of the last sentence, cf. Li Disheng 1979, p. 533.
25. *Mengzi* 6A14 and 6A15, p.p. 199–200 below.
26. *Mengzi* 6A10.
27. *Xunzi* 3, p. 24 (Knoblock I, p. 174). Cf. also *Zhongyong* 10, p. 108 above.
28. Cua 1985, p. 66.
29. Ibid., pp. 96–97.
30. Ibid., p. 23.
31. Ibid., p. 79, italics added.
32. Ruskola brings forward a similar argument against Graham (Ruskola 1992, p. 293).
33. Cf. p. 193 below.
34. Cua 1984, p. 230.
35. Ibid., pp. 230–31.
36. *Mengzi* 3B2, cf. p. 172 below.

37. *Mengzi* 4A18[17]. For the remainder of the passage, cf. p. 186 below. For Chunyu Kun's question, cf. *Liji* 30, p. 1622c (Legge II, p. 299).

38. *Chunqiu fanlu* 2.3, pp. 3a–4a, referring to *Chunqiu Zuozhuan* Xuangong 15.2, pp. 202–3 (Legge pp. 327–28), and *Lunyu* 15.36.

39. Cf. *Zhuangzi* 29, p. 435 (Watson p. 334, Graham p. 238). For Upright Gong cf. Chapter 8 above. Student Wei waited for a girl under a bridge in spite of a flood.

40. Cf. *Xunzi* 3, pp. 25–26, p. 189 below.

41. Cf. *Zhuangzi* 22, p. 319 (Watson p. 235), and *Laozi* 38.

42. *Huainanzi* 13, pp. 221–23.

43. *Xunzi* 11, p. 142.

44. Cf. Chapter 12 below. Cf. also Roetz 1993c, point E.

45. *San jun*, "three armies," according to *Zhouli* 28, p. 830a, the army of a great state.

46. *Lunyu* 7.22 and 7.28.

47. *Mengzi* 2A3.

48. *Xunzi* 21, p. 265 (Dubs p. 269, Watson p. 129).

49. *Xunzi* 8, p. 90.

50. *Kongzi jiayu* 15, p. 100, *Shuoyuan* 3, p. 94.

51. *Ji* is a pronoun meaning "self," *shen* a noun with the basic meaning "body." Both words are often used synonymically, for example in parallel passages in *Lunyu* 1.4 / *Xunzi* 1, p.1, and *Mengzi* 2A7 / *Zhongyong* 14.

52. Above all in the *Lisao*, the *Jiu zhang*, and the *Yufu*.

53. Cf. Mead 1967, Chapters III and IV *passim*, and pp. 167–68. It seems to me a Platonic ideosyncracy, therefore, to take, as Weber-Schäfer has suggested, the very linkage of self-formation to the existence of the "second one," which he discerns in the *Lunyu*, as an indication of "cosmologically bound anthropology" (Weber-Schäfer 1968, p. 33). Cf. pp. 228–29 below.

54. Cf. pp. 145–46 above.

55. Cf. the excellent description in Tu Weiming 1976, pp. 34–39.

56. *Lunyu* 4.25.

57. Nakamura has stated that the "concept of alienation is alien to Asians" (quoted in Gray and Plott 1979, p. 11). This opinion is widely accepted. Yet, any transcending of conventional morality without the experience of alienation is hardly conceivable. The Daoist revolt against convention, too, can only be understood from here.

58. From here on, the seeming contradiction between the two usages of "self" (*ji*) in *Lunyu* 12.1 explains itself. The contradiction has a *fundamentum in re* and does not rule out the above translation, as Zhao Jibin has argued. Following Qing commentators, Zhao reads *ke* as *neng* (be able). *Ke ji*, then, would mean "to understand to unfold one's self." While this would still fit in with a postconventional reading of the *Lunyu*, it prompts Zhao to reproach Confucius of "idealistic subjectivism" (1976, pp. 291–96).

59. Li Zhi writes (*Fenshu*, Li Zhi 1975, part 1, p. 16), "Confucius has never taught others to study him. Suppose that he taught others to study him, why then did he answer Yan Yuan that 'humaneness can only come from the self' and does not 'come from others'? And why did he say, 'the ancients learned for themselves' (*Lunyu* 14.23), and 'the gentleman seeks in himself' (*Lunyu* 15.21)?" Hence, to "abandon one's self and by all means study Confucius" (Li 1975, part 1, p. 17), for Li Zhi would mean betraying the spirit of the "Master" himself. His conclusion (ibid., p. 18): "That it cannot

be a sufficient criterion for me what the contemporaries regard as right or wrong, I know for long." Cf. de Bary 1970, pp. 197–204.

60. According to *Hanshu* 27 B 1, p. 1353, *gong* refers to the "inner"—the personal attitude—and *jing* to the "outer"—the task to be fulfilled, in the given case governmental affairs. He Yin, on the other hand, relates *gong* to the outer appearance and *jing* to the "heart" (quoted in *Liji* 1, p. 1231c), perhaps following the *Yijing* which likewise relates *jing* to the "inner" (*Wenyan* p. 4a). Both terms are often interchangeable.

61. *Lunyu* 5.16.

62. *Lunyu* 15.5 and 14.42.

63. *Lunyu* 13.19.

64. *Mengzi* 3B1, similarly 5A7.

65. *Xunzi* 8, pp. 83 and 82 (Dubs pp. 104 and 102).

66. *Xunzi* 29, p. 350.

67. *Lunyu* 1.1 and 15.19 (similarly 1.16 and 14.30). Cf. also *Lüshi chunqiu* 14.8, p. 158: "The attitude of a gentleman is such that he respects the others, but he is not necessarily respected by them. He loves the others, but is not necessarily loved by them. To respect and love the others, this lies with oneself. But to be respected and loved, this lies with the others. A gentleman relies on that which lies with himself, and not on that which lies with the others."

68. *Lunyu* 2.14, 15.22, 13.23.

69. *Lunyu* 4.9, 15.33, 7.16.

70. *Hanfeizi* 45, pp. 315 and 314 (Liao II, pp. 231 and 230).

71. *Hanfeizi* 6, p. 24 (Liao I, p. 42).

72. Ibid.

73. *Hanfeizi* 34, pp. 236 (Liao II, p. 95). Taigong Wang is Wen Wang's teacher.

74. *Lunyu* 19.17.

75. Cf. *Lunyu* 3.4 (similarly *Liji* 3, p. 1285a [Legge I, p. 141]): "Lin Fang asked what is the most fundamental with ritual (*li*). The Master said, 'A great question, indeed! With ritual, sparingness is better than splendor. And in mourning, grief is better than a perfect arrangement.'"

76. During the mourning period of twenty-seven months, the sons lived each for himself in a hut, retired from official life, and reduced the contact with their surroundings to a minimum. For a detailed description cf. De Groot 1894, pp. 479–88. For the topic cf. also Bauer 1985, p. 165. Canetti comments on the Chinese mourning rites (1979, p. 176): "In all civilizations, that is the only attempt I know of to wipe out the lust for survival."

77. *Xunzi* 20, cf. Plato, *Republic* 398c–402a. The old music alone is beneficial for character formation, while "licentious" and "depraved sounds," which are basically identical with the "new" music from Zheng and Wei, should be forbidden (*Xunzi* 20, p. 254 [Dubs p. 252, Watson p. 116]; cf. *Liji* 19, pp. 1538b–1540b [Legge II, pp. 116–17], *Lunyu* 15.12, *Mengzi* 7B37). The dissolution of the old musical forms obviously counts as a symbol for the disintegration of order as such (cf. for the Greeks Hösle 1984, n. 235 and 575). With regard to music, too, the Confucians fight against the trends of the time. Old music, in the meantime, is felt to be boring, while new music is "in" (*Liji* 1538b [Legge II, p.117], *Mengzi* 1B1). Mengzi, however, who perhaps lacks an aesthetic vein, does not see a real difference between old and new music. In 1B1, at least, he treats both as goods. What matters is merely to enjoy them, like other goods, collectively.

78. The quotation is from *Shijing* 34.1.

79. *Zhuangzi* 28, pp. 420–21 (Watson pp. 315–17, Graham pp. 228–29).

80. Ibid., p. 422–23 (Watson p. 318, Graham p. 230), *Shiji* 47, p. 1930.

81. Cf. *Zhuangzi* 6, p. 120 (Watson p. 86, Graham p. 89), and *Zhuangzi* 18, p. 271 (Watson p. 192). Other Daoists reject music.

82. *Zhongyong* 29. A textured program to exercise a moral effect on the world from the vantage point of the self is formulated in the *Daxue*. It describes the dependence of the "pacification of the world" on the "cultivation of the person," which in turn is based on "getting into contact with things," "achieving knowledge," "making one's motivation sincere," and "rectifying one's heart." "Getting into contact with things" links the formation of the self to the world in which it lives, avoiding the more radical inwardness which is represented by Mengzi's teaching of the pure innate roots of morality.

83. Cf. Socrates' sentence "the life which is unexamined is not worth living" (Plato, *Apology* 38a).

84. *Lunyu* 15.21, cf. *Liji* 30, p. 1620a (Legge II, p. 289).

85. *Mengzi* 4A4, cf. also 3B1, 4A28, 5A7, and 7A19.

86. *Xunzi* 4, p. 36 (Knoblock I, p. 188). Cf. also *Xunzi* 30, p. 352.

87. Cf. *Lunyu* 3.7.

88. *Mengzi* 2A7.

89. *Zhongyong* 14.

90. *Lunyu* 2.7, quoted p. 54 above, and *Lunyu* 3.4, quoted above n. 75.

91. Trauzettel 1977, pp. 352 and 351. Cf. also Bloom 1977b, p. 78 (quoted p. 15 above), Stover 1974, p. 244 ("The probing of motives is repugnant to Chinese sensibilities. The Chinese want to know *what* the other person is going to do, not *why* he does it."), and Baum 1982, p. 1177.

92. Cf. Piaget 1932, Chapter II *passim,* especially pp. 119–20. The child's "moral realism" implies a "conception objective de la responsibilité" and "conformité matérielle avec les règles posées." It does not take in account the personal intention, but only the "résultat matériel" (p. 146). Later, together with the "why" question, the importance of the intention is discovered (pp. 160, 203–4, note).

93. Cf. Ch'ü 1961, pp. 44 and 47, Santangelo 1988, pp. 6–7.

94. Cf. p. 38 above.

95. *Mozi* 44, pp. 245, 246 (Graham 1978 p. 249, EC 3).

96. *Lunyu* 4.2, cf. p. 144 above.

97. *Liji* 32, p. 1639a (Legge II, p. 333).

98. Cf. p. 64 above.

99. *Mengzi* 4B11.

100. *Shiji* 47, p. 1932.

101. The Confucian yearning for esteem and success is overstressed, to me, in Metzger 1987. Metzger argues that because the conception of an other-worldly justice was missing, "tension-resolution" depended largely on this-worldly acknowledgment of the virtuous person. Although Metzger also points out that "to be unperturbed by receiving disesteem" was regarded as a virtue itself (ibid., p. 104), he presents being unacknowledged rather as a lack to be remedied than as a normal expectation.

102. *Xunzi* 28, p. 345.

103. Cf. above, pp. 51–52.

104. There are appeals to Heaven in early Confucianism, especially in the writings of Mengzi, but on the whole they remain secondary to self-reflection. The popular belief in ghosts repaying evil, brought into play by Mo Di (*Mozi* 31, p. 151 [Mei p. 170]) and *Zhuangzi* 23 (p. 345 [Watson p. 255]), does not gain entry into the Confucian teaching. Confucius already dismisses the ghosts from ethics (cf. below p. 195).

105. Cf. Diehls/Kranz 1961, 87 B 44, A 1–2, and Barnes 1982, pp. 509–10 (Antiphon); Diehls/Kranz 1961, 68 B 244 and 264 (Democritus); Plato, *Republic* 359b–360d (about the Ring of Gyges); Epicurus 1926, p. 103 (Principle Doctrines 35).

106. Cf. *Lunyu* 12.20, pp. 51–52 above.

107. *Zhongyong* 1, too (similarly *Xunzi* 3, p. 28), recommends being "watchful when alone," pointing out that "nothing is more visible than the hidden and more manifest than the minute."

108. Santangelo 1988, p. 5.

109. Cf. Bauer 1985, pp. 177–80.

110. Xie 1969, p. 50 (Hsieh 1967, p. 315).

111. *Lunyu* 1.4. The final question can also be rendered, "Have I not practiced myself what I have transmitted?," with an interpretation in terms of the Golden Rule. Cf. *Xunzi* 1, p. 1 (Dubs p. 31, Knoblock I, p. 135): "If the gentleman broadens his learning and daily examines himself on three things, his awareness will become discerning, and his actions will be without fault."

112. Zhu Xi, *Sishu jizhu, Lunyu jizhu*, p. 32.

113. Kant, *Metaphysik der Sitten, Tugendlehre*, § 13, in: *Werke*, vol. 7, p. 573. The court metaphor plays an important role in the Ming era; cf. Wu Pei-yi 1979. Wu neither mentions, however, that the *Lunyu* is the source of the idea of "self-indictment," nor that the expression *zi ze* ("self-reproach") also goes back to the Zhou. As the *Zhuangzi* says (25, p. 389, Watson pp. 287–88), "The rulers of antiquity attributed success to the people and failure to themselves. They likewise attributed everything which was correct to the people and everything which was wrong to themselves. Therefore, if only a single being lacked its due, they retired and reproached themselves (*zi ze*)." The *Lüshi chunqiu* (18.8, p. 252) expects a gentleman to "reproach himself according to the yardstick of justice (*zi ze yi yi*)." — For the examination of conscience under the Ming cf. also Gernet 1982, pp. 194–96, Tu Wei-ming 1985, and Santangelo 1991, pp. 158–67.

114. Cf. Ricoeur 1969, pp. 100–08.

115. Cf. pp. 199–200 below.

116. *Mengzi* 7A15, quoted p. 130 above.

117. Rüdiger 1976.

118. Nelson 1974, p. 475.

119. According to Nelson, in the Cultural Revolution for the first time "older particularisms are giving ground to the newer universalities implicit in the notions of nation, people, and pure and strict science" (1973, p. 89). Meanwhile, reports have described the pitiful cultural provincialism of the period (cf., e.g. Yue Daiyun and Carolyn Wakeman 1985).

120. Nelson 1974, p. 465.

121. Nelson 1973, p. 91.

122. For Egypt cf. Breasted 1976, for the Jews Szondi 1973, for Greece and Rome Zucker 1928, for some remarks on India Nakamura 1975, p. 284.

123. Conscience is "the ground of the modern world" in the sense of "the deepest inward solitude with oneself where everything external and every restriction has disappeared—this complete withdrawal into oneself" (Hegel 1952, § 136, addition). Socrates' "daimonion," however, has not yet completely cast off the external nature of the oracle (Hegel 1941, pp. 94–96 and 106–7).

124. Cf. Piaget 1932, pp. 223 and 441–42.

125. *Xunzi* 2, p. 16 (Dubs p. 47, Watson p. 27, Knoblock I, p. 154).

126. Cf. *Lunyu* 15.32.

127. *Mengzi* 2A2. For comparison, cf. the analysis in Riegel 1980.

128. *Hanfeizi* 50, p. 352 (Liao II, p. 300).

129. The parallel between Beigong You and Confucius' disciple Zixia is not clear. Xunzi gives a hint, when he says that Zixia rejected office because of the arrogance of the feudal lords (*Xunzi* 27, p. 337). Zixia, then, had a special pride. In the *Lunyu* he is presented as a pedant, which reminds one of Beigong You's sensitiveness (cf. also *Xunzi* 6, p. 66 [Knoblock I, p. 229]). Cf. also Guo Moruo 1954, p. 338, where Zixia is seen as the progenitor of Legalism.

130. Cf. p. 146 above.

131. The negativity of the formulation, which probably reflects the idea that the main ethical task is the omission of bad acts, reminds one of Socrates, whose *daimonion* tells him what he should *not* do (Plato, *Apology* 31c–d).

132. Wang Yangming to his disciple Chen Jiuchuan, *Chuanxilu* 3, in: Wang 1976, vol. 1, p. 76, cf. Wing-tsit Chan 1963, p. 193.

133. I use the expression "principle of logos" in accordance with Socrates' dictum to "obey to nothing else of myself but to the *logos* (argument) which upon reflection appears to me the best" (Plato, *Crito* 46b).

134. *Chuanxilu* 2, Wang 1976, vol. 1, p. 62, cf. Wing-tsit Chan 1963, p. 159. Cf. *Lunyu* 15.23: "The gentleman will not promote a man simply on account of his words, nor will he dismiss words because of the man."

135. *Mengzi* 3B2. "Wide house" and "great path" are metaphors for humaneness and justice respectively (cf. *Mengzi* 4A10). "Correct position" is perhaps a metaphor for propriety.

136. Cf. *Übelhör* 1986, pp. 68–69.

137. Cf. *Xunzi* 3, p. 25 (*gua li*), *Liji* 41 *Ru xing*, p. 1670c (*te li du xing*) (Legge II, p. 408), *Kongzi jiayu* 5, p. 22 (*te xing du li*), *Zhuangzi* 23, p. 345 (*du xing*) (Watson p. 255). The *Houhanshu* contains a "Biography of men of independent conduct" (*Duxing liezhuan*). In this chapter, "independence" is, unlike the meaning of the term in the axial age, to a great extent made to serve the purpose of political loyalty. Later histories have likewise dedicated a chapter to the "solitary persons" (cf. Bauer 1985, p. 159). When *Xunzi* 28, p. 342 (similarly *Kongzi jiayu* 2, p. 7), *reproaches* Confucius' opponent Shaozheng Mao of "taking an independent standpoint" (*du li*), this means falling behind the principle of independence in *Mengzi* 3B2, *Xunzi* 23 (see below), and the *Ru xing*.

138. *Hanfeizi* 51, p. 360 (Liao II, p. 315).

139. *Xunzi* 23, pp. 298–99 (Dubs pp. 315–16, Watson pp. 169–70).

140. *Xunzi* 4, p. 35 (Knoblock I, p. 188, with a very different translation). Xunzi earlier distinguishes three other kinds of courage: that of the animals, that of traders and robbers (!), and that of the "mean man."

141. Bloch 1986, vol. 3, pp. 1224 and 1223.

142. For the distinction of "shame-cultures" and "guilt-cultures" cf. Benedict 1954. "Tradition-directed" and "inner-directed" are two of three types of character (next to the "other-directed") distinguished by Riesman. They relate to specific forms of culture which are in turn based on demographic factors. China for Riesman counts among the tradition-directed cultures. "The tradition-directed type," he writes (1969, p. 24), "feels the impact of his culture as a unit, but he is nevertheless mediated through the specific, small number of individuals with whom he is in daily contact. These expect of him not so much that he is a certain type of person but that he behave in the approved way. Consequently, the sanction for behavior tends to be fear of being *shamed*." An "inner-directed" person, however, knows the "feeling of guilt" (ibid.).

143. Cf. Benedict 1954, p. 223. For guilt, cf. Ricoeur 1969, pp. 100–8.

144. Piers and Singer 1953, pp. 48–54, cf. also Wilson 1973, and Ng 1981.

145. Fingarette 1972, p. 30, Hall and Ames 1987, p. 174. Cf. also Hall and Ames 1984, p. 8.

146. Metzger 1977, p. 241. Sun Longji, to give an example, maintains that China, since she lacks "transcendence" and hence "principles transcending conventional (*shisu*) relations" (a claim obviously taken over from Weber), has remained a "shame-culture," where the personal attitude only takes its orientation from the judgment of others. Sun has obviously overlooked that precisely the "conventional" (*shisu*) which he attacks is a concept used with contempt already in Zhou China. Eberhard does not really distinguish between external and internal shame either when he acknowledges the existence of "internalized shame" in Confucianism, but relates it to the maintenance of status (1967, p. 124). For the general topic of shame and guilt in China, especially in Neo-Confucianism, cf. the comprehensive analysis in Santangelo 1991.

147. Cf. Hu Hsien Chin 1944, Stover 1974, pp. 247–52, Baum 1982, p. 1177, Cheng Chung-ying 1986.

148. Trauzettel 1977, pp. 349–50.

149. Hegel 1956, p. 111.

150. Ibid., p. 128, trans. Sibree modified after the original.

151. Ibid.

152. Hansen 1985c, pp. 377, 373, 377, and 378.

153. Cf. Kant, *Metaphysik der Sitten, Tugendlehre* A1 (*Werke*, vol. 7), and Tugendhat 1990, pp. 9–10.

154. Cf. p. 284 above, n. 43.

155. *Shujing, Gaoyao mo*, p. 139b (Karlgren p. 9), and *Shujing, Tang shi*, pp. 160a–b (Karlgren p. 20).

156. *Lunyu* 13.3.

157. *Lunyu* 17.17.

158. *Mengzi* 7A20, quoted p. 86 above.

159. Trauzettel 1977, p. 350.

160. Cf. Chapter 8, n. 11.

161. *Lunyu* 2.3 and 12.19.

162. *Lunyu* 13.11.

163. Mengzi advocates the death penalty under the condition that all citizens demand the execution of the culprit (1B7). Xunzi does not disapprove of the death penalty either, but his ideal is the regime of the early Zhou kings under which, as he

says, there were no or only a few executions (*Xunzi* 7, p. 68 [Dubs p. 84], *Xunzi* 27, p. 331. Cf. Creel 1970, pp. 190–91). The fate of Zhòu, the last king of the Shang, Xunzi says, shows that even severe punishment will bring about nothing if the ruler himself is immoral (*Xunzi* 15, p. 188).

164. *Mengzi* 1A7 and 3A3, quoted p. 78 above.

165. Cf. *Mengzi* 7B4.

166. Cf. *Mengzi* 7B4 and 4A14. Cf. also *Mengzi* 6B9.

167. Cf. *Lunyu* 20.2.

168. *Xunzi* 28, p. 342, similarly *Kongzi jiayu* 2, p. 8.

169. *Xunzi* 18, pp. 228–29, see below.

170. *Shangjunshu* 5, p. 10 (Duyvendak p. 206).

171. Cf. *Mengzi* 1A5, *Hanfeizi* 37, p. 274 (Liao II, p. 159).

172. Cf. Ricoeur 1969, pp. 25–29.

173. *Shujing*, *Yue ming*, p. 176a.

174. *Guanzi* 1, p. 1 (Rickett 1985, pp. 53–54).

175. *Mengzi* 4B18, cf. *Lunyu* 14.27.

176. *Xunzi* 6, p. 64 (Knoblock I, p. 228).

177. For this argument cf. also Schwartz 1985, p. 107.

178. Cf. Rawls 1972, pp. 256 and 443–46.

179. I consider *you chi* a misrepresentation for *zi chi* at the end of the passage.

180. *Shenjian* 5, p. 28, cf. Ch'en Ch'i-yün 1980, pp. 195–96.

181. Cf. p. 245 below.

182. *Mengzi* 2A4, cf. 4A9.

183. *Xunzi* 4, p. 36 (Knoblock I, p. 189).

184. His work of eighteen books (*Hanshu* 30, p. 1744) is not extant. Guo Moruo (1957, pp. 245–71) attributes to him the writings *Xin shu* and *Nei ye* (now Chapters 36, 37, and 49 of the *Guanzi*).

185. Forke 1964, p. 558.

186. *Zhuangzi* 33, p. 468, and 1, p. 9 (Watson pp. 368, 31, and 32, Graham pp. 278 and 44).

187. Song Xing's and Yin Wen's maxim (*jian wu bu ru*) is frequently mentioned in Zhou literature; cf. *Xunzi* 18, p, 227 (Dubs p. 206), *Xunzi* 22, p. 279 (Dubs p. 287, Watson p. 145), *Zhuangzi* 33, p. 468 (Watson p. 368, Graham p. 278), *Hanfeizi* 50, p. 352 (Liao II, p. 300), *Lüshi chunqiu* 16.8, pp. 196–97. Xunzi reproaches Song Xing of confusing language, too (22, p. 279, Dubs pp. 287–88, Watson p. 145), and contests that his maxim would put and end to struggle and war. The natural weaknesses of man, he argues, cannot be reduced to vanity, and struggle normally emerges because of material reasons (*Xunzi* 18, pp. 227-228, Dubs pp. 206–7).

188. *Xunzi* 18, pp. 228–29 (Dubs pp. 208–9).

189. *Mengzi* 6A16, p. 196 below.

190. Cf. Roetz 1986, p. 219.

191. Kohlberg 1971, p. 171.

192. Rawls 1972, p. 256. Rawls also interprets Kant in this sense (ibid.).

193. Cf. Reiner 1974, §§ 34–36.

194. *Mozi* 2, p. 6 (Mei p. 7), cf. also *Lüshi chunqiu* 13.5, p. 132, and 21.3, p. 278.

195. *Guanzi* 64, p. 330 (Rickett 1985, p. 78). Cf. also *Guanzi* 35, p. 197, and 53, p. 291.

196. *Ethica Nicomachea* 1123b 35.
197. *Lunyu* 15.20, cf. also *Xunzi* 4, p. 38 (Dubs p. 59, Knoblock I, p. 191), *Xunzi* 5, p. 47 (Dubs p. 69, Knoblock I, p. 204), *Xunzi* 11, p. 132, *Mozi* 9, p. 38, and 12, p. 54 (Mei pp. 47 and 68).
198. Hobhouse 1956, p. 529.
199. *Zuozhuan* Xiang 24.1, p. 302 (Legge p. 507).
200. Gehlen 1964, p. 63.
201. *Shijing* 247.1.
202. *Mengzi* 6A17.
203. The Legalists, by contrast, try to functionalize the greed for fame for the state (*Shangjunshu* 6, p. 13) [Duyvendak pp. 218–19]). At the same time, as advocates of institutionalized distrust, they warn the ruler not to be tricked by people with name and fame (*Hanfeizi* 19, p. 91 [Liao I, pp. 163–64]).
204. *Zhuangzi* 29, p. 434 (Watson pp. 332–33, Graham p. 240). Cf. p. 245 below.
205. *Lunyu* 12.20, quoted pp. 51–52 above.
206. *Mengzi* 7B11.
207. *Lunyu* 13.24, cf. p. 51 above.
208. *Lunyu* 6.11. Cf. also Mengzi 4B29, *Lunyu* 1.15 and 7.16.
209. Kant, *Metaphysik der Sitten* (*Werke* 7),Tugendlehre A 177.
210. *Mengzi* 7A4. For a similar statement of Kant, see his *Kritik der praktischen Vernunft*, A 157.

NOTES TO CHAPTER 12

1. Apel 1988, pp. 361, 456–69.
2. Cf. ibid., p. 363.
3. Cf. Hall and Ames 1984, pp. 8–9 and 14–15, 1987, pp. 95 and 127, Cua 1989a, p. 281, Perenboom 1990, pp. 25–26.
4. Cua, 1989a, p. 281. The principled morality which I defend here is not a "tyrannical" one. It is rather to prevent the *tyranny of contexts* which to this day has marked human history. Cua accepts principles as subjective and personal maxims (1989a, p. 274) whose interpersonal significance is "essentially contestable by fellow agents" (p. 277). In Cua 1978, it is furthermore argued that these interpretations take place "within a given moral practice" (p. 83), that is, within "a cultural way of life . . . as a system of rules recognized as binding upon the conduct of a community of persons" (p. 79). Thus we have a double restriction on principles: They are *personal* maxims within a *specific cultural context*. Nevertheless, Cua regards *objective* principles in terms of "transcultural principles of adjudication" necessary as "*groundrules*" for international ethical discourse, wherein conflicting ideals of the good life or substantive normative proposals compete for universal acceptance, and thus call for adjudication" (1989a, pp. 186 and 285). From where to derive these principles in the case of China is a problem for Cua, since, as he says, the preferred Confucian mode of conflict resolution is not adjudication but arbitration. Adjudication decides the rights or wrongs of parties, while arbitration, in line with "the Confucian conception of ethical argumentation as . . . aiming at securing agreement among participants" (ibid., p. 285), aims at repairing human relationships and reestablishing harmonious intercourse (ibid., p. 281) based on virtues rather than

principles. Nevertheless, adjudication may become necessary also within the Confucian context if arbitration should fail, and this would provide a way to win the principles in question (ibid., p. 284).

I doubt that Cua's separation of, on the one hand, preference for arbitration/virtues/ Confucian way of life, and, on the other hand, adjudication/principles/intercultural relations as the main field of application, is tenable. Is successful arbitration morally valid if it does not stand the test of principled standards? Is not arbitration, too, a way to handle intercultural conflicts? How can adjudication, as a *legalistic* procedure, decide on the "universal acceptance" of "substantive normative proposals"? To my mind, the difference between arbitration and adjudication appears to be secondary here in relation to the more fundamental issue that in both cases the achieved solution must not be at the expense of a *third party*, thus violating a *moral principle*. I do not see how Cua, because of the above-mentioned restrictions on moral principles, can do justice to this problem. He stresses the *participant* perspective of the members of a community. The context-bound participant/member viewpoint, however, is deficient unless supplemented by the perspective of all those who are possibly *affected* by the settlement in question, which is a crucial problem of both contractualism (cf. Apel 1982, pp. 88–89) and "communitarian" ethics. This would mean that the ethical (*Sittlichkeit*-related) and way-of-life standpoint of *culture* from the very beginning has to be confronted with the moral and principled standpoint of the *other*, or the *alien*, in general.

5. Hall and Ames 1987, p. 266. For a critique of the aesthetic interpretation of the *Lunyu* by Hall and Ames cf. Paul 1990, pp. 43–55.

6. *Gesinnungsethik* (also translated as "ethics of mind") and *Verantwortungsethik* (ethics of responsibility, taking into regard the *consequences* of action or nonaction) are distinguished by Weber (1921), who advocates the latter against Kant. Schwartz's distinction of "pure ethics" and "concern with the good sociopolitical results" (1985, p. 110–111) in the *Lunyu* comes very close to the distinction I make here with Weber.

7. Cf. *Lunyu* 12.7: "Zigong asked about politics. The Master said, 'Provide food, provide military defense, and win the confidence of the people.' — Zigong said, 'If one had to dispense with one of these three things, which of them should be given up first?' — The Master said, 'The military.' — 'And if one had to dispense with one of the remaining two, which of them should be given up?' — 'Food! From ancient times, death has been the lot of all. But if the people have no confidence, nothing will endure.'" Wang Chong objects (*Lunheng* 28, p. 92) that the idea of confidence (*xin*) becomes absurd if the people starve, for hunger means the loss of all morals (which actually is also a Confucian conviction, cf. p. 78 above). Although Confucius himself elsewhere demands "solidarity with the needy" (*Lunyu* 6.4) and speaks of the necessity to "make the population rich" (*Lunyu* 13.9), he accepts the paradox in the quoted passage, when confronted with radical alternatives, in order to underline the priority of morals.

8. *Mengzi* 7A41. Cf. *Mozi* 47, p. 267 (Mei p. 224): "If one is not able to practice justice, the *Dao* yet must not be abandoned, just as the measuring line must not be abandoned if the carpenter is not able to chop wood [straight]."

9. *Mengzi* 4B23.

10. *Mengzi* 4A18[17].

11. Cf. p. 156 above.

12. *Mengzi* 3B1.

13. Ibid.

14. *Mengzi* 6B13.

15. A typical representative of such an attitude is Qu Yuan (340–278, death by suicide). Fallen into disgrace and repudiated as a minister, he deplores in his lyrics the wickedness and ignorance of his contemporaries. The resentment of the unappreciated finally increases to the abrupt rejection of the "dirt" of the world by the "pure" (*Chuci, Yufu*, pp. 296–97, *Shiji* 84, p. 2486): "The world is just a swamp, and I alone am pure. . . . I have heard that he who has freshly washed his hair will dust his cap, and he who has freshly bathed will shake out his clothes. How could I expose myself with the utmost cleanliness of my self (or: body) to the filth of things? I would rather throw myself into the floods of the Xiang and find an end in the bellies of the fish of the Jiang. How could I let myself with my radiant whiteness be soiled with the dust of the vulgar world!"

16. Cf. also *Lunyu* 5.19: After the assassination of the Duke of Qi, (481 B.C.) the noble Chen Wenzi turns his back on the country. But in the other states it does not hold him either, because they appear like Qi to him. Confucius calls him morally "clean" (*qing*), but denies that he is "humane" (*ren*).

17. Cf. above all *Chuci, Yuanyou* 67 (p. 282): "I want to cross the borders of the world and forget about returning. My thoughts roam freely and rise high." The *Yuanyou* is an outstanding example of the Daoist version of withdrawal, which does not aim at a subsequent reconciliation with the world. Cf. the comprehensive analysis of the poem under the aspect of withdrawal in Keindorf 1992.

18. For these movements, which hold a crucial place in my analysis, cf. what Toynbee (1951, pp. 248–63) has described as the "Withdrawal-and-Return motif."

19. Cf. for this argument Apel 1988, pp. 361–62 and 454.

20. *Xunzi* 3, pp. 25–26 (Knoblock I, pp. 175–76). The quotation is from *Shijing* 214.4.

21. Cf. also *Wenzi* 7, p. 8b (a Daoist text, probably from the Han): "A man who has got the *Dao* changes without, but not within. In doing so, he [shows that he] knows men. Not to change within is a means to fully preserve his self. Therefore, he has a steadfast attitude within, and can bend and straighten without. He moves with things, and in ten thousand cases does not fail."

22. Cf. *Lunyu* 15.3 and 4.15, quoted in Chapter 9 A.

23. *Xunzi* 17, p. 212 (Dubs p. 183, Watson p. 87).

24. Read *gui* for *wei* (conjecture of Wang Huaizu). In the first sentences, I follow the reading of the *Yanzi chunqiu*, which is more intelligible to me than that of the *Kongzi jiayu*.

25. Cf. the dilemma of Nanrong Zhu, quoted in Chapter 11, n. 22.

26. Or: " . . . if the gentleman has no keen perception of the listener."

27. *Kongzi jiayu* 9, pp. 53–54, cf. *Yanzi chunqiu* 4.30, p. 121.

28. *Yijing, Xici xia*, p. 48, vi (Legge pp. 398 and 189–91).

29. *Liji* 9, *Liyun*, p. 1414a (Legge I, pp. 365–66).

30. *Hanfeizi* 49, quoted p. 258 below.

31. *Liji* 9, p. 1414b (Legge I, p. 366–67).

32. *Lüshi chunqiu* 19.8, p. 252.

NOTES TO CHAPTER 13

1. *Lunyu* 7.1.

2. There is, nonetheless, a tension in Mengzi's thought between following innate and historical standards. Cf. for this topic Ivanhoe 1990b, pp. 36 and 91–101.

3. *Xunzi* 21, pp. 259 and 263 (Dubs pp. 260 and 265, Watson pp. 122 and 126).

4. Cf. *Xunzi* 8, p. 90 (Dubs p. 113): "Hearing something is not as good as seeing it." *Xunzi* 5, p. 51 (Dubs p. 73, Knoblock I, p. 207): "If you wish to see a thousand years, count the present day! If you wish to know ten thousands and millions, examine one and two! If you wish to know the ancient times, examine the way of the Zhou! . . . By the near you know the distant, by one you know ten thousand. . . . " *Xunzi* 8, p. 89 (Dubs p. 111): " . . . grasp the past through the present (following Yang Liang's conjecture), grasp ten thousand through one. . . . "

5. For the different arguments cf. Roetz 1993b.

6. *Zuozhuan* Zhao 18.2, p. 395 (Legge p. 671). Cf. Roetz 1984, pp. 199–200.

7. *Xunzi* 8, p. 77 (Dubs p. 96). Xunzi plays with different meanings of the word *dao* here.

8. *Xunzi* 12, p. 156.

9. *Lunyu* 15.29.

10. Cf. *Lunyu* 18.6: "If the world were in possession of the *Dao*, I would not have to take part in changing its state." Cf. p. 48 above.

11. *Lunyu* 9.5, quoted p. 48 above.

12. Mo Di already implicitly calls Confucius an atheist (*Mozi* 48, p. 274 [Mei pp. 233–34]). In the West, the dispute on Chinese atheism is as old as the encounter with China. The Dominicans and Franciscans tried to discredit the accommodative missionary work of the Jesuits by reproaching the Confucians with atheism (cf. Wolff 1740, pp. 68–72, n. 27, and pp. 112–22, n. 54). Many representatives of Enlightenment, like Wolff himself, more or less shared this view or were sympathetic with it, though for another reason. For them, the atheism of the educated Chinese was a welcome proof that morality was possible by means of "natural reason" without any religious revelation or authority (cf. Roetz 1984, pp. 8–9; for the more recent discussion of this topic cf. ibid., p. 204). That Confucianism, prior to the adoption of the Daoist view of nature by Xunzi, had a religious background is, for example, emphasized by Th. Hang (1988) and, similarly, by J. Ching (Kung and Ching 1989). Cf. also C. K. Yang 1957.

13. *Lunyu* 6.22. Since Confucius and his contemporary Guanyi Fu, gods and ghosts have become subject of an "as if"-fiction. Cf. *Guoyu, Chuyu* B2, p. 567 (Roetz 1984, p. 190), *Lunyu* 3.12, *Xunzi* 19, pp. 250–51 (Dubs pp. 245–46, Watson pp. 110–11).

14. Jonas 1984, p. 48.

15. *Mengzi* 3A5, 5A7, 6A6

16. *Mengzi* 6B15, 5A6.

17. *Mengzi* 2B13.

18. *Mengzi* 5A7.

19. Rowley 1956, p. 127. For Rowley, the ancient Confucians, in contrast to the biblical prophets, have no "very rich or satisfying doctrine of God" (ibid.). Only their opponent Mo Di has a real sense of religion. Of the ancient Chinese philosophers, he, therefore, "stands the highest" (ibid., p. 132).

20. *Mengzi* 2A4, 4A9[8], *Shujing, Taijia*, p. 164c.

21. *Mengzi* 2A4, 2A6, 4A11[10], 4A9[8].

22. Hsiao 1979, p. 148.

23. *Mengzi* 2A7.

24. Its main representatives are Plato, the Jewish-Christian tradition, Augustine, Luther, and Kant, and it has certainly influenced Weber's transcendence hypothesis.

25. *Mengzi* 7A1.

26. *Lunyu* 17.2.

27. Cf. Munro 1969, pp. 18–19.

28. *Mengzi* 6A6.

29. Qidiao Kai and Mi Zijian are disciples of Confucius of the first generation, Shi Shi and Gongsun Nizi are disciples of the second generation. Their writings (cf. *Hanshu* 30, pp. 1724–25) are no longer extant except for scattered quotations (compiled in *Yuhan jiyi* 64).

30. *Lunheng* 13, pp. 28–32. For Wang Chong's own view see also *Lunheng* 8, p. 17.

31. Graham 1967, pp. 224–25.

32. In view of these political implications, Mengzi's teaching of the good human nature may have been inspired by the proto-democratic idea of the Chunqiu era that the people are the "representatives of the gods" (*shen zhi zhu*, *Zuozhuan* Huan 6.1, p. 31 [Legge p. 48]; cf. Roetz 1984, pp. 182–83).

33. *Mengzi* 1A7 and 3A3, quoted p. 78 above.

34. Cf. *Mengzi* 5A1, 7B35.

35. *Mengzi* 2A2 (cf. p. 170 below) and 6A8. Cf. Schwartz 1985, pp. 270–78.

36. *Mengzi* 7B24.

37. *Mengzi* 7A38.

38. This biological aspect of *xing* is in accordance with etymology. The character *xing* contains the phonetic *sheng*, "be born," "give birth," "live." Both terms are intimately related with one another. For Gaozi, *xing* is *sheng*, just as white is white (see below). Fu Sinian's thesis that in Zhou texts originally *sheng* was used instead of *xing* counts as refuted (cf. Xu Fuguan 1963, chapter 1).

39. *Mengzi* 5A6.

40. Cf. *Mengzi* 6A10, quoted pp. 153–54 above.

41. *Mengzi* 6A14 and 6A15.

42. Cf. Tang Junyi 1979, pp. 20–28, Xu Fuguan 1963, pp. 170–74, Cai Renhou 1982, p. 66. Cf. also *Mengzi* 7A21: "What the gentleman has as his true nature— humaneness, justice, propriety, and knowledge—is rooted in his heart."

43. The standard interpretation of *bu rěn rén*, which goes back to the Han commentator Zhao Qi, is "not to endure *rěn* the suffering of others." For this rendering, however, one would expect another object of *rěn* (endure) than merely *rén* (men, others). For my rendering of *rěn*, cf. *Shijing* 257.11 ("hard-hearted," *rěn xin*), *Xinshu*, *Daoshu*, p. 928 (defining *rěn* as the antonym of "kindness," *ci*), and *Xunzi* 8, p. 92 (Dubs p. 117) ("suppressing [*rěn*] selfishness").

44. Or: the bad "reputation" of not having helped the child (Zhao Qi).

45. *Mengzi* 2A6.

46. The text does not explicitly state that the child is rescued. Lau comments (1963, p. 549), "It is worth noticing that Mencius does not say that this feeling of apprehension and pity would necessarily lead to any action at all. This serves to show that this feeling is only literally a 'beginning,' which needs cultivation before it can become a strong motive force." The hypothetical considerations concerning possible nonmoral motives such as establishing relations with the child's parents or gaining praise, however, would hardly make sense if they would not refer to the result of an actual effort of rescuing the child. Moreover, an emotional impulse without the power to evoke action surely could not serve as the natural basis which Mengzi seeks for his moral voluntarism.

47. *Mengzi* 7A15, quoted p. 130 above.

48. For the relationship of rationality and emotion cf. Yearley's remarks on "intelligent dispositions" and the "intelligent guidance of natural movements" in Mencius (1990, pp. 106–10 and 71). For the "undifferentiated use" of *xin*, cf. also Hang 1991. As Hang points out, this undifferentiatedness should not simply count as a disadvantage. It has guarded the Chinese from the "psychological fragmentation and compartmentalisation" which is, above all, typical of Western behaviorism (ibid., p. 29).

49. *Renyi*, lit. "humaneness and justice," normally a composite for "morality" in the *Mengzi*. As Gaozi later states, he regards *yi* as external, but *ren* as internal, thus exempting *ren* from being artificial. *Renyi* should, therefore, be translated as a composite here.

50. Cf. Popper's comments on the "attitude of social engineering" (1952, pp. 22–24), and Arendt 1958, § 31.

51. *Mozi* 26–28, pp. 122, 128–29, 133 (Mei pp. 140, 149–50, 156).

52. *Xunzi* 23, pp. 289 and 294 (Dubs pp. 302 and 309, Watson pp. 157 and 164). "Crooked wood" is used as a metaphor for man also by Aristotle (*Ethica Nicomachea* 1109b 5) and Kant (*Die Religion innerhalb der Grenzen der bloßen Vernunft*, III. 4, in: *Werke*, vol. 7, p. 760).

53. *Hanfeizi* 40, p. 300, and 50, p. 355 (Liao II, pp. 205 and 307), and *Hanfeizi* 46, p. 319 (Liao II, p. 239).

54. *Hanfeizi* 7, p. 36, and 48, p. 330 (Liao I, p. 46, and II, p. 258).

55. I advisedly speak of an "intuitive" rejection, because Mengzi is probably not fully aware of the real dimensions of the problem. In 4A1, he uses technical metaphors himself.

56. *Mengzi* 6A6.

57. *Mengzi* 2A2.

58. Cf. Schwartz 1985, p. 275, and Lai 1984, p. 150. For other interpretations of *yan* cf. Shun 1991. Nivison's suggestion to take *yan* as meaning "philosophical doctrines" or "moral maxims" in general (1980, p. 106, similarly Shun 1991) does not take into account the obviously heteronomous, external nature of the norms in question. Not all moral maxims must contradict the intuitions of the heart.

59. Cf. p. 170 above.

60. Lai 1984, p. 150. Lai defends Gaozi against Mengzi's "ethics of motivation." Gaozi, he maintains, advocates an ethics like that which Fingarette has rediscovered in Confucius—an ethics that "can do without the assumption of individualism or the burden of ego" (ibid.). I would like to call this a typically "American" topos.

61. The existence of such an idea of autonomy in Mengzi is also stressed by Li Minghui in his comprehensive study on Confucianism and Kant (Li 1990, pp. 64–68).

62. If we follow Lau, however, Mengzi has proven Gaozi guilty of a performative self-contradiction. According to Lau (1970, p. 238), Gaozi's argument implies that "it is bad to make man moral." Gaozi, then, would make a "moral judgment" himself, thus disproving his own claim that man is by nature amoral. Gaozi, however, does not say that it is "bad" to make man moral, just as it is not "bad" to make cups and bowls out of wood. The negative and moral evaluation of these acts is solely Mengzi's. Gaozi could answer that they are necessary and even desirable for a number of reasons. The fact that the *Mengzi* does not record any answer of Gaozi does not necessarily show that he "must have accepted Mengzi's objection as valid" (Lau, ibid.)—the text, after all, speaks

pro domo. "It is bad," moreover, would not per se be a moral judgement, since "bad," like "good," also has a nonmoral meaning.

63. *Mengzi* 6A2.

64. Cf. Lau 1970, Appendix 5, Cikoski 1975, Scharfstein and Daor 1978, Reding 1986.

65. Cf., for example, *Mengzi* 1B6.

66. *Mengzi* 6B1.

67. Aristotle, *Analytica posteriora*, Book I.7, 75a 37–38: "It follows that we cannot in demonstrating pass from one genus to another."

68. *Mozi* 41, p. 196: "[Things] of different categories cannot be compared. The explanation lies in measuring (in the absence of a common measure)." *Mozi* 43, p. 216 (Graham 1978, p. 357, B 6), illustrates, "What is longer—wood or the night? What is more—knowledge or millet?" etc. *Mozi* 45, p. 251 (Graham 1978, p. 483, NO 12), states, "If things have something in common, it does not follow that they have everything in common. The comparison of propositions can only be correct within a certain limit."

69. *Mengzi* 6A3.

70. Scharfstein and Daor 1978, p. 172.

71. For some interpretations cf. Richards 1932, pp. 25–27, Xu Fuguan 1963, p. 189, Graham 1967, pp. 247–48, Chen Daqi 1976, pp. 118–23, Lau 1970, pp. 241–43, Scharfstein and Daor 1978, pp. 172–73, and 1979, p. 47–48, Gao Baoguang 1982, p. 191, Mou Zongsan 1985, pp. 5–7, Schwartz 1985, p. 265.

72. Lau 1970, p. 242.

73. Lau, ibid., Wen Gongyi 1983, pp. 233–34.

74. Mou Zongsan 1985, p. 9. Lao Siguang (1984, vol. 1, p. 166) thinks that Mengzi's argument is sound, since the equation of *xing* and *sheng* would make it impossible to "distinguish the specific natures" of beings. Gaozi's equation of *xing* and *sheng*, however, as I understand it, only means that "nature" is something biological and nothing higher in a moral meaning. It does not mean that the biological constitution of all beings is identical. Identity is only implied with regard to the amorality of the various "natures."

75. I regard B as an attempt to specify A. According to Mou Zongsan, however (1985, p. 8), Mengzi is already committing the first mistake here, because "white is white" is analytical, but "*sheng* is *xing*" is not. Yet, Gaozi obviously *does* understand "*sheng* is *xing*" as analytical. Otherwise, there would be only one explanation why he answers Mengzi's question B in the affirmative: he has not understood his own claim (an imputation also found in Lau 1970, p. 241).

76. As is held by Lau (1970, pp. 241–42).

77. Or, adding *bai*: "[The case of justice] is different from the case of white."

78. Or: " . . . between treating an old horse as old and treating an old man as old."

79. Or: " . . . to the one who treats them as old."

80. The assignment of humaneness and justice to "internal" and "external" respectively can also be found in *Guanzi* 26, p. 156 (Rickett 1985 p. 379): "Humaneness comes from within (*zhong*), justice comes from without." (For Graham (1967, pp. 227–28), *Guanzi* 26 is a document of Gaozi's school. Lai (1984, pp. 150 and 152) opposes this view.) I suppose that a similar differentiation underlies the gentle treatment which naturalist Daoism grants to family morality in contrast to the other positive virtues. This

at least applies to *Laozi* 19 (*Laozi* 18 evaluates family virtues as a symptom of decay): "Eliminate humaneness, throw away justice, and the people will return to filial piety and parental kindness." However, the demarcation line here is not drawn between *ren* and *yi*, but between the two virtues on the one hand and family virtues on the other.

81. I admit that in his first argument concerning the externality of "white," Gaozi probably confuses a virtue and a property of things, as Bosley (1988) has noted. But I rather feel that this is a miscarried attempt to express the idea which is more clearly brought out in Gaozi's second argument. Moreover, if Gaozi's point is that a virtue is "the essence or the property of external things" (Bosley p. 11), why does he maintain the internality of humaneness, then?

82. Cf. *Mozi* 43, p. 233 (Graham 1978, pp. 450–51, B 76): "*Ren* means love, and *yi* means benefit. Here is love and benefit, and there is the loved and the benefited. Neither love and benefit nor the loved and the benefited relate to each other as internal and external. To suppose that *ren* is internal and *yi* external means to refer to love on the one hand and to the benefited on the other. This is referring arbitrarily, as if the left eye comes out of the socket and the right eye falls into it."

83. Mou Zongsan 1985, p. 15.

84. *Mengzi* 6A7: "As regards taste, all mouths share the same relishes. As regards sound, all ears share the same preferences. As regards beauty, all eyes share the same ideal. Should the heart alone be without anything which is approved of by all? What is it, then, which is approved of by all hearts? It is the basic [moral] pattern, and it is justice."

85. Cf. Roetz 1993a, pp. 79–80.

86. Hume 1886, pp. 245–46. Cf. also Kant 1981, 441–43, Popper 1952, pp. 62–66.

87. Moore 1956 (1903), Chapter 2. Cf. Frankena 1939.

88. Cf. *Mengzi* 1A1 and 6A4.

89. *Mengzi* 6A10, quoted pp. 153–54 above.

90. *Mengzi* 7B25.

91. Mengzi's explication of "good," therefore, does not fit in with the Mohist utilitarian understanding of morality (as is maintained by Graham 1978, p. 51). According to Moore, the "naturalistic fallacy" consists in the assumption that "good" can be given yet another meaning than "good." It can then be defined "by reference to a *natural object*" (1956, p. 39). This is above all the case if "good" is defined as "willed" or "desired" (ibid., p. 40).

92. *Ke* here expresses normative admissibility. It can also express objective possibility.

93. *Mengzi* 7A25.

94. This is the context in which the formulation "can will" ("*wollen können*") appears in Kant. Kant's categorical imperative demands to act according to that maxim "whereby you can at the same time will that it should become a universal law" (1981, 421).

95. *Mengzi* 7A17, cf. p. 146 above.

96. *Mengzi* 7A21, quoted p. 86 above.

97. *Mengzi* 4A16.

98. Cf. Hess 1975. Pupillometrics measures pupillary dilations, however, not the "cloudiness" which Mengzi claims to have observed. By talking about the pupils' cloudiness, he invites the counterargument of the determinist Wang Chong. Whether the pupils are clear or cloudy, Wang Chong says, is simply congenital (*Lunheng* 13, pp. 28–29).

99. For the importance of this perspective cf. Strawson 1974, p. 10, and Habermas 1983, pp. 57–58.

100. *Mengzi* 6A10, quoted pp. 153–54 above.

101. Ibid.

102. Cf. Strawson 1974, p. 14.

103. *Mengzi* 2A6, quoted p. 200 above.

104. Lorenz 1982, pp. 164–65. According to Eibl-Eibesfeldt (1987, pp. 704–5), the alert on hearing the cry of emergency of a child can count as innate, too.

105. Jonas 1984, pp. 39 and 130.

106. Cf. Wickler and Seibt 1981 on the "principle of selfishness."

107. *Hanfeizi* 46, p. 319, quoted p. 258 below.

108. *Mengzi* 1A7.

109. Cf. *Lunyu* 2.7, quoted p. 54 above.

110. *Dadai Liji* 52, p. 181.

111. *Mengzi* 2A6. Cf. also *Mengzi* 1A4, 3B9, 4B28, and 6A8, and the following passage from *Liji* 1, p. 1231b (Legge I, p. 64): "The parrot can speak, and yet remains a bird. The ape can speak, and yet remains a brute. If, as a man, one does not know propriety, is one's heart not that of a brute, then, though one can speak? It is only because brutes do not know propriety that among them father and son share the mate. Therefore, the sages arose and made propriety in order to teach men, and enable them, by their possession of propriety, to distinguish themselves from brutes."

112. Cf. Roetz 1984, *passim*.

113. This would also hold true in case Mengzi's sentence "the gentleman keeps away from slaughterhouse and kitchen" does not recommend an attitude, but only reminds the king of an existing one.

114. Gehlen 1969, p. 59.

115. Cf. Rawls 1972, pp. 463–65 (referring to J.-J. Rousseau).

116. Cf. Kohlberg 1971, pp. 191–92, Gehlen 1969, pp. 88–93.

117. *Mengzi* 7B31; cf. 7B1, p. 130 above.

118. *Mengzi* 6A6. In rendering *ruo* as "approve," I follow its basic meaning "accord with," "submit to." The graph show a kneeling man with his hands up. Zhao Qi reads *ruo* as *shun*, "follow."

119. Cf., e.g., *Mengzi* 1A4 and 1A7, quoted p. 78 above.

120. Read *nai* for *zhi*.

121. Cf. *Yijing*, *Xici xia*, p. 47b (Legge p. 393).

122. *Xunzi* 22, p. 274 (Dubs p. 281, Watson p. 139).

123. *Xunzi* 22, p. 284 (Dubs p. 295, Watson p. 151). The distinction of *xing* and *qing*, nature and emotions, is not found in Mengzi. Mengzi uses *qing* for the "essence" of something. It is in this sense that *qing* denotes *xing* in *Mengzi* 6A6 (quoted p. 213 above). For Xunzi, the emotions *qing* are so intimately connected with *xing* that he can speak of "emotional nature," *qingxing*. In the later discussion, *qing* and *xing* are often juxtaposed, *xing* denoting the good in man, and *qing* the seat of proneness to evil.

124. *Xunzi* 23, p. 290 (Dubs p. 303, Watson p. 158).

125. *Xunzi* 23, p. 289 (Dubs p. 301, Watson p. 157).

126. Cf. for example Xu Fuguan 1963, pp. 237–38, Lao Siguang 1984, vol. 1, pp. 333–36, Graham 1989, pp. 246 and 250.

127. *Xunzi* 23, pp. 290–91 (Dubs p. 304, Watson pp. 159–60).

128. *Mengzi* 2A6, 1A7, 6A10, 4A16.

129. I would thus explain the co-occurrence of *li* and *yi* by the underlying conventional reading of the two concepts. For other explanations cf. Cua 1989b.

130. *Xunzi* 23, p. 292 (Dubs p. 306, Watson p. 161).

131. For a such a reproach, cf. Long Yuchun 1987, pp. 62–63.

132. *Xunzi* 22, p. 283 (Dubs p. 294, Watson p. 150). Cf. Roetz 1984, p. 381.

133. For the translation of *gù* as "purposefulness" cf. *Zhuangzi* 15, p. 239 (Watson p. 168, Graham p. 265): "The sage discards knowledge and purpose (*gù*) and follows the pattern of heaven."

134. *Xunzi* 23, p. 291 (Dubs p. 305, Watson p. 160).

135. *Xunzi* 23, p. 290 (Dubs p. 303, Watson p. 158).

136. *Xunzi* 22, p. 274 (Dubs pp. 281–82, Watson pp. 139–40).

137. Commentary to Hu Yuan (993–1059), *Xunzi bian*, in: *Song Yuan xuean* 1, p. 7b. Huang Baijia is the son of Huang Zongxi (1610–95), who began the compilation of the *Song Yuan xuean*.

138. *Xunzi bian*, p. 7a. Hu Yuan's objection against using the term "art" (*wei*) instead of "producing" (*sheng*) is presumably because of the negative connotation of *wei* (artificial = false).

139. *Xunzi* 19, p. 243 (Dubs pp. 234–35, Watson pp. 102–3).

140. Cf. Roetz 1984, p. 335.

141. *Xunzi* 18, p. 221 (Dubs p. 199), *Xunzi* 23, p. 290 (Dubs p. 302, Watson p. 158), *Xunzi* 8, p. 82 (Dubs p. 103).

142. *Xunzi* 8, p. 91 (Dubs p. 114).

143. *Xunzi* 23, p. 292 (Dubs p. 306, Watson p. 161).

144. *Xunzi* 23, p. 295 (Dubs p. 310, Watson p. 165).

145. *Xunzi* 22, p. 279 (Dubs p. 287, Watson p. 144). Cf. *Mozi* 41, p. 194 (Graham 1978, pp. 214 and 295, A 45, Roetz 1984, p. 330). This "weak" definition of *hua* fits in with the etymology of the character which depicts a somersault.

146. Cf. Roetz 1984, pp. 288–93.

147. Cf. ibid., pp. 316–47.

148. *Xunzi* 22, p. 274 (Dubs p. 281, Watson p. 139).

149. *Xunzi* 22, p. 283 (Dubs p. 293, Watson p. 150), similarly *Xunzi* 23, p. 290 (Dubs p. 302, Watson p. 158). Cf. Roetz 1984, p. 381. According to Yearley (1990, p. 158), Mengzi pursues a similar idea, which might, then, have influenced Xunzi.

150. *Zhuangzi* 9, pp. 150–51 (Watson p. 104, Graham p. 204).

151. *Xunzi* 23, p. 294 (Dubs p. 310, Watson p. 164).

152. Ibid.

153. Chen Daqi, however, thinks that Xunzi is addressing exactly this question (1954, p. 53). This interpretation would presuppose changing "nature of the potter" and "nature of the workman" into "nature of clay" and "nature of wood"—an arbitrary and unnecessary conjecture, which, moreover, does not make Xunzi's argument more convincing.

154. Guo Moruo (1954, p. 217) objects to Xunzi that "it is the nature of clay that a tile can be made out of it . . . , and it is the nature of man that he can make a tile out of clay." Zhou Shaoxian (1977, pp. 5–6) points out that man possesses an "ingenious nature" which provides him with his specific technical skill.

155. Hu Yuan, *Xunzi bian*, p. 6a.

156. Cf. Munro 1969, pp. 77–78. For the unfoundedness, to me, of such claims cf. Roetz 1984, pp. 356–57, and Schwartz 1985, pp. 291–92.

157. In this sense I understand the following passage from *Xunzi* 27, p. 330: "Man has both justice and profiteering. Even [sages like] Yao and Shun cannot remove the people's desire for profit. But they can bring about that their desire for profit does not triumph over their fondness for justice. Even [tyrants like] Jie and Zhòu cannot remove the people's fondness for justice. But they can bring about that their fondness for justice does not triumph over their desire for profit." The two tendencies in man probably refer to his "nature" on the one hand and his intellectual faculty on the other.

158. Similarly Plato, *Statesman* 266e.

159. *Xunzi* 5, p. 50 (Dubs pp. 71–72, Knoblock I, p. 206).

160. *Xunzi* 23, pp. 293 (Dubs p. 307, Watson p. 162).

161. *Xunzi* 23, pp. 294 (Dubs p. 309, Watson pp. 163–64).

162. Cf. the criticism in Long Yuchun 1987, p. 74, and Roetz 1984, p. 355.

163. *Chunqiu fanlu* 10.36, p. 6a.

164. Cf. Chapters 11 B and E.

165. *Xunzi* 4, pp. 40 and 38 (Dubs pp. 61 and 59, Knoblock I, pp. 192 and 191).

166. *Xunzi* 23, p. 296 (Dubs p. 313, Watson p. 167).

167. *Xunzi* 12, p. 151.

168. Consider for example Xunzi's legitimation of tyrannicide (p. 75 above), his criticism of collective punishment and heritability of rank (p. 97 above), and his demand to "follow the *Dao* and not the ruler, follow justice and not the father" (pp. 65 and 82 above).

169. Aristotle, *Ethica Nicomachea* 1096a 14–16 (referring to his teacher Plato): "While both are dear, piety requires us to honor truth above our friends."

170. *Xunzi* 2, p. 12 (Dubs p. 43, Watson p. 24, Knoblock I, p. 151). When Xunzi later in this chapter recommends to "speak as the teacher speaks" and comdemns "not to hold right the teacher" (p. 20, Dubs p. 51, Watson p. 30, Knoblock I, p. 157), this presupposes, then, that the teacher is "right," and is not necessarily a proof for Xunzi's authoritarianism (as is held by Creel 1960b, p. 113).

171. Cf. Chapter 7 A.

172. I say advisedly "also" and not "primarily" or "merely." Graham, however, argues that for Xunzi "the desires in their natural state are bad *only* in the sense of being anarchic" (1989, p. 251, italics added). "But since disordered desires frustrate one another," he writes (ibid., p. 248), "the intelligent man as he learns will spontaneously come to desire the order which will make it possible to satisfy them. Love of the right is not incompatible with the badness of man's nature, on the contrary may be claimed to confirm it." Graham ignores that Xunzi not only speaks of the "contradictory and chaotic," but also of the "envious" and "biased and vicious," and thus of the *morally* "evil" in human nature (*Xunzi* 23, p. 289 [Dubs pp. 301 and 302, Watson pp. 157 and 158]). Moreover, even a robber will "desire the order that will make it possible to satisfy his desires," which has nothing to do with "love of the right." Graham has read his own preoccupation with spontaneity into a text which clearly distrusts the spontaneous impulses of man, knowing their moral ambiguity. Cf. Roetz 1991, p. 413 and *passim*.

173. *Xunzi* 19, p. 231 (Dubs p. 213, Watson p. 89).

174. Cf., Diehls/Kranz 1961, 21 B 18, and Kerferd 1981 p. 140 (Xenophanes), and Plato, *Protagoras* 321c (Protagoras). In China, the motif also appears in the *Sun Bin bingfa* (9, p. 93: "He who has no natural weapons must take precautions himself. This was the occupation of the sages."), in the *Lüshi chunqiu* (20.1, p. 255, quoted p. 69 above), and in the *Liezi* (7, p. 85 [Graham p. 153]: "In man, nails and teeth do not

suffice to provide protection, and muscles and skin do not suffice for self-defence and resistance. His quickness does not suffice to pursue his advantage (cf. Yang Bojun 1979, p. 234) and to escape harm. He has no fur or feathers to ward off cold and heat. He must rely on other things to be beneficial for him. By nature he must entrust himself to his intelligence and not rely on physical strength.")

175. *Xunzi* 23, pp. 292–93 (Dubs pp. 306–07, Watson pp. 161–62).

176. Hu Yuan, Xunzi bian, p. 7b.

177. Huang Baijia, comentary to Hu Yuan, *Xunzi bian*, p. 76.

178. Xunzi is viewed as a utilitarian, for example, by Chen Daqi (1954, pp. 6–7).

179. Cf. pp. 159–60 above.

180. Cf. pp. 64, 154, and 173 above.

181. Cf. pp. 161–62 above.

182. In *Xunzi* 23, p. 291 (Dubs p. 305, Watson pp. 160–61), Xunzi says that "the heart is fond of profit" due to "man's emotional nature." A similar statement can be found in *Xunzi* 11, p. 137. In *Xunzi* 22, however, the heart is presented as controlling the desires (quoted p. 219 above).

183. Cf. for example Tan Sitong 1954, p. 54 (Chan Sin-wai 1984, p. 150), Liang Qichao 1984, p. 84, Liang Shuming 1922, p. 146.

184. *Xunzi* 6, p. 58 (Dubs p. 78, Knoblock I, p. 223).

185. Weber 1951, pp. 152–53.

186. Granet 1934, quoted p. 10 above, Gernet 1982, pp. 219–20.

187. Trauzettel 1977, p. 353, Weber-Schäfer 1974, p. 422.

188. Eisenstadt 1986, pp. 292–93.

189. Eisenstadt himself recognizes this contradiction when he continues (ibid., p. 293), "Seemingly such stress could be seen as simple, traditional, ritual upholding of the existing social arrangement. . . . Yet in principle this was not the case. The major thrust of the Confucian orientations was the conscious taking out of these social relations from their seemingly natural context and idelogization in terms of the higher transcendental orientations. . . . " It remains unclear, however, what is won if social relations are taken out of their natural contexts just in order to be "ideologized" afterwards in the name of cosmic harmony.

190. For the existence of this separation in Chinese thought cf. Roetz 1984 *passim*.

191. Smith 1967, p. 192.

192. Cf. for example Liu Shu-hsien 1972, P. Jiang 1988, and Metzger 1977.

193. This criticism, nota bene, does not concern the concept of an *inner* transcendence located within human reason. Cf. p. 273 below.

194. Hall and Ames 1987, pp. 195, 199, 239.

195. Cf. p. 194 above, and Roetz 1984, §§ 14–15.

196. There is a cosmological statement in *Zuozhuan* Zhao 25.2, p. 414 (Legge p. 708), attributed to Zichan which contradicts his reservedness on such matters reported in other passages. Cf. Roetz 1984, p. 201.

197. Weber-Schäfer 1968, p. 33.

198. Cf. pp. 160–61 above.

199. *Zhongyong* 25.

200. *Zhongyong* 24 and 20.

201. *Zhongyong* 20.

202. *Zhongyong* 1, cf. p. 107 above.

203. *Liji* 19, pp. 1530b and1531b (Legge II, pp. 100–101 and 103).
204. *Liji* 29, p. 1617b (Legge II, p. 281). Cf. p. 117 above.
205. *Liji* 19, p. 1531b (Legge II, pp. 103–4).
206. *Dadai Liji* 42, p. 50.
207. *Xunzi* 19, p. 239 (Dubs p. 223, Watson p. 94). Cf. Roetz 1984, p. 299.
208. Cf. Roetz 1984, § 21.
209. Cf. ibid., pp. 299–308. Cua has interpreted the cosmological passages in the *Liji* in a similar way (1983, p. 12): "The cosmological passages in the *Li chi* . . . are more profitably construed as exaltations to this Confucian vision rather than an embodiment of an ethical cosmology." Cf. also Cua 1989b, pp. 132–33, n. 45: "These passages (in the *Xunzi*, H.R.), from the point of view of coherent explication, are best construed . . . as emotive rather than cognitive expressions."
210. For a comprehensive discussion of the "cosmologists" cf. Graham 1989, Chapter IV/1. The merging of ethics and ontology remains valid also for Neo-Confucianism; cf. for example Graf 1970, Metzger 1977, P. Jiang 1988, and the sharp criticism in Paul 1990, Chapter 3.
211. *Chunqiu fanlu* 12.53, pp. 5b–6a.
212. Ibid., 8.30, p. 11a.
213. It is this regression which Weber had in mind when he wrote that "the belief in spirits and their way of functioning was the one and only very effective Magna Charta of the masses in China" (1951, p. 170).

NOTES TO CHAPTER 14

1. *Zhuangzi* 33, pp. 464 and 462 (Watson pp. 364, Graham p. 275). Cf. *Xunzi* 21, p. 258 (Dubs p. 259, Watson p. 121), *Xunzi* 22, p. 281 (Dubs p. 291, Watson p. 148), *Xunzi* 25, p. 306. Yu Yingshi (1987a, pp. 27 and 91) interprets the disruption of the *Dao* as a metaphor for the breakthrough in thought.
2. *Mozi* 39, p. 178 (Mei p. 200).
3. *Mengzi* 3B9 and 3A5, cf. p. 128 above.
4. *Mozi* 16, pp. 70–71 (Mei pp. 87–88).
5. *Mozi* 25, p. 104 (Mei p. 123).
6. *Mozi* 40, p. 191 (Graham 1978 p. 270, A8).
7. *Mozi* 15, pp. 65–66 (Mei p. 83).
8. *Mengzi* 7A26.
9. When Rowley (1956, p. 71, cf. also ibid., pp. 91–93) calls it "not fair" to Mo Di to represent him as a utilitarian, he does not distinguish between Mo Di's own motivation and the way he tries to ground his ethics (nor does Graham [1989], cf. Roetz 1991, p. 411). This differentiation, however, allows us to do justice to Mo Di's altruism without having to play down his naive appeal to utility. Ahern, too, has rejected the interpretation of Mo Di as a utilitarian because this would mean to neglect his belief in Heaven (1976). Yet, Mo Di says that to follow the will of Heaven is beneficial, and to violate it is detrimental. Moral action, although rooted in Heaven, in the final analysis is not advocated for its own sake, but for reasons of utility.
10. *Mengzi* 3B1, cf. pp. 186–87 above, and *Mengzi* 1A1.
11. Cf. p. 252 below.

12. *Guanzi* 65, p. 338 (Rickett 1985, p. 110).

13. *Shangjunshu* 18, p. 33 (Duyvendak pp. 293–94).

14. *Mozi* 27, pp. 123–24 (Mei pp. 142–43).

15. *Mozi* 26, p. 119 (Mei p. 136), *Mozi* 27, p. 124 (Mei p. 144).

16. *Mozi* 27, p. 124 (Mei p. 144).

17. *Mozi* 48, p. 280 (Mei p. 240).

18. *Mozi* 31, pp. 138–39 (Mei pp. 160–61).

19. *Mozi* 31, p. 154 (Mei p. 173).

20. Cf. p. 57 above.

21. *Mozi* 16, pp. 79–80 (Mei p. 97).

22. I quote the first of the three extant versions, which is not necessarily the earliest one. The title *Shang tong* can also be translated as "to conform with superiors."

23. With Wang Yinzhi, I read *er* as *yu*.

24. *Mozi* 11, pp. 44–45 (Mei pp. 55–57).

25. It remains unclear how the duty of remonstrating with the superiors fits into this system. Rubin (1976, p. 42) speaks of "the greatest of absurdities." Yet, in the Legalist state, too, remonstration is accepted to a certain degree, inasmuch as it can be utilized for strengthening the system.

26. Cf. the sharp critique in Rubin 1976. Etiemble (1966, p. 156) draws a parallel between Mo Di and fascism.

27. Cf. *Mozi* Chapters 8–10.

28. The similarity of Mo Di and Hobbes has above all been maintained by Liang Qichao (1971, p. 38, 1978, p. 28, 1984, p. 127).

29. Cf. for example Mei 1929, p. 59, Ren Jiyu 1956, p. 55, Weber-Schäfer 1968, p. 54, Hsiao Kung-chuan 1979, pp. 241–42.

30. Cf. *Mozi* 26–28. In *Mozi* 11–12, the authority of Heaven complements the political one.

31. Mei Yi-pao's claim that the subject "Heaven" "becomes explicit" in *Mozi* 13 (1929, pp. 71 and 56; Hsiao Kung-chuan 1979, p. 236, accepts this view) is simply wrong. Mei does not refer to the transmitted text (cf. *Daozang* 306, 3, 11b), but to a conjecture by Sun Yirang. In *Mozi* 12, p. 52 (Mei p. 65) we read that "in ancient times Shangdi (the God on high of the Shang) and the ghosts and spirits established the states and capitals and set up political leaders." Mo Di, however, is interpreting a "book of the ancient kings" here.

32. Rawls 1972, pp. 12–13.

33. Hsiao 1979, p. 241. Cf. Chapter 7, n. 22.

34. For the aporias of contractualism, cf. Apel 1982, pp. 88–89.

35. Cf. Hobbes, *Leviathan* 13.

36. Ibid., 17 and 18.

37. Ibid., 13, 14, and 17.

38. Ibid., 17.

39. Cf. Apel 1982, p. 88.

40. *Mozi* 15, pp. 68–69 (Mei pp. 85), speaks of Chinese and "barbarians" in one breath. In *Mozi* 49, p. 285 (Mei p. 257), Mo Di rejects condemning the cannibalism of the Yi barbarians, as long as the Chinese themselves do not follow humaneness and justice.

41. Cf. *Xunzi* 21, p. 261 (Dubs p. 264, Watson p. 125): "Mozi was obsessed by utility and did not know culture (*wen*)."

42. *Mozi* 25, pp. 115–16 (Mei pp. 132–33).

43. *Lunyu* 7.1. Cf. *Mozi* 39, p. 181 (Mei p. 203).

44. *Mozi* 46, p. 262 (Mei p. 219).

45. Cf. *Lunyu* 13.24, quoted p. 51 above.

46. For Mo Di's step forward in the method of argumentation cf. also Metzger 1987, pp. 76–84.

47. Cf. *Hanfeizi* 32, pp. 198–99 (Liao II, p. 33). Han Fei defends Mo Di. Mo Di, he says, deliberately did not make his words eloquent, because otherwise the reader might merely look at the style and forget the utility of his writings.

48. Propositions, according to Mo Di, must have a "base" (*ben*, a confirmation by documents and reports from the past), a "source" (*yuan*, the sensory perceptions of the majority), and "utility" (*yong*, practical efficacy). Cf. *Mozi* 35, p. 136 (Mei p. 183), *Mozi* 36, p. 169 (Mei p. 189), similarly *Mozi* 37, p. 172 (Mei p. 194). Cf. also Roetz 1993a, p. 98.

49. *Mozi* 39, p. 182 (Mei p. 204).

50. Cf. *Mengzi* 3B9 and 7A26.

51. *Lüshi chunqiu* 17.7, p. 213, *Huainanzi* 13, p. 218.

52. Other accounts are primarily anecdotical. Cf. Gao Heng 1933, pp. 579–85.

53. In Daoist literature, the "true" or "genuine" (*zhen*) often denotes inborn nature as against artificiality (cf. Wang Yu 1979, pp. 433–35). It can also stand for the individual life, as in *Zhuangzi* 20, p. 305, cf. Chang Tsung-tung 1982, pp. 259 and 273, n. 4.

54. *Liezi* 7, p. 86 (Graham p. 156).

55. *Liezi* 7, pp. 83–84 (Graham pp. 150–51). For a similar argument brought forward against Mo Di, cf. *Mozi* 47, p. 256 (Mei p. 222).

56. *Liezi* 7, p. 84 (Graham p. 151).

57. *Liezi* 7, p. 78 (Graham p. 140).

58. Several forms can be distinguished (cf. also Roetz 1984, pp. 140–41): The *argument of delay* says that Heaven will punish a crime not immediately, but within a surveyable period of time, as in *Zuozhuan* Xiang 20.6, p. 292 (Legge p. 486): "If the clan Qing has not perished within five years, there is no Heaven!" (Cf. also *Zuozhuan* Xi 2.4, p. 89 [Legge p. 137], *Zuozhuan* Zhao 1.4, pp. 342–43 [Legge p. 579]). The *argument of accumulation* adds that Heaven's punishment is delayed for the reason to increase the guilt of the culprit and punish him the more severely afterwards, as in *Zuozhuan* Zhao 11.4, p. 374 (Legge p. 634): "When Heaven borrows the assistance of the bad it is not to their blessing. It is to increase their evil and wickedness, and then send down punishment upon them." We moreover find the belief in *family karma* which also stands behind the theory of the mandate of Heaven. If an evildoer remains untroubled, his family perhaps has a bonus from former generations (cf. *Zuozhuan* Cheng 8.6, p. 226 [Legge p. 367]). Reversely, offsprings may have to pay for the misdeeds of their progenitors. For the continuing popularity of this idea cf. Yang Lien-sheng 1957, pp. 298–303.

59. Cf. p. 218 above.

60. *Liezi* 7, pp. 80–81 (Graham pp. 143–46).

61. *Liezi* 7, pp. 85–86 (Graham pp. 154–55).

62. Cf. the Greek dispute between Thrasymachos and Kallikles on the one hand (Plato, *Republic* 343–44, *Gorgias* 483) and Plato on the other (*Republic* 354 and 579–80, *Laws* 662–63).

63. *Liezi* 7, p. 79 (Graham pp. 141–42).

64. Schleichert 1990, p. 113.

65. Other representatives of hedonism are Tuo Xiao and Wei Mou (*Xunzi* 6, pp. 57–58 [Dubs p. 78, Knoblock I, p. 223]), Zihuazi (*Lüshi chunqiu* 2.2, p. 15), and probably Wumazi (*Mozi* 46, p. 262 [Mei p. 438], cf. Hou Wailu 1980, vol. 1, p. 345). Cf. also *Guanzi* 4, p. 12, and 65, p. 338 (Rickett 1985, pp. 110–11). For hedonism in the *Zhuangzi* cf. Chapter 14 C. Cf. also Xu Fuguan 1963, p. 428.

66. Cf., e.g., Ren Jiyu 1979, vol. 2, pp. 226–28, and Shen Shanhong and Wang Fengxian 1985, p. 658–63, who point out that Yang Zhu's teaching even "under our present conditions has still a considerably pernicious influence and must therefore be severely criticized" (p. 663). Cf. also Xu Fuguan 1963, p. 429.

67. As is argued by Men Qiming 1933, p. 601.

68. Linguistic arguments (Yang Bojun 1984, pp. 143–63, cf. also ibid. pp. 234–35, and Graham 1961), therefore, do not necessarily affect the authenticity of the content of the chapter. As far as the content is concerned, parallels from Buddhist scriptures alone could prove the chapter as a late forgery. The thesis that the *Liezi* is influenced by Buddhism and, for this reason, is a late text, dates back to the Tang dynasty (cf. Ji Xianlin 1982, pp. 312–22). However, it hardly concerns the *Yang Zhu* chapter. Ji Xianlin, who lists parallels between the *Liezi* and Buddhist passages, does not give a single example from the *Yang Zhu*, and the material collected by Chen Dan (1984) is more than scanty. The genuineness of the *Yang Zhu* has also been claimed by Hu Shi 1920, p. 176, Xu Fuguan 1963, pp. 427–30 (with the reservation that the chapter is not by Yang Zhu himself, but by later Zhou hedonists), and Qu Wanli 1983, p. 497.

69. In order to distinguish the Daoist concept of *de* from that of the other schools which usually refers to positive virtues, I translate *de* as "primordial virtue."

70. *Zhuangzi* 12, p. 199 (Watson p. 138). In many translations from the *Zhuangzi*, I am indebted to Chang Tsung-tung's comprehensive study of the Daoist classic (1982).

71. *Laozi* 10, Mawangdui B: "In concentrating breath and reaching [the state of] weakness—can you be like a child?" In the following, I prefer the reading of Mawangdui A to B and the transmitted versions. For comparison, see the translations of Henricks (1989) and Mair (1990) which I have consulted.

72. Cf. *Laozi* 36, 76, and 78.

73. *Zhuangzi* 23, pp. 342–43 (Watson p. 253).

74. The transmitted text has "flattery" instead of "being scolded."

75. Following the wording of Mawangdui B.

76. *Laozi* 20, Mawangdui A completed by B.

77. According to Kohlberg (1971, p. 204), to stand "beyond good and evil" is characteristic of Stage $4^1/_2$.

78. It can also be found, in negative terms, in the *Hanfeizi*. Han Fei calls the people stupid like children. In order to shave their heads, children must be held fast, because they do not know what is beneficial for them. For the same reason, the people must not be handled with velvet gloves (*Hanfeizi* 50, p. 356 [Liao II, pp. 309–10]).

79. *Mengzi* 7A15 and 4B12.

80. *Zhuangzi* 8, p. 148 (Watson p. 103, Graham pp. 202–3). The point in question is also brought out in Chang Tsung-tung's translation (1982, p. 179): "What I call good is not morals, but what is good for one's own primordial virtue. What I call good is not morals, but to yield to the hidden essence of one's life."

81. *Zhuangzi* 7, p. 139 (Watson p. 97, Graham p. 97). Cf. Girardot 1983, p. 81.

82. For a detailed analysis of the *hundun* allegory cf. Roetz 1984, pp. 255–59. Cf. also the comprehensive discussion of different interpretations in Girardot 1983, Part 2, Chapter 3. For other implications of facelessness cf. ibid., Part 4, Chapter 8.

83. Cf. Roetz 1984, pp. 260–69.

84. *Zhuangzi* 16, p. 244 (Watson p. 173).

85. Schiller 1978. Cf. Roetz 1986.

86. Hegel 1940 (*Geschichte der Philosophie* I), p. 82.

87. Schiller 1978, p. 88.

88. *Laozi* 2, Mawangdui A.

89. *Laozi* 38.

90. *Zhuangzi* 22, p. 319 (Watson p. 235, Graham p. 159).

91. *Laozi* 18, Mawangdui A and B.

92. *Huainanzi* 11, p. 169.

93. *Zhuangzi* 24, p. 373 (Watson p. 276).

94. *Zhuangzi* 24, p. 372 (Watson p. 275).

95. *Zhuangzi* 10, pp. 156–57 (Watson pp. 108–9, Graham pp. 207–8).

96. The robber argument of the Daoists is the reverse of the robber argument of Plato (*Republic* 351). According to Plato, the fact that even a gang of robbers cannot do without justice speaks in favor of justice and not against it. Injustice is parasitic on justice. However, the problem of group morality is not taken seriously in Plato. The radical Daoist view of morals is probably based on the transference of ontological "pandaoism" to ethics.

97. I have used the robber argument myself in Chapters 10, p. 145, and 13, n. 172. "Gang of robbers," of course, should not be understood in a too literal and narrow sense. It can refer to any well-organized social unit which one-sidedly maintains its existence at the expense of others.

98. *Zhuangzi* 29, pp. 429–30 (Watson p. 327, Graham p. 237).

99. *Zhuangzi* 29, p. 434 (Watson p. 332, Graham p. 240).

100. *Zhuangzi* 10, pp. 154–55 (Watson p. 107).

101. *Zhuangzi* 10, pp. 158–59 (Watson pp. 109–10).

102. Cf. Chang Tsung-tung 1982, pp. 326–32.

103. *The City of God*, Book IV, Chapter IV.

104. *Zhuangzi* 11, p. 172 (Watson p. 118), similarly *Zhuangzi* 10, p. 160 (Watson p. 110, Graham p. 208), *Laozi* 19.

105. *Zhuangzi* 10, pp. 160–61 (Watson p. 111).

106. *Laozi* 3, Mawangdui B. Many of the eighty-one paragraphs of the *Laozi* probably contain different layers, the strategical one being the youngest of them. It must not be forgotten, however, that the *Laozi* is strategical not least in order to prevent the worst of all strategies—war.

107. *Laozi* 65, Mawangdui A completed by B.

108. *Zhuangzi* 11, p. 171 (Watson p. 118).

109. *Zhuangzi* 32, p. 456 (Watson p. 358). The sentence is attributed to Confucius, but it sounds thoroughly Daoist.

110. Cf. *Zhuangzi* 2, p. 41 (Watson p. 44, Graham p. 57): "In discussion something remains hidden. The great *Dao* cannot be named. The great discussion consists in not speaking."

111. *Mozi* 41, p. 201 (Graham 1978, p. 445, B 71). Cf. also *Mozi* 42, p. 202 (Graham 1978, p. 453, B 79): "To reject rejection is contradictory. The explanation lies in not

rejecting [the own rejection]." and *Mozi* 41, pp. 201–2, and 43, pp. 233–34 (Graham 1978, p. 452, B 77): "That learning is useful is explained by those who reject this."—"If you think someone does not know that learning is of no use, and therefore inform him [of this], this means letting him know that learning is useless. But this is teaching. To think that learning is useless and to teach [this], is contradictory." Cf. Roetz 1993a, pp. 93–95.

112. Cf. Roetz 1984, pp. 279–81.

113. *Zhuangzi* 2, p. 41 (Watson p. 44, Graham p. 57).

114. Cf., e.g., *Zhuangzi* 8, pp. 142–43 (Watson pp. 100–1, Graham p. 201), *Zhuangzi* 18, p. 274 (Watson pp. 194–95). Cf. also Roetz 1984, pp. 246–50.

115. *Lüshi chunqiu* 1.4, p. 8.

116. Cf. Chang Tsung-tung 1982, pp. 258–60. Cf. also Graham 1981, pp. 176–80.

117. *Zhuangzi* 12, pp. 202–3 (Watson pp. 140–41).

118. *Zhuangzi* 29, p. 432 (Watson pp. 330–31, Graham p. 239).

119. *Zhuangzi* 3, p. 55 (Watson p. 50, Graham p. 62).

120. *Zhuangzi* 33, pp. 470–71 (Watson p. 370, Graham pp. 279–80). Cf. Chang Tsung-tung 1982, p. 292.

121. Xunzi, too, rebukes Shen Dao, together with Tian Pian, for opportunism (*Xunzi* 6, p. 58 [Knoblock I, pp. 223 and 302, n. 37]). But Shen Dao also has close connections with the Legalist camp. As *Xunzi* says (*Xunzi* 21, p. 262 [Dubs p. 264, Watson p. 125]), "Master Shen was obsessed with law . . . " (cf. also *Hanfeizi* 40 and the *Shenzi*). If we follow *Xunzi* 6, the *Zhuangzi* perhaps reports the esoteric side of Shen Dao's teaching, while his legalism represents the exoteric side. For, says Xunzi (*Xunzi* 6, p. 58 [Dubs p. 79, Knoblock I, p. 223]), Shen Dao and Tian Pian "exalt law, but are themselves without law." This paradox reflects the difference between their own postconventional conviction and the authoritarian morality which they propose for society (the "law" which they disdain need not be read as "the law of *li*," then, as Schwartz 1985, p. 319, has suggested). Cf. p. 264 below.

122. The robber and the opportunist regress to Stage 1, the hedonist of the *Yang Zhu* chapter and the advocate of the child regress to Stage 2.

123. The Daoist ideal is "small countries with few people" without communication (*Laozi* 80, *Zhuangzi* 10, p. 162 [Watson p. 112]). For the connection of Daoist spontaneity and this kind of primitivism, cf. Roetz 1991, pp. 413 and 414.

124. *Hanfeizi* 46, p. 319 (Liao II, p. 239).

125. *Lunyu* 13.18, cf. Chapter 8 above.

126. *Hanfeizi* 49, pp. 344–45 (Liao II, p. 286).

127. *Shangjunshu* 4, p. 8, and 13, p. 23 (Duyvendak pp. 199 and 256).

128. Cf. pp. 55–56 above.

129. *Hanfeizi* 49, pp. 339 and 340–41 (Liao II, pp. 276 and 278).

130. This not only distinguishes Han Fei's theory from Xunzi's. In the *Mozi*, the *Shangjunshu* (7, p. 15 [Duyvendak p. 225]) and the *Guanzi* (31, p. 174) [Rickett 1985, p. 412]), too, the beginning of history is marked by quarrel.

131. *Hanfeizi* 49, p. 339 (Liao II, p. 276).

132. Ibid.

133. Cf. Rubin 1976, pp. 72–74.

134. *Hanfeizi* 19, p. 93 (Liao I, p. 168).

135. *Hanfeizi* 48, p. 330 (Liao II, p. 258).

136. For a comparison of Legalism and behaviorism cf. also Schwartz 1985, Chapter 8 *passim.*

137. *Hanfeizi* 35, p. 254 (Liao II, pp. 126–27).

138. Shang Yang recommends a ratio of 1:9 for rewards and punishments (*Shangjunshu* 4, p. 9, 5, p. 11, and 7, p. 17 [Duyvendak pp. 201–2, 211 and 230]). Cf. Rubin 1976, pp. 66–67.

139. *Shangjunshu* 7, p. 17 (Duyvendak p. 229).

140. *Shangjunshu* 7, p. 18, 13, p. 24, and 17, p. 30 (Duyvendak pp. 233, 259, and 282), *Hanfeizi* 30, p. 168 (quoting Shang Yang) (Liao I, p. 295), and *Hanfeizi* 53, p. 365 (Liao II, p. 325). Cf. also *Shujing, Da Yu mo*, p. 135 c.

141. *Shangjunshu* 5, p. 11 (Duyvendak p. 210).

142. The term *de* is ambiguous, in fact, as are its Western counterparts. In ancient China, a horse, too, can have *de*, and in Greek, *arete* can be attributed to either a moral person or a knife. The German *Tugend* is related to *Tüchtigkeit*, and the English *virtue* to *virtuosity*. To distinguish the moral from the nonmoral meaning of these word (like of the words "good" and "bad") reflects a progress in moral development.

143. *Hanfeizi* 50, p. 355 (Liao II, pp. 306–7).

144. *Shangjunshu* 5, p. 10 (Duyvendak p. 206). I presume that humaneness and kindness refer to public as well as to family virtues here.

145. Cf., e.g., *Shangjunshu* 13, p. 23 (Duyvendak p. 256).

146. *Hanfeizi* 35, p. 249 (Liao II, p. 117).

147. For a similar statement cf. *Shenzi* pp. 4–5 (Thompson 1979, pp. 260–61).

148. *Hanfeizi* 5, p. 19 (Liao I, p. 32).

149. Cf. above all *Hanfeizi* chapters 5, 7, and 8.

150. *Hanfeizi* 7, p. 28 (Liao I, p. 49).

151. *Shangjunshu* 5, p. 10 (Duyvendak p. 207).

152. *Hanfeizi* 49, p. 350 (Liao II, p. 297).

153. *Shangjunshu* 2, p. 3 (Duyvendak p. 178).

154. *Hanfeizi* 49, p. 347 (Liao II, p. 291). Cf. *Shiji* 6, p. 255.

155. Cf. *Hanfeizi* 40, p. 300 (Liao II, pp. 204–5).

156. Cf. *Shenzi* p. 6 (Thompson p. 267).

157. Cf. p. 223 above.

158. *Hanfeizi* 5, p. 17 (Liao I, p. 30).

159. Whether Han Fei himself is the author of the corresponding chapters of the *Hanfeizi* is controversial (cf. Graham 1989, p. 285). The question does not affect the Daoist-Legalist fusion as such which I am interested in here.

160. According to H. Wang and L. Chang, the fact that Han Fei "sought to ground his political philosophy on the most important concept in Chinese philosophy, namely, Tao" and moored his theory on Daoism, shows his "intellectual honesty" (1986, p. 79). However, if by integrating the *Dao* into his theory Han Fei partakes in the alleged "ancient Chinese philosophical insight that the natural world and the human world are one continuum" (ibid., p. 8), this would show the normative emptiness of such a continuum, rather than give a justification for Han Fei's standpoint.

161. Cf. *Hanfeizi* 19, p. 93 (Liao I, p. 167).

162. *Hanfeizi* 5, p. 20, and 6, p. 26 (Liao II, pp. 35 and 45). Cf. also *Shiji* 130, p. 3291.

163. Cf. n. 121 above.

164. *Shangjunshu* 1, p. 1 (Duyvendak p. 171), and *Shiji* 68, p. 2229.

NOTES TO CHAPTER 15

1. Cf. also Roetz 1989, 1993b, and 1993c.

2. The classic form of religious transcendence is Jewish-Christian religion. The metaphysical form is typically represented by the Platonic assumption of a realm of ideas beyond the empirical world of change. It cannot be ruled out, however, that Plato's dualism was, through the Pythagoreans, influenced by Zoroastrism, thence by religion.

3. Schwartz 1975, p. 3. The transcendent principle, then, might, for example, either be "the Mandate of Heaven or the dictates of one's moral will," as Tu Wei-ming has put it (1986, pp. 365–66).

4. And not merely the general cognitive potential of China, as Habermas, with Needham, has argued (1984, pp. 209–10).

5. For the Confucian and especially Xunzi's attitude towards discussion cf. Paul 1990.

6. The theoretical compatibility of Chinese philosophical thought and democracy has often been discussed; cf. for example Creel 1960a, pp. 164–69, Paul 1990, pp. 154–64, and Nathan 1990.

7. Cf. Schleichert's remarks on this point (1990, pp. 370–402).

8. Without a notion of the human person and its intrinsic value, there will be no consistent grounding for republican institutions (I prefer the notion of republic to that of democracy here, in order to preclude the misunderstanding of democracy as mere popular majority rule; cf. for this topic Creel 1960a, pp. 166–67). An autonomous notion of the "self" does not necessarily entail a republic, but it delivers its foundation and is more than a merely additional support for a "once initiated democraticization," as Paul writes in his discussion of "Confucian concepts of the self and democraticization" (1990, p. 162). Why should there be an institutionalized check on power unless, in the final analysis, for the sake of the dignity of the human person?

Bibliography

A. ZHOU AND HAN TEXTS AND CLASSICAL HISTORIES

Baihutong. Chen Li. *Baihutong shuzheng.* Huainan shuju 1875. In Zhongguo zixue mingzhu jicheng bianyin jijinhui, ed., *Zhongguo zixue mingzhu jicheng,* vol. 86. Taipei: 1978.

Chuci. Hong Xingzu. *Chuci buzhu.* (*Sibu congkan*). Reprint Kyoto: 1964.

Chunqiu. Harvard-Yenching Institute Sinological Index Series. *Combined Indexes to Ch'un-Ch'iu, Kung-yang, Ku-liang and Tso-chuan.* Reprint Taipei: Chinese Materials and Research Aids Center, 1966.

Chunqiu fanlu. In *Sibu beiyao.* Reprint Taiwan: Zhonghua, 1975.

Dadai Liji. Gao Ming. *Dadai Liji jinzhu jinyi.* Taipei: Shangwu, 1975.

Daxue. See *Liji.*

Fayan. Yangzi *Fayan.* In *Zhuzi jicheng,* vol. 7. Hong Kong: Zhonghua, 1978.

Gongyangzhuan. See *Chunqiu.*

Guanzi. Dai Wang. *Guanzi jiaozheng.* In *Zhuzi jicheng,* vol. 5. Hong Kong: Zhonghua, 1978.

Guliangzhuan. See *Chunqiu.*

Guoyu. Shanghai shifandaxue guji zhenglizu, ed., *Guoyu.* Shanghai: Guji, 1978.

Hanfeizi. Wang Xianshen. *Hanfeizi jijie.* In *Zhuzi jicheng,* vol. 5. Hong Kong: Zhonghua, 1978. (Page references for comparison are to Liao 1939.)

Hanshi waizhuan. Lai Yanyuan. *Hanshi waizhuan jinzhu jinyi.* Taipei: Shangwu, 1972. (Page references for comparison are to Hightower 1952.)

Hanshu. Peking: Zhonghua, 1962.

Houhanshu. Peking: Zhonghua, 1965.

Huainanzi. In Zhuzi jicheng, vol. 7. Hong Kong: Zhonghua, 1978.

Kongzi jiayu. Chen Shike. *Kongzi jiayu shuzheng.* Shanghai: Shanghai shudian, 1987.

Laozi. Wang Bi. *Laozi zhu.* In *Zhuzi jicheng,* vol. 3. Hong Kong: Zhonghua, 1978.

————. Guojia wenwuju guwenxian yanjiushe, ed. *Mawangdui hanmu boshu,* vol. 1. Peking: Wenwu, 1980.

Liezi. In *Zhuzi jicheng,* vol. 3. Hong Kong: Zhonghua, 1978. (Page references for comparison are to Graham 1960.)

Liji. Liji zhengyi. In Ruan Yuan, *Shisanjing zhushu.* Reprint Peking: Zhonghua, 1980. (Page references for comparison are to Legge 1895a.)

Lunheng. In *Zhuzi jicheng,* vol. 7. Hong Kong: Zhonghua, 1978.

Lunyu. Harvard-Yenching Institute Sinological Index Series. *A Concordance to the Analects of Confucius.* Reprint Taipei: 1972.

Lüshi chunqiu. In *Zhuzi jicheng,* vol. 6. Hong Kong: Zhonghua, 1978.

Mengzi. Harvard-Yenching Institute Sinological Index Series. *A Concordance to Meng Tzu.* Reprint Taipei: 1973.

Mingshi. Peking: Zhonghua, 1974.

Mozi. Sun Yirang. *Mozi jiangu.* In *Zhuzi jicheng,* vol. 4. Hong Kong: Zhonghua, 1978. (Page references for comparison are to Mei 1929.)

Shangjunshu. Yan Wanli. *Shangjunshu xin jiaozheng.* In *Zhuzi jicheng,* vol. 5. Hong Kong: Zhonghua, 1978. (Page references for comparison are to Duyvendak 1928.)

Shangshu dazhuan. In *Baibu congshu jicheng, Gujingjie huihan.* Taipei: Yiwen.

Shenjian. In *Zhuzi jicheng,* vol. 8. Hong Kong: Zhonghua, 1978.

Shenzi. In *Zhuzi jicheng,* vol. 5. Hong Kong: Zhonghua, 1978. (Page references for comparison are to Thompson 1978.)

Shiji. Hong Kong: Zhonghua, 1969.

Shijing. Harvard-Yenching Institute Sinological Index Series. *A Concordance to Shih Ching.* Peking: 1945.

Shizi. In *Sanshiliu zi quanshu,* vol. 33. Shanghai 1923.

Shujing. Shangshu zhengyi. In Ruan Yuan, *Shisanjing zhushu.* Reprint Peking: Zhonghua, 1980. (Page references for comparison are to Karlgren 1950.)

Shuowen jiezi. Hong Kong: Zhonghua, 1977.

Shuoyuan. Lu Yuanjun. *Shuoyuan jinzhu jinyi.* Taipei: Shangwu, 1979.

Suishu. Peking: Zhonghua, 1973.

Sun Bin bingfa. Xu Peigen and Wei Rulin. *Sun Bin bingfa zhushi.* Taipei: Liming, 1976.

Wenzi. In *Zhengtong Daozang,* vol. 187 (*Tongxuan zhenjing*). Taipei: Yiwen, 1962.

Xiaojing. Huang Deshi. *Xiaojing jinzhu jinyi.* Taipei: Shangwu, 1972.

Xinshu. Qi Yuzhang. *Jiazi Xinshu jiaoshi.* Taipei: Zhongguo wenhua zazhi she, 1974.

Xinxu. Xinxu jinzhu jinyi. Taipei: Shangwu, 1977.

Xunzi. Wang Xianqian. *Xunzi jijie.* In *Zhuzi jicheng,* vol. 2. Hong Kong: Zhonghua, 1978. (Page references for comparison are to Dubs 1928, Watson 1963, and Knoblock 1988.)

Yantielun. In *Zhuzi jicheng,* vol. 7. Hong Kong: Zhonghua, 1978.

Yanzi chunqiu. Zhang Chunyi. *Yanzi chunqiu jiaozhu.* In *Zhuzi jicheng,* vol. 4. Hong Kong: Zhonghua, 1978.

Yijing. Harvard-Yenching Institute Sinological Index Series. *A Concordance to Yi Ching.* Reprint Taipei: 1966. (Page references for comparison are to Legge 1899.)

Yinwenzi. In *Zhuzi jicheng,* vol. 6. Hong Kong: Zhonghua, 1978.

Zhanguoce. Shanghai: Guji, 1978.

Zhongyong. See *Liji.*

Zhouli. Zhouli zhushu. In Ruan Yuan, *Shisanjing zhushu.* Reprint Peking: Zhonghua, 1980.

Zhuangzi. Guo Qingfan. *Zhuangzi jishi.* In *Zhuzi jicheng,* vol. 3. Hong Kong: Zhonghua, 1978. (Page references for comparison are to Watson 1968 and Graham 1981.)

Zhushu jinian. Fang Shiming and Wang Xiuling. *Gujin Zhushujinian jizheng.* Shanghai: Guji, 1981.

Zuozhuan. See *Chunqiu.* (Page references for comparison are to Legge 1895b.)

B. OTHER LITERATURE

AHERN, DENIS M. 1976. "Is Mo Tzu a Utilitarian?" *Journal of Chinese Philosophy* 3, no. 2: 185–93.

ALLINSON, ROBERT E. 1985. "The Confucian Golden Rule: A Negative Formulation." *Journal of Chinese Philosophy* 12, no. 3: 305–15.

APEL, KARL-OTTO. 1971. "Szientistik, Hermeneutik, Ideologiekritik. Entwurf einer Wissenschaftslehre in erkenntnisanthropologischer Sicht." In K.-O. Apel et. al., *Hermeneutik und Ideologiekritik*, pp. 7–44. Frankfurt/M.: Suhrkamp.

———. 1980a. "Geschichtliche Phasen der Herausforderung der praktischen Vernunft und Entwicklungsstufen des moralischen Bewußtseins." *Funkkolleg praktische Philosophie/Ethik*, Studienbegleitbrief 1. Weinheim, Basel: Beltz.

———. 1980b. "Zur geschichtlichen Entfaltung der ethischen Vernunft in der Philosophie." *Funkkolleg praktische Philosophie/Ethik*, Studienbegleitbrief 2. Weinheim, Basel: Beltz.

———. 1982. "Normative Ethics and Strategical Rationality: The Philosophical Problem of a Political Ethics." *Graduate Faculty Philosophical Journal* 9, no. 1: 81–105.

———. 1988. *Diskurs und Verantwortung*. Frankfurt/M.: Suhrkamp. (English edition *Discourse and Responsibility* forthcoming in Columbia University Press.)

ARENDT, HANNAH. 1958. *The Human Condition*. Chicago: University of Chicago Press.

ARISTOTLE. 1946. *The Works of Aristotle*, ed. W. D. Ross. Oxford: Clarendon.

AUGUSTINE. 1945. *The City of God*, trans. John Hearley. London: Dent.

BAIER, KURT. 1969. *The Moral Point of View*, 6th ed. New York: Random House.

BARNES, JONATHAN. 1982. *The Presocratic Philosophers*, 2d ed. London, Boston, Melbourne, and Henley: Routledge & Kegan Paul.

BAUER, WOLFGANG. 1971. *China und die Hoffnung auf Glück*. München: Hanser.

———. 1985. "The Hidden Hero: Creation and Disintegration of the Ideal of Eremitism." In D. Munro, ed., *Individualism and Holism: Studies in Confucian and Taoist Values*, pp. 157–98. Ann Arbor: Center for Chinese Studies, University of Michigan.

———. 1990. *Das Antlitz Chinas*. München: Hanser.

BAUM, RICHARD. 1982. "Science and Culture in Contemporary China: The Roots of Retarded Modernization." *Asian Survey* 22, no. 12: 1166–86.

BEHR, WOLFGANG. 1993. *Die Darstellung der zehn Buddhatitel in Fayuns "Fanyi mingyi ji" von 1157*. Monumenta Serica Monographs, Nettetal: Steyler Verlag, forthcoming.

BEN YOSEF, I. A. 1988. "Confucianism and Taoism in The Star of Redemption." *Journal for the Study of Religion* 1, no. 2: 25–36.

BENEDICT, RUTH. 1935. *Patterns of Culture*. London: Routledge.

———. 1954. *The Chrysanthemum and the Sword: Patterns of Japanese Culture*. Rutland and Tokyo: Tuttle.

BERTALANFFY, LUDWIG VON. 1968. *General Systems Theory*. New York: Braziller.

BLOCH, ERNST. 1986 [1959]. *The Principle of Hope*, trans. N. Plaice, St. Plaice, and P. Knight. Oxford: Blackwell.

BLOOM, ALFRED H. 1977a. "Two Dimensions of Moral Reasoning: Social Principledness and Social Humanism in Cross-Cultural Perspective." *The Journal of Social Psychology* 101: 29–44.

———. 1977b. "A Cognitive Dimension of Social Control: The Hong Kong Chinese in Cross-Cultural Perspective." In A. A. Wilson, S. L. Greenblatt, R. W. Wilson, eds., *Deviance and Social Control in Chinese Society*, pp. 67–81. New York and London: Praeger.

BODDE, DERK. 1953. "Harmony and Conflict in Chinese Philosophy." In A. F. Wright, ed., *Studies in Chinese Thought*, pp. 19–80. Chicago: University of Chicago Press.

BOODBERG, PETER A. 1953. "The Semasiology of Some Primary Confucian Concepts." *Philosophy East and West* 2, no. 4: 317–32.

BOSLEY, RICHARD. 1988. "Do Mencius and Hume Make the Same Mistake?" *Philosophy East and West* 38, no. 1: 3–18.

BREASTED, JAMES HENRY. 1976 [1933]. *The Dawn of Conscience*. New York: Macmillan.

BÜNGER, KARL. 1952. "Die Rechtsidee in der chinesischen Geschichte." *Saeculum* 3: 192–217.

CAI RENHOU. 1982. "Mengzi xin xing lun zhi yanjiu." In Wu Kang, ed., *Mengzi sixiang yanjiu lunji*, pp. 59–74. Taipei: Liming.

CAI SHANGSI. 1983. "Kongzi sixiang wenti de baijia zhengming." *Zhexue yanjiu*, no. 1: 72–75.

———. 1984. *Kongzi sixiang tixi*, 2d ed. Shanghai: Renmin.

CANETTI, ELIAS. 1979. *The Conscience of Words*, trans. J. Neugroschel. New York: Farrar Straus Giroux.

CASSIRER, ERNST. 1969. *Philosophie der symbolischen Formen*, vol. II. Darmstadt: Wissenschaftliche Buchgesellschaft.

CHAN SIN-WAI. 1984. *An Exposition of Benevolence: The Jen-hsueh of T'an Ssu-t'ung*. Hong Kong: Chinese University Press.

CHAN, WING-TSIT. 1963. *Instructions for Practical Living and Other Neo-Confucian Writings by Wang Yang-ming*. New York: Columbia University Press.

———. 1969. *Neo-Confucianism Etc.: Essays by Wing-tsit Chan*. Hong Kong: Oriental Society.

———. 1975. "Chinese and Western Interpretations of Jen (Humanity)." *Journal of Chinese Philosophy* 2, no. 2: 107–29.

———. 1988. "Rujia lunli lianglun zhexue yu xiandaihua." *Zhexue yu wenhua* 165: 77–86.

Chāndogya Upanishad. 1965. Trans. Swāmi Swāhānda, Madras: Math.

CHANG TSUNG-TUNG. 1970. *Der Kult der Shang-Dynastie im Spiegel der Orakelinschriften*. Wiesbaden: Harrassowitz.

———. 1982. *Metaphysik, Erkenntnis und praktische Philosophie im Chuang-Tzu*. Frankfurt/M.: Klostermann.

CH'EN CH'I-YÜN. 1980. *Hsün Yüeh and the Mind of Late Han China: A Translation of the Shen-chien*. Princeton: Princeton University Press.

CHEN CHUN. 1983. *Beixi ziyi*. Peking: Zhonghua.

CHEN DAN. 1984. "Liezi Yang Zhu pian wei shu xin zheng." In Zheng Liangshu, ed., *Xu weishu tongkao*, vol. 2, pp. 1348–53. Taipei: Xuesheng.

CHEN DAQI. 1954. *Xunzi xueshuo*. Taipei: Zhonghua wenhua chuban shiye.

———. 1976. "Mengzi yu Gaozi de biannan." In Xiang Weixin and Liu Fuzeng, eds., *Zhongguo zhexue sixiang lunji: Xian qin pian*, pp. 117–38. Taipei: Mutong.

CHEN GUYING. 1988. "Laozi xian yu Kong xue." *Zhexue yanjiu*, no. 9: 40–48.

CHEN QUE. 1979. *Chen Que ji*. Peking: Zhonghua.

CHEN ZIANG. 1961. "Fuchou yizhuang." In *Qinding Quan Tang wen* 213, pp. 18b–20a (vol. 9, pp. 2729–30). Taipei: Huiwen.

CHENG CHUNG-YING. 1972. "On Yi as a Universal Principle of Specific Application in Confucian Morality." *Philosophy East and West* 22, no. 3: 269–80.

———. 1977. "Towards Constructing a Dialectics of Harmonization: Harmony and Conflict in Chinese Philosophy." *Journal of Chinese Philosophy* 4, no. 3: 209–45.

———. 1986. "The Concept of Face and its Confucian Roots." *Journal of Chinese Philosophy* 13, no. 3: 329–48.

CHENG YI. 1984. "Henan Chengshi jingshuo." In *Er Cheng ji*, vol. 4. Peking: Zhonghua.

CH'IEN CHUNG-SHU. 1935. "Tragedy in Old Chinese Drama." *T'ien Hsia Monthly* 1: 37–46. (See also Qian Zhongshu.)

CHOW TSE-TSUNG, ed. 1968. *Wen-lin, Studies in Chinese Humanities.* Madison, Milwaukee, and London: University of Wisconsin Press.

CH'Ü T'UNG-TSU. 1961. *Law and Society in Traditional China.* Paris: Mouton.

CIKOSKI, J. 1975. "On Standards of Analogical Reasoning in the Late Chou." *Journal of Chinese Philosophy* 2, no. 3: 325–57.

COOPER, EUGENE. 1982. "The Potlatch in Ancient China." *History of Religions* 22, no. 2: 103–28.

CREEL, HERRLEE G. 1960a. *Confucius and the Chinese Way.* New York: Harper & Brothers.

———. 1960b. *Chinese Thought from Confucius to Mao Tse-tung.* New York: Mentor.

———. 1970. *The Origins of Statecraft in China*, vol. 1. Chicago and London: University of Chicago Press.

———. 1977. "Comments on Harmony and Conflict." *Journal of Chinese Philosophy* 4, no. 3: 271–77.

CUA, ANTONIO S. 1971. "Reflections on the Structure of Confucian Ethics." *Philosophy East and West* 21: 125–40.

———. 1978. *Dimensions of Moral Creativity: Paradigms, Principles, and Ideals.* University Park: University of Pennsylvania Press.

———. 1983. "Li and Moral Justification: A Study in the Li Chi." *Philosophy East and West* 33, no. 1: 1–16.

———. 1984. "Confucian Vision and Human Community." *Journal of Chinese Philosophy* 11, no. 3: 227–38.

———. 1985. *Ethical Argumentation: A Study in Hsün Tzu's Moral Epistemology.* Honolulu: University of Hawaii Press.

———. 1989a. "The Status of Principles in Confucian Ethics." *Journal of Chinese Philosophy* 16, no. 3: 273–96.

———. 1989b. "The Problem of Conceptual Unity in Hsün Tzu, and Li Kou's Solution." *Philosophy East and West* 39, no. 2: 115–34.

Daedalus. 1975. *Wisdom, Revelation, and Doubt: Perspectives on the First Millenium B.C.*, no. 104.

DAHMER, MANFRED. 1988. *Die große Solosuite Guanglingsan, das berühmteste Werk der frühest notierten chinesischen Instrumentalmusik.* Frankfurt/M.: Peter Lang.

DAWSON, RAYMOND. 1981. *Confucius.* Oxford University Press.

DE BARY, WM. THEODORE. 1970. "Individualism and Humanitarianism in Late Ming Thought." In Wm. Th. de Bary, ed., *Self and Society in Ming Thought*, pp. 145–248. New York: Columbia University Press.

———. 1983. *The Liberal Tradition in China.* Hong Kong: Chinese University Press.

DE BARY, WM. THEODORE, CHAN WING-TSIT, AND WATSON, BURTON. 1960. *Sources of Chinese Tradition.* New York and London: Columbia University Press.

DE GROOT, J. J. M. 1894. *The Religious System of China*, vol. II, book I. Leyden: Brill.

DIEHLS, HERMANN, AND KRANZ, WALTHER. 1961. *Die Fragmente der Vorsokratiker*, 10th ed. by W. Kranz. Berlin: Weidemannsche Verlagsbuchhandlung.

DIEN, DORA SHU-FANG. 1982. "A Chinese Perspective on Kohlberg's Theory of Moral Development." *Developmental Review* 2: 331–41.

DIHLE, ALBRECHT. 1962. *Die Goldene Regel: Eine Einführung in die Geschichte der antiken und frühchristlichen Vulgärethik.* Göttingen: Vanderhoek & Ruprecht.

DÖBERT, RAINER. 1973. "Zur Logik des Übergangs von archaischen zu hochkulturellen Religionssystemen." In K. Eder, ed., *Seminar: Die Entstehung staatlich organisierter Gesellschaften*, pp. 330–63. Frankfurt/M.: Suhrkamp.

DOBSON, W. A. 1968. "Some Legal Instruments of Ancient China: The Ming and the Meng." In Chow Tse-tsung, ed., *Wen-lin, Studies in Chinese Humanities*, pp. 269–82. Madison, Milwaukee, and London: University of Wisconsin Press.

DUBS, HOMER H. 1928. *The Works of Hsuntzu*. London: Probsthain.

————. 1951. "The Development of Altruism in Confucianism." *Philosophy East and West* 1, no. 1: 48–55.

DUYVENDAK, J. J. L. 1928. *The Book of Lord Shang*. London: Probsthain.

EBERHARD, WOLFRAM. 1967. *Guilt and Sin in Traditional China*. Berkeley and Los Angeles: University of California Press.

EDER, KLAUS. 1980. *Die Entstehung staatlich organisierter Gesellschaften*. Frankfurt/M.: Suhrkamp.

EIBL-EIBESFELDT, IRENÄUS. 1987. *Grundriss der vergleichenden Verhaltensforschung*, 7th ed. München and Zürich: Piper.

EISENSTADT, SHMUEL N., ed. 1986. *The Origins and Diversities of Axial Age Civilizations*. Albany: State University of New York Press.

ELFENBEIN, DONALD. 1973. *Moral Stages in Societal Evolution*. B. A. thesis, Harvard.

ELIADE, MIRCEA. 1959. *Cosmos and History*. New York: Harper Torchbooks.

ELVIN, MARK. 1973. *The Pattern of the Chinese Past*. Stanford: Stanford University Press.

————. 1986. "Was There a Transcendental Breakthrough in China?" In S. N. Eisenstadt, ed., *The Origins and Diversities of Axial Age Civilizations*, pp. 325–59. Albany: State University of New York Press.

EPICURUS. 1926. *Epicurus: The Extant Remnants*, trans. Cyril Bailey. Oxford: Clarendon.

Ershisi xiao. 1978. In Laogu chubanshe bianjibu, *Guoxue chuji rumen*. Taipei: Laogu.

ETIEMBLE. 1966. *Confucius*. Paris: Gallimard.

FANG, THOMÉ H. 1980. *The Chinese View of Life*. Taipei: Linking.

FEHL, NOAH. 1971. *Li: Rites and Propriety in Literature and Life: A Perspective for a Cultural History of Ancient China*. Hong Kong: The Chinese University of Hong Kong.

FELBER, ROLAND. 1973. *Die Entwicklung der Austauschverhältnisse im alten China*. Berlin: Akademie.

FENG YOULAN. 1957. "Zhongguo zhexue yichan de jicheng wenti," and "Guanyu zhongguo zhexue yichan jicheng wenti de buchong yijian." In Zhexueyanjiu bianjibu, ed., *Zhongguo zhexueshi wenti taolun zhuanji*, pp. 273–85. Peking: Kexue.

————. 1961. *Zhongguo zhexue shi fubu bian*. Hong Kong: Kaiming. (English translation see Fung Yu-lan).

————. 1962. *Zhongguo zhexueshi lunwen er ji*. Shanghai: Renmin.

FINGARETTE, HERBERT. 1972. *Confucius: The Secular as Sacred*. New York: Harper Torchbooks.

————. 1979a. "The Problem of the Self in the Analects." *Philosophy East and West* 29, no. 2: 129–40.

————. 1979b. "Following the 'One Thread' of the Analects." *Journal of the American Academy of Religion* 47 Three S, Thematic Issue: Studies in Classical Chinese Thought: 373–406.

————. 1980. "Reply to Professor Hansen." *Journal of Chinese Philosophy* 7, no. 2: 259–66.

————. 1991. "Reason, Spontaneity, and the *Li:* A Confucian Critique of Graham's Solution to the Problem of Fact and Value." In Henry Rosemont, ed., *Chinese Texts and Philosophical Contexts: Essays Dedicated to Angus C. Graham,* pp. 209–25. La Salle: Open Court.

FORKE, ALFRED. 1927. *Die Gedankenwelt des chinesischen Kulturkreises.* München and Berlin: Oldenbourg.

————. 1964 [1927]. *Geschichte der alten chinesischen Philosophie.* Hamburg: De Gruyter.

FRANKENA, WILLIAM K. 1939. "The Naturalistic Fallacy." *Mind* n.s. 48: 464–77.

FREEDMAN, MAURICE. 1977. "Marcel Granet, 1884–1940, Sociologist." Introductory essay to Marcel Granet, *The Religion of the Chinese People,* pp. 1–29. New York: Harper Torchbooks.

FREEMAN, KATHLEEN. 1959. *The Pre-Socratic Philosophers,* 2d ed. Oxford: Basil Blackwell.

FU SINIAN. 1980 [1938]. "Xing ming guxun bianzheng." In *Fu Sinian quanji,* vol. 2, pp. 161–404. Taipei: Lianjing.

FUNG YU-LAN. 1952. *A History of Chinese Philosophy,* trans. D. Bodde. Princeton: Princeton University Press.

GAO BAOGUANG. 1982. "Mengzi duiyu xing de zhengbian." In Wu Kang, ed., *Mengzi sixiang yanjiu lunji,* pp. 187–98. Taipei: Liming.

GAO HENG. 1933. "Yang Zhu xuepai." In Luo Genze, ed., *Gushibian,* vol. 4, pp. 578–52. Reprint Hong Kong: Taiping shuju, 1963.

————. 1980 [1962]. *Wenshi shulin.* Peking: Zhonghua.

GARBERN LIU, LISA. 1985. "Reasoning Counterfactually in Chinese: Are There Any Obstacles?" *Cognition* 21: 239–70.

GASSMANN, ROBERT H. 1985. "Sinologie, Chinakunde, Chinawissenschaft. Eine Standortbestimmung." *Asiatische Studien* 39, nos. 1–2: 147–68.

GEHLEN, ARNOLD. 1964. *Urmensch und Spätkultur.* Frankfurt/M. and Bonn: Athenäum.

————. 1969. *Moral und Hypermoral.* Frankfurt/M. and Bonn: Athenäum.

GERNET, JACQUES. 1982. *Chine et christianisme, Action et réaction.* Paris: Gallimard.

GIELEN, UWE P. 1987a. "The Sino-American Colloquium on Moral Cognition." (Conference Report). In *Moral Education Forum* 12, no. 1: 27–32.

————. 1987b. "Perceived Parental Behavior and the Development of Moral Reasoning in Students from Taiwan." Paper presented to the 45th Annual Convention of the International Council of Psychologists, New York, August 1987.

————. 1990. "Some Recent Work on Moral Values, Reasoning, and Education in Chinese Societies." *Moral Education Forum* 15, no. 1: 3–22.

GIRARDOT, NORMAN J. 1983. *Myth and Meaning in Early Taoism: The Theme of Chaos (hun-tun).* Berkeley, Los Angeles, and London: University of California Press.

GRAF, OLAF. 1970. *Tao und Jen: Sein und Sollen im sungchinesischen Monismus.* Wiesbaden: Harrassowitz.

GRAHAM, ANGUS C. 1960. *The Book of Lieh-tzu.* London: Murray.

————. 1961. "The Date and Composition of the Liehtzyy." *Asia Major* n.s. 8, no. 2: 139–98.

————. 1967. "The Background of the Mencian Theory of Human Nature." *Tsing Hua Journal of Chinese Studies* n.s. 8, nos. 1–2: 215–71.

————. 1978. *Later Mohist Logic, Ethics and Science.* Hong Kong: Chinese University Press.

————. 1981. *Chuang-tzu: The Seven Inner Chapters and Other Writings from the Book Chuang-tzu.* London: Allen & Unwin.

———. 1983. "Daoist Spontaneity and the Dichotomy of 'Is' and 'Ought'." In V. H. Mair, ed., *Experimental Essays on the Chuang-tzu*, pp. 3–23. Honolulu: University of Hawaii Press.

———. 1989. *Disputers of the Tao: Philosophical Argument in Ancient China.* La Salle: Open Court.

GRANET, MARCEL. 1919. *Fêtes et chansons anciennes de la Chine.* Paris: Leroux.

———. 1934. *La pensée chinoise.* Paris: La Renaissance du Livre.

GRAY, WALLACE, AND PLOTT, JOHN. 1979. *New Keys to East-West Philosophy.* Hong Kong: Asian Research Service.

GUO MORUO. 1956. *Shi pipan shu.* Peking: Renmin.

———. 1957. *Qingtong shidai.* Peking: Kexue.

HABERMAS, JÜRGEN. 1981. *Philosophisch-politische Profile*, 3d ed. Frankfurt/M.: Suhrkamp.

———. 1982. *Zur Rekonstruktion des historischen Materialismus*, 3d ed. Frankfurt/M.: Suhrkamp.

———. 1983. *Moralbewußtsein und kommunikatives Handeln.* Frankfurt/M.: Suhrkamp.

———. 1984. *The Theory of Communicative Action, Vol. One: Reason and the Rationalization of Society*, trans. Thomas McCarthy. London: Heinemann.

HALL, DAVID L., AND AMES, ROGER T. 1984. "Getting it Right: On Saving Confucius from the Confucians." *Philosophy East and West* 34, no. 1: 3–23.

———. 1987. *Thinking through Confucius.* Albany: State University of New York Press.

HANG, THADDEUS T'UI-CHIEH. 1987. "The Historical and Philosophical Import of Hung-fan." *The Asian Journal of Philosophy* 1, no. 1: 1–16.

———. 1988. "The Unity of Yin and Yang: A Philosophical Assessment." In Liu Shu-hsien and R. E. Allinson, ed., *Harmony and Strife: Contemporary Perspectives, East & West*, pp. 211–24. Hong Kong: The Chinese University Press.

———. 1991. "Psychological Aspects of Confucian Moral Philosophy." In Tran Van Doan, Vincent Shen, and George F. McLean, ed., *Chinese Foundations for Moral Education and Character*, pp. 29–42. Washington D.C.: The Council for Research in Values and Philosophy.

HANSEN, CHAD. 1972. "Freedom and moral responsibility in Confucian ethics." *Philosophy East and West* 22, no. 2: 169–86.

———. 1976. Review article on Fingarette, *Confucius: The Secular as Sacred. Journal of Chinese Philosophy* 3, no. 2: 197–204.

———. 1983. *Language and Logic in Ancient China.* Ann Arbor: University of Michigan Press.

———. 1985a. "Chinese Language, Chinese Philosophy, and 'Truth.'" *Journal of Asian Studies* 44, no. 3: 491–519.

———. 1985b. "Individualism in Chinese Thought." In D. Munro, ed., *Individualism and Holism: Studies in Confucian and Taoist Values*, pp. 35–56. Ann Arbor: Center for Chinese Studies, University of Michigan.

———. 1985c. "Punishment and Dignity in China." In D. Munro, ed., *Individualism and Holism: Studies in Confucian and Taoist Values*, pp. 359–84. Ann Arbor: Center for Chinese Studies, University of Michigan.

HARBSMEIER, CHRISTOPH. 1981. *Aspects of Classical Chinese Syntax.* London and Malmö: Curzon Press.

———. 1989. "Marginalia Sino-Logica." In R. Allinson, ed., *Understanding the Chinese Mind*, pp. 125–66. Hong Kong: Oxford University Press.

————. 1991. "The Mass Noun Hypothesis and the Part-Whole Analysis of the White Horse Dialogue." In H. Rosemont, ed., *Chinese Texts and Philosophical Contexts: Essays Dedicated to Angus C. Graham*, pp. 49–66. La Salle: Open Court.

HARRELL, STEVAN. 1985. "Why Do the Chinese Work So Hard? Reflections on an Entrepreneurial Ethic." *Modern China* 11, no. 2: 203–26.

HARTMANN, EDUARD V. 1879. *Phänomenologie des sittlichen Bewußtseins*. Berlin: C. Duncker.

HAWKES, DAVID. 1964. "Chinese Poetry and the English Reader." In R. Dawson, ed., *The Legacy of China*, pp. 90–114. London, Oxford, and New York: Oxford University Press.

HE XINYIN. 1981. *He Xinyin ji*, ed. Rong Zhaozu. Peking: Zhonghua.

HEGEL, G. W. F. 1940. *Vorlesungen über die Geschichte der Philosophie*, I. In *Sämtliche Werke*, vol. XVII, ed. H. Glockner, Stuttgart-Bad Cannstatt: Frommann.

————. 1941. *Vorlesungen über die Geschichte der Philosophie*, II. In *Sämtliche Werke*, vol. XVIII, ed. H. Glockner, Stuttgart-Bad Cannstatt: Frommann.

————. 1952. *The Philosophy of Right*. In *Great Books of the Western World*, vol. 46. London: Encyclopaedia Britannica.

————. 1956. *The Philosophy of History*, trans. J. Sibree. New York: Dover.

————. 1962. *Hegel on Tragedy*, ed. A. and H. Paolucci. New York: Harper Torchbooks.

————. 1987. *Lectures on the Philosophy of Religion*, vol. II, *Determinate Religion*, ed. Peter C. Hodgson. Berkeley, Los Angeles, and London: University of California Press.

HENRICKS, ROBERT G. 1989. *Lao-tzu: Te-tao-ching*. New York: Ballantine.

HESS, ECKHARD H. 1975. *The Tell-Tale Eye*. New York: Van Nostrand Reinhold.

HIGHTOWER, JAMES ROBERT. 1952. *Han shih wai chuan*. Cambridge: Harvard University Press.

HOBBES, THOMAS. 1962. *Leviathan*. London: Dent.

HOBHOUSE, LEONARD T. 1956 [1915]. *Morals in Evolution: A Study of Comparative Ethics*. Reprint London: Chapman & Hall.

The Holy Bible (King James version). New York: American Bible Society.

HÖSLE, VITTORIO. 1984. *Wahrheit und Geschichte*. Stuttgart-Bad Cannstatt: Frommann-Holzboog.

HOU WAILU et. al. 1980. *Zhongguo sixiang tongshi*, 5th ed. Peking: Renmin.

HSIAO KUNG-CHUAN. 1979. *A History of Chinese Political Thought*, trans. F. W. Mote, vol. 1. Princeton: Princeton University Press.

HSIEH YU-WEI (see also XIE YOUWEI). 1967. "Filial Piety and Chinese Society." In Ch. A. Moore, ed., *The Chinese Mind: Essentials of Chinese Philosophy and Culture*, pp. 167–87. Honolulu: East-West Center Press, University of Hawaii Press.

HSU CHO-YUN. 1965. *Ancient China in Transition: An Analysis of Social Mobility. 722–222 B.C.* Stanford: Stanford University Press.

HSU CHO-YUN AND LINDUFF, KATHERYN M. 1988. *Western Chou Civilisation*. New Haven and London: Yale University Press.

HSÜ DAO-LIN. 1970/71. "The Myth of the 'Five Human Relations' of Confucius." *Monumenta Serica* 29: 27–37.

HU CHUSHENG. 1986. *Ruxing yanjiu*. Taipei: Huazheng.

HU HSIEN CHIN. 1944. "The Chinese Concept of 'Face.'" *American Anthropologist* n.s. 46: 45–64.

HU JIACONG. 1981. "Jixia xueguan shi gouchen." *Wen shi zhe*, no. 4: 25–33.

HU SHI. 1920. *Zhongguo zhexueshi dagang*. Shanghai: Shangwu.

————. 1963. "The Right to Doubt in Ancient Chinese Thought." *Philosophy East and West* 12, no. 4: 295–300.

HU YUAN. 1944. *Xunzi bian.* In Huang Zongxi et. al., *Song Yuan xuean* 1, pp. 5b–8b. Shanghai: Shangwu (*Sibu beiyao*).

HUANG ZONGXI et. al. 1944. *Song Yuan xuean.* Shanghai: Shangwu (*Sibu beiyao*).

HUCKER, CHARLES O. 1959. "Confucianism and the Censorial System." In D. Nivison and A. F. Wright, eds., *Confucianism in Action,* pp.182–208. Stanford: Stanford University Press.

HULSEWÉ, A. F. P. 1955. *Remnants of Han Law,* vol. 1. Leiden: Brill.

HUMBOLDT, WILHELM V. 1906 [1826]. "Über den grammatischen Bau der chinesischen Sprache." In Humboldt, *Gesammelte Schriften,* 5. Band 1823–26. Berlin: Behr.

————. 1971 [1836]. *Linguistic Variability & Intellectual Development,* trans. G. C. Buck and F. A. Raven. Coral Gables: University of Miami Press.

HUME, DAVID. 1964. *A Treatise of Human Nature.* In David Hume, *The Philosophical Works,* eds. Green and Grose, vol. 2. Reprint Berlin: Scientia.

IVANHOE, PHILIP J. 1990a. "Reweaving the 'One Thread' of the Analects." *Philosophy East and West* 40, no. 1: 17–33.

————. 1990b. *Ethics in the Confucian Tradition: The Thought of Mencius and Wang Yang-ming.* Atlanta: Scholars Press.

JASPERS, KARL. 1953. *The Origin and Goal of History,* trans. M. Bullock. New Haven: Yale University Press.

————. 1958. *Über das Tragische.* München: Piper.

————. 1959. *Die großen Philosophen,* Erster Band. München: Piper.

JI XIANLIN. 1982. *Zhong Yin wenhua guanxi shi lun.* Peking: Sanlian.

JIANG GUOZHU. 1981. "Wenhua zhuanzhi de yi li: Zhu Yuanzhang de 'Mengzi jiewen.'" *Liaoning daxue xuebao,* no. 3: 17–19.

JIANG, PAUL Y. M. 1988. "Ethics in Cosmology: Variations on the Theme of the 'Unity of Heaven and Man' in Neo-Confucianism." In Liu Shu-hsien and R. E. Allinson, eds., *Harmony and Strife: Contemporary Perspectives, East & West,* pp. 271–93. Hong Kong: The Chinese University Press.

Jinsilu. See Zhu Xi 1967.

JONAS, HANS. 1984. *The Imperative of Responsibility: In Search of an Ethics for the Technological Age.* Chicago and London: University of Chicago Press.

KACHI, YUKIO. 1990. Review article on A. C. Graham, *Reason and Spontaneity. Philosophy East and West* 40, no. 3: 389–398.

KANG YOUWEI. 1984 [1902]. *Lunyu zhu.* Peking: Zhonghua.

KANT, IMMANUEL. 1968. *Werke in 10 Bänden,* ed. W. Weischedel. Darmstadt: Wissenschaftliche Buchgesellschaft.

————. 1981. *Grounding for the Metaphysics of Morals,* trans. J. W. Ellington. Indianapolis and Cambridge: Hackett.

KARLGREN, BERNHARD. 1950. *The Book of Documents.* Stockholm (Reprint from BMFEA 22).

KEINDORF, RITA. 1992. *Die mystische Reise im Chuci: Qu Yuans Yuanyou vor dem Hintergrund der zeitgenössischen Philosophie und Dichtung.* Doctoral dissertation, J.W. Goethe-Universität, Frankfurt/M.

KERFERD, G. B. 1981. *The Sophist Movement.* Cambridge: Cambridge University Press.

KESSLER, HANS. 1990. *Das Stöhnen der Natur.* Düsseldorf: Patmos.

KEYSERLING, HERMANN. 1919. *Das Reisetagebuch eines Philosophen.* Berlin: Duncker und Humblot.

KNOBLOCK, JOHN. 1988. *Xunzi: A Translation and Study of the Complete Works*, vol. I. Stanford: Stanford University Press.

KOHLBERG, LAWRENCE. 1971. "From Is to Ought." In Th. Mischel, ed., *Cognitive Development and Epistemology*, pp. 151–235. New York: Academic Press.

———. 1981. *The Philosophy of Moral Development. (Essays on Moral Development*, vol. 1). San Francisco: Harper & Row.

———. 1984. *The Psychology of Moral Development. (Essays on Moral Development*, vol. 2). San Francisco: Harper & Row.

KOHLBERG, LAWRENCE, LEVINE, CHARLES, AND HEWER, ALEXANDRA. 1983. *Moral Stages: A Current Formulation and a Response to Critics*. Basel, München: Karger.

KÖHLER, LOTTE, AND SAHNER, HANS, eds. 1985. *Hannah Arendt — Karl Jaspers: Briefwechsel 1926–1969*. München and Zürich: Piper.

KROLL, J. L. 1987. "Disputation in Ancient Chinese Culture." *Early China* 11–12: 118–45.

KUANG YAMING. 1985. *Kongzi pingzhuan*. Jinan: Qilu shushe.

KUNG, HANS, AND CHING, JULIA. 1989. *Christianity and Chinese Religions*. New York: Doubleday.

LAI, WHALEN. 1984. "Kao Tzu and Mencius on Mind: Analyzing a Paradigm Shift in Classical China." *Philosophy East and West* 34 , no. 2: 147–60.

LANG, HERIBERT. 1981. *Die chinesische Sprache und das "sprachliche Relativitätsprinzip."* Doctoral dissertation, J.W. Goethe-Universität, Frankfurt/M.

LAO SIGUANG. 1984. *Xinbian zhongguo zhexueshi*, rev. ed. Taipei: Sanmin.

LAO YUNG-WEI (Lao Siguang). 1988. "On Harmony: The Confucian View." In Liu Shuhsien and R. E. Allinson, eds., *Harmony and Strife: Contemporary Perspectives, East & West*, pp. 187–210. Hong Kong: The Chinese University Press.

LAU, D. C. 1963. "Theories of Human Nature in Mencius and Shyuntzzy." *Bulletin of the School of Oriental and African Studies* 15: 541–65.

———. 1970. *Mencius*. Harmondsworth: Penguin.

———. 1979. *The Analects*. Harmondsworth: Penguin.

LEE SHUI CHUEN. 1987. "A Confucian Critique of Kohlberg's Theory." Paper presented to the Colloquium on Moral Education and Character Development, 22. July 1987, School of Education, Chinese University of Hong Kong.

LEGGE, JAMES. 1893. *The Chinese Classics*, vol. 1, *Confucian Analects, The Great Learning, and The Doctrine of the Mean*. Oxford: Clarendon.

———. 1895a. *The Li Ki. (The Sacred Books of the East*, vols. XXVII and XXVIII). Oxford: Clarendon.

———. 1895b. *The Chinese Classics*, vol. 5, *The Ch'un Ts'ew, with the Tso chuen*. London: Oxford University Press.

———. 1899. *The I Ching*, 2d ed. *(The Sacred Books of the East*, vol. XVI). Oxford: Clarendon.

———. 1971. *Shu ching, Book of History*. Modernized edition by Clae Waltham. Chicago: Gateway.

LEI TING, AND LIU SUYUN. 1991. "Being and Becoming Moral Men in a Chinese Culture: Unique or Universal?" Paper presented at the Debrecen Conference of the International Association for Cross-Cultural Psychology, 4–7 July 1991.

LEIBNIZ, GOTTFRIED WILHELM. 1959. *Nouveaux essais sur l'entendement humain*. In Wolf von Engelhardt and Hans Heinz Holz, eds., *Leibniz, Philosophische Schriften*. Darmstadt: Wissenschaftliche Buchgemeinschaft.

LÉVI-STRAUSS, CLAUDE. 1949. *Les structures élémentaires de la parenté*. Paris: Presses Universitaires de France.

LI DISHENG. 1979. *Xunzi jishi*. Taipei: Xuesheng.

LI MINGHUI. 1990. *Rujia yu Kangde*. Taipei: Lianjing.

LI ZEHOU. 1986. *Zhongguo gudai sixiang shi lun*. Peking: Renmin.

LI ZHI. 1975. *Fenshu, Xu Fenshu*. Peking: Zhonghua.

LIANG QICHAO. 1922. "Lun Laozi shu zuo yu zhanguo zhi mo." In Luo Genze, ed., *Gushibian*, vol. 4, pp. 305–7. Reprint Hong Kong: Taiping shuju, 1963.

————. 1938. *Yinbingshi quanji*. Shanghai: Dawen.

————. 1971 [1936]. *Zimozi xueshuo*. Taipei: Zhonghua.

————. 1978 [1921]. *Mozi xuean*. Taipei: Zhonghua.

————. 1981 [1936]. *Kongzi*. Taipei: Zhonghua.

————. 1984 [1923]. *Xian Qin zhengzhi sixiang shi*. Taipei: Zhonghua.

LIANG SHUMING. 1922. *Zhongxi wenhua ji qi zhexue*. Reprint Taipingyang tushugongsi.

LIAO, W. K. 1939. *The Complete Works of Han Fei Tzu*. London: Probsthain.

LIN YÜ-SHENG. 1974/75. "The Evolution of the Pre-Confucian Meaning of *Jen* and the Confucian Concept of Moral Autonomy." *Monumenta Serica* 31: 172–204.

LIN YUN. 1965. "Shuo 'Wang'." *Kaogu* 1965, no. 6: 311–12.

LIU SHU-HSIEN. 1972. "The Confucian Approach to the Problem of Transcendence and Immanence." *Philosophy East and West* 22, no. 1: 45–52.

LIU SHU-HSIEN AND ALLINSON, ROBERT E., eds.1988. *Harmony and Strife: Contemporary Perspectives, East & West*. Hong Kong: The Chinese University Press.

LIU SHUXIAN (Liu Shu-hsien). 1986. "Rujia lunli zai xiandai shehui de yiyi." *Mingbao* 250: 13–19.

LIU ZONGYUAN. 1961. "Bo fuchou yi." In *Qinding Quan Tang wen* 572, pp. 12a–14b (vol. 24, pp. 7348–49). Taipei: Huiwen.

LOCKE, JOHN. 1823a. *An Essay Concerning Human Understanding. (The Works of John Locke*, vol. I). Reprint Aalen 1963.

————. 1823b. *Two Treatises of Government. (The Works of John Locke*, vol. V). Reprint Aalen: 1963.

LOHMANN, JOHANNES. 1965. *Philosophie und Sprachwissenschaft*. Berlin: Duncker & Humblot.

LONG YUCHUN. 1987. *Xunzi lunji*. Taipei: Xuesheng.

LORENZ, KONRAD Z. 1982. *The Foundations of Ethology*, trans. K. Z. Lorenz and R. W. Kickert. New York: Touchstone.

MCELDERRY, ANDREA. 1986. "Confucian Capitalism? Corporate Values in Republican Banking." *Modern China* 12, no. 3: 401–16.

MACINTYRE, ALASDAIR. 1981. *After Virtue: A Study in Moral Theory*. Notre Dame: University of Notre Dame Press.

The Mahabharata. 1981. Trans. Kisari Mohan Ganguli, vol. XI, *Anusasana Parva*, part II. New Delhi: Munshiram Manoharlal.

MAHOOD, G. H. 1971. "Socrates and Confucius: Moral Agents or Moral Philosophers?" *Philosophy East and West* 21, no. 2: 177–88.

MAIR, VICTOR H. 1990. *Tao te ching: Lao tzu*. New York: Bantam Books.

MAO TING. 1984. "Kongzi de zhishilun chutan." In Zhongguo zhexueshi yanjiu bianjibu, ed., *Zhongguo zhexueshi luncong* 1, pp. 82–90. Fuzhou: Fujian renmin.

MARUYAMA, MASAO. 1974. *Studies in the Intellectual History of Tokugawa Japan*, trans. Mikiso Hane. Princeton and Tokyo: Princeton University Press and University of Tokyo Press.

MASSON, MICHAEL C. 1985. *Philosophy and Tradition: The Interpretation of China's Philosophical Past: Fung Yu-lan, 1939–1949*. Taipei, Paris, and Hong Kong: Institut Ricci.

MAUSS, MARCEL. 1966. *The Gift: Forms and Functions of Exchange in Archaic Societies*, trans. Ian Cunnison. London: Cohen & West.

MEAD, GEORGE HERBERT. 1967. *Mind, Self, and Society*. Chicago and London: University of Chicago Press.

MEI YI-PAO. 1929. *The Ethical and Political Works of Motze*. London: Probsthain.

MEN QIMING. 1963 [1933]. "Yang Zhu pian ho Yangzi zhi bijiao yanjiu." In Luo Genze, ed., *Gushibian*, vol. 4, pp. 592–610. Reprint Hong Kong: Taiping shuju.

METZGER, THOMAS A. 1977. *Escape from Predicament*. New York: Columbia University Press.

———. 1987. "Some Ancient Roots of Modern Chinese Thought: This-Worldliness, Epistemological Optimism, Doctrinality, and the Emergence of Reflexivity in the Eastern Chou." *Early China* 11–12: 61–117.

———. 1990. "Continuities between Modern and Premodern China: Some Neglected Methodological and Substantive Issues." In P. A. Cohen and M. Goldman, eds., *Ideas across Cultures: Essays on Chinese Thought in Honor of Benjamin I. Schwartz*, pp. 263–92. Cambridge, Mass., and London: Harvard University Press.

MONTESQUIEU. 1949. *The Spirit of the Laws*, trans. Thomas Nugent. Two vols. in one. New York: Hafner.

MOORE, GEORGE EDWARD. 1956 [1903]. *Principia Ethica*. Cambridge: University Press.

MOTE, F. W. 1961. "The Growth of Chinese Despotism." *Oriens Extremus* 8, no. 1: 1–41.

MOTEGI, M. 1963. "Meson and Chung-yung." Yokohama 1963. (Reprinted from *The Bulletin of the Yokohama University Society* XIV, Spiritual Science No. 1).

MOU ZONGSAN. 1985. *Yuanshan lun*. Taipei: Xuesheng.

MUNRO, DONALD J. 1969. *The Concept of Man in Early China*. Stanford: Stanford University Press.

NAKAMURA, HAJIME. 1975. *Parallel Developments: A Comparative History of Ideas*. Tokyo and New York: Kodansha.

NATHAN, ANDREW J. 1990. "The Place of Values in Cross-Cultural Studies: The Example of Democracy and China." In P. A. Cohen and M. Goldman, eds., *Ideas across Cultures: Essays on Chinese Thought in Honor of Benjamin I. Schwartz*, pp. 293–314. Cambridge, Mass., and London: Harvard University Press.

NEEDHAM, JOSEPH. 1954ff. *Science and Civilization in China*. Cambridge, London, New York, and Melbourne: Cambridge University Press.

NEGT, OSKAR. 1988. *Modernisierung im Zeichen des Drachen: China und der europäische Mythos der Moderne*. Frankfurt/M.: Fischer TB.

NELSON, BENJAMIN. 1973. "Civilizational Complexes and Intercivilizational Encounters." *Sociological Analysis* 34, no. 2: 79–105.

———. 1974. "Sciences and Civilizations, 'East' and 'West.'" *Boston Studies in the Philosophy of Science* 11: 445–93.

NG, NANCY N. 1981. "Internal Shame as a Moral Sanction." *Journal of Chinese Philosophy* 8, no. 1: 75–86.

NIVISON, DAVID S. 1960. "Protest against Conventions and Conventions of Protest." In A. F. Wright, ed., *The Confucian Persuasion*, pp. 177–201. Stanford: Stanford University Press.

———. 1980. "On Translating Mencius." *Philosophy East and West* 30, no. 1: 93–122.

OPITZ, PETER J. 1990. "Konfuzius." In S. Krieger and R. Trauzettel, eds., *Konfuzianismus und die Modernisierung Chinas*, pp. 506–34. Mainz: v. Hase und Köhler.

PANG PU. 1984. *Rujia bianzhengfa yanjiu.* Peking: Zhonghua.

PARSONS, TALCOTT. 1956 [1937]. *The Structure of Social Action*. New York: Free Press.

PAUL, GREGOR. 1990. *Aspects of Confucianism*. Frankfurt/M.: Peter Lang.

PERENBOOM, R. P. 1990. "Confucian Justice: Achieving a Humane Society." *International Philosophical Quarterly* 30, no. 1: 17–32.

PHILIPPIDIS, LEONIDAS JOH. 1929. *Die "Goldene Regel" religionsgeschichtlich untersucht.* Leipzig: A. Klein.

PIAGET, JEAN. 1932. *Le jugement moral chez l'enfant*. Paris: Alcan.

PIERS, GERHART, AND SINGER, MILTON B. 1953. *Shame and Guilt: A Psychoanalytical and a Cultural Study*. Springfield, Ill.: Charles C. Thomas.

PLATO. 1887. *The Dialoges of Plato*, trans. B. Jowett. New York: Scribner's.

POPPER, KARL. 1952. *The Open Society and Its Enemies*, vol. 1, *The Spell of Plato*, 2d ed. London: Routledge & Kegan Paul.

PRUSEK, JAROSLAV. 1970. *Chinese History and Literature*. Dordrecht: Reidel.

PULLEYBLANK, E. G. 1958. Review article on K. A. Wittfogel, *Oriental Despotism. The Journal of Economic and Social History of the Orient* 1, part 3: 351–53.

PYE, LUCIAN W. 1968. *The Spirit of Chinese Politics*. Cambridge, Mass., and London: MIT Press.

QIAN ZHONGSHU. 1979. *Guanzhuibian.* Peking: Zhonghua.

QU WANLI. 1983. *Xian Qin wenshi ziliao kaobian.* Taipei: Lianjing.

QUESNAY, FRANÇOIS. 1965. *Le Despotisme de la Chine.* In *Œuvres économiques et philosophiques*. Francfort s/M: Baer, 1888. Reprint Aalen: Scientia.

RAO ZONGYI. 1978. "Tianshenguan yu daode sixiang." *Zhongyang yanjiuyuan lishi yuyan yanjiusuo jikan (Academia Sinica. Bulletin of the Institute of History and Philology)* 49, no. 1: 77–100.

RAWLS, JOHN. 1972. *A Theory of Justice.* Oxford: Clarendon.

REDING, JEAN-PAUL. 1986. "Analogical Reasoning in Early Chinese Philosophy." *Asiatische Studien* 40, no. 1: 41–56.

REINER, HANS. 1974. *Die Grundlagen der Sittlichkeit.* Meisenheim am Glan: Hain.

REN JIYU. 1956. *Mozi.* Shanghai: Renmin.

———. 1979. *Zhongguo zhexueshi.* Peking: Renmin.

RICHARDS, IVOR A. 1932. *Mencius on the Mind.* New York: Harcourt, Brace & Co.

RICKETT, W. ALLYN. 1965. *Kuan-tzu: A Repository of Early Chinese Thought*, vol. 1. Hong Kong: Hong Kong University Press.

———. 1985. *Guanzi: Political, Economic, and Philosophical Essays from Early China*, vol. 1. Princeton: Princeton University Press.

RICOEUR, PAUL. 1969. *The Symbolism of Evil*, trans. Emerson Buchanan. Boston: Beacon.

RIEGEL, JEFFREY. 1980. "Reflections on an Unmoved Mind: An Analysis of *Mencius* 2A2." *Journal of the American Academy of Religion* 74, no. 3, Thematic Issue S: 433–57.

RIESMAN, DAVID. 1969 [1950]. *The Lonely Crowd: A Study of the Changing American Character.* New Haven and London: Yale University Press.

ROETZ, HEINER. 1984. *Mensch und Natur im alten China: Zum Subjekt-Objekt-Gegensatz in der klassischen chinesischen Philosophie*. Frankfurt/M., Bern, and New York: Peter Lang.

———. 1986. "'Naives' und 'Sentimentalisches' in Chinas Philosophie und Dichtung." In R. Ptak and S. Englert, eds., *Ganz allmählich. Festschrift für Günther Debon*, pp. 216–34. Heidelberger Verlagsanstalt.

———. 1989. "Grundzüge der chinesischen Achsenzeit im Lichte der Entwicklungslogik Lawrence Kohlbergs." *Synthesis Philosophica* (Zagreb) 7, vol. 4 no. 1: 269–87.

———. 1991. Review article on A. C. Graham, *Disputers of the Tao*. *Bulletin of the School of Oriental and African Studies* 54, no. 2: 410–14.

———. 1992. "The Tragic Motif in Zhou Literature." In *Proceedings of the 33rd International Congress of Asian and North African Studies*. Montreal: McMullin.

———. 1993a. "Validity in Zhou Thought. On Chad Hansen and the Pragmatic Turn in Sinology." In H. Lenk and G. Paul, eds., *Epistemological Issues in Classical Chinese Philosophy*, pp. 69–112. Albany: State University of New York Press.

———. 1993b. "The Cognitive-Developmental Theory in Phylogenesis: A Greek/Chinese Comparison." *Behavior Science Research*, forthcoming.

———. 1993c. "Kohlberg and Chinese Morality: A Philosophical Perspective." In Uwe P. Gielen, Ting Lei, Emely Miao, eds., *Moral Values and Moral Reasoning in Chinese Societies*, submitted.

ROSEMONT, HENRY, JR. 1970/71. "State and Society in the *Hsün Tzu:* A Philosophical Commentary." *Monumenta Serica* 31: 38–78.

———. 1976. "Notes from a Confucian Perspective: Which Human Acts Are Moral Acts?" *International Philosophical Quarterly* 16, no. 1: 49–61.

———. 1986. "Kierkegaard and Confucius: On finding the Way." *Philosophy East and West* 36, no. 3: 201–12.

———. 1988. "Against Relativism." In G. J. Larson and E. Deutsch, eds., *Interpreting across Boundaries: New Essays in Comparative Philosophy*, pp. 36–70. Princeton: Princeton University Press.

ROSENBERG, SHAWN W., WARD, DANA, AND CHILTON, STEPHEN. 1988. *Political Reasoning and Cognition: A Piagetian View*. Durham and London: Duke University Press.

ROSENZWEIG, FRANZ. 1972 [1930]. *The Star of Redemption*, trans. W. W. Hallo. Boston: Beacon.

ROWLEY, H. H. 1956. *Prophecy and Religion in Ancient China and Israel*. London: University of London, The Athlone Press.

RUBIN, VITALY A. 1976. *Individual and State in Ancient China*. New York: Columbia University Press.

RÜDIGER, DIETRICH. 1976. "Der Beitrag der Psychologie zur Theorie des Gewissens und der Gewissensbildung." In J. Blühdorn, ed., *Das Gewissen in der Diskussion*, pp. 461–87. Darmstadt: Wissenschaftliche Buchgesellschaft.

RUSKOLA, TEEMU H. 1992. "Moral Choice in the Analects: A Way without a Crossroad?" *Journal of Chinese Philosophy* 19, no. 3: 285–96.

RUSSELL, BERTRAND. 1922. *The Problem of China*. London: Allen & Unwin.

———. 1951. *New Hopes for a Changing World*. London: Allen & Unwin.

SAHLINS, MARSHALL DAVID. 1972. *Stone Age Economics*. Chicago: Aldine Atherton.

SAID, EDWARD W. 1978. *Orientalism*. New York: Pantheon.

SANTANGELO, PAOLO. 1988. "The Concept of Moral Responsibility in Late Imperial China."

Paper presented to the 31st Conference of the European Association of Chinese Studies, Weimar, September 1988.

———. 1991. *Il "peccato" in Cina*. Bari: Laterza.

SCHARFSTEIN, BEN-AMI, AND DAOR, DAN. 1978. *Philosophy East/Philosophy West: A Critical Companion of Indian, Chinese, Islamic, and European Philosophy*. Oxford: Blackwell.

———. 1979. "In Answer to Antony Flew: The Whiteness of Feathers and the Whiteness of Snow." *Journal of Chinese Philosophy* 6, no. 1: 37–53.

SCHELLING, F. W. J. 1957 [1856]. *Philosophie der Mythologie*, Erster Band. Reprint Darmstadt: Wissenschaftliche Buchgesellschaft.

SCHILLER, FRIEDRICH. 1978 [1795]. *Über naive und sentimentalische Dichtung*. Stuttgart: Reclam.

SCHLEICHERT, HUBERT. 1990. *Klassische chinesische Philosophie*, 2d ed. Frankfurt/M.: Klostermann.

SCHMIDT-GLINTZER, HELWIG. 1983. "Viele Pfade oder ein Weg? Betrachtungen zur Durchsetzung der konfuzianischen Orthopraxie." In W. Schluchter, ed., *Max Webers Studie über Konfuzianismus und Taoismus. Interpretation und Kritik*, pp. 298–341. Frankfurt/M.: Suhrkamp.

SCHOPENHAUER, ARTHUR. 1977. *Über die Grundlage der Moral*. Zürcher Ausgabe vol. VI. Zürich: Diogenes.

SCHWARTZ, BENJAMIN I. 1975. "The Age of Transcendence." *Daedalus* 104, no. 2: 1–7.

———. 1985. *The World of Thought in Ancient China*. Cambridge, Mass., and London: Belknap.

SEIWERT, HUBERT. 1984. "Ethik in der chinesischen Kulturtradition." In Peter Antes et. al., *Ethik in nichtchristlichen Kulturen*, pp. 136–67. Stuttgart: Kohlhammer.

SERVICE, ELMAN R. 1975. *Origins of the State and Civilization*. New York: W. W. Norton.

———. 1977. *A Century of Controversy: Ethnological Issues from 1860 to 1960*. Orlando: Academic Press.

SHEN SHANHONG AND WANG FENGXIAN. 1985. *Zhongguo lunli xueshuo shi*. Hangzhou: Zhejiang renmin.

SHUN KWONG-LOI. 1991. "Mencius and the Mind-inherence of Morality: Mencius' Rejection of Kao Tzu's Maxim in *Meng Tzu* 2A:2." *Journal of Chinese Philosophy* 18, no. 4: 371–86.

SHWEDER, RICHARD A. 1982. "Liberalism as Destiny." Review article on L. Kohlberg, *The Philosophy of Moral Development. Contemporary Psychology* 27, no. 6: 421–24.

SINGER, MARCUS GEORGE. 1963a. *Generalization in Ethics*. London: Eyre & Spottiswoode.

———. 1963b. "The Golden Rule." *Philosophy* 38, no. 146: 293–314.

SMITH, HUSTON. 1967. "Transcendence in Classical China." *Religious Studies* 2, no. 2: 185–96.

Song Yuan xuean. See Huang Zongxi 1944.

STAIGER, BRUNHILD. 1969. *Das Konfuzius-Bild im kommunistischen China*. Wiesbaden: Harrassowitz.

STANGE, HANS O. 1950. "Chinesische und abendländische Philosophie, ihr Unterschied und seine geschichtlichen Ursachen." *Saeculum* 1: 380–96.

STOVER, LEON E. 1974. *The Cultural Ecology of Chinese Civilization*. New York: Pica.

STRAWSON, PETER F. 1974. *Freedom and Resentment*. London: Methuen.

SUN LONGJI. 1983. *Zhongguo wenhua de shencengjiegou*. Hong Kong.

SZONDI, L. 1973. *Moses. Antwort auf Kain.* Bern, Stuttgart, Wien: H. Huber.

TAN SITONG. 1954 [1897]. *Ren xue.* In *Tan Sitong quanji*, pp. 3–90. Peking: Sanlian.

TANG JUNYI. 1979. *Zhongguo zhexue yuanlun: Yuan xing pian*, 3d ed. Taipei: Xinya yanjiusuo.

THOMPSON, P. M. 1979. *The Shen Tzu Fragments.* Oxford: Oxford University Press.

TÖNNIES, FERDINAND. 1922. *Gemeinschaft und Gesellschaft*, 4th and 5th ed. Berlin: Curtius.

TOYNBEE, ARNOLD. 1951. *A Study of History*, 5th ed., vol. III. London, New York, and Toronto: Oxford University Press.

TRAUZETTEL, ROLF. 1977. "Individuum und Heteronomie: Historische Aspekte des Verhältnisses von Individuum und Gesellschaft in China." *Saeculum* 28, no. 3: 340–64.

————. 1979. "Modernisierung der Logik und Logik der Modernisierung. Zu einer philosophischen Diskussion in China." *Saeculum* 30, no. 3: 304–15.

TRIMBORN, HERMANN. 1950. "Die Privatrache und der Eingriff des Staates." In *Deutsche Landesreferate zum III. internationalen Kongress für Rechtsvergleichung in London 1950*, 1. Teil, pp. 133–48.

TSCHARNER, EDUARD V. 1973 [1932]. "Chinesische Gedichte in deutscher Sprache." In H. J. Störig, ed., *Das Problem des Übersetzens*, pp. 223–41. Darmstadt: Wissenschaftliche Buchgesellschaft.

TU WEI-MING. 1976. *Centrality and Commonality: An Essay on Chung-yung.* Honolulu: The University Press of Hawaii.

————. 1979. *Humanity and Self-Cultivation: Essays in Confucian Thought.* Berkeley: Asian Humanities Press.

————. 1981. "The 'Moral Universal' from the Perspectives of East Asian Thought." *Philosophy East and West* 31, no. 3: 259–77.

————. 1985. "Subjectivity in Liu Tsung-chou's Philosophical Anthropology." In D. Munro, ed., *Individualism and Holism: Studies in Confucian and Taoist Values*, pp. 215–38. Ann Arbor: Center for Chinese Studies, University of Michigan.

————. 1986. "The Structure and Function of the Confucian Intellectual in Ancient China." In S. N. Eisenstadt, ed., *The Origins and Diversities of Axial Age Civilizations*, pp. 360–73. Albany: State University of New York Press.

————. 1990. "Der industrielle Aufstieg Ostasiens aus konfuzianischer Sicht." In S. Krieger and R. Trauzettel, eds., *Konfuzianismus und die Modernisierung Chinas*, pp. 41–56. Mainz: v. Hase und Köhler.

TUGENDHAT, ERNST. 1990. "The Necessity for Cooperation between Philosophical and Empirical Research in the Clarification of the Meaning of the Moral 'Ought.'" In Th. E. Wren, ed., *The Moral Domain*, pp. 3–14. Cambridge, Mass., and London: MIT.

ÜBELHÖR, MONIKA. 1986. *Wang Gen (1483–1541) und seine Lehre.* Berlin: Reimer.

VERVOORN, AAT. 1990. *Men of the Cliffs and Caves: The Development of the Chinese Eremitic Tradition to the End of the Han Dynasty.* Hong Kong: Chinese University Press.

VINE, IAN. 1986. "Moral Maturity in Socio-Cultural Perspective: Are Kohlberg's Stages Universal?" In S. and C. Modgil, eds., *Lawrence Kohlberg: Consensus and Controversy*, pp. 431–50. Philadelphia and London: Falmer Press.

WALEY, ARTHUR. 1938. *The Analects of Confucius.* London: Allen & Unwin.

WALLERSTEIN, IMMANUEL. 1974. *The Modern World-System: Capitalist Agriculture and the Origins of the European World-Economy in the Sixteenth Century.* New York: Academic Press.

WANG ANSHI. 1974. *Wang Wengong wenji.* Shanghai: Renmin.

WANG HSIAO-PO AND CHANG, LEO S. 1986. *The Philosophical Foundations of Han Fei's Political Theory.* Honolulu: University of Hawaii Press.

WANG YANGMING. 1976. *Wang Yangming quanji.* Taipei: Zhengzhong.

WANG YU. 1979. *Lao Zhuang sixiang lunji.* Taipei: Lianjing.

WATSON, BURTON. 1963. *Hsün Tzu: Basic Writings.* New York and London: Columbia University Press.

———. 1968. *The Complete Works of Chuang Tzu.* New York: Columbia University Press.

WAWRYTKO, SANDRA A. 1982. "Confucius and Kant: The Ethics of Respect." *Philosophy East and West* 32, no. 3: 237–57.

———. 1986. "Meaning as Merging: The Hermeneutics of Reinterpreting *King Lear* in the Light of the *Hsiao-ching.*" *Philosophy East and West* 36, no. 4: 393–409.

WEBER, ALFRED. 1943. *Das Tragische und die Geschichte.* Hamburg: Goverts.

WEBER, MAX. 1920. *Gesammelte Aufsätze zur Religionssoziologie,* I. Tübingen: Mohr.

———. 1921. "Politik als Beruf." In Weber, *Gesammelte politische Schriften.* München: Drei Masken.

———. 1951 [1920]. *The Religion of China,* trans. Hans H. Gerth. New York: Free Press.

WEBER-SCHÄFER, PETER. 1968. *Oikumene und Imperium: Studien zur Ziviltheologie des chinesischen Kaiserreiches.* München: List.

———. 1974. "Symbole der Politik in China und Hellas." In Abteilung für Ostasienwissenschaften der Ruhr-Universität Bochum, ed., *Ostasienwissenschaftliche Beiträge,* pp. 406–22. Wiesbaden: Harrassowitz.

WEGGEL, OSKAR. 1985. "Bürokratie contra Reform? Hypotheken und Chancen des nachmaoistischen Reformkurses." *CHINA aktuell* 14, no. 5: 303–17.

WEN GONGYI. 1983. *Xianqin luoji shi.* Shanghai: Renmin.

WHEATLEY, PAUL. 1972. *The Pivot of the Four Quarters.* Chicago: Aldine.

WICKLER, WOLFGANG, AND SEIBT, UTA. 1981. *Das Prinzip Eigennutz.* München: dtv.

WIEGER, L. 1913. *Moral Tenets and Customs in China.* Ho-kien-fu: Catholic Mission Press.

WILLIAMSON, H. R. 1937. *Wang An Shih.* London: Probsthain.

WILSON, RICHARD W. 1973. "Shame and Behaviour in Chinese Society." *Asian Profile* 1, no. 3: 431–47.

WIMMER, REINER. 1980. *Universalisierung in der Ethik.* Frankfurt/M.: Suhrkamp.

WITTFOGEL, KARL AUGUST. 1957. *Oriental Despotism.* New Haven: Yale University Press.

WOLFF, CHRISTIAN. 1740. *Rede von der Sittenlehre der Sineser. Gesammlete kleine philosophische Schrifften,* vol. 6. Halle (Wolff's own translation of his *Oratio de Sinarum philosophia practica*).

WRIGHT, ARTHUR F. 1978. *The Sui Dynasty.* New York: Knop.

WU, JOSEPH S. (Wu Sen). 1979. "The Son Bore Witness against the Father." In J. Wu, *Clarification and Enlightenment: Essays in Comparative Philosophy,* pp. 103–18. Taipei: Tunghai University Press.

WU KUANG-MING. 1987. "On Chinese Counterfactuals." *Philosophy East and West* 37, no. 1: 84–94.

WU PEI-YI. 1979. "Self-Examination and Confession of Sins in Traditional China." *Harvard Journal of Asian Studies* 39, no. 1: 5–38.

WU YU. 1985. *Wu Yu ji,* ed. by Zhao Qing and Zheng Cheng. Chengdu: Sichuan renmin.

XIE WULIANG. 1920. *Zhongguo zhexue shi.* Shanghai: Zhonghua.

XIE YOUWEI. 1969. *Zhongxi zhexue lunwen ji.* Hong Kong: Xinya yanjiusuo.

XU FUGUAN. 1963. *Zhongguo renxinglun shi: Xian Qin pian.* Taipei: Sili Donghaidaxue.

———. 1983. *Zhongguo sixiangshi lunji.* Taipei: Xuesheng.

YANG BOJUN. 1965. *Lunyu yizhu.* Peking: Zhonghua.

———. 1979. *Liezi jishi.* Peking: Zhonghua.

———. 1984. *Yang Bojun xueshu lunwenji.* Changsha: Yueli shushe.

YANG, C. K. 1957. "The Functional Relationship between Confucian Thought and Chinese Religion." In J. K. Fairbank, ed., *Chinese Thought and Institutions,* pp. 269–90. Chicago: University of Chicago Press.

YANG LIEN-SHENG. 1957. "The Concept of *Pao* as a Basis for Social Relations in China." In J. K. Fairbank, ed., *Chinese Thought and Institutions,* pp. 291–309. Chicago: University of Chicago Press.

YEARLEY, LEE H. 1990. *Mencius and Aquinas: Theories of Virtue and Conceptions of Courage.* Albany: State University of New York Press.

YU YINGSHI. 1987a. *Shi yu zhongguo wenhua.* Shanghai: Renmin.

———. 1987b. *Zhongguo jinshi zongjiao lunli yu shangren jingshen.* Taipei: Lianjing (also in Yu 1987a).

YUE DAIYUN AND WAKEMAN, CAROLYN. 1985. *To the Storm. The Odyssey of a Revolutionary Chinese Woman,* recounted by Yue Daiyun, written by Carolyn Wakeman. Berkeley, Los Angeles, and London: University of California Press.

ZHANG DAINIAN. 1981. "Kongzi zhexue jiexi." In Zhongguo shehuikexueyuan zhexue yanjiusuo zhongguo zhexueshi yanjiushi, ed., *Zhongguo zhexue shilun,* pp. 48–63. Taiyuan: Shanxi renmin.

ZHANG HENGSHOU. 1980. "Kong Qiu." In Xin Guanjie, Ding Jiansheng, and Meng Dengjin, eds., *Zhongguo gudai zhuming zhexuejia pingzhuan,* vol. 1, pp. 3–68. Jinan: Qilu shushe.

ZHANG TAIYAN. 1977. *Zhang Taiyan zhenglun xuanji,* ed. Tang Zhijun. Peking: Zhonghua.

ZHANG XINCHENG. 1954. *Weishu tongkao.* Shanghai: Shangwu.

ZHAO JIBIN. 1976. *Lunyu xintan.* Peking: Renmin.

———. 1983. "'Lunyu xinlun' daoyan." *Zhongguo zhexue* 10: 49–62. Peking: Sanlian.

ZHENG SHI. *Nü xiaojing.* In *Baibu congshu jicheng: Jindai mishu.* Taipei: Yiwen.

ZHEXUEYANJIU BIANJIBU, ed. 1957. *Zhongguo zhexueshi wenti taolun zhuanji.* Peking: Kexue.

ZHOU FAGAO. 1975. *Jinwen gulin.* Hong Kong: Xianggang zhongwen daxue.

ZHOU SHAOXIAN. 1977. *Xunzi yaoyi.* Taipei: Zhonghua.

ZHOU YUTONG AND HE ZHUOJUN. 1979. "Guanyu Kongzi de jige wenti." *Zhonghua wenshi luncong* 9: 5–18.

ZHU BOKUN. 1984. *Xianqin lunlixue gailun.* Peking: Beijing daxue.

ZHU XI. 1869. *Xiaoxue jizhu.* Shunde.

———. 1872. *Zhuzi yulei.* Yingyuan shuyuan cangban.

———. 1967, comp. *Jinsilu.* Taipei: Shangwu.

———. 1968. *Sishu jizhu.* Hong Kong: Taiping shuju.

ZUCKER, FRIEDRICH. 1928. *Syneidesis—Conscientia: Ein Versuch zur Geschichte des sittlichen Bewußtseins im griechischen und griechisch-römischen Altertum.* Jena: G. Fischer.

Index

363

34181403R00233

Made in the USA
Columbia, SC
13 November 2018